# Table of Contents

SECOND EDITION

# Programming Interactivity

*Joshua Noble*

O'REILLY®

Beijing · Cambridge · Farnham · Köln · Sebastopol · Tokyo

**Programming Interactivity, Second Edition**

by Joshua Noble

Copyright © 2012 Joshua Noble. All rights reserved.
Printed in the United States of America.

Published by O'Reilly Media, Inc., 1005 Gravenstein Highway North, Sebastopol, CA 95472.

O'Reilly books may be purchased for educational, business, or sales promotional use. Online editions
are also available for most titles (*http://my.safaribooksonline.com*). For more information, contact our
corporate/institutional sales department: (800) 998-9938 or *corporate@oreilly.com*.

| | |
|---|---|
| **Editors:** Shawn Wallace and Brian Jepson | **Indexer:** Ellen Troutman Zaig |
| **Production Editor:** Melanie Yarbrough | **Cover Designer:** Karen Montgomery |
| **Proofreader:** Kiel Van Horn | **Interior Designer:** David Futato |
| | **Illustrator:** Robert Romano |

| | |
|---|---|
| July 2009: | First Edition. |
| January 2012: | Second Edition. |

**Revision History for the Second Edition:**
   2012-01-10      First release
See *http://oreilly.com/catalog/errata.csp?isbn=9781449311445* for release details.

ISBN: 978-1-449-31144-5

[LSI]

1326213584

# Preface

This book is broken into three parts. The first introduces the three projects that will be used throughout this book, the second introduces some of the most common themes in creating interaction in designs and applications, and the third introduces some of the more advanced topics that you may want to explore further. Also included with some of the chapters are interviews with programmers, artists, designers, and authors who work with the tools covered in this book. Covering such a massive range of topics means that this book doesn't go into great depth about most of them, but it is filled with references to other books, websites, designers, and artists that you may find helpful or inspiring.

## What Is—and Isn't—in This Book

My excitement about the ideas and rapid growth of the field of interaction design is hard to contain. However, as exciting and far-reaching as interaction design is, the limitations of time and physical book size dictate that I be selective about what is and isn't covered in this book.

### What's In

This book covers Processing, Arduino, and openFrameworks. To help novice programmers, it covers some of the core elements of programming in C and C++ for Arduino and openFrameworks and also covers the Processing language. We introduce dozens of libraries for openFrameworks and Processing—too many to list here. Some of these are official libraries or add-ons for the two frameworks, and some are simply extensions that have been created for this book or provided by altruistic coders.

We also introduce some of the basics of electronics and how computer hardware functions, as well as many tools and components that you can use with an Arduino. The Arduino and Processing IDEs are covered, as are two different IDEs for openFrameworks, namely, Code::Blocks, and Xcode. The Arduino Uno and Mini are covered in depth, and we discuss other boards only briefly. We cover many electronic components that have designed expressly for the Arduino, called *shields*, in depth as well.

## What's Not In

While this book shows how to create some circuits, it doesn't cover a great deal of the fundamentals of electronics or hardware, how to create circuits, or electronics theory. Chapter 17 lists some excellent tutorials and references. While the book does cover the Processing subset of the Java programming language, to conserve space and maintain focus, it doesn't cover Java. The book doesn't cover many aspects of C++, such as templates, inline functions, operator overloading, and abstract classes. Again, though, listed in Chapter 17 are several excellent resources that you can use to learn about these deeper topics in C++.

There are so many Arduino-compatible boards now that it's almost impossible to cover them all in depth; the book mentions the Mega, the Nano, Fio, and several other boards only in passing and leaves out many of the Arduino-compatible boards that are not created by the Arduino team. Quite a few components and other tools that we would have liked to discuss in depth could not be included to maintain scope and to save space.

Many topics that we would have liked to include have been left out because of space considerations: artificial intelligence, data visualization, and algorithmic music, among others. Though these are all potentially interesting areas for artists and designers, the focus of the book is on teaching some of the theory and techniques for interaction design as well as the basics of hardware and programming. The resources listed at the end of the book can provide the names of some materials that might help you explore these topics.

## Conventions Used in This Book

The following typographical conventions are used in this book:

*Italic*
> Indicates new terms, URLs, email addresses, filenames, and file extensions.

`Constant width`
> Used for program listings, as well as within paragraphs to refer to program elements such as variable or function names, databases, data types, environment variables, statements, and keywords.

**`Constant width bold`**
> Shows commands or other text that should be typed literally by the user.

*`Constant width italic`*
> Shows text that should be replaced with user-supplied values or by values determined by context.

This icon signifies a tip, suggestion, or general note.

 This icon indicates a warning or caution.

# Companion Website

All the code included in this book is available for download from the book's companion website, *http://www.oreilly.com/catalog/9781449311445*.

# Using Code Examples

This book is here to help you get your job done. In general, you may use the code in this book in your programs and documentation. You do not need to contact us for permission unless you're reproducing a significant portion of the code. For example, writing a program that uses several chunks of code from this book does not require permission. Selling or distributing a CD-ROM of examples from O'Reilly books does require permission. Answering a question by citing this book and quoting example code does not require permission. Incorporating a significant amount of example code from this book into your product's documentation does require permission.

We appreciate, but do not require, attribution. An attribution usually includes the title, author, publisher, and ISBN. For example: "*Programming Interactivity, Second Edition* by Joshua Noble (O'Reilly). Copyright 2012 Joshua Noble, 978-1-449-31144-5."

If you feel your use of code examples falls outside fair use or the permission given above, feel free to contact us at *permissions@oreilly.com*.

# Safari® Books Online

 Safari Books Online is an on-demand digital library that lets you easily search over 7,500 technology and creative reference books and videos to find the answers you need quickly.

With a subscription, you can read any page and watch any video from our library online. Read books on your cell phone and mobile devices. Access new titles before they are available for print, and get exclusive access to manuscripts in development and post feedback for the authors. Copy and paste code samples, organize your favorites, download chapters, bookmark key sections, create notes, print out pages, and benefit from tons of other time-saving features.

O'Reilly Media has uploaded this book to the Safari Books Online service. To have full digital access to this book and others on similar topics from O'Reilly and other publishers, sign up for free at *http://my.safaribooksonline.com*.

## How to Contact Us

Please address comments and questions concerning this book to the publisher:

O'Reilly Media, Inc.
1005 Gravenstein Highway North
Sebastopol, CA 95472
800-998-9938 (in the United States or Canada)
707-829-0515 (international or local)
707-829-0104 (fax)

We have a web page for this book, where we list errata, examples, and any additional information. You can access this page at:

*http://shop.oreilly.com/product/0636920021735.do*

To comment or ask technical questions about this book, send email to:

*bookquestions@oreilly.com*

For more information about our books, courses, conferences, and news, see our website at *http://www.oreilly.com*.

Find us on Facebook: *http://facebook.com/oreilly*

Follow us on Twitter: *http://twitter.com/oreillymedia*

Watch us on YouTube: *http://www.youtube.com/oreillymedia*

## Acknowledgments

I need, first and foremost, to thank the wonderful engineers, artists, programmers, and dreamers who created the platforms that I've covered in this book. It is to all of them that I would like to dedicate this book. A woefully short list has to include Massimo Banzi, Tom Igoe, David Cuartielles, Gianluca Martino, David A. Mellis, Ben Fry, Casey Reas, Zach Lieberman, Theo Watson, Arturo Castro, and Chris O'Shea, the creators of the frameworks covered in this book. There are dozens, if not hundreds, of other names that should be on this list, but space is too limited to list them all. All I can say is thank to you to all the creators of these frameworks and to everyone who uses them to inspire, invent, amaze, and enrich the dialogue about design, technology, and art. This book is a humble attempt to thank you all for everything you've given to me—and to every other programmer, artist, or designer interested—for working with computing in novel and interesting ways and bringing more people into the conversation. I would also like to extend my deepest thanks to all my interviewees for taking the time to respond to my questions and enrich this book and for so enriching the world of interaction design and art. To everyone who provided code for this book as well, created open source code, or answered questions on any of the forums for beginners: thank you for your efforts to create a community.

This book is as much my effort as it is the sum of the efforts of the editorial team that worked on it. My technical editors, Michael Margolis, Adam Parrish, Matt Obert, Jeff Crouse, and Jeremy Rotzstain, have been absolutely fantastic. Their expertise, suggestions, and fresh look at what I was working on shaped not only this book but enlightened me, showed me new ways of solving problems, introduced me to new tools and techniques, sharpened my thinking, and broadened my horizons for the better. This book is a collaboration among all four of us in every sense of the word. I cannot pay them enough thanks for their excellent work. I would also like to thank Justin Hunyh and Mike Gionfriddo from LiquidWare as well as Nathan Seidle from Sparkfun for all of their help. My editors—Shawn Wallace, Robyn Thomas, and Kim Wimpsett—have been incredible, helping me with my sometime torturous grammar and patiently working with my propensity for sending in extremely rough drafts to bounce ideas off of them. They have made this book better than it ever could have been without their watchful eyes and guidance. Finally, I need to thank Steve Weiss for listening to my idea when I first proposed it and helping guide it through to completion.

I need to thank all of my friends in New York, Portland, Amsterdam, Geneva, London, Zurich, Boston, Paris, Copenhagen, and Toulouse for their support, their ideas, their Internet, and their encouragement. I would like to thank my family as well, and particularly my mother, for their support and humor.

# CHAPTER 1

# Introducing Interaction Design

The scientist and philosopher Alfred Korzybski once remarked, "The map is not the territory," and it's in that spirit that this book was written. The map may not be the territory, but it is helpful for getting around the territory and for finding where you are and where you want to go. This book covers a vast range of topics from programming to electronics to interaction design to art, but it doesn't cover any one of them in great depth. It covers all of these topics because they are part of an emerging territory that is often called *interaction design*, and that territory encompasses art, design, psychology, engineering, and programming. It's also a territory that is becoming more and more accessible thanks to excellent projects like the ones that we'll be exploring in the book— tools that have been created to make code and coding easier to do.

You should use this book like a map to see what technologies exist and the areas in interaction design that you might want to explore. This isn't a cookbook or an in-depth technical manual, but it will point you in the direction of other books, researchers, designers, projects, and artists as you go along. This book will also give you the technical understanding to know how to find information on almost any kind of project that you want to explore and what to do with that information once you find it.

## What This Book Is For

This book was created under the premise that technology and code are not tools solely for computer scientists or engineers to create applications and that no one be intimidated by or shy away from working with and exploring electronics, hardware, and code. Artists and designers can be interested in enabling interaction between users and between applications in ways that can be accentuated by the addition of custom computer applications or that can be realized only through the use of custom computer applications. You can focus on creating applications that emphasize their technological nature or on creating applications that feel very high-tech or use familiar metaphors like a keyboard and mouse or touchscreen. You can also choose to accentuate other aspects of the interaction or hide the technology behind a more organic interface. This book is specifically about the interactions that users or viewers can have with computers, electronics, tools, and the platforms that artists and designers can use to create applications and electronics that users can interact with. You'll be learning about three tools: Processing, openFrameworks, and Arduino.

These frameworks are designed specifically for artists and designers and as such are perfect for discussing how we can begin to create interactive designs and artworks. Each of them has a different background and uses different kinds of technology, but all of them are created with the goal of helping you explore and create applications more painlessly and quickly. In addition to showing you specifics of those three tools, this book focuses on three slightly more abstract concepts: code, interaction design, and ideas. Creating code is a similar activity whether you're writing something in C++ for openFrameworks or you're creating some logic in a circuit with Arduino. In both cases, you're creating a process that will run many times, perhaps even thousands of times, and that will generate the outcome you want.

This book also makes a few assumptions about you, the reader. I assume that you don't have a deep, or even any, programming or technical background. I also assume that you're a designer, artist, or other creative thinker interested in learning about code to create interactive applications in some way or shape. You might be a designer wanting to begin playing with interactive elements in your designs, wanting to create physically reactive applications to explore some interaction design concept, or wanting to prototype an idea for a product. You might be an artist wanting to begin working with interactive installations or with interactive computer graphics. You might be an architect wanting to get a basic understanding of programming and hardware to explore reactive architecture. You might be none of these at all, which is fine, too, as long as you're interested in exploring these themes while you learn about the three frameworks this book describes.

You'll explore the nature of interaction through common tools and techniques as well as through some discussions with designers, engineers, and artists working with interaction. In all likelihood, this book will not radically alter your perception of what interaction is, nor will it introduce you to radically new modes of interaction. This book will introduce to you to methods of creating common interactive elements that you can then use to explore further techniques of facilitating interactions between users or creating interactive elements that a user or viewer can experience.

## Programming for Interactivity

This book is called *Programming Interactivity* because it's focused primarily on programming for interaction design, that is, programming to create an application with which users interact directly. There are many styles of programming, and some techniques and ways of thinking about code are better suited to programming servers or databases than interaction. In this book, we're going to concentrate explicitly on things you can use to tell users something or to have users tell your application something.

One of the great challenges in interaction design is actually creating real interactions between what you're designing and the user who will be using it.

## The Nature of Interaction

So then, what exactly is *interaction*? Interaction could be defined as the exchange of information between two or more active participants. The writer and video game designer Chris Crawford describes interaction as "an iterative process of listening, thinking, and speaking between two or more actors." Generally, when we're talking about interaction and programming it's because one element in the interaction is a computer system of some sort or some control element that a person is trying to get to do something. The person for whom the computer or mechanical system is being designed is called the *user*, and what the user is using is called the *system*. There are many different terms floating around today, such as *human computer interaction*, *computer human interaction*, or *experience design*. All mean more or less the same thing: designing a system of some sort that a person can interact with in a way that is meaningful to them. As an interaction designer, you're trying to understand what the user wants to do and how the system that you're creating should respond. That system can be almost anything: a game, a menu, a series of connected sensors and lights, a complicated physically interactive application, or even a group of other people.

There is another key concept in interaction design that you should understand: the *feedback loop*. The feedback loop is a process of an entity communicating with itself while checking with either an internal or external regulatory system. That sounds a little more complex than it actually is. You're actually already quite familiar with biological regulatory systems; sweating keeps your body cool, breathing keeps oxygen flowing through your body, and blinking keeps your eyes from drying out. When you need more oxygen, your body breathes harder. This isn't something you have to tell your body to do; it simply does it. To maintain a constant level of oxygen, it sends out signals to breathe more and more deeply or frequently until it reaches the correct level. It feeds back on itself, sending signals to itself to breathe more again and again until it doesn't need to send those signals anymore. You can also think of the feedback that you give yourself while staying upright on a bicycle. You're constantly adjusting your balance minutely, with your brain feeding data to your body and your body feeding data back in a constant loop that helps you stay balanced. These loops are important in the notion of a system that does something constantly. Without feedback, systems can't regulate themselves because they won't know what they're doing.

Let's start at *messaging* and work our way up to *interaction*. While one participant certainly may be more active than the other, the "interaction" doesn't really apply when we use it to describe a *transmission*, that is, a message sent to someone with no way of handling a response. Think of a television commercial or a radio broadcast: it's simply a signal that you can listen to if you're in the right place at the right time and you have the right equipment. These broadcasts flow on regardless of whether you or anyone else is listening, and they occur on their own time, in their own tempo.

When you give a user a way of *rewinding* or controlling the tempo of information, an extra layer of user control is added. You can't really *interact* with a book or a static web page, or even the vast majority of dynamic web pages, but you can control the speed at which you read them, and you can rewind information that you're not sure about. These are really guided transmissions in that they give you a chunk of information that is more or less established and ask you which part of it you want to view. Scrolling, linking, fast-forwarding, and rewinding are all the techniques of guided transmissions.

When you give a user a way to accomplish a task or input data into the system that changes it in a substantial way and you create a means for that system to respond to what the user is doing, then you're creating interaction. Reactive interaction is really the beginning of interaction because it gets you started thinking about what the user will do and how your system or object will react. For everything that user does, the system or object needs to have a response, even if that response is "I didn't understand" or another kind of error message. This can also be built into a single system. Many kinds of applications monitor their own performance, checking the state of a property in the system or the number of boxes available in a warehouse, for instance. If you imagine this as being an interaction between two people, then you might imagine a parent giving a child an order.

A somewhat more complex model of interaction is one where the system is constantly doing a task and the users' input regulates that task. Many industrial monitoring systems function this way, as do the underlying parts of game engines, and many interactive installations. The difficulty of creating this kind of interaction is ensuring that users always know what the system is doing at any given time, understand how they can modify it, and understand exactly how their modifications to one aspect of the system might affect another. If you imagine this between two people, then you might imagine a parent helping a child walk, ensuring that she doesn't fall over as she goes. You can also imagine how a regulatory system might function, where the system regulates the user as they're executing a task. This isn't really two entities fully communicating because the regulated system doesn't respond—it simply changes its behavior—but it does involve continuous systems. Systems can perform this task on their own as well, monitoring a process and providing regulation of an ongoing process.

This last mode of interaction blends into another. It is a very similar but slightly more complex model of creating interaction that might be described as the *didactic*, or learning, mode of interaction. Here, the system is still running continuously, and the user can see into the system, but instead of regulating the behavior, the user is learning from the output data. A lot of monitoring applications function this way, providing a view into relevant data and data points that the user can use to learn about a process. Again, the system isn't actively conversing with a user; it's just running and reporting information to the user. The user also has his process driven by the reporting from the system but not really modified by it, which is why it's a learning model. Both systems and people are more than capable of learning from themselves, albeit in quite different ways.

A more complex mode of interaction is a management type model where the user communicates something to a system and the system communicates something back that allows the user to carry on with a secondary task. This is where you begin to see the real complexities of communication between users and systems. The user is communicating with a system and asks the system to perform some task. The system responds in a way that allows a user to continue with a secondary task. The system continues to run, and the user continues to run even while she has her own internal feedback loop occurring. One can find this in many real-time monitoring applications in fields from finance to medicine.

Finally, we have the most complex mode of interaction: a full-fledged conversation. This is something that humans have mastered doing amongst one another, but it's another matter altogether to create this between a human and a machine because of how complex the notion of a conversation really is. When you think about how much data is communicated in a conversation through words, tone of voice, facial expressions, body posture, subtext, and context, you realize it's a substantial amount of information being exchanged and processed at extremely high rates. Most user-system conversations are a great deal less complex.

A simple but good example of this is navigating using a mobile device: the device is constantly updating its position and displaying that back to the user and providing directions, while the user is actively traveling and querying the device for information. Enabling this conversational mode of interaction between users and systems is one of the most pressing challenges in interaction design and engineering. These modes of interaction all present different challenges and help users do different kinds of things. You'll find that the appropriate mode depends on the users, the task, and the context in which the interaction is taking place.

## Messages and Interaction

Interaction happens via messages sent from systems to users, and vice versa. These messages can be text, speech, colors, visual feedback, or mechanical and physical input or feedback. Depending on the kind of application, winking can be just as clear and important a message as pushing a button. One thing that interaction designers talk about a great deal is how to construct and receive messages in a way that is simple and unambiguous for users and for the system.

One of the most difficult tasks in creating interactive applications is to understand how the system sees messages from users and how the user sees messages from the system. With applications that have a great degree of interactivity, allow more tasks for the user and the system, and allow for more sophisticated messages, it is easy for a conversation to become unclear to one party. When a message isn't understood, it's quite important to help the other party understand not just what wasn't understood but also how it can be fixed. If I don't understand something that someone says to me, I ask that person to repeat it. If I ask for a web page that doesn't exist, the server responds with an error page that tells me the page doesn't exist. The more freedom each party has, the greater the possibility of erroneous, unintended messages, and the greater the need for educating one party about what the other party understands and how that understanding is being constructed.

Think for a moment about a conversation between two adults. Communicating like this requires years of what could be described as *user training*: learning a language, learning appropriate and inappropriate behavior, learning a value system, and so on. It is because of this that the interaction between two humans can be as rich as it is. This idea of training the user to understand what messages the system understands and what a message from the system means is a tricky process. Creating a program with a datagrid where a user can select items is quite simple for the user to begin to understand because most computer literate users are familiar with the notion of a datagrid. We see datagrids quite frequently, and we generally have an understanding of what they can do, what they can't do, a rough understanding of what error messages coming from datagrids might mean, and how to use them. If you're using a new kind of control or interface, you'll have to make sure that you provide ways for users to learn what your system is, how it works, and what they can do with it.

There is a correlation between the richness of interactive systems and the difficulty of creating it: the richer the interaction, the more that can go wrong. This is part of why designers spend so much time and energy attempting to create *anticipatable experiences*: interactive experiences where a user or viewer can leverage other realms of knowledge or other experiences interacting. Popular slogans in design, like "principle of least surprise," express the notion that the familiar interaction is the preferable interaction because the learning curve for the user is much more shallow than a truly novel interaction. Users must learn how feedback is returned to them and how to modify their behavior based on the feedback, both of which can be a lengthy process.

## Interfaces and Interaction

One part of the feedback from a system is actual messages sent back and forth—text prompts, for example—but the interface is another important part of the communication of an interaction. An interface sits between two actors and facilitates their communication. This can be a screen, a control panel, an interactive wall, or simply a microphone and a pair of speakers. The interface is whatever shared materials the user and the system use to send and receive messages. Interface design is a very large topic unto itself, but it gets a little more manageable if you consider it in terms of what it means for designing an interaction.

The interface is the medium of the communication between the user and the system. It drives a lot of what is possible and what is not possible, what is efficient and what isn't, and what the tone of the interaction is. If you think about how you talk to someone on the phone versus how you talk to them in person, you're probably using more hand gestures, facial expressions, and other forms of nonverbal communication in person and being more direct and using your tone of voice more when you are on the phone. What we use to do something affects a lot of how we do that thing. Having a functional, expressive, and attractive interface is very important in creating the means for an interaction to occur. The attractiveness of an interface is an important part of making an interaction pleasant to a user; the colors, text, symmetry, sounds, and graphics are important and are communicative elements that shape a great deal about what a user thinks about your system. This shouldn't come as a great surprise to anyone, but users prefer good-looking interfaces. What makes those interfaces attractive is largely a matter of context, both for your users and for the task that they're trying to accomplish with your system. While users *prefer* attractive interfaces, they *need* functional interfaces. The functionality of an interface is part of what makes a system good for a task and what makes a user able to use your system. Even if what that system does is rather opaque, the user still needs a functional interface that shows him what his input does and gives him feedback.

It's important to remember that interaction is more than the use of an interface. When we consider the most common interactions between a user and a machine—for example, a cell phone call—they're quite simple in terms of the interaction between the user and the object. For a cell phone, you simply dial numbers to find someone else in a system; it alerts you if you're being sought, and it sends and receives sound. This relatively simple interaction is important for reasons other than the interaction between the person and the object; it's important because of the context of that interaction: you can make a cell phone call from almost anywhere. Before cell phones, you needed a phone line available to you, but now, with a cell phone, you simply need a phone and an account. You can reach people while both of you are away from home, and you can be reached when you are away from your home or office. When the cell phone first emerged, cell phone users already understood how to make and receive telephone calls, and the general pattern of the user interface was already established. True innovations in user interfaces are very difficult to realize because they often require very substantial engineering efforts and serious thinking by the interaction designer to ensure that the interface will function properly. Also, they require a lot of user training and retraining. There aren't a great deal of true revolutions in user interfaces: the creation of the keyboard, Doug Engelbart's mouse (the prototype of the mouse we know today), Ivan Sutherland's sketchpad, the desktop GUI, and now the capacitive touchscreen. These were technological changes and impressive feats of engineering, and they were also shifts in the way people used computers. Revolutionary interfaces shape more than just the way that a tool appears; they redefine the possibilities of how a tool can be used.

## Languages of Interaction

All interactions have a certain vocabulary that they use. If you think of how you delete something from the desktop with a mouse, you might say, "I select the file and drag it to the trash." The actual actions that you're performing when you do this are a little different from what the system understands you to be doing, but that's not really what's important. What's important is that you understand what the actions you can perform are and you know that the system understands those actions in the same way and will perform them in the same way that you expect. Having a meaningful, efficient, and productive interaction, just like creating a language or a code, requires that both parties agree on the meaning of the symbol and the meaning of the order in which actions occur. Those particular understandings are going to be quite different depending on the interface and type of interaction that the user undertakes.

In this book, we'll examine some of the many different kinds of interactions, but don't take this next section as a list of categories. Considering the pervasiveness of computing and interactions that exist with computing, there are so very many kinds of interaction between humans and computers that it is difficult to even reference some of the most common modes of interaction without some overlap among categories.

*Physical manipulation*

These are the first interfaces that were created for electronics and some of the first designed multifunction man/machine interactions. Typically, before the advent of the car and radio, which were the first two common machines with multiple interface elements, a machine had a single switch or use. The user's attention was focused on a single task at a time. Radios and automobiles presented novel challenges because both required multiple actions by nonspecialists; in the case of the automobile, this included speed and direction at all times and other tasks at irregular times. The interface might be a control that represents either a state that can be activated by flipping a switch or pushing a button or a range that can be set by turning a knob or pushing a slider. The interface lets users not only control the values that they are setting but also check values via labeling of sliders, knobs, dials, and switches. Dials, oscilloscopes, and other feedback interface elements let users verify information more quickly without referring to the actual interface element that they were manipulating. This requires that the user monitor multiple sources of information at a given time while manipulating controls. Physical manipulation of a control is one of the most important and interesting ways of creating interaction with a system.

*Input using code*

At the dawn of the age of computing, the classic user interaction model was a terminal where a user input code commands that were then run and the results were reported to the screen in the form of text. The driving interactive concept was to command the machine via a system of commands that the computer had been preprogrammed to recognize. The user had to be knowledgeable or at the very least comfortable with requesting help from a very bare interface. This is certainly not the end of keyboard-based interactive behaviors, though. Consider the notion of the *hot key*, for instance Ctrl+Z for undo, beloved by so many programmers and ubiquitous in all applications from word-and image-processing applications to browsers. The hot key is no different from the command line but accentuates the user interface by allowing the user to automate repetitive tasks or perform a task quickly without diverting their attention from another task.

*Mouse manipulation*

This is the most common method of interacting with a computer at this moment and the interface for which almost all commonly used applications have been designed. Consider the language of working with the mouse, the techniques that have been implemented by designers and learned by users: drag-and-drop, double-click, and click-and-hold. These movements and the meanings behind them in different applications are not completely standard, nor are they entirely fixed. One application may use a given gesture in many different ways in a single application and rely on the user understanding the feedback given to them by the application to know which meaning of the gesture will be used in the current context.

*Presence, location, and image*

The use of the presence and absence of the participant or user is an extremely simple but profoundly intuitive way of interacting. This can be detected by weight, motion, light, heat, or, in certain cases, sound. The reaction to simple presence or absence acts as a switch, begins a process, or ends a process. The presence of the body, though simple, is a powerful basis of interaction; it engages users and asks users to engage with their presence, their position, and their image. This can be as simple as an automatic door sliding open as we approach, or as complex as Theo Watson's *Audio Space*, where visitors don a headset equipped with earphones and a microphone and record messages that are then placed in the spot where they were recorded. As another user enters the location where a message was left, the message is played back along with any recorded by previous visitors. Each message sounds as if it is coming from the spot where it was recorded. We can imagine the body as a switch, or we can imagine the body as the image of the body and analyze this using photos or videos in any great number of ways. This theme of embodiment drives a great deal of fascinating interactions using what is called *computer vision*, that is, the analysis of images input using a camera, turned into pixels, and then analyzed. Later in this book, we'll examine using computer vision to detect movement in an image and even to detect the location of a human face within an image.

*Haptic interfaces and multitouch*

At the time of the writing of this book, Apple iPhone, Microsoft Surface, and a great number of new tools for multiple touch-based interfaces have already been introduced. Given the excitement around these technologies, the speed of change and innovation will likely outstrip any attempts by myself or my editors to keep this text abreast of the most cutting edge products or technologies. Nevertheless, the fundamentals of designing and structuring interactions using these gesture-based interfaces will likely not change. These essentials are based on what will be familiar gestures to anyone who has used any of these products: using two fingers to expand or contract, turning two fingers to rotate, tapping to select. These are not used simply for software applications, either. Consider how often the waving gesture is used in an airport bathroom with sinks to turn on the water, paper towel dispensers, and hand driers. The language of these gestures becomes a language that we can use to enable interaction much as a common natural language, an icon, or a pattern of buttons pressed on a video game controller.

*Gesture*

The gesture is a fascinating interactive model because it so readily associates itself with signs, writing, and physicality. This notion of the interaction that is not driven by a keyboard or a mouse is particularly powerful because mouse and key interaction is often nonintuitive for certain kinds of tasks. Gestures are often implemented with touchscreen interfaces or mouse movements or pens and are very often used for drawing applications, simple navigation elements, adaptive technologies, or applications for children. There are many different cutting edge interactive approaches that are being explored, from writing recognition systems and novel key input strategies like Swype to hand motion recognition systems via video.

*Voice and speech recognition*

Voice recognition is the programming of a computer to recognize certain words or phrases and perform certain tasks based on those commands. Commands can be as simple as voice activation, that is, having the voice act as a switch to turn something on, and as complex as recognizing different words as commands. For a computer, words or commands are recognized as patterns of sounds that are then strung together and compared with a dictionary of patterns to determine what the command could be. Speech recognition is a much more advanced topic, using roughly the same approach as a simple command recognition engine, but with a far larger dictionary and more powerful tools to determine the input. Beyond speech, the voice itself can be used to provide input, volume, tone, and duration, and can be used to drive the interaction between users and applications.

This is just a short list of some of the most prevalent themes in interaction design. In this book, there won't be space to cover all of these approaches to interactivity, but you will learn some of the basics behind each of them and get information about further resources that you can use for your own design work.

---

## Interview: Matt Cottam

Matt is the CEO and cofounder of Tellart and provides both inspiration and direction for the company through involvement in conferences, lectures, academia, and design culture worldwide. He has been teaching studio courses at RISD on topics ranging from design for extreme environments to physical computing since 1999. Matt holds the position of Adjunct Professor at Umeå Institute of Design (UID Sweden). He is also a Visiting Teacher each year at Copenhagen Institute for Interaction Design (CIID, Denmark), Oslo School of Architecture and Design (AHO, Norway), and The Central Academy of Fine Arts, Beijing (CAFA, China).

*What does it mean to sketch in hardware?*

**Matt Cottam:** When I was a freshman at Rhode Island School of Design (RISD) in the early nineties, only doctors had car phones (the size of shoe boxes) and the web felt

---

like a clickable fax machine with a screen. By the time I graduated just five years later, all of my student peers had mobile phones and we all had multiple email addresses and were using browsers with color pictures, animation, and sound. It was overwhelmingly clear that digital and networked technology was going to change the way we use, perceive, and design products.

We had spent the past five years shaping blocks of wood and foam to look like digital products, representing onscreen content by gluing printouts under acetate to the models, role playing with fellow students to explore and communicate the behavior of interactive systems. This was good and we were after all at a very traditional, hands-on, craft-based school, but something critical was missing. When you design a chair, you can go to a workshop and play around, cutting, shaping, and connecting lots of different materials: steel, aluminum, leather, plywood, plastic, cork, foam; pipe, rod, sheet, resin. You can explore the capabilities of particular tools like a spot-welder or thermal former, see when they burn, melt, stretch, scratch, and when they seem to work without friction-when creating nice things seems effortless. You can work directly at the intersection of a particular tool and particular material to find the size and shape of an object that shows off their unique strengths; you can create a form that feels to be in harmony—because it was born directly from the intrinsic qualities of the medium and method.

When I was a student it was impossible for a designer to sketch directly and fluidly with the materials and tools of software and electronics. This led to an inability for the designer to create physical product forms and software interfaces that felt synthesized. There was no way to feel the real behavior, unlike the chair that you could just sit in.

When we started Tellart in 1999, we set out to create a studio of industrial and graphic designers as well as electrical and software engineers that could work closely together and quickly sketch a model of interactive with the real stuff products. We have been active in the "sketching in hardware" or "physical computing" community since the early days and have developed many hardware and software tools during our work with students and clients. Now there are hundreds if not thousands of tools designed specifically to close the gap between design and engineering—some of the most important of which are taught in this book. Now the things Tellart makes not only have physical form, including graphical and tangible user interfaces, but we are designing the content and service layers holistically.

*Do you see a relationship in being able to prototype and research? Or, I suppose, assuming that you do see at least some relationship there, how do they fit together optimally? How have you handled that in your design practice?*

**Matt:** Just the other day I received a letter saying that I had been on the faculty at RISD for 12 years, and I've been teaching at Umeå Institute of Design (UID) for 6 years and Copenhagen Institute of Design for 3. Almost everyone at Tellart teaches at least a little each year and we have lead courses in as far away places as China and Taiwan. People often ask me how I make time for both teaching and Tellart, and the answer is simple: they are a symbiotic relationship. We work with students who are always looking over the horizon, always aiming to invent. We work closely, shoulder to shoulder in the workshops with them, at table saws and APIs trying to constantly understand what the modern designer needs to do their work in optimal conditions. We create new hardware and software toolkits—a constantly evolving suite we call Sketchtools—and test them out with students. They get a new, experimental way of working and we get to see what is possible when some of the brightest minds create with Sketchtools. We then take documentation of our work together with the students and show it at international conferences and to our clients. Almost our entire team is composed of former students. I hesitate to call the work we do at schools "research" since it is not really academic or even conceptual—it is really very tactical.

*What tools do you find most influential and useful to you and your design practice on a day-to-day basis?*

**Matt:** The beautiful thing about working at Tellart and with students is that we switch hardware and software tools like colors of paint. You can rarely work successfully with just one, and learning how to mix them is where real talent comes in.

*What does open source mean to you? What does sharing and communicating mean for your practice?*

**Matt:** We have always open sourced all of our Sketchtools and plan to keep doing so. We have a handshake contract with our students to the effect of: the only way I can share 100 percent openly with you is if you do the same with me—any ideas exchanged in our class, including our toolkits, are up for grabs in for anyone involved any form and at any time. I find that people who are possessive and competitive about their knowledge tend to be insecure and fall behind quickly—the people who share effectively know this. I'm not really interested in a magnum opus, I encourage students to be prepared to come up with new ideas every day, not once in a lifetime. Of course there is a role for client confidentiality but that is another mode of practice and the two can live in parallel and even share a symbiotic relationship.

*How do you move from a drawing or a video to a physical prototype? Also, if I can stay on that line of thinking for a moment: how do you move from a physical prototype to an electronic one (i.e, one that has at least some active element in it)?*

**Matt:** This may be a bit of an oversimplification, but I like to think that we are getting closer to having hardware and software tools that are no harder for a designer to become competent with than a milling machine or thermal-former. I see tables covered in Arduino, sensors, motors, pencil sketches, bits of plastic, fake fur, and clay. I guess it depends whether you define prototype as an exact model for manufacture or as a working sketch model. I find the term prototype problematic when used this way in courses and with clients; we prefer to talk about working sketch models at varying degrees of fidelity. If you mean developing a concept through making working sketches, then I think pencil, electronics, software, physical model sketches can all be used used simultaneously—they can be a sounding board for the designer while she gets an idea out into the world (often making discoveries along the way) and not just a process for building something predetermined.

*What tools do you find most helpful for beginners?*

**Matt:** Drawing and filmmaking. Call me old-fashioned but I believe that any professional designer worth their salt should be able to draw. I don't mean portraits; I mean being able to make their ideas visible and understandable by others. To go further, I find that being able to facilitate group work involving people from various disciplines (often marketing, business leadership, manufacturing, technology) through improvisational drawing is an essential skill—maybe more today than ever before, as things like software and services are so intangible and things like data so formless, networks so complex. Interaction designers have to concern themselves with product and service ecosystems that are experienced by users over time and often over a variety of touchpoints, so developing a visual vocabulary for expressing changes and transactions (like storyboards) is an invaluable skill. An interaction designer who can draw, build low-to-medium fidelity working sketch models involving electronics and software and also make short persuasive films that communicate how their product/service is culturally and economically relevant, has it made.

*Can you explain a little about the NADA project?*

**Matt:** NADA was the first software toolkit Tellart made, back in 2001 (Brian Hinch was the project lead). It allowed designers to use predecessors to the Arduino like Teleo, Phidgets, and all kinds of MIDI devices to be connected to Flash. Design students in 2002 were connecting RFID readers to websites, and connecting the Web to lights and motors within just a few weeks. Today this seems normal, but at the time it solved a lot for us and our students.

Flash was something we already knew from making web projects and there was a ton of books, online tutorials, and courses available on the topic aimed directly at designers.

Flash, especially back in version 4 when NADA appeared, was largely a graphical authoring environment, which meant we could draw a blue square, select it, and tell it to turn on a lightbulb when clicked (even less abstract for designers than writing HTML referencing images in a folder).

Schools already had Flash as part of their annual purchase and installation (any teacher knows that getting a new software package into that group can take years of begging).

NADA was a server written in Java. In all of our early interactive documentation, tutorials were always offered in both Java and Flash, encouraging collaboration between engineers and designers.

Our documentation had code snippets, but more importantly it provided a very visual diagnostic interface that detected which hardware you had connected and gave the values for all analog inputs and PWM outputs. It seems simple enough to just trace all of these values but I can tell you most designers working with NADA left this window open most of the time. The interface even had an interactive resistor calculator that you could adjust and see the effects directly on the outputs of your sensors.

We used NADA on countless client and classroom projects. Most of the time NADA was a way to sketch and prototype, but many times it ended up in end products.

NADA then became NADA Mobile, which was an iApp and server combination that allowed designers to make iPhone/iPod apps using just JavaScript and CSS and our custom functions. Version 2 allowed for connecting Arduino to iDevices. We also added the ability for connecting analog sensors to the headphone/mic jack of iDevices to control apps, which made the hardware side of sketching dirt simple. Our most recent courses have involved iDevices and Android devices connected to Arduino, Zigbee and relays, allowing us to sketch with controlling everyday appliances from our mobiles and tablets.

We also made several hardware toolkits and they are all part of the lineage we call Sketchtools.

NADA is now just one of dozens of options for doing the same stuff, many of which are in this book. Future versions of our Sketchtools will require less building from scratch and be more about building combinations of hardware and software tools and writing design briefs that push us, our clients, and our students to think beyond what is currently possible. We never intended to be in the toolmaking process; we were just at one of those awesome times in history when you have more ideas than ways to make them. Now, thanks to all of the amazing toolkit projects out there, many of them made by our good friends, we can focus more of our time on using the tools to make great experiences.

*I'm really intrigued by the "What Is a Switch?" course that you teach as an intro course in a few different Interaction Design programs.*

**Matt:** The "What Is a Switch?" design project brief was developed for our Designing Interactions course at RISD in 2001. We had no way to experiment with tangible user interfaces in a manner that made sense to teach in a one semester industrial design course—we wanted to explore the need, use, value of technology, not the technology itself. I asked students to go into the metal and wood and plastics shops and gather as much interesting scrap as they could. The brief was then to each create 20 examples of how a human gesture or an environmental influence (light, wind, or water flow, etc.) could close a circuit. The circuit could be two lines drawn in pen on paper and the paper then folded to connect them—there were no electronics at all; the circuits were purely symbolic of connecting two components. Even today when our students come in on the first day as Arduino experts, we still see the most inventiveness in this project. There is just no friction and students allow themselves to be influenced by the qualities of the materials they find—a pile of plastic circles or some wool strips or some perforated sheet metal. The project encourages listening to materials and forms and thinking about scale and anatomy of components. This project is always done in under 24 hours, from brief to critique—speed is a key ingredient.

The "advanced" version of "What Is a Switch?" came about when we found a pile of keyboards in the school trash. We hacked the keyboard microcontrollers into these kinds of sketch switches (now including just a bit of wire but still no batteries) and captured the keystrokes in Flash. In literally a day worth of teaching and with zero dollars in materials, the students could make something as complex as "open the door and the video on the web plays, close the door and it stops." This is still my favorite project. The great thing about the low cost is that students treat the materials like pencils or clay—they are fearless, as the materials flexible and rugged. The most amazing ideas come out.

# Design and Interaction

The great industrial designer Henry Dreyfuss called design "the measure of man." By this, he meant that the design of things is an excellent way to understand and analyze the activities of human beings. Defining the word *design* is a task better left to others, so I'll leave my contribution at this: interaction design is the creation of tools for how we do specific things. The more specific the thing, the more finely the tool can be honed for it, and the more specific the interaction design can be. Interaction is sometimes confused with "doing something with a tool," and although that's important, it's a little less specific than "how we do things with a tool." Thinking about tools in terms of *how*, rather than just *what*, *when*, or *why*, isolates those things about the interaction that define the experience of doing that task. A lot depends on the task as well. A singular task with a singular action does not foster much dissonance; therefore, it can bear a lot more dissonance before it becomes meaningless. A task of multiple actions creates much greater dissonance and can lose meaningfulness much more quickly.

The design of an interaction is a complex process that involves a lot of modeling of how a system will work, how a user will approach the goal she's trying to accomplish, and how the interface needs to be configured to allow for all of these different operations. All of these taken together create the *context of the interaction* that you're making. The context is very important to what choices you should make for the design of an interaction. You might want to make the interaction very cut and dry so that everything that the user expects is given to her as quickly as possible and in an unambiguous manner. Most business applications or very task-based applications function this way; users know what they can do in unambiguous terms, and the interaction doesn't deviate much from that initial information. There is a real pleasure in knowing what to expect and getting it so that you can make the interaction—and by extension the application or object—attractive. Or, you might want to make something much more playful, where the reward is in discovering the interaction and seeing it change throughout the use of it. Either way, a good understanding of the context of the user will help you create a better system and a better experience.

One of the tricks of interaction design is that, fundamentally, what users are trying to do when they're interacting with a system is to correlate it to something else that they're more familiar with. Anyone who has ever said or heard anyone else say "the computer is thinking" has seen a little bit of anthropomorphic thought applied to a computer. As human beings, we are very good at a few different things, and when it comes to interaction design, one of the more important things is using our understanding of the inner processes of other people. Interaction with a system doesn't really involve understanding what someone else is thinking, but it does use some of the same cognitive processes. To that end, as an interaction designer, you want to give good cues that will help users understand what's going on. They may not need to know exactly what the process of your system is, and probably shouldn't, but they do need to know more or less what your system is doing with the information that they give it.

# Art and Interaction

Interactivity in art has been a hotly discussed and debated topic for at least 20 years now, and the kinds of interactivity that you see in art pieces are constantly changing to expand the definitions of *art* and *interaction*. There are many computer games that can be considered art, many art pieces that can be considered industrial design, and a vast and ever-increasing number of projects that can fit comfortably into art galleries and design shows.

For the purposes of this book, there isn't much point in differentiating between the fields of interactive art, industrial design, interaction design, and traditional software engineering. Although these different fields might seem quite different from one another, they actually all share common goals. They all attempt to create objects and experiences for users, they use similar tools and processes, and they all share a common workflow that goes from sketch to prototype to final product to showing. You can think of a continuum, where at one end there are predictable and well-defined things that may be more suited for completing a task, and at the other end are more unpredictable and dissonant works that challenge and provoke us but may not be useful in our everyday lives. There is a curious dance between art and design in interactive art that plays on the relationship between simplicity and complexity, usefulness and uselessness, and goals and open interpretations. Deciding which end of that spectrum is more interesting to you has a lot of bearing on how you think about the interaction, but it doesn't change the code that you write or the way that you design your hardware.

Making interactive art is quite different from making noninteractive art because the real object of interactive art is the situation. In painting, the object is the painting itself; in sculpture, it is the object and the space around it; in a video piece, the object is the video projection. In an interactive artwork, the object of the art is really the interaction between the viewer and the system that the artist has created. That system can be very technologically complex, it can have a single simple technical element, or it can have none at all. This book discusses artists and artworks that make heavy use of technology, what are often called *new media artists*, because they are artists who use or develop the tools that you'll be learning how to use. I distinguish new media art from interactive art because projects that use programming (but that aren't interactive) don't have that key characteristic of being created in the situation where the viewer encounters them. There are many technologically sophisticated projects that use the tools covered in this book but that are not actually interactive. For the most part, this book covers artists who work with interactivity and projects that generate feedback in response to the actions of a user.

One of the interesting challenges of working with interactive art is that the art can be truly useful and functional in many ways while still being art. You also have a great deal of control over the context of what that art is; an artwork can be viewed or experienced in any location that the user chooses, altered to become something unrecognizable, or used in a way that it was not intended to be used when it was first created. Many designers are exploring what they call *critical design*, designed objects that not only function but exist to be thought-provoking as well, making users think in critical ways that are usually associated with art rather than with design. This overlap between the design of an object and the creation of an art experience is part of what makes interactivity such a rich topic for artists to explore because you can open the realm of what a user can experience and explore in deeply expressive ways.

## Data Exchange and Exploration

The task or goal that an interaction facilitates is as important as the way in which an interaction is carried out between a user and a system. Again, the types listed here aren't being included to make a list of types of interactive work, but to show some of the common themes that run through interactive art and design and to help you get an idea of what you'll be exploring in this book:

*Supporting data visualization*

> Data visualization is an increasingly relevant theme given the amount of data that we as members of an increasingly information-centric society must process. A well-formed data visualization is a powerful tool because it lets a user not only comprehend individual *data points* but also understand the relationship between what are called data points, detect patterns in the data, and even reconfigure and re-contextualize information. Data visualization accelerates the ability of the user to process and synthesize new information by not simply learning a fact but by locating the fact within a discourse quickly.

> As the designer and writer Frank van Ham notes, "They should be massively collaborative...not focus on analysis but on communication...it should be visual and end user driven." The goal of data visualization is to generate, for the user, a view into data. This can be a view that will help the user understand the data better, as in the work of Ben Fry, where he creates beautiful diagrams that let a viewer more quickly and more fully understand the relationships between the objects in the data. His approach is informed by aesthetic considerations and by careful cognitive and psychological research. *I Want You to Want Me (http://iwantyoutowantme .org)* by Jonathan Harris and Sep Kamvar retrieves data from online data sites and uses that information to generate interactive visualizations. While still data visualization, this piece is a far more dynamic and whimsical approach than the usual graph-and-chart approach used in standard visualizations, and yet it performs deep and meaningful data parsing and analysis.

> The interaction of the user can be a process of refining, exploring juxtaposition, mining new data, or storytelling. When designing data and the interaction with it, we must consider not only what data is presented, but also how users will interpret that data, what they might want to do with it, and how they would want to interact with it. Interaction is far easier when the view into data and the visual representation of that view are clearly related. For instance, the visual representation of the

data and the visual representation of filtering should be clear so that the user easily understands what is being filtered and how to change it.

*Organizing tasks*

Some interactions are interesting because of what they allow us to accomplish. The organization of tasks or actions or of discrete and discontinuous objects is the driving force behind much of the thinking in interface design. When you look back at the history of interfaces for machines and computers, you can see an evolution of organizing tasks, applications, information, and acts. The now ubiquitous desktop model allowed the user to organize tasks in a way that leveraged both natural cognitive abilities, like the ability to organize things spatially, and a familiar motif for any office worker, namely, the desktop.

One challenge for interaction design is to conceive of ways to effectively put working spaces and organizational tools in places other than the traditional desktop environment. Computing is everywhere, and users want access to programs and data at more places. How to enable interaction on very small screens or with no screen at all is an increasingly relevant challenge given the environments in which users are interacting with environments.

Some of the themes of exploration are how to develop novel desktop environments using new tools like multitouch screens, how to create tools for users to create their own interfaces to fit their needs at a particular time, and how to create interfaces for data visualization and tasks around data visualization.

These types of interactive applications tend much more to practical and functional concerns, enabling users to complete tasks, organize information, and save information. This certainly does not mean that they need to attempt to replicate an operating system in functionality, but rather that they draw on that vocabulary of interaction. This can be used in somewhat more subversive ways as well, as with Adrian Ward's *Auto-Illustrator (http://www.adeward.com/wiki/default/read/soft ware.net)*.

*Creating experiences*

Not all interactive designs need to rely on the traditional application model. In fact, one of the most common and powerful modes of interaction is what might be called the experiential model of interaction. These are often computer games, reactive drawings, or eye-catching graphic displays that engage and entertain without a set purpose. They often use novel connections between audio and visual stimulation and create either spectacles that entertain users or have entertaining interactions. The experiential interaction is very evident in the design of many kinds of computer games, where the user can play a character in the game and see the world through that character's eye. Many times the interaction in these kinds of games is goal oriented, whether that goal be moving to the next level, killing enemies, or scoring points in some way or another. Many interactive installations use a similar model of interaction, where the interaction is playful but often lacks the goal-driven nature of gaming and instead focuses on enabling the viewing of a spectacle or playing with some engine that creates sounds or graphics. The goal of this kind of interaction is often simply to entertain or engage.

Both games and interactive installations often allow for fast switching between multiple views, perspectives, or models within the flow of the applications. This can be useful not just in gaming but also in an architectural fly-through, to show what a building will be like to walk through, or in data visualization. Gaming-style interfaces are also quite common, with first person views onto a 3-D world or with a 2-D view onto a world with the user controlling the view onto that world. These also often involve creating an environment that is reactive to user actions and independently active when the user is inactive to create the illusion of a world. Interactive installations or more playful and less task-oriented pieces will sometimes also involve inverted mediums, where one draws a sound, a sound creates an image, a physical object becomes a virtual one, or vice versa.

*Enabling collaboration between users*

The interactiveness of an art piece most certainly does not need to be driven by data or a virtual world; it can be driven by multiple participants in concert with one another. We can conceive of this in a very straightforward way, such as in a whiteboard collaborative application, or in an unpredictable and experimental way, where the input of one user is added to the input of the others in a way that can't easily be anticipated. As with many of these topics, a range exists of predictable and consonant works to unpredictable and dissonant works. Locative gaming where the game play is driven by the users' locations is another kind of interactive application that uses collaboration between users to drive the interaction. Many network-based applications also use the model of collaboration between users to drive the interaction. The system in these kinds of interactions tends to facilitate communication and ensure that messages from one user are received by another instead of generating messages and feedback for a user like a single-player game.

These applications can use chat-based metaphors or presence-based metaphors like some of the large multiplayer games that have become popular lately, or they can create a physical manifestation of each user. As long as the user has some indication of how many other users are interacting and how their actions are affecting the environment or those other users, the interaction can be very compelling.

*Controlling mechanics*

One of my favorite teachers, writers, and engineers, Tom Igoe, wrote, "Computers should take whatever physical form suits our needs for computing." It is very limiting to think of computing strictly in terms of the computer itself and the traditional interface to the computer, that is, the screen. In fact, interactive designs and artworks can be far more. With the Arduino, we can easily create computers that control machines out in the physical world. These machines can perform tasks as simple as turning lights on and off or as complex as the control of robotics. The machine can be controlled manually by a user or by many users, or it can be reactive, controlled by a program that dictates its responses in reaction to stimulus from users or viewers or from a physical environment.

The control of mechanics can be very task-oriented with rigidly defined effects for each user action, or it can be very playful as in a collaborative application. In the latter case, the controls that the user has can be very loosely defined; that is, the user may have to play with the installation to discover the action that the control performs. In the case of task-oriented controls, the labeling and structure of the controls should be very clearly delineated.

### Using tools for performance and as performance

An application can be used as a way of creating an aspect of performance, aiding a performance, or accentuating a performance. You can think of examples as simple as the modification of an electric guitar to projects as complex as completely new interfaces for musical development. An interactive application or tool is a means to a performance or interaction, driven by a performer or driven by the audience. Some of the most interesting uses of this mode of interaction involve sharing a control between the performer and the audience, though this does require some user training to ensure that the audience understands what they are supposed to be doing. These tools don't have to be as conceptually simple as creating a new tool for a performer to use on a stage. They can allow users to create new elements in a performance, control objects from remote locations, or create performers out of the audience.

### Creating environments

Many architects are beginning to explore what is called *reactive architecture*, the marriage of architectural practices with computing to create houses and environments that react to users, environmental factors, and external commands. The model of a feedback system is quite important to this model of interaction. The environment needs to monitor itself using sensors or timers to know when to change its state and when to maintain its state. At the simplest, a timer can be used to tell a house to turn the lights on and off, a temperature sensor can be used to maintain a certain temperature, a motion sensor can detect presence, or a humidity sensor can be used to control a dehumidifier. However, by using more complex sensors and systems, you can track movement in a space by using tags, cameras, microphones, or wireless radios, and have a system use that data to make changes in the environment to make it more comfortable, to make it louder, or to configure it correctly. Many architects and technologists are designing spaces and buildings that can be configured with a command by a user to change the way a space is used or to make the space itself more interactive. These sorts of spaces are often called *smart rooms* or *enabled architecture*, and they are an important area of research for both architects and engineers. Computing doesn't have to be limited to indoor spaces, though; outdoor spaces like parks, walking trails, squares, or streets can also be sites for interesting technological interventions that can be playful, helpful, or thought-provoking. It is important, though, to always consider the appropriateness of an application for the space in which it exists and how the user engages that interaction. In a public space, this becomes especially important since a user should have the decision of whether to interact with it.

*Telling a narrative or story*

One of the more interesting themes beginning to emerge in interactive design is the notion of using interaction to tell a story or narrative. These sorts of works typically rely on the interface to allow the user to control the flow or direction of the narrative using techniques cribbed from data visualization or gaming. Despite using concepts familiar from gaming and visualization, narratives offer a different set of challenges more familiar to filmmakers and authors than to engineering concerns.

# Working Process

The actual process of creating interactive work generally follows a combination of any of the following processes:

*Conception*

Conception can consist of sketches in a notebook, a daydream, a product or process of research or something developed in consultation with a client who wants the application for commercial purposes, or any combination of the three. You should try to map out in as much detail as possible what you would like the application to do, how the interaction should feel to the user, and the goals of the application. All projects will require research and planning of some kind. You shouldn't let this suffocate you or stifle your creativity, but you should include it. Starting to sketch without a clear plan of what you're doing can often lead to great and new ideas. For most people, I dare say that starting to write code without a clear plan of what they're doing usually doesn't produce something usable.

*Research*

When you've decided what you would like your application to look like and how you would like it to function, you'll need to do the research on what components you might need and what libraries or existing code might be available that can help you create your project. If you need hardware, you should determine your budget for your application and determine which components you'll need and how they fit into your budget. It's important to ask questions either on forums or of colleagues to ensure that the components or approaches you're considering will work. Most projects will require different technologies, but almost all the requisite pieces will be available, or you will be able to leverage existing projects that have been created by you or by another artist or developer. Twenty years ago, this may not have been true, but it is now.

*Design*

The design phase is one of the more amorphous because it blends so easily into the research, conception, and actual building of your project. Sometimes you may not have a design phase, and sometimes all you will have is a design phase, depending on the requirements and nature of what you are building. At the very least, you should define all the parts of your application clearly, have a clear vision of how they will appear to a user and how they will respond to a user, and understand exactly how a user's action should correlate to an action by the system. It may help to create diagrams that show the flow of actions and responses from the user to the system and back. It may also help to create diagrams of different parts of the system and show how those will appear to the user, what the user might want to do with them, and how they relate to the interaction overall. You might not want to plan everything in your application, but the more that you can plan, the easier the actual building of your application will be.

*Build*

This is the process of actually putting together hardware and writing code. This is where you'll write, debug, probably research some more, and ultimately assemble your application.

*Test*

Once you're finished building your application, it's important to test it. Testing can be as complex as creating situations for users to use your application and observing how they use it, or it can be as simple as using the application or hardware yourself and ensuring that everything works.

After testing, you might be ready to present your project by installing it or making it available for download. If your project is a piece of hardware, then you may be ready to prepare it for manufacture, if that's your aim, or to place it in the location and environment that you mean it to be used. You'll want to make sure that everything works as intended before sending a project off, so having a good testing phase is important.

Now that you've learned a little bit about what this book is about and the different ideas that you'll be exploring, you can start learning how to code.

# CHAPTER 2

# Programming Basics

Writing code is never extremely easy; however, it is also not as difficult as you might imagine. The basis of all programming is simple logic, and programming languages use lots of simple math symbols and English words. So, if you're comfortable with things like equals signs, some very basic algebra, and a smattering of English words, you'll probably do just fine. This chapter is by necessity far shorter than it could be. Learning all of the intricacies of writing code in even a single programming language, much less multiple languages, takes years of study. However, you can easily learn some of the basics, read documents, ask questions on user forums, and use what other people have created, and then find yourself able to create projects and designs within a short amount of time. With that in mind, this chapter is a simple introduction to the fundamentals that the rest of this book relies on.

There are a few types of readers using this book. The first says, "I just want it to work." For you, this chapter will explain just enough that you'll be able to follow along with the examples in this book and the ones that you find online, and be able modify them slightly to get them to do what you need them to do. You'll definitely want to read this chapter, probably more than once, but know that I understand your predicament. I was there once myself. You should know, though, that simply copying and pasting code with no understanding of what it's doing is a very easy way to become seriously frustrated. A general understanding of at least the basics of what your code is doing will go a long way. Another kind of reader says, "I want it to work, and I want to know why it works." For you, this chapter will be an introduction. You'll probably read it, read some examples, and come back to this chapter again later. That's a good thing. You'll probably also want other books soon. Some of the best are listed in Chapter 17. Another kind of reader may be familiar with some material covered in this book but not others. For you, this chapter will probably be a review and may not even be necessary, but you might want to flip through it just in case you're not familiar with the Processing or Arduino languages or some of basics of C++. If you are familiar with the basics of these languages, you might want to skip ahead to the chapters on the tools themselves or to Chapter 5 for some more advanced material on programming.

Whichever type you are, you should read enough to understand what the code listings in the rest of the book describe.

## Why You'll Read This Chapter More Than Once

In all likelihood, the first time you read this chapter, some of it will not make sense. That's perfectly normal and to be expected. As you read through the rest of this book, when you have questions, return to this chapter. There's no substitute for seeing how code functions within the context of something interesting to you. Some of the ideas might not make sense at first, but after seeing them put into practice, being patient, and hacking at them, you'll find that none of this is wildly complicated. Don't be afraid when you don't understand something, don't be afraid to look back at this chapter, and above all, don't be afraid to copy code from this book and change it until it breaks. Hacking at code, taking stuff that works, breaking it, and then figuring out why it breaks is the best way to understand. Of course, the goal throughout this book is to try to provide code that will just work and thereby satisfy the first kind of reader, those of you who simply want it to work and be done with it. In either event, though, this is going to require some patience, because it simply won't *make sense* the first time through. With a little bit of patience, though, and the willingness to experiment, fail, and try again, you'll find that this isn't all that difficult.

## The Nature of Code

Throughout this chapter, you'll be learning about programming—writing code, to be more exact—so it's important to know not only what code *is* but how it fits into the process of creating a program. There are a few key terms that you should understand before starting to program:

*Code*

> Code is a series of instructions that a computer will execute when the code is run. It is written in a programming language that, like natural languages, is essentially a contract between two parties. In the case of code, though, the two parties are the programmer and the compiler. You'll learn more about a compiler shortly; for the moment, we'll just think of it as the listener who understands our code. Code can be as simple as adding two numbers or as complex as rendering an animation. What matters is that you write correct instructions to the compiler using a programming language and a text editor of some sort and then tell the compiler what files contain the instructions. Writing code is typing code instructions into a text file that will later be passed to a compiler of some sort. To write a program can mean writing source code from scratch, or it can mean putting several programs together and creating a way for them to communicate. This can also mean configuring prebuilt projects. Creating applications and code doesn't always require

writing code, but if you have this book, then you're probably interested in creating code.

*Files*

Code is stored in text files that usually any text editor can open. These files contain your code and nothing else. For larger and more complex projects, you can link multiple files together. Sometimes, larger projects will have many hundreds of code files that will all be linked together to create the sum of the code for the application. Arduino projects use *.ino* files and sometimes *.c* files. Processing projects use *.pde* files and sometimes *.java* files. openFrameworks projects use *.cpp* and *.h* files. In each case, the different file types do different things and have different purposes that you'll learn more about later in this book.

*Compiler*

A compiler is a program that takes a code file (or many code files) and turns it (or them) into a series of instructions that a computer will run as a program. Most modern computers do not directly process any instructions that you write; instead, you ask a compiler to turn your code into machine instructions. The compiler optimizes machine instructions for the computer to run very quickly, but they would be very difficult for a person to write, so the better step is to write code in a more human-friendly way and convert it to machine-friendly instructions. This means that when you write code for an Arduino controller or write some Java code, you don't simply run that code; you compile it and have the compiler create an executable file that your computer can run. You can imagine the process of writing code as a series of translations in which you tell the compiler what you want to do with the program that it will create in a high-level programming language like Processing or C++ and the compiler then creates a machine language file that will run that file.

*Executable*

An executable is a file that can be run as an application. It is the result of writing code and compiling it. Sometimes the terms *application* and *executable* are used interchangeably, but they're not the same. An application may consist of many executable files, or it may consist of only one. In either case, for the kinds of projects you'll be learning to build in this book, you'll always have an executable.

Now you're ready to get started writing your own code.

# Variables

Looking at variables is a good place to start. Everyone remembers variables from their first algebra classes. You might have seen something like this written on a blackboard or whiteboard:

x = 5

That says, "There's something called *x*, and it is equal to the number 5." Variables in computing are very similar. They represent something, and in fact they always represent a certain kind of something. That's a little different than the algebra example because that example didn't need to say that x is going to be a number; it just says, "x is a number." If you wanted to use code to make a number called x and use it as a variable, you would do it like this:

```
int x;
```

The int indicates (or *sets*) the type of the variable. You can't just make any type of variable; you have to make specific kinds of variables. The kind of variable is called its *type*; types are dealt with a lot more in the next section, so for right now, let's concentrate on getting the basics of variables down:

```
int x = 5;
```

This code creates a variable named x that is an integer and has the value of 5. What this means is that somewhere in your computer's memory there is something called x that is storing the value 5. You can set the value of x right away, as in int x = 5, or create it and leave it for later use, as in int x. Look at another example:

```
int y = 10;
int x = 5;
int z = x + y;
```

This snippet shows some code that creates variables, gives two of them values, and sets a third variable's value to be the sum of the first two.

## Simple Types

In the platforms covered in this book, all variables are *typed*. This means that they have a type that tells the computer what sorts of things are going to be stored in the variable. This is because numbers, letters (usually called *characters*), and true/false (called *Boolean* values) all require different amounts of space to store and move around.

Here are some of the most common types that you'll encounter in each of the programming languages in this book.

### int

This is the datatype for integers, which are numbers without a decimal point, like 2 or 20,392. Now, we're about to run into our first real problem in this chapter: there are three programming languages used in this book; they all have similar things, but they sometimes work just a little bit differently. In Processing, integers can be as large as 2,147,483,647 and as low as -2,147,483,648. In Arduino and C++, the languages that openFrameworks (oF) uses, things work a little differently, and understanding why requires a quick explanation of signed and unsigned variables. The next small section explaining signed and unsigned variables might be a bit heavy at first, so you may want to skim over it the first time, particularly if you're more interested in working with Processing.

## Signed versus unsigned

As mentioned earlier, variables need to be declared with a type because the computer needs to know how much space they will take up. That means that sometimes an int is 4 bytes or 32 bits of information all the time and that it can store 4 bytes worth of information. So, what happens when you need a negative int? Well, you have to store whether it's negative or positive, and the way you do that is by moving all the values of the int down into the negative values. For the moment, you'll see how this works in C++, the language that oF uses, and then the rest of the languages will be addressed. In C++, where the int represents a value in between -2,147,483,647 to 2,147,483,647, if you have an int that is never going to use a negative number, you can use an unsigned int that stores anything from 0 to 4,294,967,295. This is what's called having *signed* or *unsigned* variables. Unsigned variables don't store negative numbers, whereas signed variables do. The way this works requires a little bit of thinking about binary numbers.

An int is 32 binary values. Binary counting uses 1 and 0 to count instead of 0 through 9 like we're used to doing. This means that when you want to set a variable to 1, you'll actually be storing the value 1 in the place where the variable is stored. When you want to store the value 2, you'll be storing 10, which means 1 in the 2's place and nothing in the 1's place. Additionally, 3 is represented as 11, which means 1 in the 2's place and 1 in the 1's place, for 2+1, which is 3. Further, 4 is represented as 100, which is 1 in the 4's place and nothing in the 2's or 1's place. Therefore, 16 is 1,000, 17 is 1,001, 18 is 1,010, and so on. This is called *two's complement math* because it counts everything up by squaring for the next value. That's a very quick introduction to binary math, but don't worry, there's a much more comprehensive discussion of this several chapters later in this book where you begin using bits and binary.

Figure 2-1 shows the ways that signed and unsigned variables work. Remember that in C++ the int is 32 bits, so there will be 32 boxes to show what each bit stores.

In unsigned numbers, the first bit is counted like any other bit. In signed numbers, the first bit is used to store whether the number is positive or not, and this is why unsigned variables can store larger values than signed variables.

Arduino and C++ use unsigned variables, and all variables are signed unless you indicate otherwise by putting `unsigned` in front of the variable type:

```
unsigned int = 5;
```

Processing does not use unsigned variables; all numerical variables in Processing are signed.

In C++, the language you'll use with oF, signed ints are –2,147,483,647 to 2,147,483,647, and unsigned ints are between 0 and 4,294,967,295. In Arduino, the int can be between –32,768 to 32,767. Tricky? Not really. Lots of times you won't have

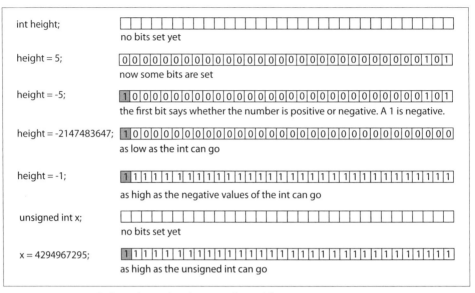

| int height; | no bits set yet |
| height = 5; | now some bits are set |
| height = -5; | the first bit says whether the number is positive or negative. A 1 is negative. |
| height = -2147483647; | as low as the int can go |
| height = -1; | as high as the negative values of the int can go |
| unsigned int x; | no bits set yet |
| x = 4294967295; | as high as the unsigned int can go |

*Figure 2-1. Setting the bits of signed and unsigned variables*

to think about what you're storing in the int. When you do have to think about how large the value you're going to be storing is, it's time to use a bigger number type, like long or double. We'll discuss these later in this section. When using Processing, you never have to think about how large the value will be at all, so it isn't a problem. Simply figure out whether you'll need a decimal point. If you do, then use a float; if you don't, then use an int.

### float

The *float* is the datatype for floating-point numbers, which are numbers that have a decimal point. Floating-point numbers are often used to approximate analog and continuous values because they have a greater range of values than integers. Signed float variables can be as large as 2,147,483,647 and as low as –2,147,483,647. Float variables aren't signed in C++ or Arduino.

### char

This type can contain characters, that is, single letters or typographic symbols such as A, d, and $. Here are two char variable declarations:

```
char firstLetter = 'a';
char secondLetter = 'b';
```

So, what is different about floats, ints, and chars? char variables can sometimes be added together like numbers, but it's not going to work the way you think it will. When working with Processing or Arduino, it's not going to work period, and with C++ in openFrameworks it will work, but not as you might expect:

```
char thirdLetter = 'a' + 'b'; // this won't become 'ab' or 'c'
```

Like I mentioned earlier, Processing and Arduino aren't going to like this at all. They're just going to throw errors at you and complain. C++, however, will work, and the next section will explain why.

# ASCII

There are a few ways that characters in a computer are stored, and one way is as numbers in a system called American Standard Code for Information Interchange, or ASCII. In ASCII, a is 97, and b is 98. That's why if you run the following snippet of code through a C++ compiler or through Processing or Arduino, it'll happily say that c is 195:

```
char a = 'a';
char b = 'b';
int  c = a+b; // notice that a+b is being stored as an int
```

You can store the result of two characters being added together *if you store the value of the result as an int* because adding the characters together is really adding the numbers that they are stored as together.

All keyboard-related things can be stored as a char. That includes particular keys on the keyboard. These are called *character escapes*, and they have a particularly special place in programming because this is how you determine when the user has clicked a key that can't be represented with a letter or number. There are other encoding systems that correlate numbers to letters, Unicode Transformation Format, or UTF, is a very popular one that you might hear mentioned. Encoding is a complex topic and the most important thing to understand is that the char is both a number and character.

## bool or boolean

*Boolean* values store two possible values: true and false. In C++ and Arduino, the true is actually a 1, and the false is actually a 0. It's usually clearer to use true and false, but you can use 1 and 0 if you like. They're very handy for storing very simple results: you received a message from the server or you didn't, the user clicked the F key or they didn't.

For Arduino and Processing, you do the following:

```
boolean b = true;
```

In C++, you do this:

```
bool  b = true;
```

Note that the Processing and Arduino version uses the word boolean, while C++ uses the word bool.

Both true and false are reserved words. That means that the compiler only recognizes them as being values that you can use to set Boolean variables. This means that you can't, for example, do this:

```
boolean true = false;
```

It will cause errors, which is something that, although unavoidable, you generally want to restrict to more interesting things that will help you create your projects.

### string

A *string* is a sequence of characters. This is both a helpful, metaphorical way to think about it and a matter of fact, and it is something that you'll investigate more closely later. The string includes helpful methods for looking at individual characters, comparing strings to see whether they're the same or different, searching strings for parts of the string (for example, finding "toast" in "toaster"), and extracting parts of strings (getting "toast" out of "toaster"). The differences between a string and a char is that a string is always defined inside double quotes ("Abc") and can consist of multiple characters, while char variables are defined inside single quotes ('A') and can consist of only one character.

Here are some strings in Processing:

```
String f = "foo";
String b = "bar";
String fb = f+b;// this will be "foobar"
```

Here are some strings in C++:

```
string f = "foo";
string b = "bar";
string foobar = f+" "+b;// this will be "foo bar" note the space w/in quotes
```

Note that Processing uses `String`, while C++ uses `string`. Why isn't there any Arduino example? Arduino doesn't have a `String` or a `string`, because it doesn't need one. We'll have to leave the explanation for this until the next section. Suffice to say, it's not a huge problem.

Since a String is defined within quotes:

```
String super = "super";
```

including quotes in a String requires the backslash character to be used preceding the quote:

```
String quoted = "He said \"It's super\"."
```

This is known as an *escape sequence*. Other escape sequences include t for the tab character, which is written \t with the escape character, and n for newline, which is written \n. A single backslash is indicated by \\ because without the \ in front, the compiler would think that you're writing an escape sequence. If you wanted to write the characters \that's great!, you'd write this:

```
String quoted = "\\that's great!";
```

Otherwise, without the double backslash, you'd end up with this:

```
"    hat's great!"
```

The compiler would assume that the \t is a tab.

## byte

The *byte* is the datatype for bytes, that is, 8 bits of information storing numerical values. In Processing, the byte stores values from –128 to 127 (a signed value), and in the Arduino it stores from 0 to 255 (an unsigned value). Bytes are a convenient datatype for sending information that can't or shouldn't be represented by strings or other kinds of numbers such as the contents of a file, data sent to or from hardware, data about the pixel of an image, or a millisecond of sound.

Here are bytes in Processing and Arduino:

```
byte firstByte = 55;
byte newByte = 10+firstByte;
```

Now, the byte newByte is just a value waiting to have something done with it. If you were to treat newByte like a char, it would be A; and if you treat it like an int, it would be 65. Because bytes are so lightweight, they often are used to represent data that needs to be read or written, or sent quickly, or as data that doesn't have an easy representation in other formats.

C++ does not have a byte type. Where you would use a byte in Processing or Arduino, you use a char in C++. Why is this? Remember that the char is an ASCII number value, that is, a number between either –128 and 127 (or 0 and 255 if the variable is an unsigned char) that represents a letter or character. The designers of C++, taking a cue from the C programming language that preceded it, recognized that this value could be used not only for characters, but for anything. In C++ you use the char more frequently than in Processing or Arduino.

## long

The long variable allows you to store very large non-floating point numbers, like an int. In C++ and Arduino, the long can store values from –2,147,483,648 to 2,147,483,647. In Processing, the maximum value is considerably larger: 18,446,744,073,709,551,615.

# Arrays

The array is a slightly more complex datatype than the ones that were shown earlier. An *array* contains one or more variables in a list. Remember one of the problems that you're going to run into in this book is that there are three different programming platforms used in this book, each of which does things slightly differently. We'll look at three different arrays filled with integers in each of our platforms to give you a feel for the similarities and differences.

The array is a list of multiple elements; in the code snippet below, it will contain integers. You're going to create an array that holds three int values: 1, 2, 3. It's nothing too thrilling, but it's a good place to start.

Note the markers above each of the elements in the array in Figure 2-2: numbers[0], numbers[1], numbers[2]. These are the array access operators. That's not a typo; they do count up from 0. We'll come back to these after we look at creating the array.

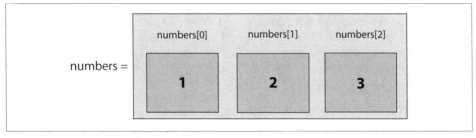

*Figure 2-2. An array with three integers*

Here's what the array looks like in Processing:

```
int[] numbers = new int[3];
numbers[0] = 1;
numbers[1] = 2;
numbers[2] = 3;
```

First, look at the declaration of the array, as shown in Figure 2-3.

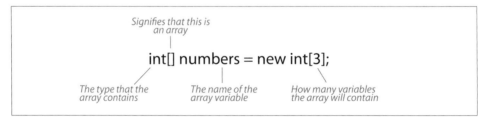

*Figure 2-3. An array containing three integers as declared in Processing*

You can declare arrays to be filled with any type, even types that you create yourself. We'll get to this later. The code snippet sets all the values of the array. When you want to access an element in the array, you use the access operators [] to access the index position in the array that is specified within the square brackets:

```
int x = numbers[0];
```

The previous sets x to 1, because the first item in our numbers array is 1:

```
int y = numbers[1] + numbers[2];
```

The previous sets y to the values of the second plus the third elements of numbers, that is, 2 + 3, which equals 5. If you use the = operator in front of the array with the access operator, it sets the value of the element in the array at that point:

```
numbers[0] = 1;
numbers[0] = 5;
```

Whereas `numbers[0]` originally was 1, it is now 5. The array is really storage, and each element in the array is like a box that can store any variable of the type declared when the array is created. When any item within the array is set, it will store that value until it is changed.

Instead of putting each number into the array on a separate line of code, the array values can be created all at once:

```
int arr[] = {1, 2, 3};
```

or:

```
int arr[3] = {1, 2, 3};
```

Note that the array does not need to have a number length assigned to it. This results in the same array as creating the array in the first example; however, it assumes that you know all the values that will go into the array. If you do not, use the first method described.

The next language to look at is the declaration of an array in Arduino. Luckily for the sake of brevity, the Arduino platform deals with arrays very similarly to Processing. Creating an array in Arduino or C++ can be done in any one of the three following ways.

Here's what the array looks like in Arduino or C++:

```
int arr[] = {1, 2, 3};
```

or:

```
int arr[3];
```

or:

```
int array[3] = {1, 2, 3};
```

Figure 2-4 breaks down the parts in the array.

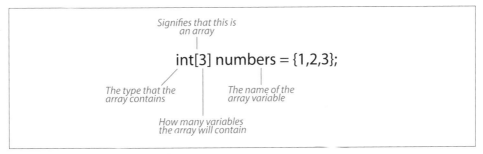

*Figure 2-4. Creating an array in C++*

The only difference between the array in Processing and in Arduino is that while Processing supports the `new` keyword when creating an array, Arduino does not. If you know all the elements when you're creating the array, do it like so:

```
int array[3] = {1, 2, 3};
```

Otherwise, you should construct an array like this:

```
int[] arr = new int[3];
```

Now that we've covered the basics of arrays, you'll look at some of the more complex aspects of dealing with the array. The first is the error that you're sure to encounter at some point, specifically, the "out of bounds access" error in all its many forms. What this means is that you've tried to access an element in the array that does not exist.

In Arduino and C++, arrays can be initialized as shown here:

```
char arr[3] = {'a', 'b', 'c'};
char badArrayAccess = arr[3];
```

When you try to do something with the badArrayAccess variable, you'll find that not only is it not a char but that accessing it will probably crash your program. The array arr contains three char variables, and you're trying to access a fourth one, which violates the number of elements established when declaring the array. Another mistake is trying to store the wrong kinds of variables in the array, as shown here:

```
char arr[3]; // an array of chars, with space for 3 variables
float f = 2.3;
arr[0] = f; // oops! arr expects chars, so will turn f into "2"
bool b = true;
arr[1] = b; // oops! arr expects chars, so will convert b into "1"
```

This won't cause an error; however, it won't return the variables correctly, because the array declared is expecting char variables, so when you place float and bool variables within that array, it automatically converts them to char, with frequently unpredictable results. Table 2-1 is a quick comparison of the datatypes and how the three languages use them.

*Table 2-1. Comparison of datatypes*

| Arduino | Processing | C++ | Use |
|---|---|---|---|
| int | int | int | A number without a decimal point, for example: 4 or −12 |
| float | float | float | A number with a decimal point, for example: 1.23 or −128.12 |
| char | char | char | A single character or number that will be treated as a character, for example: a, 1, ! |
| None (use char[] instead) | String | string | A grouping of characters together, for example: hello, 172 Cherry Street |
| byte | byte | None (use char instead) | The value of a byte, between −128 and 127 if the byte is signed and 0 and 255 if it is not signed |
| boolean | boolean | bool | A true or false value |
| double (but same as float) | double | double | A floating-point number with higher precision than float |

## Casting

What do you do if you have a number that is an integer but you need it to be a float? You *cast* it. This means that you convert it from its original type into a new type.

Here's what casting looks like in Processing, Arduino, and C++:

```
int i = 5;
float f = (float)i; // float is now 5.0
```

Why can't you simply set f to i?

```
float f = i;
```

Types won't allow you to do that, because that's the point of a type. You know what specific type values are, how much memory they require, and how they can be used. The previous code will cause an error if you try to run it. Instead, cast the variable. You can't change the type of a variable once it's declared. In this example, i will always be an int, but if you need to use it as a float, you can very easily cast it. Some other examples of casting involving char variables because they are such a fundamental datatype. For instance, if you want to cast a char to a float and then back, you do the following:

```
char ch = 'f';
int fAsInt = (int)ch;// now fAsInt is 102
char newChar = char(fAsInt); // newChar is now 'f'
```

One important thing to note is that you cannot cast an array:

```
char[] foo = {'a', 'b', 'c', 'd'};
int[](foo); // ERROR
```

To cast anything in an array, you need to cast every element of the array. We'll cover this in greater detail in the sections on loops, but for now, we'll look at this:

```
char[] foo = {'a', 'b', 'c', 'd'};
int i = int(foo[0]);
```

Here you create an array of char variables and then read one of those char values out of the array and cast it as an int.

## Operators

*Operators* are the symbols that a compiler uses to perform commands and calculations in your program. Operators let you set variables like the = operator, compare variables like the == operator, add variables like the + operator, and so on. There are three major types of operators. The first operators are the mathematical operators that perform mathematical operations. These should be familiar from any math class you've ever taken. The second are assignment operators that change values. The third are comparison operators, which determine whether two variables are equal, different, greater than, or less than another variable.

Mathematical operators work pretty much as expected, with one notable exception. + adds two values, for example:

```
int apples = 5
int moreApples = apples + 3; // moreApples is equal to 8.
```

The exception occurs when you add strings; you end up with the two strings stuck together:

```
string first = "John";
string second = "Brown";
string full = first+second; // now full is JohnBrown
```

This is because of something called *operator overloading*. If you're curious enough, you can check some of the recommended programming books from Chapter 17 for a full description, or look online because it's a more advanced topic that we're not going to have a chance to cover in this book.

The other simple mathematical operators are - (subtraction), * (multiplication), and / (division). The last mathematical operator is %, the modulo.

The modulo tells you what is left over (the *remainder*) when the value on the left is divided by the value on the right. Here are some examples:

```
8 % 2 // equals 0 since there's no remainder when 8 is divided by 2
17 % 2 // equals 1 since there's a remainder of 1 when 17 is divided by 2
19 % 5 // equals 4 since the remainder is 4 when 19 is divided by 5
12 % 11 // equals 1 since the a remainder of 1 when 12 is divided by 11
19.0 % 5 // equals 4.0 since we're dealing with floats
```

Assignment operators work from right to left. That is, the operator uses the value on the right to assign or change the variable on the left. For example:

```
int age = 6;
```

The = operator sets the variable on the left to 6. There are other types of assignment operators that change the value of the variable on the left, just like the = operator. For instance:

+=

Adds the value on the right to the value on the left:

```
int height = 6;
height += 1; // height is now 7
height += 10; // height is now 17
```

-=

Subtracts the value on the right from the variable on the left:

```
int size = 16;
size -= 8; // height is now 8
size -= 6; // height is now 2
```

++ *and* --

Add one or subtract one from the variable on the left:

---

```
int hearts = 2;
hearts++; // hearts is now 3
hearts--; // hearts is now 2 again
hearts--; // hearts is now 1
```

*= or /=

These work roughly the same as the += and -= statements, multiplying or dividing the variable on the left by the value on the right:

```
int i = 15;
i /= 3; // i is now 5
int j = 20;
j /= 2; // j is now 10
float k = 100.0;
k /= 3.333333; // k is now 30.000004
float m = 100.0;
m /= '2'; // not a good idea
i *= 4; // i is now 20
m *= 0.5; // m was 2.0 and is now 1.0
```

Comparisons are very important in programming and particularly important in using control statements, which will be discussed in the next section. Before we get to that, though, you need to become familiar with the various operators. These operators are common across all the programming languages discussed in this book and, with slight variations, across all programming languages. Comparisons allow you to determine whether variables are the same, different, greater than, or less than one another:

== (equal to)

Compares whether two things are equal. For example:

```
5 == 4 // false
'a' == 'a' // true
(12 / 3) == (2 * 2); // true
4.1 == 4 // false
char(102) == int('f') // true, because 102 is 'f' in ASCII
"duck" == 0.002 // false, because it doesn't make any sense
```

!= (not equal to)

Checks whether things are not equal, for example:

```
3 != 1 //true, they're not equal
'B' != 'b' // also true, they're not equal
```

> (greater than)

Checks whether the value on the left is *greater* than the value on the right, just like in math class:

```
4 > 3 // true
5 > 192901.2 //false
"fudge" > 8 // false, because it doesn't make any sense
```

< (less than)

Checks whether the value on the left is *smaller* than the value on the right, again, just like in math class:

```
3 < 2 // false
'g' < 106 // since 'g' is 103 in ASCII this is true
-100 < 100 // true
```

>= (greater than or equal to)

Checks whether the value on the left is *greater than or equal to* the value on the right, just like in math class:

```
3 >= 3 // true, since they're equal
0 >= -0.001 // since 0 is greater than -0.001, this is true
'?' >= 'h' // false, since '?' is 63 in ASCII and 'h' is 104
4 >= 28 // false
"happy" >= "sad" // false, because it doesn't make any sense
```

<= (less than or equal to)

Checks whether the value on the left is *smaller than or equal to* the value on the right, again, just like in math class:

```
13.001 <= 13.001 // true, since they're equal
0 <= -0.001 // since 0 is greater than -0.001, this is false
'!' <= '7' // true, since '!' is 33 in ASCII and '7' is 55
```

&&

Evaluates the statement on the left and the statements on the right and returns true if they are *both true*:

```
(4 > 3) && ('f' > '1') // true
((5 * 2) == 10) && ((6 - 3) != 4) // true
(5 < 10) && (2 > 4) // false, even though the left is true, the right isn't
```

||

Evaluates the statement on the left and the statements on the right and returns true if *either one of them is true*:

```
(4 < 3) || ('f' > 'e') // true, left isn't true but the right is
((5 * 2) == 10) || ((6 - 3) != 4) // both are true
('b'=='g') || (2 > 4) // false, none of them are true
```

You may be wondering what to do with all these evaluations and comparisons. The answer is control statements. Table 2-2 lists operators and their uses.

*Table 2-2. Operators and their uses*

| Operator | Use |
| --- | --- |
| +, -, *, / | Adds, subtracts, multiplies, and divides. |
| % | Modulo; returns the remainder of a division. |
| = | Assignment; assigns the value on the right to the variable on the left. |
| +=, -=, *=, / = | Mathematical assignment; adds, subtracts, multiples, or divides the value on the left by the value on the right and sets the value on the right to that result. |
| ++ | Adds 1 to the value to the left. |
| -- | Subtracts 1 from the value to the left. |

| Operator | Use |
| --- | --- |
| == | Compares the value on the left with the value on the right. If they are equal, then the expression is `true`. |
| != | Compares the value on the left with the value on the right. If they are not equal, then the expression is `true`. |
| >, >= | Compares the value on the left with the value on the right. If the value on the left is greater than or greater than or equal to the value on the left, the expression is `true`. |
| <, <= | Compares the value on the left with the value on the right. If the value on the left is less than or greater than or equal to the value on the left, the expression is `true`. |
| && | Checks the truth of the expression to the left of the operator and to the right; if both are true, the entire expression is `true`. |
| \|\| | Checks the expression to the left of the operator and to the right of the operator; if either is true, the entire expression is `true`. |

# Control Statements

You'll often want to control how the logic of your program flows. If one thing is `true`, then you'll want to do something different if it's `false`. You might also want to do something a certain number of times or until something becomes `false`. There are two kinds of control statements that you can use to create this kind of logic flow in your application: *conditional logic* statements, which check whether something is `true` or `false`, and *loop* statements, which do something a set number of times or until something becomes `false`.

## if/then

The `if/then` is a conditional logic statement, and it works just like it does in English: "If it's raining, then I'll bring an umbrella." These statements look like this:

```
if(condition) {
    result if the condition is true
} else {
    result if the condition is false
}
```

There must be a `true`/`false` expression in the brackets next to the `if`. Here's an example:

```
int myWeight = 72;

if(myWeight > 100) {
    print(" you're getting heavy! ");
} else {
    print(" you're still doing ok ");
}
```

You can also use the `if` statement without an `else`:

```
int myHeight = 181;

if(myHeight > 200) {
```

```
        print(" you're too tall ");
    }
```

This just means that the actions inside the brackets will execute if the statement is true; otherwise, you don't do anything. You can also check that things are not true:

```
boolean allDone = false;

if(!allDone) { // if not all done
    print(" keep going! ");
} else {
    print(" ok, quit! ");
}
```

There is one last permutation on this pattern:

```
if(age == 5){
    print(" you're 5!");
} else if(age == 25) {
    print(" you're 25!");
} else {
    print(" can't login "); // if neither of the above is true
}
```

In this example, there is a new term introduced: else if. What this does is evaluate another statement before going on to the else statement. This means that if the first statement doesn't evaluate to true, then check each else if looking for the first one that is true. If none is true, then do the else statement.

## for Loop

The for statement lets us do things over and over again, for a specified number of repetitions. Loops are frequently used to loop through arrays and examine, use, or alter each element within them. This is going to be particularly useful when dealing with the pixels in images or frames of video, as well as sounds, data from the Internet, and many other kinds of information that needs to be sorted through:

```
int i;
for(i = 0; i < 10; i++) {
    print(char(i)+", "); // this will print 0, 1, 2, 3, 4, 5, 6, 7, 8, 9,
}
```

The for statement uses three different statements, as shown in Figure 2-5.

The integer i is used to set the number of times that the loop will execute, running all the code inside the code block. In the initialization of the for loop, you set i to 0; as long as i is less than 10, you continue looping, and each time the for loop is passed, i is incremented by 1.

Of course, it is also entirely possible to use subtraction in the for loop:

```
for(int i = 5; i>-1; i--){
    print(i);
}
```

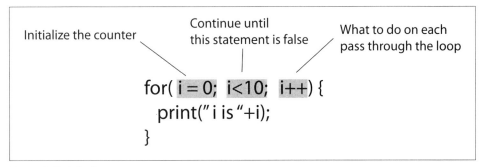

*Figure 2-5. A for loop*

Another great use of the `for` loop is to go through an array and look at each item in the array:

```
int[] intArr = {0, 1, 2, 3, 4, 5};
int sum = 0;
for(int j = 0; j < 6; j++){
    sum += intArr[j]; // we'll get the item in the array using the loop
}
```

Each time the loop executes, `sum` will be incremented using the next integer in the `intArr` array.

## while Loop

The `while` loop is similar to the `for` loop, but it is slightly less sophisticated:

```
while(trueOrFalse){
//something to do each time
}
```

As long as the expression that the `while` is evaluating each time through remains `true`, the loop will continue executing. This is important to note because if the evaluated variable does not become `false`, the loop will never exit, and your program could become locked up while the loop runs. Creating an *infinite loop*—that is, a loop that never exits—is easy and will certainly make your program unusable, so take care when using any of the control statements. Here's an example using a counter, much like in the `for` loop:

```
int j = 0;

while(j < 100) {
    print(" what's up? "+j);
    j++; // if j is not incremented we end up with an infinite loop
}
```

Each time the loop executes, the integer `j` is incremented. When `j` is no longer less than 100, the loop is exited, and the program continues on:

```
boolean ready = false;
float number = 0.0;
```

```
while(ready != true) {
    print(" we're just waiting" );
    number += 0.1;
    if(number > 1.0){
        ready = true;
    }
}
print(" we're ready ");
```

In this example, you increment a number and use a second variable, a Boolean value, to determine whether you are in fact ready. Until the **ready** variable is **true**, the loop will continue executing, and the "we're ready" message will not be printed.

## continue

The **continue** statement tells a loop to skip over any further instructions and go on to the next repetition. For instance, if you wanted to loop through a certain number of items and process only odd numbers, you could do this:

```
for(int i = 0; i< 10; i++) {
    if( i % 2 == 0){
        continue;
    }
    println(i + " is not divisible by 2");
}
```

This will print the following:

```
1 is not divisible by 2
3 is not divisible by 2
5 is not divisible by 2
7 is not divisible by 2
9 is not divisible by 2
```

The **continue** statement here starts the loop over again. If you have a complicated operation to perform, then using the **continue** statement allows you to evaluate whether you need to run that operation and to skip it if you do not. This means your code does only what is necessary.

## break

The **break** statement breaks the loop. It is a great tool to use when you're looping through an array looking for something and suddenly you find it. Once you've found it, you can quit looping easily by using the **break** statement:

```
int[] intArr = {1, 2, 3, 4, 5, 6, 2, 12, 2, 1, 19, 123, 1, 3, 13};
int counter = 0;

while(counter < intArr.length)
{
    if(intArr[counter] == 5) { // we're looking for 5
        print(" found it at ");
```

```
        break;
    }
    counter++;
}
// code will continue from here after the break
print(counter); // found the value 5 in intArr[4]
```

# Functions

What is a function?

A *function* is a name for a grouping of one or more lines of code and is somewhat like a variable in that it has a type and a name. It's very much unlike a variable in that it doesn't just store information; it manipulates it. Going back to the basic algebra analogy you saw earlier when first looking at variables, a variable is something like this:

x

A function is something more like an instruction with something that is given at the beginning of the instruction and something that is expected in return. Writing out a function in simple English, you might see something like this: "When someone gives you some money, add the amount given to you to the amount that you already have and report that number back to me."

There are a few parts there that can be broken out:

- An amount of money that you are given
- Adding the amount given to you to the amount that you already have
- Reporting that number

Those three things can be thought of in order, as follows: what the function takes or what will be passed in to it, what it does, and what it returns. Functions are set patterns of behavior in your program that take certain kinds of values, do something with those values, and return something when they are finished.

## Defining a Function

To turn the written example into code, you would define a variable to be used to keep track of all the money that you have:

```
int myBank = 0;
```

Then you create a function that takes money, adds it to myBank, and returns that value:

```
int moneyReceived(int money){
  myBank += money;
  return myBank;
}
```

Now, you have defined a function called moneyReceived(). Using pseudocode or talking though what a function is supposed to do can be quite helpful when trying to understand it. "Take an integer, add it to the money already in the bank, and return that value." Figure 2-6 is a diagram that helps walk you through what the function is supposed to do.

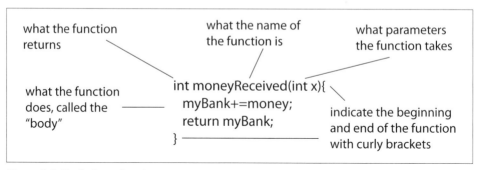

Figure 2-6. Declaring a function

Notice that the return statement is returning something that is of the same type as the type listed in front of the function name. The variable myBank is an int that the moneyReceived() function returns.

## Passing Parameters to a Function

Once the function is defined, it's time to call it. To call the function, you need to pass the correct kinds of parameters to it, which requires knowing what parameters the function requires. In the moneyReceived() function example, the required parameter is a single integer. Both of the following examples are legal:

```
moneyReceived(4);
```

or:

```
int priceOfDinner = 17;
moneyReceived(priceOfDinner);
```

This next one is not legal:

```
float f = 1.32;
moneyReceived(f);
```

because the variable being passed to the function is not the correct type. This is why being able to see the function declaration, that is, where its return type, name, and parameters are established, is so important.

The return statement indicates the type of value that the method will return, just as a type for a variable determines what kind of value the variable will store. Functions that don't return anything are declared void, and any other kind of return value needs to be declared. For example, if you created a function that would return a char, you would declare it like so:

```
char myFunction()
```

Note that the function always has the following pattern: type, function name, parentheses, and any parameters that need to be passed to the function:

```
int multiplyByTwo(int value){
    return value * 2;
}
```

This previous function takes an integer value, multiplies that value by 2, and then returns whatever that value is. When a function has a return type, it can be used to set the values of variables:

```
int x = 5;
int twoTimesX = multiplyByTwo(x); // twoTimesX is now 10
```

Here, you use a function to return a char based on the value passed into the function:

```
char convertIntToChar(int i){
    char ch = char(i);
    return ch;
}
```

New variables can be set using the values returned from a function:

```
string addExclamationPoints(string s) {
    return s+"!!!";
}
string myStr = addExclamationPoints("hello"); // myStr will be 'hello!!!'
```

That's a bit tricky to see what's going on at first, but you simply have to understand that the function is going to become equal to a string when it's all done with its operations, which means that you can treat it like a string. Your program will take care of making sure that everything within the function will be run before it gets used to set the value of the variable.

That's why having functions typed is so important. Anything typed as an integer can be used to create a new integer:

```
int squareOfEight = square(8);
```

This will work if the square() function looks like this:

```
int square(int val) {
    return val*val;
}
```

Since square() returns an int, you can use it set an int. If it returned a float or another datatype, it wouldn't work, which makes reading and understanding the return types of functions so important.

## Some Suggestions on Writing Functions

Name them well. Functions should do what their names indicate. A function called square is very well named if it takes an int or float as a parameter and returns the square of that value. It's not so well named if it doesn't do that. Generally, thinking of functions as verbs is a good way to go because it makes you think about what that thing should do in the first place and helps you remember what you meant it to do later when you have to look back at it.

Make them no smaller than sensible and no larger than necessary. A function of 200 to 300 lines of code should probably be broken down into smaller functions. This helps you reuse different parts of the code in different places, where necessary, and helps you locate problems more quickly when they occur. Being able to isolate a problem to several lines of code instead of several hundred can save you hours.

When you find yourself needing to do the same tasks repeatedly, put the code into a function and call that function. For instance, if you are frequently resizing images and saving them to a folder somewhere online, you could make a function like this:

```
resizeAndSave(int picHeight, int picWidth, String urlToSave)
```

This cleans up your code, saves you typing, and makes debugging problems easier. The less stuff you have to look at, the more quickly you'll be able to find things, locate problems, and remember where you left off in a piece of code.

## Overloading Functions

Function declarations are important for two reasons. First, the function declaration tells you what parameters to pass to the function and what kinds of things you can do with any values returned from a function. Second, the function declaration and the parameters that the function takes are unique for the function that the compiler uses. A function that accepts two strings is considered different from a function that accepts three strings, *even if those functions have the same name*. Making multiple functions with the same name that accept different parameters allows you to use the same functionality to handle different situations. This is called *overloading* a function, allowing it to accept multiple sets of parameters.

Think of a verb like "draw." It's easy for us to differentiate between "drawing a picture" and "drawing a card" because of the context. The compiler treats functions that same way, which makes it easier for us to name functions with the same functionality by the same name and rely on the compiler to differentiate between them using the context of the kinds of parameters passed. Sizes for a video could be set using int values or float values, for example. The compiler considers each of these functions to be completely separate, even if they have the same name. When the function is called, if float values are passed, then the function of that name that accepts floats is used.

Here is an example of an overloaded function in Processing:

```
char multiplyByTwo(char value){

    return char(int(value) * 2);
}

String multiplyByTwo(String value) {
```

```
    return value+value;
}

int multiplyByTwo(int value){

    return value * 2;
}

int[] multiplyByTwo(int value[]){
    for(int i = 0; i<value.length; i++) {
        value[i] *= 2;
    }
    return value;
}
```

This function accepts an int, a String, a char, and an array of ints (int[]). The version of the function that will be called is dependent on what is passed to it.

Here it is in Processing:

```
println(multiplyByTwo('z'));// this will print ô
println(multiplyByTwo(5)); // this will print 10
println(multiplyByTwo("string"));// this will print stringstring
int[] foo = {1, 2, 3, 4};
println(multiplyByTwo(foo));//this will print 2, 4, 6, 8
```

 Overloading functions is a great tool because it allows you to make a single way to do something and modify it slightly to take different kinds of variables as parameters. One thing to note is that although having different types of parameters, as shown here, is fine:

```
int function(int i) {
}

int function(float f) {
}

int function(char c) {
}
```

having different return types does not always work:

```
int function(int i) {
}

float function(float f) {
}

char function(char c) {
}
```

This will throw an error in Arduino and C++ but not in Processing. Generally, it's not the best idea, but it's your code, your project, and your call.

# Objects and Properties

So, what's an object? An *object* is a grouping of multiple properties into a single thing that represents all those different properties. That sounds wretchedly abstract, but it's actually quite simple: think of a chair. A chair has a height, a weight, and a number of legs. So, those are three different properties of a thing called a chair. If you were to think about how you'd represent that in code, you'd probably say something like this:

```
Chair myChair;
myChair.height = 22;
```

See the dot (.) after the name of the Chair instance but before the property? That's the *dot operator*, and in a lot of the most popular programming languages today it's the way that you access the properties of an object to use or set them. Let's look more at what to do with the chair:

```
myChair.legs = 4;
myChair.weight = 5;
```

So, now you've made a chair called myChair that has some different properties: legs, weight, and height. Well, that's not particularly useful. Let's think of something that might be a little bit more useful to you. The following code snippets will all be using Processing:

```
PImage img = loadImage("mypicture.jpg");
image(img, 20, 10);
img.x = 300; // set the x position of the image
img.y = 300; // set the y position of the image
```

The previous code might be a little mysterious at first, but let's look at the parts that you can make sense of right away. PImage is an object in Processing that lets you load and display image files, resize them, and manipulate their pixels. The explanation of all that needs to wait until the next chapter, which focuses on the Processing language. For the moment, you want to focus on these two lines:

```
img.x = 300; // set the x position of the image
img.y = 300; // set the y position of the image
```

What you know after looking at these lines is that the PImage has an x property and a y property. So, when you create a PImage object, like our img object created in the previous code snippet, you can get or set those properties. That means that you can tell the object where the image should be, or you can find out where the image is. It all depends on which side of the equals sign you're placing the image on:

```
int xPosition = img.x; // get the image x position
img.x = 400; // set the image x position
```

Now, let's look at another thing that an image can do, which is copy all of its pixels and return them to be used by another image. The PImage does this by using the copy function. Let's take a look at calling that function:

```
img.copy();
```

Notice the **.** operator there again? Just like the properties, the **.** operator is how you call functions as well. You might think that's confusing, but it's actually sort of helpful. The **.** indicates that you're using something within that object. So, the `PImage copy` function is another property of the `PImage`, just one that happens to be a function.

Methods versus functions: usually functions that are part of something like the `PImage`—for instance, copy—are called *methods*. The difference between them is mostly semantic and isn't something you should worry about. Just remember that if you see the term *method*, it's referring to a function that belongs to an object like `PImage`.

Now, if you happen to look at the documentation for the **copy** function on the Processing website, you'll see something that looks like Figure 2-7.

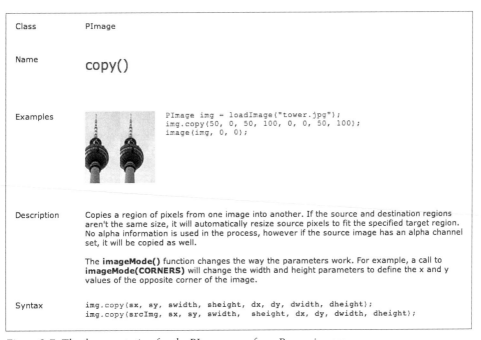

| | |
|---|---|
| Class | PImage |
| Name | **copy()** |
| Examples | `PImage img = loadImage("tower.jpg");`<br>`img.copy(50, 0, 50, 100, 0, 0, 50, 100);`<br>`image(img, 0, 0);` |
| Description | Copies a region of pixels from one image into another. If the source and destination regions aren't the same size, it will automatically resize source pixels to fit the specified target region. No alpha information is used in the process, however if the source image has an alpha channel set, it will be copied as well.<br><br>The **imageMode()** function changes the way the parameters work. For example, a call to **imageMode(CORNERS)** will change the width and height parameters to define the x and y values of the opposite corner of the image. |
| Syntax | `img.copy(sx, sy, swidth, sheight, dx, dy, dwidth, dheight);`<br>`img.copy(srcImg, sx, sy, swidth, sheight, dx, dy, dwidth, dheight);` |

*Figure 2-7. The documentation for the PImage copy from Processing.org*

So, what does this tell you? It shows you an example of using the `PImage copy`, and it shows you what the signature of the function looks like. Here it is in Processing:

```
img.copy(sx, sy, swidth, sheight, dx, dy, dwidth, dheight);
img.copy(srcImg, sx, sy, swidth, sheight, dx, dy, dwidth, dheight);
```

This tells you that the `PImage` has a function called **copy** that has two different ways it can be called. You'll need to read the rest of the `PImage` documentation on the Processing website to know what parameters you need to pass to each of these functions, but the names of those parameters should be somewhat helpful. Looking at the documentation shown in Figure 2-7 for the first function, you see several parameters with an s appended to them and several with a d appended to them. The s stands for source, and the d stands for destination, making them a little easier to understand. The function copies the pixels from one PImage object to another PImage object. Now that you have a rough idea of what sorts of parameters these functions take, you can call them on two different PImage objects:

```
PImage  p1 = loadImage("baby.jpg");
image(p1, 0, 0);
PImage p2 = new PImage(400, 400);
p2.copy(p1, 0, 0, p1.width, p1.height, 10, 10, p1.width * 2, p1.height * 2);
image(p2, 100, 100);
```

Take a moment to read the fourth line carefully. You're calling a function on the p2 PImage, on p2, and passing the height and width of p1 as parameters. Let's look at that function signature one more time:

```
img.copy(srcImg, sx, sy, swidth, sheight, dx, dy, dwidth, dheight);
```

srcImg is the PImage you want to copy pixels from, and sx and sy are where you want to copy the image from. dx and dy is where the image will be copied to and how wide and high the image will appear. You can use the properties of a PImage to pass values to a function of another PImage. You'll see this quite frequently, where properties of objects are stored, passed around, and accessed later.

Let's imagine for a moment that you've made some object that has a whole bunch of PImage objects inside it. You'll call it a PhotoAlbum. That object has a function on it called getNewestPicture. In using your PhotoAlbum class, you might have something that looks like this in Processing:

```
PhotoAlbum newAlbum;
newAlbum.getNewestPicture().filter(BLUR);
```

So, even though we haven't covered the filter function, I'd bet you can guess what doing filter(BLUR) will do. The interesting thing to note here is how a value from the getNewestPicture function has another function called on it right away. You could just as easily say this in Processing:

```
PhotoAlbum newAlbum;
PImage img = newAlbum.getNewestPicture();
img.filter(BLUR);
```

The two code snippets here will do exactly the same thing, but they'll do them in slightly different ways. It isn't important which way you do these things; it's only important that you're able to follow both the ways that they're done because you'll encounter them both.

# Scope

*Scope* is one of those nefarious things that can create some of the more difficult bugs to track down. Luckily for you, it's quite easy to keep it straight because there's a simple rule that will keep you out of trouble.

Let's first look at the following little Processing code snippet:

```
void setup() {

    if(true)
    {
        int i = 0;
    }
    i+=1;
    print(i);

}
```

OK, that was rather pointless, but if you try to compile it, you'll see something interesting pop up above the Processing console window (we'll cover how to do that in Chapter 3). You'll see this:

```
Cannot find anything named "i"
```

What was that? The scope of something means the place in your program where things are accessible. Figure 2-8 shows where in the function that each variable is accessible.

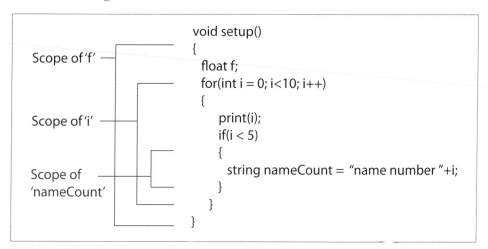

*Figure 2-8. Variable scope throughout a short function*

The general rule of variable scope is this: *all variables exist within the brackets that surround them*. If you have a variable within a function, you have this:

```
void someFunction() {
    int anInt;
}
```

The variable anInt is going to exist in that function, until the closing bracket for the function, which is the } at the end of the function. If a variable is defined within an if statement, then you have this:

```
if(something) {
    int anInt;
}
anInt = 5; // can't do this! anInt doesn't exist out here
```

In this case, anInt exists only inside that if statement, not anywhere else. Why is this? The short answer is that it makes it easier for your program to figure out what things are being used and what things aren't so that it can run more efficiently. Just remember the rule of the brackets: if there's a bracket before a variable, it exists only until another bracket closes it.

Some variables are available everywhere in a program, so they never go out of scope. These kinds of variables are called *global variables*. In a Processing or Arduino application, you can create a global variable by declaring it outside of the setup() method of your application. In an openFrameworks application, it's a little different, but we'll cover that in the oF chapters. You'll learn more about variables and global variables in each chapter relating to the specific language that you'll be looking at, because each one handles them in a slightly different fashion.

## Review

Variables represent data stored in the computer's memory for your program to access.

Variables have a type that describes what kind of information can be stored in them and specified when the variable is declared, for instance:

```
int weight = 150;
```

or:

```
float f = 1.12;
```

Variables are *declared* and then *initialized*. These can be done in separate steps:

```
int apples;
apples = 5;
```

or at the same time:

```
int apples = 5;
```

Variables can be cast to another variable type by using the name of the new type and parentheses to cast the variable:

```
float f = 98.9;
int myInt = int(f); //myInt is now the float f converted into an int
```

All variable types can be stored in arrays. These are declared with the length of the array and the type of variable stored in the array:

```
int arr[6]; // creates an array that can hold up to 6 integers
```

Accessing an array at any point within it is done by using the index, which begins at 0 and extends to the length of the array minus 1:

```
arr[0] = 1;
arr[1] = 2;
print(arr[0]); // will print '1', the first element in the array
```

Arrays can be filled when they are declared, as shown here:

```
int arr[3] = {1, 2, 3};
```

or the elements in the array can be set one at a time.

Control structures allow you to control the flow of your program. The most commonly used control structure are branching structures:

```
if(somethingTrueOrFalse){
    //if the evaluated statement is true
} else {
    //if the evaluated statement is false
}
```

and loops:

```
for(int i = 0; i<someNumber; i++) {
    //do something someNumber of times
}
```

Functions are declared with a name, a return type, and any parameter that the function requires:

```
returnType functionName(parameterType parameterName) {
    //what the function does
}
```

Using a function is usually referred to as *calling* the function. This is separate from *declaring* the function:

```
splitString(0, 10, 'hello there'); // this calls the function declared above
```

Functions can be overloaded, which means that multiple method declarations can be made with the same name and different parameters. When you call one of the functions, the compiler will determine which version of the function you meant to call.

# CHAPTER 3

# Processing

Processing was one of the first open source projects that was specifically designed for simplifying the practice of creating interactive graphical applications so that nonprogrammers could easily create artworks. Artists and designers developed Processing as an alternative to similar proprietary tools. It's completely open source and free to download, use, and modify as you see fit. Casey Reas and Ben Fry started the project at MIT under the tutelage of John Maeda, but a group of developers maintain it by making frequent updates to the core codebase and tools. It's currently at version 1.5, with tools for creating JavaScript versions of sketches, Android applications, as well as applications for online or for all the major operating systems. The Processing project includes an integrated development environment (IDE) that can be used to develop applications, a programming language specifically designed to simplify programming for visual design, and tools to publish your applications to the web or to the desktop.

One of the reasons that we brought up the Java Virtual Machine (JVM) in the introduction is that Processing is a Java application; that is, it runs in the JVM. A Processing application that you as the artist create is also a Java application that requires the JVM to run. You can take two different approaches to running Processing applications. The first is running your Processing application on the Web, which means putting your application in a Hypertext Markup Language (HTML) page where a browser like Firefox, Internet Explorer, Chrome, or Safari will encounter your application and start the JVM to run your application. The second is running your Processing application on the desktop, using the JVM that is installed on the user's machine.

What can you do with Processing? Because Processing is built in Java and runs using Java, it can do almost anything Java will do, and although Java can't quite do *everything* you'll see in computational art and design, it certainly comes close. With it you can do everything from reading and writing data on the Internet; working with images, videos, and sound; drawing two- and three-dimensionally; creating artificial intelligence; simulating physics; and much more. If you can do it, there's a very good chance you can do it using Processing.

In this chapter, we'll cover the basics of getting started with Processing, including the following: downloading and installing the environment, writing some simple programs, using external libraries that let you extend what Processing is capable of, and running applications on the Internet and on the desktop.

## Downloading and Installing Processing

The first step to installing Processing is to head to *http://processing.org* and look for the Download section. You'll see four downloads, one for each major operating system (Windows, Mac OS X, and Linux) and one for Windows users who don't want to install another instance of the JVM.

Processing includes an instance of the JVM, so you don't need to worry about configuring your computer. In other words, everything Processing needs is right in the initial download. Download the appropriate archive for your operating system, and move the files in the archive to somewhere you normally store applications. On a Windows computer, this might be a location like *C:\Program Files\Processing\*. On a Mac, it might be something like */Applications/Processing/*. On a Linux machine, it might be somewhere like *~/Applications/*.

Once you've downloaded and uncompressed the application, you're done—you've installed Processing. Go ahead and start the application, and then type the following simple program in the window.

*Example 3-1. drawARect.pde*

```
fill(0, 0, 255);
rect(0, 0, 100, 100);
print(" I'm working ");
```

Click the Run button (shown in the next section in Figure 3-1) to execute the program. This makes sure you have everything set up correctly. If this opens a new small window with a blue square in it and prints "I'm working" into the Console window, everything is good to go.

## Exploring the Processing IDE

Before we talk about the IDE in detail, it's important to understand the setup of the Processing environment. While the application is stored in your *C:\Program Files* directory (for Windows users) or in your */Applications/* directory (for Mac or Linux users), the sketches that you create in Processing are usually stored in your home documents folder. This means that for a Windows user the default location for all your different sketches might be *C:\Documents And Settings\User\My Documents\processing\*; for a Mac user it might be */Users/user/Documents/Processing/*; and for a Linux user it might be *home/user/processing/*. You can always set this to a different location by opening

Processing, opening the Preferences dialog and changing the "Sketchbook location" option to be wherever you'd like. The important thing is that you remember where it is.

Each Processing sketch you create and save will have its own folder. When you save a Processing sketch as *image_fun*, for example, a folder called *image_fun* will be created in the Processing project directory. If you're planning on working with images, MP3 files, videos, or other external data, you'll want to create a folder called *data* and store it in the project folder for the project that will use it. We'll discuss this in greater detail in the section "Importing Libraries" on page 80. You can always view the folder for a particular sketch by pressing Ctrl+K (⌘-K on a Mac) when the sketch is open in the IDE.

As you can see in Figure 3-1, the Processing IDE has four main areas: the controls, the Code window, the Messages window, and the Console window.

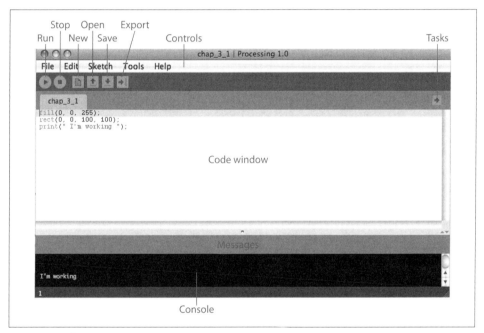

*Figure 3-1. The Processing IDE*

The controls area is where all the buttons to run, save, stop, open, export, and create new applications appear. After you've entered any code in the Code window and you're ready to see what it looks like when it runs, click the Run button, which opens a new window and runs your application in that window. To stop your application, either close the window or click the Stop button. The Export button creates a folder called *applet* within your project folder and saves all the necessary files there. You can find more information on this in the section "Exporting Processing Applications" on page 88 later in this chapter.

The Code window is where you enter all the code for the application. It supports a few of the common text editor functions, like Ctrl+F (⌘-F on a Mac) for Find and Ctrl+Z (⌘-Z on a Mac) for Undo.

The Messages window is where any system messages that might appear will be shown. It isn't widely used.

The Console window is where any trace statements or errors that occur while your application is running will be shown. Trace statements and printing messages to the console will be discussed a little later on in this chapter.

# The Basics of a Processing Application

A Processing application has two fundamental methods. These methods are the instructions for your application at two core moments. The first, setup(), is invoked when the application starts. The second, draw(), is invoked over and over again from right after startup until the application closes. Let's take a look at the first of these and dissect what a method really is.

## The setup() Method

Any instructions put in the setup() method run when the application first starts. Conceptually, you can think of this as any kind of preparation that you might be used to in daily life. Getting ready to go for a run: stretch. Getting ready to fly overseas: make sure you have a passport. Getting ready to cook dinner: check to see everything you need is in the refrigerator. In terms of our Processing application, the setup() method makes sure any information you want to use in the rest of the application is prepared properly, as shown in Example 3-2.

*Example 3-2. methods.pde*

```
void setup(){
    size(200, 200);
    frameRate(30);
    print(" all done setting up");
}
```

So, what's going on in this code snippet? Well, first you have the return type of this method, and then you have its name. Taken together these are called the *declaration* of this method. If you don't remember what a *method declaration* is, review Chapter 2. The rest of the code snippet is methods that have already been defined in the core Processing language. That is, you don't need to redefine them, you simply need to pass the correct values to them.

### The size() method

On the second line of the previous code snippet is the size() method. It has two parameters: how wide the application is supposed to be and how tall it's supposed to be, both in pixels. This idea of measuring things in pixels is very popular; you'll see it in any graphics program, photo or video editing program, and in the core code that runs all of these programs. Get inches or centimeters out of your head; in this world, everything is measured in pixels. This size()method makes the window that our application is going to run in. Go ahead and write the previous code in the Processing IDE, and click Run. Then change the size, and click Run again. You'll see that the size() method takes two parameters:

```
void size(width, height)
```

Frequently when programmers talk about a method, they refer to the *signature* of a method. This means what parameters it takes and what values it returns. If this doesn't sound familiar, review Chapter 2, specifically, the section on methods. In the setup() example, the size() method takes two integer (numbers without any decimal values) values and returns void, that is, nothing.

### The frameRate() method

The next method in the previous code snippet is the frameRate() method, which determines how many frames per second your application is going to attempt to display. Processing will never run faster than the frame rate you set, but it might run more slowly if you have too many things going at once or some parts of your code are inefficient. More frames per second means your animations will run faster and everything will happen more rapidly; however, it also can mean that if you're trying to do something too data intensive, Processing will lag when trying keep up with the frame rate you set. And how is this done? Well, the number you pass to the frameRate() method is the number of times per second that the draw() method is called.

### The print() method

The print() method puts a message from the application to the Console window in the Processing IDE. You can print all sorts of things: messages, numbers, the value of certain kinds of objects, and so forth. These provide not only an easy way to get some feedback from your program but also a simple way to do some debugging when things aren't working the way you'd like them to work. Expecting something to have a value of 10? Print it to see what it really is. All the print messages appear in the Console window at the bottom of the Processing IDE, as shown in Figure 3-2.

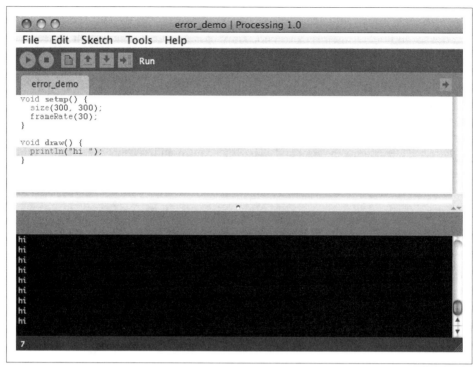

*Figure 3-2. The Console window in an application*

## The draw() Method

The draw() method is where the drawing of the application happens, but it can be much more than that. The draw() method is the heartbeat of your application; any behavior defined in this method will be called at the number of times per second specified as the frame rate of your application.

A simple example of a draw() method can be seen in Example 3-3.

*Example 3-3. methods.pde*

```
void draw() {
    println("hi");
}
```

Assuming that the frame rate of your application is 30 times a second, the message "hi" will print to the Console window of the Processing IDE 30 times a second. That's not very exciting, is it? But it demonstrates what the draw() method is: the definition of the behavior of any processing application at a regular interval determined by the frame rate, after the application runs the setup() method.

Example 3-4 is a slightly more interesting example dissected.

*Example 3-4. expanding.pde*

```
int x = 0;

void setup() {
    size(300, 300);
}

void draw() {
    // make x a little bit bigger
    x += 2;
    // draw a circle using x as the height and width of the circle
    ellipse(150, 150, x, x);
    // if x is too big, we can't see it in our window, so put it back
    // to 0 and start over
    if(x > 300) {
        x = 0;
    }
}
```

First things first—you're making an int variable, x, to store a value:

```
int x = 0;
```

Since x isn't inside a method, it's going to exist throughout the entire application. That is, when you set it to 20 in the draw() method, then the next time the draw() method is called the value of x is still going to be 20. This is important because it lets you gradually animate the value of x.

 This refers to the idea of *scope*; if that concept isn't ringing any bells for you, review Chapter 2.

To set up the application using the setup() method, simply set the size of the window so that it's big enough. Nothing too interesting there, so you can skip right to the draw() method:

```
void draw() {
```

Each time you call draw(), you're going to make this number bigger by 2. You could also write x = x+2;, but the following is simpler and does the same thing:

```
x != 2;
```

Now that you've made x a little bit bigger, you can use it to draw a circle into the window:

```
ellipse(150, 150, x, x);
```

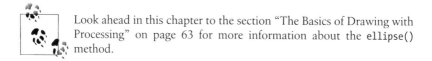
Look ahead in this chapter to the section "The Basics of Drawing with Processing" on page 63 for more information about the `ellipse()` method.

If the value of x is too high, the circle will be drawn too large for it to show up correctly in your window (300 pixels); you'll want to reset x to 0 so that the circles placed in the window begin growing again in size:

```
if(x > 300) {
    x = 0;
}
}
```

In Figure 3-3, you can see the animation about halfway through its cycle of incrementing the x value and drawing gradually larger and larger circles.

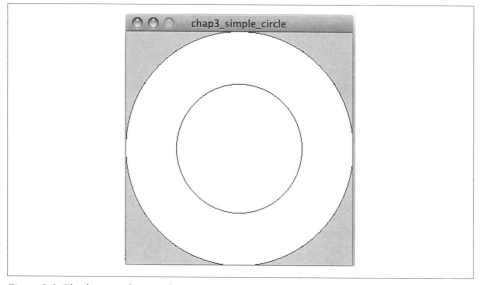

*Figure 3-3. The demo application drawing circles*

The `draw()` method is important because the Processing application uses it to set up a lot of the interaction with the application. For instance, the `mousePressed()` method and the `mouseMove()` methods that are discussed in the section "Capturing Simple User Interaction" on page 70 will not work without a `draw()` method being defined. You can imagine that the `draw()` method tells the application that you want to listen to whatever happens with the application as each frame is drawn. Even if nothing is between the brackets of the `draw()` method, generally you should always define a `draw()` method.

# The Basics of Drawing with Processing

Because Processing is a tool for artists, one of the most important tasks it helps you do easily is drawing. You'll find much more information on drawing using vectors and bitmaps in 9 and 10, and you'll find information about OpenGL, some of the basics of 3-D, and how to create complex drawing systems in Chapter 13. For right now, you'll learn how to draw simple shapes, draw lines, and create colors to fill in those shapes and lines.

## The rect(), ellipse(), and line() Methods

Each of the three simplest drawing methods, `rect()`, `ellipse()`, and `line()`, lets you draw shapes in the display window of your application. The `rect()` method draws a rectangle in the display window and uses the following syntax:

```
rect(x, y, width, height)
```

Each of the values for the `rect()` method can be either `int` or `float`. The x and y position variables passed to the rectangle determine the location of the upper-left corner of the rectangle. This keeps in line with the general rule in computer graphics of referring to the upper-left corner as 0,0 (to anyone with a math background this is a little odd, since Cartesian coordinates have the y values flipped).

The `ellipse()` method is quite similar to `rect()`:

```
ellipse(x, y, width, height)
```

Each of the values passed to the `ellipse()` method can be int or float. If you make the height and width of the ellipse the same, you get a circle, of course, so you don't need a `circle()` method.

Finally, the `line()` method uses the following syntax:

```
line(x1, y1, x2, y2)
```

The x1 and y1 values define where the line is going to start, and the x2 and y2 values define the end of the line. Example 3-5 incorporates each of the three methods.

*Example 3-5. line.pde*

```
void setup() {
    size(300, 300);
}

void draw() {
    rect(100, 100, 50, 50);
    ellipse(200, 200, 40, 40);
    line(0, 0, 300, 300);
}
```

Notice in Figure 3-4 that because the line is drawn after the rectangle and ellipse, it's on top of both of them. Each drawing command draws on top of what is already drawn in the display window.

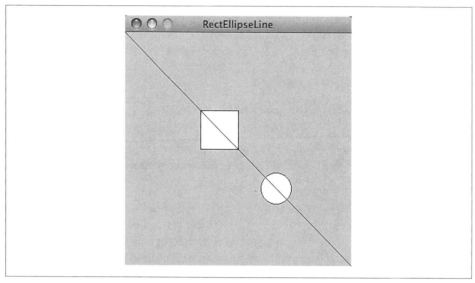

*Figure 3-4. Drawing using rect(), ellipse(), and line()*

Now, let's take a brief interlude and learn about two ways to represent color.

## RGB Versus Hexadecimal

There are two ways of representing colors in Processing in particular and computing in general: RGB and hexadecimal. Both are similar in that they revolve around the use of red, green, and blue values. This is because the pixels in computer monitors are colored using mixtures of these values to determine what color a pixel should be. In RGB, you use three numbers between 0 and 255 and pass them to the `color()` method. For example, the following defines white:

```
int fullred = 255;
int fullgreen = 255;
int fullblue = 255;
color(fullred, fullgreen, fullblue);
```

Conversely, the following defines black:

```
int fullred = 0;
int fullgreen = 0;
int fullblue = 0;
color(fullred, fullgreen, fullblue);
```

All red and no green or blue is red, all green and blue and no red is yellow, and anytime all the numbers are the same the color is a gray (or white/black).

RGB is an easy way of thinking about color perhaps, but another way is commonly used on the Internet for HTML pages and has grown in popularity in other types of coding as well: hexadecimal numbers.

What's a hexadecimal number? Well, a decimal number counts from 1 to 9 and then starts incrementing the number behind the 1. So, once you get to 9, you go to 10, and once you get to 19, you go to 20. This is the decimal system. The hexadecimal system is based on the number 16 and is very efficient for computers because computers like to process things in numbers that are cleanly divisible by 4 and 16, which 10 is not. A hexadecimal counting looks like this: 0, 1, 2, 3, 4, 5, 6, 7, 8, 9, A, B, C, D, E, F. So, that means that to write 13 in hexadecimal, you write D. To write 24, you write 18. To write 100, you write 64. The most important concept to grasp is that to write 255, you write FF, which means representing numbers takes fewer characters to represent ("255" being three characters while "FF" is only two). This is part of where the efficiency comes from; less characters means more efficient processing. Hexadecimal numbers for colors are written all together like this:

    0xFF00FF

or:

    #FF00FF

That actually says red = 255, green = 0, blue = 255, just in a more efficient way. The 0x and # prefixes tell the Processing compiler you're sending a hexadecimal number, not just mistyping a number. You'll need to use those if you want to use hexadecimal numbers.

Here are some other colors:

- 000000 = black
- FFFFFF = white
- 00FFFF = yellow

We'll cover one final concept of hexadecimal numbers: the alpha value. The *alpha value* controls the transparency of a color and is indicated in hexadecimal by putting two more numbers at the beginning of the number to indicate, on a scale of 0–255 (which is really 0–FF), how transparent the color should be.

0x800000FF is an entirely "blue" blue (that is, all blue and nothing else) that's 50% transparent. You can break it down into the following:

- Alpha = 80 (that is, 50%)
- Red = 00 (that is, 0%)
- Green = 00 (that is, 0%)
- Blue = FF (that is, 100%)

0xFFFF0000 is an entirely "red" red, that is 0% transparent, or totally opaque, with full red values and no green or blue to mix with it, and 0x00FFFF00 is a magenta that is invisible. This is why computer color is sometimes referred to as ARGB, which stands for "alpha, red, green, blue."

Now that you know the basics of colors, you can move on to using more interesting colors than white and black with shapes.

## The fill() Method

The `fill()` method is named as such because it determines what goes inside any shapes that have empty space in them. Processing considers two-dimensional shapes like rectangles and circles to be a group of points that have an empty space that will be colored in by a fill color. Essentially, imagine that setting the fill sets how any empty shapes will be *filled in*. Without a fill, Processing won't know what color you want your shapes to be filled in with. The `fill()` method lets you define the color that will be used to fill in those shapes.

Before you really dive into the `fill()` method, it's important to remember that methods can be *overloaded*; that is, they can have multiple signatures. If this doesn't seem familiar to you or you'd like a refresher on this, review Chapter 2.

The `fill()` method has many different ways of letting you set the color that will be used to fill shapes:

fill(int gray)
> This is an `int` between 0 (black) and 255 (white).

fill(int gray, int alpha)
> This is an `int` between 0 (black) and 255 (white) and a second number for the alpha of the fill between 0 (transparent) and 255 (fully opaque).

fill(int value1, int value2, int value3)
> Each of these values is a number between 0 and 255 for each of the following colors: red, green, and blue. For instance, `fill(255, 0, 0)` is bright red, `fill(255, 255, 255)` is white, `fill(255, 255, 0)` is yellow, and `fill(0, 0, 0)` is black.

fill (int value1, int value2, int value3, int alpha)
> This is the same as the previous example, but the additional `alpha` parameter lets you set how transparent the fill will be.

fill(color color)
> The `fill()` method can also be passed a variable of type `color`, as shown here:

```
void draw(){
    color c = color(200, 0, 0);
    fill(c);
    rect(0, 0, 100, 100);
}
```

fill(color color, int alpha)
> When passing a variable of type `color`, you can specify an `alpha` value:

---

```
color c = color(200, 0, 0);
fill(c, 150);
```

`fill(int hex)`

This is a fill using a hexadecimal value for the color, which can be represented by using the 0x prefix or the # prefix in the hexadecimal code. However, Processing expects that if you use 0x, you'll provide an alpha value in the hexadecimal code. This means if you don't want to pass a separate `alpha` value, use the 0x prefix. If you do want to pass a separate alpha value, use the # prefix.

`fill(int hex, int alpha)`

This method uses a hexadecimal number but should be used with the # symbol in front of the number, which can be a six-digit number only. The alpha value can be anywhere from 0 to 255.

The `fill()` method sets the color that Processing will use to draw all shapes in the application until it's changed. For example, if you set the fill to blue like so:

```
fill(0, 0, 255);
```

and then draw four rectangles, they will be filled with a blue color.

## The background() Method

To set the color of the background window that your application is running in, use the `background()` method. The `background()` method uses the same overloaded methods as the `fill()` method, with the method name changed to `background()`, of course. The `background()` method also completely covers up everything that was drawn in the canvas of your application. When you want to erase everything that has been drawn, you call the `background()` method. This is really helpful in animation because it lets you easily draw something again and again while changing its position or size without having all the previous artifacts hanging around.

## The line() Method

You can use the `line()` method in two ways. The first is for any two-dimensional lines:

```
line(x1, y1, x2, y2)
```

The second is for any three-dimensional lines:

```
line(x1, y1, z1, x2, y2, z?)
```

Now, of course, a three-dimensional line will simply appear like a two-dimensional line until you begin moving objects around in three-dimensional space; we'll cover that in Chapter 13. You need to take smaller steps first. The `line()` method simply draws a line from the point described in the first two (or three parameters) to the point. You can set the color of the line using the `stroke()` method, and thickness of the line using the `strokeWeight()` method.

## The stroke() and strokeWeight() Methods

The stroke() method uses the same parameters as the fill() method, letting you set the color of the line either by using up to four values from 0 to 255 or by using hexadecimal numbers. The strokeWeight() method, as seen in Example 3-6, simply sets the width of the lines in pixels.

*Example 3-6. strokeWeight.pde*

```
void draw(){
    stroke(0xFFCCFF00); // here we set the color to yellow
    strokeWeight(5); // set the stroke weight to 5
    // draw the lines
    line(0, 100, 600, 400);
    line(600, 400, 300, 0);
    line(300, 0, 0, 100);
}
```

This draws a rectangular shape with yellow lines, 5 pixels thick.

## The curve() Method

The curve() method draws a curved line and is similar to the line() method except it requires you to specify anchors that the line will curve toward.

You can use the curve() method in two dimensions:

```
curve(x1, y1, x2, y2, x3, y3, x4, y4);
```

or in three dimensions:

```
curve(x1, y1, z1, x2, y2, z2, x3, y3, z3, x4, y4, z4);
```

All the variables here can be either floating-point numbers or integers. The x1, y1, and z1 variables are the coordinates for the first anchor point, that is, the first point that the curve will bend toward. The x2, y2, and z2 variables are the coordinates for the first point, that is, where the line begins, in either two- or three-dimensional space. The x3, y3, and z3 parameters are the coordinates for the second point, that is, where the line ends, and the x4, y4, and z4 parameters are the coordinates for the second anchor, that is, the second point that the curve will bend toward. See Example 3-7.

*Example 3-7. curving.pde*

```
void setup(){
    size(400, 400);
}

void draw(){
    background(255);
    fill(0);
    int xVal = mouseX*3-100;
    int yVal = mouseY*3-100;
    curve(xVal, yVal, 100, 100, 100, 300, xVal, yVal);
```

```
    curve(xVal, yVal, 100, 300, 300, 300, xVal, yVal);
    curve(xVal, yVal, 300, 300, 300, 100, xVal, yVal);
    curve(xVal, yVal, 300, 100, 100, 100, xVal, yVal);
}
```

When this code snippet runs, you'll have something that looks like Figure 3-5.

*Figure 3-5. Running the curve-drawing sample*

## The vertex() and curveVertex() Methods

What is a vertex? A *vertex* is a point where two lines in a shape meet, for example, at the point of a triangle or point of a star. In Processing, you can use any three or more vertices to create a shape with or without a fill by calling the beginShape() method, creating the vertices, and then calling the endShape() method. The beginShape() and endShape() methods tell the Processing environment you intend to define points that should be joined by lines to create a shape. Three vertices create a triangle, four a quadrilateral, and so on. The Processing environment will create a shape from the vertices that you've selected, creating lines between those vertices, and filling the space within those lines with the fill color you've defined. Example 3-8 creates three vertices: one at 0, 0, which is the upper-left corner of the window; one at 400,400, which is the lower-right corner of the window; and one at the user's mouse position. The code snippet in Example 3-8 results in the shape shown inFigure 3-6.

*Example 3-8. vertices.pde*

```
void setup() {
    size(400, 400);
}
```

```
void draw(){
    background(255);
    fill(0);
    beginShape();
    vertex(0, 0);
    vertex(400, 400);
    vertex(mouseX, mouseY);
    endShape();
}
```

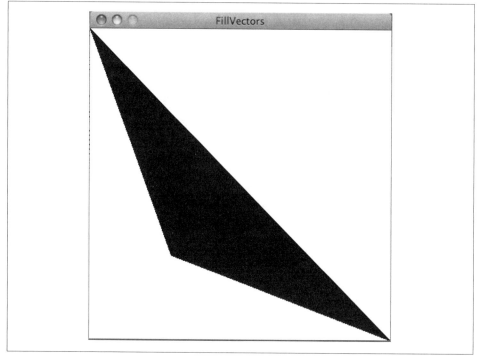

*Figure 3-6. Creating vertices and a fill*

# Capturing Simple User Interaction

To begin at the beginning, you'll see how Processing handles the two most common modes of user interaction: the mouse and the keyboard. To capture interactions with these two tools, what you really need to know is when the mouse is moving, when the mouse button has been pressed, when the user is dragging (that is, holding the mouse button down and moving the mouse), whether a key has been pressed, and what key has been pressed. All these methods and variables already exist in the Processing application. All you need to do is invoke them, that is, to tell the Processing environment that you want to do something when the method is invoked, or access the variable either when one of the methods is invoked or in the draw() method of your application.

# The mouseX and mouseY Variables

The mouseX and mouseY variables contain the position of the mouse in *x* and *y* coordinates. This is done in pixels, so if the mouse is in the farthest upper-left corner of the window, mouseX is 0 and mouseY is 0. If the mouse pointer is in the lower-right corner of a window that is 300 × 300 pixels, then mouseX is 300 and mouseY is 300. You can determine the position of the mouse at any time by using these variables. The code snippet in Example 3-9, you can determine the position of the mouse whenever the draw() method is called:

*Example 3-9. fonts.pde*

```
PFont arial;

void setup() {
    // make the size of our window
    size(300, 300);
    // load the font from the system
    arial = createFont("Arial", 32);
    // set up font so our application is using the font whenever
    // we call the text method to write things into the window
    textFont(arial, 15);
}

void draw() {
    // this makes the background black, overwriting anything there
    // we're doing this because we want to make sure we don't end up
    // with every set of numbers on the screen at the same time.
    background(0);
    // here's where we really do the work, putting the mouse position
    // in the window at the location where the mouse is currently
    text(" position is "+mouseX+" "+mouseY, mouseX, mouseY);
}
```

As you can see from the code comments, this example shows a little more than just using the mouse position; instead, it uses the text() method to put the position of the mouse on the screen in text at the position of the mouse itself. You do this by using the text() method, which takes three parameters:

```
    void text(string message, xPosition, yPosition);
```

The first parameter is the message, and the second and third parameters can be floats or ints and are for positioning the location of the text. In the previous example, you put the text where the user's mouse is using the mouseX and mouseY variables.

# The mousePressed() Method

Processing applications have a mousePressed() method that is called whenever the user clicks the left mouse button. This *callback method* is called whenever the application has focus and the user presses the mouse button. As mentioned in the previous section, without a draw() method in your application, the mousePressed() method will not work.

Let's look at Example 3-10, which uses a few drawing concepts and also shows you how to use the mousePressed() method.

*Example 3-10. mpressed.pde*

```
int alphaValue = 0;

void setup() {
    size(350, 300);
    background(0xFFFFFFFF);
}

void draw() {
    background(0xFFFFFFFF);
    fill(255, 0, 0, alphaValue);
    rect(100, 100, 100, 100);
}

void mousePressed() {
    print(mouseX + "\n");
    alphaValue = mouseX;
}
```

The mousePressed() method here sets the alpha value of the fill that will be used when drawing the rectangle to be the position of the user's mouse. The application will draw using the alphaValue variable that is set each time the mouse is clicked.

## The mouseReleased() and mouseDragged() Methods

The mouseReleased() method notifies you when the user has released the mouse button. It functions similarly to the mousePressed() method and lets you create actions that you would like to have invoked when the mouse button is released. The mouseDragged() method works much the same way, but is generally (though certainly not always) used to determine whether the user is dragging the mouse by holding the button down and moving the mouse around. Many times when looking at mouse-driven applications you'll see the mouseDragged() method being used to set a Boolean variable that indicates whether the user is dragging. In Example 3-11, though, you'll put some actual drawing logic in the mouseDragged() method.

*Example 3-11. dragged.pde*

```
int lastX = 0;
int lastY = 0;

void setup() {
    size(400, 400);
}

void draw() {
    lastX = mouseX;
    lastY = mouseY;
```

```
}
void mouseDragged() {
    line(lastX, lastY, mouseX, mouseY);
}
```

Now you have a simple drawing application. You simply store the last position of the user's mouse and then, when the mouse is being dragged, draw a line from the last position to the current position. Try running this code and then comment out the lines in the `draw()` method that set the `lastX` and `lastY` variables to see how the application changes.

An easier way to do this is to use the `pmouseX` and `pmouseY` variables. These represent the x and y mouse positions in the previous frame of the application. To use these variables, you would use the following code:

```
void mouseDragged() {
    line(pmouseX, pmouseY, mouseX, mouseY);
}
```

To extend this a little bit, you'll next create a slightly more complex drawing application that allows someone to click a location and have the Processing application include that location in the shape. This code sample has three distinct pieces that you'll examine one by one. The first you'll look at is a class that is defined in this example.

First, you have the declaration of the name of the class, `Point`, and the bracket that indicates you're about to define all the methods and types of that class:

```
class Point{
```

Next, you have the two values that are going to store the x and y values of `Point`:

```
float x;
    float y;
```

Here is the constructor for this class:

```
Point(float _x, float _y){
    x = _x;
    y = _y;
}
```

The constructor takes two values, _x and _y, and sets the x and y values of `Point` to the two values passed into the constructor. What this `Point` class now lets you do is store the location where someone has clicked.

Now that you've defined the `Point` class, you can create an array of those `Point` objects. Since you want to allow for shapes with six vertices, in order to store them you'll need an array of `Point` instances with six elements:

```
Point[] pts = new Point[6];
```

Now all that's left to do is set the `mousePressed()` method so that it stores the `mouseX` and `mouseY` positions using the `Point` class and then draws all those `Point` instances into the window. In Example 3-12, we'll break down each step of the code because this is pretty complex.

*Example 3-12. point.pde*

```
Point[] pts = new Point[6];

int count = 0;
void setup(){
    size(500, 500);
}
```

In the draw() method, the background is drawn filled in, the fill for any drawing is set using the fill() method, and a for loop is used to draw a vertex for each of the points:

```
void draw(){
    background(255);
    fill(0);
    beginShape();
    for(int i = 0; i<pts.length; i++){
```

Just to avoid any errors that may come from the Point object not being instantiated, you check to make sure that the Point in the current position in the array isn't null:

```
if(pts[i] != null) {
```

If it isn't null, you'll use it to create a vertex using Point from the pts array:

```
vertex(pts[i].x, pts[i].y);
        }
    }
```

Now you're done drawing the shape:

```
endShape();
}
```

When the user presses the mouse, you want to store their mouse position for use in the pts array. You do this by creating a new Point object, passing it the current mouseX and mouseY positions, and storing that in the pts array at the count position:

```
void mousePressed(){
    if(count > 5){
        count = 0;
    }
    Point newPoint = new Point(mouseX, mouseY);
    pts[count] = newPoint;
    count++;
}
```

Finally, you have the declaration for the Point class:

```
class Point{
    float x;
    float y;
    Point(float _x, float _y){
        x = _x;
```

```
        y = _y;
    }
}
```

So, what happens when you click in the window? Let's change the `Point` class constructor slightly so you can see it better:

```
Point(float _x, float _y){
        println(" x is: "+_x+" and y is "+_y);
        x = _x;
        y = _y;
    }
```

Now, when you click in the Processing window, you'll see the following printed out in the Console window (depending on where you click, of course):

```
x is: 262.0 and y is 51.0
x is: 234.0 and y is 193.0
x is: 362.0 and y is 274.0
x is: 125.0 and y is 340.0
x is: 17.0 and y is 155.0
```

So, why is this happening? Look at the `mousePressed(d)` method again:

```
void mousePressed(){
...
    Point newPoint = new Point(mouseX, mouseY);
    pts[count] = newPoint;
}
```

Every time the `mousePressed` event is called, you create a new `Point`, calling the constructor of the `Point` class and storing the `mouseX` and `mouseY` positions in the `Point`. Once you've created the `Point` object, you store the point in the `pts` array so that you can use it for placing vertices in the `draw()` method.

So, in the previous example, you'll use `for` loops, classes, and arrays, as well as the `vertex()` method. The last code sample was a difficult one that bears a little studying. There's a lot more information on classes in Chapter 5.

## The keyPressed and key Variables

Many times you'll want to know whether someone is pressing a key on the keyboard. You can determine when a key is pressed and which key it is in two ways. The first is to check the `keyPressed` variable in the `draw()` method:

```
void draw() {
    if(keyPressed) {
        print(" you pressed "+key);
    }
}
```

Notice how you can use the `key` variable to determine what key is being pressed. Any keypress is automatically stored by your Processing application in this built-in variable.

Processing also defines a `keyPressed()` method that you can use in much the same way as the `mousePressed()` or `mouseMoved()` method:

```
void keyPressed(){
    print(" you're pressing a key \n that key is "+key);
}
```

Any code to handle key presses should go inside the `keyPressed()` method. For instance, handling arrow key presses in a game, or the user pressing the Return button after they've entered their name in a text field.

 Note that `keyPressed()` is a method call while `keyPressed` is a property. They're not the same but they do have the same name. The `keyPressed()` method will only be called once when the key is actually pressed down, while checking the `keyPressed` variable in the `draw()` loop means that you'll trigger code *as long as the key is pressed*.

---

## Interview: Ben Fry

Ben Fry was one of the originators of the Processing project along with Casey Reas. He has lectured worldwide on data visualization, media art, and computer science; published two books, *Processing: A Programming Handbook for Visual Designers and Artists* (coauthored with Casey Reas; MIT Press) and *Visualizing Data* (O'Reilly); and has created numerous data visualizations, illustrations, and essays.

*What made you get interested in data visualization? Was it an aesthetic thought or more of a problem set that you realized wasn't being properly addressed, or some combination of the two?*

**Ben Fry:** It's the combination of the two. I'd been interested in graphic design and computer science since an embarrassingly young age: I found advertising and logos and typography interesting even in middle school and did my first BASIC programs even younger. In college I studied graphic design but especially enjoyed information design (and motion graphics and kinetic information display). For a long time I thought that UI design was the way to go and did internships and a first job in that. But it wasn't until grad school at MIT that I was able to bring the design and visualization sides together. At school my focus was primarily in graphic design actually, with a minor in computer science (at least for undergrad). Design was the primary subject because I thought it would give me more flexibility and teach me more about how to think. I was led to computational art because of how it melded these two (until then) very distinct interests together. One of the disappointments was actually being a few months in and realizing I was no longer "cross disciplinary," because my two primary disciplines of interest were now merged. The positive side was that I could focus on the combination in a more direct way, but the negative was that I could no longer play the two against one another the way I could when I was younger.

*I see a theme in your work of the role of the designer in society, in science, in computation, and in places where visual design considerations were usually taken as being secondary to other considerations. Is that an accurate evaluation? Do you see a need for visual design in other places where it's not being valued correctly?*

**Ben:** I think that's correct, and I see two sides to it. First, the society/science/computation aspects are what I'm most drawn to and curious about. Second, there's a more pragmatic point in that fewer people are interested in those issues, so I can carve out my own niche.

*Looking at your work visually, I very often have this reaction that goes something like "Wow...oh." At first the visual beauty and complexity really strike me, and then I realize what is being visualized. Is this something intentional or something you hear a lot and is something desired?*

**Ben:** People tend to separate making things beautiful or informative, and this disparity is especially wide when dealing with information. But unless you have some of both, I don't think it's particularly fulfilling. So, my hope is always that the project is still rewarding after the initial "Ooh!" Otherwise, the "pretty" part is easy to write off. On some level, I'm just making things that *I* want to look at, and I want them to be visually and intellectually stimulating. Of course, this quickly gets into highly subjective territory, and I'm unwilling to refer to my own work as "beautiful"—that's a personal opinion that may or not be shared by the viewer. I also consider it a failure if people stop at "Ooh!" If the image doesn't make people curious enough to delve deeper and curious about the subject matter, then I'm not doing my job (at least as I see it).

*A piece like the graphics piece "aligning humans and animals" is both an excellent illustration and a piece that sort of alludes to a world of information in a reasonably scientifically rigorous way. In that way, it reminds me of some contemporary artists (Carsten Nicolai jumps to mind) who work with difficult concepts and make them visible and legible. Can you talk about some of the contemporary artists or designers whom you feel inspired by?*

**Ben:** I get a lot of inspiration from typography, motion graphics, and film. But I don't have a good list of specific people or pieces, since it's always little tidbits here and there: the cinematography found in Kubrick movies, cheesy film infographics, and the balance of beauty and structure (and ubiquity) in the typographic work of someone like Matthew Carter. I started a blog (*http://benfry.com*) partly so that I could write about such things and assemble them in one place. When I find something like the scientist who's pouring molten aluminum into ant holes (*http://benfry.com/writing/archives/98*) so that he can see their structure (after letting the aluminum cool and removing the dirt), I have somewhere to post that. But those are the sort of ideas that stick with me—associating the organic shape from the ant colony and how it connects to other shapes like it, whether spindly arrangements of lakes in northern Canada or a complicated network topology diagram.

*In glancing through your writing on your blog and looking at the books you've written, the breadth of topics you cover is quite interesting—from typography to baseball players to storyboarding the government and privacy—but they all seem to have a common skein of the interpretation or misinterpretation of data. Do you or have you had a methodology for finding topics to approach?*

**Ben:** It's largely just the things I'm curious about, but it's a way for me to assemble my thoughts. I don't tend to enjoy blogs, books, and so on that seem to have a direct connection to my work (they tend to muddle my thinking), but I'd never been able to figure that out why. As I've started assembling things, it's easier to understand where my head is. It's partly to improve at writing, and it's partly therapeutic.

As for methodology, I'm desperately trying to stick to themes around information and data, though it strays a little bit into film and motion, usually as it relates to drawing (which has to do with communication) or narrative (since that's what visualization is about). It's tough for me to stay away from politics or, say, the Space Olympics skit on last week's *Saturday Night Live*, but I don't want to spiral into general interest or an online diary.

*Do you think your design work may ever lead you away from information visualization and toward something more abstractly aesthetic, or is that something you're not interested in?*

**Ben:** Nah, I think I'm too obsessed with information. It's more likely the other way around—that it might lead me away from design and into more about how we think about data in general (for instance, along the vector of all the privacy and security posts on the blog that get to the "we have all this data, now what?"). But I love the visual side equally, so I don't really think I could ever give that up completely.

*How much of the creation of Processing was simply wanting a tool for your own uses, and how much was it an interest in creating a tool for others to use, and how did these two fit together?*

**Ben:** Hmm, I think it may have been equal parts initially but then became more about the tool for others. The amount of time it takes to make a tool for yourself and to make (and support and maintain) a tool used by strangers is multiple orders of magnitude different. Even faced with that, we've chosen to continue the public part of it (often to the detriment of our own work).

That said, it's still very much driven by my personal work—specific improvements are often aligned with projects that I'm developing at one time or another. And to be honest, there are areas that we don't cover well enough (sound, for instance) because Casey and I don't make as much use of it in our own work.

I think that Processing is more of a "giving back" project. I learned programming because lots of people shared code with me (whether directly or indirectly) when I was 10 or 12 years old, so I owe them. It's also a matter of opening up this sort of work to people who are more talented and can take it further. Every once in a while I see something built with Processing that makes me want to give up on doing my own projects and just work a lot harder on Processing itself.

*As a programmer I really love the Deprocess and Revisionist pieces because they document two different processes that center around a single thing: the developing of code and the running of code.*

**Ben:** These are both about making an image of what's in one's head...that I have a general *idea* of what code changes over time look like, or what running code looks like, but I really want to *see* that. And I suspect that's what other people respond to as well—

that the images aren't particularly groundbreaking (we've seen visual diffs and code traces before), but it's a bit like seeing a dream realized or reading an article that perfectly articulates the way you feel about, say, a complicated political situation or societal phenomenon.

*Do you have a clear vision for the future of Processing, or has the community of Processing, which is large and very active, taken over guiding the project in a sense?*

**Ben:** I think the community has guided us in a lot of our decision making. If you look at our goals when we started, the project (online web delivery, plus support for features like serial I/O, hardware devices, and so on) and where we are now (full-scale applications, accelerated graphics, and dozens upon dozens of libraries), you can see how that invisible hand has pushed progress.

Some of the more recent developments have to do with using the API in other languages (JavaScript, Ruby, and Python), which is something that wasn't really feasible when we started but yet I'm really excited about. That's something where the community has really picked it up and run.

*Are there sorts of projects that people aren't really exploring with Processing that you ever think, "I wish people were doing this more"?*

**Ben:** One of Casey's and my personal goals in the project was that if we made the easy things easy, and made the hard things less painful, the overall level of quality in such work could perhaps improve a bit—or put another way, that you'd be able to get away with a lot less B.S. I don't think we've been as successful in this as I would like.

*How did you approach the idea of creating a language for nonprogrammers? Did you refer to other "friendly" languages like Ruby or Python? Or was it driven by what you imagined users would be doing with it? Was it driven by the idea of making a "teaching" language as well?*

**Ben:** It was a combination of all those things, plus all our accumulated biases and quibbles based on past experiences.

But to be sure, we haven't created an ultimate language of some sort—we simply tried to assemble what we knew and make an evolutionary jump forward toward where we thought things should be. If it were more revolutionary, I think the syntax and mental model would be quite different. But we had to balance that against the practical (how far from existing languages people were willing to diverge and how quickly software we created needed to run).

*Beyond the cognitive processes of analyzing data and understanding data, you also work with allowing users to interact with it. Do you find that the notion of interacting with data to be as rich a territory as the notion of displaying it legibly and informatively?*

**Ben:** Oh, it's absolutely a rich territory, because it gets closer to involving more of our senses and/or our bodies. There are few things in our environment that we just stare at statically—we reach and manipulate them and move them around to see what they do (look at any 6-month-old baby). The more we can do this with information, the more we'll be able to learn.

# Importing Libraries

One of the great aspects of using Processing is the wide and varied range of libraries that have been contributed to the project by users. Most processing libraries are contained within *.jar* files. JAR stands for *Java archive* and is a file format developed by Sun that is commonly used for storing multiple files together that can be accessed by a Java application. In Processing applications, the Java application that will be accessing the *.jar* files is the Processing environment. When you include a library in a Processing code file and run the application, the Processing environment loads the *.jar* file and grabs any required information from the *.jar* and includes it in the application it's building.

## Downloading Libraries

Many Processing libraries are available for download at www.processing.org/reference/libraries/index.html. The libraries here include libraries used for working with 3-D libraries, libraries that communicate with Bluetooth-enabled devices, and simple gesture-recognition libraries for recognizing the movements made by a user with a mouse or Wii remote controller.

For this example, you'll download the ControlP5 library, install it to the Processing directory, and write a quick test to ensure that it works properly. First, locate the ControlP5 library on the Libraries page of the Processing site under the Reference heading. Clicking ControlP5 on the Libraries page brings you to the ControlP5 page at *http://www.sojamo.de/libraries/controlP5/*. Once you've downloaded the folder, unzipping the *.zip* file will create the *controlP5* folder. Inside this is a *library* folder that contains all the *.jar* files that the Processing application will access.

Now that you've downloaded the library, take a look at the *libraries* folder of your Processing sketchbook. The *Processing sketchbook* is a folder on your computer where all of your applications and libraries are stored. To change the *sketchbook* location, you can open the Preferences window from the Processing application and set the value in the "Sketchbook location" field. You'll need to copy the contributed library's folder into the *libraries* folder at this location. To go to the sketchbook, you hit Ctrl+K (⌘-K on Mac OS X). If this is the first library you've added, then you need to create the *libraries* folder. For instance, on my computer the Processing sketchbook is installed at */Users/base/processing*, so I place the *controlP5* folder at */Users/base/processing/libraries/*. Your setup may vary depending on where you've installed Processing and your system type. Once the library is in the correct location, restart the Processing IDE, and type the following code in the IDE window:

```
import controlP5.*;
```

Then run the application. If a message appears at the bottom of the IDE saying this:

```
You need to modify your classpath, sourcepath,
  bootclasspath, and/or extdirs setup. Jikes could not find package
  "controlP5" in the code folder or in any libraries.
```

then the ControlP5 library has not been created properly. Double check that the folder is in the correct location. If you don't get this message, you've successfully set up ControlP5. We'll talk about it in greater depth in Chapter 7 and show you more of the libraries that you can use in Processing.

# Loading External Data into Processing

Now that we've covered some of the basics of drawing with Processing and some of the basics of capturing user interaction, you'll learn how the Processing environment loads data, images, and movies. Earlier, we mentioned the default setup of a Processing project, with the folder *data* stored in the same folder as the *.pde* file. The Processing application expects that anything that's going to be loaded into the application will be in that folder. If you want to load a file named *sample.jpg*, you should place it in the *data* folder within the same folder as the *.pde* file you're working with.

## Loading and Displaying Images

First, you'll learn how to load images. One class and two methods encapsulate the most basic approach to loading and displaying images: the `PImage` class, the `loadImage()` method, and the `image()` method.

### The PImage class

Processing relies on a class called `PImage` to handle displaying and sizing images in the Processing environment. When you create a `PImage` object, you're setting up an object that can have an image loaded into it and then can be displayed in the Processing environment. To declare a `PImage` object, simply declare it anywhere in the application, but preferably at the top of the code, as shown here:

```
PImage img;
```

Once you've declared the `PImage` object, you can load an image into it using the `load Image()` method.

### The loadImage() method

This method takes as a parameter the name of an image file and loads that image file into a `PImage` object. The name of the file can be either the name of a file in the filesystem (in other words, in the *data* folder of your Processing application home folder) or the name of a file using a URL. This means you can do something like this to load a .jpg file from the Internet:

```
PImage rocks;
rocks = loadImage("http://thefactoryfactory.com/images/hello.jpg");
```

Or you can do the following to load an image from the *data* folder within your Processing application folder:

```
PImage rocks;
rocks = loadImage("hello.jpg");
```

The `loadImage()` method lets you load JPEG, PNG, GIF, and TGA images. Other formats, such as TIF, BMP, or RAW files, can't be displayed by Processing without doing some serious tinkering.

Now that you've looked at implementing the class that helps you display images and you've seen how to load images into the application, let's look at actually displaying those images using the `image()` method.

### The image() method

The `image()` method takes three parameters:

```
image(PImage, xPosition, yPosition);
```

The first is the `PImage` object that should be displayed. If the `PImage` has not been created with `loadImage()`, then trying to put it on the screen using the `image()` method will cause an error. There are ways around this, but we'll leave those to Chapter 10. For now, let's say that until a `PImage` object has had an image loaded into it, don't try to use it with the `image()` method. The next two parameters are the *x* and *y* positions of the upper-left corner of the image. This is where the image will be displayed. See Example 3-13.

*Example 3-13. image.pde*

```
PImage img;

void setup() {
    size(400, 400);
    img = loadImage("sample.jpg");
    image(img, 0, 0);
}
```

As soon as the `setup()` method is called, the window is given a size, the *sample.jpg* file is loaded into the `PImage`, and the `PImage` is placed in the window at the 0,0 position (that is, in the upper-left corner of the window). You can also size the `PImage` using the `image()` method. Like so many methods in Processing, the `image()` method is overloaded, letting you pass optional `width` and `height` values that will size the image:

```
image(img, x, y, width, height)
```

By default, the image is displayed in the Processing window at its default height and width, but you can also set the `height` and `width` of the image. Be aware, though, that the image may have a different aspect ratio and might look stretched or squashed slightly if using a size that doesn't match the original aspect ratio.

## Displaying Videos in the Processing Environment

The Processing environment contains a `Movie` class to display videos. This class relies on the Apple QuickTime video libraries, so if your computer doesn't have the Quick-Time libraries installed on it, you'll need to download and install them for your operating system. Note that at this time, working with video in Processing on Linux is a fairly difficult and involved process. The GSVideo library is fairly new and has a somewhat difficult setup procedure; however, it does appear quite workable and allows Linux users to work with different video formats in Processing. For the sake of brevity in this book, we'll leave you to explore it on your own, if you're curious.

## Using the Movie Class

The `Movie` class lets you load QuickTime movies; load movie files with *.mov* file extensions; play, loop, and pause movies; change the speed; and tint the video. Creating a `Movie` object is somewhat similar to creating an image using the `PImage` class, with one important distinction: you need to first import all the libraries that contain the information about the `Movie` class and how it works. These are all stored in a separate location that can be accessed by using the `import` statement, as shown here:

```
import processing.video.*;
```

Next, declare a `Movie` variable:

```
Movie mov;
```

In the `setup()` method, you need to *instantiate*, or create, a new instance of that `Movie` class. You do this by calling the constructor of the `Movie` class. The constructor of the `Movie` class is another overloaded method that has four signatures:

```
Movie(parent, filename)
Movie(parent, filename, fps)
Movie(parent, url)
Movie(parent, url, fps)
```

The `parent` parameter is the Processing application that will use and display the `Movie` class. For a simpler application, the parent is almost always the application itself, which you can reference using the `this` keyword:

```
Movie(this, http://sample.com/movie.mov");
```

This isn't vital to understand, but all Processing applications are instances of a Java class called `PApplet`. The `PApplet` class handles calling the `setup()` and `draw()` methods and handling the mouse movement and key presses. Sometimes, if you're referencing a Processing application from a child object loaded into it, the parent `PApplet` will be the application that your child is loaded into. This is fairly advanced stuff and not something you'll likely be dealing with, but if you come across the parent parameter, the `this` keyword in an application, or the `PApplet`, you'll know that all these things refer to the main application class.

The `filename` and `url` parameters work much the same as they do in the `loadImage()` method. When loading a local file stored on the machine that the Processing application is running on, use the filename of the *.mov* file. When loading a file from a site on the Internet, use a URL. Finally, as an optional parameter, you can pass a frame rate that the movie should be played at, if the frame rate of your movie and the frame rate of the Processing application are different. In the `setup()` method of this application, using the reference to the Processing application and the local filename, you'll instantiate the `Movie` object:

```
void setup() {
    size(320, 240);
    mov = new Movie(this, "sample.mov");
    mov.play();
}
```

In this code snippet, take a look at the `play()` method. This is important because it tells the Processing environment to start reading from the movie file right away. Without calling this method, the Processing application won't read the frames from the movie to display them. It's important to call either the `play()` or `loop()` method whenever you want the Processing environment to begin displaying your movie.

To read a movie, you need to define a `movieEvent()` method in the application. Why? Well, as the QuickTime Player plays the movie, it streams its video in pieces or frames (not too different from the frames of a film movie) to the Processing application, which then displays them in the window. The `movieEvent()` method is the QuickTime player notifying the Processing environment that a frame is ready to be displayed in much the same way that the `mousePressed()` method is the machine notifying the Processing environment that the mouse has moved. To get the information for the frame, you want to call the `read()` method of the `Movie` class. This reads the information for the frame into the `Movie` class and prepares the frame for display in the Processing environment:

```
void movieEvent(Movie m) {
    m.read();
}
```

To draw the current frame of the movie into the window, you use the `image()` method again just the same as you did for a `PImage` that contained all the information for a picture:

```
void draw() {
    image(mov, 0, 0);
}
```

This draws the current frame of the movie into the 0,0, or upper-left, corner of the window. Figure 3-7 shows the results of the complete code listing in Example 3-14.

*Example 3-14. movie.pde*

```
import processing.video.*;

Movie mov;
```

```
void setup() {
    size(320, 240);
    mov = new Movie(this, "sample.mov");
    mov.play();
}

void movieEvent(Movie m) {
    m.read();
}

void draw() {
    image(mov, 0, 0);
}
```

*Figure 3-7. Showing a video using the Movie class*

# Reading and Writing Files

The last thing to look at is reading in files. You can read in a file in two ways, and the one you should use depends on the kind of file you want to load. To load a picture, you would use the `loadImage()` method; to load a simple text file, you would use the `loadStrings()` method; and to load a file that isn't a text file, you would use the `load Bytes()` method. Since loading and parsing binary data with the `loadBytes()` method are much more involved, we'll leave those topics for Chapter 12 and focus instead on reading and writing simple text files.

### The loadStrings() method

The `loadStrings()` method is useful for loading files that contain text and only text. This means that loading more complex text documents like Microsoft Word files isn't going to work as smoothly as you'd like because they contain lots of information other than just the text. Generally, files with a *.txt* extension or plain-text files without an extension are OK. This means that files created in Notepad or in TextEdit will be loaded and displayed without any problems. To load the file, you call the `loadStrings()` method with either the filename or the URL of the text that you want to load:

```
loadStrings("list.txt");
```

Now, that's not quite enough, because you need to store the data once you have loaded it. For that purpose, you'll use an array of `String` objects:

```
String lines[] = loadStrings("list.txt");
```

This code makes the `lines` array contain all the lines from the text file, each with its own string in the array. To use these strings and display them, you'll create a `for` loop and draw each string on the canvas using the `text()` method, as shown in Example 3-15.

*Example 3-15. loadStringsDemo.pde*

```
void setup(){

    size(500, 400);

    PFont font;
    font = loadFont("Ziggurat-HTF-Black-32.vlw");
    textFont(font, 32);

    String[] lines = loadStrings("list.txt");
    print("there are " + lines.length + " lines in your file");
    for (int i=0; i < lines.length; i++) {
        text(lines[i], 20 + i*30, 50 + i*30);//put each line in a new place
    }
}
```

As a quick reminder, the text file that you load must be in the *data* folder of your Processing application or be downloaded from the Internet.

## The saveStrings() method

Just as you can read strings from a text file with the `loadStrings()` method, you can write them out to a file just as easily. The process is somewhat inverted. First, you make an array of strings:

```
String[] lines = new String[4];
lines[0] = "hello";
lines[1] = "out";
lines[2] = "there";
lines[3] = "!";
```

After creating an array, you can write the data back to a file by passing its name to the `saveStrings()` method:

```
saveStrings("data/greeting.txt", lines);
```

This creates and saves a file called *greeting.txt* with each element from the `lines` array on a separate line in the file.

# Running and Debugging Applications

To run your application, simply click the Run button in the Processing IDE; you'll see the output shown in Figure 3-8.

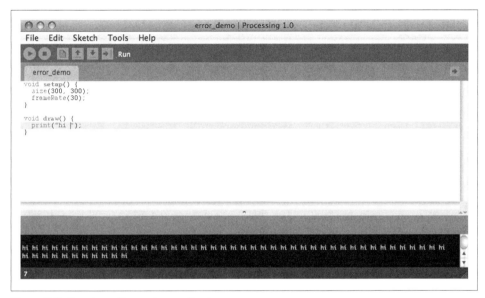

*Figure 3-8. Running a Processing application*

It couldn't be easier, could it?

What happens when it doesn't run? Look at the Message window in Figure 3-9.

Note the message, which is, in this case, very helpful:

```
The function printd(String) does not exist.
```

You see that the method you tried to call, `printd()`, doesn't exist. The Processing environment will also return deeper errors. For example, if you enter the following line in a `setup()` method:

```
frameRate(frames);
```

you may see this in the Console window:

```
No accessible field named "frames" was found in type "Temporary_85_2574".
```

This error indicates you've forgotten to define the variable frames. Change that line to this:

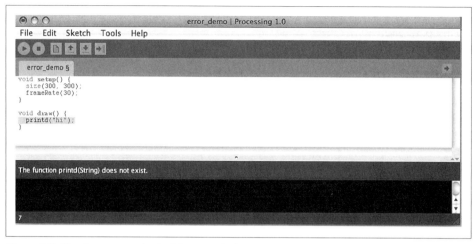

*Figure 3-9. Viewing an error in the Message window*

```
String frames = "foo";
frameRate(frames);
```

You'll see the following in the Console window:

```
Perhaps you wanted the overloaded version "void frameRate(float $1):" instead?
```

This tells you the `frameRate()` method does not accept a string as a parameter. Instead, it takes a float or an *int*. Since the Processing IDE always highlights the offending line, figuring out which line is causing the problems tends to be quite easy. Some errors, though, aren't so easy to figure out. In these cases, checking the Processing forums at *http://processing.org/discourse/yabb_beta/YaBB.cgi* is usually your best bet. Thousands if not tens of thousands of Processing users from all over the world ask and give advice on these forums. If you're having a problem, chances are someone has had it before, asked there, and gotten an answer.

## Exporting Processing Applications

Now, while running and debugging certainly helps when you want to see how the application is doing and check for errors in the code, it doesn't much help when you're trying to share it with a friend. To do that, you need to export the application.

The first step is to either select the Export Application option in the File menu or click Ctrl+E (⌘-E on OS X). This will bring up a dialog, shown in Figure 3-10, asking you what operating systems you would like to create a dialog for.

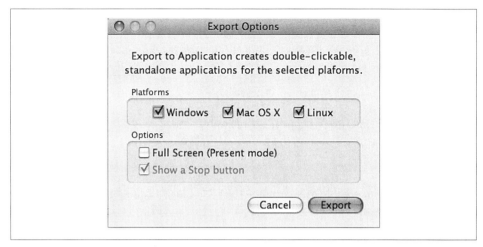

*Figure 3-10. Exporting an application*

Once you click the Export button, you'll be shown the location of your created executable files in your filesystem (see Figure 3-11). There should be four folders, one for each operating system that you've created an application for and one for an applet that can run in a web browser. Each folder for the operating system version contains your application, compiled and ready to run on a desktop machine. The fourth folder contains the file necessary to place your application in a website where it can be viewed in a browser.

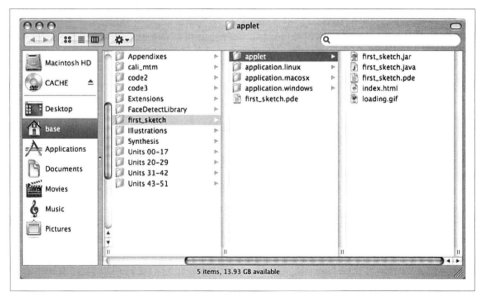

*Figure 3-11. What is created after exporting an application*

If you take a slightly closer look at what is generated by the export, you'll see four distinct folders. The first folder is the *applet* folder. This folder contains all the files that you'll need in order to put your Processing application on the Internet. You'll see each file in the order that it appears. This application is named *first_sketch*, so all the files will have that name:

*first_sketch.jar*
: This is the Java archive, or *.jar* file, that contains the Java runnable version of the sketch. When someone views the web page that contains your application, this file contains information about your application that will be used to run it.

*first_sketch.java*
: This is the Java code file that contains the code that the Java Virtual Machine will run to create your application.

*first_sketch.pde*
: This is your Processing code file.

*index.html*
: This is an HTML web page generated by the export that has the *first_sketch.jar* file embedded in it. When users open this page in a browser, if they do not have the correct Java runtime installed, a message directs them to the Sun site where they can download it. This file is created so that you can simply post the file to the Internet after you've created your application and have a ready-made page containing your Processing application.

*loading.gif*
: This *.gif* file is a simple image to show while the Java runtime is preparing to display your application.

So, in order to display your application online, simply place all the files in this folder in a publicly accessible location on a website.

The other three folders contain runnable executable versions of your processing application for each of the three major home operating systems: Windows, Mac OS X, and Linux. A Windows application for instance, has an *.exe* extension; an OS X application has an *.app* extension; and a Linux executable application doesn't have any extension. Each of these three options lets you show your application outside the browser. If you have a friend who has a Windows computer that you want to send the Processing application to, you would simply compress the folder and all the files it contains into an archive and send it to that person. They could then unzip the file and run it by clicking the executable file. Each of these folders contains somewhat different files, but they all contain the *.java* file for their application and the Processing *.pde* file within their source folder. This is important to note because if you don't want to share the source of your application, that is, the code that makes up your Processing application, remove this folder. If you want to share (remember that sharing is a good thing), then by all means leave it in and share your discoveries and ideas.

# Conclusion

If you're already thinking of exploring more about Processing, head to the Processing website at *http://processing.org*, where you'll find tutorials, exhaustive references, and many exhibitions of work made with Processing. Also, the excellent book, *Processing: A Programming Handbook for Visual Designers and Artists* (MIT Press), written by Casey Reas et al., provides a far more in-depth look at Processing than this chapter possibly could.

What next? Well, if you're only interested in working with Processing, then skip ahead to Chapter 7, where we explore different themes in computation and art and show you more examples of how to use Processing. If you're interested in learning about more tools for creating art and design, then continue with the next chapter. In Chapter 4, we discuss the open source hardware initiative that helps create physical interactions and integrates nicely with Processing.

# Review

Processing is both an IDE and a programming language. Both are included in the download, which is available at processing.org/download.

Processing is based on the Java programming language, but is simplified to help artists and designers more easily prototype visual and interactive applications.

The Processing IDE has controls on the top toolbar to run an application; stop an application; and create, open, save, or export an application. All of these commands are also available in the File menu or as hotkeys.

Clicking the Run button compiles your code and starts running your application.

A Processing application has two primary methods: the `setup()` method, which is called when the application starts up, and the `draw()` method, which is called at regular intervals.

You set the number of times the `draw()` method is called per second using the `frame Rate()` method.

The Processing drawing methods can be called within the `draw()` or `setup()` method, for example, with `rect()`, `ellipse()`, or `line()`. The method `background()` clears all drawing currently in the display window.

When drawing any shape, the `fill()` method determines what color the fill of the shape will be. If the `noFill()` method is called, then all shapes will not use a fill until the `fill()` method is called again.

Processing defines `mouseX` and `mouseY` variables to report the position of the user's mouse, as well as a `key` variable and a `keyPressed()` method to help you capture the user's keyboard input.

You can import libraries into Processing by downloading the library files and placing them in the Processing *libraries* folder and restarting the Processing IDE. Once the library has been loaded, you can use it in your application with the `import` statement to import all of its information, as shown here:

```
import ddf.minim.*; // just an example, using Minim
```

The `PImage` object and `loadImage()` method allow you to load image files into your Processing application and display and manipulate them.

The `Movie` class enables you to load QuickTime movies into your application, display them, and access their pixel data.

The `saveStrings()` and `loadStrings()` methods let you load data from text files, with a *.txt* extension, and also to save data to those files.

The `print()` method is helpful when debugging because it lets you trace the values of variables at crucial points where their values are being changed.

The Processing IDE prints any error messages to the Console window at the bottom of the IDE. These messages can be helpful when trying to determine the cause of an error or bug. This Console window is also where any print messages are displayed.

You can export a Processing application as either a standalone executable, an *.exe* file for Windows, an *.app* file for Mac OS X, or you can export it for the Web as a Java applet.

# CHAPTER 4

# Arduino

The word *Arduino* refers to three separate tools, which, bundled together, create the toolkit that we refer to as Arduino. First, there is the Arduino controller, which exists in several forms, from large to small to a freely available schematic that anyone with the requisite knowledge can assemble. Second, there is the language and compiler, which creates code for this microcontroller, and which, much like the Processing language, simplifies many of the tasks that challenge designers and developers alike when working with hardware and physical interaction. Finally, there is the Arduino programming environment, which, again like the Processing IDE, is a simple open source IDE built in Java. Therefore, because the word *Arduino* can have several meanings, I'll be quite specific when referring to a particular aspect of the environment, such as the *Arduino language*. When I simply refer to *Arduino*, I'm referring to the environment as a whole.

So, with that established, what is Arduino? It's a goal, and that goal is to simplify the creation of interactive applications or objects by simplifying the programming language used to create instructions and by providing a powerful yet basic controller that can easily be used for many common programming tasks while still being robust enough to support more complex projects. The Arduino controller is one of the most remarkable and popular open source projects because it enables so much. Programming microcontrollers can be, to the untrained, daunting and frustrating. Yet, being able to create working computers the size of a matchbox that can easily interact with hardware opens up an entirely new world of possibilities to interactive designers and artists.

> Tinkering is what happens when you try something you don't quite know how to do, guided by whim, imagination, and curiosity. When you tinker, there are no instructions, but there are also no failures, no right or wrong way of doing things. It's about figuring out how things work and reworking them.
>
> —Massimo Banzi, one of the originators of the Arduino project

What sorts of things do people make with Arduino? They create physical controls that people can interact with, including buttons, dials, levers, and knobs. They create interactive environments that use weight sensors, ultrasonic and infrared sensors, and temperature sensors. They create ways to control their appliances, control the lights in their houses, and control video cameras or still cameras, what's generally called *home automation* or a *smart house*. They create small robotics or mechanical toys. They create small autonomous programs that communicate with one another and send signals, thereby creating miniature or not-so-miniature networks. The potential of the controller, what it can do, and what it can enable you to do, is enormous. So, with little further ado, let's get started.

## Starting with Arduino

First, and perhaps most important, you'll need an Arduino controller. When you look at the Arduino home page you'll notice that there are around a dozen different Arduino controllers with several dozen more "Arduino-compatible" boards that can be used with the Arduino IDE and language. I recommend that beginners use the Arduino Uno. The Uno doesn't require anything more than a USB cable to get started, which means you can begin exploring the Arduino environment just moments after you open the box. This isn't to say that you have to use the Uno. The Arduino Mega, which provides a great deal more computational power and pins for input and output, is also an excellent choice. There is also the Arduino Nano, Pro, and the Pro Mini, all of which are smaller and easier to operate; you might explore these later after you've grown more comfortable with the Arduino. All of these are available from a great number of online electronics supply stores; a quick online search will be able to guide you to a few places.

You'll also need a USB cable with one end that is USB A and the other USB B, as shown in Figure 4-1.

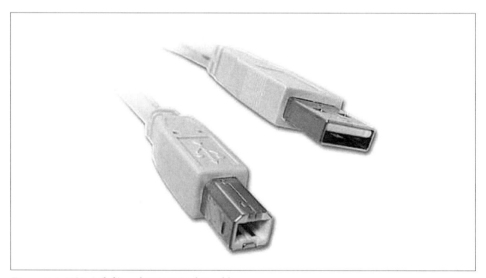

*Figure 4-1. USB A (left) and USB B (right) cables*

You'll use the USB cable to connect the Arduino controller to your computer, since the Arduino controller connects only with the USB B (the square shape), and most computers use only the USB A (the rectangular shape). If you don't have an Uno or similar board that has a built-in LED, it's also recommended that you purchase an LED light from an electronics store for testing purposes. Using a blinking light is a great way of verifying that the board is working and is a great tool for debugging code.

## Installing the IDE

The next part of the Arduino controller that you'll need is the IDE, which you can download from the Arduino website at www.arduino.cc/en/Main/Software. Select your operating system and download the zipped files. Once you've downloaded the files, unzip them. On a Mac, you should see something like Figure 4-2.

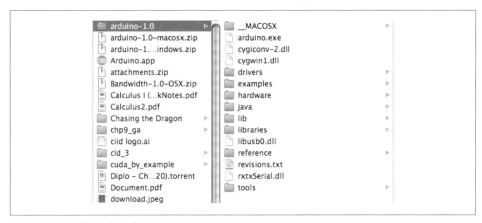

*Figure 4-2. Arduino download*

The drivers are what allow your computer to communicate with the Arduino board. Without these drivers installed, you won't be able to communicate with the Arduino, so it's important that they are installed before you try to upload any code. The file structure on a Windows or Linux computer will be the same, but the process for installing will be slightly different.

### Mac OS X

To install Arduino on OS X you simply drag the Arduino.app to your Applications folder and you're done.

### Windows

The easiest way to install the Windows drivers for the Arduino controller is simply to plug the controller in to your computer and wait for the Found New Hardware Wizard to appear. You may need to open the Device Manager, as shown in Figure 4-3.

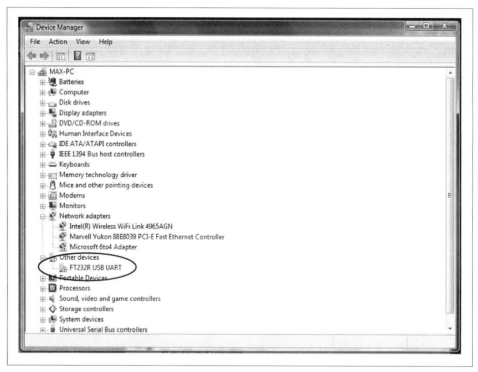

*Figure 4-3. Selecting devices*

Continue to the "Please choose your search and installation options" window, and add the location of the drivers folder to the locations that Windows will search for the driver by adding it to the "Search for driver software in this location" field, as shown in Figure 4-4.

Click Next until you get to the final screen, and then click Finish. The drivers are now installed, and you're ready to go.

### Linux

I hate to perpetuate stereotypes about Linux users, but I'm going to assume that if you're running Linux, you're clever enough to troubleshoot a lot of the difficulties and peculiarities of your particular distribution. With that in mind, here's a slightly more high-level overview of what's involved in getting Arduino running on a Linux machine, because it's a slightly more involved process. You will need to install the following programs:

- The Java Runtime Engine (called the JRE)
- avr-gcc (aka "gcc-avr")
- avr-libc

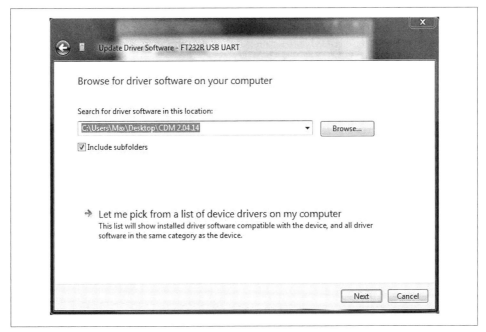

*Figure 4-4. Browsing for the installer files*

How you install these programs is going to depend on which distribution you are using. You will also need a compatible kernel. If you have `brltty` installed (the default on recent versions of Ubuntu), you'll need to remove it. Once you've done this, download the latest Arduino Linux distribution, extract these files to a directory, and run the *arduino* script. If you encounter problems, consult the Linux install instructions at www.arduino.cc/playground/Learning/Linux, where there are links to more detailed instructions for several of the most popular Linux distributions.

## Configuring the IDE

Once you've installed the drivers, you can run the IDE. On all systems, the Arduino IDE is an executable in the folder where the download was unzipped. You shouldn't move the actual executable because it requires the *hardware* folder in order to operate correctly. Once you start up the IDE, you'll need to configure it correctly. This means telling the IDE which board you're using and which serial port is connected to the Arduino controller. To select the board, go to Tools→Board, and select the board type, as shown in Figure 4-5.

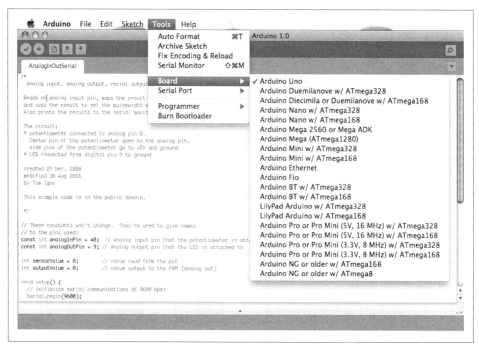

*Figure 4-5. Selecting the Arduino board*

Next, you'll need to select the port on which the board will operate. On OS X, this will be the option with the letters *tty* in it, as shown in Figure 4-6.

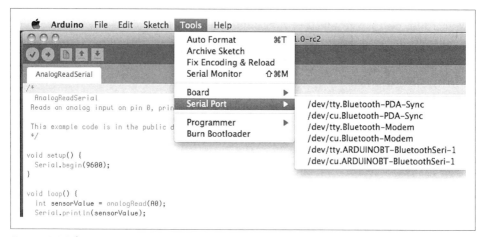

*Figure 4-6. Selecting a port on Mac OS X*

On a Windows computer, the ports will have the word *COM* in the title. You may need to do a little testing to determine which port is the correct one on your computer. Once you get the correct port, you're ready to go. If you'd like to run a simple script to check whether your board is working correctly, look ahead to the section titled "Touring the Arduino IDE" on page 105.

# Touring an Arduino Board

Now that you know how to install the Arduino IDE and drivers, you can move on to looking at the boards themselves. Since the Uno is the easiest and most straightforward of the boards, we'll contrast that one with some of the other Arduino controllers so you understand not only what the Uno is, but what makes it unique.

## The Controller

So, what is this controller? Really, it's just the same thing as your average computer, minus the hard drive and a few other things you might be used to having. The core elements are there, however. Input/Output (I/O) is done through pins and the USB port, the processor is there, and there is a small amount of random access memory (RAM) that acts much the same as RAM in a larger computer. Of course, all of these things are on a far smaller scale than a laptop or desktop computer, which means that the engineering is quite different in some respects, and there are many different issues that you need to consider with a microcontroller that you would not need to consider with a normal computer, particularly when working with powering other devices and powering the controller itself. That said, the general principles still apply, which makes working with microcontrollers a good way to learn more about the inner workings of computers and of computing.

## Uno Versus Mini Versus Mega

We'll be looking at three controllers. The Uno controller, shown in Figure 4-7, is a slightly larger controller that is a little easier to work with for beginners, since components can be attached directly to the controller.

*Figure 4-7. Arduino Uno controller*

The other Arduino controller that we'll examine is the Mini. This controller is much smaller, and that changes the types of projects that it can be used with. The Mini requires a separate USB adapter (see Figure 4-8) that allows you communicate with the controller over USB for uploading code and receiving messages over the Serial port. The Mini also requires that you purchase a prototyping board in order to wire any components to it or to power it separately from a computer using a battery. This isn't a great impediment, and you should purchase a prototyping board anyway for doing any kind of serious work with the Arduino controller.

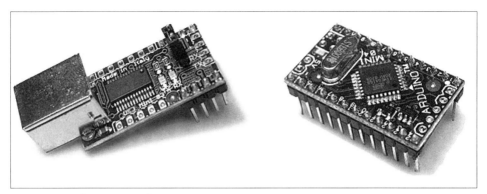

*Figure 4-8. Arduino Mini and Programmer*

The Uno comes with small LED lights that you'll find next to the USB port on the Uno. When you connect the controller to power, if there is a program currently loaded into the memory of the controller, a light should begin blinking. The Mini does not have such an easy way to tell that it's plugged in and powering up correctly, but making a small program that can turn on an LED that is connected to one of the Mini's pins is easy enough to do. We'll cover doing that a little bit later in the section "Hello World" on page 121.

Uno means *1* in Italian and was created to mark the release of Arduino 1.0. The Uno and version 1.0 will be the reference versions of Arduino, moving forward, so learning about the Uno is a great way to learn the core fundamentals of the Arduino environment. It is designed to be easy to understand and to work for those without experience in electronics. It has 20 pins (6 analog and 14 digital), 6 pulse-width modulation-enabled pins, a TX and RX pin pairing, and an I2C port. Newer boards (after revision 3) have four additional convenience headers that mirror other pins on the board. None of that makes sense? Then read on.

### What's a pin?

A *pin* provides an input or output through which the controller can communicate with components. Smallish copper wires can be inserted into the pins connectors, and you're off to the races. When you look at the Uno, you'll see a row of small black holes along either side of the controller that a wire can be inserted into.

### Digital versus analog pins

Digital pins have two values that can be read or written to them: high and low. *High* means that 5 volts (V) is being sent to the pin either from the controller or from a component. *Low* means that the pin is at 0 V. Now, start to imagine the sorts of information that this can encompass: on/off, there/not there, ready/not ready. Any kind of binary information can be read or written to a digital pin.

Analog pins are slightly different; they can have a wide range of information read or written to them. How wide a range? Well, from 0 to 255 can be written, which represents 256 steps of voltage information, once again starting with 0 V and going up to 5V. Analog values from 0 to 1,023 can be read (representing voltages from 0 to 5 V in 0.005 V increments). These pins are what we use to read and write information that has a range of values, such as the position of a dial, the distance of an object from an infrared sensor, or the brightness of an LED light. In addition to the digital and analog pins, there are connectors relating to the powering of components.

Figure 4-9 shows the Uno. Note that the digital pins are at the top of the picture. These are where you'll plug in any controls that communicate using digital signals, that is, either an on or off state. We'll talk more about this later in this chapter, but for the moment, understand that when we're referring to the digital ports, the ports at the top of the board are what we mean. Some of the ports are also enabled for pulse width modulation (PWM), which means, in essence, that they can be used to send analog information to a component. Those are ports 3, 5, 6, 9, 10, and 11, you can notice them by the tilde ~ next to the number. That means that these ports can be set to do things other than just digital communication. The possible values of these pins is IN (that is, the information is coming from the component to the control) and OUT (meaning the information is going to the component from the controller).

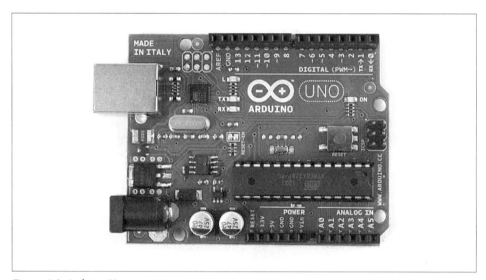

*Figure 4-9. Arduino Uno*

At the bottom of the controller, we have the power connectors that provide 5V power, provide 3.3V power, and provide two ground pins that can be used to ground any components that you attach to the Arduino controller. Power, voltage, and ground are all defined at the end of the book, so if you're not quite familiar with those terms, then make sure to read it.

Just to the right of the power pins are the Analog In pins. These allow you to receive analog information, that is, information in a range of voltage from 0 to 5V, in 4.9mV (millivolt) increments, which means that the analog information can be between 0 and 1,023. These pins are quite important, because many different types of controls send analog information in a range of values, such as a dial being turned or an infrared sensor sending range information.

Above the analog pins is the processor that the Arduino controller runs. Just above the processor is the reset button. This allows you to restart your program. This is important to know because the controller saves any program uploaded to it. So, if you write a program for your controller that is made to blink an LED on or off, it will begin running that program when you power up the Arduino. The reset button stops the program that is currently running. To change the program saved on the Arduino, you'll need to clear the memory by uploading a new program. Just to the right of the reset button are the ICSP pins, which allow you to program the Arduino without using the USB cable (handy in some situations).

As a comparison, the Arduino Mini was first introduced in 2006 and is a space-saving alternative to the larger Uno. It can be so much smaller because it uses a different processor package, does not have the same easy-access pins that the Uno has, and requires a USB adapter that can communicate with the computer over USB. That said, the size of the controller means you can use it in projects where space is truly at a premium.

### Pins on the Mini

When you turn over the Mini controller, you'll see a row of small copper pins that represent each pin. These function in the same way as the connectors on the Uno, but where you can simply insert a wire into the Uno, you'll need to insert the Mini into a prototyping board and then attach a wire to the same line on the board, as shown in Figure 4-10.

The Mini has 14 digital pins, which, as you can see in the diagram in Figure 4-10, has 8 along the left side of the board and 4 more along the bottom of the right side. Since the pins are not marked on the Mini as they are on the Uno, it's important to know which pin is which. Above the four digital pins on the right side of the controller are the four analog pins. Unlike the Uno, all of these can be set to read data in or write data out. The other four analog pins (4–7) are at the bottom of the controller in a square-shaped formation.

Next to analog pins 4–7 are a pair of power pins, a ground pin, and a +5V pin to power components. Looking at the Mini, there are 3 +5V power pins and 4 ground pins, one on each side of the board. This makes the Mini even better suited for working in tight places, because grounding pins can be accessed from all sides of the controller, a real blessing when space is at a premium.

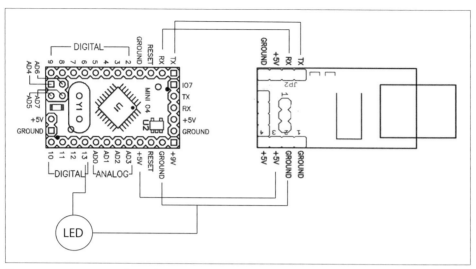

*Figure 4-10. Connecting the Arduino Mini to the Programmer*

### Pins on the Mega

For comparison, we'll take a look at the Arduino Mega now, to show what you can get for a little extra space and battery drain. The Arduino Mega 2560 has 54 digital input/output pins (of which 14 can be used as PWM outputs), 16 analog inputs, 4 UARTs (hardware serial ports), a 16 MHz crystal oscillator, a USB connection, a power jack, an ICSP header, and a reset button. So you have four times the number of PWM pins and analog in pins as the Uno, which makes the Mega a formidable tool for larger systems. You'll need to consider that it still pushes the same amount of current though, so you won't be able to drive servos on all those pins without an external power supply.

As of the writing of this book, these are just some of the other Arduino controllers:

*Nano*
> A compact board designed for breadboard use, the Nano connects to the computer using a Mini USB B cable.

*Ethernet*
> The Ethernet Arduino controller contains an Ethernet controller and port so that the board can connect to a wired network via Ethernet.

*LilyPad*
> Designed for wearable application, this board can be sewn onto fabric and is a stylish purple.

*Pro*
> This board is designed for advanced users who want to leave a board embedded in a project. It's cheaper than an Uno and easily powered by a battery, but it requires additional components and assembly.

*Pro Mini*

Like the Pro, the Pro Mini is designed for advanced users requiring a low-cost, small board and willing to do some extra work.

There are also numerous non-Arduino microcontroller boards that are quite similar to the Arduino: Teensy, Freeduino, Sanguino, Bare Bones Board, LEDuino, and Miduino, among others. The nice thing is that once you've learned the basics of using one of these boards, you can apply that knowledge to using any of the others depending on your preference and the particulars of your project.

## Touring the Arduino IDE

First, we'll take a look at the IDE, and then we'll look at the language that the Arduino controller uses. Looking around the IDE you'll notice that it's quite similar to the Processing IDE. This is no accident; the Processing project shared the code and design philosophy for the Arduino IDE, keeping a light, simple, and intuitive design with the IDE.

Before discussing the IDE, we'll explain how Arduino works. In Processing, for example, you compile and then run the code. Arduino adds an extra step to this: you compile the code, but the next step is to upload it to the Arduino controller so you can run it. Your computer doesn't run Arduino code, so you'll need to upload your code to a controller that can run the code in order to test what you've written. As soon as code is uploaded to the Arduino controller, it runs right away, so the *run* step of the Processing workflow is entirely removed and replaced by an *upload* step. Now, take a look at the buttons at the top of the controller (see Figure 4-11).

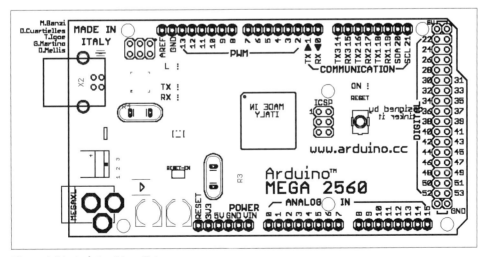

*Figure 4-11. Arduino Mega Printouts*

Clicking the *Run* button does not in fact run your code; it checks for errors and compiles your code. Still, when you're writing code, it's quite handy to know what your errors are before you've uploaded anything to the board. The *Stop* button stops the IDE from listening on the serial port. There's more information on how this works in the section "Debugging Your Application" on page 124 later in this chapter. The *New* button simply creates a new application, but note that it doesn't save it automatically. The *Open* button opens a project from your local machine. The *Save* button saves your project. The *Upload to Board* button actually uploads your code to the board, assuming that the board is properly connected and all the drivers are properly installed. Finally, the last button on the right opens the Serial Monitor window. This is quite important if you want feedback from the controller.

The Sketch menu of the toolbar (shown in Figure 4-12) contains some duplicates of the functionality in the IDE controls but also contains some other interesting options.

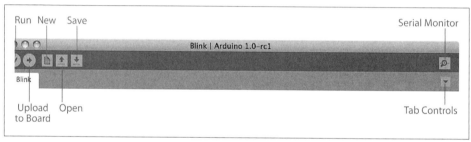

*Figure 4-12. Controls of the Arduino IDE*

The *Import Library* option allows you to import functionality from a library created for a specific purpose, for instance, working with motors or I2C communication. These can be either the default libraries that come with Arduino or a library that you have created yourself. If you select the Stepper library, for example, you'll see the following line appear in the code window:

```
#include <Stepper.h>
```

This imports the Stepper library into the project, making all of its functionality available to your application. You'll find more information on importing libraries and functionality later in this chapter. The Show Sketch Folder option is a shortcut that brings up the folder in your operating system (OS) where the application files are stored. This is helpful if you're storing other files with your application or need to copy or change a file in the file system. Finally, the *Add File* option allows you to select a file easily from anywhere in your operating system and save it to the folder where your application is located.

The *Tools* menu (shown in Figure 4-13) contains menu buttons for selecting the controller and port on which the controller is connected to your computer. Additionally, this menu item contains the *Auto Format* option, which formats all your code to standardize the indentations and spacing. It also contains a *Copy for Forum* option, which copies all the code in an application to the system clipboard of your computer in an HTML-ready format so that it can be pasted into a web page without losing its formatting. The *Archive Sketch* option simply creates a *.zip* file of your application. Finally, the *Burn Bootloader* option is a rather advanced topic. Suffice to say that you won't need to burn a bootloader with any of the controllers that we'll be looking at unless you're building your own board.

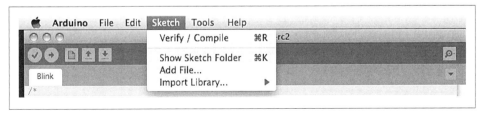

*Figure 4-13. The Sketch menu options*

So, now that we've examined the basics, let's start writing some code. The code window is the main window of the IDE, which is where all your code will go. Once you've written something, you'll want to compile the code, which you can do by clicking the *Run* button. Give the code in Example 4-1 a spin.

*Example 4-1. blink.ino*

```
void setup() {
    pinMode(13, OUTPUT);       // sets digital pin 13 as output
}

void loop() {
    digitalWrite(13, HIGH);
    delay(500);
    digitalWrite(13, LOW);
    delay(500);
}
```

For those of you with Uno controllers, if there are no errors, you can click the button to upload the code to your board. You should see the TX and RX lights on your controller blink as the code is being uploaded and the memory for the program initialized, and you'll then see a message displayed in the Console window of the IDE that says something like this:

```
Binary sketch size: 1092 bytes (of a 14336 byte maximum)
```

If that works, you'll see the LED on your board start blinking, and you're ready for the next section. If it doesn't, your controller is probably not connected properly. Check the settings for your controller and the port in the Arduino IDE, and try again.

# The Basics of an Arduino Application

We're going to jump into code now rather than wiring for one simple reason: you've already seen code, so what you learned in the previous chapter will help you understand the new things in this chapter. In fact, the Arduino language is structured quite similarly to the Processing language with regard to how the application itself is structured. There is a setup() statement, and code within that statement runs once when the application first starts up. Then there is a loop() statement, which runs over and over again. Almost all Arduino applications consist of the declaration of some variables that will be needed throughout the lifetime of the application, one-time initialization to set things up ready to run, and functions to use in the main loop.

## The setup Statement

The setup() statement is the first thing called in the Arduino application. As in a Processing application, this is where things that need to be initialized should be placed. For instance, if you're going to use the serial port for debugging your application, you'll need to start the serial connection using the Serial.begin() method in the setup() method. Some devices need to be initialized when the microcontroller starts up; other devices need to have a signal sent to them just after the device starts up but before it's used. These are the sorts of tasks that should be handled in the setup() statement. All applications must have a setup() method, even if nothing is done in them. This is because the compiler will check for this method, and if it isn't defined, an error will occur.

## The loop Method

The loop() method contains anything that needs to happen repeatedly in the application; that could be checking for a new value from a control, sending information to a computer, sending a signal to a pin, or sending debug information. Any instructions in this method will be run repeatedly until the application is terminated. Usually we want to check any values that might be input from a control or another program, determine what to do with the input, and then send any information or instructions to any other components or programs that might need them. We'll look at two examples, one simple and one more complex.

In Figure 4-14, you'll see the organization of the code for a simple program to turn a light on and off when a button is pressed. There are three distinct elements to this program:

initialization

> This element contains all the variables and values that will be used throughout the program. Recall that if a variable is declared within a method, then it exists only

within that method. This is called *variable scope*. If this doesn't sound familiar, take a look back at Chapter 2.

setup

This element contains the code to configure the pin for the button to receive information from a control and set the pin for the light to send information.

loop

This element contains the code to check the value of the button. If it is sending a LOW signal, that is, if the button is pressed, then send a signal to the light to turn on; otherwise, it tells the light to turn off.

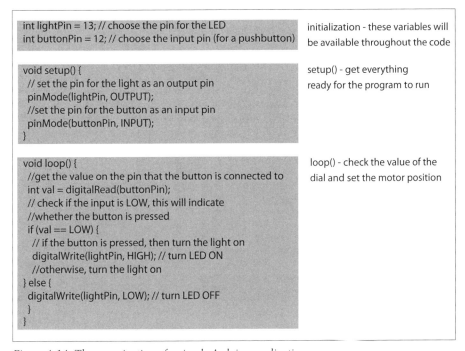

Figure 4-14. The organization of a simple Arduino application

Figure 4-15 shows how an Arduino application breaks these elements down.

*Figure 4-15. Tools menu of the Arduino IDE*

Another, slightly more complex example is to use a potentiometer (more commonly but less accurately called a dial) to set the position of a stepper motor. Stepper motors are covered in much greater detail later in this chapter and in Chapter 11, but for the moment, think of a stepper motor as being a motor that has distinct positions that it can be placed at, rather than a simple motor like a fan that simply spins. To use a stepper motor in Arduino, import the Stepper library into the application. Once again, you'll learn more about importing libraries into an Arduino application later in this chapter; for the moment, we want to familiarize you more with the structure of an Arduino application. So our steps for this application will be as follows:

1. `import`: before you do anything else, you need to import any libraries that you'll use in the application.
2. `initialization`: this initializes the variables, which in this case includes the Stepper object that you'll use to handle positioning the stepper motor correctly.
3. `setup`: this sets the speed of the Stepper object.
4. `loop`: this checks the value of the dial and sets the position of the stepper motor accordingly.

Figure 4-16 shows the organization of a more complex Arduino application.

# Features of the Arduino Language

The Arduino language is designed to support communication with electronic components. It works in a similar way to Processing, but it is structured a little bit differently because it deals with different problems. When dealing with electrical components, you are usually sending information as voltage or, in the case of I2C, sending communication in binary strings. Still, these forms of communication are at the very root and core of computing; they are, to use two very geeky terms, *low level* and *close to the metal*. When one sends an instruction as a pattern of electrical bursts, they're really working at the level that electrical components speak rather than asking a *higher-level* or more abstract programming language to do it for them.

```
#include <Stepper.h>

// create an instance of the stepper class
// this requires specifying the number of steps of the motor
//and the pins it's attached to
Stepper stepper(100, 8, 9, 10, 11);

// the previous reading from the analog input
int previous = 0;

void setup()
{
  // set the speed of the motor to 30 RPMs
  stepper.setSpeed(30);
}

void loop()
{
  // get the sensor value from the dial
  int val = analogRead(0);

  // move a number of steps equal to the change in the
  // sensor reading
  stepper.step(val - previous);

  // remember the previous value of the sensor
  previous = val;
}
```

import - import any libraries that will be used in the application

initialization - these variables will be available throughout the code

setup() - get everything ready for the program to run

loop() - check the value of the dial and set the motor position

*Figure 4-16. The organization of a more complex simple Arduino application*

The language that Arduino uses is essentially C++. Now, a quick word on C++ is relevant here because it's important to understand what C++ is and how Arduino is and isn't like C++. C++ is an old programming language, which makes it very well suited for our purposes because it was designed back when computing memory and processing power were at a premium. This means that while C++ may not be friendly to read and write for the new programmer, it certainly is stingy with its resources, making it perfect for doing things on a microcontroller where resources are more limited than on a desktop machine or laptop. The Arduino language relationship with C++ is quite similar to the relationship that the Processing language has with Java. If you understand C++, you'll understand a lot of Arduino, and conversely, if you understand Arduino, you'll understand *some* C++. Now, it's important to note that Arduino is not quite C++, which is to say that if you find some neat C++ code somewhere that you want to run, pasting it into the Arduino IDE and expecting it to work might lead to disappointment. You can do this, but it requires some planning and some serious knowledge of what you're doing.

The basics of the Arduino programming language are similar to C++ and Processing. Methods are defined with a return type and any parameters like so:

```
return methodName(params...) {}
```

Variables are defined like so:

```
variableType variableName;
```

Some of the other features of the Arduino language aren't going to be so immediately familiar, but the next few paragraphs will help explain some of the more important ones.

## Constants

The Arduino language has the following constant variables that can be used throughout any Arduino application:

true/false
> You can always use true and false just as they are. These are predefined, never change, and are always available:
>
> ```
> if(variable == true) {
> doSomething();
> } else {
> doSomethingElse();
> }
> ```

HIGH/LOW
> These define the voltage level on a digital pin, either 5V or 0V. These make your code more readable:
>
> ```
> digitalWrite(13, HIGH);
> ```

INPUT/OUTPUT
> These are constants used for setting pins that can be used either for output or for input:
>
> ```
> pinMode(11, OUTPUT);
> ```
>
> As you'll notice, the OUTPUT constant is used to set the value of the pin using the pinMode() method. This seems like a good place to segue into the core methods of the Arduino language.

## Methods

Now you should learn about some of the methods of the Arduino language:

pinMode(pinNumber, mode)
> Remember that the digital pins of the Arduino controller can be set to either input or output, which is to say that they'll send values to a controller or receive values from a controller. Before we use a digital pin, though, we need to establish in which

direction the information on that controller will be flowing. Usually you do this in the setup() method, because you'll rarely need to do it more than once in an application.

digitalWrite(value, pin)

This method sets a digital pin to HIGH if value is high or LOW if value is low, which is to say that it sends 5V or 0V through the pin. This can work only on pins that have been set to OUTPUT using pinMode(). For example:

```
pinMode(11, OUTPUT);
digitalWrite(11, HIGH);
```

If the pinMode() method hasn't been used to set the pin to be OUTPUT, then calling digitalWrite will have no effect.

int digitalRead(pinNumber)

This method reads the state of a pin that is in input mode. This can be either HIGH or LOW, that is, 5 V or 0 V, and no other value. The digitalRead method is used for reading buttons, switches, anything that has a simple on and off, and any control that returns a simple true or false, 1 or 0, or other type of binary value. It returns the value of the pin read as an integer.

analogRead(pinNumber)

This reads the value of an analog pin, returning a range from 0 to 1,023, that represents the voltage being passed into the pin. As you'll discover later, it is important that any controllers you connect to your Arduino controller send analog signals in the range between 0 and 5 V because higher values will not be read and could damage the board. This method returns an integer and so can be used as shown here:

```
int analogVal = analogRead(11);
```

This code snippet uses the value returned from the analogRead method and stores it in the analogVal integer. This is a common technique that allows you to retrieve the value from a pin and use that value later in your code.

analogWrite(pin, value)

This writes an analog value to a pin and can be any value between 0 and 255. This means that the value sent to this method can be used as an adjustable voltage and sent through the pin to any controller on the side:

```
analogWrite(11, 122);
```

delay(ms)

This method tells the program to wait for a given number of milliseconds before executing the next instruction. In practice, this means that in the following lines of code:

```
digitalWrite(13, HIGH);
delay(1000);
digitalWrite(13, LOW);
```

there will be a delay of one full second between when the first instruction and the third instruction are executed. In practice, this is often used for timing, such as controlling how long, for example, a light stays lit.

millis()

This returns the number of milliseconds since the program started running. This can be useful if you need to keep track of time, which you can do by storing the result of the millis call and then comparing with another millis call at some later point, as shown here:

```
long timer = 0;
void setup() {
    timer = millis();// get the timer the first time
}
void loop() {
    int lengthOfALoop = millis() - timer; // compare it
    timer = millis(); // now set the timer variable again
}
```

Of course, you might want to do something more interesting with millis, but it's a start.

## Arrays

Arduino treats arrays in much the same way as C++ and somewhat like Processing, though you cannot use the constructor with an array as with Processing. The same rules about what can be stored in the array apply:

```
int intArray[10]; // now the array is ready, no need to call new Array()
intArray[4] = 4;
intArray[3] = "hello!"; // doesn't work!
```

You can also declare and initialize an array at the same time:

```
int preinitialized[3] = {1, 2, 3};
```

## Strings

Working with strings in Arduino is different from working with strings in Processing or openFrameworks because the Arduino language doesn't use a String class like C++ and Processing. This might seem like a big deal at first, but you'll realize after working with Arduino for a little while that the types of things that you do with Arduino don't require strings or text as frequently. If you do need to work with a String class, you need to make an array of characters, as shown here:

```
char name[5] = {'j', 'o', 's', 'h', 0};
```

or

```
char name[] = "josh";
```

If you need to, for example, store multiple strings in an array, you can create an array with multiple char arrays stored within it:

```
char* multichar[4];
char name1[5] = {'j', 'o', 's', 'h',0};
char name2[5] ={'t', 'o', 'd', 'd',0};
```

or

```
char * multichar[] = {"josh", "todd"};
```

OK, so what's going on here? You'll notice that there's a pointer being used in a somewhat non standard way to store the arrays. Pointers are covered in greater detail in Chapter 5. When you declare the array, you're declaring that it will store pointers to char variables. Though this may seem a little strange at first, it isn't hard to get used to, and generally, in Arduino, you're not dealing very extensively in Strings.

## Interview: David Cuartielles

David Cuartielles was one of the creators of the Arduino project along with Massimo Banzi. He currently teaches and mentors at the University of Malmo in Sweden. You can find more information about his work and thoughts at www.0j0.org.

*What sorts of things are you most excited about working on?*

**David Cuartielles:** We take projects that we consider challenging. We could say that we don't do this for the money but for the pleasure of making things the best way possible. We are in a constant learning process. For example, today I am in Seoul (Korea) to teach about generative music using Arduino boards, a topic I have been researching for the last months, just for fun. Now it is time to see if this research was worth the effort!

*Can you explain the history of the Arduino controller and what the original motivations for it were?*

**David:** For the individual people in the team, the motivations were a little different. To me, the important thing was to create an educational tool that would be so cheap that people could afford giving it away inside their pieces.

We made it in a couple of days of hacking during after-work hours at Interaction Design Institute Ivrea (IDII) in Italy. Massimo Banzi and I were discussing the need of something like this. A couple of his students joined the discussion, and one of them, David Mellis, started to craft the software in a very neat way, wrapping functionality together in a way that was very easy for people without a true technical background to understand. We were trying to create a new way to prototype and a new way to think about prototyping things.

*How did you begin working with electronics and coding?*

**David:** I burned my first computer at the age of 9. It was a Commodore 64, and I was trying to make an LED screen. It was fun and sad at the same time. It took a couple of months until I could get replacement parts to fix it. I use all the Arduino controllers extensively; it is very powerful when used in, I guess, "expert mode." I like to code aloud, letting people around me look at the code while I write it...I guess that is why I became a teacher.

*You run a toy-making company (according to a bio I found of you online). Can you talk a little bit about making toys and how you began doing that and what sorts of toys you find yourself making.?*

**David:** Right now we are focusing on sound. Everything you see around has the shape of a keyboard, as if we didn't know how to play with any other tools. Our first toy collection is dealing with this issue. At the same time, we are documenting all our processes, and we are trying to make the first open source toy collection in the world.

*What is the philosophy of open hardware? How is it different/same as the open source software philosophy?*

**David:** To me the only difference is that one of those two happens to have a physical representation. Hardware costs money beyond the personal effort of creation. Software can be given completely for free; hardware cannot.

*You do a lot of workshops and teaching. What sorts of things do you try to focus on with beginning students?*

**David:** I focus on learning. Many people come to me with a motor in one hand or a screen or whatever weird gadget and ask, "Can I hook this up to Arduino?" Then I answer, "Yes, what for?" I don't fancy technology. To me, it is just a way to understand more about our current way of living.

For me, it is more important that people understand how it works than them making the fanciest project in the world. On the other hand, once people understand, it becomes much easier to make fun projects.

*This is a very broad question, so feel free to answer however you would like: how are interactions developed? What sorts of processes do you go through, from envisioning a project to creating a rough prototype to creating a finished piece?*

**David:** There is a lot of value in knowing what may or may not work while developing a piece. However, many times we give a try to things we don't fully believe in just because we can try them easily, and we can clarify our potential doubts by actually physically interacting with the object.

To me, the idea of "designing an interaction" is based either in the concept of aesthetically pleasant interaction or, sometimes, in the more functionalist concept of meaningful interaction. The issue for me is, "Is it really possible to anticipate the audience's feelings toward whatever object or experience we produce?" Shall we then "design the interaction" or just make something that is pleasant for us?

*You very often work with other designers, engineers, and artists. Can you talk a little bit about how you find it best to work with others on a particular art piece? Is this different from how the core Arduino team has collaborated on the design of the various Arduino controllers?*

**David:** Yes, with Arduino we have kind of a higher mission than making just one piece. We want to help people make their own pieces, and that requires an extra effort in documentation and community building. Working on making a piece for/together with someone means solving technical issues and accommodating as much as possible the project's expectations. Making Arduino means trying to set up a quality standard in how to speak about things.

*How do you see the relationship between industrial design and engineering and fine arts and more visual design changing now and also in the next few years?*

**David:** Right now we are experiencing a revival of the craft, not only in design but also in the arts. Conceptual art is being left behind, and artists are going back to the galleries bringing illustrations and beautifying our lives with objects. It is a cycle that in my opinion was a logical step to take after postmodernism. Visual design (understood as graphic design) is in my eyes a very powerful tool for artists to express their ideas and point controversial topics. Illustration is a technique to do so.

Industrial design and engineering are experiencing some kind of similar romance. Now we are seeing new tools that allow industrial designers to jump from conceptualizing to actually crafting the objects to a certain extent. They don't just do boxes and let us imagine the rest; they prototype the interaction and start to give extra thoughts to the physical affordances of objects in terms of how they will be used as digital artifacts.

*Do you see a difference between "interactive art" and "interactive design"?*

**David:** Yes and no. I jump from one to the other constantly, because I come from the line of action of "critical design" where we create objects to express existential conflicts. This ends up being very close to art. On the other hand, during the last few years, I have gotten to know a lot of people coming from the conceptual arts and moving toward electronic art, and their theoretical framework is so much heavier than mine. There is where I think that art and design differ a little. Design has sometimes that quality of not needing to express anything, and just entertain instead.

*What do you see as the most exciting areas or themes of exploration in physical computing?*

**David:** Now that we have both Wii Remote and iPhone, anything else is rediscovering the wheel…just kidding, of course. I think there is a lot to do. The field of *haptics* (touch-based feedback) is still in an early stage. There is no common language for physical programming of objects. We have to learn about new smart materials—not just textiles, but all sorts of intelligent plastics, and so on.

As I see it, considering the state of the art of technology, projects are constructed from either physical computing objects with embedded intelligence or computer vision installations, or hybrids. Knowing about one of the fields is a must for interaction designers. Many times there are two ways of solving the same issue, and those two ways can be framed within these two categories.

*What are some of the projects or designs that you've seen that you feel best embody the idea of an interactive device?*

**David:** I love the Wii Remote because it has everything people have been discussing physical computing should be. It is nothing but a magic wand, a link to the infrastructure that does almost nothing by itself, but it has a very good cause-effect relationship (thanks to the well-crafted software). I also like that it is hackable; it is a property of digital technologies to be hackable, modifiable, and copyable.

On the other hand, there is a project by some of my students called *Table Talk* that anyone can find on YouTube (created by Marcus Ericsson et al.; see *http://tabletalk .se/*); it shows the idea of subtle interaction that happens without having to jump on things or dance or clap your hands. It is the total opposite of the Wii Remote, and it best expresses this second category of devices that do things without demanding users to be crazily active.

# How to Connect Things to Your Board

Of course, the one thing that we haven't talked about much yet is how to actually connect things to your board. To connect a component to your board, you need to create an electrical connection between the correct pin on your board and the correct corresponding pin on the component. There are two ways of getting this done: using a project board and solder or using a prototyping board.

Soldering should be used once your designs are really ready. Prototyping boards save time and solder because they allow you to fix mistakes easily. Just pop the wires out, and connect them in the right place; it's much easier than needing to undo a bunch of solder and resolder it all. There are lots of situations in electronics where you don't want to use a prototyping board because they can allow stray current to leak around places you might not want it, but since the controller of the Arduino is already somewhat protected, a breadboard is fine to use. Figure 4-17 shows a prototyping board.

To connect the controller to the board, you can use either solid 24-gauge wire or jumper wires like the kind shown in Figure 4-18.

Both the prototyping board and the wires can be procured from an electronics store and will make your Arduino experimenting life a lot easier. A prototyping board has two different directions for its rows. The rows on the edge of the board travel the length of the board, as you can see in Figure 4-19.

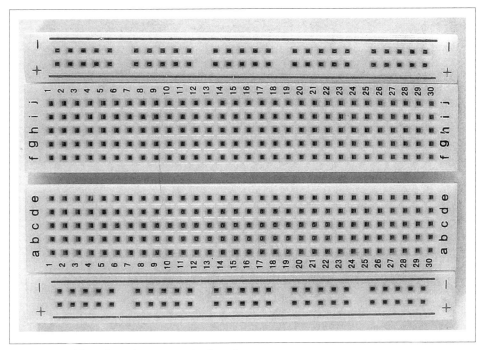

*Figure 4-17. A breadboard or prototyping board*

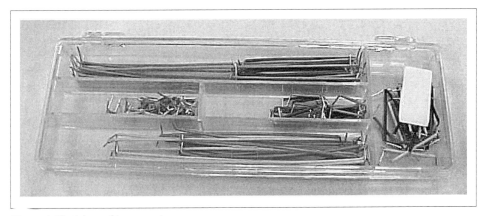

*Figure 4-18. A box of jumper wires*

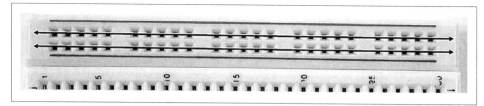

*Figure 4-19. Top of a breadboard with lengthwise rows*

The top two rows are usually used with one row providing access to power for all components and the other providing a ground for all components on the board. The middle of the board is a little different, as shown in Figure 4-20.

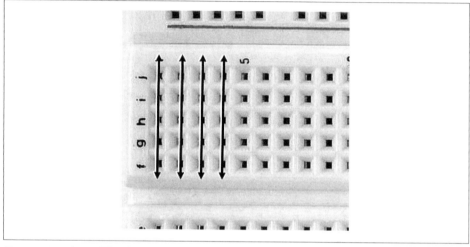

*Figure 4-20. The middle of the board runs widthwise*

The middle of the board is where you connect components and controllers together. Each row can be connected to the others using either 24-gauge wire or jumper wires. Connecting two rows together makes them share a circuit.

Once you have your design ready to go, you can easily pick up a drilled breadboard, some solder, and a soldering iron and get started making a more permanent version of your project. Until then, though, it's easier to use the prototyping board. There's one more thing you'll need to connect things to your board: a resistor.

## Resistors

The resistor is one of the most important electrical components that you'll use, and for that reason we should explain why they get their own section. Resistors do one thing: resist the flow of electrical current, hence the name resistor. By resisting current, not letting it flow, they control where and how fast electrons flow.

Everyone, from high school physics teachers to electrical engineers, uses the current-as-water metaphor, and for consistency sake, I'm going to stick with it. Imagine that electrical current is water, a stream flowing along. Now imagine that you force the water through a pipe that is slightly smaller than the stream bank. This will cause some of the water to not get through; you'll be limiting the amount of water flowing. Smaller the pipe, the less water gets through. This, in essence, is the resistor. The resistor only allows a certain amount of the electrical current to pass through it. It has a special relationship to the voltage and the current that you'll see a little farther down the page. To continue with our water metaphor: with a fire hydrant, you want low resistance, with a water fountain, you want high resistance. Mix up the two pipe sizes and you can't put out a fire and hurt yourself trying to get a small sip of water. Most electrical components are the same: they can only handle certain amounts of current or they use certain amounts of current to signal states or modes. Resistors are the way to do both of these.

Now we move on to the more scientific explanation. Resistance is measured in ohms, written as the Omega symbol $\Omega$. The larger the resistance value, the less current it allows. Resistors generally range from 1 ohm at the smallest to 1 mega-ohm (1.0 M$\Omega$) at the largest. You can read the resistor by looking at the colored stripes on the body of the resistor, called the resistor color code, but they're difficult to understand at first. Luckily a quick online search will show you mobile phone apps, reference tables, calculators, and other tools to help you understand which resistor you have in your hand.

Now the math: the ratio of the voltage applied across resistor's terminals to the intensity of current flowing through the resistor is called resistance. This relation is represented with something called Ohm's law:

```
voltage = current * resistance
```

often written as

```
V = IR
```

That means that the current can be found by dividing the voltage by the resistance.

```
I = V/R
```

LEDs can only handle certain amounts of current. The 5V of your Arduino passed through a 1K ohm resistor means that there are 0.005 amps passing through the LED. That's perfectly safe for the LED. Allow more current to pass through and the LED will burn out, allow less and it will glow less brightly. There's more to know about resistors, but we'll leave it at that for the moment.

# Hello World

The "Hello World" of the Arduino controller is a blinking light. For this to work, you'll need to do your first little bit of wiring with the Arduino controller, attaching an LED to pin 13 of your controller with a 5K resistor as shown in Figure 4-21. To get this to work properly, you'll need to add a new element to the wiring scheme, the 1k resistor. We're using the resistor to prevent the Arduino from burning out the LED, since the Arduino can send more current than an LED can handle.

Once you've attached the pin to the controller, put the following in the code window of the IDE, and click Run. After the IDE has finished compiling the code, click Upload. It should take a few seconds to upload the code to the controller, and then you should see the LED blink on and then off in a syncopated rhythm.

*Example 4-2. brightness.ino*

```
int ledPin = 9;
int brightness = 0;
boolean increase;

void setup() // run once, when the application starts
{
  pinMode(ledPin, OUTPUT); // sets the pin where our LED is as an output
  increase = true;
}

void loop() // run over and over again
{
  if(increase)
    brightness++;
  else
    brightness--;

  if(brightness == 1023 || brightness == 0)
    increase != increase;

  analogWrite(ledPin, brightness);    // sets the LED on
}
```

That's not too exciting yet, is it? In the spirit of interactivity, let's give you some control over that LED. We're going to use the INPUT mode of the pin that a button is connected to so we can send a signal and control the LED with the button, as shown in Example 4-3.

*Example 4-3. buttonOn.ino*

```
int lightPin= 13; // choose the pin for the LED
int buttonPin = 10;    // choose the input pin (for a pushbutton)

void setup() {
    // set the pin for the light as an output pin
    pinMode(ledPin, OUTPUT);
    // set the pin for the button as an input pin
    pinMode(buttonPin, INPUT);
}

void loop() {
    // get the value on the pin that the button is connected to
```

```
    int val = digitalRead(buttonPin);
    // check if the input is LOW, this will indicate
    // whether the button is pressed
    if (val == 0) {
        // if the button is pressed, then turn the light on
        digitalWrite(lightPin, HIGH);  // turn LED ON
        // otherwise, turn the light on
    } else {
        digitalWrite(lightPin, LOW);  // turn LED OFF
    }
}
```

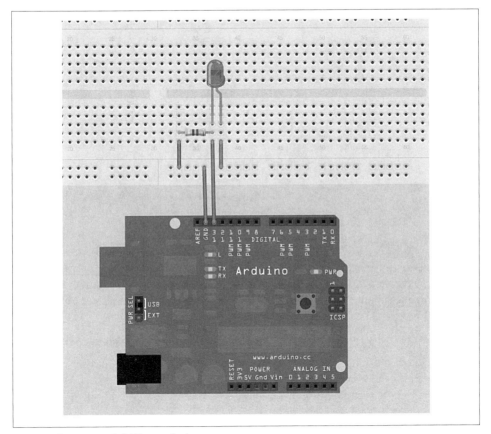

*Figure 4-21. Uno with LED attached*

When the circuit is completed, flowing all the way through, the value from pin 10 will read LOW, and the light will be given power to turn it on. Create the circuit in Figure 4-21.

This is where using a breadboard pays off. Plug the +5V pin into one of the connection lines that runs the length of the board and a ground pin into the other connection line. Next, use the 10K resistor to create a connection between one pin of the button and

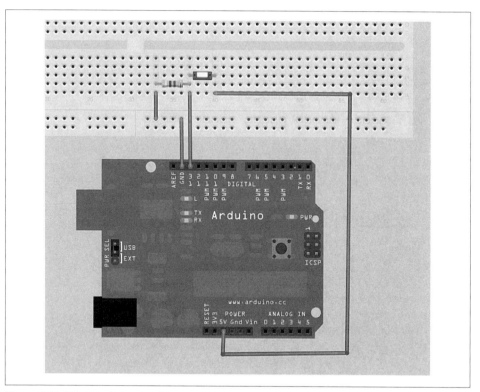

*Figure 4-22. Wiring a button to the Uno*

the connection line that carries the 5V. The button will have two connection points, so one gets connected with the resistor and the other gets connected to the ground connection line. Then, connect the LED to the ground connection line and pin 13. Take a look at Figure 4-22.

To upload the code, simply click the Upload button, as shown in Figure 4-23.

You should see the LEDs on the board begin flashing, and you should see a message printed out in the console window. Your Arduino controller may take a second or two to begin running the code, but you'll be able to turn the light on and off.

## Debugging Your Application

So, what do we do if we need to know the value being sent back from a sensor to a controller? Or, what if there's something going wrong that you can't quite sort out? You'll use the Serial library to send messages—character strings actually—back from the controller to the computer so you can see what's happening. This lets you send messages to know that something is working or not working and to monitor the values being passed around in your application. Whenever you have some code that you need

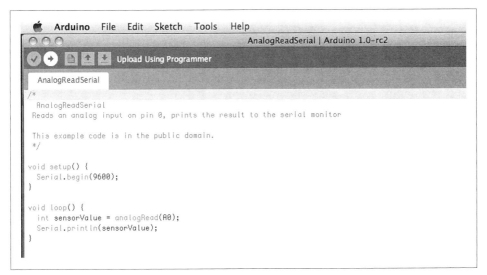

*Figure 4-23. Uploading code to the Arduino board*

to monitor, you can use the `Serial print()` method to allow you to check the values of variables or the execution of code and see those messages in real time using the Serial window of the Arduino IDE.

Use the `begin()` method of the `Serial` class in the `setup()` method of your application to set the communications speed:

```
int speed = 9600;

void setup() {
    Serial.begin(speed)
}
```

This sets the data rate in bits per second (baud) for serial data transmission. For communicating with the computer, use one of these rates: 300, 1200, 2400, 4800, 9600, 14400, 19200, 28800, 38400, 57600, or 115200. The higher the number, the faster the Arduino controller will send messages to the computer, but also the higher demand you'll make on your controller. Note, too, that the speed needs to be the same on the sending and receiving, so if you're trying to read data on the Serial Monitor of your Arduino IDE, you'll need to make sure that you're using the same speed in the IDE as you've set in the `begin()` method. Once you've called the `begin()` method of the serial, you can send data from your Arduino controller to your computer using the `print()` method:

```
Serial.print(data)
```

The `print()` method is more or less like the Processing `print()` method that you encountered in Chapter 3 and the `printf()` you'll encounter in Chapter 6, but it is optimized to save space for Arduino and so works slightly differently. By default, the `print()` method, with no format specified, prints an ASCII string. For example, the following:

```
int b = 79;
Serial.print(b);
```

prints the string 79 to the Serial Monitor window. The little application in Example 4-4 will print the message every two seconds.

*Example 4-4. serialTalking.ino*

```
int i = 0;

void setup() {
    Serial.begin(9600);
}

void loop() {
    Serial.print(" hey there, just saying hi for the ");
    Serial.print(i);
    Serial.print("th time. \n");
    delay(2000);
    i++;
}
```

Once you've uploaded the application to the board, you start monitoring the output of the serial by clicking the Serial Monitor button, as shown in Figure 4-24.

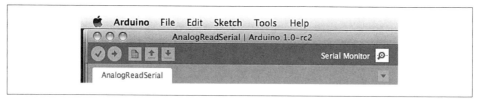

*Figure 4-24. Starting the Serial Monitor*

Once the Serial Monitor is started, you can see the output in the bottom of the Arduino IDE, as in Figure 4-25.

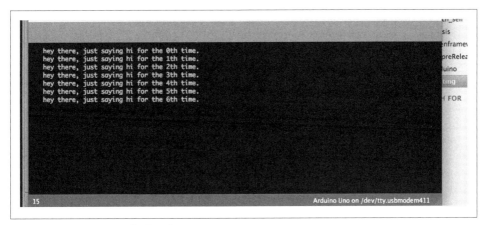

*Figure 4-25. Monitoring the Serial output*

You'll need to make sure that the baud rate selected in the drop-down list above the output window matches the rate that you passed to the serial `begin()` method, or the Serial Monitor won't be listening at the same rate that the controller is sending.

You can also pass additional parameters to the `print()` method to get the output to be formatted a specific way:

```
int b = 79;
Serial.print(b, HEX);
```

This prints the string **4F**, which is the number 79 in hexadecimal. Table 4-1 lists most of the format specifiers for the serial `print()` method.

*Table 4-1. Output with the serial print() method*

| Format specifier | Output |
| --- | --- |
| DEC | Prints the value as an decimal |
| HEX | Prints the value as a hexadecimal |
| OCT | Prints the value as an octal value |
| BIN | Prints the value as a binary number |
| BYTE | Prints the value as a single byte using ASCII characters |
| (No format specified) | Prints the value as a string |

# Importing Libraries

There are many extremely useful libraries for the Arduino controller that help you do things like work with LED lights, control motors, use LCD screens, or even control certain kinds of cell phones.

For this section, we'll primarily use the Stepper library for demonstrations. The Stepper library comes with the Arduino download and allows you to reduce the number of connections required by a stepper motor from four to two. We won't get into why this is good and what this allows us to achieve in any great detail until Chapter 8, focusing here instead on how the library functions in the Arduino environment.

An Arduino library is generally made up of four parts:, an *.h* file, a *.cpp* file, a *keywords.txt* file that highlights Arduino library words in the IDE, and the actual binary library code. Arduino uses *.h* files to contain the information about a library, the variables it contains, the methods that it has, and so forth. The *.cpp* file contains the definitions for those methods and variables and is compiled into the binary library files used at runtime by the Arduino controller. For those of you experienced working with C or C++ already (which, after you read through the sections on openFrameworks, will be all of you), you'll recognize the *.h* file and what it does. The *.h* file is what is imported into the Arduino application using the #include statement. If you want to know what is in a library, glancing at the *.h* file will tell you. For example, looking at the *Stepper.h* file, you'll see the following:

```
// constructors:
Stepper(int number_of_steps, int motor_pin_1, int motor_pin_2);
Stepper(int number_of_steps, int motor_pin_1, int motor_pin_2, ¬
    int motor_pin_3, int motor_pin_4);
// speed setter method:
void setSpeed(long whatSpeed);
// mover method:
void step(int number_of_steps);
int version(void);
```

This tells you that to create a new instance of the stepper, you pass it the number of steps, the pin that the first motor is connected to, and the pin to which the second motor is connected. Once you've created the stepper, you can call two methods on it: setSpeed() and step(). Learning to read *.h* files is a great asset in working with Arduino, openFrameworks, C, and C++, because it saves you the time of digging through documentation, and helps you get acquainted with the inner workings of the programming languages and the libraries that are written in them. There will be plenty more on *.h* files later on in this book.

So, now that you've had a crash course in *.h* files, you'll look at importing some functionality. It's actually quite simple; you add the following line to the top of the application file:

```
#include <Stepper.h>
```

This will import all the stepper functionality, allowing you to create new **Stepper** objects and call their methods. For instance, take Example 4-5.

*Example 4-5. stepper.ino*

```
#include <Stepper.h>
```

```
Stepper stepper(100, 8, 9, 10, 11); // note that we don't use = new Stepper();

void setup()
{
    // set the speed of the motor to 50 RPM
    stepper.setSpeed(50);
}

void loop()
{
    stepper.step(1);
    delay(500);
    stepper.step(2);
    delay(500);
    stepper.step(2);
    delay(500);
}
```

The Arduino download comes with a few core libraries that we'll outline in a rough way, just to give you an idea what's out there:

*EEPROM*

Depending on the board, the microcontroller on the Arduino board has 4 kilobytes, 1 kilobyte, or 512 bytes of EEPROM, which is permanent memory, like an extremely small hard drive that you can save information to. So, how big is 512 bytes? It's 128 integers, or 512 Boolean values; so it's not a lot, but it's enough.

So, you ask what you might do with it. You can save the last values input by a user, save the last state of a controller, save the highest reading ever for a component, save just a tiny bit of GPS data, or store a URL or some other kind of valuable information.

*Stepper*

This library allows you to control stepper motors. To use it, you will need a stepper motor and the appropriate hardware to control it.

What you might use it for: making things that use stepper motors, of course, such as making small robot arms, rotating cameras, manipulating toys, pointing things, or driving things.

*Wire*

Two-Wire Interface (TWI/I2C) is for sending and receiving data over a net of devices or sensors. This library allows you to communicate with I2C/TWI devices. On the Arduino, SDA (data line) is on analog input pin 4, and SCL (clock line) is on analog input pin 5.

So, you ask what you might use it for. You can read GPS sensors, read from RFID readers, control accelerometers, and in fact do many of the things that we're going to do later in this book.

# Running Your Code

Once you have loaded your program onto the board, it is saved in the program memory of the board whether the board is being powered or not. There's no worry about the controller *forgetting* its program. When the controller starts up again, it will automatically run the last program that it had loaded into it.

You can clear the RAM memory of the board either by grounding the reset pin, which works on the Uno and the Mini, or by simply pressing the reset button, which works only on the Uno. This restarts the board and the program that is saved on the board, but doesn't clear the program. That will happen only when a new program is uploaded to the board.

## Running Your Board Without a USB Connection

There are two ways to run your Arduino, both of which are available to you with the Uno controller, and one of which is available to you with the Mini controller. The first is to plug the controller directly in to a wall using a 9V or 12V DC adapter, and this can be done only with the Uno. Most electronics supply shops will have one of these adapters with the correct attachment end that will fit in the Uno DC port.

The other option, which is available on both controllers, is to simply use a 9V battery with a snap-on cap that allows you to get two wires from the battery to send to the controller. On the Mini, attach the positive lead (the red wire) of the battery cap to the +9V pin and the ground lead (the black wire) of the battery cap to the ground pin. On the Uno, attach the positive lead to the 9V Voltage In (Vin) pin and the ground lead to the ground pin. You're now wireless and free to wander around with your Arduino.

 When connecting to a power source, be careful. You can fry your controller by sending voltage to the wrong pin. If working with a battery, always connect the ground first and the positive lead after.

You've seen the beginnings of the Arduino; now you can either flip ahead to Chapter 8, where you will work with the Arduino to create some real interactivity, or you can read the next chapter, which delves a little deeper into programming to get you ready for openFrameworks and C++.

# Review

The Arduino project is several different components: a microcontroller board, a simplified version of C and C++ for nonengineers to use in programming their microcontroller, and an IDE and compiler used to create and load code onto the microcontroller board.

To get started with the Arduino, you'll need to download the Arduino IDE and compiler from the *http://arduino.cc* website and purchase a board from one of the online suppliers.

Once you have the board and the IDE ready, you'll need to configure the IDE correctly for your board by plugging the board in and then, in the IDE, going to the Tools menu, selecting the board option, and selecting the board that you're using.

You can run a simple blinking light script to ensure that your board is working properly.

Pins can either input, which means they will read values from a control, or output values to a control. Communication between the Arduino and any controls attached to it is done via the amount of voltage being sent either to or from the Arduino. Arduino controllers have two kinds of pins: analog pins that can read and write analog values, from 0 to 5V, and digital pins that simply read or write binary values represented as 0V or 5V.

Running an Arduino program has two steps: the first is to compile the code on your computer in the Arduino IDE. You can do this by pressing Ctrl-R (⌘-R on OS X). Once your code compiles, you upload it to the Arduino board using the Upload to I/O Board button on the Arduino IDE or by pressing Ctrl-U (⌘-U on OS X).

An Arduino application has two required methods: the `setup()` method that is called once when the application first starts up, and the `loop()` method that is called over and over.

To attach an LED to your Arduino, connect the first lead of the LED to a resistor, connect the resistor to any digital pin, and connect the second lead of the LED to Ground. Once you use the `digitalWrite()` method to set that pin to `HIGH`, the LED will light up.

To connect a button to your Arduino, attach a button with a resistor to a digital pin and the other end of the button to the 5V pin of the Arduino. Buttons are an easy way to get started creating some physical interactivity in your designs.

To debug your application, you can use the `Serial.print()` method to send messages from your Arduino controller to the console of the Arduino IDE at critical junctions to help you see what your application is doing.

The `Serial.print()` method can be formatted by passing a second parameter to the `print()` method to specify what format should be used.

You can import libraries to your Arduino application using the Sketch menu item of the toolbar at the top of the Application menu and then selecting the Import Library option. You can also write the name of the *.h* file that the library uses, if you've placed it in the *libraries* folder of your Arduino installation, like so:

```
#include <Wire.h>
```

Other Arduino libraries allow you to work with stepper motors, Two-Wire Interface, the memory of the Arduino controller, and many other techniques or controls.

Once you've written a working program and have uploaded it to the Arduino, the board will save the code in program memory and begin executing the program. The code will start as soon as the board is powered up again.

# CHAPTER 5

# Programming Revisited

In this chapter, we'll cover several more advanced topics that you will need to understand to use some of the other code samples in this book. First among these is *object-oriented programming* (OOP), that is, programming using classes and objects as the fundamental units to organize your code. This topic is a fundamental part of the nature of C++, which is quite important to understand if you're going to work with openFrameworks (oF) in any meaningful way. We will cover file structure and how to create classes and objects in C++. Finally, we will cover pointers and references, which are quite advanced topics but important ones if you plan on doing any serious work with openFrameworks. It also helps a lot when looking at libraries created for Arduino or if you decide to build your own library.

## Object-Oriented Programming

To work with oF—and, in many cases, to work with Processing—you need to understand object-oriented programming, which is a way of organizing and assembling your code that is used in many different kinds of programming languages and for many different purposes. Hundreds of programming languages support OOP, and the principles don't vary too greatly across languages, so once you understand the basics of it, you'll find yourself better able to follow along with code that you encounter and better able to construct your own code when you're working on a project. At its core, OOP is the philosophy of creating *classes* that represent different tasks or objects in your application to delegate responsibility and organize the structure of your application. Classes can handle specific functionality like reading data from a camera and displaying it to a screen, they can represent a data object like a file, and they can be events for one part of an application to tell another about something that has happened. The class is the blueprint for what kind of object the class will create. When you create one of these classes to use in your application, you call that particular instance of the class an *object*. There may be unfamiliar terms in that previous sentence, but there probably aren't any unfamiliar concepts. My favorite analogy is the car analogy.

Imagine a car. What are the abstract qualities of a car? Let's stick with four right now: doors, windows, wheels, and the motor. So, we have a really basic abstract car that has a few different characteristics that we can identify. We're not talking about any *particular* car; we're talking about *any car*. Now, let's picture a particular car. I'm thinking of the red 1975 Volvo 240L station wagon that my parents had when I was a kid; you're most likely thinking of a different car. We can both identify our particular cars as being two instances of the abstract kind-of-thing car that share all the common characteristics of a car as well as having their own particular characteristics that make them unique objects. If you can handle that leap of taxonomic thinking, objects and classes should be fairly easy for you. Let's go forward.

## Classes

All three tools profiled in this book—Arduino, Processing, and openFrameworks—provide a wide and rich variety of data types and methods. That said, it is inevitable that as you work with these tools you'll need to add your own constructions to these frameworks to create the works that you envision. These things that you need to add can be different kinds, but in all likelihood, they'll consist of some data and some functionality. In other words, they will probably consist of some variables and some methods. Once again, we need to approach this with the three distinct programming languages discussed in this book in mind. Arduino doesn't use classes as much as Processing or oF. This is because sending and receiving bytes from a microcontroller or from hardware tends to be a very "low-level" operation; that is, it doesn't frequently require the use of classes and new types. Arduino, and the C++ programming language on which it is based, can use something called a *struct*, which is a collection of properties with a name, but we won't be discussing the *struct* in this book. This isn't because structs aren't important, but rather because they aren't particularly important in the common tasks that are done in Arduino. Lots of times in Arduino when you need to do new things, you write new functions. This isn't always the case; when you're creating a library, for instance, you'll end up creating classes. However, for beginners, OOP isn't something that you'll be doing a lot in Arduino. In Processing and C++, however, the kinds of things that these languages are good at frequently require new data types and new objects with their own methods. In Processing and C++, when you need to create a new different type to do something in your application or to store some data, you create a class.

Why do you use classes? The short answer is that you use classes to break functionality into logical pieces that represent how you use them, how the application regards them, and how they are organized. An application that handles reading data from multiple cameras and saving images from those cameras as pictures will probably have a Camera class, a Picture class, and maybe a File class. A game with spaceships might have the classes Spaceship, Enemy, Asteroid, and so on. Using classes helps make the code for an application easier to read, modify, debug, and reuse.

## The Basics of a Class

The concept of a class is a difficult one for many people at first; however, with a little bit of patience, you'll find that it's not all that different from the way you see the world. A *class* is a grouping of variables and methods into an object that contains and controls access to them all. Think of a very simple description of dog. A dog has a breed, an age, and a weight, for example. These are all traits that, if you were trying to describe the dog in code, you would use variables to describe. A dog also has some actions it can perform; it can run, it can eat, or it can bark. If you were to describe these actions in code, you would make methods to describe them. Let's go ahead and make a simple class in Processing that shows what this Dog class might look like:

```
class Dog{

    String breed;
    int age;
    int weight;

    Dog(){} // we'll talk about this one much more
    void run(){}
    void bark(){}
    void eat(){}
};
```

In C++, that class will look exactly the same. The differences between Processing and C++ are going to become more apparent later.

That's all. When you want to create a Dog in your application, just like when you make a string, you create a new instance of a Dog, declare the variable, and call the constructor:

```
Dog rover = new Dog();
```

Now that you've made **rover**, you can describe **rover** and call his methods:

```
rover.breed = "shepherd"; // set the breed of the dog
rover.age = 3; // set his age
rover.weight = 50; // set his weight
rover.run(); // tell him to run
rover.bark(); // tell him to bark
```

That was nothing terribly challenging, was it? So the concept of classes really isn't that difficult, because the idea was created to make programming easier for people, to make writing code mimic the way that people perceive and classify the world. Classes have properties (variables), like the **breed** property of the **Dog**, and methods (behaviors), like the run() method of the **Dog**. All methods of a class are created equal, except one, which we call the *constructor*. Let's revisit making the **Dog** variable **rover** once again:

```
Dog rover = new Dog();
```

Let's look more closely at = new Dog(). This calls the constructor, performing any actions that you want to perform when the **Dog** is first created. This will be the first thing that this instance of the **Dog** does, because this is where the **Dog** really begins, in the constructor call. The Dog() method is a special method, which is why it doesn't return anything; that is, it doesn't declare a return type. Let's continue thinking about the Dog example. A Dog, rover in particular, has to have an age. It's impossible to have a dog without an age, so let's go ahead and say that when the Dog is created, you set its age:

```
Dog() {
    age = 1;
}
```

This means now that by default whenever you make a Dog, its age will be 1:

```
Dog rover = new Dog();
println(rover.age); // prints 1, because the dog is 'just born' ;)
```

So now, you've created a simple class that you can use to create objects possessing all of the properties that you require. A well-written class lets you group functionality and data together in logical objects that allow you to focus on what the code needs to do, rather than how it is structured. This topic will be revisited many times in the following chapters.

## Class Rules

Classes can be declared in files outside your primary code file. To work with a class or multiple classes that have been defined in separate files, those files and classes need to be imported. This is handled slightly differently in each of the different programming environments discussed here, so we'll discuss it in the chapter relevant to each of these languages. The filenames that these classes should be saved in are particular to each environment and language as well. In C++, classes are saved across two file types: *.cpp* files and *.h* files. The reason for this and the way that it works will be discussed in Chapter 6. In Processing, these external class files are saved in *.pde* files that are then imported. There are also *.java* files that can be imported into the Processing environment.

Both in Processing and in C++, the class declaration must always look like this:

```
class ClassName{
    // all the things the class has
};
```

Note that the class declaration is followed by curly brackets (that enclose the definition of the class) and are followed by a semicolon. In C++ this is very important. In Processing and Java, the semicolon isn't required, but the brackets function the same way.

Classes should have a declared constructor unless they're just for storing data. For example:

```
class Point{
    int xPosition;
    int yPosition;
};
```

---

This doesn't require a constructor, but when you use your code, you'll have to use it like this:

```
Point pt = new Point();
pt.xposition = 129;
pt.yposition = 120;
```

If a constructor is provided for this class, as shown here:

```
class Point{

    int xPosition;
    int yPosition;
    // this is the constructor for this class
    Point(int xPos, int yPos){
        xPosition = xPos;
        yPosition = yPos;
    }
};
```

then the class can be used as follows:

```
Point pt = new Point(129, 120);
```

This saves you some typing and makes your code more compact. It also avoids the classic problem that you might run into later where you have `Point` objects that don't have any values because none were set. This way, all `Point` objects will have an *x* and *y*. In this case, the problem is taken care of, and you can concentrate on your project and not hunting down bugs.

A class generally should have good method names linked to the job that class is supposed to do. A good rule of thumb is to say that classes should be nouns and methods should be verbs. This isn't for the compiler; the compiler doesn't care what you call your class, variable, or method. This is more for you, the person writing the code. Remembering what you were thinking when you wrote a class or what the class should be used for is far easier if you have names for the class and the methods that make sense to you. For instance, a `Dog` should have `run()`, `bark()`, and `eat()` methods, but not a `paper()` method. A method called `fetchThePaper()` would be far more appropriate, but ultimately, your code is your own, and you can do whatever you like with it.

# Public and Private Properties

A class has a name, and it has two basic kinds of properties: public and private. *Public* ones are available to the outside world, which means that other classes can use those properties and methods. *Private* properties are not available to the outside world, only to methods and variables that are inside the class, which means that other classes cannot use those properties and methods. When we create a class, we have the following shell in C++:

```
class Dog {
    public:
```

```
        // all public stuff goes here
    private:
        // all private stuff goes here
}; // a closing bracket and a ; to mark the end of the class
```

To give the Dog class some methods, you simply put the method definitions underneath the public and private keywords, depending on whether you needed that method to be public or private like so:

```
class Dog {
    public:
    void bark() {
        printf("bark");
    }

    void sleep() {
        // sleep() can call dream, because the dream() method
        // is within the Dog class
        dream();
    }

    private:
    void dream() {
        printf("dream");
    }
};
```

In Processing, you do not need to use the public: keyword on top of all the public variables. Instead, each method is marked as public and private separately, like so:

```
class Dog{

    public void bark(){
        println("bark");
    }

    // sleep() can call dream, because the dream() method
    // is within the Dog class
    public void sleep() {
        dream();
    }

    private void dream() {
        println("dreaming");
    }

};
```

Now, if you create a Dog, called **rover**, and try to call the **dream()** method on him, you'll get an error because **dream()** is private and cannot be accessed by external operations, that is, operations that are not going on inside the class itself:

```
Dog d;
d.bark();
d.dream(); // this doesn't work
```

Now, that may not make a ton of sense right away: why make things that we can't use? The answer to that is design and usage. Sometimes you want to make certain methods or properties of a class hidden to anything outside of that class. Generally, you want a class to expose the interface that something outside of your class can access and have the class do what it is supposed to do. Methods or properties that aren't necessary for the outside world to use or manipulate can be declared private to keep objects outside the class from accessing them or using them inappropriately. You might not ever make methods private, but if you work with C++ and Processing long enough, you're guaranteed to run into methods and variables that have been marked private when you're looking at other people's code. Now you'll understand what it is and why they might have done it.

# Inheritance

Discussing public and private brings us to inheritance. This is a big part of OOP, and, like many of the other topics in OOP, seems tricky at first but ends up being fairly easy and commonsensical. We'll look at some simple examples using Dog and then some more complicated examples using shapes later to help you get the hang of it.

*Inheritance* means that a class you're making extends another class, getting all of its variables and methods that have been marked public. Imagine there is a general kind of Dog and then specialized kinds of dogs that can do all the things that all dogs can do, such as run, bark, smell, *plus* some other things. If I were to make a class called Retriever, I could rewrite all the Dog stuff in the Retriever class, *or* I could just say this: a Retriever *is a* Dog with some other special stuff added on. Let's say the Retriever does everything the Dog does *plus* it retrieves.

Here's the code in Processing:

```
class Retriever extends Dog{ // note the "extends"; that's important

    public void fetch() {
        println("fetch");
    }

}
```

Here's the code in C++:

```
class Retriever : public Dog { // note the " : public "; that's important
public:
    void fetch() {
        printf("retrieve");
    }

private:

};
```

Does this mean that you can have the `Retriever` bark? Since the `Retriever` is a `Dog`, the answer is yes, because all the methods and variables from the `Dog` are available to the `Retriever` class that extends it.

Here's the code in Processing:

```
Retriever r = new Retriever();
r.bark(); // totally ok, from the parent class
r.fetch();
```

Here's the code in C++:

```
Retriever r; // note, you don't need to do = new...()
r.bark(); // totally ok, from the parent class
r.fetch();
```

In Figure 5-1, you can see how the methods of classes are passed down what is sometimes called the *chain of inheritance*.

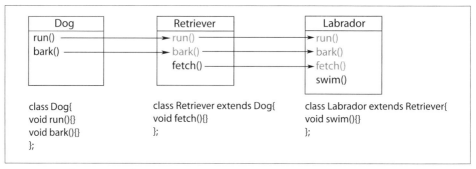

*Figure 5-1. Inheritance in classes*

The `Dog` class defines two methods: `run()` and `bark()`. The `Retriever` logically extends the `Dog`, since the `Retriever` is a dog, but it is also a specific kind of dog, namely, the kind of `Dog` that can fetch things. So, the `Retriever` defines only one method, but actually it has three because it inherits from the `Dog`. The `Labrador` is a kind of `Retriever` and hence is a `Dog` as well. A `Labrador` can do all the things a plain old `Retriever` can do because it extends the `Retriever`, but it also can `swim`. So, even though the class for the `Labrador` class has only one method, it can do four things, `run()`, `bark()`, `fetch()`, and `swim()`, because it always inherits all the methods of its parent classes.

Why is this important? Well, if you're going to make interactive designs and artwork that use code, you're going to end up reading a lot of code. You're inevitably going to run into a class that is calling methods that you won't see anywhere when you look at the code listing. It's probably defined in one of the parent classes that the class extends. You also might start making types of things that you realize share some common characteristics. If you're making an application that draws lots of things to the screen, it might make sense to put a `draw()` method on them all. If at some point later in writing code you want to change some core aspect of the `draw()` method, you would go through every class and change it. It would make things easier if the `draw()` method was in one place, like a parent class, for instance. This is another one of the advantages of creating class structures: to avoid duplicating code unnecessarily and make your code simpler to read, change, and share.

There's a caveat to using inheritance with your classes, which is that *only methods and variables marked as public* will be inherited. You heard right: anything marked private doesn't get inherited. There's one small catch to this: in both C++ and Java, there are a few additional levels of privacy for methods and objects, but they're not as important for the purposes of this book. So, in the class shown in Figure 5-2, again using the `Dog` and `Retriever` analogy, the `Retriever` will have a `bark()` method that it will inherit from the `Dog` class, but it will not have a `dream()` method because the `Dog` has that method marked as private.

*Figure 5-2. Inheritance with public and private methods*

The same would go for any variables defined in the `Dog` class; the `Retriever` will inherit *all public* variables and *no private* ones. This is a good thing to know when reading through the code of libraries that you might want to use, like the `ofImage` or `ofVideoGrabber` classes in openFrameworks or some of the libraries available in Processing.

## Processing: Classes and Files

In Processing, classes often are defined within the main file for the application that you see when you're working with a Processing application. If you open the folder that your application is saved in, you'll see that this main file is a *.pde* file that has the name of your application. This is the main file of your application, and lots of times if you want to make a new class, you'll just add it to this file. However, in a complex application, you may want to make multiple classes, and you want to break them apart into separate files so they're easier to read and maintain, or so you can use a file from another place. To do this, all you need to do is create a new *.pde* file in the same folder and put your class declaration and description into that file.

To create a new *.pde* file within your application folder that will automatically be imported into your application, click the New Tab icon at the right of the Processing IDE, as shown in Figure 5-3.

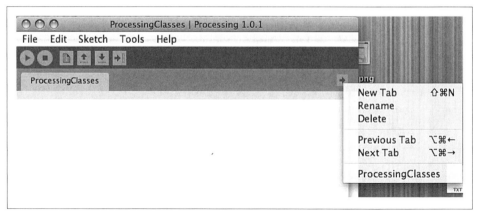

*Figure 5-3. Creating a class in Processing*

This opens a small dialog box asking you to name your new file (see Figure 5-4).

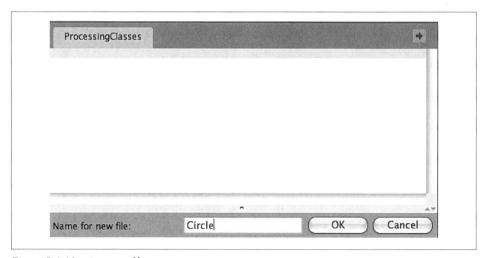

*Figure 5-4. Naming your file*

After you've given your file a name, Processing automatically creates the new *.pde* file in your sketch folder. You can begin adding your class to the file and then using it in your main application file, that is, the file that contains the draw() and setup() methods (see Figure 5-5).

What do you get for putting this extra work into creating new files and classes? There are two distinct advantages to creating files and separate classes: it makes organizing

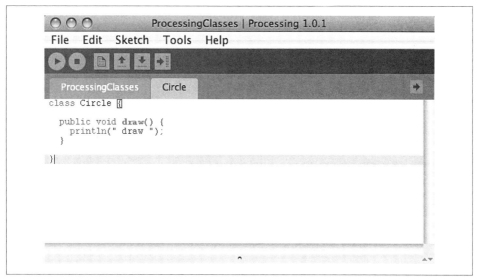

*Figure 5-5. The newly created Circle class file*

your code and debugging your application easier, and once you've written some classes that work well and do something that you'd like to use again, it's easy to copy and paste the file into a new project and reuse all your code from the class. This last bit is, although oversimplified, a lot of the basis of the Processing, Arduino, and openFrameworks projects: providing reusable code to speed up creating your projects.

# C++: Classes and Files

C++ is an object-oriented language. It's quite difficult to write anything in C++ without creating at least a few classes. And as you work with oF, you'll find classes and class files all over the place. If you've read this chapter up to this point, you should have a fairly good idea of what a class is and what it does.

So, now we're going to define an absurdly simple class called Name:

```
class Name {
public:
        string firstName;
        string secondName;

        Name(string first, string second) {
                firstName = first;
                secondName = second;
        }
};
```

Next up is creating an instance of `Name`. Somewhere else in our code, we create an instance of `Name`, like so:

```
Name name("josh", "noble");
```

That's it. We've made a class, and we've instantiated an instance of it. We're sort of off to the races.

So, what are some things that are commonly created and stored as classes? A good example is one of the oF core classes, the `ofSoundPlayer` class. This class represents what it sounds like it would represent: a sound player. It has methods to play, stop, set the volume, and set the position that the player reads from. We wouldn't expect it to do anything else, and in fact it doesn't. It also provides lots of useful properties that help us determine whether a sound is currently playing and whether there was a problem loading the sound.

Why do we use classes? In the short answer, we use classes to break functionality into logical pieces that represent how we use them, how the application regards them, and how they are organized. It makes sense to think of a spaceship game having spaceships, enemies, asteroids, planets, high scores, and so on. For example, we use classes to organize all the functionality that an enemy would need into one place so that when we need to make an enemy, we know we're always getting the same characteristics, and when we need to make a change to the enemies, we can do it in just one place. It's far more difficult to introduce classes later than it is to simply begin with them. The theory of how to best organize classes is a serious topic that has spawned many a serious nerd-spat. We're not going to delve into it deeply, but in Chapter 17, there are some pointers to introductory texts as well as heavy classics.

## .cpp and .h

*.cpp* and *.h* shall now forever be burned into your mind as *the two file formats of a C++ class*. That's right: two file formats and two separate files. The why of this is a bit irrelevant; what's important is that you follow how the two work together and how you'll use them. We're going to take this slowly because it's important.

In an oF application, there will be two types of files: *.cpp* and *.h* files. The *.cpp* files contain the implementation of a class, while the *.h* file contains the prototype of that class. The prototype of that class, the *.h* file, is going to contain the following:

- Any `import` statements that the class needs to make
- The name of the class
- Anything that the class extends (more on this later)
- Declarations of variables that the class defines (sometimes referred to as *properties*)
- Declarations of methods that the class defines

The definition of the class, the *.cpp* file, will contain the following:

- The actual definition of any methods that the class defines

So, why are there so few things in the *.h* file and so many in the *.cpp*? Well, usually the definition of a method takes up a lot more space than the declaration of it. If I want to define a method that adds two numbers and returns them, I define it like so:

```
int addEmUp(int a, int b);
```

This is the kind of thing that you'll see in a *.h* file—methods with signatures but no bodies. Take a moment to let that sink in: the method is being *declared*, not *defined*. Now, if I want to do something with this method, I need to actually define it, so I'll do the following:

```
int addEmUp(int a, int b){
    return a+b;
}
```

Here, you actually see the meat of the method: add the two numbers and return it. These are the kinds of things that you'll see in the definition of a class in the *.cpp* files.

If you want to have your class contain a variable, and you will, then you can define that in the *.h* header file as well. Just remember that the declarations go in the *.h* file and the definitions go in the *.cpp* file, and you'll be OK. When you're working with oF, you'll frequently see things that look like Figure 5-6.

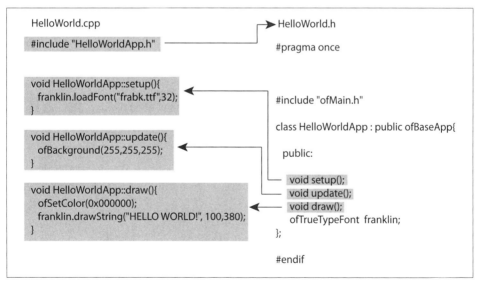

*Figure 5-6. How methods are spread across .h and .cpp files*

Don't worry about all the specifics of this diagram; we're going to return to it in Chapter 6 when we discuss oF in greater detail. For now, just notice how the setup(), update(), and draw() methods are declared but not defined in the *.h* file, and how they are defined in the *.cpp* file with the name of the class in front of them. This is going to be a wonderfully familiar pattern for you by the end of this book.

## A Simple C++ Application

Example 5-1 is your first C++ class, helpfully named `FirstClass`. First up, you have the *.h* file where all the definitions are made:

*Example 5-1. FirstClass.h*

```
// make sure we have one and only one "First class"
#pragma once

// give the class a name
class FirstClass{
// declare all the public variables and methods, that is, all the values that can
// be shared
public:
    FirstClass();
    int howManyClasses();
// declare all the private variables and methods, that is, all the values that are
// only for the internal workings of the class, not for sharing
private:
    int classProperty;
};
```

We'll talk this through, because the first thing you see is this really odd `#pragma`. Don't let this scare you away, because it actually has a perfectly good explanation. Frequently, in a larger project, you'll have a single class that is referenced in lots of other classes. Going back to our little space game example, our `Enemy` class is going to be needed in more than one place. When the compiler is compiling our classes, we don't want it to compile `Enemy` multiple times; we want it to compile the enemy only once. Compiling it multiple times would mean that multiple versions of the class would be stored in the final program file causing all kinds of problems. This weird little `#pragma` statement tells the compiler to only compile the file once, not multiple times, saving us headaches later on. The rest of it is much more straightforward. The `class` keyword goes in front of the name of the class and a {. All the class data is contained within the opening class statement { and the closing class statement };.

Inside of that you can see the word `public`. This means that after the `public` keyword, everything will be publicly accessible, which means that it is available to other classes that have access to instances of `FirstClass`. Everything up until the `private` keyword will be `public`, and, logically, everything after the `private` keyword will be `private`.

So, by looking at the *.h* file, you know the name of the class, what properties your class defines, what methods it defines, and whether those properties and methods are public or private. That's great, but it's not quite everything, so we'll list the *.cpp* file so you can see how all these methods are actually defined in Example 5-2.

*Example 5-2. FirstClass.cpp*

```cpp
// first import our header file
#include "FirstClass.h"
// then import the file that contains the 'print' method
#include <iostream>


// this is our constructor for the FirstClass object
FirstClass::FirstClass()
{
    // this is a little magic to get something printed
    // to the screen
    cout << " FirstClass " << endl;
    classProperty = 1; // initialize our property
}

int FirstClass::howManyClasses()
{
    // once again, just a little message to say 'hello'
    cout << " howManyClasses method says: 'just one class' " << endl;
    // note that we're returning classProperty, take a look at the method
    // declaration to understand why we're doing this (hint, it says 'int')
    return classProperty; // do something else with our property
}
```

Note that for each of the methods that are declared in the *.h* file, there is a corresponding definition in the *.cpp* file. Here, you can see how each of the methods of the class is put together with both a definition in the *.cpp* file and a declaration in the *.h* file. So far, so good. You have an instance of a class, but you aren't creating an instance of it anywhere yet. That's about to change with the final file. This last file is not a class but is a single *.cpp* file called *main*. There is a rule in C++ that says you must have one file that has a method called `main()`. When your application is launched, this is the method that will get called, so it's where all your initialization code goes. In an oF application, this is just creating an instance of your application and running it; this will all be covered in greater detail in Chapter 6. There is no rule that says you must have a file called *main* in order to run your application, but it's the way it's done in oF, and that means it's the way we'll demonstrate in Example 5-3.

*Example 5-3. main.cpp*

```cpp
#include "FirstClass.h"

// all applications must have a 'main' method
int main() {
    FirstClass firstClass; // here is an instance of our class
    firstClass.howManyClasses(); // here we call a method of that inst.
    return 0; // here we're all done
}
```

So, is this the only way to make a simple C++ application (see Figure 5-7)? The answer is no; however, this is the way that oF is set up, so this is the way that we'll show.

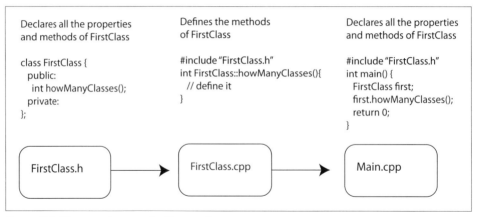

| Declares all the properties and methods of FirstClass | Defines the methods of FirstClass | Declares all the properties and methods of FirstClass |

```
class FirstClass {
  public:
   int howManyClasses();
  private:
};
```

```
#include "FirstClass.h"
int FirstClass::howManyClasses(){
  // define it
}
```

```
#include "FirstClass.h"
int main() {
  FirstClass first;
  first.howManyClasses();
  return 0;
}
```

FirstClass.h → FirstClass.cpp → Main.cpp

*Figure 5-7. The organization of a C++ application*

There are many more tricks to classes in C++ and many more wonderful mysterious things that you can do. If you want to learn more, you're in luck, because there are dozens of good manuals and guides to help you learn C++. If you don't really want to learn more, you're in luck, because oF hides much of the complication of C++, allowing you to concentrate on other parts of your project.

## Pointers and References

C++ is a very powerful and very fast programming language because it is very "low-level." That is, it doesn't hide the inner workings of the computer nearly as much as a language like Processing. This has upsides and downsides. To follow many of the openFrameworks examples in this book, you'll need to have at least a cursory familiarity with two concepts: the *pointer* and the *reference*. If you're not interested in working with openFrameworks and C++ right now, then feel free to skip this section and move on. You might come back to it later; you might not. Above all, this book is meant to be helpful to you, not to shove things at you that you're not interested in.

The pointer and the reference are complementary concepts that are inextricably linked. To understand how they work, though, you need to first understand what happens when a variable is declared and see how the memory of a computer works. Take a look at this:

```
int gumballs = 6;
```

What you're doing here is telling the computer to store something the size of an int with a value of 6 and a variable name of gumballs. It's important to understand that the value and the variable name are separate. They are exchanged for one another when needed. One example is when you add 5 to gumballs:

```
int moreGumballs = gumballs + 5; // "gumballs" is replaced with 6
```

This is easy to do because gumballs is really representing a part of memory. That section of memory is represented by hexadecimal numbers like 0x2ac8 that simply stand for the beginning of the location in the computer's memory where the value of gumballs is stored. The variable gumballs simply stores that location so that you can access it easily. When you set gumballs to 8:

```
gumballs = 8;
```

you're changing the value that is stored in the section of memory that gumballs represents. When you *set* gumballs, you set that section of the computer's memory. When you *get* gumballs, you read that section of the computer's memory. You're reading the bytes stored in the computer's memory by location. That location is referred to by the *friendly* variable name, but in reality, it's a location in memory. It really doesn't matter a ton, until you start to deal with pointers and references, because the pointer and the reference let you declare up front whether you want to work with a pointer to a location in memory, or whether you want to deal with that memory explicitly. We'll talk more about when and why you would do each of those things later.

Here's a simple example that you can run with any C++ compiler to see how this works:

```cpp
#include <iostream>
int main () {
    int gumballs = 6;
    int gumdrops = 12;
    // here's where we make the magic
    cout << " the variable gumdrops has the value of " << gumdrops
        << " and the address of " << &gumdrops << endl;
    cout << " the variable gumballs has the value of " << gumballs
        << " and the address of " << & gumballs << endl;

}
```

This will print out something that might look like this:

```
the variable gumdrops has the value of 12 and the address of 0xbffff998
the variable gumballs has the value of 6 and the address of 0xbffff99c
```

Notice two things. First, notice the & in front of the two variables:

```
&gumdrops
&gumballs
```

These are both references, which indicate that you want the name of the location in memory where these are stored. When you use the variable name, you just get back what's stored there. When you use the reference, though, you get the name of the location where the actual value is stored. Second, notice the actual location in memory: 0xbffff998. That's just on my computer at one particular moment in time, so if you run the code, your output will almost certainly look different. This is interesting because this is the place that gumdrops is stored. What is stored there is an integer, 12, and the way you get at that integer is by using the variable name gumdrop.

# Pointer

Pointers are so called because they do in fact point at things; in particular, they point at locations in memory much like you just saw in the discussion of references.

The pointer, like a variable and a method, has a *type*. This is so you know what kind of thing is stored in the memory that the pointer is pointing at. Let's go ahead and make a pointer to point at `gumdrops`:

```
int* pGumdrops = &gumdrops;
```

There are two important things to notice here. First is that when the pointer is created, the `pGumdrops` variable uses the same type as the variable whose address the pointer is going to point to. If you are making a pointer to point to a float, then the pointer must be of type `float`; if you are making a pointer to point to an object of a class called `Video`, then the pointer must be of type `Video` (assuming that `Video` is a class). The second is that the pointer is marked as a pointer by the presence of the * after the type declaration. A pointer to a float would look like this:

```
float* pointerToAFloat;
```

In the preceding code snippet, you have *declared* the pointer, but have not *initialized* it. This means that it doesn't point at anything yet:

```
pointerToAFloat = &someFloat;
```

Now you have initialized the pointer, which means that it can be passed around in place of the variable itself, which is all well and good, but it doesn't help you do things with the pointer. To do things with the pointer, you need to *dereference* the pointer:

```
int copyOfGumdrops = *pGumdrops;
```

To dereference the pointer—that is, to get the information that is stored in the location that the pointer points to—you dereference the pointer by using the * symbol in front of the name of the pointer. Think of the * as indicating that you're either telling the pointer to point to some place in particular, initializing it, or getting what it points at. Here's another example showing how dereferencing the pointer works:

```
int gumdrops = 12;
int* pGumdrops = &gumdrops;

cout << " pGumdrops is " << *pGumdrops << endl;  // will be 12
gumdrops = 6;
cout << " pGumdrops is " << *pGumdrops << endl;  // will be 6
gumdrops = 123;
cout << " pGumdrops is " << *pGumdrops << endl;  // will be 123
```

Any time you change the value of `gumdrops`, the value that `pGumdrops` points to changes. Figure 5-8 illustrates the relationship between the variable and the pointer. You create the relationship shown in Figure 5-8 when you do the following:

```
int gumdrops = 12;
int* pGumdrops = &gumdrops;
```

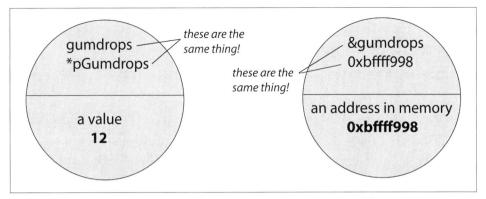

*Figure 5-8. The relationship between a pointer and a reference, two sides of the same coin*

The biggest difference between a pointer and a reference can be shown in the following lines:

```
void checkPointer(char* c)
{
    if(c) {
        cout << "pointer is good!";
    } else {
        cout << "no pointer";
    }
}
```

A pointer though can and should be checked for being null, which is what the `if` statement does there. No valid pointer? No problem. However, you can't check a reference for null, so you have to always assume that they're ok, that they've had something assigned to them and are ready to use.

## Reference

The reference, as mentioned earlier, is the location in memory where a variable is stored. Any variable's address can be accessed using the reference operator (&). This means that whatever you do to the reference happens to the memory that the reference refers to.

It's important to realize that this can go bad quickly if something happens to the variable that you referenced. Remember the idea of scope? That becomes very important because while a reference allows you to access the memory of a variable, it also assumes that you have the right stuff in the right location with that variable.

 Because you can't make a reference, you can only point it to something that already exists, you're probably going to work with pointers more than references, though you'll see both quite a bit.

A reference can be created, though you'll probably never see it done, like this:

```
int i = 4;
int &r = i; // you'll probably never see this
```

Usually you'll see references used like this:

```
void method(int& r) {
    // stuff done to r actually changes the memory indicated by r
}
```

This allows you to alter the actual memory of an object without creating a point. As with a pointer, if you pass a variable that hasn't been properly constructed, things will blow up. Unlike a pointer though, you don't know if it's going to be correctly constructed or not. That's the downside of a reference: you can't test it for null like a pointer.

The wonderful thing about a reference is that it lets you change the object itself. Let's take a look at an example:

```
void swap(int i, int j) {
    int tmp = i;
    i = j; // this doesn't change i
    j = tmp;
}
```

In this code snippet, we're not actually changing the value of i or j because they're being passed by value. Instead of getting the location where the value is stored, you're getting a copy of what that storage space contains, so a 5 or 12. When we do the following, it doesn't actually work:

```
int a = 1;
int b = 2;
swap(a, b);
cout << a << " " << b << endl; // still 1 and 2
```

Let's change the swap() method to use references:

```
void swap(int& i, int& j){
    int tmp = i;
    i = j;
    j = tmp;
}
```

In this case you're getting the actual location where the integer is stored, so just like the pointer, when you change i or j, you're changing what that reference holds:

```
int a = 1;
int b = 2;
swap(a, b);
cout << a << " " << b << endl; // now they're swapped. awesome!
```

## When to Use Pointers

As you may recall from the earlier discussion on methods, when something is passed to a method, a copy of it is used for manipulation. This generally means that when you pass something to a method, it doesn't alter the original variable:

```
void addExclamation(string s){
    s.append("!");
}

string myName = "josh";
addExclamation(myName);
printf( myName ); // will still be 'josh', not 'josh!'
```

What we want is to have the **string** passed into the method *by reference*, that is, the memory of the location where the actual value is, not a copy of what the value is when it's passed into the method. Calling methods on pointers is done with the -> operator, not the . operator. If you wanted to alter the variable that is passed in to the **addExcla mation()** method, you would pass a pointer to the method and use the -> operator to add the exclamation point:

```
void addExclamation(string* s){
    s->append("!"); // note the -> operator
}

string myName = "josh";
string* pName = &myName;
addExclamation(pName); // we're passing the memory of pName, not the value of it
printf( myName ); // will now be 'josh!', not 'josh'
```

When you pass a pointer you are passing an object that points to the actual memory, and dereferencing the pointer allows you to change what is actually in memory. If you have a very large picture that you want to alter, you want to alter the picture, not create a copy of the picture and alter that. Why not? Because the picture might be really large and altering might take up too much memory or because you might want to pass that same picture on to something else. Pointers let you do things like this:

```
void addExclamation(string* s){
    s->append("!");
}

void addQuestion(string* s){
    s->append("?");
}

void addQandE(string* s) {
    addExclamation(s);
    addQuestion(s);
}

string myName = "josh";
string* pName = &myName;
addQandE(
```

Since pointers and references are linked together, you may see the following used sometimes:

```
void retrieve(Retriever* retriever) {
    retriever->retrieve();
}
Retriever r;
retrieve(&r); // makes sure we're passing the pointer, not the value.
```

The & operator creates a temporary pointer from the variable, so you'll sometimes see this instead.

## When to Use References

In general, you should only use references in method signatures, like:

```
void addOne(int& i) {
    i += 1;
};
```

This method can do essentially the same thing as a pointer version: alter the actual memory of the variable instead of altering a copy of the variable. Using the addOne() method as shown in the following would actually increment the variable:

```
int i = 1;
addOne(i); // i is now 2! reference magic!
```

The reference is used a lot in oF code and in most proper C++ code. You can always count on those doing the right thing with the variables you're passing to them, so in a lot of respects a reference makes things easier on you as you write code and use libraries that make frequent use of pointers and references.

## Some Rules for Pointers

If you have a video file, a huge photo, or a lot of sound data, you don't want to be making copies of that all over your program, though you'll probably need to access it all over the place. The judicious use of the pointer is a way to allow different parts of a program to access a variable and alter that variable without multiple copies of it.

There are several very important rules to pointers. Write these down somewhere, commit them to memory, or otherwise preserve them:

- Don't try to access a pointer before it has been initialized. This:

    ```
    int* pInt;
    printf(" printing out pInt %i ", *pInt);
    ```

    will not print anything meaningful.

- Check whether a pointer is NULL before doing anything with it:

```
if(ptr != NULL) {
    // now you can use the pointer
}
```

- If you try to use the pointer and it isn't assigned to anything, then your application won't do what you want it to do and might crash.

- Although you can do this:

```
int* ptInt = 212;
```

you really shouldn't. This can create bugs that are really difficult to track down. When using a pointer, unless you're very confident in your skills, brave, or just very smart, you should set pointers to initialized variables. If you're comfortable with dynamically allocating memory, it can be a very powerful tool.

- You might come across code that looks like this:

```
FirstClass* fc = new FirstClass();
```

- This creates a new `FirstClass` and keeps a pointer to the object that can be used to access that object.

- If you dynamically create an object, you have to clean up after yourself by calling `delete` on the pointer:

```
FirstClass* fc = new FirstClass();
// do some things with fc
...
// now we're all done with it, so clean up
delete fc;
```

- If you don't delete pointers that you've dynamically allocated when you're done using them, and especially if you assign them in a method and don't delete them before the method is finished, you're creating what's called a *memory leak*. These can cause your application to run slowly or crash.

- You access the properties of a pointer using the `->` operator, like so:

```
Dog* d = new Dog();
d->bark();
```

## Some Rules for References

- A reference is an *alias* (an alternate name) for an object. When you make a pointer you're making another object that points to the object. A reference is the object itself. When you have a reference inside a method, it only exists inside that method.

- Use references when you can, and pointers when you have to.

- If you want to have a property of a class changed by another class or other piece of code, return a reference to that property in a method like this:

```
class dog {
public:
    int& getAge() { return age; }
private:
```

```
    int age;

};
```

- Never return a reference to a local variable. This will crash your program:

```
dog& app::createNewDog() {
    dog d;
    return d;
}
```

## Pointers and Arrays

Pointers and arrays have a very close relationship. An *array* is in fact either a pointer to a section of memory or a pointer to a bunch of pointers. Really, when you make an array of `int` variables:

```
int gumballs[10];
```

what you're saying is that there are going to be a list of 10 integers next to one another. It's the same thing as this:

```
&gumballs[0]
```

How's that? Take a look at what declaring the array actually does in Figure 5-9.

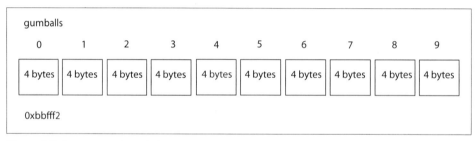

*Figure 5-9. An array and a pointer*

What you are doing is making a series of 10 integers, all in a row, within memory. Nothing links them together, except that they are all right next to one another. When you get the second element in the array, what you're doing is *getting the next integer after the initial integer*. The array itself is just a pointer to the location in memory where the first element of the array is stored, along with a number to indicate how many more places are stored for the array. In this case, there are 9 after the initial place, for a total of 10. So, if the beginning of the array is the location of the first element in memory, how do we get the next element in memory? By adding one to the pointer. Don't let this throw you for a loop, because it's deceptively simple:

```
int myInt = 4;
int* ptInt = &myInt;
int* nextPointer = ptInt + 1;// point to the next piece of memory
```

Imagine a row of shoe boxes. Imagine that you make a metaphorical pointer to the second shoe box by saying "that red shoe box there." Saying "the next shoe box" is like saying "the shoe box to the right of the red shoe box." You're not doing anything with the shoes inside those shoe boxes; you're just getting the next shoe box. That's exactly what adding to the pointer does. You're not adding to the value that the pointer is pointing to, you're adding to the location in memory that you're interested in accessing. Going back to our gumballs array of integers, when you get the second element in the array, what you're doing is this:

```
gumballs + 1
```

because gumballs is a pointer to the location of the first element in the array. You can do some really clever things with pointer arithmetic, but they aren't particularly important at the moment.

## When Are You Going to Use This?

If you follow along with this book, you're going to encounter pointers first when getting sound data in an openFrameworks application. The main application class in oF is called ofBaseApp, and it has an audioReceived() method that you can use to get data from the sound card of a computer. The audioReceived() method looks like this:

```
void audioReceived (float * input, int bufferSize, int nChannels)
```

That pointer to float is a pointer to the beginning of an array of sound samples. All the data of a sound is stored in a computer in an array of floating-point variables. When you want to work with the sound that your computer's sound card has captured, you'll get a pointer to an array and a bufferSize variable that tells you how large the array is. To use that sound data, you simply loop through the values in that array using a for loop:

```
for (int i = 0; i < bufferSize; i++){
    cout << "left channel is " << input[i*2] << " and right channel is "
    << input[i*2+1] << endl;
}
```

The reasoning behind the way the elements are accessed from the input array will be explained in Chapter 7. For the time being, just rest assured that, if you've followed everything in this chapter and the previous section in particular, you're going to be able to put it to use to make some interesting stuff. If you didn't really follow that last bit, don't sweat it too much, because you're not going to really need to work with pointers if you don't want to quite yet. You'll find that as you spend more time around these things and see how they're used more, they'll start to make a lot more sense to you.

# Review

A class is a group of variables and methods that are stored together within a single object. For example:

```
class Point{
    int xPosition;
    int yPosition;
};
```

Once classes are defined, they can be used like other variable types. First defined, then initialized:

```
Point pt = new Point();
```

Classes can define multiple methods and variables. One of the special methods that a class defines is the *constructor*. The constructor is a method that has the same name as the class and is called when the class is instantiated:

```
class Point{
    int xPosition;
    int yPosition;
    Point(){
        // anything to do when the object is first constructed
    }
};
```

The constructor is the only method that does not use a return type.

Pointers are a special type that exists in C++ that point to a location in memory where a value is stored. They are declared with a type, like any other variable, but use the * immediately after the type declaration to indicate to the compiler that the variable is a pointer:

```
int* intPt;
```

A reference refers to the actual location in memory where the value of variable is defined and is indicated by the & in front of the variable. Once the pointer is declared, it can be set to point to the reference of a variable:

```
int apples = 18;
intPt = &apples;
```

Pointers can be set only to the reference of a variable or a value but should usually be set only to the reference of a variable.

Pointers can be incremented and decremented using the addition and subtraction operators. This moves the location in memory to which the pointer points.

# openFrameworks

openFrameworks (oF) is the third and last tool you'll learn about in this part of the book. As you may have guessed from its name, oF is a *framework*, which is a collection of code created to help you do something in particular. Some frameworks are designed for working with databases, and others are designed for working with Internet traffic. Frameworks don't provide you with a prebuilt tool in the way that Processing and Arduino do, but they provide you with code that you can use to create your own programs.

Specifically, oF is a framework for artists and designers working with interactive design and media art. That sounds simple enough, right? It is written in C++ and expects that you write programs in C++. As mentioned in Chapter 2, C++ is a big, powerful, old, and (again for emphasis) powerful programming language. You can create features using oF that would not be possible in Processing because the underlying language is so much more flexible and low-level. Although this isn't always ideal or necessary, when it is, you'll appreciate it. It isn't always necessary to use oF, though. Sometimes Processing will work just as well. Let's take a quick look at some tasks you can do in Processing that aren't as easy to do in oF, and vice versa:

*Make a project visible on the Internet*
Use Processing; this is much trickier to do with oF.

*Make a project that renders a lot of 3-D graphics*
Use oF; this is where C++ really shines.

*Make a project that can run on many different computers without a lot of configuration*
Use Processing; this is rather tricky to do with oF.

*Make a project that uses a computer vision library like OpenCV*
Use oF; Processing doesn't communicate with a C++ library like OpenCV as easily as oF.

*Make a project that interfaces with the Arduino controller*
Use either, depending on what you need to do with the information from the Arduino controller.

openFrameworks is developed by Zach Lieberman, and Theo Watson, Arturo Castro, and Chris O'Shea, along with help from collaborators at Parsons School of Design, MediaLabMadrid, and Hangar Center for the Arts, as well as a far-flung network of developers, artists, and engineers. The framework originated in the Design and Media Arts program at Parsons School of Design, where Lieberman was a student. He found himself needing increasingly more power for his projects and began to learn C++. As he worked, he realized that although thousands of different libraries were available to C++ developers, nothing provided the same kind of ease of use and low barrier to entry for artists like Processing does for Java development. Hence, openFrameworks was born.

# Your IDE and Computer

Your computer and its operating system are about to become very important for a moment. That's because oF, unlike Arduino and Processing, does not have an integrated development environment (IDE). It requires that you use another IDE, and that IDE depends on your platform and what's available to you. So, we'll break it down by operating system. Because the requirements and instructions for getting your IDE set up may change without warning, the following sections are going to be less of step-by-step instructions and more of a general overview of what is involved. The openFrameworks website (www.openframeworks.cc) will have the most current instructions, and you can probably resolve any problems you run into on its forums.

Roughly, each of these OS and IDE combinations requires two steps. The first is to install and configure the IDE correctly, and the second is to download the appropriate oF package. Since oF really is just a collection of C++ code, you simply put the code files in the appropriate location for the IDE. You can then get started running the sample programs that come with oF, or you can start building your own programs.

## Windows

Those wanting to work with Windows are well taken care of. The structure and philosophy of oF work well with Windows, and several major Windows-based projects have been built in oF on Windows already.

### Visual Studio

Visual Studio is probably the most popular development environment for Windows. It's developed by Microsoft and is very powerful, and after some serious attention by the oF community, plays quite well with oF. It's a well-designed IDE that provides a lot of tools for developers and a host of extensions that can be used to beef up the core IDE. Visual Studio doesn't use the GNU Compiler Collection, which means that it compiles code slightly differently than the other IDEs listed here. That's sometimes a good thing and sometimes not, but it's probably not anything you need to worry about right away. The current version of Visual Studio is Visual Studio 2010. There is a commercial edition that can be bought and also a free version called Visual Studio C++ Express Edition.

### Code::Blocks for Windows

Code::Blocks is an open source IDE for C++ development. Currently, it is the preferred tool for working with oF on Windows. Code::Blocks comes bundled with a compiler system called MinGW that replicates the free and open source GNU Compiler Collection. If you don't really follow that last bit, don't worry about it—just know that because of MinGW, Code::Blocks is free. To get started with Code::Blocks, first download the IDE from www.codeblocks.org and install it. Once you've gotten Code::Blocks set up, download the oF for Windows Code::Blocks project files. Once you've downloaded the packages, you'll be able to open any one of the example programs and run them. Simply navigate to the *apps/examples/* section of the download and open up any one of the applications in the Code::Blocks IDE to get started.

## Mac OS X

Anyone with a Mac will have access to Xcode, which means you have access to an excellent IDE. Take a look at the top-level directory on your main hard drive. If you see a folder called *Developer*, then you're set. Otherwise, you'll need to install the Developer Tools packages. You can do this in two ways: insert the operating system DVD that came with your computer and install the Developer Tools, or go to *http://developer.apple.com/technology/xcode.html* and download and install the Developer Tools from the *.dmg* file you've downloaded. You'll need admin privileges on the computer to do this.

Once you've gotten set up with Xcode, you can download the Xcode oF package and get started by opening any one of the *xcodeproj* files in the example *apps/examples* folder. There is also a template for Xcode that you can install that allows you to generate new oF projects from Xcode.

## Linux

### Code::Blocks for Linux

When you download the Linux version of oF you'll see that there is a scripts folder with scripts for different distributions (Debian, Fedora, Ubuntu) to help you get set up. The first thing you'll do is run the *install_codeblocks.sh* script for your distribution that will install the most recent version of Code::Blocks. Next, look for the script called *install_dependencies.sh* and run that to install all the libraries needed to use openFrameworks on Linux. After that you're good to go. There is a template for Code::Blocks that allows you to generate new oF projects from the IDE by clicking a button, which makes generating new projects a cinch. You'll find it in your oF download in *scripts/*

*linux/codeblocks_wizard* along with a *readme* file that shows you how to install the template. In the *scripts/linux* folder you'll also find a lot of scripts using the Python language to create, update, edit, and compile projects.

### Using makefiles

Ah, the makefile—the classic build tool. While the Linux download of oF may look like it's oriented entirely towards Code::Blocks, it isn't. Each of the projects is actually built using a makefile inside the project folder. You can easily run this file from the command line without needing to open up the IDE at all. You'll notice that there are two or three makefiles, depending on whether add-ons are being used: *makefile*, the main file; *config.make*, where you'll add any customizations you want; *addons.make*, where all the included add-ons are listed. This allows you to use any text editor that you'd like with oF. Now it's time for a little review of C++.

## Taking Another Quick Tour of C++

In the previous tools you looked at in this book, Processing and Arduino, you learned about the more popular language that each of those languages extends and resembles: Java in the case of Processing, and C in the case of Arduino. In both those cases, however, we had to note that although the tools' languages were similar and derived from Java and C, respectively, they were not quite the same. You cannot just use Java code in a Processing program; you need to take certain steps for that to happen. oF is different because oF is C++, end of story. Anything you can do with C++, you can do with oF, because oF is simply a C++ library that was built with the intention of making C++ easier to use. This has a wonderful upside to it, in that oF is very straightforward, incredibly extensible, and is as powerful as C++. Which is to say, it's about as powerful as programming languages get.

The downsides, though, are that C++ can be difficult to learn and that the tools across platforms aren't completely standardized. So, in order to get you an appropriate tour of oF, you'll need to take a rudimentary tour of C++. Now, as with many other things in this book, this tour is an introduction, not a complete guide. Hundreds of C++ books exist for a reason: C++ is a massive topic. This quick tour is intended to provide you with the information you'll need to get started with oF C++, and creating interactive programs using them. At some point, though, you'll need to refer to another resource, be it the oF forums, an online reference (of which there are many good ones), or another book. That said, oF makes working with C++ easy and relatively painless while letting you (once you're comfortable) reach into some pretty tricky territory.

Bjarne Stroustrup developed C++ in 1979 at Bell Labs as an enhancement to the C programming language and named it C with Classes. In 1983, it was renamed C++. The idea of creating a new language originated from Stroustrup's experience in programming for his Ph D thesis. C++ is one of the most widely used programming languages, and is used to create programs and systems, from video games to software for the space shuttle to other programming languages.

## Basic Variable Types

The basic variable types in C++ are more or less the same as the variable types in Arduino with one fairly crucial difference: where Arduino uses the `byte` type, C++ uses the `char`. This is worth mentioning because at some point you'll probably encounter some code that does something strange like get all the bytes from a JPEG file into a char array. The reason that the bytes of a JPEG are stored in `char` variables is that the `char` stores exactly 1 byte of information, which can be a character like *B* (hence the name *char*); a small number, up to 255; or some bytes, like a pixel in a JPEG. Just be aware that you'll see the `char` type used in some places where the information being represented isn't an alphanumeric character.

These are the other most common C++ variable types:

`bool`
> For storing `true`/`false` values

`int`
> For storing integer numbers, for example, `1` or `89`; in all likelihood, this has a maximum value of `32767` on your computer

`long`
> For storing large integer values, for example, `3831080`; in all likelihood, this has a maximum value of `2147483647` on your computer

`float`
> For storing floating-point numbers, for example, `3.14` or `0.01`

`char`
> For storing character values, for example, `'f'` or `'g'`

`string`
> For storing strings of characters, for example, `"C++"` or `"openFrameworks"`

## Arrays

Arrays in C++ are identical to arrays in Arduino because Arduino is written in C++. To create an array, give the type of object that the array will store and a length for the array:

```
int arr[5] = { 5, 10, 15, 20, 25 };
```

One thing to note is that you can't initialize an array like this in the class declaration in your *.h* file. You need to declare the array first, int arr[5], and then assign values to it in the setup() method of your application. There are other ways to create an array using static variables, but this is probably the most common approach. This should be pretty familiar; if it isn't, refer to the discussion of arrays in Chapter 2.

## Methods

Methods have signatures:

```
returnType methodName(params) { }
```

Methods can be overloaded:

```
String overloadedMethod(bool b);
String overloadedMethod(char c);
String overloadedMethod(String s);
```

Each of these methods will be treated as a separate method, although this isn't extremely common. In oF, it does crop up now and again, and it's important to know what's going on if you see it.

Methods can be scoped to an object or be static. This might be a little complex; then again, it might be a cinch for you to understand. It isn't a vital aspect of working with oF, but it is something you might come across, and it is helpful to understand. To start, think back to the idea of scope. Sometimes methods or variables are scoped to a class. This means you can't call the method without an instance of a class. For instance, an oF program has a draw() method. You can't call draw() without having a program in which to draw. That's fairly simple, isn't it?

```
ofBaseApp myApp;
myApp.draw();
```

So far, so good. Imagine you have a method you want to call without making any objects at all, for instance, the local date and time. You don't want to have to make a date object just to get the time; you just want to know what time it is. In those cases, you use what are called *static methods*. Now, this is a sticky topic with a lot of nuances to it, but *generally* (and for our purposes) this means a method is available without being called on an object. This means that calling a static method is *not like* the previous example where the draw() method of a particular instance of ofBaseApp (you'll learn exactly what this class is a little later on in this chapter) is called:

```
myApp.draw(); // calling a method of an *instance*
```

Sometimes, however, you'll see a method called like this:

```
NameOfClass::nameOfMethod();// calling a method of a *class*
```

For instance, this might be something like the following:

```
// this calls the static method of the ApplicationTime class
// the method is the same for every ApplicationTime instance
```

```
// and it always does the same thing
ApplicationTime::staticTimeMethod();
```

You look around and don't see any instance of `ApplicationTime` anywhere, but the method is being called and works fine. What gives? This means the `ApplicationTime` class has a static method called `staticTimeMethod()` that can be called anywhere, at any time, without having to create an instance of the `ApplicationTime` class.

The `ApplicationTime` class would probably look like this:

```
class ApplicationTime {

    public :
    static int staticTimeMethod();   // can be accessed from anywhere
};
```

The `static` keyword in front of that method marks it as being accessed from anywhere by using the name of the class, followed by two colons:

```
ApplicationTime::staticTimeMethod()
```

You might not ever need to use static methods in your code, but you probably will run into them at some point. As with many other things in this book, static methods have a lot of very subtle and complex nuances, and this book isn't the place to cover them.

## Classes and Objects in C++

If you skipped over it, or weren't aware that it existed, now would be an excellent time to review the section "C++: Classes and Files" on page 143 in Chapter 5. Generally, and particularly in oF, a class is stored in two separate files, an *.h* file that *declares* all the variables and methods of the class, and a *.cpp* file that *defines* all the methods of a class.

A class is declared in the *NameOfClass.h* file, as shown here:

```
class NameOfClass {
public:
    void publicMethod(int);
private:
    int privateMethod();
}
```

In the *NameOfClass.cpp* file, the class is defined as follows:

```
// we have to include the header file
#include "NameOfClass.h"

// all class declarations require the name of the class
// followed by :: to ensure that the method is included
// with the class
void NameOfClass::publicMethod(int i) {
//do some stuff
}
int NameOfClass::privateMethod() {
```

```
//do some other stuff
}
```

You should make note of four elements here: the class is declared in the *.h* file, the methods are declared but not defined in the *.h* file, the *.h* file is included in the *.cpp* file, and all the methods in the class use the name of the class and double colons before the method definition. If this seems unfamiliar at all, review Chapter 5.

At this point, you're ready to start exploring openFrameworks. Again, although C++ is complex and sometimes a bit obtuse, openFrameworks is designed to make working with C++ as easy and straightforward as possible so that you can get started experimenting and making your projects quickly.

# Getting Started with oF

Getting started with oF is as simple as downloading the appropriate package for your computer, compiling it, and starting to look through the sample programs that have been built by the oF team. These should appear in something like the configuration shown in Figure 6-1.

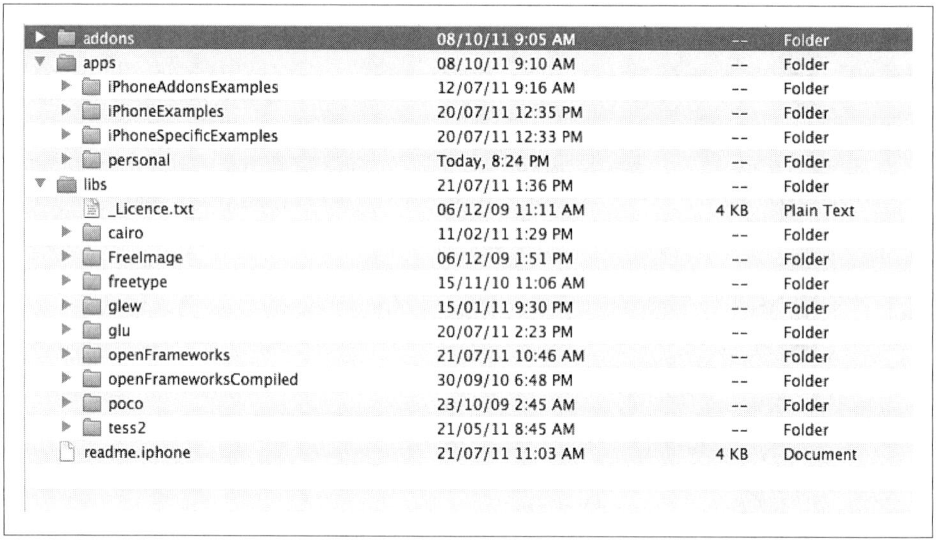

| | | | |
|---|---|---|---|
| ▶ 📁 addons | 08/10/11 9:05 AM | -- | Folder |
| ▼ 📁 apps | 08/10/11 9:10 AM | -- | Folder |
| ▶ 📁 iPhoneAddonsExamples | 12/07/11 9:16 AM | -- | Folder |
| ▶ 📁 iPhoneExamples | 20/07/11 12:35 PM | -- | Folder |
| ▶ 📁 iPhoneSpecificExamples | 20/07/11 12:33 PM | -- | Folder |
| ▶ 📁 personal | Today, 8:24 PM | -- | Folder |
| ▼ 📁 libs | 21/07/11 1:36 PM | -- | Folder |
| 📄 _Licence.txt | 06/12/09 11:11 AM | 4 KB | Plain Text |
| ▶ 📁 cairo | 11/02/11 1:29 PM | -- | Folder |
| ▶ 📁 FreeImage | 06/12/09 1:51 PM | -- | Folder |
| ▶ 📁 freetype | 15/11/10 11:06 AM | -- | Folder |
| ▶ 📁 glew | 15/01/11 9:30 PM | -- | Folder |
| ▶ 📁 glu | 20/07/11 2:23 PM | -- | Folder |
| ▶ 📁 openFrameworks | 21/07/11 10:46 AM | -- | Folder |
| ▶ 📁 openFrameworksCompiled | 30/09/10 6:48 PM | -- | Folder |
| ▶ 📁 poco | 23/10/09 2:45 AM | -- | Folder |
| ▶ 📁 tess2 | 21/05/11 8:45 AM | -- | Folder |
| 📄 readme.iphone | 21/07/11 11:03 AM | 4 KB | Document |

*Figure 6-1. Directory structure of openFrameworks*

Figure 6-1 shows the Mac OS X Finder, so obviously if you're on Windows or Linux, you'll see something different, but the general idea is the same. The oF folder contains the following folders:

*addons*

This contains all the added-on features for openFrameworks that have been contributed by users over the past year or so. These libraries change often, and new ones are added frequently, so it's important to remember that these are dynamic because you need to explicitly include them in your program if you're planning on using these libraries in a program.

*apps*

This is where your programs should be stored. If you have a strong preference, you can organize them in other ways, but that would go against the flow and would break some of your code. The example programs that use the core oF libraries are stored here, as are the example programs that show you how to use each of the add-on libraries. These are some of your best learning resources because they give you wonderful starting points for exploring oF and C++, and because they're usually well commented and documented.

*libs*

This is where the libraries that oF relies on are stored. These range from external libraries like fmodex, which is used for two- and three-dimensional sound manipulation, to the GLee library, which is used for OpenGL graphics. Most important, you'll see the core *openFrameworks* folder, which stores the header files that define all the core oF functionality in six folders. As you find your ideas and techniques becoming more and more sophisticated, you'll probably need more libraries than those provided here.

*openFrameworks*

The *openFrameworks* folder contains the core of the oF framework within twelve folders. The *app* folder contains the header file for the ofBaseApp class, which is the base program class of any oF program. The ofBaseApp class lets you easily toggle between full-screen and window views, set up code to handle mouse movements and keyboard presses, and integrate the simplified drawing routines with the graphics environment of your operating system. The *communication* folder contains tools for communicating over serial ports that can be used to communicate with the Arduino controller. The events folder contains *ofEvents*, which handles sending and receiving events in an oF application.

The *graphics* folder contains five classes, each of which is broken into a *.h* and *.cpp* file: *ofBitmapFont*, for working with bitmapped fonts, *ofGraphics* for working with 2-D drawing, *ofImage* for working with bitmapped image data, *ofTexture* for working with OpenGL textures, and *ofTrueTypeFont* for working with fonts.

The *sound* folder contains two classes for working with sound: the ofSoundPlayer that is a more simplified class for creating and playing sound files, and the ofSound Stream class that provides more low-level access to the sound capabilities of your computer.

The *video* folder contains code for capturing video from a video camera and for playing back captured video or video files loaded from your computer. We'll talk more about all these topics in later chapters, which are organized thematically.

Finally, the *utils* folder contains useful code for helping you work with math, useful code to get and measure time, and some core data types that are used throughout the program.

One of the first steps you'll want to take after you've downloaded oF is to go to the *apps/examples* folder and try running one or two of these programs. After you've run a program, open the code files, and explore how the program is put together. Keep an eye out for the references to `ofBaseApp`, and in the *.h* header file, look at the `#import` statements. You might not understand everything in these sections, but exploring these files is a good way to get familiar with what the libraries are, how they are imported, and how an oF program is structured.

oF is built out of multiple layers of libraries and code that uses those libraries. As you grow more comfortable with oF and with C++, you'll probably delve deeper into the official oF libraries and the underlying third-party libraries that they use. At the beginning though, you'll just want to focus at the top. The diagram in Figure 6-2 shows the structure of an oF application.

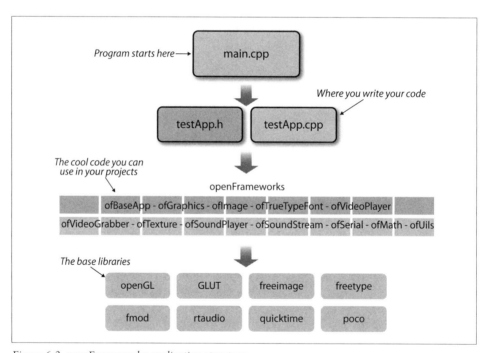

*Figure 6-2. openFrameworks application structure*

As you can see, your application sits atop the openFrameworks libraries, which sit atop a series of third-party libraries. As you learn more and more about oF and how all the libraries interrelate, you'll be delving deeper into both the oF and third-party libraries to do more.

# Interview: Theo Watson

Theo Watson, along with Zach Lieberman, is head of the openFrameworks project. Theo's work ranges from creating new tools for artistic expression, experimental musical systems, and immersive environments with full-body interaction. He lives in Amsterdam, the Netherlands.

*Can you talk a little bit about how you got started programming and working with interactive art?*

**Theo Watson:** Before I was doing programming work, I was really obsessed with sound. I was at Parsons, and I was skipping a lot of classes because I was so interested in working with music and, more particularly, with making instruments. I started off doing Max/MSP and was creating synthesizers that would take radio signals and use them to modulate the sounds that the synthesizers would make. That way, the synthesizers wouldn't just be making the sounds that you thought they would be making, but would also be driven by where you were based on which radio stations could be picked up in that area. I was very stubborn about doing any visual work; I wanted to keep everything based in sound.

Later, I had a class with Zach Lieberman called Audio Visual Synthesis. I had lost the use of my arms over the summer because of carpal tunnel syndrome, so I couldn't use a computer, and I wanted to make something that I didn't need to actually touch—something I could control using just my voice. That got me thinking...what if I didn't even need to control it at all? It would create a performance for itself, and then it could not only create a performance for itself but appreciate itself as well. It remembers what it has played so it builds up an interpretation of that. And because the microphone information is imperfect, it creates these very subtle variations that were stored and carried into the next performance.

When I played it back through MIDI using the information as a piano, it sounded very much like a jazz pianist. It totally blew my mind. It wasn't anything intentional, because of the feedback loop that was delayed and imperfect; what it was hearing was quite different from what it was playing.

*Do you see your artistic work and your work on oF as being distinct from one another, or are they part of the same project for you?*

**Theo:** We approached openFrameworks and our own work from the perspective of having an idea and really wanting to make it. I'm really taken with the idea of learning the skills as you go and doing whatever it takes to achieve your vision. I really firmly believe that you can get something unexpected back as feedback from your art.

From the process of making something, I can have something that I want to do in an art project and not have any idea how to accomplish that and then treat that as a process of learning how to do something. As something that shapes my ideas about what I'm doing, there's this constant back and forth and feedback. Neither Zach nor I are engineers; we're just people with funny ideas who have a bit of a nerdy background and a technical fascination with learning what we need to know.

*What kinds of things have you done with openFrameworks?*

**Theo:** It's really good that both Zach and I make projects; it gives us a real impetus to make sure that everything works because we're using oF ourselves. In my latest project, for example, I put it together in about two weeks, and if it weren't for oF, it would have taken about two months to make. It wasn't something that I was always excited about, but it's beginning to become more appealing to me now.

There were things that I had never used in oF. For example, I was trying to figure out how to use 3-D vector rotations, and then I just happened to glance into `ofVector Math`, and there was a bunch of code to help me. I was sitting there with a pencil and a piece of paper, and then it hit me: "Oh, yeah, I know there's something like this." I looked, and there it was, so I didn't have to figure out. I could spend time on the more interesting stuff. So, it's not like we're just making sure the code compiles and then putting it out there; we're using it in installations that have to run sometimes for weeks straight without crashes, so oF is just as important to us as it is to anyone using it.

Zach and I worked together on L.A.S.E.R. Tag. L.A.S.E.R. Tag was a really nice project because it reached so many people—both people who played with it and people who downloaded the software, set up the projector, and used the project themselves. It's working at a different scale both in terms of physical size and in terms of audience size. It's something that people are getting really excited about, and that's really amazing to me. I want to push those ideas and put people into situations where they can shape their environment and experience their environment. I think Zach and I are going to perhaps collaborate on something else soon, aside from oF, of course.

*Can you talk a little bit about the philosophy of openFrameworks?*

**Theo:** The motive of oF is to get rid of all the frustration of getting a window, getting something drawn in the window, and getting an image displayed in it. For some people first starting out, getting a window displayed and getting a shape drawn in it are really big deals. You have to deal with all this stuff that really isn't going to be interesting to you at all. You really should be thinking about how to make your idea richer, not "Why am I having this strange windowing error?"

When learning to code, you can start anywhere. My entry was with PHP and with Max/MSP. What I loved about Max/MSP that is a bit underrated was that in some ways it teaches you to be a good programmer because it teaches you how to break a problem into discrete parts. So, it helps you visualize how to break something into parts. Lots of times when I run into people who've never programmed before, a big hurdle is that they frequently don't know how to break something into the correct kinds of parts or they underestimate what it means to make something.

*How did openFrameworks get started?*

**Theo:** The idea of oF came about because Zach was teaching these classes, and in every class he was essentially trying to do the same thing every time—to get people up to speed, so to speak, with programming, with building an application, with being able to understand graphics and how graphics are drawn on the computer screen, with playing a sound, with capturing a sound, and so forth.

It actually started that summer, and I wasn't involved in it at all, because I was working on my thesis all that year. On that project, I was very determined that I write every line of code myself, and I ended up writing all the computer vision code for my project. I wrote every single function—including contour detection—that I used in that project. I mean everything, so I was very much busy at that point, working on my own stuff.

But then what happened was, after Parsons, we had a very rough outline of oF that was in use, and it was great for these students, so you could say "use ofCircle" instead of needing to work with cosine and sine, for example, and your class could be more interesting. It became something where we were incorporating more and more functionality, and it was stuff that was more and more interesting to me. When someone asked, "How do I do this?" and we didn't know, we would end up spending three or four days trying to solve the problem, and it would be a really valuable thing to learn. Later I'd find myself using that same information or knowledge in my own work, so it became something I was doing to teach myself as much as because it was something we wanted to add to oF.

*What kinds of people have you found using oF?*

**Theo:** The forums have sprung up in a really interesting way, because there's such a wide range of kinds of things that people are talking about and backgrounds that people are coming from. A lot of people who are a lot smarter than us are participating, which is great because it's really helping to lower the barrier to entry, because not only is there this framework that we've put together but additionally there are people other than us to answer questions. For example, there's Arturo Castro. We wanted to do a Linux version of oF, but neither of us really knew a lot about Linux, especially video and audio capture in Linux. But he did, so he really took over that part of it, which is amazing because the community around this project is allowing us—all of us involved with oF or using oF—to make and use things that maybe we aren't as familiar with as we'd need to be without it. So, we're very lucky.

We really want people to use it in the most unusual way they can imagine. We don't want it to be just about using computer vision, where people are going to say, "OK, I need to do computer vision, so I'll use oF." We're quite interested in things that use machinery, sound, or nontraditional means of interacting. I want to take it away from computer vision, graphics, and installation work and allow people to work more richly with sound.

*Are there particular types of projects that you want to see people using openFrameworks for, or particular ways you want to see people using it?*

**Theo:** We don't want to have to tell people, "This is the way you have to use it." We just want to see it used in new and different ways, so every time there's a new project, I feel like there's very often a new plug-in for that project that's born out of it. As long as people don't claim they wrote oF, we're fine with anything they do with it. If that is something having to do with maximizing profits in a design project, we're fine with that. We don't want to force people to share their code; we won't use GPL, because we don't want to restrict what people can do with it. We want them to feel they can do whatever they want with it. We think it should be up to the end user—to the people playing with it—to decide what they need.

# Touring an oF Application

The core of an oF program is the main application class, ofBaseApp. Since oF is a bare-bones C++ library, the best way to understand it is to look at the code, and the first place to look is the program. Everything you make in oF will have an ofBaseApp class somewhere in it.

## Methods

All the methods in the ofBaseApp class are event-handling methods. This means they are triggered in response to events that happen within your program, such as the user moving the mouse, the user pressing a key, the program quitting, or your program redrawing. At its simplest, working with oF is adding new code to the appropriate method and waiting for the program to call your methods. If you want to work with the user's mouse actions, add some code to the mouseMoved() method of the ofBaseApp. The core oF framework handles creating the window and adding the appropriate code behind the scenes. To do something when these events occur, you simply need to create a class that extends ofBaseApp and add the appropriate methods. If that sounds a little intimidating, don't worry, because we'll walk you through it after looking at each of the methods in the ofBaseApp class.

The setup() method is called when the program first starts up, the same as in Arduino and Processing. If something has to run only once or it is important to run at the beginning of your program, it should be in setup(). Also, if you're defining variables in your .h file, you should initialize them. For instance, in an .h file you might have:

```
int numberOfVideos;
```

In your setup method, you should initialize that if you're going to need it once your application starts running:

```
numberOfVideos = 5;
```

The update() method is called just before the draw() method. This is important because in oF you generally want to put any data processing you need to do in the update() method so you're drawing with new data. If you need to check and see, for example, whether any new sound is coming from a microphone before you draw the sound wave, you'll want to do that in the update() method.

The draw() method is called when the program draws its graphics, much like in Processing. In contrast with Processing, however, in oF you should have drawing code only in your draw() method to keep your program running smoothly.

The exit() method is called when the program exits and closes down. If you want to do any final processing or data logging in your program, or to free memory, which we'll discuss later, this is the place to do it.

The keyPressed() and keyReleased() methods are callbacks that handle any key actions that the user makes:

- keyPressed(int key) sends the code of the key just pressed as an integer
- keyReleased(int key) sends the code of the key just released as an integer

The ofBaseApp class defines four callback methods to handle mouse movements. You can add any code to handle these events to these methods. The mouseMoved() method passes in the current x and y position in pixels of the mouse. The mouseDragged() and mousePressed() methods pass in the x and y positions and also the button that has been pressed. The mouseReleased() method is triggered whenever either mouse button is released:

```
mouseMoved(int x, int y)
mouseDragged(int x, int y, int button)
mousePressed(int x, int y, int button)
mouseReleased()
```

The audioReceived() method is a little more complex than the other methods because it receives a pointer to the stream of audio data and because dealing with a pointer is a little tricky. This requires that you remember what a pointer really is—a piece of information that tells you the location of something:

```
audioIn(float * input, int bufferSize, int nChannels)
audioOut(float * output, int bufferSize, int nChannels)
```

Imagine you get some data in the audioIn() callback. That data represents the waveform of the sound that the computer's microphone has captured in a list of floating-point numbers, maybe something like 0.000688 or –0.000688 for a loud noise, or 0 for silence. The numbers represent the waveform of the sound, just like a waveform display that you might see on an oscilloscope or in recording software. Instead of sending all the data—all those floating-point numbers—to ofBaseApp, the program sends just a single value: the location in memory where all this data is stored. That means instead of needing to send a few hundred values, the program needs to send only one (see Figure 6-3), saving the space that would be needed if it had to copy all the data every time.

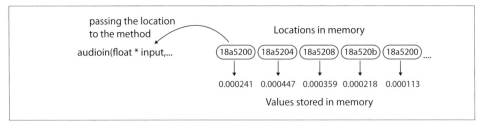

*Figure 6-3. Passing a pointer to an array of data for sound processing*

So, you simply pass the location of the first item in the array of sound data and then start processing the data in the `audioIn()` method. You'll learn more about this in Chapter 10, so we'll leave it be for the moment. You might also want to look back at Chapter 5 in the section "Pointers and References" on page 148.

## Variables

The two variables that `ofBaseApp` defines are the `mouseX` and `mouseY` values:

```
int mouseX, mouseY;
```

`mouseX` and `mouseY` let you always determine the location of the user's mouse. Since we're talking about the mouse position, we'll point out two very handy methods you can call to figure out the size of the screen where your program is being displayed. This might not be as important if you always know the computer that your program is going to be running on, but if you're going to be moving it around or you don't feel like measuring your screen, you can use these methods to find the height and width of the screen in pixels:

```
int ofGetScreenHeight();
int ofGetScreenWidth();
```

You'll be using these later in this chapter to help control the speed of a movie file with the mouse position.

Now that you have a basic idea of what is included in an oF program, you'll create one of your own.

## Creating "Hello, World"

In this section, you'll create a simple program that will print the words "Hello oF World" to the screen. As described in Chapter 5, your program will be spread across three different files, *HelloWorldApp.h*, *HelloWorldApp.cpp*, and *main.cpp*. In all the oF downloads, you can use the empty project templates so you don't have to create a new project yourself. You should generally keep the *apps/examples* folders clean, so it might be better to make your own folder in the *apps* directory. Simply copy the *emptyPro-*

*ject* template and give it a new name, and you have all the classes, libraries, and paths you need to create your program.

All oF programs extend the **ofBaseApp** class. Any methods you want your program to use will be defined in the *.h* file of your application class. In this case, you need to use only the **setup()** and **draw()** methods. Any methods you do not extend in your program are simply left as they were in the original program.

Example 6-1 show the *HelloWorldApp.h* file.

*Example 6-1. HelloWorldApp.h*

```
#pragma once

#include "ofMain.h" // we need to include all the oF files, linked here

class HelloWorldApp : public ofBaseApp{

    public:

        void setup(); // we need this to start the application
        void draw(); // we need this to draw something on the screen

};
```

This line may jump out at you from *HelloWorldApp.h*:

```
#pragma once
```

This is what is called *preprocessor instructions* and it's important to the compiler that's going to create your oF program from your code, because it tells the compiler to make the class only once. In a simple program like the one you have here, this isn't a big deal, but in more complicated programs, the compiler may try to compile the class multiple times, which would cause all kinds of problems.

Now the *.cpp* file:

```
#include "HelloWorldApp.h"

void HelloWorldApp::setup(){
    // no need to do anything here
    cout << " just get started here " << endl; // just saying hello
}

void HelloWorldApp::draw(){
    ofBackground(255, 255, ?55); // background white
    ofSetColor(0, 0, 0); // text black
    cout << " say hello " << endl;
    ofDrawBitmapString("HELLO WORLD!", 100,380);
}
```

The **setColor()** method sets the color of any drawing that the program will do, and in this case, that drawing is going to be the text. Since you're passing 0, 0, 0, which is RGB black, the text will appear in black. The `drawString()` method writes the text to the location on the screen specified by the *x* and *y* coordinates.

Now that the program is ready, you need to run it. In C++, as you may recall, you do this in a `main()` method, which is a special method that the compiler looks for when it starts compiling your code. In an openFrameworks program, this method is always in the *main.cpp* file. For an oF program, the `main()` method should set up the window size and then start the program. The framework handles everything else.

The first step you'll see here is the setup of the window. You can specify a window with a size, or you can just say `oF_FULLSCREEN` to make the program fill the screen of the computer that it's being run on. The next line of code contains the call to the `ofRunApp()` method that starts the program. You pass it a new instance of the program, and the `ofRunApp()` method takes care of starting the program and calling its `update()` and `draw()` methods.

Here's the *main.cpp* file:

```
#include "ofMain.h"
#include "HelloWorldApp.h"

int main(){

    // can be OF_WINDOW or OF_FULLSCREEN
    // pass in width and height too:
    ofSetupOpenGL(1024,768, OF_WINDOW);// <-------- setup the GL context
    // this kicks off the running of my app
    ofRunApp(new HelloWorldApp);

}
```

And that's the "Hello, World" of openFrameworks. Now you'd probably like to learn how to draw something a little more significant.

## Drawing in 2-D

To begin, drawing in oF is quite similar to drawing in Processing; you set the color that the drawing will use, set the fill mode of the drawing (whether the shape will be filled in with color), and then use one of the predefined drawing methods to draw the shape to the screen. For example, to draw two circles to the screen, you would simply add calls to `ofCircle()` to the `draw()` method of a program. `ofCircle()` uses whatever the last color that you set using the `ofSetColor()` method to draw the circle. Like in Processing, when you set the color, you're setting how all the drawing will be done until the end of the `draw()` method. Let's take a look at tweening through colors first and then walk through how colors work in oF. Take a look at Example 6-2.

*Example 6-2. SimpleGraphics.cpp*

```
#include "simpleGraphics.h"
```

```
void simpleGraphics::setup(){
    ofSetCircleResolution(100);
    ofBackground(255,255,255);
    ofSetVerticalSync(true);

    fillColor.set(255, 0, 0); // red

}
```

Here's where we're actually going to tween through the colors using HSB instead of RGB. Read on to see what that means:

```
void simpleGraphics::update()
{
    fillColor.setHue(fillColor.getHue()+1);
    if(fillColor.getHue() > 254) fillColor.setHue(0);
}

void simpleGraphics::draw(){

    ofBackground(255,255,255);
    ofSetColor(fillColor);
    ofFill(); // draw "filled shapes"
    ofCircle(100,400,100);

    // now just an outline
    ofNoFill();
    ofSetLineWidth(10);
    ofSetColor(fillColor);
    ofCircle(400,400,200);

}
```

The *.h* header file for the class would look like the code in Example 6-3.

*Example 6-3. SimpleGraphics.h*

```
#pragma mark once

#include "ofMain.h"

class simpleGraphics : public ofBaseApp{

    public:

    void setup();
    void update();
    void draw();

    ofColor fillColor;

};
```

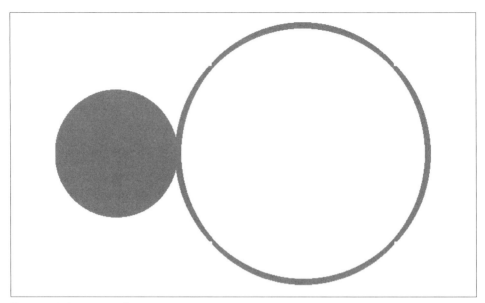

*Figure 6-4. Tweening colors in oF*

Since you're not overriding any of the other methods of the **ofBaseApp** class, you don't need to include them in the header file for your class. The result will look something like Figure 6-4.

Setting color in oF is similar to the way you set it in Processing. The **ofSetColor()** method takes either RGB values, RGB and alpha values, hex color values, or an **ofColor** object. If you take a look at the *ofGraphics.h* file in *lib/openFrameworks* you'll see the following:

```
// color options
void ofSetColor(int r, int g, int b); // 0-255
void ofSetColor(int r, int g, int b, int a); // 0-255
void ofSetColor(const ofColor & color);
void ofSetColor(const ofColor & color, int _a);
void ofSetColor(int gray); // new set a color as grayscale with one argument
void ofSetHexColor( int hexColor ); // hex, like web 0xFF0033;
```

That's a lot of different ways to set a color. The most interesting of these is the **ofColor** object, which allows you to work with RGB and HSB color. HSB stands for Hue Saturation Brightness (sometimes also called HSL, or Hue Saturation Lightness) and it's a way of representing colors that might be familiar from the color wheel. The hue is the location on the color wheel, the saturation is how far away from grey it is, and Brightness is how far from white it is. The reason we're using it here is that we want to shift between colors easily. HSB makes that easy because you simply increment the hue value until you reach 255, and then go back to 0. This creates a smooth transition between colors without any of the complex math that doing this in the RGB color spaces would require.

## Setting Drawing Modes

The drawing mode of a program indicates whether lines or shapes should have fills. In oF, you set these drawing modes using one of two methods. If you want your drawing to have a fill, that is, a color that fills in the shape, you call the method ofFill() before doing any drawing; if not, then call ofNoFill():

```
ofSetColor(0xCCCCFF); // set our color to light blue
ofFill();        // drawing will use "filled shapes"
ofRect(100, 100, 200, 200); // draw a rectangle 200x200 pixel

// now just an outline
ofNoFill();
ofRect(400, 100, 200, 200);
```

This code draws two rectangles that will sit next to one another. You'll see what that looks like in a few moments after you add a little more detail to the rectangles. oF provides quite a few convenient drawing methods for drawing simple 2-D shapes:

```
void ofTriangle(float x1,float y1,float x2,float y2,float x3, float y3);
void ofCircle(float x,float y, float radius);
void ofEllipse(float x, float y, float width, float height);
void ofLine(float x1,float y1,float x2,float y2);
void ofRect(float x1,float y1,float w, float h);
```

Putting a few of these methods together, you can make a simple drawing (as shown in Figure 6-5) that overlaps squares and circles with varying alpha values.

## Drawing Polygons

The Open Graphics Language (OpenGL) handles all the drawing in oF. Chapter 13 in this book is dedicated to OpenGL, so in this chapter you'll learn how to get oF to draw without touching any actual OpenGL code. Sometimes you don't want to draw a circle, square, ellipse, or triangle, and you don't want to delve into OpenGL. For this, you can use several polygon-drawing functions in oF to draw shapes by placing points and setting fills. This works much the same as drawing vectors in Adobe Flash, Adobe Illustrator, and many other paint programs: you place three or more points, and the program creates the fill between those points that defines the shape. In oF, you tell the program to begin to draw a polygonal shape, you add points (*vertices* in oF) that define the edges of the point, and then you close the shape, which triggers the filling in of your shape.

This method is called before the shape is drawn, telling the oF application that you're starting to draw a shape:

```
void ofBeginShape();
```

This method is called after the shape is drawn, telling the oF application that you're finished drawing the shape:

```
void ofEndShape(bool bClose);
```

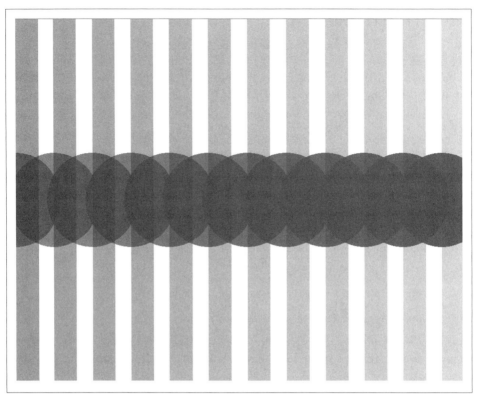

*Figure 6-5. Drawing in oF using alpha*

This method takes a single parameter: a Boolean that indicates whether the shape should be closed, that is, whether any space between the first point and the last point should just be closed up by OpenGL. The default is `true`.

The following places a vertex at the position on the screen indicated by the *x* and *y* values passed into it:

```
ofVertex(float x, float y);
```

When you place a vertex, OpenGL automatically connects the previous point (if one exists) and the next point (when one exists) via the location of the just added point with two straight lines.

If you don't want to draw straight lines (and sometimes you just won't), then you might want to use the `ofCurveVertex()` method:

```
ofCurveVertex(float x, float y);
```

This method places a vertex that a line will curve to from the previous point and that will be curved from to the next vertex. `ofCurveVertex()` has one tricky part: for reasons that have to do with the way OpenGL draws vertex curves, you need to add the first and last vertices in the shape twice. The following code snippet shows how to use the ofCurveVertex() method:

```
ofSetColor(0xffffff);
ofFill();
ofBeginShape();
    ofCurveVertex(20, 20);// that's not a typo; you need to add the first
    ofCurveVertex(20, 20); // point twice
    ofCurveVertex(220, 20);
    ofCurveVertex(220, 220);
    ofCurveVertex(20, 220);// that's not a typo; you need to add the last
    ofCurveVertex(20, 20);// point twice as well
        ofCurveVertex(20, 20);
ofEndShape(false);
```

One drawback to the ofVertexCurve() method is that you have no control over how curved the curve is. To control the curviness of the curve, you'll want to use the ofBezierVertex() method, which lets you set the starting point of the curve and then define two control points (see Figure 6-6) that will be used to define the shape of the line on its way to the next vertex:

```
ofBezierVertex(float x1, float y1, float x2, float y2, float x3, float y3)
```

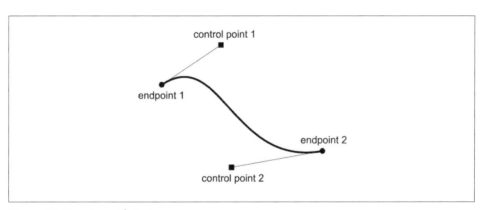

Figure 6-6. Drawing with Bezier curves

In the ofBezierCurve() method, the first two floats, x1 and y1, set the location of the line; the next two, x2 and y2, set the location of the first control point; and the last two, x3 and y3, set the location of the second control point. This lets you create quite complex shapes by combining multiple Bezier curves. Take Example 6-4: the code snippet in the draw() method of an oF program creates two moving Bezier curves.

Example 6-4. bezierGraphics.cpp

```
void bezierGraphics::draw(){

    float bez1X1 = 400 + (100 * cos(ofGetElapsedTimef()));
    float bez1Y1 = 500 + (100 * sin(ofGetElapsedTimef()));
    float bez1X2 = 600 + (100 * cos(ofGetElapsedTimef()));
```

```
    float bez1Y2 = 500 + (100 * sin(ofGetElapsedTimef()));

    float bez2X1 = 400 - (100 * cos(ofGetElapsedTimef()));
    float bez2Y1 = 500 - (100 * sin(ofGetElapsedTimef()));
    float bez2X2 = 600 - (100 * cos(ofGetElapsedTimef()));
    float bez2Y2 = 500 - (100 * sin(ofGetElapsedTimef()));


    ofFill();
    ofSetHexColor(0xffffff - fillColor.getHex());
    ofBeginShape();
        // first we create the point from which to begin drawing
        ofVertex(0,300);
        // then create the Bezier vertex
        ofBezierVertex(bez1X1,bez1Y1,bez1X2,bez1Y2,900,300);
        ofBezierVertex(bez2X1,bez2Y1,bez2X2,bez2Y2,100,300);
        // finish the shape
        ofVertex(1000,300);
    ofEndShape();

    ofFill();
    ofSetColor(fillColor);
    ofBeginShape();
        ofVertex(0,300);
        ofBezierVertex(650,300,bez2X2,bez2Y2,900,300);
        ofBezierVertex(100,300,bez1X2,bez1Y2,100,300);
        ofVertex(1000,300);
    ofEndShape();

}
```

Figure 6-7 shows what the previous code will look like when run.

# Displaying Video Files and Images

Now that you can draw some simple shapes with oF, you might be interested in loading and displaying video files and images.

## Images

You can display images in an oF program by using the ofImage class, which handles most of the dirty work of loading an image into memory and displaying it on the screen. Though, as with all things, you can do this work yourself, but it's often easier to have oF do it for you until you really need to do it for yourself.

The ofImage class is a core class of oF, which means you don't have to use any import statements to include this class in your program. Simply declare an instance of the ofImage class in the header file of your program, and you're ready to go. Example 6-5 shows a header file for an oF program that will use an ofImage class.

*Example 6-5. imageApp.h*

```
#pragma mark once
#include "ofMain.h"

class imageApp : public ofBaseApp{

    public:

        void setup();
        void update();
        void draw();

        ofImage milkShakeImg;
        ofImage friesImg;

        ofVec2f friesPosition;
        ofVec2f shakePosition;
};
```

Most of the time when you're dealing with an image, you're dealing with image files: JPEG, PNG, and so on. To load an image from a file, call the `loadImage()` method, and pass the relative or absolute name of the file that you want to load as an argument. The *relative* filename is the file path from the program to the location of the image. The *absolute* name is something that starts with *C:\...* if you're using Windows and */Folder/...* if you're using OS X or Linux. Generally, you'll want to use the *data* folder within your oF program:

```
void loadImage(string fileName);
```

This loads the image into memory so that you can display it or manipulate it as you see fit.

 openFrameworks assumes that a folder called *data* is in the same directory as your program. Whenever you load an image, font, QuickTime movie, or other kind of file, by default your oF program will look in the *data* folder. Unless you have a good reason to do so, you should always store data within this folder to leverage the work that the creators of oF have put into the framework.

Once you've loaded the image, you need to draw it into the graphics window. You do this using one of the `draw()` methods of the `ofImage` class, like so:

```
void draw(float x, float y); // use the images default size
void draw(float x, float y, float w, float h); // specify image size
```

In the previous code, the *x* and *y* parameters dictate where the image will be drawn in the program window. This overloaded method also lets you either use the default size of the image file you've loaded or set a new height and width for the image:

```
void resize(int newWidth, int newHeight);
```

To dynamically resize an image, in an animation for example, use the `resize()` method to change the size of the image:

```
void saveImage(string fileName);
```

The `saveImage()` method lets you save an image to a file that you pass in as a string to the method name. You might want to do this if you're manipulating an image or creating a new image from a screen capture. You'll learn how to use a screen capture later in this chapter. If you want to look at doing pixel-level manipulations with an image file, look ahead to Chapter 10.

## Video

You can work with video from a prerecorded movie file and from a live video source. The first option is to display a video that has been saved in a QuickTime, WMV, or MPEG file. You might want to load the file, play it, rewind it, speed it up, or even grab and manipulate the individual pixels that make up the image. oF helps you do all these tasks with its `ofVideoPlayer` class, which you'll learn about in this section. The second option for working with video is using a camera attached to your computer. You might want to display the video from your camera, resize the display, or manipulate the pixels of your video to create new images. oF helps you do all these tasks with its `ofVideoGrabber` class, which you'll learn about in Chapter 10.

Working with video is a huge topic, and because oF lets you do so many things by extending its functionality and integrating so many different libraries, this chapter is only scratching the surface of the topic. We'll save the majority of the other functionality for the later chapters in this book and concentrate on the basics in this chapter.

Creating a program that loads a movie is a cinch. Simply declare an instance of the `ofVideoPlayer` class in an *.h* file for the program, and then load the movie in the `setup()` method of the program. See Example 6-6.

*Example 6-6. videoApp.h*

```
#pragma mark once

#include "ofMain.h"

class videoApp : public ofBaseApp{

    public:

        void setup();
        void update();
        void draw();

        ofVideoPlayer player;
        float screenHeight;
        bool isPaused;
```

```
        void mouseMoved( int x, int y );
        void keyPressed  (int key);
};
```

Once you have declared all the methods and variables of the videoApp class, you can move on to defining it in the *videoApp.cpp* file. You'll use two very important methods here. The first is the draw() method for ofVideoPlayer that draws the pixels from the current frame of the movie onto the screen. This needs to be called in the draw() method of your program. The second is the idleMovie() method, which in essence tells the movie to load the next chunk of data from the file and prepare to display itself. This is called in the update() method of the oF app, keeping with the philosophy of doing all nondrawing-related processing in the update() method before the draw(). If you omit this method, the movie will play fine, but skipping around in the movie won't work, so it's important to remind the player to do its internal housekeeping. See Example 6-7.

*Example 6-7. videoApp.cpp*

```
#include "videoApp.h"

void videoApp::setup()
{
    ofBackground(255,255,255);
    screenHeight = float(ofGetScreenHeight());
    //player.loadMovie("something.mov");// this loads from the data folder
    player.loadMovie("fingers.mov"); // this loads from a website
    player.play();
    isPaused = false;
}

void videoApp::update()
{
    player.idleMovie();
}

void videoApp::draw()
{
    player.draw(20, 20);
}

void videoApp::mouseMoved( int x, int y )
{
    float yPos = (mouseY / screenHeight ) * 2.0;
    player.setSpeed(yPos);
}

void videoApp::keyPressed  (int key)  {
    if(    isPaused ) {
        isPaused = false;
    } else {
        isPaused = true;
    }
    player.setPaused(isPaused);
}
```

You won't recognize a few methods here unless you've done a little creative investigation into the header files already. The ofVideoPlayer class uses the loadMovie() method to load a video file into memory:

```
bool loadMovie(string name);
```

Remember that, by default, oF expects you're either

loading files from the *data* folder of your program, so the value of name you pass into the loadMovie() method should be relative location of your movie file. loading files from the Internet.

I went with the Internet so you could see the movie, if you didn't have anything in the *data* folder.

To control the speed of the movie, you use the setSpeed() method; 1.0 is normal speed, which means 0.5 is half speed, and 2.0 is double speed:

```
void setSpeed(float speed);
```

Next, try using the setPosition() method of the ofVideoPlayer class:

```
void setPosition(float pct)
```

This sets the position of the video as a percentage of its total length, so 0.5 is halfway through the movie file, and 1.0 is the end of the movie file.

This concludes your brief introduction to working with video in oF, though you'll find plenty more information in Chapter 10.

# Compiling an oF Program

Depending on the IDE you use, compiling your program is a little bit different.

## Compiling in Xcode

If you're using a Mac with OS X, you'll be using Xcode. To build your program in Xcode, select Edit Scheme from the Product menu as shown in Figure 6-7.

In your scheme browser and set the Build Configuration to Release, as shown in Figure 6-8.

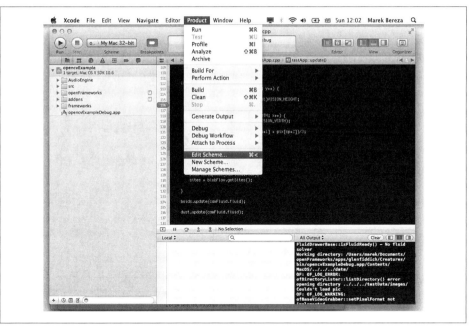

*Figure 6-7. Opening the Scheme browser*

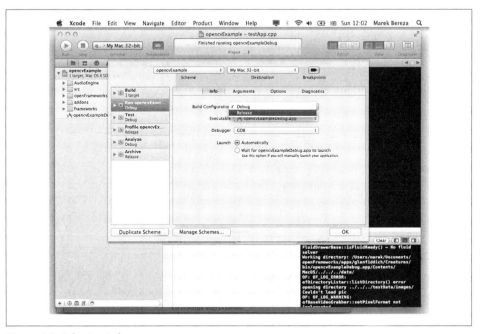

*Figure 6-8. Selecting Release*

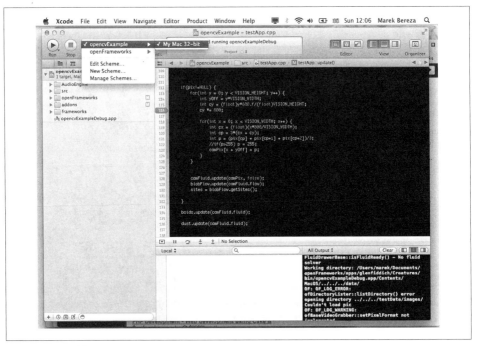

*Figure 6-9. Building your project*

Then, choose the example to build as shown in Figure 6-9. Note that there are two projects, the core oF project and the project that you're actually running. Be sure to build your project, not the openFrameworks project.

## Compiling in Code::Blocks

If you're on Linux or Windows, you'll probably be using Code::Blocks (unless you're using the makefile approach). To build and run your project in Code::Blocks, click F9, or click the Build and Run button, as shown in Figure 6-10.

You can also change the configuration of your project, whether you're preparing it for build or for release, by using the "Build target" drop-down menu shown in Figure 6-10. To just build your project and check it for errors, click Ctrl+F9. This won't run your program, but it will tell you whether you have any errors, which is often quite useful.

## Debugging an oF Application

Invariably, things will go wrong with the code you write. Luckily, you can use several tools to figure out what went wrong and how to fix it. The following sections highlight some strategies to use when writing code to help make debugging easier and faster.

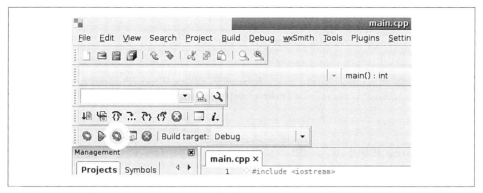

*Figure 6-10. Building your project in Code::Blocks*

## Using the cout Statement

The cout statement is one of the greatest tools available to you when working with code. Anywhere you have code that might be executing in an unexpected way or you have a variable that isn't behaving as expected, you can use the cout statement and pass it the variable name to determine the value of the variable at a given point in time. The cout method is a bit of a strange one because it requires what you might think of as the binary shift operator from Chapter 4. If you use the << on a number, it's a binary shift; if you use it with the cout command, it's simply putting together a string. That's because of something called operator overloading, which is a bit of an advanced topic and isn't something you have to worry about at this stage:

```
int widthOfSomething = 5;
cout << " this is the width of something: " << widthOfSomething << endl;
```

This prints the following:

```
this is the width of something: 5
```

The cout concatenates all the values passed to it and puts a carriage return, that is, makes a new line, if you put the endl statement at the end of the line. Say, for instance, that you have an ofVideoPlayer object with a variable height and width that you want to check at a vital point in your program. You would use the following:

```
cout << " video is " << player.width << " by " << player.height << endl;
```

which would print this:

```
video is 240 by 320
```

As long as you always remember to put the <<, all your messages and variables will be neatly put together and logged to the console of your application.

## Using the GNU Debugger

Beyond cout, both Xcode and Code::Blocks provide a debugger that interfaces with the GNU Debugger, which is a wonderful tool that lets you pause in the middle of your program, examine values, and move to the next line of code. This book doesn't have enough space to permit going deeply into debugging, but you'll learn how to get a debugging session started in Xcode and Code::Blocks; the rest of the discovery is left to you.

## Using the Debugger in Xcode

First, set a breakpoint anywhere in your code by double-clicking a line number to the left of your code in your code view (see Figure 6-11).

Then, make sure your project is set to Debug mode, as shown in Figure 6-12.

Initiate a debugging session by clicking the Build and Go button and selecting the Build and Debug option, as shown in Figure 6-13.

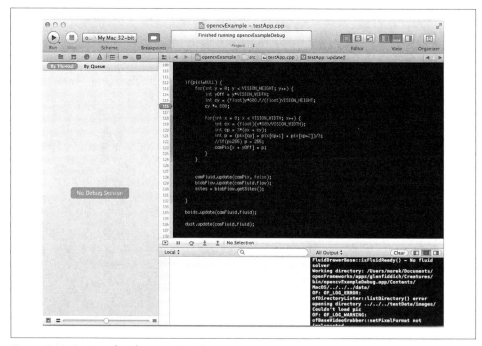

*Figure 6-11. Setting a breakpoint in Xcode*

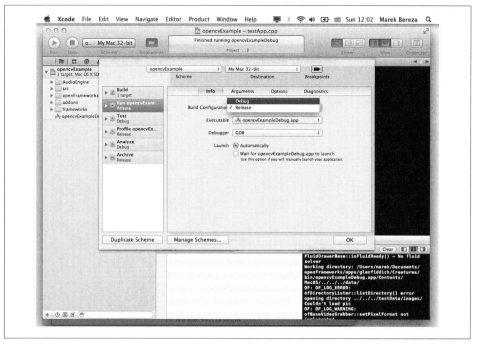

Figure 6-12. Setting your build configuration to Debug

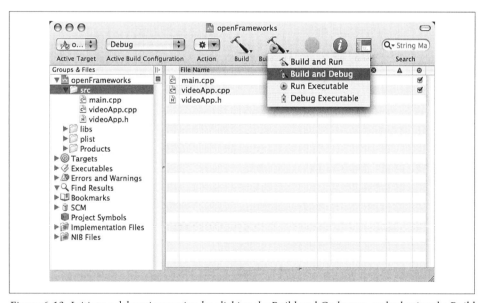

Figure 6-13. Initiate a debugging session by clicking the Build and Go button and selecting the Build and Debug option

Once you've started a debugging session, the debugger will run your code until it encounters the line where you've set a breakpoint, as shown in Figure 6-14.

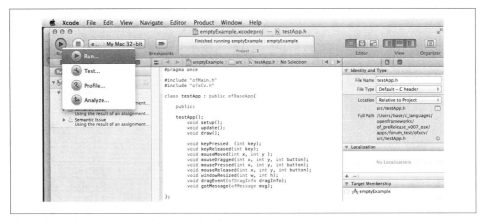

*Figure 6-14. Running your code up to a breakpoint*

By clicking the Step Over button that you see above the variable, you can *step through* the code, which means you can advance the debugger line by line to see what is going on in your code. If you encounter a variable that contains a value you didn't expect, set a breakpoint in front of where that variable is altered, and step through the code. This helps you understand the flow of your program and how values are being passed around.

You may find that certain methods aren't doing what you expect them to do. If you know that the logic inside the method is sound, you can set breakpoints just inside the method to see what's getting passed in when the method gets called. This can help you understand how the program is calling that method and what's going on outside it. There are many other tricks to using debugging effectively; what's most important to understand is that the debugger lets you check the value of a variable at a given point in time.

## Using the Debugger in Code::Blocks

Setting breakpoints in Code::Blocks is similar to setting a breakpoint in Xcode; simply click on a line number. A bright red circle appears. This tells you where the debugger will stop when it is executing code. Next, you simply start the debugging session. From the Debug menu, select Debug→Start (see Figure 6-15) or press F8.

*Figure 6-15. Starting the debugger in Code::Blocks*

Once the debugger is running, you can check the values of your variables by looking at the variables in the Watches window (see Figure 6-16).

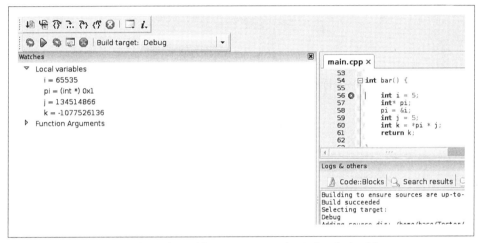

*Figure 6-16. Viewing the values of variables at runtime in the Code::Blocks debugger*

By clicking F7, you can step through the code line by line to see what is going on in your code. Of course, you can do many other things with the Code::Blocks debugger, but we'll leave that to you to discover if you're interested.

# Importing Libraries

One of the wonderful things about the community that has grown up around oF is that new libraries are being developed all the time to fit not only the needs of the people developing them, but also the needs of the community of people who are using oF. While oF includes libraries to do many of the simpler things that you might want to do, you might be interested in working with more complex kinds of functionality. For this, you can look at the add-ons to oF that oF users have created.

These libraries are all stored in the *addons* folder of the file you downloaded. Each of those folders contains an add-on that has been created with a specific purpose. An add-on isn't included in your program by default, so to include one, you simply tell the compiler you want to include that add-on, and away you go. The ofxOpenCV add-on is a great example. With the ofxOpenCV library, you can use the OpenCV computer vision library created by Intel in your oF program. You can do motion tracking, face detection, and much more with this library, but you have to include it first. To do that, look at the *ofxOpenCv* directory in the *addons* folder; you'll see a file called *ofxOpenCv.h*, which contains all the import statements needed for the add-on to run correctly. Opening the *ofxOpenCv.h* file, you see the following:

```
#ifndef OFX_CV_H
#define OFX_CV_H


//--------------------------
// constants
#include "ofxCvConstants.h"

//--------------------------
// images
#include "ofxCvImage.h"
#include "ofxCvGrayscaleImage.h"
#include "ofxCvColorImage.h"
#include "ofxCvFloatImage.h"
#include "ofxCvShortImage.h"

//--------------------------
// contours and blobs
#include "ofxCvContourFinder.h"


#endif
```

When you include the *ofxOpenCv.h* file in your application, you're including everything that *ofxOpenCv.h* includes. You still need to add all the files to your project in your IDE but you only need to change one line of code in your application. This means that the whole library is being imported, allowing you to get it all with only one statement: `#include "ofxOpenCv.h"`. Now your application is ready to go:

```
// standard defining of app
#pragma mark once

#include "ofxOpenCv.h"

// everything else as usual
class opencvApp : public ofBaseApp{
// rest of our app
};
```

And that's it.

Here are some of the add-ons you might want to use.

## ofxOpenCv

Computer vision is a huge and fascinating topic that can open all kinds of new possibilities, from face detection to analyzing movement to blue screening images. We'll discuss the ofxOpenCv package in great detail in Chapter 14.

You might use ofxOpenCv for tracking motion, detecting faces in a video screen, recognizing user gestures, or compositing images in real time.

## ofxVectorGraphics

Generally speaking, you'll encounter two kinds of graphics in computer programming: bitmap and vector. Vector graphics are defined by paths, lines, and fills that create shapes and are a lot more lightweight than bitmaps because an image can simply be some mathematical information that the graphics card will use to create an image. The size of a vector image doesn't matter as much, because it's only the values that describe the shape. Bitmaps are defined by data about each pixel in the image, which means that as the image gets bigger, the number of pixels gets bigger, and the amount of data that your program needs to work with gets much larger. Vectors are perfect for quickly drawing graphics that use basic shapes.

You might use ofxVectorGraphics for creating large animations, creating an EPS file, creating precise curves and lines, and graphing data.

## ofxAssimpModelLoader

This add-on enables you to load 3-D models from a wide variety of programs. It wraps functionality from a well-known library called Open Asset Import Library (always shortened to "Assimp"), which is a portable open source library. Assimp and therefore the `ofxAssimpModelLoader` also allow you export the 3-D files again, so you essentially have a general-purpose 3-D model converter at your disposal.

## ofxNetwork

This add-on helps you send and receive data over a network. With it, an oF program can act as a client and read data from another computer, a server, or another device altogether. A program can also act as a server and send information to a series of client programs.

You might use ofxNetwork for sending data to a website, creating a program that runs in multiple geographic locations at the same time and communicates across those locations, or storing or saving data from a program.

## ofxOsc

Open Sound Control (OSC) is a protocol for communication between computers, sound synthesizers, and other multimedia devices. OSC is used to create robotics, help programs communicate with one another, and help devices communicate with a computer. OSC is really just a message format that ensures that devices creating OSC messages and devices receiving OSC messages are all using the same specification.

You might use ofxOsc for communicating with a keyboard, drum pad, or other MIDI device; having an oF program communicate with non-Arduino hardware; or communicating with a Processing or Flash program.

# Review

openFrameworks is a C++ framework created to simplify advanced graphics and sound programming for artists and designers.

openFrameworks does not supply an IDE and requires that you use one of the available IDEs for your operating system. Xcode is recommended for Mac OS X, and Code::Blocks is recommended for Linux and Windows.

All oF programs use a base class called `ofBaseApp`. To create an oF program, you create your own application class that extends this `ofBaseApp`.

A very basic oF program consists of three files: the *.cpp* file for the `ofBaseApp` class, the *.h* file for the `ofBaseApp` class, and the *main.cpp* file.

The `ofBaseApp` class has three primary routine methods: `setup()`, which is called when the program starts up; `update()`, which is called just before `draw()` and should be where you put any code that changes data; and `draw()`, which is where the program does its actual drawing.

The `ofBaseApp` class defines callback methods for letting your program know when the user has moved a mouse or clicked a key. You can find all these methods in the *ofBaseApp.h* file.

A few simple 2-D drawing methods are provided in oF that you can use to create images and animations; they're all stored in the *ofGraphics* files. These methods help you easily draw circles, lines, rectangles, and curves.

To load images into an oF program, declare an object of the `ofImage` class in your *.h* file. Then, in your `setup()` method, load an image source into your `ofImage` using the `load()` method of `ofImage`. In your program's `draw()` method, call the `draw()` method of the image to display the pixels from the images on the screen.

To play videos, declare an object of the `ofVideoPlayer` class in your *.h* file. Then, in your startup method, load a video file into your `ofVideoPlayer` using the `load()` method `ofVideoPlayer`. In your program's `draw()` method, call the `draw()` method of the image to display the pixels from each of the videos on the screen.

To import add-on libraries into your program, add the definition for that add-on into the *.h* file of your ofBaseApp class.

The easiest way to debug your program is to use the cout statement and check the values of your program as it executes your code.

If you're using Xcode or Code::Blocks, you can use the built-in debugger to set breakpoints by clicking the line numbers of the code in which you're interested. When you start a debugging session, the debugger will stop once it reaches that line of code; this lets you see the values of your variable during runtime. This is a fairly advanced operation, so consult the manual for your IDE to learn more.

# CHAPTER 7

# Physical Input

Interaction design opens new possibilities of interaction between humans and technology. Physical computing is a particular type of interaction design that centers on the interaction between the human body and the computer. All the types of interaction explored in this chapter are driven by physical actions, both the sending of information out into the physical world and the sending of information from the physical world into the digital world. The power of physical interaction is in the connection of a physical action to an abstracted result, be that an auditory or visual result.

Some of the controls explored in this chapter are instantly familiar, such as knobs, buttons, and sliders, and some aren't so instantly familiar, such as accelerometers and infrared sensors. All the code will be Arduino, and we'll include diagrams to help you get your components connected to your board.

## Interacting with Physical Controls

Human beings are flat perceivers; that is, we perceive the world as a flat 2-D space. This is advantageous, evolutionarily speaking, because it's a natural limit to the amount of information humans can accept. However, humans are quite skilled at mentally manipulating a series of two-dimensional images into a fully realized three-dimensional space, assembling it piece by piece. To record information, we are accustomed to drawing flat representations, maps and diagrams, with which a three-dimensional mental model can be mentally assembled. The classic way of turning two-dimensional information into three-dimensional information is to physically manipulate the object or environment. You want to see how it fits together, so you turn it over; you want to see the other side, so you walk around it. This physicality is an inseparable aspect of information gathering, and as anyone who has spent time interacting with alternative interfaces like a multitouch user interface or any other kind of haptic interface can attest, varying the physical interaction frequently leads to new experiences, new realizations, and new ways of thinking.

One of the great strengths of using physical interaction is the ability to separate the feedback from the action that the user takes. Anyone who has spent time making music can relate to the intuitiveness of turning knobs to speed or slow a beat or change a pitch. We have tools that help us physically and cognitively understand and work with an interface using physical objects that we manipulate with our hands.

In the simplest model of physical input: you press a button, and a light goes on. In a more complex model, you tilt and turn a sensor, and the tone a computer plays changes; you turn a pair of dials, and a camera pans and rotates. What these all have in common, of course, is that they're physically driven by controls that are instantly recognizable as controls. In this chapter, we'll focus on such controls. An entirely separate realm of physical computing uses implicit interfaces and focuses on gathering physical or environment data in ways that aren't directly controlled by the user, and we'll cover some of those later in this book. When you think about an explicit interface, you're dealing with quite different challenges than when you're dealing with an implicit interface.

All controls require some discovery to use—some instruction given to us by a combination of the controls and the labels around the controls. With anything that we make for others to use or that we ourselves learn to use, the creator must provide a discovery process that the participant actively takes part in. When we are faced with a new control or a new series of controls, those controls have unknown consequences and side effects. To understand those consequences and side effects, we have to discover how to work the equipment. How we approach engendering this discovery process, and specifically, how we engineer the discoverability of an object, is one of the most important decisions in making an application or device.

Any equipment that we interact with via controls has three elements to it: the things that we touch, the electricity that powers and communicates with the system, and the software that handles that communication. While you as the developer and creator will, of course, be concerned with all three, you have to remember that the user will deal only with the first.

## Thinking About Kinetics

Here's an interesting question: is kinetic movement thinking? Well, yes. To paraphrase the psychologist Scott Kelso, it's important to remember that the brain and the mind that it engenders didn't evolve just to picture and analyze the world. The brain and mind are both parts of a larger system that always exists within a physical realm. A lot of research suggests that the ways in which humans think is an extension of their existence as embodied minds. The way that we think is driven by our physicality, and our physicality drives the way that we think. Your goal in interaction design is to tailor the design of your application to your users' capabilities and to the way that they process information and make decisions—in short, to the way that they think. Interacting with physical controls allows users to act and react kinetically.

We've all seen muscle memory in action, abstractly. An experienced guitarist isn't consciously aware of each finger. They see through the action to the task. In a sense, this is the goal of industrial interaction design: to allow workers to perform their action instinctively and without the need to consider each action but to instead consider its larger consequence. A task itself is often an impediment to seeing through it to the desired result. Most often when making an interactive system, the goal should be enabling the user to realize a goal or see through the interaction to the system below it. When we speak or listen to our native language, we don't have to actively think to process and produce the information. Physical interaction is much the same; we're adept with our hands, and we learn certain movements quickly and well enough that we can perform them before our conscious mind is fully aware of what we are doing. Tapping into this fundamental human ability lets your users engage your system more fully and develop habits around that system more quickly.

Muscle memory is more than the movement of the body. Many linguists have noted how native Chinese speakers frequently "write characters in the air" with their fingers when attempting to recall the stroke order for a particular character. This is a linguistic example, but it extends to other tasks. Ask a piano player to write down the keys that they hit in a piece of music they know. Usually, unless they can sit at the piano and use their muscle memory of the order of the keys, they can't do it. This is because the memory isn't a visual memory; it's isolated in the act of finger movements. A great many tasks are far easier to accomplish with a kinetic or physical interface.

# Getting Gear for This Chapter

This chapter, and the rest of the Arduino chapters, will be a bit challenging because of all the controls and components you'll use. For each type of control we discuss, parts may go in and out of production and in and out of stock at popular electronics stores. Updates may be made to a component that may necessitate minor changes in the code shown here. But the controls we discuss are common and classic enough that they will likely remain consistent for several years. What follows is a list of essential gear that *all* the examples will use:

*Arduino board*
> This chapter and its diagrams assume that you're using or referring to the Arduino Diecimila or Duemilanove board. If you're using the Mini or the Nano, you can still run all the code in this chapter, but you'll need to check the differences between the two boards to make sure you're making connections to the correct pins.

*Prototyping board*
> This is just a board with electrical conductive metal and a plastic grid atop it that allows circuits to be created easily without soldering, saving you time, solder, and the pain of having to unsolder mistakes.

*10 KiloOhm resistors (always written as 10K)*
> You can find these at any hobby electronics shop and even at some hardware stores.

*22- or 24-gauge single-core plastic-coated wire*
>   *Wire gauge* refers to the thickness of the wire. The smaller the gauge, the larger the wire; the thinner the wire, the easier it is to bend and turn. Getting several different colors of wire lets you follow what you're doing more easily when you create circuits with a prototyping board.

For everything else, please refer to the later section "Review" on page 244, which will include names, models, manufacturers, and likely sources for all the controls and components in this chapter.

# Controlling Controls

We've already discussed how to attach a button to an Arduino controller, but now let's talk about what attaching a button to an Arduino controller "really does." The "really does" is in quotation marks because any element in any interactive object exists as several different things. Even the simple button is rather complex.

## The Button As an Electrical Object

A button works by completing a circuit external to the controller. The Arduino board sends a small amount of electricity to the button. When the button itself is pressed, the circuit is completed, and the input pin to which the button has been connected detects the change in voltage, alerting the controller that the button has been pressed.

## The Button As an Interactive Object

Buttons are far more commonly encountered in the digital age than knobs, largely because buttons define a binary operation that shape a user's behavior so quickly: on/off, start/stop. The button guides behavior by breaking down all the possible interactions, even a complex series of interactions, into a set of binary oppositions. Even when the button controls a range, it controls the range in fixed increments. You push a button to increase or decrease the temperature of an oven 5 degrees for each click, or the volume of a stereo increases in fixed amounts with a click.

## Reading the Value of a Button

The Arduino controller registers the button press as voltage passing to a pin on the controller. In Chapter 4, you saw how the button is wired to the Arduino controller: the button has two wires, voltage is passed through one wire, and the other is connected to a port that listens for a 5-volt signal. When the button is pressed, the circuit is completed, and the Arduino controller registers the voltage change. You can check this by using the `digitalRead()` method. All the controls that the Arduino interfaces with send electrical signals that the controller reads and processes in an application.

# Turning Knobs

Buttons operate using a digital signal, which indicates two things: we read the button using the `digitalRead()` method (see Chapter 4), and the possible values for the button are HIGH or LOW, or 0 and 1. A button can't be anything other than pressed or not pressed. Analog signals, in contrast, can be a range of values. In Arduino, you read the analog values as integers from 0 to 1,023 using the `analogRead()` method. These analog values correlate to the amount of voltage sent into the analog pin on the analog input of the controller. Any value from 0 to 5 volts means that each 4.8 millivolts correlates to an increase or decrease of an integer value.

## The Dial As an Interactive Object

A dial fully represents a range and allows for a smooth transition from one value in the range to the next. Although buttons allow for greater precision in setting the value, they jarringly move from one state to the next. Imagine a stereo suddenly turned on or an engine roaring to life. Think of the dial for the volume of an old stereo or the hands of a clock.

Each turn of the dial increments or decrements a value in a fixed amount, but we tend to experience these amounts as fluid changes. The hour hand of a clock seems to turn imperceptibly; turning the volume on a mixing console changes the volume subtly enough that the music seems to simply rise in volume.

## Potentiometers

*Potentiometers*, perhaps known to you as knobs or dials, work by receiving a current and increasing or decreasing the amount of voltage on a pin as it's turned. For the Arduino controller, this means that the potentiometer is connected to three places on the board (see Figure 7-1) to provide the three things that the potentiometer needs to communicate with the board:

- Voltage (in this case, 5 volts from the +5V pin),
- A ground (from the ground bus),
- An analog input to read how much voltage is being returned (in this case, the An In 0 pin).

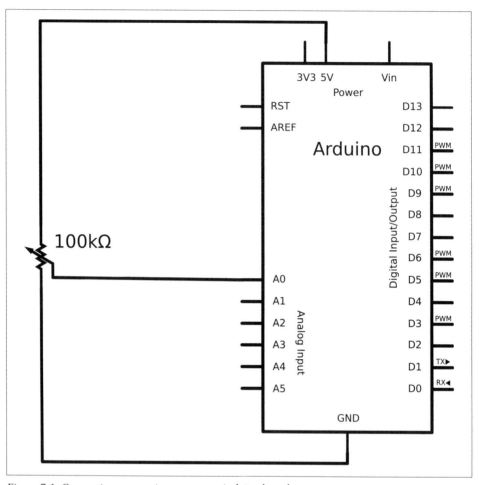

*Figure 7-1. Connecting a potentiometer to an Arduino board*

You can configure the Arduino board to read data from the analog pins by using the analogRead() method. This method, like the digitalRead() method, takes the number of the port that should be read and returns the value that is read from the port. In the case of analog data, that value can be from 0 to 1,023.

Example 7-1 shows the analog value sets the blinking rate of an LED.

*Example 7-1. PotentiometerBlink.ino*

```
int potentiometerPin = 0;
int ledPin = 13;
int val = 0;

void setup(){
    pinMode(ledPin, OUTPUT);
    Serial.begin(9600);
```

```
}

void loop(){
    val = analogRead(potentiometerPin);
    Serial.println(val);
    digitalWrite(ledPin, HIGH);
    delay(val);
    digitalWrite(ledPin, LOW);
    delay(val);
}
```

To use the value from the potentiometer to set the brightness of the LED, you need to remember that analog output can be any value from 0 to 255, so you divide the analog input value by 4, converting the 0 to 1,023 range to the 0 to 255 range (see Example 7-2):

*Example 7-2. AnalogWrite.ino*

```
int potentiometerPin = 0;
int ledPin = 9;
int val = 0;

void setup(){
    // setup isn't doing anything, but we still need it here
}

void loop(){
    val = analogRead(potentiometerPin);
    Serial.println(val);
    analogWrite(ledPin, val/4);
}
```

A slightly different twist on the potentiometer is the 0.5-millimeter-tall soft potentiometer that provides a very different form factor that you can use for flatter, fingertip-tactile interfaces.

The soft potentiometer shown in Figure 7-2 is manufactured by Spectra Symbol and is widely available. A few other suppliers are creating them, so checking at any of the recommended suppliers should give you an idea of what's available for your region and price range. This particular soft potentiometer can be wired the same as a standard dial potentiometer, while providing a much different appearance and experience for a user.

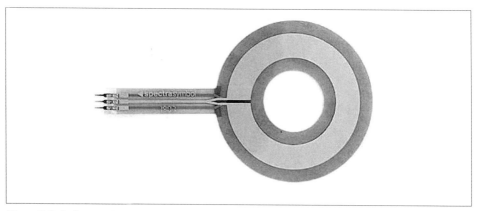

*Figure 7-2. Soft potentiometer*

# Using Lights

A light is generally used as a feedback mechanism to tell users that something is on or has changed, to inform them of progress by blinking, or to warn them. When a light blinks, you instinctively pay attention to it. When a light suddenly comes on, you notice it. When a light goes off, you tend not to notice. If a light is always on, you'll notice only if you're searching for the cause of something gone wrong.

Lights are one of the oldest electronic feedback mechanisms because they're simple to engineer, easy to comprehend with a well-placed label or icon, and cheap.

## Wiring an LED

Attaching a small light to the Arduino board is quite easy. Create a circuit with a 220 Ohm resistor to the 5-volt pin of the Arduino and then connect that to the longer leg of the LED. Connect the shorter leg of the LED to the ground pin of the Arduino.

Figure 7-3 shows the electrical diagram.

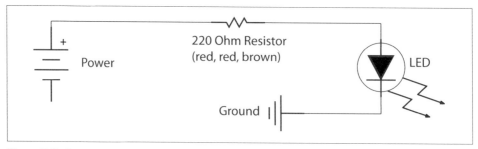

*Figure 7-3. Connecting an LED*

The LED simply requires a complete circuit and enough voltage to turn it on. Depending on the color, an LED turns on anywhere between 2 to 3.5 volts. The resistor is placed in series with the LED to limit the current and to drop the 5V down to the operating range of the LED. An LED can be controlled by hooking either side of the circuit up to one of the Arduino's digital pins, as shown in Figure 7-4.

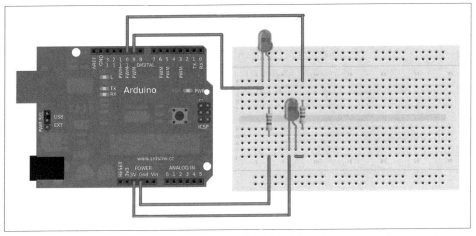

*Figure 7-4. Wiring multiple LEDs to an Arduino board (all breadboard and schematic diagrams created with Fritzing.org)*

When the light is wired to the digital out, it turned on or off by the digital port either sending a HIGH value or sending a LOW value. You can also send analog values to the lights by using the `analogWrite()` and using any one of the pins marked PWM to power the lights. See Example 7-3.

*Example 7-3. AnalogWrite2.ino*

```
int ledPin = 9;
int amountOfLight = 0;

void setup(){
}

void loop(){
    if(amountOfLight > 254) {
        amountOfLight = 0;
    }
    analogWrite(ledPin, amountOfLight);
    amountOfLight+=1;
    delay(10);
}
```

Since the `loop()` method is going to repeat every 10 milliseconds, you can use that loop to slowly increase the amount of power that is sent to the lights, creating a slowly increasing glow. Of course, the next thing you might want to do is add multiple lights and control them independently. While this is fairly easy to do with a limited number of lights by using the same number of lights as digital out or analog out ports that the Arduino controller possesses, using more lights in more complex configurations is an entirely different matter. Chapter 11 will cover more complex ways of using LEDs in your applications.

## Detecting Touch and Vibration

A *piezoelectric* sensor (*piezo* sensor for short) is a device that uses the piezoelectric effect to measure pressure, acceleration, strain, or force by converting these factors to an electrical signal. Piezo sensors use a phenomenon called *piezoelectricity*, the ability of some materials (notably crystals and certain ceramics) to generate an electric potential in response to physical stress. What this means is that the material of a piezo sensor, usually a crystalline coating over metal, returns more current when bent or otherwise disturbed. This lets you detect very slight changes in the sensor, for example, a breeze or the touch of a finger.

The principles behind the piezo sensor should give you an idea of how the sensor connects to the Arduino board. A certain amount of current is sent through the sensor, and that current is fed through the sensor. When the sensor is bent, the resistance of the sensor increases, and the amount of current returned from the sensor is reduced. Many electrical supply stores carry small hobbyist piezo sensors (see Figure 7-5) that have two wires attached to them.

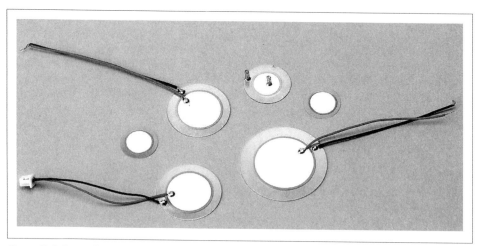

*Figure 7-5. Piezo elements*

To connect the piezo sensor, you'll want to connect 5 volts to the input of the sensor, the red wire, and connect the output of the sensor, the black wire, to an Analog In pin on the Arduino controller.

# Reading a Piezo Sensor

The code in Example 7-4 will detect vibration in a piezo sensor attached to your Arduino with 5 volts of power (+5V pin) connected to the red wire of the piezo and the other end of the piezo sensor connected to Analog In pin 2.

*Example 7-4. Piezo.ino*

```
int piezoPin = 2;     // input for the piezo
int ledPin = 13;    // output pin for the LED
int val = 0;         // variable to store the value coming from the sensor

void setup() {
    pinMode(ledPin, OUTPUT);  // declare the ledPin as an OUTPUT
}

void loop() {
    val = analogRead(piezoPin);     // read the value from the sensor
    // a nice even number that could represent a little bit of change
    if(val < 100) {
        // if there's resistance on the piezo, turn the light on
        digitalWrite(ledPin, HIGH);
    } else {
        // otherwise, turn the light off
        digitalWrite(ledPin, LOW);
    }
}
```

Detecting force in a piezo sensor can also detect the amount of force up to a certain range; however, the piezo sensor reaches a maximum value quickly. If you want to detect more force than the piezo sensor allows, you can use a flexible pressure sensor. These sensors read the amount of force that is exerted on a flexible piece of electro-conductive material and commonly range from 1 to 100 pounds of maximum force detection. The sensor in Figure 7-6, manufactured by FlexiForce, is accurate from 0 to 25 pounds of pressure and is about 0.2 millimeters thick, making it unobtrusive and easy to conceal inside levers, soft objects, punching bags, and shoes, among other possibilities.

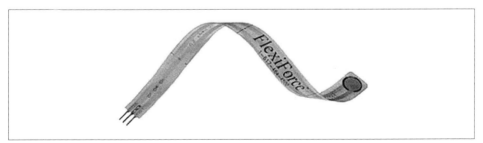

*Figure 7-6. FlexiForce sensor*

## Getting Piezo Sensors

RadioShack stocks a small piezo sensor kit that consists of a piezo sensor held inside a small plastic case. Carefully open the case to remove the sensor, or simply leave it inside the case. It's easier to work with the sensor outside of the case, but it's also more delicate, so be careful not to disconnect the wires from the back or to tear the material of the piezo element itself. You can also buy piezo sensors from a well-stocked electronics supplier.

# Detecting Proximity

Proximity is another interactive concept that gives you ways to determine what someone is doing and create a response to their movement. Pairing multiple proximity sensors together allows you to begin to create simple gestures. Even three simple proximity sensors arranged in a small triangle allows you to detect eight simple gestures that a user can perform to send a message to your system. Proximity is different than distance (which we'll look at later in this chapter), since it tends to be measured in millimeters or centimeters rather than meters and that means that the interactions can be more precise.

## Proximity Through Capacitance

As someone brings their hand or finger or other part of their body closer to the sensor, you get a stronger reading. If you've used a smartphone with a touch screen you've probably used a capacitive sensor. It's not the pressing on the screen that registers the capacitance, it's bringing your finger in proximity to the capacitive sensor that's underneath the screen that does it. Capacitance is usually measured in farads, which is a measure of how much electrical potential exists between two surfaces. In the case of a touch sensor, these two surfaces are the sensor and your fingertip. As you bring your finger closer to the sensor, the capacitance increases and you can get an estimation of whether you're touching the sensor or not. Capacitive values are analog, not digital, so there's no on/off. Instead, you're reading an analog value representing the capacitance on the sensor and making a guess as to whether it's being touched or not. There are several microchips that make capacitive sensing more robust and accurate and provide extra filtering, but you can create a simple capacitive sensor with just an Arduino, wire, and aluminum foil.

There are two ways to wire up the foil to your Arduino. The first is with a capacitor and the second is without. So your first decision is whether you want to use the capacitor or not. Your second decision is what size resistor you want to use because the size of the resistor affects what distances the capacitive sensor detects at. A 1 megohm resistor requires an absolute touch to the foil to activate it, while using a 10 megohm resistor means that the sensor will start to respond when your finger is as far as 4–6 inches away from the foil. See Figure 7-7.

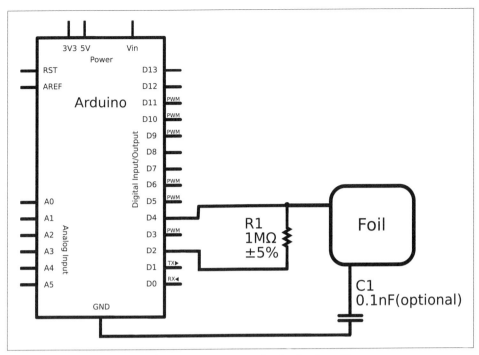

*Figure 7-7. Using foil to sense changes in capacitance for the CapSense library*

You'll also want to download the CapSense library that can be found on the Arduino site and then place it in your *libraries* folder that lives inside your Arduino application folder. Check back to Chapter 4 if you're not sure what I'm referring to. Once you're done put the CapSense library in the right place, you're ready to go. See Example 7-5.

*Example 7-5. CapSensing.ino*

```
#include <CapSense.h>

CapSense cSensor(4,2);

void setup()
{
    Serial.begin(9600);
}

void loop()
{
    long sensor =  cSensor.capSense(30);
    Serial.print(" Reading ");
    Serial.println(sensor);
    delay(50);
}
```

And that's all there is to it. You have a simple way of creating touch-enabled applications. You can put the foil underneath thin plastics or fabrics without compromising the capacitance, which means that you can hide your hardware under an exterior.

---

### Interview: Tom Igoe

Tom Igoe is the author of *Making Things Talk* (*http://shop.oreilly.com/product/0636920010920.do/*) (Make Books) and *Physical Computing* (Course Technology). He teaches at the Interactive Telecommunications Program at New York University.

*You wrote a great post on your blog (http://www.tigoe.net/blog/) about the themes that emerge again and again in physical computing. Why do you think artists and designers are drawn to these themes?*

**Tom Igoe:** I think people return to the same ways of creating interaction because of the technology involved. Certain things like gloves, interactive mirrors, mechanical pixels, tilt controllers, and so on, all come up a lot because they're easy to do and they're things that are already popular. People tend to build what they already know exists. If you look at that list of themes and ideas from that blog post you mention, one of the things that really strikes me is that the interaction in almost all of them is quite vague. In other words, with the theremin, for example, you're waving your hands to make this "wooooo" sound. Your body is a kind of cursor, and as a result, people don't have to mess with the nuances of interactive design as much. You seldom see a class in an art school or a design school that focuses on designing a control panel or control surface, because, frankly, it's kind of boring to artists and designers who are just learning how to think about interaction design. They think, "Why would I want to design a power plant control system?" The thing is that power plant control systems are really cool, and there are a lot of interesting problems there, but you can't see that by looking at it purely aesthetically. It's only when you get people to think about it in a performative sense—how the needs of system and the needs of the users map to a set of controls—that you realize it's quite complex and quite interesting.

*One of the biggest difficulties in beginning to work with interactive design is deciding which skills are important to you. I think people often don't realize how important being able to design an interaction is. Being able to design the functionality of a control panel is a real skill.*

**Tom:** It's true—I think it's a skill-born experience. I think that you're always learning new skill sets, and a woodworker is always learning new tools and new variations on tools, too. But what I think you're referring to in terms of the practice of craft for years is that you do have to repeat and hone a skill. People who work a lot with their product, whether their product is a physical interface or software interface, have gained a craft that you can't teach easily. That's a natural extension from dealing with all the limitations that you run into. Often people who come from an industrial design background or an art background are used to the idea that they're making an object or product that does one thing. They're the ones who have the most trouble establishing the boundaries of their project when they start to do physical computing projects. It's because it's the first time they use software, and software always makes them want to do too many things. For them to suddenly have the ability to do almost anything is a little mind-

---

blowing for them. There's a difference between an application and a platform. When you're making something, you have to decide whether that thing is a platform or whether it's an application. I think if anything is the craft of building applications, it is having an understanding of the limitations that a particular task needs.

*What are the most important and/or difficult things for students to learn when it comes to physical interaction?*

**Tom:** I think that one of the biggest challenges in physical computing is learning to think specifically. If a designer can't describe the action that they want to bring about, then they can't really design for that action. The ones who can do it best are those who come from theater and performance—those who've taken an acting class—because they know that you can't get up on stage and think. You have to get up on stage and take an action, and that action has to communicate something. So, often I see students who say, "Well, then I'm going to make it possible for them to interact." I'll try to push them to be very specific, and they respond, "Well, you know, they're gonna make the thing happen." And that just doesn't work. I think that a lot of people who deal with physical interaction don't understand that you have to be that specific when you think about the interaction because at the guts of that "thing," somewhere there's a piece of software that's going to be looking for that series of actions.

*How do you teach students how to make an interaction that can be understood by the user...that the interaction is appropriately discoverable?*

**Tom:** People like to use the dirty word *intuitive* for that, and I always tell them that there's no such thing as intuition when it comes to user interface. I make students read the first two chapters of Donald Norman's *Design of Everyday Old Things* (Basic Books). They read it and realize that there is this idea of a mental model and of affordances and that you can lead a person to a decision. You should be leading people to the next thing to do, and there are some good "next" things to do. You have to organize things in a way that allows a user to read the interface and follow it along. It's really interesting to just sit down and analyze physical interfaces. The writer and designer Dan Safer does this quite a bit, as do I. If you do figure out how to lead people in the physical design of a layout and the performance of it, you solve a lot of your software and electronic problems because you don't have to write code to listen to every sensor in the system. The user is going to pay attention to the switch that's blinking, so you can stop checking the other 16. Someone else who's very bright about these things is Chris Crawford. His book *Art of Interactive Design* (No Starch Press) talks about conversational error messages. Recognizing that all device interaction is a conversation, it's an iterative loop of thinking and speaking. So often, artists, more so than designers, get really good at the speaking side of the conversation and don't develop the listening skills. This is the area where I find the great difference between people who are attempting to make interactive art as opposed to those who are attempting to make interactive design. The distinction comes in that art is primarily an act of self-expression, whereas design is primarily an act of facilitating communication. Artists have to make things that do something or say something. This is one of the reasons *interactive art* is kind of a fallacy. I always tell students, look, it doesn't matter which side of the divide between art and design you fall on, but be clear on the distinction, and when you make your choices, be clear on which of the two is governing your choices.

*You attended the Interactive Telecommunications Program at NYU as a student and now you teach there. What and why are things different now as opposed to when you were there as a student?*

**Tom:** This program is often jokingly described as the center for the study of the recently possible. What that means is that we don't necessarily do bleeding-edge technology. We look at what's being done and say, "OK, how can this be applied?" It has to change every three years. When I first heard about the program, people were working on interactive video with laser discs and Mac Pluses. One of the interesting things here when I was a student was you had a lot of people trying to be the next Nam June Paik and doing big video installations. Over the years there was a shift from space-based applications like installations to device-based applications—partially out of its immediacy and partially out of recognition that you don't always get to build a space to show your work in. You might have to make things that don't need a space to be presented in. The cell phone really changed how people think about devices and communication. Streaming media has really been a constant line of research. What has stayed constant is the question of how you communicate with a user through the limitations of a device.

*As someone who does physical computing and interactive design, in what sort of role in society do you see yourself? How do see yourself or refer to yourself?*

**Tom:** I don't know what I call myself. I use the word *designer* a lot. It gets overused a bit and abused a bit. It has a lot of baggage, but I still find it useful because for me designers facilitate communication and facilitate action. I come from a theater design background where your role is to serve the action, and everything else is secondary. And nobody remembers your name. People in industrial design and people in architecture of course wouldn't necessarily agree with me. I very much doubt Santiago Calatrava feels that it's his role for everybody to forget his name. But nonetheless, he's still there to facilitate you getting things done.

Recognizing that a designer's job is to make it easier for people to do things through tools is another big part of it. *Facilitator* I think comes up a lot, too, because, again, what you're really doing is figuring out how to get this person to talk to that person. How do you get people interested in something? The answer is that you start with something that they're already interested in. Games are a great example of this, too. So, facilitation, direction, and engagement, all of that; ultimately my feeling is that whatever we are as technologists or designers, our role should be to serve, and to make people's lives better in some way.

*Do you think there are fundamental things that everyone who wants to do things with interactive design or art has to learn?*

**Tom:** Yes, but I can't say that there are specifics. So, for example, I think that everyone doing this should learn some programming regardless of the language. It doesn't mean you have to get good at it; you just have to know and understand it. In fact, some of the best people coming out of the ITP program are crappy programmers, but they know what can be achieved through programming.

I think everybody should get his or her hands on digital hardware at some point. Understanding the connection between code and physical reality is huge. At the end of the day, everything we do is grounded in our physical reality, and you need to have a handle on that. An understanding of formative communication is the key, and that means a lot of different things. You need to understand that the communication is the performance. You need to have an understanding of what hardware can do and how it interfaces with a person, and you need to understand that physical interaction is always a performance by the user.

*How did you get involved with the Arduino project?*

**Tom:** I got involved in 1995 when I visited the Ivrea school. Massimo Banzi told me that they were working with this board called Arduino, and I already knew Wiring at that point, which was Hernando Barragan's project. Massimo and David Cuartielles were using the Arduino in the workshop that we did. I saw it and I thought that I'd use it in my own classes and knew a lot of other people would use it in their classes, too. Later, they decided they needed a core team of developers, and I joined. What I do on the team is be opinionated. David Mellis does the software work; David Cuartielles, Massimo, and Gianluca Martino do the hardware work. I do a lot of the beta testing and looking at the design of the board. Occasionally, I'll contribute real hardcore technical things. I guess I'm a bit like the fifth wheel in that way; I remind them about things they may have forgotten.

*What are the things that you find the most exciting in physical computing right now?*

**Tom:** In the past couple of years, I've gotten interested in communication between things, and specifically between physical things, which is more possible than it has ever been. When I first started teaching physical computing, you just didn't do wireless, right? Now, you can spend 40 bucks and buy two XBee wireless controllers, and in 15 minutes you have wireless communication. So, that's huge, and I think that changes things in terms of interactive design, too, because even the people who are the most technology obsessed now are interested in tackling the problem of getting two things to talk to each other. So, they're designing a conversation. It's easy to step from there to "Now why don't you design a conversation between two people?" What's gone on with social networking is huge. I think it's interesting when people start to think about the information flow of social networking. How can we incorporate that flow of information in the everyday environment for use by other people because we're already letting it be used when it's online. What happens when my daily thoughts are on the wall, what happens when it's on my car, or anywhere else?

On a technological level and on an ecological level, it's still not simple and cheap to do WiFi from a microcontroller. When it is, in terms of both money and electrical power, that's a change I'm very interested in.

The other one is sustainable technology development. I'm curious to see that get easy; by that, I mean I want it to be so easy to think not only about how to make something but also how to unmake it that people automatically think about this stuff ecologically. By that I mean they think about the destruction of the thing as a fuel for technical nutrients. That's still a ways off, but I think it's essential, and I think it's really interesting. There's such an obsession with how to make things, and it's almost seductive to get hooked into how to make it, not even worrying about what it does. I'd love to see that same kind of seductive energy linked into how to recycle it.

# Detecting Motion

Motion detection is one of the most immediately satisfying experiences to create for a user or viewer, and it's also quite simple to implement. You can use motion detection in an environmental way, with the motion detection not being apparent to the user, or you can use it more like a control to signal the computer. The difference between being apparent or hidden for the user is determined by the placement and obviousness of the control. A motion detector for security should not be apparent to the user, or it will not be as effective in securing the area around it. A motion detector to detect whether a person is putting their hands under a faucet to start the flow of water, while not readily visible, is a control that the user is aware of, for example.

## PIR Motion Sensor

You provide motion detection for your application in several ways. One is a passive infrared (PIR) motion sensor, shown in Figure 7-8.

*Figure 7-8. A Parallax PIR motion detector*

If your PIR sensor comes with a connector like the one shown in Figure 7-8, you may need to cut this off so you can connect the sensor to the Arduino controller, as shown in Figure 7-9.

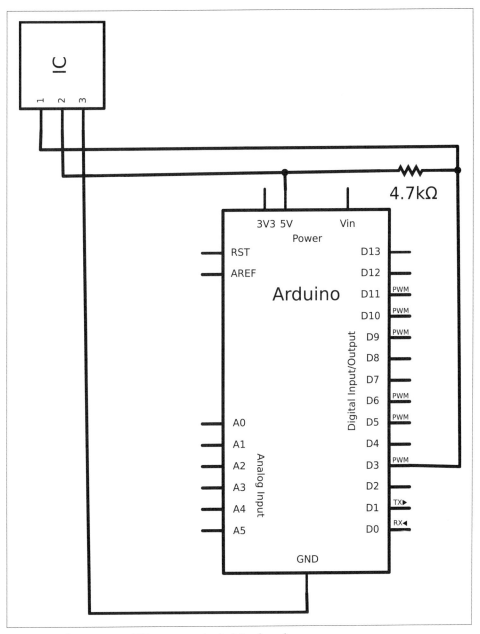

Figure 7-9. Connecting an PIR sensor to the Arduino board

The code in Example 7-6 will light the LED on the Arduino controller when motion is detected by the PIR sensor. The source code is quite simple:

*Example 7-6. PIR.ino*

```
int alarmPin = 3;      // motion alarm output from PIR
int ledPin = 13;       // output pin for the LED
int motionAlarm = 0;

void setup(){
    pinMode(ledPin, OUTPUT);
    digitalWrite(ledPin, LOW);
}

void loop(){
    motionAlarm = digitalRead(alarmPin);
    // this is a very simple loop that lights an LED if motion detected
    if(motionAlarm == HIGH){
        digitalWrite(ledPin, HIGH);// we've detected motion
        delay(500);
        digitalWrite(ledPin, LOW); // turn off the light
    }
}
```

The kind of motion detection offered by the PIR motion detection sensor is really useful only for very simple interactions. Combined with another system, though, it can be quite powerful. Applications or machines that turn on or enter a ready state when a user approaches create a powerful affordance: preparedness. Other, more precise ways exist for not only detecting motion but also gathering more information about the motion and position of an object; you'll learn about these methods in the next section.

## Reading Distance

Some sensors provide information about the distance to an object, and these are extremely useful because they detect presence and distance. While a simpler motion sensor can tell you whether something has moved within its range, a distance sensor will also tell you how far away that thing is. They're used extensively in hobbyist robots because they're simple to program, do not require a great deal of power, and provide very important information, such as how far away objects are. With that sort of information, you can go further than simply giving a user or audience binary feedback (such as you're moving or you're not) and give them analog feedback (such as you're this far away, now this far, now this far). It creates a more fluid interaction and experience because, while it may start rather suddenly when a person comes into range of the sensor, it does not end there.

You'll see two technologies widely used: ultrasonic and infrared. *Ultrasonic* sensors work by detecting how long it takes a sound wave to bounce off an object. The sensor provides an output that indicates the amount of time it takes for the echo signal to return to the sensor, and the magnitude of the echo delay is proportional to distance.

One of the most popular lines of ultrasonic sensors is the Daventech Range Finder series, which has several different models varying in price and the range at which they function. The two most common are the SRF04 and SRF08. The SRF04 is a good and cheap sensor that is accurate to about 4 meters. The SRF08 is a little more expensive and has a range of about 8 meters.

Daventech sensors provide an output signal that has a pulse width proportional to distance. Using the Arduino `pulseIn()` method, this signal can be measured and used as a distance value, as shown in Example 7-7.

*Example 7-7. UltraSonic.ino*

```
long echo = 0;
int usPin = 9; // Ultrasound signal pin
long val = 0;
void setup() {
    Serial.begin(9600);
}

long ping(){
    pinMode(usPin, OUTPUT); // Switch signalpin to output
    digitalWrite(usPin, LOW); // Send low pulse
    delayMicroseconds(2); // Wait for 2 microseconds
    digitalWrite(usPin, HIGH); // Send high pulse
    delayMicroseconds(5); // Wait for 5 microseconds
    digitalWrite(usPin, LOW); // Holdoff
    pinMode(usPin, INPUT); // Switch signalpin to input
    digitalWrite(usPin, HIGH); // Turn on pullup resistor
    echo = pulseIn(usPin, HIGH); // Listen for echo
```

Now the value returned from the `pulseIn()` method can be used to determine how far away the object is in centimeters from the ultrasonic sensor by multiplying the echo by 58.138. This value comes from the manufacturer's specifications sheet, so you might want to check your sensor before assuming that this code will work. If you want the value in inches, you can multiply the value by 0.39:

```
        long ultrasoundValue = (echo / 58.138);
        return ultrasoundValue;
}

    void loop() {
        long x = ping();
        Serial.println(x);
        delay(250); // delay 1/4 seconds.
    }
```

Try adding a video or audio application written in Processing or openFrameworks that uses an ultrasonic sensor to control the speed of a video or audio file. Another common use of distance sensing is to detect presence or the absence of presence: starting an application or device when motion is detected within a certain range or when something that the device is programmed to expect is absent. An alarm on a door or window could function this way, as could a simple trip wire type of interaction. Motion detection is also an interesting possibility for mobile or handheld devices if you indicate to the user how to direct the sensor. This allows them to point the device at an object or surface to activate a reaction to it based on distance. Used in tandem with an accelerometer within the same handheld device or as part of a large set of controls, buttons, or potentiometers, a distance sensor can be a rich input for an interface to utilize.

Another way to measure distance, which uses technology borrowed from autofocus cameras, is *infrared*. The infrared sensor has two lenses, the first of which emits a beam of infrared light and the second of which detects any infrared light reflected back. If the second lens detects any light, then the angle of the beam is measured by an optical sensor and used to determine the distance. The greater the angle, the greater the distance. The Sharp Ranger line is a popular choice, particularly for measuring accurate distances up to a meter.

Figure 7-10 shows how to wire an infrared sensor to your Arduino board.

## Reading Input from an Infrared Sensor

To read data from an IR sensor, you need to initialize the pin that will be connected to the IR sensor and use the `analogRead()` method to read values from the sensor.

Generally, the sensor will report slight differences in readings from the sensor. You can smooth out your reading using the average of several readings. This may not be necessary, but if you find that your readings are slightly erratic, then using an average may be the answer. The snippet in Example 7-8 is an example of averaging the readings from 10 IR sensor readings:

*Example 7-8. IRReader.ino*

```
#define NUMREADINGS 10

int readings[NUMREADINGS];           // the readings from the analog input
int index = 0;                       // the index of the current reading
int total = 0;                       // the running total
int average = 0;                     // the average

int inputPin = 0;

void setup()
{
    Serial.begin(9600); // start serial communication
    for (int i = 0; i < NUMREADINGS; i++)
        readings[i] = 0; // initialize all the readings to 0
}

void loop()
{
    total -= readings[index]; // subtract the last reading
    readings[index] = analogRead(inputPin); // read from the sensor
    total += readings[index]; // add the reading to the total
    index++;
```

```
    if (index >= NUMREADINGS) {// if at the end of the array
        index = 0; // start again at the beginning
    }
    average = total / NUMREADINGS;// calculate the average
    Serial.println(average); // send it to over the Serial
}
```

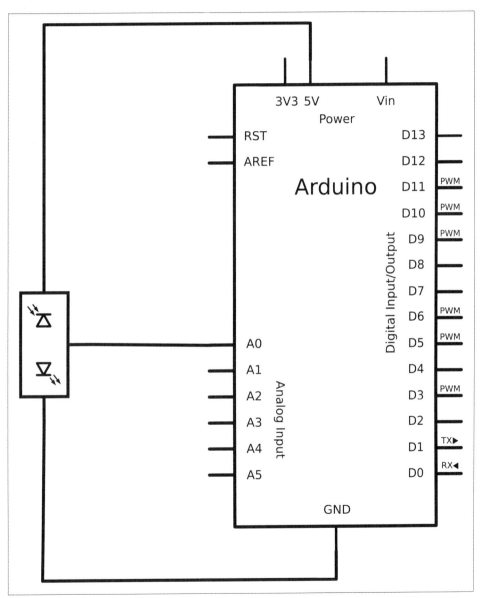

*Figure 7-10. Connecting an infrared sensor to the Arduino board*

# Understanding Binary Numbers

As you may have heard at some point, computers and electronic components do not generally use decimal numbers. That means values like 17, 4, and 1,977—while certainly recognizable and usable in any computer program—aren't recognizable by the computer at runtime in that decimal form. Instead, computers and some sensors use binary counting. What follows is a quick introduction to binary numbers and, more importantly, how binary numbers and bit shifting work.

## Binary Numbers

When you count from 1 to 13, you'll notice that you're counting up to 9 and then shifting a 1 over; then, you're continuing counting until you get to the next 9:

> 9, 10, 11....19, 20, 21....29, 30, 31...99, 100, 101...999, 1,000, 1,001

Notice how every time a 9 appears in the last place, you increment the value on the left and put a 0 on the right, and if all the numbers are 9, you add a 1 to the front. This counting system is called *decimal*. It's something so automatic that it takes a moment to realize that this is just one counting system among many. A binary counting system is similar to a decimal counting system, but instead of using 10 numbers to count, it uses only 2, which is why it's called *bi*nary.

When you count in binary numbers, the numbers reset every two values, so to count to four, you do the following:

> 1, 10, 11, 100

Notice how every time you have a 1 in the right column, you add another 1 on the left and transform the number on the right to a 0. Replicating the counting that you did in decimal system would look like this:

> 1001, 1010, 1011...10011, 10100, 10101...11101, 11110, 11111...1100011, 1100100, 1100101, 1100110...1111100111, 1111101000, 1111101001

That requires more numbers for certain, but why? Remember that underneath all the niceties that a computer provides to make it easier for us to work with code and numbers, the computer represents everything by the presence or absence of an electrical current. For representing values simply by a presence or an absence, what could be better than a numbering system with two values: 0 and 1?

## Bits and Bit Operations

Now that you have a rough idea of how counting in binary works, let's look at using objects that are represented in binary using bit shifting.

*Bit shifting* means shifting bits around by places. Although the uses of it are a little tricky to understand, the principles behind it aren't. Consider a situation where people are discussing salaries. Since they all make salaries that are measured in the thousands, they might say things like "52K" or "65." What they're doing, really, is shifting the numbers by three places so that 48,000 becomes 48. Now, some information isn't explicitly expressed, but if you know you're talking in thousands, then no information is actually lost. If you know that when you say "70" you really mean 70,000, it isn't a big deal, because you can always mentally "shift" those three places. The same works with percentages. Everyone knows that the "50" in a 50/50 chance is really 0.5. You just shift the value up two places to make it easier to think about because percentages use nice round numbers and those are easier to think and talk about. Bit shifting is essentially the same principle, except that shifting in binary is a bit more natural for a computer than for a human so it looks a bit strange at first.

Let's say you have the integer 3, bit shifting looks like this:

```
int val = 3;
```

You know that as an int this variable has 16 bits available to it, so that, as far as your computer is concerned, you're really storing this:

    0000 0000 0000 0011

and all those extra zeros are just placeholders. The only things doing anything are the last two numbers. Normally, this isn't a big deal at all, because computers have enough memory that wasting a few extra spaces is nothing to get bent out of shape about. That's fine for a laptop or an Arduino controller, but sometimes for very small sensors that's not fine, and they might do something like send you an integer in two pieces. And that could be a problem. Why? Well, what if you had a relatively big integer, for example, 30,000?

    0111 0101 0011 0000

If you had to send that integer as two pieces in binary the first time, you'd get the following:

    0111 0101

This is 117 in decimal, and the second time you'd get the following:

    0011 0000

and this is 48 in decimal. Now, even if you know that you're supposed to be getting something kind of like 30,000, how are you going to turn those two numbers into what you're expecting back? The answer lies in the magic of shifting. Let's say that you're getting a value from an accelerometer sensor that sends information in two pieces. Since you know that the sensor is sending the first 8 bits of the number and then the second 8 bits (that is, the two halves of the integer), just shift the first 8 bits over and then put the next 8 bits behind it. To do this, use a bit shift operator:

<<

Returns the value on the left *up* by the number of places indicated on the right.

*<<= and +=*

Sets the variable on the left by shifting up by the number of bits indicated on the right, the same way that += adds the value on the right to the value on the left:

```
int val = 3;
val <<= 1;
```

In the code snippet above, the variable val is now 6, because 3 in binary is 11, so moved over 1, it's 110, or 6.

Back to the sensor example, say that the total is 30,000, or 0111 0101 0011 0000 in binary. To shift the integer values over correctly so you get the first half of the number, you'd do the following:

```
int valueFromSensor = firstHalfOfValue; // this is 0111 0101
valueFromSensor <<= 8; // now our value is shifted over correctly
// since the second half won't affect the top, just add it
valueFromSensor += secondHalfOfValue;
```

Another bit shift operation is the right shift, which works the opposite of the left shift. It's not used as commonly in the types of code that you'll encounter because there isn't as much of a need to make big numbers into small ones, but it's available, and it's good to know:

*>>*

Shifts the value on the left *down* by the number of places indicated on the right.

*>>=*

Shifts the value on the left *down* by the number of bits indicated on the right, just like += adds the value on the right to the value on the left:

```
int val = 100;// val is 1100100
val >>= 2; // removing the last two digits, val is now 11001 or 25
```

So, to recap in a slightly more academic fashion, you have this:

```
00010111 << 1 =  00101110
00010111 >> 1 =  00001011
```

In the first case, the left digit is shifted out, and a new 0 was shifted into the right position. In the second case, the last digit, a 1, was shifted out, and a new 0 was placed into the left position. Multiple shifts are sometimes shortened to a single shift by some number of digits. For example:

```
00010111 << 2 =  01011100
```

A word of warning and a word of explanation as well: for the Arduino controller, an integer is 16 bits, that is, a binary number with 16 places. It's very important to note that *the first of those digits indicates whether the number is negative or positive*, so the number is only 15 digits long, with a final bit to indicate either a positive or negative number. Here's a few integer values:

```
0111111111111111 = 32767
```

Now, you would think that the value of that number if it was shifted to the left would be 65,534. But it's not, because the first bit says whether the number is negative or positive. It would actually be the following:

```
1111111111111110 = -32766
```

Why is that important? When you start bit shifting numbers around, you may encounter some surprise negative numbers. This would be one source of those sorts of errors.

## Why Do You Need to Know Any of This?

The complete answer lies at the end of the section "Introducing I2C" on page 237, where you begin working with I2C. Beyond that, though, this section was an excellent introduction to how the fundamentals of a computer actually function. It's also good to understand how bits and bit shifting actually works, because when working with sensors and the Arduino controller, you'll frequently see the bit shifting operators used in example code. As mentioned earlier, frequently, smaller electrical components do not use larger numerical values and so will assume that any controller accessing their data can assemble those larger values using bit shifting. Now that you've read this section, you'll be able to follow along with how those controls send data.

# Communicating with Other Applications

So far, we've covered getting input, which is one half of the interaction or conversation; however, at some point, you'll probably want to use the input from the Arduino to communicate with other applications built in Processing and openFrameworks. Communicating with Processing and openFrameworks is done via the serial port. In Chapter 4, we looked at using the `Serial` class in an Arduino application to send debugging information to the Arduino IDE. So, thinking about that for a moment, you're sending a message from the Arduino controller to the computer and listening to that message. That's not some magic in the Arduino IDE; it's something that all modern computers are able to do. Therefore, you can use the same `Serial` methods to communicate with a Processing or openFrameworks application.

So, what is the `Serial` object and what is serial communication? It's a way of sending information from your computer to another machine that could be another computer but is more frequently another kind of device. Serial communication uses a protocol called RS-232. This protocol dictates how messages are sent and received using the serial port. Many devices use serial communication to communicate with a parent computer: Bluetooth-enabled devices, GPS sensors, older printers and mice, bar-code scanners, and, of course, the Arduino board. How do you do it? Well, it's pretty low-level and can be pretty simple or quite complex. To send a message from a Processing application to the Arduino board, the event flow is like the one in Example 7-9.

*Example 7-9. P5Serial.ino*

```
import processing.serial.*;

// Declare the serial port that we're going to use
Serial arduinoPort;

void setup() {
    // uncomment the next line if you want to
    // see all the available controllers
    // println(Serial.list());
```

Now you set up the communication between the Arduino and the Processing application. The following line may need to be changed if the Arduino isn't connected on the first serial port of your computer:

```
    arduinoPort = new Serial(this, Serial.list()[0], 9600);
}

void draw() {}

void keyPressed() {
    // Send the key that was pressed
    arduinoPort.write(key);
}
```

When you send the key, it will be the ASCII representation of the key, which means that on the Arduino side, you need to listen for a number, not a character. This is important.

The constructor of the Serial object has a few different signatures:

```
Serial(parent, name, rate)
Serial(parent)
Serial(parent, rate)
Serial(parent, name)
```

parent:PApplet

Is the Processing application that owns the Serial object. You usually just use this.

rate:int

Is the serial rate at which you're communicating; 9,600 is the default, so if you've set your Arduino controller to communicate at a different rate, you'll want to change this.

name:String

Is the name of the port. If you uncomment the Serial.list() call in the previous code snippet, you'll see the names of all the available ports.

You can create the serial port in some other ways, but we'll leave those for you to explore, because at the moment, we need to move on to the Arduino code.

The new stuff here is all in the loop() method of the Arduino application, as shown in Example 7-10.

*Example 7-10. ArduinoSerial.ino*

```
int message = 0;     // for incoming serial data
int ledPin = 13;

void setup(){
    pinMode(ledPin, OUTPUT);
    Serial.begin(9600);    // opens serial port, sets data rate to 9600 bps
}

void loop() {
```

The Serial objects available() method tells how much data has arrived and is available on the serial port from the Processing application. This is important because were you to not wait until you were sure that all the messages had been received, you might get incorrect data. It's important to always make sure that there is something in the buffer before you try to use it. In the following example, you'll turn the light on if you get a ! from the Processing application, and you'll turn the light off if you get a ?. Otherwise, just ignore it:

```
        // do something only when we receive data:
        if (Serial.available() > 0) {
            // read the incoming byte:
            message = Serial.read();
             if(message == '!') {
                 digitalWrite(ledPin, HIGH);
             }

             if(message == '?') {
                  digitalWrite(ledPin, LOW);
              }
        }
    }
```

In openFrameworks, you send messages to an Arduino controller by using the ofSe rial object. It's quite similar to the Serial object that Processing contains, so the methods that it defines should be familiar to you:

bool setup(string portName, int baudrate)
: Starts up the communication between the openFrameworks application and the Arduino board using the name of the port, something like "/dev/tty.usbser ialA6004920" if you're on OS X or "COM1" if you're on Windows.

bool setup(int deviceNumber, int baudrate)
: Starts up the communication between the openFrameworks application and the Arduino board using the device number. This can be problematic if you have anything else plugged in to your computer and don't know the device number of the Arduino port.

int readBytes(unsigned char * buffer, int length)
: Reads multiple bytes from the Arduino into a character array.

```
int writeBytes(unsigned char * buffer, int length)
```
Writes multiple bytes out to the Arduino.

```
bool writeByte(unsigned char singleByte)
```
Writes a single byte out to the controller.

```
int readByte()
```
Reads a single byte from the controller. This is an int, so if the controller sends a character, you'll get its ASCII representation.

In the previous Processing application, you simply sent the ASCII key number over the serial port to the Arduino board. To duplicate the same functionality in openFrameworks, you'd simply do what's shown in Example 7-11:

*Example 7-11. OFSendSerial.h*

```
#pragma mark once

#include "ofMain.h"

class OFSendSerial : public ofBaseApp{

    public:
        void setup();
        void keyPressed(int key);
        ofSerial serial; // here's our ofSerial object that we'll use
};
```

You would implement it as shown in Example 7-12:

*Example 7-12. OFSendSerial.cpp*

```
#include "OFSendSerial.h"

void OFSendSerial::setup(){
    serial.setup("/dev/tty.usbserial-A6004920", 19200);

}

void OFSendSerial::keyPressed  (int key){
    serial.writeByte(key);
}
```

And that's all there is to it.

# Sending Messages from the Arduino

To have a Processing or openFrameworks application receive messages from Arduino, you need to make sure that something is listening in the application. In Example 7-13, you send a message to the serial port if digital pin 13 is HIGH, which could be any digital signal, a button press or something similar.

---

*Example 7-13. ArduinoSender.ino*

```
int buttonPin = 13;

void setup() {
    // open the serial port at 9600 bps:
    Serial.begin(9600);
}

void loop() {
    if(digitalRead(buttonPin ) == HIGH) {
        Serial.print("!");
    } else {
        Serial.print("?");
    }
    delay(200);
}
```

In the following Processing code (see Example 7-14), you listen on the port for any incoming information from the serial port and print the data that you receive from the Arduino controller. Of course, you can do far more sophisticated things with the data you receive, but for this demonstration, let's keep it simple.

*Example 7-14. ProcessingReceiver.ino*

```
import processing.serial.*;

Serial arduinoPort;
void setup() {
    // set up the communication between the Arduino and the Processing app
    arduinoPort = new Serial(this, Serial.list()[0], 9600);
}

void draw() {
    // Expand array size to the number of bytes you expect
    byte[] inBuffer = new byte[7];
    while (arduinoPort.available() > 0) {
        inBuffer = arduinoPort.readBytes();
        arduinoPort.readBytes(inBuffer);
        if (inBuffer != null) {
            String myString = new String(inBuffer);
            println(myString);
        }
    }
}
```

# openFrameworks

Communication between an Arduino board and an openFrameworks application uses the ofSerial object. The ofSerial class defines the following methods:

void enumerateDevices()
    Prints out to the console all the devices that are connected to the serial port.

```
void close()
```
Stops the openFrameworks application from listening on the serial port.

```
bool setup()
```
Is the setup method without the port name and rate; by default it uses port 0 at 9,600 baud.

```
bool setup(string portName, int baudrate)
```
Uses the `portName` to set up the connection.

```
bool setup(int deviceNumber, int baudrate)
```
Uses the `devicenumber` if there are multiple devices connected.

```
int readBytes(unsigned char * buffer, int length)
```
Reads any bytes from the buffer that the Arduino controller has sent.

```
int writeBytes(unsigned char * buffer, int length)
```
Writes some data to the serial buffer that the Arduino controller can receive.

```
bool writeByte(unsigned char singleByte)
```
Writes a single byte to the serial buffer for the Arduino controller.

```
int readByte()
```
Reads a single byte from the buffer; it returns –1 on no read or error.

```
void flush(bool flushIn, bool flushOut)
```
Flushes the buffer of incoming serial data; you can specify whether both the incoming and outgoing data are flushed. If there's some data in the serial buffer, it will be deleted by calling `flush()`.

```
int available()
```
Returns 0 if the serial connection isn't available and another number, usually a 1, if it is.

We show a common pattern for working with the `ofSerial` application here. First, define the number of bytes that you're expecting. A Boolean value, like a button being pressed, would just be a single byte. The values from a potentiometer would be integers and so would be 2 bytes. Example 7-15 is the header file for the application.

*Example 7-15. SerialDemo.h*

```
#pragma once

#define NUM_BYTES 2
```

Next, define the application:

```
class SerialDemo : public ofBaseApp {
    public:
        void setup();
        void update();
```

Next, use a Boolean value to determine whether you should try to read from the buffer. An openFrameworks application runs faster than the serial protocol can send and receive information, so you should try to read from the serial buffer only every five frames or so. This value will be set to true when you're ready to read from the serial port; otherwise, it remains false:

```
bool bSendSerialMessage;      // a flag for sending serial
// this will be used to count the number of frames
// that have passed since the last time the app reads from the serial port
int countCycles;
```

Here's the ofSerial object:

```
ofSerial serial;
};
```

In the *.cpp* file for your application, shown in Example 7-16, the setup() method of your application will need to call the setup() method of the ofSerial object.

*Example 7-16. SerialDemo.cpp*

```
void SerialDemo::setup(){
    bSendSerialMessage = false;
    serial.enumerateDevices(); // this will print all the devices
    // this is set to the port where your device is connected
    serial.setup("/dev/tty.usbserial-A4001JEC", 9600);
}
```

The update() method of ofApplication should do all the reading from and writing to the serial port. When the bSendSerialMessage flag is set to true, the openFrameworks application sends a message to the Arduino board telling it that it's ready to receive data:

```
void SerialDemo::update(){
    if (bSendSerialMessage){

        // send a handshake to the Arduino serial
        serial.writeByte('x');
        // make sure there's something to write all the data to
        unsigned char bytesReturned[NUM_BYTES];
        memset(bytesReturned, 0, NUM_BYTES);
```

The openFrameworks application reads bytes from the serial port until nothing is left to read:

```
        // keep reading bytes, until there's none left to read
        while( serial.readBytes(bytesReturned, NUM_BYTES) > 0){}
    }
```

Once you've read all the data out of the serial port and into the bytesReturned variable, set the bSendSerialMessage flag to false:

```
        // wait a few cycles before asking again
        bSendSerialMessage = false;
    }
```

Now you can use the signal sent from the Arduino however you'd like. The countCycles variable is incremented until it hits 5; then the bSendSerialMessage variable is set to `true`, and the next time the `update()` method is called, the openFrameworks application will read from the serial port:

```
        countCycles++;
        if(countCycles == 5) {
            bSendSerialMessage = true;
            countCycles = 0;
        }
    }
```

# Detecting Forces and Tilt

*Accelerometers* are sensors that detect forces acting upon them, specifically, the force of acceleration. Much the same way as you can detect the acceleration of your car when you press on the gas by the feeling that you have of being pushed back into the seat, the accelerometer detects the force of any acceleration onto it by detecting the shift in the forces acting on the internals of the sensor and reporting how much they've changed. Two-dimensional accelerometers detect forces registering changes in the *x*- and *y*-axes, and three-dimensional accelerometers detect changes in the *x*-, *y*-, and *z*-axes.

In this example, you're going to use a SEN-00849, which is a simple board that holds the accelerometer and provides easy access to its *x*, *y*, and *z* pins. Later in this chapter, we'll look at another accelerometer, but for now, the SEN-00849 is easy to use; match the pin to an Analog In, and you're off to the races.

Figure 7-11 shows the wiring diagram to connect to an accelerometer.

Example 7-17 demonstrates reading from an accelerometer using the `analogRead()` method to read the value for the plane that the accelerometer reports values for:

*Example 7-17. ArduinoTilter.ino*

```
int xpin = 2;        // x-axis of the accelerometer
int ypin = 1;        // y-axis
int zpin = 0;        // z-axis (only on 3-axis models)

void setup()
{
    Serial.begin(9600);
}

void loop()
{
    Serial.print(analogRead(xpin));
    Serial.print(" ");
    Serial.print(analogRead(ypin));
    Serial.print(" ");
    Serial.println(analogRead(zpin));
    delay(50);
}
```

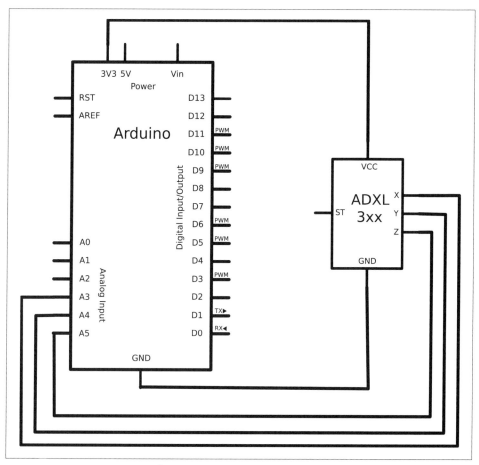

Figure 7-11. Connecting an accelerometer to the Arduino controller

Although this is a simple application, it's an effective one. Once you get the values from the accelerometer, you can do all kinds of things with them, such as create a drawing tool, create a pointer, control a sound, change a game, or rotate in a 3-D world.

In the following example, you're going to send a message from an accelerometer to an openFrameworks application. First up is the code for the Arduino application. You'll see a few familiar things here, including the averaging of data from the controller, just like in the sketch with the infrared sensor. As you'll notice after working with an accelerometer for any length of time, the data from the accelerometer is jumpy, varying quite quickly by as much as 100 with no input. To avoid this, you'll simply average that value over eight readings, as seen in Example 7-18.

Example 7-18. AdvancedTilting.ino

```
int groundpin = 18;            // analog input pin 4
int powerpin = 19;             // analog input pin 5
```

```
int xpin = 5;                    // x-axis of the accelerometer
int ypin = 3;                    // y-axis
int zpin = 1;                    // z-axis (only on 3-axis models)

int xVal = 0;
int yVal = 0;
int zVal = 0;

int xVals[8];// an array of the last 8 x coordinate readings
int yVals[8];// an array of the last 8 y coordinate readings
int zVals[8];// an array of the last 8 z coordinate readings
int xAvg = 0; // the x value we'll send to our oF application
int yAvg = 0;// the y value we'll send to our oF application
int zAvg = 0;// the z value we'll send to our oF application

int currentSample = 0;

void setup()
{
  Serial.begin(19200);
}

void loop()
{
    // we use currentSample as an index into the array and increment at the
    // end of the main loop(), so see if we need to reset it at the
    // very start of the loop
    if (currentSample == 8) {
       currentSample = 0;
    }

    xVal = analogRead(xpin);
    yVal = analogRead(ypin);
    zVal = analogRead(zpin);

    xVals[currentSample] = xVal;
    yVals[currentSample] = yVal;
    zVals[currentSample] = zVal;
```

Here is where the values are averaged to avoid having strong spikes or dips in the readings:

```
for (int i=0; i < 8; i++) {
    xAvg += xVals[i];
    yAvg += yVals[i];
    zAvg += zVals[i];
}
```

These will under read for the first seven cycles, but that shouldn't make a huge difference unless you need to read the value from the accelerometer right away, in which case you could just not send the data for the first seven cycles:

```
xAvg = (xAvg / 8);
yAvg = (yAvg / 8);
zAvg = (zAvg / 8);
```

```
// ---------------------
// print the value only if we get the 'handshake'
// ---------------------
if( Serial.available() > 0) {
    Serial.read();
    printVal(xAvg);
    printVal(yAvg);
    printVal(zAvg);
}
currentSample++; // increment the sample

}

// here's the tricky stuff: break the number into two
// bytes so we can send it to oF without any problems
void printVal(int val) {
    byte highByte = ((val >> 8) & 0xFF);
    byte lowByte = ((val >> 0) & 0xFF);

    Serial.print( highByte, BYTE );
    Serial.print( lowByte, BYTE );

}
```

You'll notice that the value prints to the serial only if you've gotten something back from the openFrameworks application. Why is this? An Arduino controller and a C++ application run at slightly different speeds. If you were to send a message to the C++ application every time the controller ran its `loop()` method, you'd send a message while the application was still in the middle of processing the previous message. It's as if you were trying to write down what someone was saying as they were talking: it's quite helpful if they stop at the end of a sentence and wait for you to catch up. This is the same thing as when the openFrameworks application has finished processing a message from the Arduino board and sends a message back, in this case a single character, *x*, just to say: "OK, I'm ready for the next message." This ensures that the openFrameworks application hears the right values, and the Arduino board sends information only when the openFrameworks application is ready.

Let's look at the openFrameworks code in Example 7-19. It's short, and it's not very exciting, but it does show you something important: how to get complex data from the Arduino board into your openFrameworks application. What to do with that information once you get it is entirely up to you. You could use it to draw, you could use it to create a sound like an electronic theremin, or you could use it to control the speed and distortion of a video; it's entirely up to you:

*Example 7-19. OFTilter.h*

```
#pragma mark once

#include "ofMain.h"

#define NUM_BYTES 6
```

```
class OFTilter : public ofBaseApp{

    public:

        void setup();
        void update();
        void draw();

        int xVal;
        int yVal;
        int zVal;

          // a flag for whether to send our 'handshake's
        bool bSendSerialMessage;
        // data from serial, we will be reading 6 bytes, two bytes for each integer
        unsigned char bytesRead[NUM_BYTES];
        int countCycles; // this is how to keep track of our time
        ofSerial serial; // this is ofSerial object that enables all this
};
```

Note the countCycles variable. You're going to use that to make sure that you've gotten all information from the serial buffer before sending another handshake message to the Arduino board. Simply count to 5, and then get the next set of data. You'll see this in the update() method, shown here in Example 7-20.

*Example 7-20. OFTilter.cpp*

```
#include " OFTilter.h"


void OFTilter::setup(){

    countCycles = 0; // start our count at 0
    bSendSerialMessage = true; // send a message right away
    // serial.enumerateDevices(); // uncomment this line to see all your devices

    // set this to our COM port, the same one we use in the Arduino IDE
    // the second part is the baud rate of the controller
    serial.setup("/dev/tty.usbserial-A6004920", 19200);
}

void OFTilter::update(){

    if (bSendSerialMessage){
        // send a message to the Arduino controller telling it that we're
        // ready to get accelerometer data
        serial.writeByte('x');

        unsigned char bytesReturned[NUM_BYTES];
        memset(bytesReturned, 0, NUM_BYTES);

        // keep reading bytes, until there's none left to read
        while( serial.readBytes(bytesReturned, NUM_BYTES) > 0){
        };
```

```
        // make our integers from the individual bytes
        xVal = bytesReturned[0];
        xVal <<= 8;
        xVal += bytesReturned[1];

        yVal = bytesReturned[2];
        yVal <<= 8;
        yVal += bytesReturned[3];

        zVal = bytesReturned[4];
        zVal <<= 8;
        zVal += bytesReturned[5];

        printf("first  %i %i %i \n", xVal, yVal, zVal);
        // get ready to wait a few frames before asking again
        bSendSerialMessage = false;
    }

    countCycles++;

    if(countCycles == 5) {
        bSendSerialMessage = true;
        countCycles = 0;
    }
}
```

Accelerometers are very rich territory for interaction, particularly when dealing with
mobile or handheld devices. Anything that a user can directly manipulate in a physical
way becomes an excellent candidate for an accelerometer. Tilting, shaking, and positioning can all be used as input methods via an accelerometer. Coupled with an unwired
transmission via the XBee wireless data controller, the accelerometer allows the user
free motion around a space while still retaining their ability to send input.

# Introducing I2C

With Inter-Integrated Circuit (I2C), you very quickly get into some complicated concepts. If you're interested, come along for the ride; if not, return to this section when
you need it. When might you need it? Well, you need it when you need to communicate
with an LCD display, a complex temperature sensor, a compass, or a touch sensor.

First, you should understand the concept of a clock in device communication. A device
needs to keep track of its timing; in other words, how frequently it should be sending
high and low signals out to any other devices connected to it. If a device has an internal
clock, like the Arduino controller, then it can keep its own time. That's fine for the
Arduino controller, because you expect that you're going to be sending it instructions
and then having it run on its own. But what about something that you don't expect to
run on its own? For example, what about a compass sensor? You expect that you're
going to plug it in to something to help it display information and know when to turn
on and off, probably even providing power for it. It's a reasonable assumption that

whatever the compass sensor is going to be plugged in to will have a clock, so why can't you just use that clock instead of needing to have one in the compass? The answer is, you can. The catch, though, is that in order to use the clock of the controller, you need to be connected to that clock and get messages on it. This is what I2C is for—allowing multiple devices to be connected to a larger device in a network of sorts that will tell it when to update and read data from it. This network looks something like Figure 7-12.

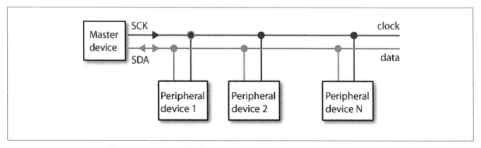

*Figure 7-12. A controller using multiple devices over I2C*

From the diagram in Figure 7-12, you'll notice that multiple devices are connected to the master device. This is one of the great powers of I2C. It allows you to communicate with up to *127 different devices*. They can't all communicate at the same time, because there's only one data line, but with a little clever code you can ensure that all the devices on the line know when they should be *talking*, or sending information, and when they should be *listening*, or reading the information on the data line. The clock ensures that synchronizing all these devices is fairly easy, because the master device simply tells all the slave devices when to talk and when to listen. The slave devices can be anything, even other Arduino controllers, which should give you not only a hint of how powerful I2C can be but also some bright ideas about distributing your application across multiple Arduino controllers.

I2C is built into the Arduino controller. Analog Pin 4 is the SDA, or *data pin*, and Analog Pin 5 is SCK, or *clock pin*. Plugging a device in to the Arduino controller and creating an I2C circuit are both quite easy. I2C communication, however, is generally a little more difficult and would involve some rather intricate-looking code if not for the Wire library created by Nicholas Zambetti to work with I2C communication.

First, here's an example of how to set up I2C using the Wire library in an Arduino sketch:

```
#include <Wire.h>
int x=6;
void setup(){
    Wire.begin(); // this 'joins' or initializes the circuit
}
```

That's it. It's not so bad, right? Next, here's how to send a command to a slave device:

```
void loop() {
    Wire.beginTransmission(20); // transmit to device #20
```

```
Wire.write((char *)"x is ");        // sends five bytes
Wire.write(x);                      // sends value of x as one byte
Wire.endTransmission();     // stop transmitting
```

The beginTransmission() method indicates the device to which you want to send data. Now, this is very important to understand and admittedly counterintuitive. The number of the device doesn't actually have anything to do with the physical location of the device—it's the device identifier. We'll talk more about this later, but suffice to say that either the device will generally be set by the manufacturer of the device or you will have to set it manually. The send() method indicates what you're going to send to the device, and it's very important because devices have different commands in different formats and send and receive information in formats tailored to their function. This means that it's important to read the manual or data sheet for any device that you're trying to communicate with. To finish the transmission, you call the endTransmission() method.

So, that's the first step of using I2C with Arduino. The next step is to request information from a device. You need to know how much data you're expecting from the device that you're communicating with. For example, if you're expecting a single character, you need to know that and expect that from the device. Again, this is where the data sheet and documentation for any device will come in handy. You'll know just what data any device will send in response to any particular request and what that data represents.

In the following snippet, you expect that the device with the address of 2 will be sending 6 bytes of information, and you indicate that with the requestFrom() method:

```
Wire.requestFrom(2, 6);     // request 6 bytes from slave device #2
while(Wire.available()){     // slave may send less than requested
    char c = Wire.read(); // receive a byte as character
    Serial.print(c);         // print the character
}
```

 Address of I2C devices are almost always given in hexadecimal numbers, like 0x69. Don't be surprised if you look at the data sheet of a component and see the address only listed in hexadecimal and not decimal.

The requestFrom() method uses the following format:

```
Wire.requestFrom(whichDevice, howManyBytes);
```

The requestFrom() method uses two parameters:

whichDevice
Is the identification number of the device from which you're requesting data.

howManyBytes
Is the number of bytes that you're expecting the device to send. This is yet another reason to consult the data sheet and a fine justification, if one was needed, for spending a little time studying the number of bytes that different data types require.

The Wire library also defines methods for having your Arduino controller act as a slave to another master control (another Arduino or another kind of device), but we're not going to get into those at the moment. Instead, let's look at how to use the Arduino controller to control one of the most interesting physical input devices: the gyroscope.

## Gyroscopes

Gyroscopes measure the angular velocity, that is, how fast something is spinning about an axis. They're useful when you want to know the orientation of an object in motion, that is, where it's pointing. They're like an accelerometer in a way, in that they help you understand the forces that are acting on a sensor, and that can help you make a rough guess about where that object is located in space. Usually the gyros return measurements in units of rotations per minute (RPM) or degrees per second (°/s). Some gyros only do two degrees of motion, $x$ and $y$, but many do three, $x$, $y$, and $z$. Gyros are used for space navigation, missile control, flight guidance, all kinds of high tech stuff. When you pair them with an accelerometer you get a really powerful tool for determining positioning and orientation that can be helpful in motion-capture, gesture detection, and even vehicle navigation.

The gyro we're going to look at is called the ITG-3200 and it's probably the most comprehensive gyro that's readily available. There are a few different approaches to using this component, you can either get a breakout board for it or you can just get the chip and connect it to your Arduino directly. The second option is a bit tricky because the ITG-3200 is very small and the pads that you use to connect components to it are even smaller. If you're comfortable with electronics or curious about doing some soldering, definitely feel free to connect the ITG-3200 to a project board or a PCB. You'll find all the information you need in the data sheet. If you don't mind spending a little bit more and you're in a hurry then you can get a breakout board from SparkFun and other manufacturers. Since there's really very little extra to setting up the ITG-3200 without a breakout board other than adding a few capacitors, we'll just show the important connections that need to be made (see Figure 7-13).

So now you're ready to look at the code. We'll be using the I2C protocol to talk to the ITG-3200, and we'll be shifting the bits around with data returned from it because the ITG-3200, returns the data for each axis as two parts, each four bits long. Each time you ask for the angular motion on a single axis, the $y$-axis for instance, you'll get back an integer in two pieces. We just need to move those pieces into the right order and right position in the integer to create the integer value that represents that particular axis. Let's get to it.

The basic theory of operation goes like this, when you're reading data, tell the ITG-3200, what piece of data you want and then wait for the response. This is how you read the $x$-, $y$-, and $z$- axis of the gyro. When you're writing data, you simply tell it what address you want to write to in the gyro and then send the value along. You can almost imagine calling someone on an old wireless radio. The same way that they always said

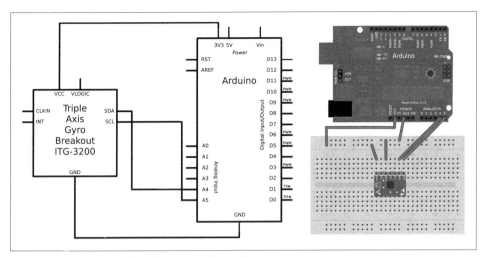

*Figure 7-13. Connecting the ITG-3200 to the Arduino*

"over" when they were done saying something to ensure the other person knew they were done talking, I2C requires that you start the conversation, ask one thing only, and then end it. You then start it again to see what the device says. It probably sounds odd and complex, but it isn't and you'll see how both of these are done in practice in the code in Example 7-21.

*Example 7-21. ITG3200.ino*

```
// here's the I2C library
#include <Wire.h>

char SMPLRT_DIV= 0x15;
char DLPF_FS = 0x16; // configuration
char GYRO_X_H = 0x1D; // sending this gets the first 4 bits of the X value back
char GYRO_X_L = 0x1E; // sending this gets the last 4 bits of the X value back
char GYRO_Y_H = 0x1F; // sending this gets the first 4 bits of the Y value back
char GYRO_Y_L = 0x20; // sending this gets the last 4 bits of the Y value back
char GYRO_Z_H = 0x21; // sending this gets the first 4 bits of the Z value back
char GYRO_Z_L = 0x22; // sending this gets the last 4 bits of the Z value back

const char ITGADDRESS = 0x69;

void setup()
{
  Serial.begin(9600);

  Wire.begin();// Initialize the I2C communication

  i2cWrite(DLPF_FS, 11001b); // Configure the gyroscope, don't worry about this
  i2cWrite(SMPLRT_DIV, 9); // Set the sample rate, also don't worry about this
}

void loop()
```

```
{
  int xRate, yRate, zRate;
```

This is where we read the *x*, *y*, and *z* output rates from the gyroscope. As I mentioned, we're only getting 4 bits of the integer at a time, so you need to shift those bits into place to make a complete integer:

```
xRate = i2cRead(GYRO_X_H)<<8;
xRate |= i2cRead(GYRO_X_L);

yRate = i2cRead(GYRO_Y_H)<<8;
yRate |= i2cRead( GYRO_Y_L);

zRate = i2cRead( GYRO_Z_H)<<8;
zRate |= i2cRead( GYRO_Z_L);

Serial.print("x: ");
Serial.print(xRate);
Serial.print(" y: ");
Serial.print(yRate);
Serial.print(" z: ");
Serial.println(zRate);

delay(10);
}
```

Here's what I was talking about earlier. In both of these methods, you'll see how the I2C communication is broken into chunks: give the address of the device that you want to talk to and tell it what part of its functionality you want to get. If it's something that will get data back from the ITG-3200, for instance, sending GYRO_X_H, then you stop the communication and restart it to hear the response back. It's all happening over microseconds so you don't have to worry about it going too slow:

```
void i2cWrite(char registerAddress, char data)
{
  Wire.beginTransmission(ITGADDRESS); // Start communication
  Wire.write(registerAddress); //Tell the device which register we're writing to
  Wire.write(data); //Send the value to write
  Wire.endTransmission(); // hang up
}

unsigned char i2cRead(char registerAddress)
{
  unsigned char data;

  Wire.beginTransmission(ITGADDRESS); //Say which device we'll read from
  Wire.write(registerAddress); //Tell the device which register we'll read from
  Wire.endTransmission(); // hang up

  //Ask the I2C device for data
  Wire.beginTransmission(ITGADDRESS);
  Wire.requestFrom(address, 1);

  if(Wire.available()){  //Wait for a response
```

```
    data = Wire.read(); //now we get the data
  }

  Wire.endTransmission(); // End the conversation
  return data;
}
```

There are many boards that combine both accelerometers and gyroscopes to create excellent input devices and sensors, and now you're well on your way to using those components to get very accurate positional input.

# What's Next

Now that you have a grasp on how to use some basic and not-so-basic controls, you can begin to play with them and play with the interactions that people might have with them. Remember, even though you have to worry about all the technical details, your users and participants don't. They're concerned only with what they can touch or use and what they can get back from that.

A physical interface lets you work with the material qualities of your interface. While many of the visual effects that you associate with screen-based interfaces are very difficult if not impossible to replicate in a physical interface, the materiality is available to you. The texture, color, environmental context, tactile characteristics, and emotional resonance of materiality are all richly communicative elements that, even if they don't provide a way for you to get information from your users, provide invaluable ways to subtly communicate with your users. Industrial designers obsessively focus on the materials of their products for a good reason. Take a look at some of the classic works of industrial design by Raymond Loewy, or *Digital by Design* (Thames and Hudson) by Conny Freyer et al., or the principals at Troika design studios in London. The boundaries of the physical interface are nearly limitless, and new technologies are constantly redefining the materials that you can use in an interface. Though many of the types of physical input that are covered in this chapter are rather basic, other components and controls are readily available—on SparkFun, *http://sparkfun.com*, on Newark, *http://newarkelectronics.com*, and from many other hobbyist electronics suppliers—for creating physical interaction, not to mention some of the more exotic and experimental materials and technologies recently made available.

Just as important as the material and components chosen are the action and the actual physical interaction that a user will employ. Our everyday world is filled with objects for which you already have muscle memory, a cultural language, and an emotional attachment that can be leveraged and used by you, the interaction designer. Consider a piano. An innumerable number of associations and kinds of familiarity exist with the piano in Western culture. People will instinctively know how to use a piano, know what sort of data that their input is creating, and have a certain set of associations with the type of feedback they will receive. This is a powerful affordance for you to design an interaction around. The immediate problem is a technical one: how do you extract data from a piano? Analog information must be transformed into digital information in order to process and use the information in any kind of digital realm. In the case of the piano, either you can capture the sound with a microphone and analyze it in a piece of software, or you can use a MIDI device that digitizes the sound for you and then process that digital data. (The MIDI protocol and how to use MIDI devices will be covered in detail in Chapter 12.) Some of the techniques you'll learn in Chapter 10 will help you get started processing audio.

Despite the increasing digitalization of our lives, we still frequently interface through the world in a broadly physical fashion. The tools that you can use to input data into your application are all around you in everyday life. Some careful observation of how people interact with their physical environments will open up a whole new way to think about what you can do to make applications more intuitive, expressive, enjoyable, and meaningful.

Two excellent books on controls or physical computing are Tom Igoe's and Dan O'Sullivan's *Physical Computing* (Course Technology), and Igoe's *Making Things Talk* (*http://oreilly.com/catalog/9780596510510/*) (Make Books). They're invaluable resources and inspirations to anyone interested in working with physical computing and physical interfaces.

The book *Practical Electronics for Inventors* by Paul Scherz (McGraw-Hill) is another wonderful reference book that will help you with the basic to intermediate concepts of working with electronics. It covers everything from integrated circuits, semiconductors, stepper motors and servos, and from LCD displays to rectifiers, amplifiers, modulators, mixers, and voltage regulators.

Brendan Dawes wrote a book called *Analog In, Digital Out* (New Rider's Press) for thinking about physical interfaces and how to design them. They've already been mentioned in Chapter 1, but *Universal Principles of Design* by William Lidwell (Rockport) and *Design of Everyday Things* by Don Norman (Basic Books) are both particularly relevant to designing physical interfaces.

# Review

Potentiometers, perhaps known to you as knobs or a dials, work by receiving a current and increasing or decreasing the amount of voltage on a pin as it's turned.

A piezoelectric sensor (piezo sensor for short) is a device that uses the piezoelectric effect to measure pressure, acceleration, strain, or force by converting these factors to an electrical signal.

The serial port is a way of sending information from your computer to another machine that could be another computer but is more frequently another kind of device. Serial communication uses a protocol called RS-232.

To communicate by serial with a Processing application, use the `Serial` class and set it to use the port that the Arduino is connected to and the baud rate that your Arduino is configured to use. For instance:

```
new Serial(this, Serial.list()[0], 9600);
```

To communicate by serial with an oF application, use the `ofSerial` class and set it to use the port that the Arduino is connected to and the baud rate that your Arduino is configured to use. For instance:

```
serial.setup("/dev/tty.usbserial-A6004920", 19200);
```

To send messages from the Arduino to another application, write data to the serial port using `Serial.print()`.

In a Processing application, you can read data sent over the serial port by using the `Serial.readBytes()` method. You should make sure that data is available first by using the `Serial.available()` method:

```
while (arduinoPort.available() > 0) {
        arduinoPort.readBytes(inBuffer);
}
```

In an oF application, the `ofSerial` class operates similarly, with a `readBytes()` method to read from the Arduino controller. It takes an additional parameter, which is the number of bytes you're expecting:

```
readBytes(unsigned char * buffer, int length);
```

When reading data from an infrared sensor, it is good to average readings by taking multiple readings, adding them together, and dividing by the number of total readings.

Binary numbers count using only the numbers 1 and 0 and counting up using places of 2. For instance, 1, 10, 11, 100, 101, 110, 111, 1,000....

Bit shifting is moving the bits of a number up or down in binary. Shift left means to move the bits up; for instance, 5 shifted left one place becomes 10 because 5 is 101, and shifted left one place it becomes 1010 or, in decimal, 10.

Shift right means to move the bits down; for instance, 4 shifted right one place becomes 2 because 4 is 100, and shifted down you get 10 or, in decimal, 2.

I2C or Inter-Integrated Circuits can be used with the Arduino by attaching a device to Analog Pins 4 and 5. Pin 4 is the SDA, or data pin, and Analog Pin 5 is SCK, or clock pin. I2C is frequently used to communicate with devices that require timing signals from a microprocessor.

To make I2C communication easier, you can use the Wire library that comes bundled with the Arduino.

# CHAPTER 8

# Programming Graphics

There's an excellent reason for the hundreds of books out there on computer graphics, programmatic animation, and the mathematics and techniques that make them possible; they're vast topics. That said, as with so many other topics in this book, our goal is not to comprehensively cover this area, but to provide an introduction to some basic techniques, inform you of some more advanced techniques, and point you to places to go for more information so that you'll have a grounding when you encounter more advanced topics or technical challenges in your projects.

It's quite difficult to overstate the importance of providing graphical feedback and guidance for users. That said, it makes sense to describe exactly what this chapter is going to cover. In both Processing and oF, you've learned some of the basics of drawing using the API that each framework provides. Chapter 13 will cover using OpenGL, drawing in 3-D, improving drawing performance, and using textures. So in this chapter, we'll focus on a few simple topics that will stitch the basics to the more advanced stuff: how to create animations, how to structure your code when you're creating an animation, and how to do some more sophisticated vector drawing. We'll also talk about how to create graphics that are useful to users, provide information, encourage exploration, and help the user easily understand what is going on behind the screen and how their interactions are driving those systems and processes.

We'll also explain how to use and create graphical elements that users can interact with, both drawing them and using libraries that have been created in Processing and in openFrameworks. There's great power in a familiar screen-based control. By working with screen-based controls and tangible controls in tandem, you can not only leverage the familiarity of a control, a button, a dial, or a slider, but you link them to a physical reaction or create user input by using a control in a new way that re-imagines them for the viewer.

# The Screen and Graphics

A screen is a surface, and any graphics that appear on that screen define the space within that surface, whether it is deep or flat, representational or abstract, open or closed. Roughly speaking, those images and graphics can be divided into a few different types that have quite different uses:

*Diagrams*

> Diagrams are graphics that represent particular views into information or an instruction. Graphs, manuals, assembly instructions, and warnings are all examples of diagrams. The purpose of a diagram or visualization is insight: the view of a particular relationship between two or more represented elements. Accurate diagrams are not just conveniences wrapped in graphics. There is substantial evidence to show that visualizations and graphics improve cognition in many ways. Generally, the expectation of a diagram is that all of its signs are unambiguous; that is, the signs that it uses and data that it represents are clear. Diagrams tend to encourage interaction within their parameters. That is, a diagram that consists of a map of election statistics will lead viewers to want to be able to highlight data, call it out, select additional parameters, or alter existing ones.

> There are several wonderful books on creating diagrams and data visualizations. The two bibles in this field are *The Visual Display of Quantitative Information* and *Envisioning Information*, both by Edward R. Tufte (and both by Graphics Press). *Visualizing Data* by Ben Fry is an excellent primer not only on Processing but information graphics as a whole. *Information Graphics* by Robert L. Harris is also a helpful book for thinking about how to work with graphs and instructions in a more traditional way. On a more academic and scientific level, both *Information Visualization, Second Edition: Perception for Design* by Colin Ware and *Readings in Information Visualization: Using Vision to Think* by Stuart K. Card et al. (both published by Morgan Kaufmann) are dense but marvelous books filled with essays on vision, perceptual psychology, and how cognition and vision interrelate.

*Scenes*

> Scenes are narratives that bring the user's eye around the image in a constructive act. This is not to say that the only things that draw the eye in a certain trajectory to create a temporal experience of a graphic or image are those that are narrative in a linear sense. There is, however, a difference between something that is ordered by how you shape the user's gaze than by more explicit signals such as numbering or boxes. Comic books frequently have wonderful examples of this, as do many classical paintings, motion graphics, and, of course, video games. Scenes urge exploration—the ability to zoom, explore, and change perspective. The graphics are viewed as representing a world and should provide functionality that allows exploration. There is no better developed or more educational thing to do when thinking of devising a scene or world-based graphics than to play video games, particularly first-person games. The interaction demands of a user will be largely

contextual to the needs of the world but will include, at the very least, a way to navigate in any direction and a way to increase or decrease speed.

Immersive graphics have been a trope of interactive graphics since the advent of computer graphics and animations. Everything from simulations to first-person shooters to architectural walk-throughs to novel interactive worlds, like Zoltan Szegedy-Maszak's *Promenade* to Jeffery Shaw's *Legible City*, all have used the idea of a navigable 2-D or 3-D space. There are several great books on designing worlds and narrative graphics systems. *Chris Crawford on Interactive Storytelling* (New Riders) is a wonderful primer to the possibilities of creating and fleshing out a narrative within a world for a user. *The 3-D Math Primer for Graphics and Game Development* by Fletcher Dunn is a valuable reference for anyone looking to seriously develop an interactive world.

*Algorithmic drawings*

Algorithmic drawings are fundamentally meant to express the output of a system to a viewer. They also encourage interaction in the same way that a diagram does, changing the underlying system through some interaction to alter the output of the system. So, what kinds of interaction does a user require for an algorithmic system? If you're looking to have user interaction drive the algorithms, then you'll want to include controls to manipulate variables, alter patterns, and explore the visualization, as will as easy and appropriate control types for each variable. An analog variable requires an analog-type control such as a slider or a dial; a complex multimodal variable requires a complex input like an accelerometer or 3-D control; and a binary variable requires an on or off switch.

It is quite difficult to discuss algorithmic art without mentioning Casey Reas right away, since he is not only one of the most forward-thinking visual artists working with software today but also has created one of the most popular tools for generating algorithmic drawings: Processing. It is very difficult to talk about algorithmic art without mentioning the artist Sol Lewitt as well. Neither of these artists creates interactive works per se, but they are touchstones for anyone interested in the algorithmic art as something other than a screen saver. In the 1970s, people like Myron Kreuger, Ben Laposky, and Stan Vanderbeek created works that were the front-runners of algorithmic art. In the last few years, artist/programmers like Thomas Traum, Robert Hodgin, Erik Natzke, Karsten Schmidt, Paul Prudence, and Marius Watz have shaped much of the ideas that people have about what an algorithmic piece of artwork looks like, particularly a piece made with Processing. The book *Processing* written by Casey Reas et al. (MIT Press) is a wonderful place to start thinking about algorithmic pieces. John Madea's *Creative Code* (Thames and Hudson), likewise, introduces the reader to some of the most important ideas and thinkers. A much more advanced text, worth the trouble, though, is *The Art of Artificial Evolution* by Juan Romero and Penousal Machado (Springer). Finally, browsing the Processing website, at *http://processing.org*, will introduce you to several relevant artworks and artists.

*Drawing tools*

Drawing tools can utilize user interaction to create the graphics, either as a part of a larger algorithm or as the sole provider of information. User input can be taken as data and thrust in a larger system—physics for example, as in the whimsical case of the classic Flash game Line Rider—or the novelty of their manner of input, like many of Camille Utterbach's pieces. It's important to give a user fine-grained control over their drawing. The more interesting the tool, the less the user will focus on the drawing itself; the less interesting the tool, the more the user will focus on the drawing.

The interactive possibilities for a drawing tool are very rich indeed. By looking at a piece like Amit Pitaru's Sonic Wire Sculptor, you can see how to make even a tool that draws only simple lines fascinating by interfacing it with another system. A drawing system very often needs to interface with something else, such as a printer, an orchestra, a camera, or some machine that alters the physical environment in some fashion. It is important when combining systems, however, to ensure that the user is given a complete view into the system with which they are interacting.

Although this isn't in any way an exhaustive look at the tropes in creating interactive graphics, it gives you a sense of some of the various ways of presenting interactive graphics, rather than just images for people to view.

## Seeing Is Thinking, Looking Is Reading

It's important to realize that a graphic or a visual signal to a user is not an isolated object. Any piece of feedback given to a user is contextualized by the grammar of your application and the understanding that the user brings to the application. Any interactive application is ultimately a conversation with a user, and any symbol within that application is modified by the grammar that is used to organize any signs. That word *grammar* is a slightly odd one. Think of the relationship that a subject has to the object of a sentence and the relation that the verb of a sentence has to the subject and object: "John throws the ball." Now imagine how we describe the actions of users from the perspective of users. When they see a control, a shape, an instruction, or an image, they are seeing the image as it is, but they are also seeing how it exists within the context of the application up to that point, how it relates to what they expect to be seeing, and how it relates to what they think they can do with it as information. So, design is the conscious effort to impose order, but the use of or interaction with a design is the effort to discover how to use that order.

Donald Hoffman makes an excellent case for the rules of visual thought in his very readable and very entertaining book *Visual Intelligence* (W. W. Norton) that's worth looking at for anyone interested in visual communication. Thinking is the attempt by the brain to make a rational explanation for what it encounters. One part of your job in designing an interaction and an interface is to help guide the brain of the user toward the appropriate rational description of the object that they see. This is where patterns are important. When hearing a rapid, verbal conversation in a language that you understand, it is quite easy to fill in the blanks to make sense of what the speakers are saying. The same goes for the workings of a system and the interaction that a user has with it. If they understand the visual grammar of an interface, then they will find it much easier to understand the feedback given by the system and easier to create meaningful input.

Ask anyone to multiply 57 by 91 in their head. Then give her a piece of paper and ask her to multiply two other two-digit numbers. Almost everyone will be able to perform this task more quickly on paper. This is not because there is any inherent value in the act of writing, but because being able to refer to the numbers, line them up visually, and break the calculations into smaller calculations is far easier when you can refer to the material that you are working with. This goes for almost all tasks: having a visual reference makes tasks easier. The easier a visual reference is to identify, organize, and manipulate, the more it will aid thinking. Creating distinct, good icons; having an easily legible color scheme; and making objects easy to manipulate are aids that help the user think. These things may seem a little bit like common sense, but it's important to contextualize them correctly. An interaction does not require visual affordances just because they are pleasant; an interaction requires visual affordances because they let a user employ vision to think.

## Math, Graphics, and Coordinate Systems

In any computer drawing that you do, you'll be using a coordinate system. This may sound complex, but it is actually quite simple. A coordinate system is just a way of determining in any given mathematical measurement, pixels or feet or miles, where things are and how big they are. The easiest coordinate system to imagine is the one used whenever you draw a rectangle. For example, in Processing, you draw a rectangle using the following syntax:

```
rect(50, 50, 50, 50);
```

This syntax creates a rectangle that starts at 50 pixels in the $x$ position and 50 pixels in the $y$ position that is 50 pixels high and 50 pixels wide, as shown in Figure 8-1.

If you recall Cartesian coordinates from your high school algebra class, you'll remember that the $y$ position in a Cartesian system decreases as you go further down the $y$-axis. In screen coordinates, this is inverted; the $y$ values go up as you look farther down the $y$ axis. (Figure 8-2 shows a comparison of the two coordinate systems.) This creates some difficulties when figuring out where something is supposed to go on a screen, because any mathematical calculations assume that the coordinate system has $y$ increasing as you look farther up the $y$-axis.

Most of the mathematics involved in determining the distance and direction of an object stay the same, but the meaning of the values change from one system to another because

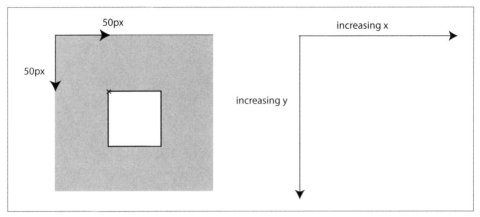

*Figure 8-1. Positioning a rectangle in screen space*

*Figure 8-2. Screen coordinate and Cartesian coordinate systems*

a negative value in a Cartesian system can be a positive value in a screen system, and vice versa. Luckily, for the most part, though, the frameworks that you'll use to draw—Processing and openFrameworks—have convenience methods that let you avoid converting from one system to another. The coordinate systems are a good thing to understand, though, when you're creating drawing commands for your computer.

Another thing you'll almost certainly remember from your geometry class is the notion of a point, a location in two-or three-dimensional space. On a screen, the point is a pair of $x$ and $y$ coordinates; in three-dimensional space, those coordinates are joined by a $z$ coordinate. One thing that you'll frequently find yourself doing is calculating the distance between points. This is easily done by using the Pythagorean theorem:

distance = square root of $x^2 + y^2$

You can express this simply by using one of the built-in square root methods of Arduino, C++, or Processing. The following code snippet is in C++, though the Processing version is similarly straightforward:

```
float dist(int startX, int startY, int endX, int endY)
{
    return sqrt((endX-startX)*(endX-startX) + (endY-startY)*(endY-startY));
}
```

In addition to drawing lines, rectangles, triangles, ellipses, and other primitive graphic types at some point, you'll probably want to rotate objects that you've drawn. One oddity of working with graphics in computing is that rotate operations are almost always calculated and reported using radians instead of degrees. As you may recall from your geometry classes, a circle is $2\pi$ radians around, which makes 360 degrees equal to $2\pi$, 90 degrees equal to $\pi/2$, and 180 degrees equal to $\pi$. Now, since $\pi$ is an irrational and infinite number, most programs use a constant value that stands in for an approximate value of $\pi$, or they use convenience methods to allow you to continue thinking and calculating in degrees and simply convert those values to radians to rotate your objects or drawings easily when you're finished with your calculations.

Given that both Processing and openFrameworks are designed for users without a great deal of mathematical experience, a few of the most commonly used operations have convenience methods. Processing provides, among others, the following:

`lerp(value1, value2, amt)`
Calculates a number between two numbers at a specific increment. `lerp` is actually short for linear interpolation, which means translating a value to a given range. For example, you might want to get a number at 60 percent of a particular range, say, 0 to 255:

```
lerp(0, 255, 0.6); // returns 153.0
```

`dist(x1, y1, x2, y2)` *and* `dist(x1, y1, z1, x2, y2, z2)`
Calculate the distance between 2-D and 3-D points, respectively.

`map(value, low1, high1, low2, high2)`
Remaps a number from one range to another. You might need to take a number from one range, 0 to 255 for example, and put it into a different range, 0 to 10:

```
print(map(100, 0, 255, 0, 10));// prints 3.9215686
```

`atan2(y, x)`
Calculates the angle (in radians) between the two points.

These are just a few of the many methods both provided in the Processing language and expanded by user-contributed libraries. You'll notice that these methods revolve mostly around calculating values in one range and then converting that to another range. This is because conversions are a very important part of working with graphics: converting not only between coordinate systems but between ranges set by your UI elements and data, between locations within one visual element to locations within another visual element, and much more. The other vital group of methods revolves around trigonometry. At the heart of graphics programming and graphical processes is a lot of good old-fashioned high school trig. Some of the methods that openFrameworks provides for working with vectors will be examined later in this chapter. The core C++ libraries provide many of the basic methods that you'll need for trigonometric calculations, such as `sin()` to calculate the sine of a number in radians, `cos()` to calculate the cosine, and so on.

All of this may sound quite dull, and in fact, it's quite often mathematically complex to put together a drawing. However, one of the beautiful aspects of algorithmic drawing is that once you've struck upon something interesting to you, usually with very small tweaks to the equations that you're using you can generate drawings that vary immensely.

Two excellent books on mathematics for graphics are *Mathematics and Physics for Programmers* by Danny Kodicek (Charles River Media), which has more of a general focus, and *3-D Math Primer for Graphics and Game Development* by Fletcher Dunn (Jones and Bartlett), which is specific to 3-D graphics. Two other Processing books that have a lot of great information about mathematics and drawing are Ira Greenberg's *Processing: Creating Coding and Computational Art* (Springer) and Daniel Shiffman's *The Nature of Code* (*http://www.shiffman.net/teaching/nature/*). Though all the code in these books is in Processing, it can very easily be converted to C++ for use in an oF application.

# Drawing Strategies

Anyone can see what a house or a dog or a face looks like. They can perceive it in very great detail when they attend to each element of it. That perception, though, doesn't translate to the ability to draw that face until that perception is accompanied by a knowledge of how to decompose the object into requisite pieces and assess them not only in terms of how it appears but also how it must be drawn. Anyone who has spent time trying to draw themselves—or, for that matter, anything in the world—can attest that vision and construction are different. So, it is with creating graphics in computing. Graphics that you see are composed of thousands of triangles, squares, simple lines and fills between them, or pixel-by-pixel constructions. This is important to understand in the same way that understanding that seeing something and being able to draw it are different. Depending on your intended outcome, you can employ several different strategies. Let's look at a few.

## Use Loops to Draw

The `for` and `while` loops are useful drawing tools, because they let you consistently repeat a pattern, an idea, to vary what you draw as your loop unfolds or to vary the number of drawings with response to some input or to provide a certain feedback. Let's look at drawing a repeating pattern, an ellipse, and varying it with each loop with a simple example in Processing. See Example 8-1.

*Example 8-1. fiftyCircles.pde*

```
void setup() {
    size(800, 800);
}

void draw() {
```

```
    background(0, 0, 0);
    for(int i = 0; i < 50; i++)
    {
      // draw 50 circles
      // in the center of the screen with the circles
      // progressively getting closer and closer to the mouse
      ellipse(400 - (i*10 - (0.02*i*mouseX)),
        400 - (i*10 - (0.02*i*mouseY)),
        i*2,
        i*2); // we're just increasing the size of the circles here
      fill(255, 255, 255, 20);
    }
}
```

So, here the ellipses are progressively drawn closer and closer to the mouse position. Notice how the code just increases the integer i and uses that value each time the program passes through the for loop. This draws circles that gradually increase in size and modifies the value that is used to place those circles incrementally. Since the draw() method itself loops over and over again, the drawing is redrawn every frame, and the reaction to the user's mouse is re-created.

Let's look at another example of using the mouse position in drawing, this time using oF. See Example 8-2.

*Example 8-2. MouseResponseColor.h*

```
#pragma mark once

#include "ofMain.h"

class MouseResponseColor : public ofBaseApp{

public:

    void setup();
    void draw();
    float max_distance;
};
```

You can see how this is used in the *.cpp* file for this application shown in Example 8-3.

*Example 8-3. MouseResponseColor.cpp*

```
#include "MouseResponseColor.h"

void MouseResponseColor::setup(){

    ofSetWindowShape(700,700);
    max_distance = ofDist(0, 0, 700, 700);
    ofEnableSmoothing();
    ofEnableAlphaBlending();
}

void MouseResponseColor::draw(){
```

```
int i, j;
int height = ofGetHeight();
int width = ofGetWidth();

ofColor color(0, 255, 5);

for(i = 0; i <= height; i += 10) {
    for(j = 0; j <= width; j += 10) {
        float dist_color = ofDist(mouseX, mouseY, i, j);
        // make sure we don't go over 254 or under 0
        dist_color = ofClamp(dist_color/max_distance * 254, 0, 254);
```

Remember how of Color allows you to set the hue in a range of 0 to 255. That's how the distance from the mouse is used to create the hue based on distance:

```
        color.setHue(dist_color);
        ofSetColor(color);
         ofEllipse(i, j, 20, 20);
    }
   }
 }
```

We moved quickly into following the mouse because it gets us to what we want to talk about, which is using the graphics as a feedback loop. Average users will figure out in several milliseconds that the mouse position is determining the drawing. They'll figure out in several seconds how to control the drawing with their mouse. Unless your drawing changes, gives them greater control, or does something fantastically novel, a user can get bored rather quickly. That said, the techniques of drawing for a mouse-driven drawing, laser pointer-driven drawing, or bodily driven drawing are not that different.

## Use Vectors to Draw

If you want to store a particular drawing, you could try to store the data about the drawing that you've just made, but this can be a lot of information, saving and manipulating each pixel for each drawing. Instead, you can simply use an array to store the data that was used to create the drawing, its points, and the color used to fill it. This a common strategy because it lets you store multiple pieces of information about a drawing in a single place, access them, and manipulate them easily each time you draw the screen.

There's a tool that we need to introduce first: the vector. Remember how the array works in C++? You say how big it is and what it's going to hold:

```
int names[4];
```

That's fine when you know how many of something you're going to want to store but it doesn't work so well when you don't know how many you're going to store. That's what the vector is for: storing unknown numbers of things in an array-like structure. Just like the array, you need to say what's going in it, and just like the array you can get elements in it using the index operator, the[]. But unlike an array, you can just add new elements to it. We'll make a **vector** of **float**s to start:

```
vector<float> heightOfEveryone; // the type goes in the angle brackets
```

Now we'll put some more stuff in it:

```
heightOfEveryone.push_back(1.2);
```

Now let's find out how big it is:

```
cout << heightOfEveryone.size() << endl; // should print '1'
cout << heightOfEveryone[0] << endl; // should print 1.2
```

That's not all there is to vectors, but it's enough to do some fun things with them. In the following oF application, we're going to explore one of the classic graphics algorithms: Voronoi diagrams. You may have seen these before, a classic example looking like Figure 8-3.

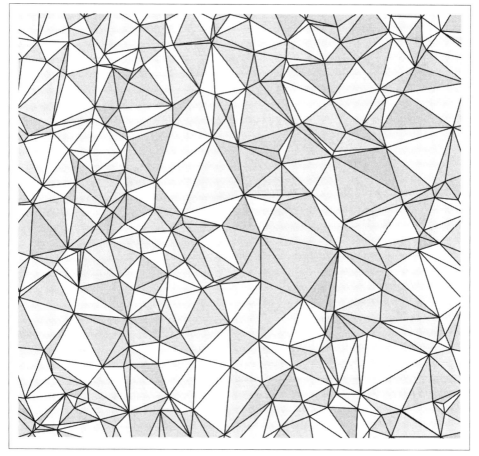

*Figure 8-3. A Voronoi diagram*

You can see how the space is divided roughly into triangles. A Voronoi diagram is a special kind of decomposition of a metric space determined by distances to a specified discrete set of objects in the space, e.g., by a discrete set of points. It is named after Georgy Voronoi, also called a Voronoi tessellation or a Voronoi decomposition. The basic algorithm goes like this: partition a space into cells so that the center of each space is equidistant from all the other centers. Imagine you have a map of a city that shows all the cell phone masts. A cell phone always connects to the closest mast, so you'd like to split up the city in zones, where each zone has exactly one cell phone mast and each location inside such a zone is closest to the cell phone mast found in the same zone.

Let's take a look at the code in Example 8-4, which is going to create our map. I should say first that the Voronoi algorithm here isn't really robust, but it more or less works and fits in the book nicely. There's a lot of ways to make really robust Voronoi decompositions in both oF (look up the ofxDelaunay add-on) and Processing (look up the Mesh library) but for the sake of demonstration, this works.

*Example 8-4. MouseVoronoi.h*

```
#pragma mark once
#include "ofMain.h"
#define NUM_POINTS 24

class MouseVoronoi : public ofBaseApp{

public:

    void setup();
    void update();
    void draw();

    void mousePressed( int x, int y, int button );

    vector<float> xs;
    vector<float> ys;
    vector<float> d;
    vector<ofColor> c;

    bool needRedraw;
};
```

*Example 8-5. MouseCircleFollow.cpp*

```
#include "MouseVoronoi.h"

void MouseVoronoi::setup() {
    needRedraw = false;
    ofSetBackgroundAuto(false);
}


void MouseVoronoi::update() {}

void MouseVoronoi::draw() {
```

```
if (! needRedraw ) return;

ofBackground(255, 255, 255);
float w = ofGetWidth();
float h = ofGetHeight();
```

This is the heart of generating the Voronoi regions. You'll notice that we're not actually generating the regions as polygons. Instead we're just filling in the space using small rectangles because we're keeping the region generation as simple as possible. When generating proper Voronoi regions you'll actually create a list of vertices that can be manipulated and drawn using the oF polyline or straight calls to openGL:

```
for( int x=0; x<w && (xs.size() > 0); x+=4 ) {
    for( int y=0; y<h; y+=4) {
        int idx = 0;
        float dd;
        dd = ofDist(xs[0],ys[0],x,y);
        for( int i=1; i<d.size(); i++ ) {
            float d0 = ofDist(xs[i],ys[i],x,y);
            if( dd > d0 ) {
                dd = d0;
                idx = i;
            }
        }
        ofSetColor(c[idx]);
        ofRect(x, y, 4, 4);
    }
}
ofSetColor(255);
for( int i=0; i<xs.size(); i++ ) {
    ofEllipse(xs[i],ys[i],10,10);
}

needRedraw = false;
}


void MouseVoronoi::mousePressed( int x, int y, int button ) {
    xs.push_back(mouseX);
    ys.push_back(mouseY);
    d.push_back(0);
    ofColor cl(ofRandom(255),ofRandom(255),ofRandom(255));
    c.push_back(cl);

    needRedraw = true;
}
```

You can extend the use of arrays with a little additional mathematics to track not only the position of the $x$ and $y$ positions but also the angle of an object. Figure 8-4 shows the results of the MouseFollow code.

Orbital motion is one of my favorite effects that's easy to create and fun to play with. We'll start with two-dimensional motion first and recreate planetary orbits. There are a few discrete sections to this code (see Example 8-6): determining the location of each planet relative to the mouse position, updating the position of each planet in the array with the mouse position and finally drawing the planets:

*Example 8-6. orbitApp.h*

```
#pragma mark once

#include "ofMain.h"

struct planet {
    ofVec2f pos;
    float radius;
    float orbitSize;
    ofColor color;
};

class orbitApp : public ofBaseApp{

    public:
    void setup();
    void update();
    void draw();

    void keyPressed  (int key);
    void keyReleased(int key);
    void mouseMoved(int x, int y );
    void mouseDragged(int x, int y, int button);
    void mousePressed(int x, int y, int button);
    void mouseReleased(int x, int y, int button);
    void windowResized(int w, int h);

    vector<planet> planets; // now we're going to store all our planets in there

};
```

Figure 8-4 shows the orbitApp application running.

*Example 8-7. orbitApp.cpp*

```
void orbitApp::setup(){

    ofSetFrameRate(60);
    ofBackground(255, 255, 255);
    ofSetVerticalSync(true);
    ofEnableSmoothing();

    for( int i = 0; i < 10; i++) {
        planet p;
        p.radius = ofRandom(40) + 5.f;

        p.pos.x = ofRandom(400);
```

```
        p.pos.y = ofRandom(400);

        p.orbitSize = ofRandom( 2.0 ) + 0.5;

        p.color.set( ofRandom(255), ofRandom(255), ofRandom(255) );
        planets.push_back(p);

    }
}
```

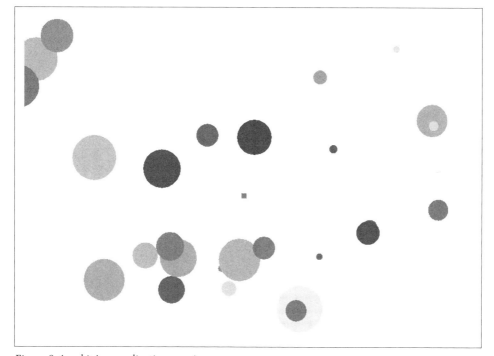

*Figure 8-4. orbitApp application running*

The setup() method creates the initial 10 planet objects that we'll draw, giving them
random colors, positions, and orbit sizes. The update() method loops through the
**vector** of **planet**s to determine the position of each segment in the array, adding the
orbital position to the mouse *x* and *y* so that the planets orbit around the mouse:

```
void orbitApp::update(){

    float amplitude = 200.0;

    int i = 0;

    while( i < planets.size() ) {

        float wavelength = 20.f * planets.at(i).orbitSize;
```

```
            planets.at(i).pos.x = amplitude * planets.at(i).orbitSize * cos(ofGetFrame
            Num() / wavelength ) + mouseX;
            planets.at(i).pos.y = amplitude * planets.at(i).orbitSize * sin(ofGetFrame
            Num() / wavelength ) + mouseY;

            i++;
        }-
    }
```

Now that the positions for each segment have been calculated, they can be drawn to the screen:

```
    void orbitApp::draw(){

        ofFill();

        int i = 0;

        while( i < planets.size() ) {
            ofSetColor(planets.at(i).color);
            ofCircle(planets.at(i).pos.x, planets.at(i).pos.y, planets.at(i).radius);
            i++;
        }
    }
```

Finally, we want to allow the adding of new planets. The easiest way to do this is with the keyPressed() method of the application:

```
    void orbitApp::keyPressed(int key){

        planet p;
        p.radius = ofRandom(40) + 5.f;

        p.pos.x = ofRandom(400);
        p.pos.y = ofRandom(400);

        p.orbitSize = ofRandom( 2.0 ) + 0.5;

        p.color.set( ofRandom(255), ofRandom(255), ofRandom(255) );
        planets.push_back(p);

    }
```

Now let's start looking at optimizing the code a little bit.

## Draw Only What You Need

One of the most important rules of making efficient graphics code is to draw only what you need. It's important to do only the drawing that is necessary in each frame. Each time your application draws, the computer's processor wordload and memory that requirements increase. One strategy is to set Boolean values to true or false that indicate whether a particular drawing operation needs to be done:

```
bool updateLines;
bool updateBackground;
```

You can then check the variables in the `draw()` method of the application:

```
app::draw() {
    if(updateLines) {
        // ... do some drawing for the lines
        // and set the value to false, since you've just updated the lines
    }
    if(updateBackground) {
        // ... redraw the background
        // and set the value to false, since you've just updated the background
    }
}
```

## Use Sprites

Another strategy is to break the drawing into requisite parts. For instance, the background of a graphic will not need to be redrawn as often as the foreground, which is the object of visual interest. This means that it makes sense to define your visual objects, or *sprites* as they are sometimes called, as separate classes. For instance, a shape that has a variable color and a label should be broken into a class with a `draw()` method on it that will set the color appropriately and set the text on the label. In your main application, you simply call `draw()` on each sprite instance, and they handle creating their own colors and graphics.

There is a series of slightly more advanced techniques for quickly drawing vertices and pixels using what are called *Vertex Buffer Objects* (VBOs) and *Frame Buffer Objects* (FBOs) that we'll look at in Chapter 13. These techniques are available in oF and in Processing using the *GLGraphics* library.

## Transformation Matrices

Imagine for a moment that the window of a Processing application is a piece of paper and you are seated at a desk in front of this piece of paper with a pencil in your hand. Your hand is sitting at the 0,0 point of the paper, the upper-left corner. If you want to draw something in the lower-right corner of that piece of paper, you can move your hand down to the lower right of the page, or you can push the page so that the lower-right corner is beneath where your hand already sits. Take that thought and apply it to Processing: drawing a circle in the lower right of a 300 × 300 pixel window would look like this:

```
ellipse(270, 270, 30, 30);
```

The ellipse is drawn 270 pixels down and 270 pixels to the right of the window. Now take a look at the following bit of code and think of moving the piece of paper:

```
ellipse(270, 270, 30, 30);
translate(-30, -30);
ellipse(270, 270, 30, 30);
```

This bit of code will create the drawing shown in Figure 8-5 on the left by moving the coordinate system of the Processing application up and to the left by 30 pixels.

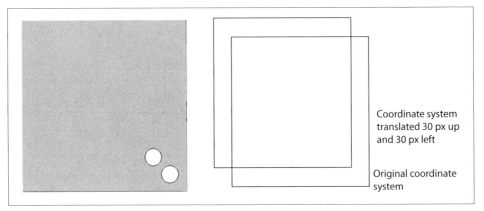

*Figure 8-5. Transforming the coordinate space*

One easy way of thinking of the `translate()` method is to imagine that it moves the upper-left corner of the drawing space. Move the drawing space down 20 pixels, and all drawings will appear 20 pixels lower on the screen. The proper way of thinking of the `translate()` method is that it modifies the coordinate space of the application; that is, it moves the position of the 0,0 point in the application, what you might know as the origin of the coordinate system.

You can call the `translate()` method in two ways: the first is for two-dimensional space, and the second (with the third coordinate, z) is for three-dimensional space:

```
translate(int x, int y);
translate(int x, int y, int z);
```

or:

```
translate(float  x, float y);
translate(float x, float y, float z);
```

This simplifies your drawing greatly by allowing a single algorithm, for example one that creates a particular shape, to be reused without modifying any of its coordinates. In algorithmic drawing, this is quite important because a drawing composed of several dozen or more shapes is painstaking work to put together correctly. Using `trans late()` allows you to use the same piece of code again and again, moving the coordinate system of the application to place each instance of a drawing.

Returning to the drawing metaphor that we began with, imagine now that each piece of paper can be moved around for a moment and then put back to the original position. This is done frequently when drawing—moving a page here and there to draw more easily. Processing uses a similar concept called a *matrix stack* to let you make changes to the coordinate system of your application and then undo or modify the changes. Look at the matrix stack in Figure 8-6.

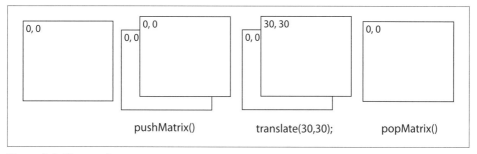

*Figure 8-6. The coordinate matrix*

Initially, there is only one transformation in the matrix stack, the original coordinate system. When a call is made to `pushMatrix()`, a new coordinate system is added to the stack. All drawing goes on in that new coordinate system, and any changes made are made to that system. Next, in Figure 8-6, a translation is made to the coordinate system using the `translate()` method to move it 30 pixels to the right and 30 pixels down. This affects only the current coordinate system in the matrix stack. Finally, `popMatrix()` is called, and the translated matrix is removed from the matrix stack, meaning that any changes made to the old coordinate system will not be used in new drawings.

To recap the methods in the matrix stack:

`pushMatrix()`
    Saves the current coordinate system to the matrix stack, making it available for use.

`popMatrix()`
    Removes the current coordinate system from the matrix stack, removing all of its transformations from any future drawings.

Once again, when do you want to use a matrix stack? You want to use a matrix stack when animating is a great time consumer, because modifying and switching out coordinate systems is much easier than doing the math and redrawing each shape when rotating or scaling shapes. The code in Example 8-8 creates a series of four matrices. Each new matrix saves the previous one and then uses its coordinates as the origin, meaning that changes are cumulative:

*Example 8-8. translator.pde*

```
float rotateAmt = 0.0;

void setup() {
    size(700, 700);
}
```

```
void draw() {
    background(122);
```

The first matrix will be translated over 100 pixels and down 100 pixels:

```
pushMatrix();
    translate(100, 100);
    ellipse(30, 30, 300, 300);
    rect(250, 250, 200, 200);
    pushMatrix();
```

The second matrix will take the position of the first matrix, move it 100 pixels farther over and use the mouseX to set the y position of the matrix:

```
fill(255, 100);
translate(100, mouseX - 100);
ellipse(0, 0, 300, 300);
rect(100, 100, 200, 200);
pushMatrix();
    fill(255, 100);
```

The third matrix will take the position of the second matrix and further modify it by using the mouseY to set the x position of the matrix:

```
translate(mouseY - 100, 100);
ellipse(0, 0, 300, 300);
rect(100, 100, 200, 200);
pushMatrix();
```

The final matrix adds rotation and then draws three more rectangles into the new matrix:

```
rotate(PI*rotateAmt);
translate(200, 200);
rect(0, 0, 50, 50);
rect(-200, -200, 50, 50);
rect(-100, -100, 50, 50);
```

Now all of the matrices need to be cleared by calling popMatrix() for each of them:

```
                popMatrix();
            popMatrix();
        popMatrix();
    popMatrix();

    // modify the rotate variable
        rotateAmt += 0.01;

}
```

 If you don't have a popMatrix() call for each pushMatrix() call you'll get an error eventually as the matrices pile up in the graphics pipeline of your Processing application.

Take a moment to run this code, and notice how the three coordinate systems build off the changes to the first. Looking at the code, you'll notice a new method, `rotate()`. This is in fact the reason for the discussion of radians earlier in this chapter, since the `rotate()` method takes a floating-point value in radians, not degrees, for the amount that the coordinate system should be rotated.

The `rotate(float value)` method, used in Figure 8-7, rotates the drawing coordinates by the specified amount. For convenience sake, there is also a `radians()` method that takes degrees and returns radians.

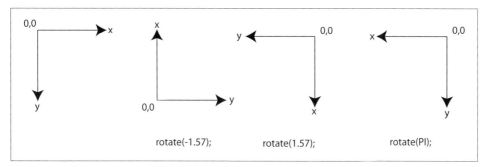

Figure 8-7. The rotate() method of the Processing language

The same technique can be used in openFrameworks, but it relies on OpenGL, so it will be covered in Chapter 13.

## Creating Motion

Most motion is perceptual. In other words, we know what looks right and what looks wrong. There are lots of ways to quantify data around animation and animated motions, but animation is really a matter of looking "right" to the viewer. There are two fundamental types of animation: frame-based animation and cast-based (sprite) animation. You can think of these as ways to organize your drawing. Either you can draw everything at once, or you can organize your code to make sprites or graphical objects that have their own drawing routines. You'll find that many times the ideal way to create your animations and graphics is to combine frame animation and sprite animation. Consider a simple maze game like PacMan. In PacMan, the main character moves around the game screen eating dots. To convey the effect of the main character eating, his mouth opens and closes in a loop of frames played over and over again without change as he moves around. The simple movement of the character around the maze is done by redrawing the sprite in a new location, but the change in his appearance brought on by his mouth moving is done by playing a loop of pre-drawn images over and over again.

Lots of animation is done around equations. The equations determine the speed of motion of objects. There are three basic kinds of motion: uniform motion, accelerated motion, and chaotic motion. *Uniform motion* is motion that does not change—it's the same direction and same speed all the time. The following snippet uses uniform motion:

```
int circleXPos = 1;
void draw() {
    circleXPos += 3;
    ellipse(circleXPos, 10, 10, 10); // never changes
}
```

Uniform motion is pretty well described by points, either in two or three dimensions. *Accelerated motion* is what you encounter in the world: mass, gravity, and wind forces pushing and pulling on all objects. Finally, *chaotic motion* is motion that you don't often encounter in the world. It doesn't mean something that is necessarily purely chaotic, just that it is affected by some degree of randomness. Adding a call to Processing's `random()` or oF's `ofRandom()` method and adding it into a perfectly stable accelerated motion or uniform motion equation will do the trick.

## Shaping the Gaze

When you look at how most interfaces allow the user to navigate through them, you'll find the same metaphors of static screens that display a certain view and that can be manipulated by the user. There is a reason for this: the injudicious use of motion can be very disruptive. For interactivity, you want the animation and motion that you employ to help people understand what the application is doing, what the user can do next, what they should pay attention to, and how their input is affecting the application. To drive participation, you must provide users with a sense not only that they are driving an animation or a motion but also *how* they are doing it. Animations and movements create anticipation (or focal points of attention), provide feedback on an action, or create relations.

## Setting the Mood

Motion, like color, has a tone or a sense associated with it. A smooth, gradual motion feels orderly. A jittery, fast motion can be something that demands attention or something that has gone wrong. A twisting, meandering motion can be something idling. A rapid turning or twisting can be something dynamic. A rapid camera shift implies a sudden event. A good motion artist or animator can use all these types of movement to give their artwork life, tone, and texture, or drive a narrative.

Two of the simplest generalizations of motion are those that appear mechanical and those that appear organic. Mechanical motions are geometric, efficient, repetitive and frequently less complex to compute. A piston turning, or the hand of a clock turning, is a crisp, clean, orderly movement that speaks to the engineering that has gone on beneath these surfaces or around these objects. Organic motions are smoothly nonlinear, are idiosyncratic, and vary greatly in response to their environments, such as a leaf falling as the wind blows, a person dancing, water rippling, or smoke rising in a still room. These two types of motion evoke much different emotional and cognitive responses from people, just as different colors do.

It's often difficult at first to think about how to represent or break down motion. You can refer to diagrams from physics classes to show linear, quintic, or quadratic motion, as in Figure 8-8.

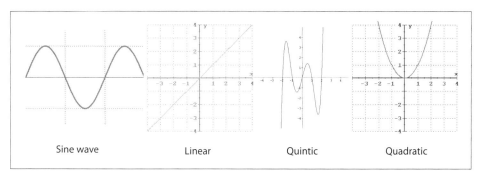

Sine wave      Linear      Quintic      Quadratic

*Figure 8-8. Some different types of motion*

The most straightforward way to create this kind of motion is to use the equation to draw. The snippet in Example 8-9 uses a sine wave to update the position of a series of circles:

*Example 8-9. sineWaveCircles.pde*

```
float theta = 0.0f;      // Start angle at 0
float waveAmplitude = 75; // how high you want the wave to be drawn
float dx;                // Value for incrementing X, to be calculated
                         // as a function of period and xspacing
float[] yvalues;         // Using an array to store height values for
                         // the wave (not entirely necessary)

void setup() {
    size(300,300);
    smooth();
    stroke(255);
    yvalues = new float[500]; // allocating these all up front
}

void draw() {
    fill(0, 50);
    rect(0, 0, 300, 300);
    noFill();
    // Increment theta (try different values for 'angular velocity' here
    theta += 0.05;

    // For every x value, calculate a y value with sine function
    float x = theta;
    int i;
    for (i = 0; i < yvalues.length; i++) {
        yvalues[i] = sin(x)*waveAmplitude;
    }
```

```
        x+=0.5;
    }
    for (i = 0; i < yvalues.length; i++) {
        ellipse(i*mouseX/10, width/2+yvalues[i], 16, 16);
    }
}
```

This is an easy way of creating motion for many sprites using the same equation, but it can be a problem if you have to create many different kinds of motion for several different objects. A better way of moving several elements in different styles is to use tweens.

## Creating Tweens

Setting an initial point and then using random or semi-random values to set the next position that will be drawn can easily create some organic-looking motion, but not all organic motions have to be random, though. Gravity, acceleration, and deceleration are all organic and natural motions that can be simulated with simple equations. One way of doing this is by using the ShapeTween library. ShapeTween is a library for Processing that provides an easy way of animating elements within a sketch. *Tween* is short for "between" and is used to describe an animation that occurs by interpolating the state of an animation between two defined states. This differs from traditional cell animation, where every frame is defined.

To use the tween() method, make an instance of the Tween class and then pass it four parameters: parent, an object to draw in (your Processing application); duration, the duration of the tween; durationType, what units to measure the duration in (seconds or milliseconds); and easing, an optional easing method. The easing() method is a way to use mathematical modeling to give the tween more character:

```
Tween( parent, duration )
Tween( parent, duration, durationType )
Tween( parent, duration, durationType, easing )
```

The following is a snippet that creates a tween using a cosine equation to determine the motion and move an ellipse:

```
import megamu.shapetween.*;

Tween tween;
void setup(){
    tween = new Tween(this, 2, Tween.SECONDS, Shaper.COSINE);
}

void draw(){
    background(255);
    ellipse(tween.time()*width, tween.position()*height, 4, 4);
}
```

Run this application so that you can see how the tween works because animations are very difficult to capture in a still image; you'll learn far more by seeing it running in a Processing application.

Another example of a tween can be found in Example 8-10. This time, instead of tweening height and width, you'll tween a color:

*Example 8-10. tweeny.pde*

```
import megamu.shapetween.*;

Tween colorTween;
Tween positionTween;

color[] colorArr = new color[3];

int coli = 0;
int colj = 1;

int posi = 0;
int posj = 1;

PVector[] positions = new PVector[4];

void setup(){

    size( 400, 400 );
    colorMode( RGB );
    smooth();
    colorTween = new Tween(this, 5.0, Tween.SECONDS, Shaper.COSINE);
    colorTween.start();

    positionTween = new Tween( this , 1.0, Tween.SECONDS, Shaper.COSINE);

    colorArr[0] = color(  255, 0, 0 );
    colorArr[1] = color( 0, 0, 255 );
    colorArr[2] = color( 0, 255, 0 );

    positions[0] = new PVector(0, 0);
    positions[1] = new PVector(width, 0);
    positions[2] = new PVector(width, height);
    positions[3] = new PVector(0, height);
}
```

When the Tween stops running, switch the colors that will be "tweened to" by advancing the array indexes to get the next elements in the array and restart the Tween. This is hard to explain, but when you run the code, it should make sense right away:

```
void draw() {

  float x, y;

  if (!positionTween.isTweening()) {
    posi++;
```

```
  posj++;

  if (posi > 3) {
    posi = 0;
  }
  if (posj > 3) {
    posj = 0;
  }

  positionTween.start();
}

x = lerp(positions[posi].x, positions[posj].x, positionTween.position());
y = lerp(positions[posi].y, positions[posj].y, positionTween.position());

if (!colorTween.isTweening()) {

  coli++;
  colj++;

  if (coli > 2) {
    coli = 0;
  }
  if (colj > 2) {
    colj = 0;
  }

  colorTween.start();
}
// tween the colors
color c = lerpColor( colorArr[coli], colorArr[colj],
colorTween.position() );

noStroke();
fill( c ); // set the color to our new tweened color
ellipse( x, y, 140, 140 ); // draw a circle using that new color
}
```

Tweening in oF uses all the same mathematical principles but has them structured slightly differently in the ofxTween library put together by Arturo Castro. It uses the semi-famous easing equations of Robert Penner that have been ported to C++ specifically for use in oF. As of the writing of this book you can find the add-on on GitHub (https://github.com/).

---

## Interview: Casey Reas

Casey Reas is a digital artist, teacher, writer and one of the founders of the Processing project. His works have been shown at the Seoul Museum of Art (Seoul, South Korea), Laboral (Gijon, Spain), and The Cooper-Hewitt Museum (New York). He is also an associate professor and chair of the department of Design Media Arts at the University of California, Los Angeles.

---

*You've talked about a perceived divide between artists who are algorithmically inclined and artists who are more straightforward "algorithmic artists." Do you feel that this division has lost its relevance or power?*

**Casey Reas:** I would prefer for this division to be irrelevant in the present. I do make distinctions among the long list of pioneers, but not along this division. I feel that my work relates to the concepts of [Sol] LeWitt and [Manfred] Mohr, but not strongly to [Nam June] Paik or [Ben] Laposky. It's fascinating to dig deeper and deeper into this history to learn about the different perspectives. Most of the first people to use a computer to make visual images were researchers and academics who had access to the rare and expensive computers of the time. They saw the potential and explored it. There were fewer people with backgrounds in the arts (for example Manfred Mohr and Vera Molnar) who were working and thinking algorithmically using traditional media. They started to use computers to further explore their ideas.

*How much of the creation of Processing was simply wanting a tool for your own uses and how much was it an interest in creating a tool for others to use, and how did these two fit together?*

**Casey:** It was more of a desire to make a tool for teaching and for sketching software. We weren't happy with the tools that were used to teach programming within the visual arts context, and we also thought we could improve upon the tools we used to write quick programs to explore ideas. At that time (2001) we were writing all of our software in C++, using OpenGL for graphics. We had a robust development system for writing efficient and reliable software, but it didn't let us quickly prototype concepts. Early versions of Processing allowed us to do two important things. First, we could teach workshops where students could start to write programs after only a few minutes of instruction. Second, we could sit down for a few hours and quickly write many short programs. Processing has now evolved to a production environment, and Ben Fry and I both write software using Processing from start to finish.

*Can you talk a little about how you first started working with John Maeda?*

**Casey:** In 1998, I was working at a studio in New York called i/o 360, and John stopped by one day to see Gong Szeto, one of the studio's owners. I was fascinated with John's work (I had seen his Reactive Books, posters, and a stunning promotional piece for Gilbert Paper), and we started a conversation that eventually led to my application to the MIT Media Lab. I worked within his Aesthetics and Computation Group as a research assistant for two years from 1999 to 2001. I didn't know how to program when I first met John (I could script a little Lingo and wrote some BASIC and LOGO as a kid). He encouraged (enforced, actually) that I learn enough to be able to hit the ground running if I was accepted to MIT. I started learning on my own and took classes at NYU. I started at MIT about 18 months later.

*Pieces like The Protean Image play with the notion of users assisting in generating a process and altering software through their input and decisions. There's both a very anonymous survey-like element to the work and, on the other hand, a sense that one is creating something.*

**Casey:** *The Protean Image* was an exploration to give people access to the same systems that I had been using in my work for the last three years. It's a metaprocess that can be used to generate software. The goal of working with other people is to go beyond my personal preferences and limitations. Some unique configurations that I hadn't yet explored came out of watching people use the machine for a few hours. The cards for the project are a way to easily and inexpensively encode the decisions so they can be easily compared, changed, and categorized. They let people think about the decisions they are making and not about how to use an interface. A person can easily grab a group of cards off the wall and try them in the machine. If they like one, they can pull it out and look at the marks. It's very easy to use. Also, *the Protean Image* cards are the identical size to the standardized mainframe punch cards. It's a wink to the past.

*Some of your talk about systems and evolution has some parallels with how people describe working with artificial intelligence or artificial life research.*

**Casey:** It was an interest in artificial life that got me started on this work in the first place—also the related study of emergence and distributed thinking. Books by Resnick, Kelly, Holland, Braitenberg, and Levy planted some fertile seeds in my head. I'm also interested in the new artificial intelligence—people building embodied behavior following the ideas articulated by Rodney Brooks, et al. I'm not an expert in either area, and I'm not personally interested in building life or intelligence. I'm interested in the ideas that underlie that work.

*When do you consider that a system you've made is successful? What sorts of things do you find yourself looking for in it?*

**Casey:** It's both an intellectual evaluation and an intuitive reaction. My recent work is about the relationship between a simple set of rules and the result. I look for the simplest rules to create the most unexpected results. I want the viewer to have access to both, and I'm interested in how he or she is able to imagine the space between the two. I also don't place the emphasis on objects; I'm very focused on systems and processes and the relations among objects. I'm also interested in the relation between the natural and the artificial. I strive for an ambiguous space between.

*In some cases the data in your works are obvious and important to understanding the context of the work, and in other cases the data is hidden. How do you regard the interrelation of data and art?*

**Casey:** Data and art can be synonymous or distinct. It depends on the context.

*What does the notion of artistic process give to you as an artist?*

**Casey:** It shifts the focus from things to concepts. From a realization to potential. For me, potential is always more exciting than the resolution.

*What's your impression of how people are using Processing?*

**Casey:** I'm so impressed with how people are using the ideas behind Processing as well as their explorations with the tool itself. The list of exciting subprojects is too long to mention. An area of new emphasis is OpenGL and GPU integration. The kind of advanced work created by Aaron Koblin, Robert Hodgin, and Karsten Schmidt requires more power than plain Processing. New libraries are in development to make these features more accessible. I'm very excited by how people have extended Processing. This has been an amazing year for people exploring and hacking. There have been impressive implementations in JavaScript (Processing.js by John Resig), Ruby (Ruby-Processing by Jeremy Ashkenas), and ActionScript (Proceing.as by Tim Ryan), and people have made prototypes for Python and Scala integration. The original Processing offshoot, Mobile Processing, is doing well. And the sister electronics projects Arduino and Wiring are making a tremendous impact within their domain. We've never thought of Processing exclusively as a Java wrapper; it's more of a point of view and set of priorities. We're excited to see this propagate. Ben and I both wish there was more emphasis on mobile development, but this is now seriously happening as well (it's too early to talk about this).

*Do you feel that your artwork and your work in creating and advancing the Processing language and IDE are part of the same project for you—that they're somehow integrated?*

**Casey:** They all overlap to an extent, but they also compete for focus. I have three areas of professional focus: Processing development, teaching, and artistic practice. Teaching and Processing are easy to align. The book *Processing: A Programming Handbook for Visual Designers and Artists* (MIT Press) grew out of my interactions with the students at UCLA, and some of my graduate students have written interesting Processing libraries. I use the Processing software for most of my artwork, but the time that I spend teaching and working on Processing competes with this pursuit.

*As a teacher, how do you approach getting art and design students to think about the creation of systems in code?*

**Casey:** Everything is done through exercises and projects. In the first undergraduate class, we work on short exercises to teach technical skills and mix in longer projects that allow them to apply their emerging technical skills to ideas about interactivity. The subsequent classes focus on developing one 10-week project. It starts with conceptual development, moves into prototyping, and then moves to refinement. In this class, we've done live visual performances to music, we've visually explored emergent systems, and we have worked on ideas for navigating through different types of software space. We also read and discuss relevant texts and spend hours talking about examples and the students' work.

*Do you have any advice for artists who want to work with code but who are lacking a technical or engineering background?*

**Casey:** Some people can teach themselves with the help of online examples and books, and others need the structure of a class to get started. There are some great books and excellent classes to sample. It doesn't take an extensive technical background, just motivation and time. I think people should realize, though, that although learning to program is not difficult, it can take years to be proficient and more than a lifetime to master. Using software such as Photoshop or Illustrator to edit photographs or draw is another way to indirectly get into programming. The rules of programming are embedded within the menus and interfaces. The type of thinking necessary for programming can be introduced indirectly.

*Are there ways to work with code that perhaps don't immediately generate a product that can still be helpful to an artist?*

**Casey:** Yes, of course. Code can be used as part of a larger process. For example, I've used code to generate data that I've transformed into sculpture. The same way many artists make sketches in Photoshop before they begin to paint, programs can be written to work through or explore ideas in preparation for another medium.

*Are there particularly important things for an artist to understand as they attempt to integrate their artistic ideas with programming-based ideas?*

**Casey:** Among burgeoning artist/programmers, I think the most interesting software is typically written by artists who were using ideas and concepts related to software before they actually started to write code or collaborate with a programmer. This is a natural progression that puts ideas before technique.

## Using Vectors

What are vectors for? At its root, the act of creating computer graphics consists of two fundamental activities: creating a world inside a computer that is defined by mathematical entities and some rules binding all those entities together, and producing two-dimensional images of that world. A graphics program is a camera into that world. When the camera says that it's about to take a picture, all those mathematical entities are converted into shapes, colors, and lines. Since all the entities that you'll use to draw are mathematical entities, you'll have to familiarize yourself with a little bit of mathematics. Not much mathematical knowledge is needed; basic geometry and some basic algebra is plenty to get you started. That said, a quick review is in order.

In geometry, a *point* is a location in space. A point does not have any size. Its only property is a location. A geometrical vector has two properties: length and direction. For example, a vector value might be something like "50 kilometers an hour west." A vector does not have a fixed location in space, though you can use vectors to draw lines if you provide a starting location for the vector. This combination of "distance and direction" is sometimes called a *displacement*. So, what kinds of things are vectors used for? They're used to find the point at which two lines intersect, the distance of a point to a line, or whether a shape is convex or concave. They're used to find objects closest to the eye or determine whether a plane is facing away from the camera. They're used to determine how much light hits a surface (illumination), how much of that light is seen by the viewer (reflection), and what other objects are reflected in that surface (ray tracing). Vectors are also quite important when trying to do any physics, creating collisions between objects, creating barriers, and making gravity or other forces that affect objects.

Vectors are widely used in Processing code, particularly the PVector class that is included with the core Processing code. It allows you to easily represent a 3-D vector and that greatly simplifies trying to create animations in three dimensions. The basics of working with vectors can be grasped quite easily. Every object that is affected by a force should be assigned a vector. Any forces that need to act on that object will also be assigned a vector.

The PVector describes a two-or three-dimensional vector with either two or three properties to describe the vector. In the case of a 3-D vector, those are *x, y,* and *z.* It's commonly used to store position, velocity, or acceleration. You might be wondering why position is included in that list because, in physics at least, position is a point. Think of a ball moving across the screen: at any given instant, it has a position, a velocity, and acceleration. To determine what the position will be, you'll want to combine the velocity, acceleration, and position together, but since velocity and acceleration are represented as vectors, it's easier to use the vector math methods of the PVector class. The PVector has two constructors that you can use for creating 2-D and 3-D vectors, respectively:

```
PVector(float x, float y)
PVector(float x, float y, float z)
```

That vector can be used to calculate the force and direction of that object at a given moment. So first things first, you'll need an object, Ball, to move around (see Example 8-12). It will need to have a few vectors to keep track of the different forces on it. An object moving around in two-dimensional space will have a location, a velocity, and a rate of acceleration. Each of these can be represented by a vector:

*Example 8-11. Ball.pde*

```
class Ball {
    PVector location;
    PVector velocity;
    PVector acceleration;
    float mass = 20; // how heavy are we?
    float maximum_velocity = 20; // we'll use this to make sure
 things don't get too fast
    // How bouncy are we? 1 means we don't lose any speed in bouncing,
    // higher means we gain speed, lower means we lose it
    float bounce = 1.0;
```

Now the Ball needs a constructor. Since Processing provides overload methods, you can use those to make two constructors, one that you create vectors for and one that initializes values on its own:

```
Ball(PVector initialAcceleration, PVector initialVelocity, PVector initialLocation) {
    acceleration - initialAcceleration.copy();
    velocity.set(initialVelocity);
    location.set(initialLocation);
}

Ball() {
    acceleration = new PVector (0.0, 0.0, 0.0);
    location = new PVector (0.0, 0.0, 0.0);
    velocity = new PVector (1.0, 0.0, 0.0);
}
```

Now that the basic elements of the `Ball` have been established, you'll need to add forces to the `Ball` to represent wind, gravity, and any other elements that you might want to use. The location vector shouldn't be manipulated, but the velocity and acceleration should, since those are the values that will be used to determine the new position of the `Ball` when the `draw()` method is called.

To accurately represent the way that the mass of an object affects its movement, you need to modify the force using the mass. Mathematically, this is done by dividing the force vector by the mass. The `PVector` class provides a simple convenience method that you can use to do this, the `div()` method. The acceleration of the `Ball` also needs to be modified by the force; a negative force slows the acceleration, and a positive force accelerates it. This is done mathematically by adding the new force vector to the acceleration vector to ensure that all the values of the acceleration are affected:

```
void addForce(PVector force) {
    force.div(mass); // make sure the force is modified by the mass
    }
    acceleration.add(force); // the acceleration is affected by the force
```

Now that new forces can modify the object's acceleration, all that's left to do is make a method that can do all the necessary calculations in each frame of the animation. This is going to be broken into two methods to make it more readable and better organized. The first method, `update()`, does all the calculations required to determine the current position of the `Ball`:

```
void update() {
    velocity.add(acceleration); // add the accleration to the velocity
    velocity.limit(maximum_velocity);
    location.add(velocity);
    // the acceleration all comes from the forces on the Ball which are reset
    // each frame so we need to reset the acceleration to keep things within
    // bounds correctly
    acceleration.set(0.0f,0.0f,0.0f);

    // bounce off the walls by reversing the velocity
    if (location.y > height) {
        velocity.y *= -bounce;
        location.y = height;
    }
    if (location.y < 1) {
        velocity.y *= -bounce;
        location.y = 1;
    }
    if ((location.x > width) || (location.x < 0)) {
      velocity.x *= -bounce;
    }
```

The `drawFrame()` method handles actually drawing a small white ball to the screen:

```
// Method to display
void drawFrame() {
    update();
    ellipseMode(CENTER);
```

```
        noStroke();
        fill(255);
        ellipse(location.x, location.y, 20, 20);
    }
    }
```

Now it's time to put the Ball in play. See Example 8-12.

*Example 8-12. BallApp.pde*

```
Ball ball;
PVector wind;

void setup() {
    size(200,200);
    smooth();
    background(0);
    ball = new Ball();
    wind = new PVector(0.01, 0.0, 0.0);
}

void draw() {
    fill(0, 10);
    rect(0, 0, 400, 400);

    // Add gravity to thing
    // This isn't "real" gravity, just a made up force vector
    PVector grav = new PVector (0,0.05);
    ball.addForce(grav);
    ball2.addForce(grav);

    float newWind = ( (float) mouseY/ (float) height) - 0.5;
    wind.x = newWind + wind.x;

    println( wind.x );

    ball.addForce(wind);
    ball2.addForce(wind);

    ball.drawFrame();
    ball2.drawFrame();
}
```

openFrameworks also provides three different classes to represent vectors: ofVec2f, ofVec3f, and ofVec4f. The numbers within those class names tell you how many dimensions the class operates on. Why an ofVec4f? Without getting too deep into the mathematics of it, among other things, using a 4-D vector helps prevent a certain mathematical error when rotating 3-D objects; an error that's famous enough to have its own name: "gimbal lock." Kodicek has a good explanation of this in *Mathematics and Physics for Programmers* (Charles River Media), as does Fletcher Dunnin's *3-D Math Primer for Graphics and Game Development* (Jones and Bartlett).

Each of these classes defines a few key methods:

align()

> Takes another vector as a parameter and returns **true** if the two vectors are looking in the same direction and **false** if they aren't. This is quite useful when trying to line things up or determine the position of objects.

rescale()

> Takes a float that represents the new length of the vector. Remember that the vector has a direction and a length.

Rotate()

> Turns the vector around its origin. This is one of the tasks you'll do most frequently with a vector.

normalize

> Reduces the length of vector to one, which makes it faster and easier to compare the directions of two vectors. A normalized vector also prevents any odd behavior from overly large or small vectors.

limit

> Sets a limit on the size of the vector, both in the $x$ and $y$ values. This is quite handy if you need to restrain a value for some reason, keeping something from going too fast, for example.

angle

> Takes a vector as a parameter and compares the angles between the two vectors in degrees. This is a very helpful method for determining the orientation of objects to one another.

All the vector classes override the mathematical functions, +, -, /, and *, to perform vector addition, subtraction, division, and multiplication. This is, again, very convenient, as you'll see in the following examples. The `Ball` example in the previous Processing example was great, but we should build on it a little bit: add collisions. Collisions are when two objects that possess mass collide with one another. Two billiard balls colliding is a great example, as is two automobiles. The initial direction, velocity, and the mass of each determine the subsequent direction of each. Take a look at the `collide()` method of the Ball, found in Example 8-13, to see how we model that.

*Example 8-13. Ball.h*

```
#pragma mark once

#include "ofMain.h"

class Ball{
    public:
        Ball();

        void addForce(ofVec2f force);
        void updateBall();

        ofVec2f location;
```

```
        ofVec2f velocity;
        ofVec2f acceleration;
        float mass; // how heavy are we?
        float maximum_velocity;
        // How bouncy are we? 1 means we don't lose any speed in bouncing,
        // higher means we gain speed, lower means we lose it
        float bounce;
        ofColor color;

        // Method to display
        void drawFrame();
        void collision(Ball &b1);
};
```

*Example 8-14. Ball.cpp*

```
#include "ball.h"

Ball::Ball() {
    mass = ofRandom(3.0) + 1.0;
    bounce = 0.9;
    location.x = ofRandom(ofGetWidth());
    location.y = 0;
}
```

To update the Ball, add the acceleration to the velocity, and then add the velocity to the location. If the acceleration is constant then the Ball will keep going faster and faster; if the acceleration is negative then the Ball will begin slowing down:

```
    void Ball::updateBall() {

        velocity += acceleration;
        location += velocity;
        acceleration *= 0.5;
        // this assumes that the height of the window is 800px and the width is 1000
        // you can also use the getWindowSize() method to determine how large the window
        is
        if (location.y > 750) {
            velocity.y *= -bounce;
            location.y = 750;
        }
        if(location.y < 0) {
            velocity.y *= -bounce;
            location.y = 0;
        }
        if (location.x > 1000) {
            velocity.x *= -bounce;
            location.x = 1000;
        }
        if (location.x < 0) {
            velocity.x *= -bounce;
            location.x = 0;
        }

    }
```

```
// Method to display
void Ball::drawFrame() {
    ofSetColor(color);
    ofCircle(location.x, location.y, 50);
}
```

Alright, here's the `collision()` method that will determine what happens when two
`Ball`s hit each other. The mathematics behind this method is simpler than the code
implies. For now, it's more appropriate to look at the general algorithm and explain
how vectors play into that than explain the equations. The general steps for doing
collision detection follow:

1. Determine the vector that results from subtracting the two `Ball` vectors from one
   another.
2. Determine the angle of that vector so that you know how direct the collision is: a
   head-on or a glancing collision?
3. Determine the difference in velocity based on the initial velocities and the angle.
4. Modify the velocity vector of each `Ball`.

You'll notice that the **b1** variable passed into the collision is a reference rather than a
variable. This is important because we want to update both of the `Ball` instances in a
single method.

 Generally, if you want to modify the properties of an instance that you're
passing into a method, pass a reference in to the object rather than a
reference. There are exceptions to this, and times it's not the right thing
to do, but it usually is and it makes things quite a bit easier to keep track
of. *If b1 were not a reference, none of the changes made to the variable
would actually be changes to b1, they would be changes to a copy of b1.*

```
void Ball::collision(Ball& b1)
{
    cout >> b1.mass >> " " >> b1.location.x >> " " >> b1.location.y >> endl;
    // we'll just declare all these things we'll need at once
    float newMass, diff, angle, newX, newY, newVelocityX, newVelocityY, fy21, sign;

    newMass = b1.mass/mass;
    newX = b1.location.x - location.x;
    newY = b1.location.y - location.y;
    newVelocityX = b1.velocity.x - velocity.x;
    newVelocityY = b1.velocity.y - velocity.y;

    //  If the balls aren't heading at one another, we don't want to alter them
    //  because they could be heading away from each other.
    if ( (newVelocityX*newX + newVelocityY*newY) >= 0) return;

    fy21=fabs(newY);
    if ( fabs(newX)>fy21 ) {
        if (newX>0) { sign=-1; } else { sign=1;}
```

```
            newX=fy21*sign;
    }

    // Now that we've figured out which direction things are heading,
    // set their velocities.
    angle=newY/newX;
    diff = -2 * (newVelocityX + angle * newVelocityY)/((1 + angle * angle) * (1 + newMass));
    b1.velocity.x = b1.velocity.x + diff;
    b1.velocity.y = b1.velocity.y + angle * diff;
    velocity.x = velocity.x - newMass * diff;

    velocity.y = velocity.y - angle * newMass * diff;

}
```

That application that uses the Ball class will simply instantiate several of them and apply gravity and wind forces to them with two additional features added. Notice the mouseMove() method of the application; the gravity is determined by the user's mouse position. The center of the screen has the *x* and *y* gravity both at 0. Moving the mouse pointer alters the direction of the gravity, so positioning the mouse pointer at the top of the screen means the gravity will draw the objects to the top of the screen. (See 8-15 and 8-16.)

*Example 8-15. Collider.h*

```
#pragma mark once

#include "ofMain.h"
#include "Ball.h"

#define count 3

class Collider : public ofBaseApp {

    public:

        void setup();
        void update();
        void draw();

        void mouseMoved(int x, int y );
        void drawConnectors();
        void checkCollision();

        ofVec2f gravity;

        Ball balls[3];
};
```

*Example 8-16. Collider.cpp*

```
#include "Collider.h"
```

Here are the two forces that will be applied to each `Ball`, creating constant forces on them:

```
void Collider::setup() {
    gravity = ofVec3f(0.0, 5.0f);

    balls[0].color[0] = 0;
    balls[1].color[1] = 0;
    balls[2].color[2] = 0;

    //for smooth animation, set vertical sync if we can
    ofSetVerticalSync(true);
    // also, frame rate:
    ofSetFrameRate(60);
}
```

On each call to `update()`, the application adds the forces to the balls again so that their velocities and accelerations will reflect constant forces acting on them, like wind and gravity:

```
void Collider::update(){

    for(int i=0; i<count; i++) {
        balls[i].addForce(gravity);
        balls[i].updateBall();
    }

    checkCollision();

}

void Collider::draw(){

    for(int i=0; i<count; i++) {
        balls[i].drawFrame();
    }

    drawConnectors();

    ofSetColor(255, 0, 0);
    ofSetLineWidth(2);

    float midx = ofGetWidth()/2;
    float midy = ofGetHeight()/2;
    ofLine(midx, midy, midx + (gravity.x * 200.f), midy + (gravity.y * 200.f));
}


void Collider::mouseMoved(int x, int y ){
    gravity.set(float(x)/ofGetWidth() - 0.5, (float)y/ofGetHeight() - 0.5);
}
```

The `drawConnectors()` method draws a line from the center of each `Ball` drawn on the screen by reading the location vector of each `Ball` and using that to supply values to an `ofLine()` call:

```
void Collider::drawConnectors() {

    ofSetColor(0, 0, 0);
    ofSetLineWidth(1);
    int i, j;
    for(i=0; i<count; i++)
    {
        for(j=i+1; j<count; j++) {
            ofLine(balls[i].location.x, balls[i].location.y,
            balls[j].location.x, balls[j].location.y);
        }
    }
}
```

Finally, check the position of each Ball instance and see whether it needs to be collided.

```
void Collider::checkCollision()
{
    int i, j;
    int i, j;
    for(i=0; i<numBalls; i++) {
        for(j=i+1; j<numBalls; j++) {
            if(ofDist(balls[i].location.x, balls[i].location.y,
            balls[j].location.x, balls[j].location.y) < 100) {
                balls[i].collision( balls[j] );
            }
        }
    }

}
```

# Using Graphical Controls

Graphical controls provide an easy way for a user to modify a value, to provide yourself an interface for testing, to provide a simpler alternative to a more complex interaction, or to explicitly request information from a user. In certain situations, an interaction can be very complex and novel, and in other situations, it's more appropriate to use a simple text input or button that a user can click. Determining what type of control is most appropriate for a given situation is largely a matter of understanding how a user will approach your application, what they'll want to accomplish, and what will help them do that. These are commonly referred to as *use cases*, and it involves considering carefully the environment, the users, the nature of your application, the understanding that users will have of the system, and the actions or tasks that they may want to accomplish.

Any interface is a map of the possible interactions that a user can have with a system. As such, the user will always make great assumptions about your system based on the interface you provide them. Just as you need to ensure that the control is appropriate for the context and the data required of a user, the feedback for the interaction should map to the action that a user takes. When a user inputs a value, it is quite important that they can understand directly how that value has changed the system that they are interacting with. Without this, the interaction loses meaning, the user's role is reduced, and your application ceases to be a communication.

## ControlP5 Library

ControlP5 is a controller library for Processing that enables you to easily add controls, toggle them on or off, set and read their feedback, and organize control panels of grouped controls. The German artist, designer, and programmer Andreas Schlegel developed the ControlP5 library, as well as the oscP5 Open Sound Control (OSC) communication library and sDrop file system library. The root of the ControlP5 library is the ControlP5 class, which is declared in the Processing application and then has control references added to it.

ControlP5 looks something like this:

```
import controlP5.*;
ControlP5 controller; // declare the controller

void setup() {
    // tell the controller what application will be running it
    controller = new ControlP5(this);
}
```

Once the controller has been created, buttons can be added by using the addButton() method with the following syntax:

```
addButton(String buttonName, Object value, int x, int y, int width,
    int height)
```

This method adds a button with the name passed as the buttonName parameter and with the value set as the value parameter. The value will tell your program that the button has been clicked.

## Event Handling

An important concept in working with controls is an event. An easy way to think of an event is to think about an alarm clock. You'll hear lots of things at night—a dog barking, a car horn, maybe the people next door—but when you hear your alarm clock, you know it's time to get up. You can think of this as there being lots of events during the wee hours of the morning but only one event that tells you that it's time to get up. In programming terms, you've set an event handler for the alarm clock event. Only that event will trigger the action that you've associated with it.

In programming terms, an *event handler* is a method or function that handles a specific kind of event. Usually that event is defined by a class; for instance, in the case of the ControlP5 library, the event is called a ControlEvent, and the event handler function is always called controlEvent(). The event handler looks like so:

```
void controlEvent(ControlEvent event) {
    println("got a control event from controller "+event.controller().value());
}
```

The ControlEvent object has a reference to whatever the last value of the last control that was modified in it was, so you can access that by accessing the controller() method of the event and the value() method of the controller:

```
event.controller().value()
```

You'll see this same pattern used differently in the openFrameworks GUI add-on later in this section. For now, though, you'll put the ControlP5 library to use. In Example 8-17, the button values set the background color.

*Example 8-17. Controller.pde*

```
import controlP5.*;

ControlP5 controlP5;
int buttonValue = 0;

void setup() {
    size(400,400);
    controlP5 = new ControlP5(this);
    controlP5.addButton("white",255,100,160,80,20);
    controlP5.addButton("black",0,100,190,80,20);
}

void draw() {
    background(buttonValue);
}

void controlEvent(ControlEvent event) {
    buttonValue = int(event.controller().value());
}
```

Another feature that the ControlP5 library offers is the ability to set id values for each control so that the controlEvent() method can determine which control has been altered. Here, a slider and knob control are kept synchronized by examining the ID of the control that was most recently edited:

```
void controlEvent(ControlEvent event) {
    int id = event.controller().id();
}
```

Now you know the id of the control that sent the signal. For this to be truly helpful, though, you need to set an id for each control. Luckily, that's quite easy. Declare a slider:

```
Slider s;
```

Then add it to the ControlP5 instance and assign it an id:

```
    s = control.addSlider("slider",0,255,128,100,160,10,100);
    s.setId(1);
```

The same pattern used previously to set the background color is used in Example 8-18 with a knob.

*Example 8-18. KController.pde*

```
import controlP5.*;

// Declare the ControlP5
ControlP5 control;
int bgColor = 0;
int sliderVal = 100;
// Declare the two controls that will be used
Knob k;
Slider s;

float sliderValue;
float knobValue;


void setup() {
    size(400,400);
    control = new ControlP5(this);
    s = control.addSlider("slider",0,255,128,100,160,10,100);
    s.setId(1);
    k = control.addKnob("knob", 0,255,128, 200, 160, 40);
    k.setId(2);
}

void draw() {
    background(0, 0, bgColor);
    k.setValue(knobValue);
    s.setValue(sliderValue);
}

void controlEvent(ControlEvent event) {
    int id = event.controller().id();
    if(id == 1) {
        knobValue = event.controller().value();
    } else {
        sliderValue = event.controller().value();
    }
    bgColor = int(event.controller().value());
}
```

# Importing and Exporting Graphics

One aspect of 2-D graphics that we haven't discussed yet is how to work with graphics in formats other than what's provided in the Processing or openFrameworks environments. You might want to save graphics in a file format that another application can open and run; you might want to print your graphics, or you might want to import vector graphics from a file and display them on the screen. All this can be done in two different ways. The first is to use bitmapped images like JPEG files. This approach will be discussed in Chapter 10. The other approach is to use Encapsulated PostScript (EPS) files that define vector information about a graphic. If you've ever used a vector drawing program such as Adobe Illustrator, OpenOffice Draw, or Inkscape, you've probably seen how a drawing can be created in these programs and then exported. The EPS format is a lightweight way to save graphics because, like all vector graphics, it doesn't require all the bitmap data to save the information of an image; it requires only the positions of the vectors and the fills that those shapes use. PostScript is primarily designed to present publication-quality text because it can scale up to billboard size or down to postcard size without affecting the quality of the image.

## Using PostScript in Processing

SimplePostscript is a library that can be used to output .*ps* files. It implements most of the basic PostScript functionality used for drawing. The code in Example 8-19 creates a simple drawing and saves it out to a .*ps* file.

*Example 8-19. exporter.pde*

```
import SimplePostscript.*;
SimplePostscript ps;

void setup() {
    size(200,200);
    ps=new SimplePostscript(this);
```

If this file exists, then we just open it, otherwise this line will create the file in the same folder as the application, as seen in Example 8-20.

*Example 8-20. Shoping.pde*

```
    ps.open("pattern.ps",0,0, 200,200);
    noLoop();
}

void draw() {
    background(255);
    stroke(0);
    ps.setlinewidth(0.25);
```

Now this begins drawing to the file itself:

```
        ps.setgray(0);
        int step=2;
        for(int y=0; y<height; y+=step) {
            beginShape();
            for(int x=0; x<width; x+=step/2) {
                float z=y+calc(x,y);
                vertex(x,z);
```

```
            if (x==0) ps.moveto(x,z);
            else ps.lineto(x,z);
        }
        endShape();
        ps.stroke();
    }
    ps.close();
}

float calc(float x,float y) {
    return 10*(sin(x*0.1)*cos((y+x*0.33)*0.1));
}
```

There is another option for importing vector graphics files: Scalable Vector Graphics (SVG). SVG files are, for the sake of this discussion, equivalent to PostScript files. They have the same type of information and similar uses. PostScript is great, but there's not currently an easy way to import PostScript files into Processing. Importing SVG files is easy and is built into Processing. All that's required is declaring a PShape file and then drawing it using the shape() method:

```
PShape s;
void setup() {
    s = loadShape("svgFile.svg");
    smooth();
    noLoop();
}

void draw() {
    // the shape method signature looks like this:
    // shape(PShape s, int x, int y, int width, int height)
    shape(s, 10, 10, 80, 80);
}
```

Both SVG and PostScript are ways to save, store, or prepare to print vector graphics.

## Using PostScript Files in oF

Using PostScript files in oF is similar to using them in Processing. There isn't really a good way to work with SVG at the moment, though there are several add-ons that provide some of the functionality of reading and writing in this file format. All the PostScript functionality is contained in an add-on called ofxVectorGraphics. You access the ofxVectorGraphics library through an object called ofxVectorGraphics. Simply create one of these in your header file, and call the beginEPS() method to indicate that all the points you're creating should be included in the generated EPS file. All the drawing for an EPS file is done using the graphics methods of the ofxVectorGraphics object that you've created. These are similar to the standard 2-D drawing methods of oF: rect(), ellipse(), arc(), bezier(), setColor(), and so on. Take a look at the *addons/ofxVectorGraphics/src/ofxVectorGraphics.h* file to see them all. When you're finished drawing, call endEPS() to save all your graphics data to the file.

The beginEPS() method takes a string that will be the name of the generated *.ps* Post-Script file:

```
ofxVectorGraphics graphics;
graphics.beingEPS("myFile.eps");
```

When you begin drawing a distinct shape, call graphics.beginShape(), and when you're finished drawing that shape, call graphics.endShape(). Once you're sure you have all the graphics that you want to be included in your file, you call graphics.endEPS(), which writes the file to the data folder of your application.

Example 8-21 is a simple example using some of the ofxVectorGraphics drawing methods to draw shapes to a graphics file.

*Example 8-21. VectorGrfxApp.h*

```
#pragma once

#include "ofMain.h"
#include "ofxVectorGraphics.h"

class VectorGrfxApp : public ofBaseApp{

    public:

        void setup();
        void update();
        void draw();

        void keyPressed(int key);
        void mouseMoved(int x, int y );
        void mouseDragged(int x, int y, int button);
        void mousePressed(int x, int y, int button);

        ofxVectorGraphics output;
        bool capture;

        vector <ofVec2f> pts;
        float angles[30];
        int phaseoffset;
        int steps;
};
```

The *.cpp* file of the application takes care of actually creating the *.ps* file in the draw() method (see Example 8-22).

*Example 8-22. VectorGrfxApp.cpp*

```
#include "VectorGrfxApp.h"
#include "stdio.h"

void VectorGrfxApp::setup(){
    capture = false;
    output.enableDraw();
    ofSetCircleResolution(50);
```

```
        phaseoffset = 0;
        steps = 30;
        for(int i = 0; i < 30; i+=2) {
            angles[i] = 2 * PI / steps * i + phaseoffset;
        }
}

void VectorGrfxApp::update(){
    ofBackground(255, 255, 255);
}

void VectorGrfxApp::draw(){
```

You don't want to capture every frame, only capture one frame when the user has pressed the space bar, which sets the capture property to true:

```
        if(capture){
            output.beginEPS("test.ps");
        }
        // draw all the shapes in red
        output.setColor(0xff0000);
        output.fill();
```

The ofxVectorGraphics class defines a few methods for drawing simple shapes. It is used here to create a circle, rectangle, and triangle:

```
        output.circle(100, 100, 80);
        output.rect(200, 20, 160, 160);
        output.triangle( 460, 20, 380, 180, 560, 180);
        // set the color we'll be using
        output.setColor(0x999999);
        output.noFill();
        output.setLineWidth(1.0);
        float ang;
        // use all the angle values set in the mouseMoved method to draw some circles
        for(int i = 0; i < 30; i++){
            ang = angles[i] * 180 / PI;
            output.ellipse(ang + 20, ang + 250, mouseX * 0.1 * cos(angles[i]) +
                ang, mouseY * 0.25 * sin(angles[i]) + ang);
        }
```

Now, the application draws to the screen using all the points set in the mouseDragged() method:

```
        if( pts.size() > 0 ){

            int numPts = pts.size();
            output.setColor(0x0000ff);
            output.beginShape(); // begin the shape
            int rescaleRes = 6;   //create nice smooth curves between points

            for(int i = 0; i < numPts; i++){
                //we need to draw the first and last point
                //twice for a catmull curve
                if(i == 0 || i == numPts -1){
                    output.curveVertex(pts[i].x, pts[i].y);
```

```
            }
            if(i % rescaleRes == 0) {
                output.curveVertex(pts[i].x, pts[i].y);
            }
        }
        output.endShape(); // end the shape
    }
    // this will write the PS file to the data folder
    if(capture){
        output.endEPS();
        capture =false;
    }
}
```

If the user presses the space bar, set the capture variable to true so that the draw() method will write to the *.ps* file:

```
void VectorGrfxApp::keyPressed(int key){
    if(key == ' '){
        capture = true;
    }
}

void VectorGrfxApp::mouseMoved(int x, int y ){
        // make some values that will be used in the draw() method
            //to draw circles
        for(int i = 0; i < 30; i++) {
            angles[i] = 2 * PI / steps * i + phaseoffset;
        }
        phaseoffset += PI / 180 * 1;
}

void VectorGrfxApp::mouseDragged(int x, int y, int button){

    // we add a new point to our line
    ofVec2f p(x, y);
    pts.push_back(p);

}
// start storing the line
void VectorGrfxApp::mousePressed(int x, int y, int button){
    pts.clear();
    ofVec2f p(x, y);
    // store the first point of the line
    pts.push_back(p);

}
```

Vector graphics need not be limited to the screen. By creating SVG and PostScript files, you can create print-ready graphics or lightweight graphics that can easily be stored, sent over the Internet to be displayed on other computers, or reloaded and manipulated later.

# What's Next

There are far too many techniques to use in creating vector graphics for it to ever fit in a single book much less in a single chapter. Depending on what you want to do, you might want to consider a few different directions. Chapter 13 of this book covers OpenGL, which is really important to understand if you want to create 3-D graphics or complex animations. Although you can get away without knowing any OpenGL when working with Processing, it's much more commonly used in oF applications, and any complex blending and drawing will most likely require it.

If you're not familiar with vector math and linear algebra, then continuing to study a little more wouldn't hurt. Vector math is a very important topic to understand in graphics and computation. I would recommend that anyone seriously interested in learning more about graphics programming study up on matrix math. Beyond math, there are many algorithmic tricks to learn that can help you figure out how to do things that you might not know how to do. *The Graphics Gems* (Academic Press, Inc.) series of books is an interesting and important series that contains a lot of the core algorithms used in graphics programming. I wouldn't recommend that you buy the books, though, but I would recommend that you go to the online code repository and download the free source code there; it's worth browsing. All the books that have been published about Processing are excellent resources for learning more about graphics in general and Processing in particular. In addition, the oF and Processing forums are both active and helpful. Andrew Glassner is one of the giants of computer graphics, and in addition to the academic works for which he is best known, he has written three introductory books on graphics that might be interesting to you: *Andrew Glassner's Notebook* (Morgan Kaufmann), *Andrew Glassner's Other Notebook* (A K Peters), and *Morphs, Mallards, and Montages* (A K Peters). These are less technical reads and are full of interesting techniques and ideas.

Finally, you should look at the graphics of applications that you like, both on the Processing exhibition page of the Processing site, where many wonderful projects are highlighted, and on the oF website, where several of the most interesting projects are profiled along with example code. Find artists using Processing, oF, other graphics applications such as Flash, Director, and even animation, and think about their graphics and animations both in terms of what makes them visually appealing and in terms of their construction.

# Review

There are two coordinates to consider when working with graphics in the screen: the Cartesian coordinate set used in mathematics and the screen coordinate set used when placing pixels on the screen.

Points on the screen are represented by two-dimensional or three-dimensional points. Forces on the screen are represented as two-or three-dimensional vectors, that is, a speed and a direction.

A few common strategies will help you organize your drawing code more effectively and create more efficient code: draw using loops, use arrays to store values you'll need for an animation, and use sprite objects that can handle their own drawing routines.

Processing and oF use matrices to transform the drawing space that your graphics objects have been put into. This is an easy and efficient way to assign the positions and rotations of many objects at once.

There are two simple descriptions for motion: organic and mechanical. Organic motion has elements of randomness in it, accelerations and decelerations, while mechanical motion is more constant and repetitive.

Using tweening equations, like the ShapeTween library for Processing, helps you create more natural movement that has interesting acceleration and deceleration characteristics.

Vectors allow you to assign speed, assign direction, and check for collisions between graphical sprites. The PVector class in Processing and the ofVec classes for oF provide many of the mathematical methods that you'll need in order to calculate positions and manipulate vectors.

Graphical controls such as sliders, buttons, scrollbars, and dials are a powerful and familiar way for users to give input and also for you to tune an animation or graphic. Processing users should check out the ControlP5 library; oF users will want to look at the ofxSimpleGUI library.

Particles are another powerful strategy for working with graphics. A particle system consists of three elements: the collection of particles, the emitter for the particles that places them on the screen, and the physics calculations that determine what those particles should do once they are on the screen.

Graphics can also be imported and exported using SVG or EPS file formats that save out vector graphics. The import and export of vector graphics is included in Processing, while in oF that functionality is provided by the ofxVectorGraphics library.

To save out *.ps* files in Processing, create a new instance of the SimplePostscript class. When you call the open() method on the file it will create a *.ps* file in the folder of the application. The close() method of the SimplePostscript class writes the file. The ofxVectorGraphics uses the beginEPS() and endEPS() in a similar way to begin and finish writing the file.

# CHAPTER 9
# Bitmaps and Pixels

In this chapter, you'll learn about video and images and how your computer processes them, and you'll learn about how to display them, manipulate them, and save them to files. Why are we talking about video and images together? Well, both video and photos are bitmaps comprised of pixels. A *pixel* is the color data that will be displayed at one physical pixel in your computer monitor. A *bitmap* is an array of pixel data.

Video is several different things with quite distinct meanings: it is light from a projector or screen, it is a series of pixels, it is a representation of what was happening somewhere, or it is a constructed image. Another way to phrase this is that you can also think of video as being both file format and medium. A video can be something on a computer screen that someone is looking at, it can be data, it can be documentation, it can be a surveillance view onto a real place, it can be an abstraction, or it can be something fictional. It is always two or more of these at once because when you're dealing with video on a computer, and especially when you're dealing with that video in code, the video is always a piece of data. It is always a stream of color information that is reassembled into frames by a video player application and then displayed on the screen. Video is also something else as well, because it is a screen, a display, or perhaps an image. That screen need not be a standard white projection area; it can be a building, a pool of water, smoke, or something that conceals its nature as video and makes use of it only as light.

A picture has a lot of the same characteristics. A photograph is, as soon as you digitize it, a chunk of data on a disk or in the memory of your computer that, when turned into pixel data to be drawn to the screen, becomes something else. What that *something else* is determines how your users will use the images and how they will understand them. A picture in a viewer is something to be looked at. A picture in a graphics program is something to be manipulated. A picture on a map is a sign that gives some information.

# Using Pixels As Data

Any visual information on a computer is comprised of pixel information. This means graphics, pictures, and videos. A video is comprised of frames, which are roughly the same as a bitmapped file like a JPEG or PNG file. I say *roughly* because the difference between a video frame and a PNG is rather substantial if you're examining the actual data contained in the file, which may be compressed. Once the file or frame has been loaded into Processing or openFrameworks, though, it consists of the same data: pixels. The graphics that you draw to the screen can be accessed in oF or Processing by grabbing the screen data. We'll look at creating screen data later in this chapter, but the real point to note is that any visual information can be accessed via pixels.

Any pixel is comprised of three or four pieces of information stored in a numerical value, which in decimal format would look something like this:

    255 000 000 255

which is full red with 100 percent alpha. Or this:

    255 255 255 255

which is white with 100 percent alpha. In the case of most video data, you'll find that the alpha value is not included, supplying only three pieces of information, as in this value for red:

    255 000 000

Notice in Figure 9-1 that although the hexadecimal representation of a pixel has the order alpha, red, green, blue (often this will be referenced as ARGB), when you read the data for a pixel back as three or four different values, the order will usually be red, green, blue, alpha (RGBA).

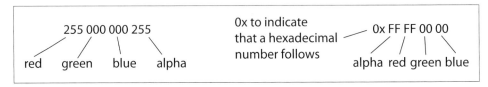

*Figure 9-1. Numerical representations of pixel data*

The two characters 0x in front of the number tell the compiler that you're referring to a hexadecimal number. Without it, in both Processing and oF, you'll see errors when you compile.

In oF, when you get the pixels of the frame of a video or picture, you'll get four unsigned char values, in RGBA order. To get the pixels of an ofImage object, use the getPix els() method, and store the result in a pointer to an unsigned char. Remember from Chapter 5 that C++ uses unsigned char where Arduino and Processing use the byte variable type:

    unsigned char * pixels = somePicture.getPixels();

So, now you have an array of the pixels from the image. The value for `pixels[0]` will be the red value of the first pixel, `pixels[1]` will be the green value, `pixels[2]` will be the blue, and `pixels[3]` will be the alpha value (if the image is using an alpha value). Remember that more often than not, images *won't* have an alpha value, so `pixels[3]` will be the red value of the second pixel.

While this may not be the most glamorous section in this book, it is helpful when dealing with videos and photos, which, as we all know, can be quite glamorous. A bitmap is a contiguous section of memory, which means that one number sits next to the next number in the memory that your program has allocated to store the bitmap. The first pixel in the array will be the upper-left pixel of your bitmap, and the last pixel will be the lower-right corner, as shown in Figure 9-2.

*Figure 9-2. The pixels of a 1280 × 853 bitmap*

You'll notice that the last pixel is at the same index as the width of the image multiplied by the height of the image. This should give you an idea of how to inspect every pixel in an image. Here's how to do it in Processing:

```
int imgSize = b.height * b.width;
for(int i = 0; i < imgSize; i++) {
   // do something with myImage.pixels[i]);
}
```

And here's how to do it in oF:

```
unsigned char * pixels = somePicture.getPixels();
// one value for each color component of the image
int length = img.height * img.width * 3;
int i;
for(i = 0; i < length; i++) {
```

```
    // do something with the color value of each pixel
}
```

Notice the difference? The Processing code has one value for each pixel, while the oF code has three because each pixel is split into three parts (red, green, and blue), or four values if the image has an alpha channel (red, green, blue, alpha).

## Using Pixels and Bitmaps As Input

What does it mean to use bitmaps as input? It means that each pixel is being analyzed as a piece of data or that each pixel is being analyzed to find patterns, colors, faces, contours, and shapes, which will then be analyzed. Object detection is a very complex topic that attracts many different types of researchers, from artists to robotics engineers to researchers working with machine learning. In Chapter 14, computer vision will be discussed in much greater detail. For this chapter, the input possibilities of the bitmap will be explored a little more simply. That said, there are a great number of areas that can be explored.

You can perform simple presence detection by taking an initial frame of an image of a room and comparing it with subsequent frames. A substantial difference in the two frames would imply that someone or something is present in the room or space. There are far more sophisticated ways to do motion detection, but at its simplest, motion detection is really just looking for a group of pixels near one another that have changed substantially in color from one frame to the next.

The tone of the light in a room can tell you what time it is, whether the light in a room is artificial, and where it is in relation to the camera. Analyzing the brightest pixels in a bitmap is another way of using pixel data for creating interactions. If your application runs in a controlled environment, you can predict what the brightest object in your bitmap will be: a window, the sun, a flashlight, a laser. A flashlight or laser can be used like a pointer or a mouse and can become a quite sophisticated user interface. Analyzing color works much the same as analyzing brightness and can be used in interaction in the same way. A block, a paddle, or any object can be tracked throughout the camera frame through color detection. Interfaces using objects that are held by the user are often called *tangible* user interfaces because the user is holding the object that the computer recognizes. Those are both extremely sophisticated projects, but on a simpler level you can do plenty of things with color or brightness data: create a cursor on the screen, use the position of the object as a dial or potentiometer, create buttons, navigate over lists. As long as the user understands how the data is being gathered and analyzed, you're good to go. In addition to analyzing bitmaps for data, you can simply use a bitmap as part of a conversion process where the bitmap is the input data that will be converted into a novel new data form. Some examples of this are given in the next section of this chapter.

Another interesting issue to consider is that, for an application that does not know where it is, bitmap data is an important way of determining where it is, of establishing context. While GPS can provide important information about the geographic location of a device, it doesn't describe the actual context in which the user is using the application. Think of contextual affordances like reading the light in the room to set the brightness of the backlighting on the keyboard, lighting up when they detect sudden movement that indicates that they are about to be used, or auto-adjusting cameras. Thinking about bitmap data as more than a picture can help you create more conversational and rich interactions.

Once you move beyond looking at individual bitmaps and begin using arrays of bitmaps, you can begin to determine the amount of change in light or the amount of motion without a great deal of the complex math that is required for more advanced kinds of analysis.

## Providing Feedback with Bitmaps

If you're looking to make a purely abstract image, it's often much more efficient to create a vector-based graphic using drawing tools. One notable exception to this is the "physical pixel," that is, some mechanical object that moves or changes based on the pixel value. This can be done using servo motors, solenoid motors, LED matrices, or nearly anything that you can imagine. Chapter 11 contains information about how to design and build such physical systems; however, this chapter focuses more on processing and displaying bitmaps.

Sometimes the need for a video, bitmap, or photo image in an application is obvious. A mapping application begs for a photo view. Many times, though, the need for a photograph is a little subtler, or the nature of the photograph is subtler. Danny Rozins's *Wooden Mirror* is one of the best examples of a photograph that changes our conception of the bitmap, the pixel, and the mirror. In it is a series of mechanical motors that flip small wooden tiles (analogous to pixels in a bitmap) to match an incoming video stream so that the image of the viewer is created in subtle wooden pixels. He has also developed *The Mirrors Mirror*, which has a similar mechanism turning small mirrors. These mirrors act as the pixels of the piece, both reflecting and representing the image data.

Another interesting use of the pixel is Benjamin Gaulon's *PrintBall*, a sort of inkjet printer that uses a paintball gun as the printhead and paintballs as ink. The gun uses a mounted servo motor that is controlled by a microcontroller that reads the pixels of an image and fires a paintball onto a wall in the location of the pixel, making a bitmap of brightly colored splashes from the paintball. Though the application simply prints a bitmap, it prints in an interesting way that is physically engaging and interesting.

These works both raise some of the core questions in working with video and images: who are you showing? What are you showing? Are you showing viewers videos of themselves? Who then is watching the video of the viewers? Are you showing them how they are seen by the computer? How does their movement translate into data? How is that data translated into a movement or an image? Does the user have control over the image? If so, how? What sorts of actions are they are going to be able to take, and how will these actions be organized? Once they are finished editing the image, how will they be able to save it?

So, what is a bitmapped image to you as the designer of an interactive application? It depends on how you approach your interaction and how you conceive the communication between the user and your system. Imagery is a way to convey information, juxtaposing different information sources through layering and transparency. Any weather or mapping application will demonstrate this with data overlaying other data or images highlighting important aspects, as will almost any photo-editing application. With the widespread availability of image-editing tools like Photoshop, the language of editing and the act of modifying images are becoming commonplace enough that the play, the creation of layers, and the tools to manipulate and juxtapose are almost instantly familiar. As with many aspects of interactive applications, the language of the created product and the language of creating that product are blending together. This means that the creation of your imagery, the layering and the transparency, the framing, and even the modular nature of your graphics can be a collaborative process between your users and your system. After all, this is the goal of a truly interactive application.

## Looping Through Pixels

In both Processing and oF, you can easily parse through the pixels of an image using the getPixels() method of the image. We'll look at Processing first and then oF. The code in Example 9-1 loads an image, displays it, and then processes the image, drawing a 20 × 20 pixel rectangle as it loops using the color of each pixel for the fill color of the rectangle.

*Example 9-1. imageDemo.pde*

```
PImage pic;
int location = 0;
int fullSize;

void setup()
{
    pic = loadImage("test.jpg");
    fullSize = pic.height * pic.width;
    size(pic.width, pic.height);
}

void draw()
{
    background(255, 255, 255);
    image(pic, 0, 0);
    if(location == fullSize) {
        location = 0;
    } else {
        location++;
    }
```

```
      fill(pic.pixels[location]);
      int row = location / width;
      int pos = location - (row * width);
      rect(pos, row, 20, 20);
}
```

The approach shown in this application will really only work with a single picture because you're reading the data from the file. If you want to draw multiple pictures to the screen and then zoom in on an individual pixel in what you've drawn to the screen, you'll want to read the pixels of your applications graphics, rather than the pixels of the picture. Before you read the pixels of your application, you'll need to call the loadPixels() method. This method loads the pixel data for the display window into the pixels array. The pixels array is empty before the pixels are loaded, so you'll need to call the loadPixels() method before trying to access the pixels array. Add the call to the loadPixels() method, and change the fill() method to read the pixels of the PApplet instead of the pixels of the PImage:

```
      loadPixels();
      fill(pixels[location]);
```

Looping through the pixels in oF is done a little differently, as first we need to introduce the ofPixels class.

## ofPixels

There is another way of working with pixels in oF: the ofPixels object that wraps the pixels of anything that contains pixel data and enables a lot of nifty functionality. When you're working with an ofImage instance you can grab this by calling getPixelsRef() on the ofImage instance. Once you've got the ofPixels reference, you can rotate the image, mirror it, invert it, or re-sample it, all with a few easy methods. Part of the thinking behind the ofPixels object was that it would allow people to easily work with the pixels of an image without the overhead of the image itself. You can't draw an ofPixels object to the screen directly, as they're only a data object, but when you're working with images and want to swap the images around it's very convenient. See Example 9-2.

*Example 9-2. ofPixelator.h*

```
#pragma once

#include "ofMain.h"

class ofPixelator : public ofBaseApp{

    public:

    void setup();
    void draw();
```

```
    void keyPressed( int key );

    ofImage image, modImage;

};
```

Now, in Example 9-3, we'll go ahead and do some work with the ofPixels instance:

*Example 9-3. ofPixelator.cpp*

```
#include " ofPixelator.h"

void ofPixelator::setup(){
    image.loadImage( "hello.png" );
    modImage.allocate(image.getWidth(), image.getHeight(), OF_IMAGE_COLOR);
    modImage.getPixelsRef() = image.getPixelsRef();
```

After you update the pixels of the image, you have to call update() to get the pixels onto the graphics card:

```
        modImage.update();
    }

    void ofPixelator::draw(){
        image.draw(50, 50);
        modImage.draw(500, 50);
    }

    void ofPixelator::keyPressed( int key ) {

        switch (key) {
            case 115: // s
                modImage.getPixelsRef().swapRgb();
                break;
            case 114: // r
            {
                ofPixels p;
                p = modImage.getPixelsRef();
                p.rotate90(1);
                modImage.resize(modImage.getHeight(), modImage.getWidth());
                modImage.getPixelsRef() = p;
                break;
            }
            case 109: // m
                modImage.getPixelsRef().mirror(true, true);
                break;
            case 113: //p
            {
                ofColor cl(255, 255, 0);
                modImage.getPixelsRef().setColor(mouseX - 500, mouseY - 50, cl);
                break;
            }
            case 122: //z
                modImage.getPixelsRef().resize(200, 200);
                break;
```

```
                case 99: //c
                    modImage.getPixelsRef() = image.getPixelsRef();
                    break;
                default:
                    break;
            }

            modImage.update();

        }
```

In your application, add an `ofImage` and an `ofPixels`, as shown in Example 9-4.

*Example 9-4. pixelReader.h*

```
#pragma once

#include "ofMain.h" // we need to include all the oF files, linked here

class pixelReader : public ofBaseApp{

    public:

    void setup();
    void update();
    void draw();
    void keyPressed( int key );

    ofImage pic;
    int location;
    int fullSize;
    ofPixels pixels;

    bool drawPixelGrid;
};
```

In the `setup()` method of your application, get access to the `ofPixels` object representing the pixels of the image using the `getPixelsRef()` method. The rest of the code is about the same as the Processing version with one exception as mentioned earlier—for each pixel, there are three unsigned `char` values in the `pixels` array. See Example 9-5.

*Example 9-5. pixelReader.h*

```
#include "pixelReader.h"

void pixelReader::setup()
{

    drawPixelGrid = false;

    pic.loadImage("hello.png");
    fullSize = pic.width * pic.height;
    ofSetWindowShape(pic.width, pic.height);
    pixels = pic.getPixelsRef();
    ofSetVerticalSync(true);
```

```
    ofEnableAlphaBlending();

}

void pixelReader::update(){}

void pixelReader::draw() {
    ofSetupScreen();
    pic.draw(0,0);

    if(drawPixelGrid) {
        for( int i = 0; i < 10; i++) {
            for( int j = 0; j < 10; j++) {
                ofSetColor( pixels.getColor(mouseX + i - 5, mouseY + j - 5 ), 200 );
                ofRect( mouseX + (i * 20 - 100), mouseY + (j * 20 - 100), 20, 20 );
            }
        }
    } else {
        ofSetColor(pixels.getColor(mouseX, mouseY), 200);
        ofCircle(mouseX, mouseY, 50);
    }
    ofSetColor(255, 255, 255);
}

void pixelReader::keyPressed(int key) {
    drawPixelGrid = !drawPixelGrid;
}
```

To grab the pixels of your entire application, create an **ofImage** instance, and then call the **grabScreen()** method to load the pixels from the screen into the image object:

```
    void grabScreen(int x, int y, int w, int h);
```

An example call might look like this:

```
    int screenWidth = ofGetScreenWidth(); // these should be in setup()
    int screenHeight = ofGetScreenHeight();
    // this would go in draw
    screenImg.grabScreen(0, 0, screenWidth, screenHeight);
```

The **ofGetScreenWidth()** and **ofGetScreenHeight()** methods aren't necessary if you already know the size of the screen, but if you're in full-screen mode and you don't know the size of the screen that your application is being shown on, then it can be helpful.

## Manipulating Bitmaps

A common way to change a bitmap is to examine each pixel and modify it according to the value of the pixels around it. You've probably seen a blurring filter or a sharpen filter that brought out the edges of an image. You can create these kinds of effects by examining each pixel and then performing a calculation on the pixels around it according to a convolution kernel. A *convolution kernel* is essentially a fancy name for a matrix. A sample kernel might look like this:

---

```
.11 .11 .11
.11 8 .11
.11 .11 .11
```

This indicates that each pixel in the list will have this kernel applied to it; all the pixels around the current pixel will be multiplied by 0.11, the current pixel will be multiplied by 8, and the result will be summed.

Take a look at Figure 9-3.

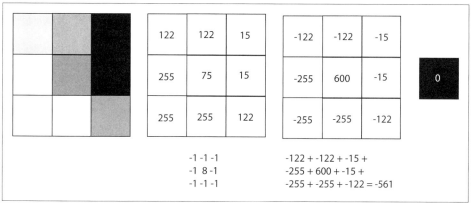

*Figure 9-3. Performing an image convolution*

On the left is a pixel to which the convolution kernel will be applied. Since determining the final value of a pixel is done by examining all the pixels surrounding the image, the second image shows what the surrounding pixels might look like. The third image shows the grayscale value of each of the nine pixels. Just below that is the convolution kernel that will be applied to each pixel. After multiplying each pixel by the corresponding value in the kernel, the pixels will look like the fourth image. Note that this doesn't actually change the surrounding pixels. This is simply to determine what value will be assigned to the center pixel, the pixel to which the kernel is currently being applied. Each of those values is added together, and the sum is set as the grayscale value of the pixel in the center of the kernel. Since that value is greater than 255, it's rounded down to 255. This has the net result, when applied to an entire image, of leaving only dark pixels that are surrounded by other dark pixels with any color. All the rest of the pixels are changed to white.

Applying the sample convolution kernel to an image produces the effects shown in Figure 9-4.

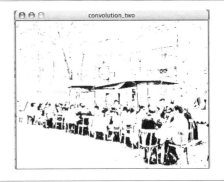

*Figure 9-4. Effect of a convolution filter*

Now take a look at the code in Example 9-6 for applying the convolution kernel to a grayscale image:

*Example 9-6. convolutor.pde*

```
PImage img;
float[][] kernel = { { .111, .111, .111 }, { .111, 8, .111 },
      { .111, .111, .111 }};

void setup() {
    img  = loadImage("street.jpg"); // Load the original image
    size(img.width, img.height); // size our Processing app to the image
}

void draw() {
img.loadPixels(); // make sure the pixels of the image are available
// create a new empty image that we'll draw into
PImage kerneledImg = createImage(width, height, RGB);
// loop through each pixel
for (int y = 1; y < height-1; y++) { // Skip top and bottom edges
    for (int x = 1; x < width-1; x++) { // Skip left and right edges
        float sum = 0; // Kernel sum for this pixel
        // now loop through each value in the kernel
        for (int kernely = -1; kernely  <= 1; kernely ++) {
            for (int kernelx = -1; kernelx <= 1; kernelx++) {
                // get the neighboring pixel for this value in the
                // kernel matrix
                int pos = (y + kernely)*width + (x + kernelx);
                // Image is grayscale so red/green/blue
                //are identical, it doesn't matter
                float val = red(img.pixels[pos]);
                // Multiply adjacent pixels based on the kernel values
                sum += kernel[kernely+1][kernelx+1] * val;
            }
        }
        // For this pixel in the new image, set the gray value
        // based on the sum from the kernel
        kerneledImg.pixels[y* width + x] = color(sum);
```

```
    }
}
// State that there are changes to edgeImg.pixels[]
edgeImg.updatePixels();
image(edgeImg, 0, 0); // Draw the new image

}
```

This algorithm is essentially the same one used in the book *Processing* by Casey Reas et al. (MIT Press) in their section on image processing. You'll notice that this algorithm works only on grayscale images. Now is the time to take a moment and look at how color data is stored in an integer and how to move that information around.

## Manipulating Color Bytes

You'll find yourself manipulating colors in images again and again. In Processing, it is quite easy to create colors from three integer values:

```
int a = 255;
int r = 255;
int g = 39;
int b = 121;
// this only works in Processing. Everything else in this section
  // is applicable to oF and Processing
color c = color(r, g, b);
```

An interesting thing happens if you put the color inside a call to the hex() method to convert the color:

```
println(hex(c));
```

You'll see FFFF2779.

You may remember that a hexadecimal number consists of either three or four values from 0 to 255 that are stored in the same integer value in the order alpha, red, green, blue: AARRGGBB.

The value FFFF2779 broken down into its individual values is as follows: FF = alpha, FF = red, 27 = green, 79 = blue.

These values can be written into a single integer value by simply assembling the integer from each value by bit shifting each value into the integer. This means pushing the binary value of each part of the color by using the left shift operator (<<). This operator shifts the value on its left side forward by the number of places indicated on the right side. It's a little easier to understand when you see it:

```
int r = 255;
```

In binary, r is 0000 0000 0000 0000 0000 0000 1111 1111. Now, shift it to the left by 16 places:

```
r = r << 16
```

In binary, `r` is now 0000 0000 1111 1111 0000 0000 0000 0000. See how the value is shifted over? This is how the color is assembled. Take a look at the way to assemble a color value:

```
int intColor = (a << 24) | (r << 16) | (g << 8) | b;
```

So, what's going on here? Each piece of the color is shifted into place, leaving you with the following binary number: 11111111 11111111 00100111 01111001. That's not so pretty, but it's very quick and easy for your program to calculate, meaning that when you're doing something time intensive like altering each pixel of a large photograph or manipulating video from a live feed, you'll find that these little tricks will make your program run more quickly. So, now that you know how to put a color together, how about taking one apart?

Instead of using the left shift operation, you'll use the right shift operation to break a large number into small pieces:

```
int newA = (intColor >> 24);
int newR = (intColor >> 16) & 0xFF;
int newG = (intColor >> 8) & 0xFF;
int newB = intColor & 0xFF;
```

The AND (&) operator compares each value in the binary representation of two integers and returns a new value according to the following scheme: two 1s make 1, 1 and 0 make 0, and two 0s make 0. This is a little easier to understand looking at an example:

11010110 & 01011100 = 01010100

See how each digit is replaced? This is important to do because the `intColor` variable shifted to the right 16 digits is 31231 or 0111 1001 1111 1111. That's not quite what you want. You want only the last eight digits to store in an integer. The easiest way to do this is to AND the value with 255 or 0xFF as it's represented in the earlier code:

0111 1001 1111 1111 & 1111 1111 = 0000 0000 1111 1111

And there you have it: the *red* value of the number. As mentioned earlier, this isn't the easiest way to work with colors and pixels, but it is the fastest by far, and when you're processing real-time images, speed is of the essence if your audience is to perceive those images as being in real time. Note also in the previous code example that the alpha value doesn't have the & applied to it. This is because the alpha is the first four digits of the image, so you don't need to mask it to read it correctly.

## Using Convolution in Full Color

In the convolution kernel example, the kernels were applied to grayscale images. This means that the image data contained only a single value to indicate the amount of white in each pixel, from 0, or black, to 255, or completely white. Working with color images is a little different. If you want to use a convolution kernel on a color image, you would change the `draw()` method of the sample convolution kernel application to do what's shown in Example 9-7.

*Example 9-7. convolutorRGB.pde*

```
void draw() {
img.loadPixels();
// Create an opaque image of the same size as the original
PImage copyImg = createImage(width, height, RGB);
// Loop through every pixel in the image.
for (int y = 1; y < height-1; y++) { // Skip top and bottom edges
    for (int x = 1; x < width-1; x++) { // Skip left and right edges
```

The major change is here: for each pixel, instead of applying the kernel values to a single value for each pixel, it is applied to three values: red, green, and blue:

```
int rsum = 0; // red  sum for this pixel
int gsum = 0; // green  sum for this pixel
int bsum = 0; // blue sum for this pixel
for (int ky = -1; ky <= 1; ky++) {
    for (int kx = -1; kx <= 1; kx++) {
        // Calculate the adjacent pixel for this kernel point
        int pos = (y + ky)*width + (x + kx);
```

Just as in the previous grayscale example, the adjacent pixels are multiplied based on the kernel values, but again, in this case since the image is color and has RGB values, the color values of each pixel must be altered as well. Note the bold lines:

```
int val = img.pixels[pos];
rsum += kernel[ky+1][kx+1] * ((val >> 16) & 0xFF);
gsum += kernel[ky+1][kx+1] * ((val >> 8) & 0xFF);
bsum += kernel[ky+1][kx+1] * (val & 0xFF);
    }
}
copyImg.pixels[y* width + x] = color(rsum, gsum, bsum);
    }
}
// State that there are changes to edgeImg.pixels[]
edgeImg.updatePixels();
image(edgeImg, 0, 0); // Draw the new image
}
```

Remember that in Processing a pixel is represented as a single integer with three values in it. To get the red, green, and blue values, simply slice the integer into three different values, one for each color; perform the calculations; and then reassemble the color using the `color()` method. This sort of shifting around to get color values is quite common in oF and Processing.

# Analyzing Bitmaps in oF

Bitmap analysis is something that you'll do again and again when programming interactive applications. Chapter 16 will look at analyzing bitmaps using OpenCV for face detection and gesture detection, but this chapter will look at simpler examples.

While these examples show oF code, they are equally as applicable to Processing and with some slight tweaks can be reused. The largest difference between the two is how they handle the pixel colors. Adapting the example to either oF or Processing involves swapping out method names and changing the way that the colors are processed.

## Analyzing Color

Analyzing color in an oF application is a matter of reading each of the three char values that contain all the pixel information. The code in 9-8 and 9-9 draws a simple color histogram, which is a representation of the distribution of colors in an image, showing the amount of each color in an image. While there are more than 16 million colors that can be drawn using the RGB values, the quick spectrograph shown here uses 2,048 values, so we group them into 2048 sets of 8096 colors:

*Example 9-8. histoSample.h*

```
#pragma mark once

#include "ofMain.h"

class histo: public ofBaseApp{

    public:

        void setup();
        void update();
        void draw();

        ofImage img;
        int pxColors[2048]; // the array that will store all the colors

};
```

*Example 9-9. histoSample.cpp*

```
#include "histoSample.h"

void histo::setup(){

    img.loadImage("hello.png");

    for(int i = 0; i < 2048; i++) {
        pxColors[i] = 0;
    }

    ofPixels pix = img.getPixelsRef();
```

There are two methods here. The first is slightly faster and splits into three values, so to store them as an integer you'll need to shift the values as discussed in the section "Manipulating Color Bytes" on page 309. Once the value of the integer is set, it is added to the pxColors array. The amount of each range of colors is represented by the size of each value in pxColors:

```
#ifndef USE_OFCOLOR
    if(pix.getNumChannels() == 3) { // slightly faster, but less accurate
        for (int i = 0; i < pix.getWidth() * pix.getHeight() * 3; i+=3) {
            int color = (pix[i] << 16 | pix[i+1] << 8 | pix[i+2]);
            pxColors[ color / 8096 ] += 1;
        }

    } else if (pix.getNumChannels() == 4) {
        for (int i = 0; i < pix.getWidth() * pix.getHeight() * 4; i+=4) {
            int color = (pix[i] << 16 | pix[i+1] << 8 | pix[i+2]);
            pxColors[ color / 8096 ] += 1;
        }
    }
#endif
```

The second uses the ofColor object and the getColor() method of ofPixels. Simply pass the location that you would like a color for and use the hue retrieved from getHue() to find which hue should be incremented:

```
#ifdef USE_OFCOLOR
    for (int i = 0; i < pix.getWidth(); i++) {
        for(int j = 0; j < pix.getHeight(); j++) {
            ofColor color = pix.getColor(i, j);
            pxColors[ int (color.getHue() * 8.0) ] += 1;
        }
    }
#endif

}

void histoSample::update(){ }
```

Since the pxColors array contains integer values, those need to be broken into the individual color values. Those values are then used to set the color that will be drawn with the line:

```
void histo::draw(){

    ofBackground(255, 255, 255);

#ifndef USE_OFCOLOR
    for(int i = 0; i < 2048; i++) {
        int il = i * 8096;
        int r = (il & 0xFF0000) >> 16;
        int g = (il & 0xFF00) >> 8;
        int b = il & 0xFF;
        ofSetColor(r, g, b);
        ofLine( i/2, 0, i/2,  pxColors[i] / 4 );
    }
#endif
#ifdef USE_OFCOLOR
    ofColor cl;
```

```
            cl.setHsb(255, 255, 255, 255);
            for(int i = 0; i < 2048; i++) {
                float ind = ofClamp((float) i / 8.f, 0.f, 255.f);
                cl.setHsb( ind, 255, 255, 255);
                ofSetColor(cl);
                ofLine( i/2, 0, i/2,  pxColors[i] / 8 );
            }
        #endif
        }
```

Again, the first method is ever-so-slightly faster, but doesn't look nearly as nice, since the colors aren't smoothly displayed across the hue spectrum.

## Analyzing Brightness

Brightness is another valuable and simple way of analyzing a bitmap. You can easily find the brightest pixel by looping through each pixel grabbed from a video and comparing it to the brightest pixel found (see Example 9-10 and Example 9-11):

*Example 9-10. OFBrightness.h*

```
#pragma mark once

#include "ofMain.h"

#define grabbedVidWidth 320
#define grabbedVidHeight 240

class OFBrightness : public ofBaseApp
{
    public:

        void setup();
        void update();
        void draw();

        unsigned char* drawingPixels;
        int brightestLoc[2];
        ofVideoGrabber videoIn;

};
```

*Example 9-11. OFBrightness.cpp*

```
#include "OFBrightness.h"

void OFBrightness::setup(){

    videoIn.initGrabber(grabbedVidWidth ,grabbedVidHeight);
}

void OFBrightness::update(){

    videoIn.grabFrame();
```

```
    int brightest = 0;
    int index = 0;

    if (videoIn.isFrameNew()) { //check to make sure the frame is new
        drawingPixels = videoIn.getPixels();
        int length  = grabbedVidWidth*grabbedVidHeight*3;
        for (int i = 0; i < length; i+=3) {
            unsigned char r = drawingPixels[i];
            unsigned char g = drawingPixels[i+1];
            unsigned char b = drawingPixels[i+2];

            if(int(r+g+b) > brightest) {
                brightest = int(r+g+b);
                brightestLoc[0] = (i/3) % grabbedVidWidth;
                brightestLoc[1] = (i/3) / grabbedVidWidth;
            }
        }
    }
}

void OFBrightness::draw(){
    ofSetColor(0xffffff);
    videoIn.draw(0, 0);
    ofEllipse(brightestLoc[0],brightestLoc[1], 10, 10);
}
```

Using the brightest point in an image or camera feed is an easy way to enable a user to create a cursor from a flashlight, an LED laser, or any other light source. If you can control the environment that will be used to generate the pixels, then other kinds of data can be used: most red, darkest, and so on.

## Detecting Motion

To detect motion in an oF or Processing application, simply store the pixels of a frame and compare them to the pixels of the next frame. 9-12 and 9-13 are pretty simple. If the difference between the pixels is greater than an arbitrary number (70 in the following example), then the pixel to be displayed is colored with a color that's changed on each frame. This highlights the movement in any frame:

*Example 9-12. OFMovement.h*

```
#pragma mark once

#include "ofMain.h"

#define GRABBED_VID_WIDTH 320
#define GRABBED_VID_HEIGHT 240

class moveTracker : public ofBaseApp{
```

```
    public:

        void setup();
        void update();
        void draw();

        ofPixels drawingPixels, dataPixels;

        ofVideoGrabber videoIn;
        ofTexture text;
        ofTexture history[40];
        int latestTexture;
        ofColor latestColor;
        float hue;
    };
```

*Example 9-13. OFMovement.cpp*

```
#include "moveTracker.h"


void moveTracker::setup(){

    videoIn.initGrabber(GRABBED_VID_WIDTH ,GRABBED_VID_HEIGHT);

    for( int i = 0; i<40; i++) {
        history[i].allocate(GRABBED_VID_WIDTH, GRABBED_VID_HEIGHT, GL_RGBA);
    }

    drawingPixels.allocate(GRABBED_VID_WIDTH, GRABBED_VID_HEIGHT, 4);

    latestTexture = 0;

    ofEnableAlphaBlending();

}

void moveTracker::update(){

    videoIn.grabFrame();

    if (videoIn.isFrameNew()){

        ofPixels tempPixels = videoIn.getPixelsRef();

        hue += 30.f;
        if(hue > 255.f) hue = 0;

        latestColor.setHsb(hue, 255, 255, 255);
        ofColor clear(0, 0, 0, 0.f);
```

If the difference across all three color components is greater than 40, it sets the pixel to our new color; otherwise just set it to clear:

```
for( int i = 0; i < GRABBED_VID_WIDTH; i++) {
    for( int j = 0; j < GRABBED_VID_HEIGHT; j++) {
        int r = fabs(tempPixels.getColor(i, j).r - dataPixels.getColor(i, j)
        .r);
        int g = fabs(tempPixels.getColor(i, j).g - dataPixels.getColor(i, j)
        .g);
        int b = fabs(tempPixels.getColor(i, j).b - dataPixels.getColor(i, j)
        .b);
        int diff = r+g+b;

        if( diff > 40 ) {
            drawingPixels.setColor(i, j, latestColor);
        } else {
            drawingPixels.setColor(i, j, clear);
        }
    }
}
```

Now that all the changed pixels have been colored, they are loaded into an ofTexture
object:

```
    // copy all the pixels over
    dataPixels = tempPixels;

    history[latestTexture].loadData(drawingPixels);
    latestTexture++;
    if(latestTexture > 39) {
        latestTexture = 0;
    }
    }
}
```

Now draw the video and all the history textures and you have a rainbow-hued history
of movement:

```
void moveTracker::draw(){


    videoIn.draw(20,20);

    for( int i = 0; i<40; i++)
    {
        history[i].draw(340, 20);
    }

}
```

Figure 9-5 shows the application in action.

*Figure 9-5. Detecting the changed pixels between images*

## Interview Zachary Lieberman

*Can you explain just a little bit of your background and more specifically how you, conceptually and philosophically, went from printmaking and painting to, for lack of a better term, interactive media art-making?*

**Zachary Lieberman:** My background is in fine arts: I studied painting and printmaking and it was accidental that I wound up working with technology. As I was approaching the end of undergraduate school, I had to find a job. At that time, it was very popular to be doing web design, so I bluffed my way into an interview. They wanted to see a design portfolio, and I actually brought slides of my painting. Somehow they saw something in me and decided to give me a shot. I was learning on the job, keeping books about Photoshop and Illustrator in my backpack as a reference. This was 1999. As the economy slid, we had a great amount of free time in the office, and I started to learn about folks doing amazing work in animation via Flash, online, like Yugo Nakamura, Amit Pitaru, and Joshua Davis. I had always loved animation, and for me, this medium seemed really promising. So I decided to jump into it.

*Looking at a lot of the work you make, it's very playful, it's very user driven, and it's very instantly understandable. Whereas a lot of times when I see people working with technology in art-making what they make is very wrapped up in "being technological." How do you keep your vision intact, even when dealing with what must have been fairly substantial engineering challenges at different points?*

**Zachary:** Thanks! That's an important part of the work that I do. I actually don't know how to answer this question. I want to say something like, "The trick to making work that is not technologically obsessed is to make work that is not technologically obsessed." For me, the answer has been to focus on the human—human nature, human gesture—and that helps get you past the technology.

*I was talking to Regine Debatty and she was bemoaning the great number of interactive pieces where, as she said: "You do something, and the machine does something, and that's it," I was thinking of how in a really reductive sense, the interaction in your pieces is really simple—you poke at things, or make shapes with your hands—but that the kinds of things that you can do with these simple interactions is really amazing. I was thinking that instead of making pieces for people to play with, you're quite often in essence making tools for people to make their own things, their own experiences, or sounds, or objects. Do you think of it this way as well?*

**Zachary:** While to some point I agree with Regine, I think the goal of the work is to overcome that. In many of the projects, we are asking participants to become performers, and because many of the works have a second life as a performance tool (like MIS, Messa, Drawn) they have a certain amount of depth to them. They can be expressive, and in that they hopefully offer the user more than just an input-leads-to-output-type result.

*This is, again, perhaps an odd question, but do you see yourself as being a part of a tradition in the way that, say, my friend who is a poet, sees a clear lineage of sorts from Gertrude Stein to herself? Is that important to you or not?*

**Zachary:** Yes, very clearly. First to the other generation of media artists, such as Masaki Fujihata, David Rokeby, Myron Krueger, and their peers, but also to abstract animators, like Norman McLaren, Oscar Fischinger, Mary Ellen Bute, and Len Lye. Their work is the inspiration for mine, and it's important to understand the historical precedents and the great lineage. I always argue that artistic practice is research, a sort of R&D for humanity, and if that's the case, it's important (like a scientist) to understand and absorb the research that's been done before you.

*Do you see your work in creating tools for artists to use and creating interactive artworks for participants/viewers/spectators as being aspects of the same project in a sense or as being quite different projects?*

**Zachary:** I see the toolmaking as an extension of the art-making process. I always like art that leads to art. You go to a museum, you get inspired, you buy a sketchbook and start drawing. It's not always like that, but when it is, it's one important facet. I see the toolmaking in the same way: can I use my artistic practice to make something that leads to more art?

I think the sharing is also in relation to the level of technique and how hard it is. The more sharing we do, the more understanding we have. There is a significantly higher level of complexity in the medium of computational arts, and therefore, the more we can illuminate the process, the quicker we can use the medium to express our voice.

*In the design world, you're paid by a client; in the art world, you're paid by a buyer or museum or gallery. There are quite clear channels for compensation that makes for clear venues for critical discussion, training, publicity, communication. How do you see the ecology around new media art: the opportunities for exhibition, for interaction with other artists, for publicity, for financial gain, for the critical discussion around it? Do you see these things as important in the same way that they're important in the other spheres?*

**Zachary:** The works I am involved are typically not objects (I describe them as systems), and therefore, they don't function very easily in the traditional art scene. Fortunately, there is a very healthy system of museums and festivals that are curious and experiment with exhibiting these kinds of projects. It seems that the more exposure people have to good work, the more risk taking that happens, which is good for the art form.

*One thing I like about oF is how it works with so many libraries, weaving them together in a very open way. That is a really C++ thing, philosophically, back all the way to Soustroup, and it's something that really differentiates oF from Arduino and Processing, which are also library based, but in a much more hidden way. Did you consciously think "we'll make this thing where people can learn C++ and this philosophy of assembling open source tools," or is that just a really wonderful side effect?*

**Zachary:** No, this was really conscious—because one of the hardest parts of programming, especially C++, is knowing how pieces can fit together. We want that to be totally transparent, so that beginners and experts alike can jump in and alter, fix bugs, etc. In making it open, we hoped to be able to teach a bit of the process too, so that others can either take that energy into add-ons, or on to other toolkits, if oF doesn't fit their needs. We want the code and library to be a bit of an education, and the public discussion about it has been supremely illuminating, especially for the developers.

*I know that oF came in some part from your teaching experiences at Parsons. Can you talk a little bit about other contexts in which you've used oF as a teaching tool, how you've structured it to be teachable or accessible for self-teaching.*

**Zachary:** Yes, it began as a teaching tool. It shares lineage with Processing, in that processing came out of the Aesthetics and Computation Group at MIT, led by John Maeda. That group, which ran from 96–03, had extremely prolific and talented students, like Ben Fry, Casey Reas, Golan Levin, Peter Cho, Elise Co, David Small, and so on. They are an amazing group. "And" in house, they had developed a closed source, C++ library called acu, which was their toolkit for making works. I learned C++ on this toolkit when I started to collaborate with Golan. acu in turn became p5. At the same time, when I started to teach, I realized that I couldn't give my students the acu tool to work from, so I started from scratch (and a great deal of inspiration) to create a new tool, for my own work and for my students. oF came out of that process.

It was funny, too, because I was sort of battling my department, which is an amazing one, at Parsons School of Design in New York, to let me teach C++. They kept saying, "These are art students; they won't be able to handle it." That kind of response only inspired me more, and once I started teaching it, my students proved the naysayers wrong. I saw the amazing projects that students made, like Evan Roth's *Graffiti Analysis Project,* or Theo Watson's *Audio Space,* and I realized that this was a necessary tool to have out there.

I use it in workshops, short ones that look at oF and how to make works that leave the screen, and larger ones like "Interactivos?" where students spend two weeks making a fully realized project.

As for structuring the library to be useful in those situations, there are a few simple things we did—made code that is its own best documentation, chose simple design patterns that made it easy for non-C++ experts, tried to envision what skills people had and what they might need to pick up from the examples, and made everything work at both a high level and low level, so it's easy to get into but also provides room for experimentation.

*Do you envision oF being a tool that people can use in commercial projects, and would you feel at all conflicted about that?*

**Zachary:** Yes, it always is being used for commercial projects, including my own, and I know there is not a fine line between artistic and commercial practice. I am super glad if we put out something that helps someone bring home the bacon. I don't feel conflicted one bit.

*Are there particular things that you hope to see designers and artists using oF for that you aren't seeing at the moment?*

**Zachary:** We are really seeing a wide range of work, where you can clearly see people's voices coming through. It doesn't feel like a "tool," which is something I'm really proud of. As for what I'd like to see, we are starting to push a bit this next release with the hardware integration, via firmata, so I hope that leads to more interesting hardware/software connections. But besides that, we've been overwhelmed with all the great ideas that have come from the community.

*As you've been working on oF, have you found its audience changing, or your goals for it changing, or have these things remained fairly consistent over the years?*

**Zachary:** It's funny, but new audiences bring new changes. For example, I went for a year to work on oF in Barcelona, and everyone there was a huge Linux fanatic (and gave me a hard time for using Windows). That really pushed us to support Linux in a major way. Now, when we just went to Japan, we met a new set of really advanced users and understood what they were interested in, which will push us for a new set of features. As the user base expands, our job is to listen, to take requests, and to try to make a tool (and a platform) that is flexible for as many people as possible.

One thing that's been extremely helpful in this, which I can't stress enough, is meeting people face to face. We've been trying to do that as much as we can now—through the knitting circles (informal get togethers, held now in New York, Madrid, Stockholm, and Barcelona), the oF Lab (a research lab we held at Ars Electronica), and through workshops—and the result is a much tighter community.

*Do you have any big, long-term plans for oF? Are there things you want it to do or provide that are different than what it does and provides at present?*

**Zachary:** The long-term plan is to keep pushing and refining the tool, keep strengthening the community and keep providing better ways for people to get involved or put their energy in. Our primary goal is always the same, and hasn't changed one ounce: to have as much fun as we can making work (and the tools), and to do the best we can to help others make work, too.

# Using Edge Detection

Another interesting piece of information that pixels can tell us is the location of edges in the image. This verges on the territory that will be covered in Chapter 14, but it's a nice way to think a little more in depth about what you can do when processing pixels.

Edges characterize boundaries between objects, which makes them very interesting and important in image processing. *Edges* in images are areas with strong intensity contrasts, a jump in intensity from one pixel to the next. The goal in edge detection is to reduce the amount of data and filter out any nonedge information from an image while still preserving the important structural properties of an image, which is the basic shape of what is displayed in the image. This is done in much the same way as in the bitmap filtering example. Though the Processing code in that example filtered the image, increasing the contrast, the fundamental way that the operation works is the same: we create a 3 × 3 array that will serve as the kernel, process each pixel according to that kernel, and set the value of the pixel to the result of multiplying it by the kernel.

Two of the most popular edge-detection algorithms are called Sobel and Prewitt. These are named after their respective authors, Irwin Sobel and JMS Prewitt. They operate in very similar ways: by looping through each pixel and comparing the amount of change across the surrounding nine pixels in both the *x* and *y* directions. Then the algorithm sums the differences and determines whether the change is great enough to be considered an edge. Whichever algorithm you choose, once it has done its job by returning the amount of change around a given pixel, you can decide what you'd like to do with it. In the following example, if the change in a pixel isn't great enough to be considered an edge, then it's painted darker by darkening the color values of each pixel. If it is an edge, then it's painted lighter by lightening the pixel. This way, an image where the edges are white and the nonedges are dark can be produced. You are of course free to use these detected images in whatever way you like.

First, here's the EdgeDetect header file for the oF application (see Example 9-14):

*Example 9-14. EdgeDetect.h*

```
#pragma mark once
#include "ofMain.h"


class EdgeDetect : public ofBaseApp{

public:

    void setup();
    void update();
    void draw();
    int setPixel(unsigned char* px, int startPixel, int dep,
                int depthOfNextLine, int depthOfNextNextLine,
                const int matrix[3][3]);

    void edgeDetect1Channel(); // this is for grayscale images,
    // with only gray pixels
    void edgeDetect3Channel(); // this is for color images with an RGB

    void keyPressed(int key);

    int sobelHorizontal[3][3]; // here's the sobel kernel
```

```
    int sobelVertical[3][3];

    int prewittHorizontal[3][3]; // here's the prewitt kernel
    int prewittVertical[3][3];

    unsigned char* edgeDetectedData;
    ofImage img;
    ofImage newImg;

    int dwThreshold;
    bool updateImg;

    string imagePath;

};
```

*Example 9-15. EdgeDetect.cpp*

```
#include "EdgeDetect.h"

void EdgeDetect::setup(){
```

The following code sets up the different kernels that will be used for the edge detection:

```
        sobelHorizontal[0][0] = -1; sobelHorizontal[0][1] = 0; sobelHorizontal[0][2]= 1;
        sobelHorizontal[1][0] = -2; sobelHorizontal[1][1] = 0; sobelHorizontal[1][2] = 2;
        sobelHorizontal[2][0] = -1; sobelHorizontal[2][1]= 0; sobelHorizontal[2][2] = 1;

        sobelVertical[0][0] = 1; sobelVertical[0][1] = 2; sobelVertical[0][2]= 1;
        sobelVertical[1][0] = 0; sobelVertical[1][1] = 0; sobelVertical[1][2] = 0;
        sobelVertical[2][0] = -1; sobelVertical[2][1]= -2; sobelVertical[2][2] = -1;
```

This is the matrix for the Prewitt edge detection that will be used with color images:

```
        prewittHorizontal[0][0] = 1; prewittHorizontal[0][1] = 1; prewittHorizontal[0][2]= 1;
        prewittHorizontal[1][0] = 0; prewittHorizontal[1][1] = 0; prewittHorizontal[1][2] = 0;
        prewittHorizontal[2][0] = -1; prewittHorizontal[2][1] = -1; prewittHorizontal[2][2] = -1;

        prewittVertical[0][0] = 1; prewittVertical[0][1] = 0; prewittVertical[0]
        [2]= -1;
        prewittVertical[1][0] = 1; prewittVertical[1][1] = 0; prewittVertical[1]
        [2] = -1;
        prewittVertical[2][0] = 1; prewittVertical[2][1] = 0; prewittVertical[2]
        [2] = -1;
```

Next, load an image. If you want to use a color image, then you can load the *test.jpg* image that is included with the downloadable code file for this chapter. Otherwise, you can use the grayscale image, *test.bmp*, also included in the code file. The difference between the two is rather important—the bitmap image has one byte per pixel because each pixel is only a grayscale value, and the JPEG image has three bytes per pixel because it contains the red, green, and blue channels:

```
        imagePath = "hello.jpg"; // there's also a hello.bmp to test 1 channel

        img.loadImage(imagePath);
```

```
// set aside memory for the image
edgeDetectedData = new unsigned char[img.width * img.height * 3];

updateImg = true;
dwThreshold = 100;
}
```

Here the type of edge detection is set. If the image is color, then you'll want to use the edgeDetect3D() method; otherwise use the edgeDetect1Channel() method:

```
void EdgeDetect::update(){
    ofBackground(255, 255, 255);
    if(updateImg) {
        if(img.getPixelsRef().getNumChannels() == 3) {
            edgeDetect3Channel();
        } else {
            edgeDetect1Channel();
        }
        updateImg = false;
    }
}
```

The simple part is drawing the images: first the original image and then the edge-detected image that's been created from running the edge-detection algorithms:

```
void EdgeDetect::draw(){
    img.draw(0, 0);
    newImg.draw(img.width, 0);
}
```

This is the edge detection for images that are grayscale, that is, that have only one byte per pixel, which is why there's an "1Channel" at the end of the method name. It loops through each pixel of the image and multiplies it by the Sobel kernel, just like you've seen in the other convolution kernel examples from earlier in this chapter:

```
void EdgeDetect::edgeDetect1Channel() {
    int xPx, yPx, i, j, sum, sumY, sumX = 0;

    unsigned char* originalImageData = img.getPixels();

    int heightVal = img.getHeight();
    int widthVal = img.getWidth();

    for(yPx=0; yPx < heightVal; yPx++)  {
        for(xPx=0; xPx < widthVal; xPx++)  {
            sumX = 0;
            sumY = 0;
```

If you're analyzing the image boundaries, then just set sum to 0, because there won't be surrounding pixels on at least one side to run the algorithm correctly:

```
if( yPx == 0) {
    sum = 0;
} else if( xPx == 0) {
    sum = 0;
} else   { // Convolution starts here
```

Here, you find the change on the x-axis and the y-axis by multiplying the value of each pixel around the current pixel being examined by the appropriate value in the Sobel kernel. Since there are two kernels, one for the x-axis and one for the y-axis, there are two `for` loops that loop through each pixel surrounding the current pixel:

```
for(i=-1; i<=1; i++)  {
        for(j=-1; j<=1; j++)  {
            sumX = sumX + (int) originalImageData [(yPx + j) *
            img.width + xPx + i] * sobelHorizontal[i + 1][j + 1];
        }
    }
```

Now find the amount of change along the y-axis:

```
    for(j=-1; j<=1; j++)  {
        sumY = sumY + (int) originalImageData[(yPx + j) * img.width
        + xPx + i] * sobelVertical[i + 1][j + 1];
    }
}
// add them up
sum = abs(sumX) + abs(sumY);
}
```

Here the values are *thresholded*; that is, results that are less than 210 are set to 0. This makes the edges appear much more dramatically:

```
if(sum>255) sum=255;
if(sum<210) sum=0;
```

Now all the edge-detected pixels are set to white by taking the `sum` value and subtracting it from 255 to make a white pixel out of any values that are 0:

```
edgeDetectedData[ yPx * img.width + xPx ] = 255 - (unsigned char)(sum);
    }
}
```

Now that the application has loaded the data into the `edgeDetectedData` array, copy the values from `edgeDetectedData` into the `newImg` instance for `ofImage`:

```
    newImg.setFromPixels(edgeDetectedData, img.width, img.height,
                                    OF_IMAGE_GRAYSCALE, false);
}
```

```
void EdgeDetect::edgeDetect3Channel() {

    unsigned char* imgPixels = img.getPixels();
    unsigned int x,y,nWidth,nHeight;
    int firstPix, secondPix, dwThreshold;
```

Now determine the number of pixels that are contained in a single horizontal line of the image. This will be important because as you run through each pixel, you'll need to know the locations of the pixels around it to use them in calculations:

```
    int horizLength = (nWidth * 3);
    long horizOffset = horizLength - nWidth * 3;
```

```
nHeight = img.height- 2;
nWidth  = img.width - 2;
```

Now, as in the `edgeDetect1Channel()` method, loop through every pixel in the image. Since this method is supposed to be checking all three values of the pixel, R, G, and B, you'll notice there are three different values being set in the `edgeDetectedData` array. The code is a little more compact than the `edgeDetect1Channel()` method, because the actual multiplication of each surrounding pixel by the appropriate value in the kernel is now in the `setPixel()` method, making things a little tidier:

```
for( y = 0; y < nHeight;++y) {
    for( x = 0 ; x < nWidth; ++x) {
```

It's important to keep track of where the locations of the pixels around the current pixel are. This code will be the location above the current pixel in the array of pixels. `center` is the value of the pixel currently being calculated, and `below` is the value of the pixel below the pixel being calculated:

```
long above = (x*3) +(y*horizLength);
long center = above + horizLength;
long below = center + horizLength;
```

Next, compare the red values of the pixels:

```
firstPix = setPixel(imgPixels, 2, above, center, below, prewittHorizontal);
secondPix = setPixel(imgPixels, 2, above, center, below, prewittVertical);
edgeDetectedData[5 + center] = max(dwThreshold, min( (int)sqrt(pow(firstPix,
2.f)+pow(secondPix,2.f)), 255 ));
```

Compare the blue values of the pixels:

```
firstPix = setPixel(imgPixels, 1, above, center, below, prewittHorizontal);
secondPix = setPixel(imgPixels, 1, above, center, below, prewittVertical);
edgeDetectedData[4 + center] = max(dwThreshold, min( (int) sqrt(pow(firstPix,
2.f)+pow(secondPix,2.f)), 255 ));
```

Compare the green values:

```
firstPix = setPixel(imgPixels, 1, above, center, below, prewittHorizontal);
secondPix = setPixel(imgPixels, 1, above, center, below, prewittVertical);
edgeDetectedData[3 + center] = max(dwThreshold, min( (int) sqrt(pow(firstPix,
2.f) + pow(secondPix,2.f)), 255 ));
```

```
    }
}
```

Now set the bitmap data for the new image:

```
newImg.setFromPixels(edgeDetectedData, img.width, img.height,
    OF_IMAGE_COLOR, true);
}
```

Last up is multiplying the value of the pixel and the pixels around it by the kernel to get the value that the pixel should be set to:

```
int EdgeDetect::setPixel(unsigned char* px, int
  startPixel, int above,      int center, int below, const int matrix[][3]) {
    return (
        (px[startPixel + above] * matrix[0][0]) +
            (px[startPixel + 3 + above] * matrix[0][1]) +
        (px[startPixel + 6 + above] * matrix[0][2]) +
            (px[startPixel + center] * matrix[1][0])+
        (px[startPixel + 3 + center ] * matrix[1][1]) +
            (px[startPixel + 6 +center] * matrix[1][2]) +
        (px[startPixel + below]* matrix[2][0]) +
            (px[startPixel + 3 +below]* matrix[2][1]) +
        (px[startPixel + 6 + below]* matrix[2][2])) ;
}

void EdgeDetect::keyPressed(int key) {
    if(key == '+')
        dwThreshold += 10;

    if(key == '-')
        dwThreshold -= 10;

    updateImg = true;
}
```

Figure 9-6 shows the result of running the edge detection on a photo.

*Figure 9-6. Edge-detection results on a photo*

The most famous and one of the most accurate edge-detection algorithms is called the
Canny edge-detection algorithm after its inventor John Canny. The code is a little more

complex and lengthy than there is room for here but there are easy implementations for Processing and oF that you can find by looking on the Processing and oF websites.

## Using Pixel Data

We've been discussing pixels as data, and that extends beyond manipulating the pixels on the screen. Those pixels are valid data to use as physical information as well on controls like an LED matrix. An LED matrix is simply an array of LED lights that come in 8 × 8, 12 × 12, or even larger configurations. One of my favorite ways to connect an LED matrix to an Arduino is the LoLShield, made by Jimmie Rodgers.

The LoLShield has 14 rows of 9 LED columns, meaning 126 LEDs that can be individually addressed using a technique called Charlieplexing. The particulars of how this technique works are a little lengthy for this chapter (feel free to look it up online) but you can think of it as a very clever way to drive a lot of LEDs without a lot of pins. To be more specific, for $N$ pins, you can $N * (N–1)$ pins. In the case of the LoLShield, 12 of the Arduino's digital pins are taken up powering the 126 LEDs, but it doesn't require any additional power. You'll need to grab the LoLShield library from its Google Code repository at *code.google.com/p/lolshield/*. Note, this is *not* the Charlieplexing library from the Arduino site; it's a similar but different library from the LoLShield site.

Once you've installed the LoLShield library, start by including the library, as shown in Example 9-16.

*Example 9-16. LEDMovement.ino*

```
#include "Charlieplexing.h"
```

Now declare some variables to store the incoming variables:

```
int incomingRow, incomingColumn;

void setup() {
  Serial.begin(57600);
}

void loop() {
```

If information is being sent, then clear the display by looping through each LED and turn it off:

```
for(uint8_t y = 0; y < 9; y++) {
  for(uint8_t x = 3; x < 11; x++) {
    LedSign::Set(x,y,0);
    }
}

// read the incoming byte:
```

Now to read and turn on LEDs based on the indices sent from the oF application:

```
        while(Serial.available() > 0) {
          if(Serial.read() == 'x') {
            incomingRow = Serial.read();
              incomingColumn = Serial.read();
            LedSign::Set(incomingRow, incomingColumn, 1);
          }
        }
    }
```

Now take a look at the oF code in Example 9-17.

*Example 9-17. LEDMovement.h*

```
#include "ofMain.h"

#define GRABBED_VID_WIDTH 320
#define GRABBED_VID_HEIGHT 240

class LEDMovement : public ofBaseApp{

    public:

        void setup();
        void update();
        void draw();

        int motionVals[126];
        int totalPixels
        unsigned char dataPixels[GRABBED_VID_WIDTH * GRABBED_VID_HEIGHT * 3];
        ofVideoGrabber videoIn;
        ofSerial serial;
};
```

The oF code is much the same as the motion detection code shown earlier in this chapter. The incoming pixels from the **ofVideoGrabber** instance are compared to the pixels of the previous frame. Since the LED matrix has only 64 LEDs, one way to fix the pixels of the video into those 64 values is to divide the screen into 64 pieces. Create an array of 64 value and increment the appropriate value in the array if there is movement in that quadrant of the frame (see Example 9-18):?

*Example 9-18. LEDMovement.cpp*

```
#include "LEDMovement.h"

void LEDMovement::setup() {

    videoIn.initGrabber(GRABBED_VID_WIDTH ,GRABBED_VID_HEIGHT);
    serial.setup("/dev/tty.usbserial-A4000Qek", 57600);
    totalPixels = GRABBED_VID_WIDTH*GRABBED_VID_HEIGHT*3;
}

void LEDMovement::update() {

    videoIn.grabFrame();
```

```
if (videoIn.isFrameNew()) {
    unsigned char * tempPixels = videoIn.getPixels();
    int i;
    for(i = 0; i < 126; i++) {
        motionVals[i] = 0;
    }

    for (i = 0; i < totalPixels; i+=3) {
        unsigned char r = abs(tempPixels[i] - dataPixels[i]);
        unsigned char g = abs(tempPixels[i+1] - dataPixels[i+1]);
        unsigned char b = abs(tempPixels[i+2] - dataPixels[i+2]);

        int diff = r+g+b;
        if (diff > 70)  {
            motionVals[totalPixels/610]++;
        }

        tempPixels[i] = dataPixels[i];
        tempPixels[i+1] = dataPixels[i+1];
        tempPixels[i+2] = dataPixels[i+2];

    }
```

For each value in the array, check whether the motion in that quadrant of the frame is above an arbitrary amount (in this case, 100), and if it is, then send it to the serial port for the Arduino to read:

```
    for(i = 0; i < 126; i++)
    {
        if(motionVals[i] > 70) {
            serial.writeByte('x');
            serial.writeByte(i % 8);
            serial.writeByte(i / 8);
        }
    }
  }
}

void LEDMovement::draw(){
    videoIn.draw(20,20);
}
```

This is just the tip of the iceberg, as they say. A few other more playful ideas that come to mind are: connecting multiple household lights to an Arduino and turning them on or off based on some pixel data; attaching a servo to a USB web camera and using the motion analysis to turn the camera toward whatever is moving in the frame; and creating a simple system of notation that uses color and edges to play the notes of the musical scale. On a more practical level, pixel analysis is the start of computer vision techniques. What you've learned in this chapter isn't quite enough to begin to develop gestural interfaces that a user interacts with via a touchscreen, or simply by using their hands, or using marked symbols as UI objects (these are called *fiducials*). It is, however, a start on the road to being able to do that and should give you some ideas as you consider how to create the interaction between your users and your system.

# Using Textures

Textures are a way of using your bitmaps in a more dynamic and interesting way, particularly once they're coupled with OpenGL drawing techniques. You've already used textures without knowing it because the ofImage class actually contains a texture that is drawn to the screen when you call the draw() method. Though it might seem that a texture is just a bitmap, it's actually a little different. Textures are how bitmaps get drawn to the screen; the bitmap is loaded into a texture that then can be used to draw into a shape defined in OpenGL. I've always thought of textures as being like wrapping paper: they don't define the shape of the box, but they do define what you see when you look at the box. Most of the textures that we've looked at so far are used in a very simple way only, sort of like just holding up a square piece of wrapping paper. Now, we'll start to look at some of the more dynamic ways to use that metaphorical paper, curling it up, wrapping boxes, and so on. Textures are very much a part of learning OpenGL, and as such we're going to need to tread lightly to avoid talking too much about things that you'll learn in Chapter 13.

Processing and oF both use textures, but in very different ways. oF draws using the Graphics Language Utility Toolkit (GLUT) library, which in turn uses OpenGL. Processing draws to OpenGL optionally, and it uses textures only when you use the OpenGL mode. You set this mode when declaring your window size, which we'll see later. Now, on to the most important part: when you draw in OpenGL, any pixel data that you want to put on the screen must be preloaded into your graphics card's RAM memory before you can draw it. Loading all this pixel data to your graphics card's RAM is called *loading* your image into a texture, and it's the texture that tells the OpenGL engine on your graphics card how to draw those pixels to the screen.

The Processing PImage is a good place to start thinking about textures and bitmaps. The PImage is often used to load picture files into a Processing application:

```
PImage myPImage; // allocate space for variable
// allocate space for pixels in ram, decode the jpg, and
// load pixels of the decoded sample.jpg into the pixels.
myPImage = loadImage("sample.jpg");
image(myPImage,100,100); // draw the texture to the screen at 100,100
```

The PImage is a texture object that has a built-in color array that holds pixel values so that you can access the individual pixels of the image that you have loaded in. When you call loadImage(), you're just pointing to the file, loading the data from that file into an array of bytes, and then turning that array of bytes into a texture that can be drawn to the screen.

Remember how you access the individual pixels of the screen? You first call loadPix els(), make your pixel changes, and then call updatePixels() to make your changes appear. Although you use a different function altogether, what happens is the same as what happened in the previous Processing application with PImage: Processing is loading your pixels from the screen into a texture, essentially a PImage, and then drawing that texture to the screen after you update it. The point here is that you've already been working with textures, those drawable arrays of bitmap data, all along.

The ofImage class also has a texture object inside it. The oF version of the previous Processing application code is shown here:

```
ofImage myImage;
// allocate space in ram, then decode the jpg, and finally load the pixels into
// the ofTexture object that the ofImage contains.
myImage.loadImage("sample.jpg");
myImage.draw(100,100);
```

The ofImage object loads images from files using loadImage() and images from the screen using the grabScreen() method. Both of these load data into the internal texture that the ofImage class contains. When you call the draw() method of the ofImage class, you're simply drawing the texture to the screen. If you wanted to change the pixels on the screen, you would also use an ofImage class to capture the image and then load the data into an array using the getPixels() method. After that, you could manipulate the array and then load it back into the image using setFromPixels():

```
ofImage theScreen; // declare variable
theScreen.grabScreen(0,0,1024,768); // grab at 0,0 a rect of 1024×768.
                                     // similar to loadPixels();
unsigned char * screenPixels = theScreen.getPixels();
// do something here to edit pixels in screenPixels
// ...
// now load them back into theScreen
theScreen.setFromPixels(screenPixels, theScreen.width, theScreen.height,
    OF_IMAGE_COLOR, true);
// now you can draw them
theScreen.draw(0,0); // equivalent to the Processing updatePixels();
```

You can edit the pixels of an ofImage because ofImage objects contain two data structures: an array of unsigned char variables Array is singular all the colors of every pixel in the image, and a texture (which is actually an ofTexture object, the next thing that we'll discuss) that is used to upload those pixels into the GPU RAM after changes.

## Textures in oF

Textures in openFrameworks are contained inside the ofTexture object. This can be used to create textures from bitmap data that can then be used to fill other drawn objects, like a bitmap fill on a circle. Though it may seem difficult, earlier examples in this chapter used it without explaining it fully; it's really just a way of storing all the data for a bitmap. If you understand how a bitmap can also be data, that is, be an array of unsigned char values, then you basically understand the ofTexture already. The ofTexture creates data that can be drawn to the screen. A quick tour of the methods of the ofTexture class will give you a better idea how it works:

## void allocate(int w, int h, int internalGlDataType)

This method allocates space for the OpenGL texture. The width (w) and height (h) do not necessarily need to be powers of two, but they do need to be large enough to contain the data you will upload to the texture. The internal datatype describes how OpenGL will store this texture internally. For example, if you want a grayscale texture, you can use GL_LUMINANCE. You can upload whatever type of data you want (using loadData()), but internally, OpenGL will store the information as grayscale. Other types include GL_RGB and GL_RGBA.

## void clear()

This method clears/frees the texture memory if something was already allocated. This is useful if you need to control the memory on the graphics card.

## void loadData(unsigned char * data, int w, int h, int glDataType)

This method loads the array of unsigned chars (data) into the texture, with a given width (w) and height (h). You also pass in the format that the data is stored in (GL_LUMINANCE, GL_RGB, GL_RGBA). For example, to upload a 200 × 100 pixels wide RGB array into an already allocated texture, you might use the following:

```
unsigned char pixels[200*100*3];
for (int i = 0; i < 200*100*3; i++){
    pixels[i] = (int)(255 * ofRandomuf());
}
myTexture.loadData(pixels, 200, 100, GL_RGB);
```

## void draw(float x, float y, float w, float h)

This method draws the texture at a given point (x, y) using a given width and height. This can be used if you simply want to draw the texture as a square. If you want to do something a little more complex, you'll have to use a few OpenGL calls. You'll see in the following application how to draw an **ofTexture** object to an arbitrarily sized shape. This is the first look at OpenGL in this book and it might look a bit strange at first, but the calls are very similar to a lot of the drawing API methods that you've learned in both Processing and oF. Since the point here is to show how the **ofTexture** is used, we won't dwell too much on the GL calls and instead concentrate on the methods of the **ofTexture**. Chapter 13 is entirely dedicated to OpenGL and 3-D graphics, so you may want to look ahead to that chapter after you finish this one.

In the header file for this application, seen in Example 9-19, there is an **ofTexture** instance and a pointer to pixels that will be used to store data for the texture. Everything else is pretty standard:

*Example 9-19. textureDemo.h*

```
#pragma mark once

#include "ofMain.h"

class textureDemo : public ofBaseApp{
```

```
    public:

        void setup();
        void update();
        void draw();
        void mouseMoved(int x, int y );

        ofTexture colorTexture;
        int            w, h;
        ofPixels colorPixels;
         bool countUp;
        float blue;

};
```

*Example 9-20. TextureDemo.cpp*

```
#include "textureDemo.h"

void textureDemo::setup(){

    w = 500;
    h = 500;
    colorTexture.allocate( w, h, GL_RGB );
    colorPixels.allocate( w, h, 3 );

    // color pixels, use w and h to control red and green
    ofColor col;
    for (int i = 0; i < w; i++){
        for (int j = 0; j < h; j++){
            col.set( i, j, 0 );
            colorPixels.setColor( j, i, col );
        }
    }
    // this is important, we load the data into the texture,
    // preparing it to be used by the OpenGL renderer
    colorTexture.loadData(colorPixels);
    countUp = true;
}


void textureDemo::update(){
    if( countUp ) {
        blue += 0.1;
    } else {
        blue -= 0.1;
    }

    if( blue > 254 || blue < 1 )
        countUp = !countUp;
}

void textureDemo::draw(){
    ofBackground(255,255,255);
    colorTexture.draw(0, 0, mouseX, mouseY);
}
```

```
void textureDemo::mouseMoved(int x, int y ){

    ofColor col;
    // when the mouse moves, we change the color image:
    float pct = (float)x / (float)ofGetWidth();
    for (int i = 0; i < w; i++){
        for (int j = 0; j < h; j++){
            col.set( i/2, j/2, pct );
            colorPixels.setColor( j, i, col );
        }
    }
    // finally, load those pixels into the texture
    colorTexture.loadData(colorPixels );
}
```

The mouseMoved() method updates all the values in the colorPixels array to update the pixels in the texture. This will slow down the application some, but as soon as you're done loading data into the texture it's more or less free to draw it any time:

```
void textureDemo::mouseMoved(int x, int y ){

    ofColor col;
    // when the mouse moves, we change the color image:
    for (int i = 0; i < w; i++){
        for (int j = 0; j < h; j++){
            col.set( i/2, j/2, blue );
            colorPixels.setColor( j, i, col );
        }
    }
    // finally, load those pixels into the texture
    colorTexture.loadData(colorPixels );
}
```

In Chapter 13, you'll learn a lot more about some of the OpenGL calls that were used in this sample code, so for the moment we'll move on to covering textures in Processing.

## Textures in Processing

In Processing, when you use the OpenGL mode, a texture is stored inside a PImage object. To draw the PImage to the screen, either you can use the image() method to draw the PImage directly to the screen or you can use the PImage as a texture for drawing using the fill() and vertex() methods. There are five important methods that you need to understand to draw with a texture:

size(400, 400, P3D);
    When you call the size() method to set the size the application stage, you need to pass three parameters. The first two are the dimensions, and the third parameter is the P3D constant that tells the PApplet to use a 3-D renderer. That means that all the calls to vertex() and fill() need to reflect that they are being drawn into a three-dimensional space rather than a two-dimensional space.

```
textureMode(NORMALIZED);
```
This method sets the coordinate space for how the texture will be mapped to whatever shape it's drawn onto. There are two options: `IMAGE`, which refers to the actual coordinates of the image being used to create the image, and `NORMALIZED`, which refers to a normalized space of values ranging from 0 to 1. This is very relevant to how the `vertex()` method is used, because the fourth and fifth parameters are the locations of the texture that should be mapped to the location of the vertex. If you're using the `IMAGE textureMode()` method, then the bottom-right corner of a 200 × 100 pixel texture would be 200, 100. If you're using `NORMAL IZED`, then the bottom-right corner of the same texture would be 1.0,1.0.

```
texture(PImage t);
```
This method sets a texture to be applied to vertex points. The `texture()` function must be called between `beginShape()` and `endShape()` and before any calls to `ver tex()`. When textures are in use, the fill color is ignored. Instead, use `tint()` to specify the color of the texture as it is applied to the shape.

```
beginShape(MODE);
```
This shape begins recording vertices for a shape, and `endShape()` stops recording. The value of the `MODE` parameter tells it which types of shapes to create from the provided vertices; the possible values are `POINTS`, `LINES`, `TRIANGLES`, `TRIANGLE_FAN`, `TRIANGLE_STRIP`, `QUADS`, and `QUAD_STRIP`. The upcoming example uses the `QUADS` mode, and the rest of these modes will be discussed in Chapter 13. For the moment, you just need to understand that every vertex created by a call to `vertex()` will create a quadrilateral.

```
vertex(x, y, z, u, v);
```
All shapes are constructed by connecting a series of vertices. The method `ver tex()` is used to specify the vertex coordinates for points, lines, triangles, quads, and polygons and is used exclusively within the `beginShape()` and `endShape()` functions. The first three parameters are the position of the vertex, and the last two indicate the horizontal and vertical coordinates for the texture. You can think of this as being where the edge of the texture should be set to go. It can be larger than the vertex or smaller, but this will cause it to be clipped if it's greater than the location of the vertex. One way to think of this is like a tablecloth on a table. The cloth can be longer than the table or smaller, but if it's longer, then it will simply drape off the end, and if it's shorter, then it will end before the table.

In the following code, an image is used as a texture and followed by a color interpolation and the default illumination. The shading of the surfaces, produced by means of the illumination and the colors, is multiplied by the colors of the texture:

*Example 9-21. textureDemo.pde*

```
PImage a;

void setup() {
    size(400,400,P3D);
```

```
    a = loadImage("test2.png");
}

void draw() {
    background(255);
    textureMode(NORMALIZED);
    beginShape(QUADS);
    texture(a);
        vertex(0, 0, 0, 0, 0);
        vertex(200, 0, 0, 0, 1.0);
        vertex(200, 200, 0, 1.0, 1.0);
        vertex(0, 200, 0, 1.0, 1.0);
    endShape();
    beginShape();
        texture(a);
        vertex(200, 0, 0, 0, 0);
        vertex(mouseX, 0, 0, 1.0, 0);
        vertex(mouseX, 200, 0, 1.0, 1.0);
        vertex(200, 200, 0, 0, 1.0);
    endShape();
}
```

In addition to generating textures from JPEG files, you can also generate a texture
yourself. For example, the pattern of a chessboard can be generated by creating a
PImage, filling it with an empty image, and then setting the value of each pixel in the
image. See Example 9-22.

*Example 9-22. textureFromImage.pde*

```
PImage textureImg;
void setup() {

    size(300, 300);
    // dummy image colorMode(RGB,1);
    textureImg = loadImage("test.png");

    color col;
    int squareWidth = 20;
    boolean isBlack = true;
```

Look through each pixel of the image and use the area of each square on the chessboard
to determine what color the pixel should be colored. If the square being currently drawn
is black, switch to white, when the end of the square is reached and so on, until the
edge of the image:

```
        for( int i = 0; i < textureImg.height; i++) {
            for ( int j = 0; j < textureImg.width; j++) {
                if(j % squareWidth == 0) {
                    isBlack = !isBlack;
                }
                if(isBlack) {
            textureImg.pixels[ i * textureImg.width + j] = color(255);
                } else {
                    textureImg.pixels[ i * textureImg.width + j] = color(0);
```

```
                }
            }
            if(i % squareWidth != 0 && i != 0) {
                isBlack = !isBlack;
            }
        }
    }
}

void draw() {
    image(textureImg, 0, 0);
}
```

## Saving a Bitmap

You've learned how to load bitmaps, now take a look at saving them. In oF, saving an image is handled through the ofImage class. The saveImage() method allows you to write a file by default to the data folder of your oF application, though you can write it anywhere else:

```
void saveImage(string fileName);
```

This means that you can also take a screenshot and then save the image by calling the grabScreen() method and then calling the saveImage() method. You can save in all the common file formats, and if you try to save to a format that oF doesn't understand it will be saved as a bitmap file.

In Processing, the same thing can be accomplished by calling the save() method, as shown here in the keyPressed() handler of an application:

```
void keyPressed() {
    if(key == ENTER) {
        save("file.png");
    }
}
```

Images are saved in TIFF, TARGA, JPEG, and PNG format, depending on the extension within the filename parameter. If no extension is included in the filename, the image will save in TIFF format, and .tif will be added to the name. These files are saved to the sketch's folder, which may be opened by selecting "Show sketch folder" from the Sketch menu. You can't call save() while running the program in a web browser. All images saved from the main drawing window will have an opaque background; however, you can save images without a background by using the createGraphics() method:

```
createGraphics(width, height, renderer, filename);
```

The filename parameter is optional and depends on the renderer that is used. The renderers that Processing can use with the createGraphics() methods that *don't* require a filename are the P2D, P3D, and JAVA2D. There's more information on these different renderers in Chapter 13. The DXF renderer for DXF files and PDF renderer for creating PDF files both require the filename parameter. The OPENGL mode doesn't allow offscreen use, so it's not possible to use createGraphics() method with it. Unlike the main drawing surface, which is completely opaque, surfaces created with `createGraphics()` can have transparency. So, you can use `save()` to write a PNG or a TGA file and the transparency of the graphics that you create will translate to the saved file. Note, though, that with transparency, it's either opaque or transparent; there's no half transparency for saved images.

## What's Next

Now that you've learned some about textures and about how your computer creates and interprets graphics, a logical next step is to look ahead to Chapter 13 on OpenGL. If you're particularly interested in learning more about image processing, motion detection, or face detection, look ahead to Chapter 14. You can also, of course, continue reading the book straight through.

For more image-processing examples, take a look at some books, such as Casey Reas' and Ben Fry's *Processing* (MIT Press), Daniel Shiffman's *Learning Processing* (Morgan Kaufmann) and *The Nature of Code* (*http://www.shiffman.net/teaching/nature/*), and Ira Greenberg's *Processing: Creative Coding and Computational Art* (Springer). There aren't a great deal of introductory-level image-processing or signal-processing texts out there, but *Practical Algorithms for Image Analysis* by Lawrence O'Gorman et al. (Cambridge University Press) is the closest thing I've found. Be advised, though: it isn't a simple or quick read. There are also several websites that offer tutorials on image processing that are of varying quality. Some are worth a perusal. If you search for *image processing basics*, you'll come across more than one. Once you've figured out what you want to do, you'll find a wealth of information online that can help, from code snippets to algorithms to full-featured toolkits that you can put to work for yourself.

If you're looking for ideas or thoughts on how to design with images, *Graphic Design: The New Basics* by Ellen Lupton and Phillips Jennifer Cole (Princeton Architectural Press) is an excellent text for ideas. *Design Elements: A Graphic Style Manual* by Timothy Samara (Rockport) is also worth checking out. Both of these books will give you ideas for how to frame, layer, and present video and images.

## Review

All videos and photos are bitmaps once they have been read into the memory of the computer. You can read the pixel values of those bitmaps to alter them, analyze them, and save them to the user's computer.

The Processing, `PImage` can actually be a texture object that has a built-in color array that holds pixel values so that you can access the individual pixels of the image that you have loaded. Images cannot draw themselves using a `draw()` method, like in oF, but they can be drawn by the `image()` function.

In Processing, if you want to access the individual pixels of the screen, call `loadPix els()`, make your pixel changes, and then call `updatePixels()` to make your changes appear.

In openFrameworks, any image file can be loaded into the application by creating an `ofImage` object and calling the `loadImage()` method of that object, passing the name of the file to be loaded to the method.

To read the pixels from an `ofImage` object, call the `getPixels()` method. This will return an array of unsigned `char` values, with one value for each color component and, if the image has alpha values, the alpha value of each pixel. This means that for an 100 × 100 pixel image without an alpha channel, there will be 30,000 values, while an image with an alpha value will have 40,000 values.

In an oF application, you can read video from a camera attached to your computer by creating an `ofVideoGrabber` object and calling the `initGrabber()` method on it. To draw the pixels of the video to the screen, use the `draw()` method. To retrieve the pixels from the camera, call the `getPixels()` method.

A convolution kernel is a 3 × 3 matrix used to calculate how to change each pixel in an image to achieve different kinds of spatial effects on the bitmaps.

Motion detection can be done by storing each incoming bitmap of data from a video stream and comparing the next incoming frame to the previous frame. A difference of more than an arbitrary value indicates movement in that pixel of the frame.

You can do simple edge detection by creating convolution kernels and applying them to a bitmap. Two of the more well-known edge-detection algorithms are the Sobel and the Prewitt algorithms.

Textures in Processing are created and altered using the `PImage` class. You can load an image into the `PImage`, draw it to the screen, alter its pixels, and use it as a texture for OpenGL drawing.

Textures in openFrameworks are handled by the `ofTexture` class, which contains methods for loading bitmap data into a drawing-ready texture, for copying bitmap data into textures, and for drawing the pixels to the screen.

Saving images is done in Processing by simply calling the `save()` method. In oF, the `saveFile()` method of the `ofImage` class enables you to save images.

# CHAPTER 10

# Sound and Audio

Our primary experience of computing and of computers is through the screen. The feedback to the user and the input of the user are both most often communicated visually. This isn't, however, how our experience of the world works, or how our cognitive and perceptual facilities function. One of our most finely tuned and emotionally evocative senses, our hearing, is often relegated to a lesser role or is ignored altogether in interactive design. In some scenarios, sound isn't a viable method of input or feedback. We don't want to have to talk to a computer or have it making noise in a quiet office. In other situations, neglecting the possibility of aural interaction with a user is a great loss to both an art piece or a product. Video game designers have put great effort and attention into their sound engines and the quality of the sounds in their games. Architects and interior designers, stage designers, sociologists, and of course musicians and sound artists all understand how our experience of the world is shaped by sound. Sound isn't always vital to a particular task, but it's an essential component of a rich and complete experience. You don't need to hear anything to enter your credit card number into a form, but a well-crafted, logical, and sensible use of sound in an application helps you perceive the world.

When sound is married effectively with a visual element, both elements are strengthened. Imagine a ball hitting a wall, and then imagine it again without the sound. Being able to hear the sound tells you a great deal about the room, including whether it echoes, whether it's muffled, and how large it is. It tells you a great deal about the wall, about the ball, and about the strength with which the ball was thrown. These shape the mental image and shape the understanding of the world around that image. When you create applications, it's of utmost importance that you help the user understand the application. From this little thought experiment, you can begin to see how sound can shape, heighten, and enrich a user's understanding of the world.

Sound physically affects us beyond its movement of the air that surrounds us; a sound wave causes the area of the human brain that is responsible for processing audio signals to generate electrical pulses at the same frequency. The sound wave for an A note, 440 Hz, causes the brain to produce electrical pulses at 440 Hz. So, your physical reaction to sound reaches beyond the pressure on your ears and, in some extreme cases, your stomach and skin and reaches into your brain as well. Our experience of hearing is a physical phenomenon on many different levels.

The physical nature of sound also makes it a very powerful tool for input. Asking a participant to interact with a device through sound is, while not completely novel, engaging in that it asks them to draw more attention to themselves than asking them to input something through a keyboard. An application that asks you to talk to it demands your attention and your presence in a way that keyboard input does not. This kind of vocal input also tells your application a lot more about the user. An incredible amount of information is contained within the voice that can be used by application: the volume, pitch, cadence, rhythm, pauses, and starts.

In this chapter, you'll learn some of the techniques for creating and processing audio in Processing and openFrameworks, as well as learn more about how computers process audio and how you can analyze audio signals.

# Sound As Feedback

Sound can influence a person's perception of objects and information. A higher sound is in a different location than a lower one. A major chord is a different type of object than a minor chord. A sudden change in pitch signals a change in the state of your system. Typically, humans can hear any sounds between 20 Hz and 20,000 Hz. This is an immense data set; however, we'll offer a few caveats. First, the human ear is far more sensitive to certain ranges of sound than others. These ranges correlate generally to normal human vocal ranges. Second, the ear can't detect all changes in frequency. The amount of change of a frequency depends greatly on the volume of the sound and the range that it's in. Despite these limits, the amount of information that can be transmitted in audio is immense.

Here are a few general examples about how you can use sound to give a user direct feedback on an action or on information:

*As a recognition or audio icon*

> Think of an action, one without a visible indication of what has happened. If you can't provide any visual signal to a user, then a sound can signal the user. This can be a simple clicking sound that accompanies pressing a button or a small, subtle sound that acknowledges that a transaction at an ATM has completed. The sound does the same thing as a pop-up message. Given the myriad of contexts in which users interact with applications today—in a busy office, on a bus, in their cars— it's difficult to create omnicontextually appropriate sounds, so many designers avoid the use of sound altogether. This doesn't mean that using sounds as feedback isn't useful, appropriate, or even enriching. It does, however, shape a lot of the thinking about the use of sound. Some research suggests that the first time a user performs a task, audio feedback is extremely helpful, but that with repeated

performances of that same task, sonic feedback becomes a potential nuisance. It's important to consider this when designing for a task-driven activity.

*As an associative or textural message*

In more passive activities, sound becomes something quite different. Think of almost any product, and you'll probably hear a jingle dancing through your head. A sound can be, just like an image, an iconic signifier or a branding tool. Movies, television shows, commercials, radio broadcasts, and even operating systems all have musical signatures. This is because sound is a very ephemeral and, frequently, a deeply emotional experience. It's partly that ephemeral quality that makes sound such a powerful experience.

*As an aid to simulation*

In less task-driven interactions, in play, for example, or in exploratory applications, sound becomes a vital part of the feedback to the user because we experience so much of the world in a fully audiovisual environment. The experience of a world or environment without sound is at least a little limited. The higher the fidelity of the sound and the more closely the sound is appropriately related to the event, the more fully realized the environment will seem. Think of a video game that involves computer-generated enemies shooting at you. When enemies are right next to you, you would expect that the sound of their gunfire would be louder than when they are far away from you. The sound "seems right" if it matches our experiential expectation. The audio can give a user information if it's contextually correct. If you see someone walking down a hallway and you hear echoes, this is contextually correct and gives a sense of the hallway, their footsteps, and the scene as a whole. The sound of footsteps echoing in a field doesn't really give a user information because it isn't contextually accurate.

Humans are very skilled at positioning sound. This is a product of the development of our ability, via hearing, to detect danger from potential predators or enemies. This means that auditory signals can transmit spatial information. Playing any video game will bear this out. Using two or four speakers, you can experience a rich world of physical data, positioning Doppler effects, echoes, and other facts that give you so much information. You'll learn more about creating 3-D sound in openFrameworks later in this chapter.

*As a product of play or nondirected action*

Creating tools for making sound is one of the oldest endeavors. Creating instruments is a complex and vast topic. Nearly all of us have at least some experience with an instrument for creating sound, whether it's a guitar, a drum, the tapping of our foot, our own voice, a computer program, or a programming language. One of our favorite pieces for working with sound is the Sonic Wire Sculptor by Amit Pitaru. It combines the ability to visualize sound, to make something out of the most ephemeral of art forms, with a tool that gives the user the ability to create both drawings and music. The Reactable project (which Sergi Jordà et al. developed at Pompeu Fabra University of Barcelona) is another excellent example of a music- and sound-making tool.

*As a way of telling us information about the objects making the sounds*

This ties in to a certain degree to the third point, as an aid to simulation. The source of a sound is oftentimes indicated in the sound itself. Hitting a glass with a fork sounds like a glass, a person whistling sounds like air rushing past something, a rock landing in water tells you a great deal about the size of the rock, and when you hear someone's voice, you gather a great deal of information about them. You can hear what makes the sound. You also hear where the sound is coming from, the location, the echo, the shape of the room or space, and how much background noise distracts from the primary noise.

*As an emotional trigger*

The beeps, clicks, and verification sounds that you're accustomed to hearing in an application are small, subtle tones. Those small audible feedback signals are appropriate for use in a business application, an operating system, or a website. Many books and discussions of using sound in interaction are limited to these sorts of auditory signals because, on a pragmatic level, the majority of work done in interaction design is for websites and business applications. Part of the premise of this book is to consider the possibilities for communication outside these sorts of contexts.

The powerful subconscious emotional significance of sound as a signifier is almost always on display in limited and subtle ways in traditional application interaction design and surrounds us in our day-to-day lives, in the soaring strings in a poignant moment of a film, in the cheer when a goal is scored in football, or in the opening stanza of a national anthem. Because the context of interaction with programs changes rapidly and dramatically, the nature of the sound and the information that it conveys changes as well. At the dawn of the video gaming industry, the 8-bit sound employed by game designers was aimed at producing simple feedback signals to accompany visuals. Now sound design is employed in games to add emotional elements, drive the narrative, heighten tension or rewards, or alert players to events offscreen.

The best way to determine how to create the signals and understanding in your users or audience is to experiment and observe closely how the sounds you use are received. Although engineering is often the art of avoiding failure, interaction and industrial design are the art of failing and understanding the failures correctly. Sound in particular is difficult to understand in the context of an application without seeing how others react to it. A good sound design is a deeply enriching aspect to any experience that is immersive, emotionally affective, and truly communicative, and takes a great amount of practice, testing, and tweaking to get right. That said, getting it right is well worth the effort.

# Sound and Interaction

Interactive art that works with sound is bound to the interaction that the user has with the sound. That depth of interaction is determined by the control that the user or participant has over the sound.

The key element to understand is how the audience will control the sound that they will hear or that they create. If the user doesn't have any control over the sound they hear, that person is a spectator. The control that users have over the sound can vary. The acoustics of an automobile, the road noise, the sound of the engine, and the acoustic qualities of the interior are very important to the driver. All of these become elements that the driver controls and alters while driving. Spend any time with someone who loves cars, and they'll invariably tell you about the sound of an engine when it's revved up. The interaction there is simple: press on the pedal. What it communicates, though, is quite rich and complex. If it were simply a sound that the driver did not control, then it would not have the same attractiveness to the driver. It's part of the experience of driving and an element of the experience that industrial engineers pay close attention to. The industrial designer Raymond Loewy wrote, "A fridge has to be beautiful. This means it also has to sound good."

Interaction is generally processing-oriented. This means that the elements of interaction never stand on their own: they are always interrelated and linked to a temporal development. Sounds themselves are inherently bound to processes in time. As interactive systems become more and more common, where the processes of the system are more and more difficult for users to understand, providing continuous feedback becomes more important. While visual information relies on movement and color, a sound can create a more continuous signal. The idea isn't to have an application buzz or beep the entire time the user is interacting with it, because some of the aspects of sound make working with it less desirable, such as public space, low sound quality, and bandwidth problems.

Let's examine some of the most common ways of using sound as the driver of an interaction:

*The user creates a sound that she or someone else can hear*

> This is essentially a recap of using sound as feedback for play or nondirected action. In these sorts of scenarios, the user's goal is to manipulate, control, or make a sound. This doesn't have to be as directed and purposeful as playing a piano or as finely controlled as a recording studio mixing board. Helping people make novel sounds can be a sort of play, a way of communicating whether someone can control the generation of sound, or a way of sending a signal to someone else. Some sound-generating interactive instruments are the theremin, RjDj, the iPhone DJing application, and of course the classic DJ turntable setup. What these all have in common isn't just that they make sound, but that the sound is produced interactively. In the case of the theremin and turntables, the sound is produced by a user's gestures. Think of using the Wii to drive a theremin, using the accelerometer to

change the tempo of a drum, or having a painting application create different sounds based on the color and stroke that users create on a canvas.

*The user creates a sound input using a tool*

Sound is everywhere and has such a vast range of tempos, timbres, pitches, and volumes that it's nearly impossible to prune it down into neat input data, unless you know exactly what kind of sound you're expecting. You may remember rotary dial phones—the old phones that sent a series of clicks for each number. The call routing system used those clicks to determine what number you were dialing. That system was later replaced by push-button phones that used a different tone to represent each number. These are both prosaic but excellent examples of sound-creating tools that create input. Any well-known music instrument can create a very precise tone that could be used as a command. A MIDI keyboard or a tool like the Monome control board offers even more possibilities. Any sound that can be reproduced with any degree of fidelity can be mapped to a command. The sort of fidelity required for complex commands isn't well suited to the human voice, but it can be very well suited to any instrument.

*The user creates a sound that is the input*

Two different types of applications use sound that users generate on their own, that is, without an extra tool: those that use sound data and those that use speech data. While it's true that spoken words are sound data, getting a computer to recognize speech is different from having it process sound. If you're interested only in processing the sound that users make, you can use a few different approaches. The first, and perhaps more obvious, is to use a microphone. From a microphone, you can analyze the volume of the user's speech, varying some input based on how loud they are talking. You can also determine whether they have just begun talking by taking a "snapshot" of the sound in a given period of time (a second, for instance) and comparing it with the sound in the next snapshot. Big changes in sound can indicate an activation that can act like a switch. Volume is a spectrum, which means it doesn't report data that's on or off but rather data from 0 to 100. Pitch, the frequency of the user's voice or the sound he is creating, works much the same way. It can be turned into any kind of spectrum values. Another thing that you can determine from a voice is its tempo. You can do this using beat detection, which a library like Minim for Processing makes very easy. The speed of sound is another spectrum of data that you can use. Adding another microphone lets you create positional data by simply comparing which mic is louder. Finally, as mentioned earlier, sound is vibration, and many piezo elements or small microphones can be used with Arduino to create up to 10 sound and vibrational inputs. These could be used to determine the position of a user within a room, enable many different elements to communicate, or create an interface that uses highly sensitive sounds to catch taps, touches, or rattling.

*The user talks or says a word to create the input*

Speech recognition is exciting, filled with interactive possibilities, and is, at the moment, very difficult to do. *Speech recognition* doesn't mean recognizing who is talking (that's called *voice recognition*), but rather recognizing what someone is saying. As you might imagine, the difficulty of the task grows as the vocabulary grows. Recognizing a "yes" or a "no" is quite easy. Understanding a full-speed English sentence with a possible vocabulary of 25,000 words is very, very difficult. Beyond the computational difficulties, there aren't any easy ways to get started working with speech recognition. A few open source speech recognition engines exist that you can play with, but they're a little difficult to get started with. Ideally, this will change soon so that artists and designers can get started making voice-activated and speech-driven applications.

You should consider creating an application that enables sound interactions for several reasons. On a practical level, sound creates opportunities for you to let users with physical or situational mobility issues interact with your application. Sound interaction also enables communication where no keyboard or physical input can be used. On a completely different level, interacting through sound can be fun. Making noises is like play, and making noises to drive an application that does something playful in response is a fun interaction all around: the input is fun, and the feedback is fun.

## How Sound Works on a Computer

Before we can discuss a representation of sound, we need to discuss what sound actually is. *Sound* is a wave of air pressure that we can detect with our ears. That wave has both a minimum and maximum pressure that define the sound frequency. Higher sounds have a higher frequency, and lower sounds have a lower frequency, which means that the maximum and minimum values occur much more closely together. The volume of the sound is, roughly speaking, the amount of air that the sound displaces. So, a pure single tone is a single wave, which might look something like one of the two waves in Figure 10-1.

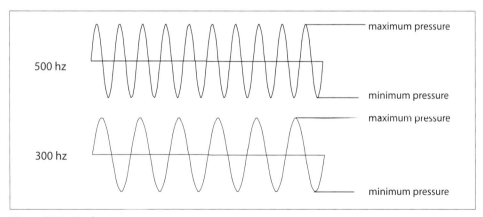

*Figure 10-1. Single tones*

It's interesting to note that when two or three tones are combined, they create a complex tone that looks like the ones in Figure 10-2.

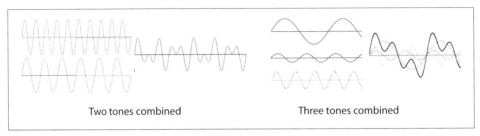

Figure 10-2. Two and three tones combined into a single tone

For you to work with sound on a computer, you or someone else needs to have captured the sound using a microphone; alternatively, you might have synthesized it using a sound synthesizer. In the case of capturing sound, you're converting the wave in the air to an electromagnetic wave. That electromagnetic signal is then sent to a piece of hardware called an *analog to digital converter*, which converts the electromagnetic wave into a series of integers or floating-point numbers. This is where one of the trickiest parts of working with sound comes into play.

A wave is a smooth curve, whereas a series of numbers trying to represent that curve needs to reduce some of the complexity of that curve. Why is that? Take a look at Figure 10-3.

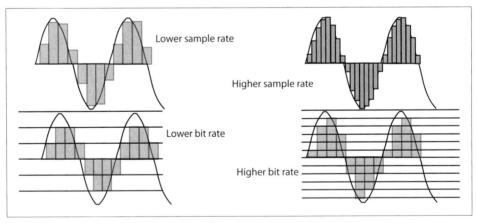

Figure 10-3. Sine wave representation of sound wave numeric values

Notice in the upper two diagrams of Figure 10-3 how a higher sampling rate means that the values of the blocks, which represent the values in the array of floating-point numbers for passing audio data around an application, more closely approximate the curves. The sample rate is actually the number of samples taken per second. In CD audio, the waveform is sampled at 44.1 kHz (kilohertz), or 44,100 samples per second. That's the most common modern sample rate for consumer audio, but it's not the only possibility. Older audio files used to go as low as 11 kHz or 22 kHz, whereas modern video uses an audio sample rate of 48 kHz. Greater sample rates mean larger data sets, and lower sample rates mean smaller data sets. Depending on your needs, one sample rate might be more appropriate than another. A nice compromise is 44.1 kHz.

In the lower two diagrams of Figure 10-3, the one on the left shows how a lower bit rate makes it more difficult to accurately approximate a sound. Specifically, 8-bit audio (256 possible values per sample) isn't a very good representation of a sound: think of the first Nintendo Entertainment System. That has its own charm, but you wouldn't want to record most music with it. CDs use 16-bit audio, allowing more than 65,000 possible values for each sample. Modern digital audio software also starts at 16-bit, but it's increasingly popular to record at 24-bit, with a massive 16 million possible values per sample.

For uncompressed audio, such as a *.wav* or *.aiff* file, sound approximation is done by measuring the wave many, many times a second and converting that measurement into a binary number of a certain size. Each measurement is called a *sample*, and the overall process is referred to as *sampling*. This creates a representation of the wave using *slices* of discrete values; the representation looks like stairs when you lay it over the sine-wave diagram. These factors (the number of measurements per second, or *sample rate*, and the precision of measurements, or *bit depth*) determine the basic quality of an uncompressed audio file. What about MP3 files? They operate in much the same way, but with an extra level of compression to save space. You'll notice that an MP3 file is smaller than the same data saved in WAV format. This saves space but also reduces quality, and means that the actual data stored in an MP3 file is different.

As you work through the examples in this chapter, you'll find arrays of floating-point numbers used again and again. This is because floating-point numbers are the root of audio processing, storing and manipulating data as numbers, and then writing the numbers to the audio card of a computer. Listed below is some of the equipment and hardware interaction used to make, capture, or play sound:

*Sound card*
    A *sound card* (also known as an *audio card*) is a computer expansion card that facilitates the input and output of audio signals to/from a computer with the help of specialized software. Typical uses of sound cards include providing the audio component for multimedia applications such as music composition, video or audio editing, presentation/education, and entertainment (games). Many computers have sound capabilities built-in, while others require additional expansion cards to provide for audio capability.

*Buffering and buffers*
    Computers grab only what you need from a file to send to the sound card. This is called *buffering*. You'll notice that much of the sound data that you receive when

working with audio is grabbed in small chunks that are often passed around, either as arrays of floating-point numbers or as pointers to arrays of floating-point numbers.

*Drivers and devices*

Most libraries enable communication between your software and your computer sound card. The average sound card handles both writing sound out to a speaker and reading and digitizing sound coming from a microphone. For most other devices, like keyboards or instruments, you'll need to have your application enable the device either by using a library for Arduino, Processing, or openFrameworks, or by having your application interface with another system. The applications that enable an operating system to communicate with other applications are called drivers and are often used to facilitate communication over USB or serial ports. This chapter explains some of the basics of how to use the MIDI and OSC protocols, which let you communicate with other systems and devices—many of which are quite relevant to processing audio signals.

# Audio in Processing

While Processing has a great deal of support for working with graphics, video, and OpenGL built into the core libraries, it doesn't provide nearly as much functionality for working with audio. Luckily, the Processing community has developed several excellent libraries for working with sound. The Minim library, developed by Damien Di Fede, is one of the best known and most complete, though several others are available as well. It's available with the Processing download as one of the core libraries.

## Instantiating the Minim Library

The philosophy in creating Minim was, as Damien puts it, to "make integrating audio into your sketches as simple as possible while still providing a reasonable amount of flexibility for more advanced users. There are no callbacks, and you do not ever need to directly manipulate sample arrays; all of the dirty work is handled for you."

The core of the Minim library is a class called `Minim`. Every time you use the Minim library, you need to instantiate a Minim object and call its constructor with the `this` keyword. You can perform four tasks with the `Minim` object: play an audio file that you load into your application, play audio that you create in your program, monitor audio and get data about it, and record audio to disk. Different classes in the Minim library handle these tasks and you can obtain instances of those classes by calling the appropriate methods of `Minim`. Take a look at Example 10-1.

*Example 10-1. fileLoading.pde*

```
Minim minim;
// remember that the 'this' keyword refers to your Processing application
minim = new Minim(this);
```

Now that you have the library initialized, you can begin doing things with it, like loading MP3 files and playing them back:

```
import ddf.minim.*;
AudioPlayer song;
Minim minim;
void setup()
{
    size(800, 800);
    // don't forget to instantiate the minim library
    minim = new Minim(this);
    // this loads song.mp3 from the data folder
    song = minim.loadFile("song.mp3");

}
```

This is a common pattern in the Minim library and in a lot of sound manipulation libraries, like the C++ Sound Object library. A core class is instantiated, and then new objects are created from that core object to do specific tasks, like playing files, creating filters, or generating tones. To load an audio file, the AudioPlayer class provides mono and stereo playback of WAV, AIFF, AU, SND, and MP3 files. AudioPlayer is instantiated by the static Minim loadFile() method. Once you've created AudioPlayer, you can pause, play, and apply filters, as well as read data from the raw audio file using the right and left arrays, all from AudioPlayer. The left and right properties of Audio Player are arrays filled with floating-point numbers that represent the left and right channels in the audio file. In the draw() method, those arrays can be used to draw a line of small ellipses. You'll be hearing the sound, and seeing a representation of it as well:

```
void draw()
{
    fill(0x000000, 30);
    rect(0, 0, width, height);
    //background(0);
    stroke(255);
    noFill();
    for(int i = 0; i < song.bufferSize() - 1; i++)
    {
        ellipse(i * 4, 100 + song.left.get(i)*100, 5, 5);
        ellipse(i * 4, 250 + song.right.get(i)*100, 5, 5);
    }
}
```

The AudioPlayer class also defines play() and pause() methods for the playback of the audio information:

```
boolean isPlaying = false;
void mousePressed()
{
    if(isPlaying) {
        song.pause();
        isPlaying = false;
    } else {
```

```
        song.play();
        isPlaying = true;
    }
  }
  void stop()
  {
    minim.stop();
    super.stop();
  }
```

In these few lines of code, you have instantiated an audio library that can load an audio file, control the playback, and read the data from the audio file to create graphics as it plays.

## Generating Sounds with Minim

Minim also defines methods to generate new sounds from equations. Four fundamental kinds of waves can generate sounds: triangle, square, sine, and sawtooth. The names are derived from the appearance of the waves when they are graphed, as in Figure 10-4.

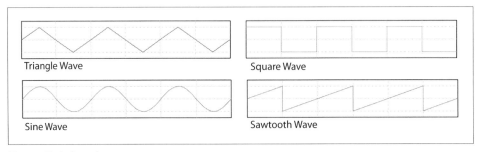

*Figure 10-4. Sound wave pattern types*

Each of these creates a slight variation of the familiar single tone that can be the base of a more complex tone. Minim simplifies generating tones for you by providing several convenience classes that generate tones and let you manipulate their frequency and amplitude in your application. While generating a sine wave may not seem useful when you need to provide feedback to a user, it's an excellent way to begin building complex layers of sound that increase in pitch or volume depending on input.

Before we go over the code for generating the waves, it's important to understand how the Minim library gets access to the sound card of the computer on which it's running. Generating a sine or sawtooth wave is really a process of feeding floating-point values to the sound card so that it can convert them into analog signals. The `AudioOutput` class is used to store information about the data being sent to the sound card for manipulation while the application is running. Though the `AudioOutput` class has several dozen methods, in the interest of space we'll discuss these two:

`addSignal(AudioSignal signal)`
  Adds a signal to the chain of signals that will be played.

```
removeSignal(AudioSignal signal)
```
Removes a signal from the chain of signals that will be played.

Additionally, the `AudioOutput` class defines the following variables:

`left`

Is an array containing all the samples for the left channel of the sound being sent to the sound card.

`right`

Is an array containing all the samples for the right channel of the sound being sent to the sound card.

`mix`

Is an array of data containing the mix of the left and right channels.

Any time you need access to the data being sent to the sound card—say you're mixing several tones together and want the final mix of all the sounds—the `mix` property of the `AudioOutput` class will give you access to that information.

You can't use `AudioOutput` before it has had all of its information set by the Minim framework. To do this, you use the main `Minim` class, which defines a `getLineOut()` method with the following four signatures:

```
getLineOut(int type)
getLineOut(int type, int bufferSize)
getLineOut(int type, int bufferSize, float sampleRate)
getLineOut(int type, int bufferSize, float sampleRate, int bitDepth)
```

You'll notice that all the methods require a type parameter, which can be one of the following:

`MONO`

Sets up a mono, or single-channel, output.

`STEREO`

Sets up a stereo, or two-channel, output.

The `getLineOut()` method instantiates and gives data to `AudioOutput`, as shown here:

```
AudioOutput out;
out = minim.getLineOut(Minim.STEREO);
```

Without calling the `getLineOut()` method, none of the audio data generated by the `SineWave` or `SquareWave` classes will be routed correctly to the sound card. Now that you know how to start the sound, take a look at generating a square wave and a sine wave in Example 10-2.

*Example 10-2. waves.pde*

```
import ddf.minim.*;
import ddf.minim.signals.*;

AudioOutput out;
```

```
SquareWave square;
SawWave saw;
Minim minim;

void setup()
{
    size(800, 800);
    //don't forget, you always need to start Minim first
    minim = new Minim(this);

    //get system access to the line out
    out = minim.getLineOut(Minim.STEREO, 512);

    // create a SquareWave with a frequency of 440 Hz,
    // an amplitude of 1 with 44100 samples per second
    square = new SquareWave(440, 1, 44100);
    // create a SawWave with a frequency of 600Hz and
    // an amplitude of 1
    saw = new SawWave(600, 1, 44100);

    // now you can attach the square wave and the filter to the output
    out.addSignal(square);
    out.addSignal(saw);
}

void draw() {
    saw.setFreq(mouseX);
    square.setFreq(mouseY);
}

void stop() {
  minim.stop();
  super.stop();
}
```

Running this program should give you an idea of what setting the frequency on a sine or square wave sounds like. In the next chapter, which covers using controls with the Arduino board, you'll learn how to use physical knobs to tune a sine wave. That is just the beginning of what is possible when you combine means of input and means of feedback.

Another thing that you'll probably want to do with the Minim library is play back and manipulate audio files. To play audio files in Minim, you use the AudioPlayer. Like many of the other objects in the Minim library, you create the object by having it returned from a method on the main Minim object. For the AudioPlayer, it looks like this:

```
AudioPlayer player = Minim.loadFile("myfile.mp3");
```

This starts the file streaming from its location. The name of the file can be just the filename, like *mysong.wav*, in which case Minim will look in all of the places Processing looks (the data folder, the sketch folder, etc.); it can be the full path to the file, or it can be a URL:

---

```
void play()
```
Starts playback from the current position.

```
void play(int millis)
```
Starts playback millis from the beginning.

One of the difficulties in working with sound in Java is that certain implementations of the JVM have small quirks. One of them affects how Minim changes the volume of the sound when you play back an MP3 file. On some machines, you'll use the set Gain() method, and on others you'll use the setVolume() method. Both take floating-point values, usually between –80 and 12 for setGain(), and 0 to 1.0 for setVolume(). The easiest way to check whether some functionality is supported is to call the hasCon trol() method of the AudioPlayer class:

```
AudioPlayer player = Minim.loadFile("myfile.mp3");
boolean hasVolume = player.hasControl(Controller.VOLUME);
```

This code snippet shown below loads up two files and then allows the user to fade between them using the movement of the mouse. The code will be broken up into the following snippets found in Example 10-3.

*Example 10-3. interactiveSounds.pde*

```
import ddf.minim.*;

AudioPlayer player;
AudioPlayer player2;
Minim minim;

boolean hasVolume;

void setup()
{
  size(512, 200);
  minim = new Minim(this);

  // load a file, give the AudioPlayer buffers that are 1024 samples long
  player = minim.loadFile("two.mp3", 1024);
  player2 = minim.loadFile("one.mp3", 1024);
  // play the file
  player.play();
  player.printControls();
  player2.play();
  hasVolume = player.hasControl(Controller.VOLUME);
}

void draw()
{
  background(0); // erase the background
  stroke(0, 255, 0);
```

```
float gain1 = 0;
float gain2 = 0;
```

If the setup on the users computer can alter the volume, then set that using the mouse position, otherwise, set the gain using the mouse position. The effect will be more or less the same.

```
if(hasVolume) {
  player.setVolume(mouseX / width);
  gain1 = map(player.getVolume(), 0, 1, 0, 50);
} else {
  player.setGain(map(mouseX, 0, width, -20, 1));
  gain1 = map(player.getGain(), -20, 1, 0, 50);
}
```

As mentioned earlier in this chapter, the sound buffer is really just a big array of floating-point numbers that represent the sound wave. To draw the sound wave to the screen, you can just loop through all the values in each channel and use the value however you'd like. Here, it's just being used to draw a line:

```
for(int i = 0; i < player.left.size()-1; i++) {
    line(i, 50 + player.left.get(i)*gain1, i+1, 50 + player.left.get(i+1)*gain1);
    line(i, 150 + player.right.get(i)*gain1, i+1, 150 + player.right.get(i+1)*gain1);
}
  stroke(255, 0, 0);
  if(hasVolume) {
    player2.setVolume(width - mouseX / width);
    gain2 = map(player2.getVolume(), 0.0, 1, 0, 50);
  } else {
    player2.setGain(map(width - mouseX, 0, width, -20, 1));
    gain2 = map(player2.getGain(), -20, 1, 0, 50);
  }
  for(int i = 0; i < player2.left.size()-1; i++) {
    line(i, 50 + player2.left.get(i)*gain2, i+1, 50 + player2.left.get(i+1)*gain2);
    line(i, 150 + player2.right.get(i)*gain2, i+1, 150 + player2.right.get(i+1)*gain2);
  }
}

void stop()
{
  // always close Minim audio classes when you are done with them
  player.close();
  player2.close();
  minim.stop();

  super.stop();
}
```

## Filtering Sounds with Minim

Filtering sounds is an important element of manipulating them. Filtering a sound can involve removing a narrow band of its sound frequency, removing the highest or lowest frequency part of a complex sound, changing its pitch, or removing popping sounds from audio to smooth it out, among other things. Being able to create and tune filters in Minim is quite simple. Example 10-4 creates a `SquareWave` tone and then applies a `LowPass` filter to it, the frequency of which is controlled by the mouse position:

*Example 10-4. minimSignal.pde*

```
import ddf.minim.*;
import ddf.minim.signals.*;
import ddf.minim.effects.*;

AudioOutput out;
SquareWave square;
LowPassSP lowpass;
Minim minim;

void setup()
{
    size(800, 800);
    // don't forget to instantiate the minim library
    minim = new Minim(this);
    // get a stereo line out with a sample buffer of 512 samples
    out = minim.getLineOut(Minim.STEREO, 512);
    // create a SquareWave with a frequency of 440 Hz,
    // an amplitude of 1, and the same sample rate as out
    square = new SquareWave(440, 1, 44100);
    // create a LowPassSP filter with a cutoff frequency of 200 Hz
    // that expects audio with the same sample rate as out
    lowpass = new LowPassSP(200, 44100);

    // now we can attach the square wave and the filter to our output
    out.addSignal(square);
    out.addEffect(lowpass);
}

void draw()
{
    try {
    if(out.hasSignal(square)) {
        out.removeEffect(lowpass);
    }
    // set the frequency of the lowpass filter that we're using
    lowpass.setFreq(mouseY);
    out.addEffect(lowpass);
    } catch(Exception e) {
    }
}
```

You'll want to make sure that you include a `stop()` method to close out the Minim library:

```
void stop()
{
    out.close();
    minim.stop();
```

```
        super.stop();
    }
```

This is very small taste of what the Minim library can do, but it is a starting place to explore how to create sophisticated sound in your Processing applications. For more information on the Minim library, go to the Minim website and look at the thorough, well written, and extremely helpful documentation by Damien Di Fede.

---

## Interview: Amit Pitaru

Amit Pitaru is an artist, designer, and researcher. He develops instruments and installations for music and animation, and has exhibited and performed at the London Design Museum, Paris Pompidou Center, Sundance Film Festival, and ICC Museum in Tokyo. He is also a designer with a particular interest in assistive technologies and universal design. In addition, he creates toys and software that are inclusively accessible to people with various disabilities. He also teaches at the ITP program of New York University and the Cooper Union in New York City.

*You've mentioned the idea of there being an infinite learning curve when learning how to make interactive art or interactive design objects. Can you elaborate on that?*

**Amit Pitaru:** Think about other crafts, for instance, photography. When the camera was introduced and it became accessible to anyone who could afford it, there were perhaps five years where people had to figure out how to use it. During these five years, much of the work that was done, if you judge from history, was more experimental than artistic. The really good stuff came afterward. There's value in the experimental new work, in finding new territory and such, but it's not the stuff that we look at today as the remastery of the medium. So, what do you do when you have a medium like new media, when a certain period of five years of technical mastery is expanded to become infinite? Do people ever snap out of the learning mode, and will artists be able to overcome this learning period? Or will they forever be dealing with technical mastery?

You can look at that a different way and say that the ultimate goal of any artist is to spark this creative feedback loop where they could get into this little tunnel of creativity and come out with something really beautiful at the end. You want to be in the zone, in the flow—whatever you want to call it. It's the same when you're writing or you're drawing, or anything. The question is, how do you start that spark? How do you spark this process with new media? Having that technical proficiency (or hiring someone who knows how to do what you can't do) is a relevant issue because of what we said before: the learning curve is infinitely expanded because the technologies keep changing all the time. Sometimes it's better to learn a single technology and then stop worrying about the technology and realize that it's better to concentrate on making your artwork than learning new skills and techniques.

*I know some people who really enjoy the process of learning everything and really thrive from exploring technical challenges, and I know other people who really want to bypass that stuff and get to the part where they make their work or their object.*

**Amit:** It's very different if you actually enjoy programming or you want to use programming as a method to do something that you know is possible. It's the bottom-up

---

versus top-down approach. You learn because you want to get somewhere, but at some point, you get new ideas because of what you just learned. For instance, say someone wants to do a motion-tracking thing that can output whatever. That's an artistic idea, but by its definition someone needs to build all of this technology. I think everyone should try to learn the technology, but I'm not sure that person should go and do everything themselves. I think the trick for people like that is to respect the craft. They need to understand that anybody who makes it look easy has had just as much practice as any other craft or sport, so just jumping into it—unless you're some sort of super-hacker—will make you understand that this craft requires practice and attention.

*How did you start programming?*

**Amit:** My background is in music, not programming. I started programming on a leap of faith, but I had some musical instruments that I wanted to play and ended up enjoying the process of learning how to program very much. I think this was because of my musical training and the analogies that I made very quickly between the type of abstractions that code has and the abstraction that a musical rotation would have or the understanding of what a musical piece would have when you're composing it. I think you'll find a lot of commonalities there.

*What do you actually learn when you want to start programming?*

**Amit:** One of the things that happens with new artists who are trying to get into this is that they still don't have a connection between what they want to see and the amount of work it requires. For example, suppose you want to do sound analysis. If all you want to do is grab the volume of the microphone, then it's something you could do with a beginner's exercise. If you want to grab the pitch of the microphone, you need a few months because it's not as straightforward. If you want to do speech recognition and you don't understand the gaps in difficulties, you won't understand the huge mountains between those three things. If you want to start programming and you're set on doing speech recognition, before you even know how to write a lot of code, you may put yourself in a bad situation, especially once you realize how big of a task this is. I think it's really important to learn a little bit of code first, understand what's possible, and come up with ideas and goals that somehow relate to the type of things you can do.

*You teach at NYU and Cooper Union. What do you teach there?*

**Amit:** I'm very interested in assisted technology, so the latest course I taught was making games, video games, and hardware for children with disabilities. We hooked up with a hospital and a school, and we actually developed games and hardware that the students are now using. Those things were delivered to them as products. So, it was an interesting exercise in constraints at the end because, as a person who does art for people to use, it is so important to understand usability. We're tapping now into a different subject, but I find that if we have to list the things that new media artists need to know—for example, if you're working on something interactive—you have to learn usability design. All the courses that I teach heighten students' sensibilities to how people use the things that they make, whether it's art or not. I pay close attention to this in any work that I do.

*What do you find that your students have the most difficulty learning, other than the basics of code?*

**Amit:** I try not to mix topics too much. If I'm teaching about disability design for a particular target or particular niche, I don't necessarily want to teach them the ABCs of code at the same time. For example, let's talk about teaching a person how to start programming. I think the most difficult thing is to be able to visualize the system that they are creating. Once they are able to control visual representation of how program flows and how program is structured, that's when they really have to simulate (if not all of the program, then parts of your program at a time) in their own brain. Basically, you can't just have the machine run the program and then look at the output and say, "OK, I know what to do." Usually, programming involves running the code together with the machine, to some extent, and that is a skill that takes time to learn, and that is a skill that needs to be learned. For example, if I draw 10 horizontal lines and I ask a painter, "What do you see?", they'll respond "I see 10 horizontal lines." What I want them to think about now is a program that creates 10 lines evenly spaced horizontally. Then it could be 10, 20, or 30. I want them to see the process that creates those lines, the computational process, and then understand how that system can be flexed and expanded and how different variables go in there.

*What do you find when you're teaching a class more centered on usability or interaction design? What are the first things you have to get people to think about?*

**Amit:** You need to start by understanding how you react to the world. In art school they would tell you, "OK, stand upside down on your hands and describe what you see," just to break the usual way of looking. Here, you have to do the same thing. Ask yourself how you perceive a certain situation if you are interacting with anything, whether it's an ATM or artwork at the mall. And break down those different things that are happening in your mind as much as you can, and try to find patterns in the way that you see things. Then, you have to look at how other people perceive the same thing, and once you are open to that, the realizations that you have to test everything that you do daily is important. At the end of the day, most of the works that are being done fall down upon the stupidest and smallest details. Art should be communicated before it's understood. You can't build a piece of art that delivers on your intentions without learning usability.

*What do you think it means to be making new media art?*

**Amit:** If you want to be a new media artist today, you are in an excellent place, almost in all aspects. First of all, the system isn't defined yet, so you're allowed to be inside of the accepted genres or on the outside, because there really is no outside; you can do whatever you want. I often see people who try to define what new media is, and I run away from that like the plague. I think it's our luxury right now not to be defined. The only time it's worth trying to define yourself and what exactly you want to be doing in this field is if you want to be a commercial new media artist and the art world has figured out a system for artists to make money, which it hasn't.

*How did you think about the making of the interface for the Sonic Wire Sculptor?*

**Amit:** When I built it, I built it for myself. The evolution of this thing started from looking at musical instruments. Musical instruments evolved over centuries to be as perfect as they are today. There's the guitar, the piano—revision after revision after revision of becoming perfect in the way we think, the way we move. It'd be really hard to make a better piano, but it's that kind of thinking that got me really interested in what is important for the interface of an instrument. Turntables in particular are enjoyable to touch, so I knew when I was making an instrument that it had to be enjoyable to touch. I realized how much I enjoy touching the instruments that I know how to play. That was an important part of learning to play them, and that's an important part of expressing myself with them.

The next step was constraining myself and saying, "Well, instead of asking what kind of sound and what kind of drawing, if I can draw a line—a simple, single wave line— what would that sound like?" Another issue in interactive art, and usability in general, is about how you map things into another, such as how you map a line to a sound.

If I wanted to hold a note, the same way as holding a note on a piano or when playing the trumpet, I don't want to move anything, but I still want that note to come out. That's one thing that must happen, so you must give a dimension there, where the note can actually visually extract, even if you're not actually moving anything.

Another thing was notation. I was really interested in notation, and I was really interested in the texture of the sound, rather than the notes themselves. I wanted the ingredient of the note, not the note. So if I made a three-dimensional sculpture of the piece and then I actually move it in space to see what happens to notation, I thought that would be interesting. So, all those things came together, and I don't know what came first, but they were all on my mind, and they made enough sense for me to put a lot of time into programming it.

Once I had created the Sonic Wire Sculptor, I got some interest from museums to show it in the context of art. When I was performing, people wanted to use it all the time, so I started the second version of the tool. I thought, "How do I make this enjoyable to the person who walks into the room and who hasn't seen this before and doesn't know what it is if I'm not there to explain it to them?"

It took me about six or seven shows to get it right. I noticed that if I just put it with the computer and the touch screen, people felt very intimidated. It just didn't work right, and it wasn't enjoyable. I couldn't break the ice and get people to touch it, without committing to it. And I noticed that when you're looking at artwork, like a drawing or painting in a museum, you control the level of engagement that you want to have with the piece. But with interactive work specifically like Sonic Wire Sculptor, it's all or nothing. So, how do you create an atmosphere where the viewer has control over the engagement? How do you create an atmosphere where the engagement pulls the viewer in and they want more of it?

Now, I have an actual device that looks like a moon crossed with a Russian missile control system that I fabricated out of wood and metal, and that wasn't arbitrary. You know, it's really retro, so when you come into the room and see this sculptural thing that's kind of heavy and bulky and weird, it makes sense. There's an embodiment to the sound, and it makes sense that sounds would come out of this. Then I put this thing in the center of the room, and I have a projection that mirrors everything that's happening on the interface of this instrument. So, you can be next to the tool, playing and looking at your little screen at the same time, and everybody sees what you're doing on the big screen. This is actually surround installation, and the sound actually spins around depending on the space of the sculpture. So, that got more people into it, and then I put couches and an air conditioner there. And the result is that now when I put it there, people will stay there, sometimes up to 40 minutes, and people will clap. The difference between the first time when no one wanted to stay in the room for more than 30 seconds and now is unbelievable! And pay mind that I almost didn't change anything in the software.

When you're in play mode, you don't mind failing, like killing yourself 50 times in a game and restarting a game, when you feel there's no consequence to failing. This is where you learn at your best. When I look at a piece of interactive art that doesn't have this learning scaffold—where you want to be playful with it, you want to engage with it, you want to try it out, and the system accommodates you to do that—I feel that that piece is lacking in soul. It's as extreme as that for me.

# Sound in openFrameworks

It's certainly not this book's intention to overwhelm you with library names and strange acronyms, but they are an important part of working with openFrameworks. For many purposes, the code included in the openFrameworks core library will do just fine. In equally as many cases, though, you'll want to work with the underlying engines to tweak something, add some functionality, get a different value to work with, or do any of several tasks. When you glance into the *libs* folder of openFrameworks, you'll see the libraries with the classes that openFrameworks uses to make an openFrameworks application, specifically ofGraphics, ofTexture, ofSoundStream, and so on. When working with sound, you'll work with two classes most of the time: ofSoundPlayer and ofSoundStream. ofSoundStream is used for more low-level access to the sound buffer and uses the RtAudio library developed at McGill University by Gary P. Scavone. RtAudio provides an API that lets you control and read data from the audio hardware of your computer. The other library used in openFrameworks for the ofSoundPlayer class is the FMOD Ex library, a commercial library developed by Firelight Technologies and is primarily used in games. It provides more high-level methods to play and manipulate sounds.

You can manipulate sound with openFrameworks using two approaches. The first option is to directly manipulate the sound data sent from the sound card by using the ofSoundStream class that is included as a part of the core oF distribution. The second option is to use a library like Maximilian, which is a flexible library that includes a wealth of tools for generating, manipulating, and mixing sounds. First, let's look at the ofSoundStream class.

The ofBaseApp class defines two callback methods that let you work with sound: audioIn() is called when the system receives any sound, and audioOut() is called before the system sends sound to the sound card. Both of these callbacks require that the ofSoundStreamSetup() method is called before they will be activated. This tells the RtAudio library to start up, begin processing audio from the system microphone (or line in), and send data to the system sound card:

```
ofSoundStreamSetup(int nOutputs, int nInputs, int
  sampleRate, int bufferSize,  int nBuffers)
```

The ofSoundStreamSetup() method has five parameters:

nOutput
: Is the number of output channels that your computer supports. Usually this will be two: left and right. If you have a surround sound setup, it might be four or five.

nInputs
: Is the number of input channels that your system uses.

sampleRate
: Is usually 44,100 kHz, or CD quality, though you may want to make it higher or lower depending on the needs of your application.

bufferSize
: Is the size of the buffer that your system supports. At the time of writing this book, on any operating system, it's probably 256 values.

nBuffers
: Is the number of buffers that your system will create and swap out. The more buffers, the faster your computer will write information into the buffer, but the more memory it will take up. You should probably use two for each channel that you're using. Here's an example call:

```
ofSoundStreamSetup(2, 0, 44100, 256, 4);
```

The previous snippet will send two channels of stereo sound to the audioIn() method each time the underlying RtAudio library sends information from the sound card. This should be called in the setup method of your openFrameworks application. Now, look at the first of two callback methods. The audioIn() method is called whenever the system microphone detects sound:

```
void audioIn(float * input, int bufferSize, int nChannels)
```

input
: Is a pointer to the array of data.

bufferSize
: Is the size of the buffer, the number of floating-point values in the input array.

nChannels
: Is the number of sound channels represented in the sound data.

The input parameter is always an array of floating-point numbers with the length given in the bufferSize variable. This sounds a little tricky to work with, but as you can see, by using a for loop with a length determined by bufferSize, it isn't that difficult:

```
float samples[bufferSize];
for (int i = 0; i < bufferSize; i++) {
    // increment the sample counter
    samples[sampleCounter] = input[i];
}
```

Remember that the pointer to a float is actually just the first element in an array. If this doesn't ring any bells, look back at Chapter 5. Also, note that this callback won't be triggered unless you call ofSoundStreamSetup() with one or two channels set as the input, like so:

```
ofSoundStreamSetup(0, 2, 44100, 256, 4);
```

Next, the audioOut() method is called when the system needs one buffer worth of audio to send to the sound card. The method sends the array of floating-point information that represents the buffer of audio data, the size of the buffer, and the number of channels:

```
void audioOut() (float * output, int bufferSize, int nChannels)
```

To have the audioOut() callback triggered by the system, you would need to call ofSoundStreamSetup() with one or two channels in the output. If you want to alter the data before it's sent to the sound buffer, you must do it within this method.

## openFrameworks and the FMOD Ex Library

The ofSoundPlayer class offers higher-level access and uses the FMOD Ex library developed by Firelight Technology. FMOD Ex is used in many major video games and is available for all the major operating system platforms: Xbox, PlayStation 3, and iPhone. If you look at the ofSoundPlayer header file, *ofSoundPlayer.h*, in the *sound* folder of *oF/ libs*, you'll see some of the core functionality that the ofSoundPlayer class enables:

```
void    loadSound(string fileName, bool stream = false);
void    unloadSound();
void    play();
void    stop();

void    setVolume(float vol);
void    setPan(float vol);
void    setSpeed(float spd);
void    setPaused(bool bP);
void    setLoop(bool bLp);
void    setMultiPlay(bool bMp);
void    setPosition(float pct);    // 0 = start, 1 = end;
```

These methods are all very straightforward to understand and use, so in this section we'll move on to a different aspect of the FMOD libraries: using the 3-D sound engine.

FMOD Ex is the low-level sound engine part of the FMOD suite of tools. This library is included with openFrameworks. FMOD Ex input channels can be mapped to any output channel and output to mono, stereo, 5.1, 7.1, and Dolby Pro Logic or Pro Logic 2 with ease. The API includes a whole suite of 14 DSP effects, such as echo, chorus, reverb, and so on, which can be applied throughout the DSP mixing network. The API can play back *WAV*, *MIDI*, *MP3*, *XMA*, *OGG*, and *MOD* files. FMOD Ex also lets you work with 3-D sound and supply 3-D positions for the sound source and listener. FMOD Ex will automatically apply volume, filtering, surround panning, and Doppler effects to mono, stereo, and even multichannel samples.

Because the implementation of FMOD Ex in openFrameworks is all contained within ofSoundPlayer, looking at the *ofSoundPlayer.h* file will give you an idea of what sort of functionality is built-in. Take note of these two methods:

```
static void initializeFmod();
static void closeFmod();
```

These methods start up and close down the FMOD Ex engine. If you glance at the definitions of these methods in *ofSoundPlayer.cpp*, you'll see the calls to the FMOD Ex engine:

```
FMOD_System_Init(sys, 32, FMOD_INIT_NORMAL, NULL);  //do we want
                                                     //just 32 channels?

FMOD_System_GetMasterChannelGroup(sys, &channelgroup);
bFmodInitialized = true;
```

It's these sorts of calls that you're going to add and modify slightly. The FMOD Ex engine isn't set up to run in 3-D sound mode the way that openFrameworks has implemented it. The solution is to create a new class that extends the ofSoundPlayer class that we'll call Sound3D.

The header file for that class looks like Example 10-5.

*Example 10-5. Sound3D.h*

```
#pragma mark once

#include "ofMain.h"

class Sound3D : public ofFmodSoundPlayer {
    public:

    Sound3D();
```

These two methods are the most interesting:

```
        static void initializeFmod();
        static void closeFmod();
        void loadSound(string fileName, bool stream = false);
        void play();
```

All the positions of the listeners and the sound emanating from the channel are positioned using FMOD_VECTOR vector objects. The FMOD_VECTOR represents a 3-D vector with an *x, y, and z* value that each represent a direction. FMOD uses four different vectors for the listener and two for the channel, as shown in Figure 10-5. The listener vectors represent the position, facing, relative up, and velocity of the listener, who is most likely the user. The channel vectors represent the position and velocity of the sound origin:

```
FMOD_VECTOR listenerVelocity, listenerUp, listenerForward, listenerPos,
    soundPosition, soundVelocity;

void updateListener(ofVec3f position, ofVec3f velocity,
    ofVec3f forward, ofVec3f up);
void updateSound( ofVec3f position, ofVec3f velocity );
void update();

};
```

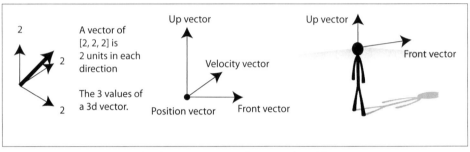

*Figure 10-5. The vectors used by the FMOD Ex to place sounds and listeners*

The definition of the Sound3D class in Example 10-6 sets up the FMOD Ex library to operate in 3-D mode:?

*Example 10-6. Sound3D.cpp*

```
#include "Sound3D.h"
#include "ofFmodSoundPlayer.cpp"

bool bFmod3DInitialized = false;

Sound3D::Sound3D(){

    listenerVelocity.x = 1;
    listenerVelocity.y = 1;
    listenerVelocity.z = 1;
    listenerUp.x = 0.f;
    listenerUp.y = 1.f;
    listenerUp.z = 0;
    listenerForward.x = 0.f;
    listenerForward.y = 0.f;
    listenerForward.z = 1.0;
    listenerPos.x = 3.f;
    listenerPos.y = 3.f;
```

```
    listenerPos.z = 1.f;
    soundPosition.x = 3.f;
    soundPosition.y = 3.f;
    soundPosition.z = 1.0;
    soundVelocity.x = 1;
    soundVelocity.y = 1;
    soundVelocity.z = 1.0;

    initializeFmod();
}

// this should only be called once
void Sound3D::initializeFmod(){

    if(!bFmod3DInitialized){
        FMOD_System_Create(&sys);
        FMOD_System_Init(sys, 32, FMOD_INIT_NORMAL, NULL);
        // do we want just 32 channels?
```

Here, the FMOD Ex engine is set to use 3-D mode. Now that the two static variables are declared, the `FMOD_CHANNELGROUP` and the `FMOD_SYSTEM` are passed to the `FMOD_Sys tem_GetMasterChannelGroup()` method. The `FMOD_SYSTEM` instance is initialized and then the `FMOD_CHANNELGROUP` is set as the channel that the system will use:

```
        FMOD_System_Set3DSettings(sys, 10.0f, 10.0f, 10.0f);
        FMOD_System_GetMasterChannelGroup(sys, &channelgroup);
        bFmod3DInitialized = true;
    }

}
```

These two methods are provided to allow access to the `channelgroup` and the `sys` variables. These are used by the oF application to set the locations of the sounds and the listeners:

```
    void Sound3D::loadSound(string fileName, bool stream)
    {
```

The listener attributes are set in the `update()` method of the oF application using the `FMOD_System_Set3DListenerAttributes()` method, and the channel attributes are set using the `FMOD_Channel_Set3DAttributes()` method. These are both rather longish methods and are filled with pointers, which means that you'll need to use the reference operator & in front of the vectors that you pass to these methods. Note also that you must pass the system needs to set the listener attributes, which is why the `getSys tem()` method was added to the `Sound3D` class. Since this example has only one listener, just pass 0 for the listener and the correct vectors for the rest of the parameters to represent the position of the listener in 3-D space:

```
    FMOD_System_Set3DListenerAttributes(FMOD_SYSTEM *system, int listener,
        const FMOD_VECTOR *pos, const FMOD_VECTOR *vel, const FMOD_VECTOR *forward,
        const FMOD_VECTOR *up);
```

Setting the properties of the channel is a little simpler. Pass the channel, which is the vector that represents the position of the sound in 3-D space, and its velocity:

```
FMOD_Channel_Set3DAttributes(FMOD_CHANNEL *channel, const FMOD_VECTOR *pos,
    const FMOD_VECTOR *vel);
```

Here are the actual calls:

```
        result = FMOD_System_CreateSound(sys, ofToDataPath(fileName).c_str(),
        FMOD_3D, NULL, &sound);
        result = FMOD_Sound_Set3DMinMaxDistance(sound, 1.f, 5000.0f);

        if (result != FMOD_OK){
            bLoadedOk = false;
            printf("ofSoundPlayer: Could not load sound file %s \n", fileName.c_str() );
        } else {
            bLoadedOk = true;
            FMOD_Sound_GetLength(sound, &length, FMOD_TIMEUNIT_PCM);
            isStreaming = stream;
        }
    }

    void Sound3D::play(){

        FMOD_System_PlaySound(sys, FMOD_CHANNEL_FREE, sound, bPaused, &channel);
        FMOD_VECTOR pos = {  0.0f, 0.0f, 0.0f };
        FMOD_VECTOR vel = {  0.0f, 0.0f, 0.0f };
```

The `FMOD_Channel_Set3DAttributes()` call makes the `FMOD_Channel` passed in to it able to have positional properties set on it:

```
        FMOD_Channel_Set3DAttributes(channel, &pos, &vel);
        FMOD_Channel_GetFrequency(channel, &internalFreq);
        FMOD_Channel_SetVolume(channel,volume);
    }

    void Sound3D::updateListener(ofVec3f position, ofVec3f velocity,
    ofVec3f forward, ofVec3f up)
    {

        listenerVelocity.x = velocity.x;
        listenerVelocity.y = velocity.y;
        listenerVelocity.z = velocity.z;

        listenerPos.x = position.x;
        listenerPos.y = position.y;
        listenerPos.z = position.z;

        listenerForward.x = forward.x;
        listenerForward.y = forward.y;
        listenerForward.z = forward.z;

        listenerUp.x = up.x;
        listenerUp.y = up.y;
        listenerUp.z = up.z;
```

Here the FMOD engine is set up with the values passed in:

```
    FMOD_System_Set3DListenerAttributes(sys, 0, &listenerPos, &listenerVelocity,
    &listenerForward, &listenerUp);

}

void Sound3D::updateSound( ofVec3f position, ofVec3f velocity )
{
    soundPosition.x = position.x;
    soundPosition.y = position.y;
    soundPosition.z = position.z;

    soundVelocity.x = velocity.x;
    soundVelocity.y = velocity.y;
    soundVelocity.z = velocity.z;

    FMOD_Channel_Set3DAttributes(channel, &soundPosition, &soundVelocity);
}

void Sound3D::update()
{
    FMOD_System_Update(sys);
}
```

Now you're ready to create an actual application that uses FMOD Ex.

In the following header file (see Example 10-7), you'll see the four vectors for the listener and the two for the sound defined as ofVec3f along with the Sound3D instance. Other than that, the rest of the header file is rather straightforward:

*Example 10-7. fmodApp.h*

```
#pragma mark once

#include "ofMain.h"
#include "Sound3D.h"

class fmodApp : public ofBaseApp{

public:

    void setup();
    void update();
    void draw();
    void keyPressed( int key );
    void keyReleased( int key );
    void mouseDragged( int x, int y, int button );
    Sound3D player;

    bool settingListener;
    bool settingSound;

    ofVec3f lposition, lvelocity, lforward, lup;
    ofVec3f sposition, svelocity;
```

```
    bool keyIsDown;
};
```

The *fmodApp.cpp* file contains a few other "newish" methods specific to the FMOD engine that require a little bit of explanation. First, all the vectors are initialized in the setup() method. Neither the listener nor sound is given a velocity here. You can experiment with changing these values on your own in Example 10-8.

*Example 10-8. fmodApp.cpp*

```
#include "fmodApp.h"

void fmodApp::setup(){

    keyIsDown = false;

    lvelocity.set(1, 1, 1);
    lup.set(0, 1, 0);
    lforward.set(0, 0, 1);
    lposition.set(0, 0, 0);

    sposition.set(3, 3, 2);
    svelocity.set(1, 1, 1);
```

Next, the player has a sound loaded from the openFrameworks application's data folder, and the play() method is called on it:

```
    player.loadSound(ofToDataPath("organ.wav"));
    player.setVolume(0.75);
    player.setMultiPlay(true);
    player.play();
}
```

When we update() we want to set all the properties of the sound and the listener and then update the player. As a side-note, the Sound3D could be set up to use the event listening mechanism, making the call to Sound3D update() unnecessary:?

```
void fmodApp::update() {
    if(!player.getIsPlaying())
        player.play();

    if ( keyIsDown )
        settingListener = false;
    else
        settingListener = true;


    player.updateListener(lposition, lvelocity, lforward, lup);
    player.updateSound(sposition, svelocity);
    player.update();
}
```

Next, ensure that the sound loops, but check whether the player is playing. If it isn't, restart the playback of the *.wav* file. Next, in the draw() method, draw circles at the positions of the listener and the sound in the application window so you have a visual representation of the sound and listener positions:

```
void fmodApp::draw(){
    ofSetHexColor(0xff0000);
    ofEllipse(sposition.x*20, sposition.y*20, 10, 10);
    ofSetHexColor(0x0000ff);
    ofEllipse(lposition.x*20, lposition.y*20, 10, 10);
}
```

Allow the user to set the sound and listener positions by dragging the mouse. This could be anything—a user's movement in a space, an accelerometer, a joystick, or almost anything else that can create three numbers. The important thing is to get the three numbers:

```
void fmodApp::mouseDragged( int x, int y, int button ) {
    if(settingListener) {
        sposition.x = float(x)/20;
        sposition.y = float(y)/20;
    } else {
        lposition.x= float(x)/20;
        lposition.y = float(y)/20;
    }
}
```

Finally, to let the user toggle between editing the sound and listener positions, make any key press change the object for which the position is being modified:

```
void fmodApp::keyPressed( int key ){
    keyIsDown = true;
}

void fmodApp::keyReleased( int key ) {
    keyIsDown = false;
}
```

This is just the bare surface of what the FMOD Ex library can do. It can create up to 16 channels and position each of them in 3-D space, navigate a listener or even multiple listeners through multidimensional space, create echoes based on the geometry of a space, simulate Doppler effects, and do a lot more. It lets you use sophisticated techniques to place, shape, and simulate sound. Having the ability to create complex and realistic sound helps with one of the main points of working with sound that was mentioned at the beginning of this chapter: sound gives us a lot of information about the world. In the case of a virtual world, correct sound goes a long way toward giving us information about a world that may not immediately be visible to the user.

# Maximilian

Audio synthesis in oF became much easier when Mick Grierson released Maximilian, a simple but powerful library for creating and manipulating audio data. While you can use the library independently of its oF add-on, we're going to, of course, focus on using it in the context of an oF application. First you'll need to download the library from *http://maximilian.strangeloop.co.uk/* and place it in your  *addons* folder, *openframe-works/addons*. Next, create an empty project and add the ofxMaxim folder to the add-ons of your project. Try adding the following line to the header of your *testApp.h* file:

```
#include "ofxMaxim.h"
```

If it compiles, you're good to go. If it doesn't, you'll want to check that you added the add-on correctly and set any necessary headers paths; take a look back at Chapter 5 for more info. Now it's time to explore Maximilian a little more.

Opening up ofxMaxim you'll see typedefs turning the names of the regular maxim classes into versions with ofx appended at the beginning. This is to conform to the naming conventions that oF uses, but it also makes for a bit of confusion when looking through the source code. In this chapter, I'll be referring to the classes and objects by their ofx-appended names, instead of by their original names, to avoid confusion.

Doing audio generation is largely a matter of mathematics performed on arrays full of floating-point numbers that will be passed to the sound card of your computer, the *audio buffers*. When you're making an oF application that uses Maximilian, you need to pass all the values in to set up all of those equations, so that applying a filter (for example) has the intended effect. To do that, you call the setup() method of the ofx MaxiSettings and tell it the sampling rate that you're using, the number of channels that you'll be using, and the buffer size. A very standard example is shown below:

```
ofxMaxiSettings::setup(44100, 2, 512);
```

That's all that's required for Maximilian to work in the set up, but it's not all that you need. You'll need to make sure that your oF application has the audioOut() method defined, and if you want to work with incoming sound as well, then the audioIn(), too. Maximilian works by adding functionality to work with the raw data the audio drivers that oF integrates with gives to the oF application. This is where you alter all the out-going sound by storing data in the output buffer. This buffer is called output and is passed into the audioOut() method. Any information you put in that array will be sent to the audio card when the audio card is ready for new audio data. When your appli-cation is sending sound data to the sound card, you'll need to do the following:

```
void testApp::audioOut     (float * output, int bufferSize, int nChannels){

    for (int i = 0; i < bufferSize; i++){
        // is where the maximilian will do it's magic
        output[i*nChannels    ] = i * 1000;
        output[i*nChannels + 1] = i * 1000;
    }
}
```

When your application is receiving sound from the sound card that you want to use, for instance, if you want to record microphone data, you'll want to store that in two arrays, one for each channel, left and right. Declare those like so:

```
float lAudioIn[BUFFER_SIZE]; // where BUFFER_SIZE is the buffer size
float rAudioIn[BUFFER_SIZE];
```

In the audioIn() method, you can store the audio coming from the audio in those buffers:

```
void testApp::audioIn     (float * input, int bufferSize, int nChannels){
    for (int i = 0; i < bufferSize; i++){
        lAudioIn[i] = input[i*2];
        rAudioIn[i] = input[i*2+1];
    }
}
```

Since Maximilian doesn't do much with incoming sound, you probably won't be working with the audioIn() all that much, though we will use it in this chapter. But it does do a lot with the outgoing sound in the audioOut() method.

 Older versions of openFrameworks used audioRequested() when the sound card was ready for data and audioReceived() when the sound card was sending data to the application. These still work, but they are deprecated in favor of the audioIn() and audioOut().

In this first demonstration application, you'll be generating several sine waves and using them to modify each other. To generate a sine wave with Maximillian, create an ofx MaxiOsc instance and call the sinewave() method, passing in the frequency that you want the wave generated with:

```
double sinewave(double frequency)
```

You'll notice that this returns a double, and that double is used to fill the outgoing audio buffer in the audioOut() method. Because the buffer is at least 512 values, the easiest way to fill it is by putting the sinewave() call in a loop within the audioOut() method. We'll also be using another method of the ofxMaxiOsc class, phasor(), to generate phase waves that start at a certain frequency and advances to the next frequency in a given time period. Sounds vague, but you'll understand it the instant you hear it. Take a look at Example 10-9.

*Example 10-9. sineJoiner.h*

```
#pragma mark once

#include "ofMain.h"
#include "ofxMaxim.h"
#include "ofGui.h" // this is included in the downloads

class sineJoiner : public ofBaseApp{

    public:

    void setup();
    void update() {}
    void draw();
```

```
    void audioOut     (float * input, int bufferSize, int nChannels); // output method

    ofSlider slider1, slider2, slider3; // just making a simple gui
    ofGuiCollection gui;

    int        initialBufferSize; // buffer size
    int        sampleRate;

    ofSoundStream soundStream;

    // begin maximilian stuff
    double outputs[2]; // this will be important later
    ofxMaxiOsc sine, phasorSine, phasor;

    int bin_number;
    float largest;

    ofxMaxiMix mix;
    ofxMaxiFilter filterlo;

    float waves[512];
    float phasors[512];

};
```

Now the *cpp* file, in Example 10-10.

*Example 10-10. sineJoiner.cpp*

```
#include "sineJoiner.h"

void sineJoiner::setup(){

    ofEnableAlphaBlending();
    ofSetupScreen();
    ofBackground(0, 0, 0);
    ofSetVerticalSync(true);

    sampleRate        = 44100;
    initialBufferSize = 512;

    slider1.setup("wave", 512.f, 0, 1024 );
    slider2.setup("phasor", 0.f, 0.f, 1024 );
    slider3.setup("filter", 0.25f, 0.001f, 0.5f);

    gui.setup("gui", 10, 10);
    gui.add(&slider1);
    gui.add(&slider2);
    gui.add(&slider3);
```

Set up both Maximilian and the ofSoundStream instance:

```
ofxMaxiSettings::setup(sampleRate, 2, initialBufferSize);
soundStream.setup(this, 2, 2, 44100, 512, 4);

}
```

For the `draw()`, we'll just draw the actual sine waves as they're generated from the `sinewave()` and `phasor()`, and draw a small circle for each value in the outgoing buffer:

```
void sineJoiner::draw(){

    ofSetColor(255, 255, 255, 255);
    int i;
    for(i = 0; i < initialBufferSize; i++) {
        ofSetColor(255, 255, 0);
        ofCircle( i * 2, ofGetHeight()/2 + phasors[i] * 100, 2, 2);
        ofSetColor(0, 255, 255);
        ofCircle( i * 2, ofGetHeight()/2 + waves[i] * 100, 2, 2);

    }

    ofSetColor(255, 0, 0);
    float h = slider3.getValue() * ofGetHeight() * 2.f;
    ofLine(0, ofGetHeight() - h, ofGetWidth(), ofGetHeight() - h);

    gui.draw();
}
```

Now the magic: the `bufferSize` tells you how many values the audio card will need, and the output is where the values need to be stored. Putting together the two sounds is as simple as adding them and then adding them to the `ofxMaxiMix` instance that creates stereo sound for the audio output. That's why the `output` array was declared:

```
void sineJoiner::audioOut(float * output, int bufferSize, int nChannels){

    for (int i = 0; i < bufferSize; i++)
    {
        waves[i] = sine.sinebuf(abs(slider1.getValue()));
        phasors[i] = phasorSine.sinewave(phasor.phasor(1.0, 0,
        abs(slider2.getValue()) ));

        float filteredOutput = filterlo.lopass(waves[i] + phasors[i],
        abs(slider3.getValue()));
        mix.stereo(filteredOutput, outputs, 0.5);

        output[i*nChannels    ] = outputs[0];
        output[i*nChannels + 1] = outputs[1];
    }

}
```

Now you're ready to walk through loading a file and controlling its playback speed. The first class to understand from a conceptual standpoint is `ofxMaxiSample`, which allows you to load audio files from your disk, play them back, and read the data into buffers to be manipulated by other procedures. We'll stretch out a loaded sound a little more effectively by using a class called `maxiTimestretch`. Actually, in this example, we'll use a pointer to a `maxiTimestretch` because we need to create it with a few initial parameters.

The `maxiTimestretch` does the stretching in a two methods. First, when you create the `maxiTimestretch` instance, you tell it where its input is going to come from:

```
maxiTimestretch(maxiSample *sample)
```

Then, when you're outputting the data from that input, you can pass in how you want that output to be modified:

```
double play(double speed, double grainLength, int overlaps, double posMod=0.0)
```

So with that out of the way, look at the application. This application requires a sound with a 44,100 sample rate. One is included in the code downloads. See Example 10-11.

*Example 10-11. wavStretcher.cpp*

```
#pragma mark once

#include "ofMain.h"
#include "ofxMaxim.h"
#include "maxiGrains.h"
#include <sys/time.h>

class wavStretcher : public ofBaseApp
{

    public:

    ~wavStretcher(); // this is a destructor, handy in this case

    void setup();
    void update();
    void draw();

    void mouseDragged (int x, int y, int button );

    void audioOut(float * input, int bufferSize, int nChannels); // output method

    int    initialBufferSize;
    int    sampleRate;

    double outputs[2];
```

Here are the objects that will load the sample, mix the result, and do the time stretching:

```
    maxiSample samp;
    maxiMix mymix;
    maxiTimestretch<hannWinFunctor> *ts;
    double speed, grainLength;
```

These will allow us to create a visualization of the sound:

```
        ofxMaxiFFT fft;
        ofxMaxiFFTOctaveAnalyzer octaveAnalyser;
        int current;
        double pos;

    };
```

Example 10-12 is the *.cpp* file.

*Example 10-12. wavStretcher.cpp*

```cpp
#include "wavStretcher.h"

wavStretcher::~wavStretcher()
{
    delete ts; // clean up after yourself!
}

void wavStretcher::setup()
{

    samp.load(ofToDataPath("organ.wav")); // this be any wav file

    ofEnableAlphaBlending();
    ofSetupScreen();
    ofBackground(0, 0, 0);
    ofSetFrameRate(60);

    sampleRate          = 44100; /* Sampling Rate */
    initialBufferSize   = 512;    /* Buffer Size. fill this buffer with sound*/

    ts = new maxiTimestretch<hannWinFunctor>(&samp);

    speed = 1;
    grainLength = 0.05;
    current=0;

    fft.setup(1024, 512, 256);
    octaveAnalyser.setup(44100, 1024, 10);

    int current = 0;
    ofxMaxiSettings::setup(sampleRate, 2, initialBufferSize);
    // Call this last !
    ofSoundStreamSetup(2,0, this, maxiSettings::sampleRate, initialBufferSize, 4);

}

void wavStretcher::update()
{
    //nada
}

void wavStretcher::draw()
{

    ofSetColor(255, 255, 255, 255);
```

```
    int i;
    ofBeginShape();
    ofVertex(50, ofGetHeight()/2);
    for(i = 0; i < octaveAnalyser.nAverages; i++) {
        // you can draw them as simple rects
        //ofRect( 50 + i * 10, ofGetHeight()/2 - (octaveAnalyser.averages[i] * 4), 10,
        octaveAnalyser.averages[i] * 8);
        // or as peaks+troughs
        ofVertex(50 + i * 10, ofGetHeight()/2 - (octaveAnalyser.averages[i] * 4));
        ofVertex(50 + i * 10, ofGetHeight()/2 + octaveAnalyser.averages[i] * 4);
    }
    ofVertex(ofGetWidth(), ofGetHeight()/2);
    ofEndShape(true);
}

void wavStretcher::audioOut(float * output, int bufferSize, int nChannels)
{
    for (int i = 0; i < bufferSize; i++)
    {
```

Here is the actual time stretching, as mentioned above:

```
    float wave = ts->play(speed, grainLength, 5, 0);
            if (fft.process(wave)) {
                octaveAnalyser.calculate(fft.magnitudes);
            }

            //play result
            mymix.stereo(wave, outputs, 0.5);
            output[i*nChannels    ] = outputs[0];
            output[i*nChannels + 1] = outputs[1];
        }
    }

    void wavStretcher::mouseDragged(int x, int y, int button )
    {
        speed = ((double ) x / ofGetWidth() * 4.0) - 2.0;
        grainLength = ((double) y / ofGetHeight() * 0.1) + 0.001;
        pos = ((double) x / ofGetWidth() * 2.0);


    }
```

For the final Maximilian application (see Example 10-13), you'll estimate a pitch that you hum into the microphone. This will work a lot better if you're wearing headphones, because you'll hear your own voice over the sound from the speakers.

*Example 10-13. pitchEstimator.h*

```
#pragma mark once

#include "ofMain.h"
#include "ofxMaxim.h"

class pitchEstimator : public ofBaseApp{
```

```
public:

~testApp();
void setup();
void update();
void draw();

void audioOut     (float * input, int bufferSize, int nChannels); // output method
void audioIn      (float * input, int bufferSize, int nChannels); // input method

int           initialBufferSize; /* buffer size */
int           sampleRate;

ofSoundStream soundStream;
```

Three sine waves to additively estimate the sound received from the microphone:

```
double outputs[2];
ofxMaxiOsc sine, sine1, sine2;

int bin_number, bin_number1, bin_number2;
float largests[3];
```

The ofxMaxiFFT will do the actual estimation of what frequency ranges the sound coming in from the microphone is loudest in:

```
ofxMaxiFFT fft;
ofxMaxiMix mix;

float *inputL, *inputR;

float estimatedPitch[3];

};
```

For the meat of the application, see Example 10-14.

*Example 10-14. pitchEstimator.cpp*

```
#include "pitchEstimator.h"

pitchEstimator::~pitchEstimator() {
    delete inputL; // clean up after yourself
    delete inputR;
}

void pitchEstimator::setup(){
    // some standard setup stuff

    ofEnableAlphaBlending();
    ofSetupScreen();
    ofBackground(0, 0, 0);
    ofSetVerticalSync(true);

    sampleRate          = 44100;
    initialBufferSize   = 512;
```

```
    inputL = new float[initialBufferSize];
    inputR = new float[initialBufferSize];

    fft.setup(16384, 1024, 512);

    soundStream.setup(this, 2, 2, 44100, initialBufferSize, 4);
    estimatedPitch[0] = estimatedPitch[1] = estimatedPitch[2] = 0.f;

}

void pitchEstimator::update(){
    //nothing
}

void pitchEstimator::draw(){

    ofSetColor(255, 255, 255, 255);
    int i;
    for(i = 0; i < fft.bins; i++) {
        ofRect(i * 11, ofGetHeight()/2 - (fft.magnitudesDB[i] * 4), 11,
        fft.magnitudesDB[i] * 8);
    }

}

void pitchEstimator::audioOut    (float * output, int bufferSize, int nChannels){

    for (int i = 0; i < bufferSize; i++)
    {
        wave = sine.sinebuf4(abs(estimatedPitch[0])) + sine1.sinebuf4(abs(estimatedPitch[1])) +
        sine1.sinebuf4(abs(estimatedPitch[2]));

        mix.stereo(wave/3.f, outputs, 0.5);

        output[i*nChannels    ] = outputs[0];
        output[i*nChannels + 1] = outputs[1];
    }

}

void pitchEstimator::audioIn    (float * input, int bufferSize, int nChannels){

    double lIn, rIn;
```

Here, the input data is sent to the FFT, which figures out how loud each different magnitude in the sound is, using the magsToDB() method. Then we look through each "loudness" registered in the magnitudesDB array and determine what the loudest three bins in that array are, so that they can be used to create sine waves:

```
    int i;
    for (i = 0; i < bufferSize; i++){

        lIn = input[i*2];
        if(fft.process(lIn)) {
```

```
        fft.magsToDB();
    }

    rIn = input[i*2 + 1];
    if(fft.process(rIn)) {
        fft.magsToDB();
    }

}

bin_number = bin_number1 = bin_number2 = 0;
largests[0] = largests[1] = largests[2] = 0.f;
for (i = 0; i < fft.bins; i++) {
    if(abs(fft.magnitudesDB[i]) > largests[0]) {

        largests[2] = largests[1];
        largests[1] = largests[0];
        largests[0] = abs(fft.magnitudesDB[i]);

        bin_number2 = bin_number1;
        bin_number1 = bin_number;
        bin_number = i;
    }
}
```

The 12.0 here simply seemed like a nice number to determine whether there was adequate volume in that bin:

```
if(largests[0] > 12.0)
    estimatedPitch[0] = ( (float) bin_number / fft.bins) * (sampleRate * 0.5);
else
    estimatedPitch[0] = 0.f;

if(largests[1] > 12.0)
    estimatedPitch[1] = ( (float) bin_number1 / fft.bins) * (sampleRate * 0.5);
else
    estimatedPitch[1] = 0.f;

if(largests[2] > 12.0)
    estimatedPitch[2] = ( (float) bin_number2 / fft.bins) * (sampleRate * 0.5);
else
    estimatedPitch[2] = 0.f;

}
```

Now let's make some sound with the Arduino.

# Physical Manipulation of Sound with Arduino

This chapter began by talking about the physical nature of sound. Yet we haven't really looked at any direct electrical manipulation of sound. We're about to rectify that. One of the most commonly used sensors for the Arduino controller is a piezo sensor. You can find a more thorough discussion of piezoelectricity and how to find these sensors in Chapter 8, so the introduction to this sensor will be brief here.

Piezo sensors are usually used to detect vibration and pressure by outputting more electricity when they are bent or altered. However, it's possible to do more with a piezo sensor than detect pressure. In fact, one of the more common uses of a piezo sensor is in a buzzer. Many older electronics and primitive speakers use piezo elements. Their output range is quite limited, but for simple tones without a great deal of depth, a piezo is quite adequate. Thanks to some excellent work by David Cuartielles, who figured out the amount of time to push a common piezo sensor HIGH to replicate each note of the common eight-note scale, you can use Table 10-1 to play notes from a piezo sensor.

Table 10-1. Piezo sensor notes

| Note | Frequency | Period[a] | Pulse width[b] |
|------|-----------|-----------|----------------|
| C | 261 | 3830 | 1915 |
| D | 294 | 3400 | 1700 |
| E | 329 | 3038 | 1519 |
| F | 349 | 2864 | 1432 |
| G | 392 | 2550 | 1275 |
| A | 440 | 2272 | 1136 |
| B | 493 | 2028 | 1014 |
| C (high C) | 523 | 1912 | 956 |

[a] Length of time it takes to make the tone.
[b] Length of the high signal in the tone.

This concept of *pulse width* is one that will require a little bit more exploration. For the Arduino, the *pulse* is a short blast of 5-volt current, and the *width* is the length of time that the controller sends those 5 volts. You'll notice on your controller (or, if you have an Arduino Mini, in the schematic for your controller) that some pins are marked PWM.

# A Quick Note on PWM

PWM stands for *pulse width modulation*, and it's important because your Arduino controller can't actually output analog voltages. It can output only digital voltages, either 0 or 5 volts. To output analog voltages, the computer uses averaged voltages, flipping between 0 and 5 volts at an appropriate interval to simulate the desired output voltage, as in Figure 10-6.

To make a tone—for example, an A—you send a 5-volt signal to the piezo sensor for 1,136 microseconds and then send a 0-volt signal or no signal to the piezo for 1,136 microseconds. In the following code, you'll see two arrays filled with the notes and their relative microsecond delays:

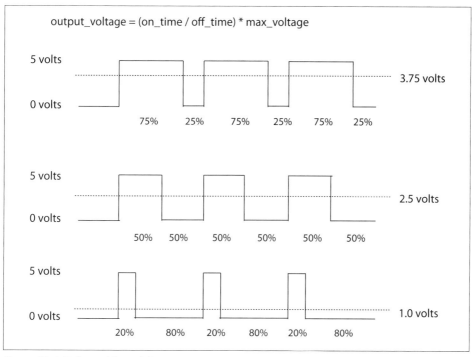

output_voltage = (on_time / off_time) * max_voltage

*Figure 10-6. Pulse width modulation*

```
// this enumerates the different notes
byte names[] = {'c', 'd', 'e', 'f', 'g', 'a', 'b', 'C'};
// enumerate the tones and the period required for them
int tones[] = {1915, 1700, 1519, 1432, 1275, 1136, 1014, 956};
```

The duration of the pulse is in *microseconds*, not *milliseconds*; 1,136 microseconds is 1.136 milliseconds and 0.001136 seconds.

A melody can be input as a series of notes with lengths in front of them, for example, 4a, which indicates a note with a length about four times the base length. Notice next that the notes in the names array correlate to the correct lengths in the tones array. For each note, the PWM value will be looked up in the tones array. The microsecond value is used to send a HIGH signal and then a LOW signal from the digital pin. The rest of the code that follows finds the correct note and adjusts the length of the note. This is because high notes will be shorter than longer notes since the amount of time in the signal required to make the sound is longer.

The piezo sensor will almost certainly have a red wire and a black wire. If not, look at the data sheet for your piezo sensor to determine which wire is the ground and which is the power. The power line is connected to digital pin 3 of the Arduino controller, and the ground is connected to the ground pin on the Arduino. The rest of this code is carefully annotated for you in Example 10-15:

*Example 10-15. piezoSound.ino*

```
int speakerOut = 3; // this is the pin that the piezo element should be connected to
// this enumerates the different notes
byte names[] = {'c', 'd', 'e', 'f', 'g', 'a', 'b', 'C'};
// enumerate the tones and the frequency required for them
int tones[] = {1915, 1700, 1519, 1432, 1275, 1136, 1014, 956};
// here's the melody we'll play, with the length of the note and the note itself
byte melody[] = "4c4d4e4f4g4a4b4C";
int eachNote = 0;
int noteLength = 0;
int findNote = 0;
int melodyLength = 8;
int theRightNote;

void setup() {
  pinMode(3, OUTPUT);
}

void loop() {
  //start our program
  digitalWrite(speakerOut, LOW);
  int correctedNoteLength;

  //loop through each notes in our melody
  for (eachNote = 0; eachNote < melodyLength; eachNote++) {
      // find the note that we're suppposed to play
      for (findNote=0;findNote<8;findNote++) {
        //store that note
        if (names[findNote] == melody[eachNote*2 + 1]) {
          theRightNote = findNote;
        }
      }

      // adjust the note because higher notes take less time to play
      // so we need to add some time to higher notes and subtract time
      // from lower notes
      int adjustmentAmt = (1450 - tones[theRightNote])*3;
      correctedNoteLength = (((melody[eachNote*2]) * 200) + adjustmentAmt) / 100;

      //make sure that we play the note for the length specified in the length
      for (noteLength = 0; noteLength <= correctedNoteLength; noteLength++) {
          digitalWrite(speakerOut,HIGH);
          delayMicroseconds(tones[theRightNote]);
          digitalWrite(speakerOut, LOW);
          delayMicroseconds(tones[theRightNote]);
      }
    }
  }
}
```

If you liked this, you can find an updated example of this code by David Cuartielles on the Arduino website (*http://www.arduino.cc/*) and a more complex example that uses an actual speaker instead of a piezo element created by Alexandre Quessy.

## Creating Interactions with Sound

Now that you've learned some basic sound generation and manipulation techniques, the question becomes, how do you create interactions with these libraries and techniques? FFT lets you do rather sophisticated analysis of sounds. Analyzing sounds lets you do things based on a pitch or on the amplitude of a sound in a particular frequency range. This lets you create an input based on the volume or pitch of people's voices, based on tones as old touch-tone telephones once did, or based on certain patterns of sounds. With all the libraries that have been presented in this chapter, we've just scratched the surface of what they can do, and all of them deserve a closer look.

Using the Minim library, you can create tones and sounds; load, play back, and process audio files; mix and loop multiple complex series of sounds; and apply effects to those sounds. With the Sound Object library, you can create tones, loops, mixes of sounds and tones, and you can perform exact manipulations of those tones. This opens up two options: first, you can programmatically create audible feedback for a user or listener, and second, you can let users create their own sounds, loops, and mixes based on an interface and input system that you devise. Applying audio effects, pitch bending, tuning, and control of the timing of sounds is rich interactive terrain both as input and as feedback. Finally, with the FMOD Ex library, you can create 3-D sound and sound effects to provide physically realized feedback that can position, respond, and inform a user.

## Further Resources

For anyone serious about making computer sound, the following four tools are invaluable: PureData, Max/MSP, Csound, and SuperCollider.

PureData, created by Miller Puckette and maintained by Puckette and a large group of collaborators, is a real-time graphical programming environment for audio, video, and graphical processing. Max/MSP shares some core ideas and lineage with PureData and has a very similar interface: a graphical programming environment bolstered by a wealth of plug-ins. It's a commercial product and must be purchased, but it provides a substantial community and a wide range of tools that make it a worthwhile investment. It's very popular with composers, sound artists, and interactive artists, and has been used to generate music by DJs, in sound installations, and in live performances of all kinds all over the world.

Csound is a system and programming environment for creating sounds, mixing, and creating filters.

Finally, SuperCollider is an environment and programming language released in 1996 by James McCartney. It consists of a server that processes commands to perform real-time audio synthesis and algorithmic composition, and a scripting language that lets you pass commands to that server. Since then, it has been evolving into a system used and further developed by both scientists and artists working with sound. It's an efficient and expressive dynamic programming language, and it's an interesting framework for acoustic research, algorithmic music, and interactive programming.

For understanding music, digital signal processing, and sound on a computer, *The Computer Music Tutorial* by Curtis Roads (MIT Press) is a must. It's a little bit dated at this point, but the explanations of fundamental concepts in signal processing, synthesizer generation, and the mathematics behind sound are invaluable.

*HCI Beyond the GUI*, edited by Philip Kortum (Morgan Kaufmann), also provides a lot of very valuable information for designers or artists thinking about working with sound as an interactive element, particularly for application development or more commercially or product-oriented design efforts. David Huron wrote a wonderful book on the topic of sound, surprise, and expectation called *Sweet Anticipation* (MIT Press) that addresses the psychology of music and sound. Leonard Meyer's *Emotion and Meaning in Music* (University of Chicago Press) is also a wonderful book on similar topics that would be well suited to anyone with a background in music.

If you're interested in working with electronics for music and audio production either by assembling components from low-level components or by repurposing other electronics, the book *Handmade Electronic Music* by Nic Collins (Routledge) is a gold mine of tutorials, information, and inspiration. It's also a fine primer for many of the basic concepts of electronics that we don't have space to cover in this book.

Voice user interfaces are one of the most tantalizing interactive elements of working with sound. Unfortunately, at this time they are also difficult to begin working with right away. In the interest of preventing this book from becoming out-of-date too quickly, we'll make only a few mentions of projects that might be of interest. A fully open source library called Sphinx, developed at Carnegie Mellon University, was primarily intended to run on Linux but has been ported to Mac OS X and Windows. The Julius library has been developed over the past dozen or so years by a rotating team of researchers at Japanese universities. Currently, the project is headed up out of Kyoto University. The Julius project is being updated frequently and has a fairly large user base. It has successfully been used in iPhone applications and seems quite promising. By the time this book is published, better documentation and resources may be available for Julius and Sphinx.

## Review

Sound is a wave of air pressure that has both a maximum and minimum pressure as well as a frequency.

The sound card is a device that converts sounds into digital signals. Devices that need to communicate with an operating system use applications called drivers to exchange information with an operating system. Buffering is the technique of storing a small portion of the audio data received from the audio card.

In a Processing application, you can use the Minim library to load sounds and play them back by using the `load()` and `play()` methods of the Minim object. The `AudioOutput` class of the Minim library allows you to output sounds through your sound card; the `AudioInput` allows you to input sounds.

The Minim library allows you to create filters, for instance a `LowPass` filter, and waves, for instance a `SquareWave` or a `SineWave`.

Sound in oF is done through two classes `ofSoundPlayer` and the `ofSoundStream`. The `ofSoundPlayer` wraps the FMOD Ex library for higher-level sound access, and the `ofSoundStream` uses the rtAudio library for lower-level access to data directly from the sound card.

Pitch shifting is a technique for changing the pitch of a sound by shifting the value of each number in the sound data up or down a certain amount. This often involves the use of a technique called windowing, which is used to create a small section of a signal for analysis.

The FMOD Ex library can also be used to create 3-D sounds that let you place both the listener and the sound origin.

To generate sounds in oF, you can use the Maximilian library to load sounds, create waves, and mix these together. The `ofxMaxim` add-on allows you to use the Maximilian library in oF easily.

To stretch a sound you've loaded, you can use the `ofxMaxim maxiTimestretch` object to time stretch a sample.

You can also play sounds with the Arduino controller by using Pulse Width Modulation to send signals to a piezo element at a specific interval to create a sound.

The *Fast Fourier Transform* is an algorithm used to determine how loud a signal is within a certain frequency range. This is often used to create equalizer views or to do rudimentary beat detection.

# CHAPTER 11

# Arduino and Feedback

Although there are projects that allow us to alter an aspect of reality as it confronts us (the *Parallel Tracking and Mapping* project at the Oxford Robots Lab or the ARToolkit library come to mind), nothing can replace the richness of the actual physical sensation of the world around us. This includes, of course, both the sound and the images of the world around us, as discussed in earlier chapters, but too often the easily manipulated senses are the only ones that interaction art and design addresses. Any industrial or product designer, architect, or sculptor can tell you about the emotional and cognitive effects that the physical product has upon us. Objects that are carried, lifted, or felt; that change the nature of space around us; or that let us change the nature of the space around us engage us differently than those that do not.

When you're thinking about creating physical feedback, you're thinking about using mechanics and about creating machines. More than any other topic in this book, physical feedback involves thinking about and using the practices of mechanical and electrical engineering and coupling them with programming. Luckily for you, the Arduino community on the bulletin boards is very knowledgeable and helpful in answering questions about these sorts of topics, and a host of other resources are available. This does require a slightly different approach and way of thinking, though, because you'll need to follow along quite closely with electrical diagrams as well as copying down code. Debugging circuits is usually done using a voltmeter or, if you're really dedicated or lucky, an oscilloscope. It's a much different process than coding, but it has some rich rewards: enabling you to create things that move and act in the world.

So, from the perspective of designing an interaction, how do you create good physical interaction? The rules are pretty much the same: spectrum feedback mechanisms usually should correlate to spectrum inputs, and binary feedback should correlate to binary input. User input that changes a state leads a user to expect a changed state. Thinking about this in terms of the physical environment that one or more viewers inhabit presents interesting challenges and wonderful opportunities to engage. You can explore a whole new range of senses and kinds of thinking with physical feedback, though. The feel of something, its actual sensation, or the changing of the physical space around us are all quite different sensory experiences than looking at a screen or hearing a sound.

The physical nature of what a user is doing is going to shape drastically their perception of what should be happening, so the digital states of a system or an application and the physical states that the user perceives should be kept synchronized when possible.

When you design a system that presents physical feedback, it is necessary to understand and plan around every possible aspect of the physical environment of the user. The vibrate setting on my cell phone works because I keep my cell phone in my pocket. Just having a blinking light to indicate to me that my turn signal is on in my car doesn't work because I might not be looking at the dashboard. Coupled with a clicking sound, I notice it.

Innumerable tools, from backhoes to bombs, alter our physical environment. Their actions in the environment are not intended to help a viewer or participant understand something that has occurred, to give or request information from them, or to further an exchange. Simple tools alter the world as the result of an action. Although the design and construction of such tools is fascinating, this chapter will focus on tools that use physical feedback to further an interaction or enable communication between a system and a user.

There is another element to some of the tools that we'll be touching on in this chapter that takes the discussion outside the realm of this book, but it's an important one nonetheless. Lots of times in physical computing there is no user, or the user really doesn't matter much. That's not often true with any of the other themes of interaction design that we've discussed so far, but it can be true with physical machines. Sometimes all the user does is watch or press a button to start a long process. That's not the focus of this book, but it is a reality in physical computing, so it's worth mentioning: lots of times the design of machines is pretty nonpeople-friendly, because the machine isn't going to be interacting with people very much. However, in this chapter, we're going to be looking at things with the assumption that someone will be actively operating or experiencing them.

## Using Motors

The motor is the primary tool for creating motion. At its simplest, you can use a motor to make something spin. With a little more mechanical work, using gears and other mechanical devices, you can use a motor to make something move, vibrate, rise, fall, roll, creep, or perform almost any other type of motion that does not require precise positioning. There are several different kinds of motors: servos, stepper motors, or unidirectional DC motors. In this chapter, you'll look at all three kinds and how you can use them. The simplest motors are good for designs that need motion forward or backward, like a remote control car or a fan, but not for things that need to move to a precise position, like a robotic arm or anything that points or moves something to a controlled position.

Motors are all around us; just look inside moving toys and you'll find a number of excellent motors and gears you can repurpose if you'd like. Any electronics supplier will have a wide range of motors that will suit many purposes, from spinning small objects to driving large loads. In Figure 11-1, you'll see two small motors that can be controlled by an Arduino controller and a diagram that shows how the internals of a brushed DC electric motor work.

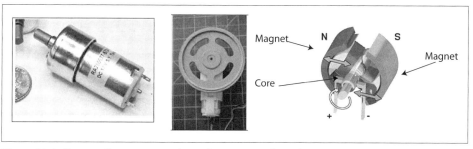

*Figure 11-1. Two small motor examples and a cutaway of another*

## DC Motors

In a motor, when current passes through the coil wound around the core, the side of the positive pole is acted upon by an upward force, while the other side is acted upon by a downward force. This creates a turning effect on the coil, making it rotate. To make the motor rotate in a constant direction, the current reverses every half a cycle, which ensures that the motor rotates in the same direction. To work through the example in this section, you'll need a DC motor that runs on low-voltage DC, somewhere between 5 V and 15 V.

This part of the example reverses the direction that the motor spins. To reverse a DC motor, you need to be able to reverse the direction of the current in the motor. The easiest way to do this is using an H-Bridge circuit. There are many different models and brands of H-Bridge. This example uses one of the most basic, an L293E from Texas Instruments (a similar chip is the SN754410). If you simply want to turn a motor on and off and don't need to reverse it—for example, if you're controlling a fan—you can simply control the motor by controlling the current sent to the motor.

The example in Figure 11-2 uses an H-Bridge integrated circuit, the Texas Instruments L293E. You can find these chips or equivalent at most large electronics suppliers. This particular chip can control two motors. It can drive up to 1 amp of current and between 4.5 and 36 V. If your motor needs more than that, you'll need to use a more powerful H-Bridge.

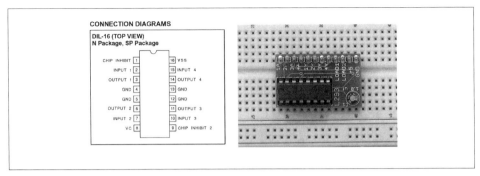

*Figure 11-2. The pinout and image of the 1293 H-Bridge chip*

There's another component included in this circuit that you'll need to understand: the capacitor. A *capacitor* is a pair of conductors (or plates) separated by an insulator (Figure 11-3), and it stores energy as an electrostatic field between the plates. *Capacitance* is a capacitor's ability to store that energy. The basic unit of capacitance is the farad (F). So, you'll see capacitors marked as 10 microFarads, or µF, as in Figure 11-4. Usually there are slight swings in the amount of current passed around a circuit. Sometimes variations in the voltages of these circuits can cause problems; if the voltages swing too much, the circuit may operate incorrectly. In the case of the motor in Figure 11-3, the capacitor smoothes the voltage spikes and dips that occur as the motor turns on and off.

*Figure 11-3. The electrical symbol for a capacitor and a representation of a polarised capacitor*

Now you're ready for the wiring diagram in Figure 11-4.

Let's break the wiring diagram down a little bit. The switch connected to the Arduino pin 2 controls which direction the motor will turn. When the switch is high or on, Arduino pin 3 will send a low signal, and pin 4 will send a high signal. This tells the H-Bridge to send the motor one direction. When the switch is low, the Arduino pin 3 will send a high signal, and pin 4 will send a low signal, telling the H-Bridge to send the motor in the other direction. See Example 11-1.

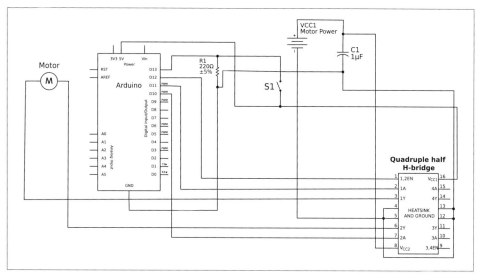

Figure 11-4. Wiring the motor and H-Bridge

Example 11-1. MotorDriving.ino

```
int switchPin = 2;      // switch input
int motorPin1 = 3;      // H-bridge leg 1
int motorPin2 = 4;      // H-bridge leg 2
int speedPin = 9;       // H-bridge enable pin
int ledPin = 13;        // LED

void setup() {
    // set the switch as an input:
    pinMode(switchPin, INPUT);

    // set all the other pins you're using as outputs:
    pinMode(motorPin1 , OUTPUT);
    pinMode(motorPin2 , OUTPUT);
    pinMode(speedPin, OUTPUT);
    pinMode(ledPin, OUTPUT);

    // set speedPin high so that motor can turn on:
    digitalWrite(speedPin, HIGH);

    // this is borrowed from Tom Igoe and is a nice way to debug
    // your circuit, if the light blinks 3 times after the initial
    // startup that's probably an indication that the Arduino has reset itself
    // because the motor caused a short
    blinkLED(ledPin, 3, 100);
}

void loop() {
```

If the switch is set to high, the motor will turn in one direction:

```
        if (digitalRead(switchPin) == HIGH) {
            digitalWrite(motorPin1, LOW);    // set 1A on the H-bridge low
            digitalWrite(motorPin2, HIGH);   // set 2A on the H-bridge high
        }
```

If the switch is low, the motor will turn in the other direction:

```
        else {
            digitalWrite(motorPin1, HIGH);   // set 1A on the H-bridge high
            digitalWrite(motorPin2, LOW);    // set 2A on the H-bridge low
        }
    }

    // this method just blinks an LED for debugging
    void blinkLED(int whatPin, int howManyTimes, int milliSecs) {
        int i = 0;
        for ( i = 0; i < howManyTimes; i++) {
            digitalWrite(whatPin, HIGH);
            delay(milliSecs/2);
            digitalWrite(whatPin, LOW);
            delay(milliSecs/2);
        }
    }
```

Now that you know how to wire a motor, you can begin to use a motor to create motion in any of your projects. If you're looking to use a motor to drive a more complex motion, you'll probably need to use some gears or wheels in different kinds of configurations. A number of websites worldwide sell tracks, wheels, and gear and axle kits.

## Stepper Motors

Stepper motors operate differently from normal DC motors. Instead of just rotating when voltage is applied to their terminals, they have multiple toothed electromagnets that are given power by an external control. To make the motor shaft turn, first one electromagnet is given power, which makes the gear's teeth magnetically attracted to the electromagnet's teeth. When the gear's teeth are thus aligned to the first electromagnet, they are slightly offset from the next electromagnet. When the next electromagnet is turned on and the first is turned off, the gear rotates slightly to align with the next, and so on, all the way around the gear. Each rotation is called a *step*, with an integral number of steps making a full rotation that lets you set the position of the motor to a precise angle.

To work with a stepper motor and an Arduino, you'll probably need to use a chip to control a stepper, called a *driver*, like the one pictured in Figure 11-5.

The driver lets the Arduino control the motion of the motor with pin 3 connected to the Step input, as marked on the diagram, and pin 2 connected to the Dir input, as marked in the diagram. To power your motor, you'll send the current to the pin on the Pololu Motor Driver marked +V. How much current you'll need to send is dependent on the motor that you're using, so check the data sheet for your motor. Figure 11-6

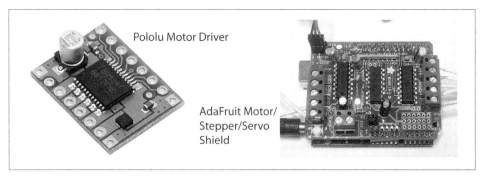

Figure 11-5. Two different motor driver shields

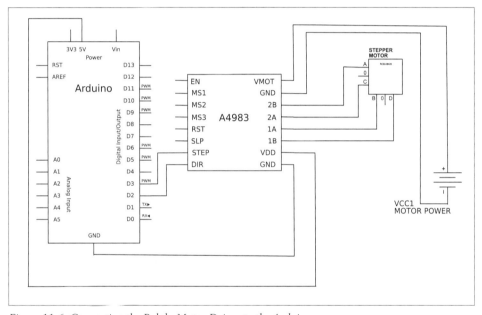

Figure 11-6. Connecting the Pololu Motor Driver to the Arduino

shows the connections that need to be made between the Pololu Motor Driver and the Arduino.

The Arduino code to control a stepper motor looks like Example 11-2.

Example 11-2. StepperViaShield.ino

```
int dirPin = 2;
int stepperPin = 3;

void setup() {
    pinMode(dirPin, OUTPUT);
    pinMode(stepperPin, OUTPUT);
}
```

```
void step(boolean dir,int steps){
    digitalWrite(dirPin,dir);
    delay(50);
    for(int i=0;i<steps;i++){
        digitalWrite(stepperPin, HIGH);
        delayMicroseconds(100);
        digitalWrite(stepperPin, LOW);
        delayMicroseconds(100);
    }
}

void loop(){
    step(true,1600);
    delay(500);
    step(false,1600*5);
    delay(500);
}
```

Another option is to use the Stepper library that comes with the Arduino IDE distribution. You can find examples of using this library both on the Arduino site and on the *MAKE* magazine site, *http://makezine.com*. Anything that you need to move a very controlled amount, such as a camera, a light, a small door, or a slide for a slide whistle, can all be controlled with a stepper motor.

In the next section, we'll look at servo motors, which are quite similar but have a few differences from a stepper motor. A servo is much smoother and better for continuous motion, while stepper motors can much more easily lock into fixed positions and can hold those fixed positions with much greater torque than a servo, making them more appropriate for moving into preset positions. You can see stepper motors at work in printers, laser cutters, tool and die machines of all flavors, as well as throughout industrial production lines.

## Motor Shields

Another option for working with stepper motors is a motor shield from Adafruit Industries, shown on the right in Figure 11-5. As of the writing of this book, the motor shield supports two smaller (5 V) servos, up to four bidirectional DC motors, and two stepper motors, as well as providing a block of connectors to easily hook up wires (10-22AWG) and power. These are worth looking into because they simplify working with multiple motors.

Pololu is a robotics supply company, who make motor drivers like the one shown on the left of Figure 11-5, that can be used to drive stepper and bidirectional motors. While the boards made by Pololu are more versatile, the Adafruit shield is much more Arduino-ready. Whether either of these tools is appropriate for your project base is dependent on how much you can spend.

# Smart Feedback

One of things that a motor can help you do is provide clever and informative haptic feedback: pushing or pulling meaningfully in a way that tells you what is going on inside the system. There are so many things that tell when they're reaching some end state by getting harder to do that it's incredibly easy to understand. One way of demonstrating that is using a motor to push against you using a lever and two Hall effect sensors.

A Hall effect sensor is a sensor that reads the strength of the magnetic field right around it, usually around 12 inches. Hall effect sensors are all rated to work with a specific strength of magnet field (measured in Gauss), which dissipates with distance from the magnet. Just like sound, it is softer when you are farther away from the source. The only reason this is important is because the distance a magnet needs to get to one of these sensors to trigger it is totally dependent on the magnet's strength. A powerful magnet will trigger the sensor from a greater distance than a weaker magnet. Hall effect sensors also have a max Gauss rating as well, so if you use too powerful of a magnet too close you'll damage or potentially break your sensor, so it pays to attend to the rating of the sensor. So what do you do with the hall effect sensor? The most common is as a digital input: is the door closed or open, is a lid up or closed, is something too close? But there are any multiple types of Hall effect sensors and multiple uses for them. The first distinction is between the type: linear Hall effect sensors output an analog signal depending on the strength and polarity of a magnet; digital Hall effect sensors latch on when a strong enough field is sensed, but won't unlatch until an equally strong, opposing field is sensed.

The Allegro A1321 is a linear hall effect sensor, meaning that it outputs an analog signal to read which when no minimum magnetic field is sensed, this sensor will output half of the source voltage—in the case of the Arduino will be 2.5V. When the north side of a magnet approaches the face of the sensor, the output voltage will linearly ramp up to the source voltage, 5V, and when the south pole of a magnet approaches the face of the A1321, the output will linearly drop to ground, 0V.

Now what you need is a way to trigger those Hall effect sensors and, for an interactive application, it would be good to have that associated with the input. Putting a magnet on a lever itself is an easy way to do that. Lay your motor on its side and attach a lever with a magnet at its end. At the nine o'clock and three o'clock positions, place the Hall effect sensor. (See Figure 11-7.) Now you have a way of creating resistance in a lever, which is a really powerful technique for giving a feel to an input through a sensor.

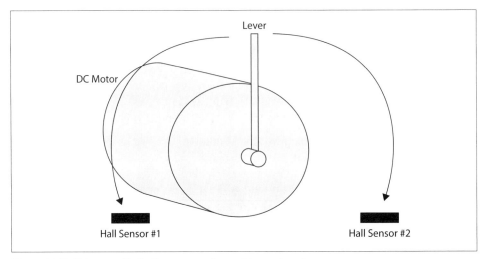

Figure 11-7. Using two Hall effect sensors for position estimation

If you're using the Adafruit Motor Shield, then the connections are very simple, as shown in Figure 11-8.

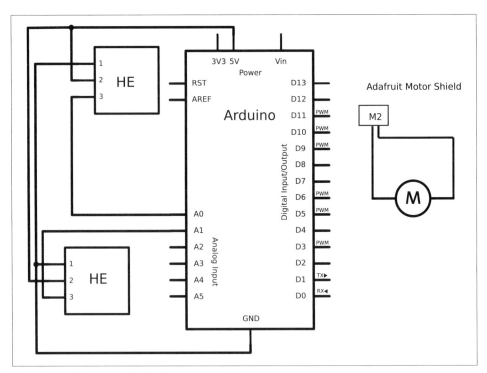

Figure 11-8. Connecting Hall effect sensors and a motor

And now the code, laid out for you in Example 11-3.

*Example 11-3. HallMotor.ino*

```
#include <MotorShield.h>

const int HALL_PINL = 1;
const int HALL_PINR = 2;

// this will depend on your sensors and setup
// but for the allegro A1321, we start at 2.5V or
// 512 on the analogRead
const int THRESHOLD = 0;

bool isStopped = true;
Motor dc(2, 48);

void setup() {
}

void loop() {
  int hallPosL = analogRead(HALL_PINR);
  int hallPosR = analogRead(HALL_PINL);

  if(hallPosL > THRESHOLD)
  {
    dc.run( FORWARD );
    dc.setSpeed( 255 - (hallPosL/2));
    isStopped = true;
  }
  else if(hallPosR > THRESHOLD)
  {
    dc.run( BACKWARD );
    dc.setSpeed( 255 - (hallPosR/2) );
    isStopped = true;
  }
  else {
    if(!isStopped) {
      dc.run( RELEASE );
      isStopped = true;
    }
  }
}
```

Now, this is a very introductory technique for creating haptic feedback directly correlated to input and has a "feel" for the user.

# Using Servos

The motor is not, on the face of it, an interactive element; it is a reactive element. For example, I turn the key and my car turns on. But motors are important and relevant to interaction and interactivity because working with motors and servos allows you to make the first step into one of the most important areas of human computer interaction and computing: robotics. Now, given the space constraints that I frequently mention, it's impossible for us to delve too deeply into robotics, but it is quite easy to show some of the basics of controlling a servo and creating *programmable motion*.

A servo is a type of motor but with a few added advantages. It, like the motor, receives a PWM signal that it uses to power itself; however, a servo reads the amount of voltage passed in to determine how far to rotate within a limited range. The most common range for a servo motor is 180 degrees, and the servo can move from any point in that range to any other point, clockwise or counterclockwise, making it a powerful tool for controlling anything that needs a controllable, repeatable movement. Robots, puppets, cars, and in fact most automated machinery make extensive use of servos. For our purposes in this chapter, we'll be looking at small servos, but you are encouraged to think big. One of the really wonderful aspects of servos is that though there are many to choose from with different sizes and performance, the signals used to control the servo are almost always the same, meaning that you could apply the same code to move a small hobbyist servo as you would to move a very large servo.

Now, although this won't quite make sense until we look at code to control the servo, it's worth mentioning here that the PWM pin on the Arduino control isn't set at the correct frequency to control a servo motor. That means that we can't write simple instructions to tell a servo to move to a certain position. We have to send the servo a 5 V pulse, where the duration of the pulse tells the servo to move to a given position. This isn't as difficult as it sounds, although it does make our code a little strange. But don't worry, because it will be explained in full.

## Connecting a Servo

To connect a servo motor to the Arduino controller, you need to provide the servo with power from the 5 V pin on the Arduino controller, you need to ground the servo, and you need to send commands to the servo PWM port. Now, as we mentioned, the PWM port of the Arduino controller doesn't operate at the proper frequency to communicate with a servo. If you're savvy with AVR microcontrollers—the chip that the Arduino uses—and C programming, you can change it, but that's beyond the scope of this book and isn't necessary to communicate with the servo.

## Communicating with the Servo

To control the servo, you send it a command every 20 milliseconds. The servo responds to a short pulse (1 ms or less) by moving to one extreme, and it moves around 180 degrees in the other direction when it receives long pulses (around 2 ms or more). The amount that the servo moves is determined by the length of time that the pulse is sent to the servo (see Figure 11-9). You should be aware that there is no standard for the exact relationship between pulse width and position; different servos may need slightly longer or shorter pulses.

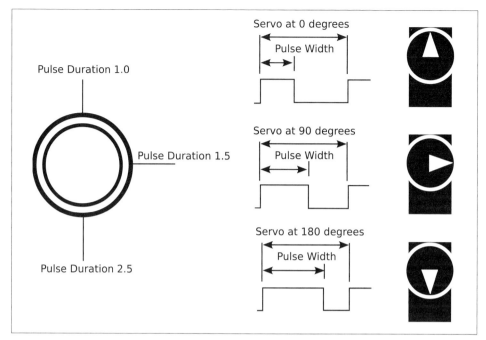

*Figure 11-9. Positioning a servo using the pulse width or duration*

Servo motors have three wires: power, ground, and signal, as Figure 11-10 shows. The power wire is typically red and should be connected to the 5V pin on the Arduino board, though some servo motors require more power than the Arduino can provide. The ground wire is typically black or brown and gets connected to a ground pin on the Arduino board. The yellow (or white) wire of the servo goes to the digital pin that you're using to control the servo. In Figure 11-10, it's digital pin 9, and the red and black wires go to +5V and ground, respectively.

## Wiring a Servo

As you'll see in the code snippet that follows, controlling a servo is really just a matter of determining how long in microseconds you need to send each command to the servo. Sending commands to the servo is a matter of writing a pulse to the motor that is the desired length. In Example 11-4, a value between 0 and 180 degrees (followed by a non-digit character) is sent using the serial connection to a computer to the servo. For example, 180 microseconds will move the servo fully in one direction, and 0 microseconds will move it fully in the other.

*Example 11-4. ServosRock.ino*

```
int command = 0;
int pulseWidth = 1500;
```

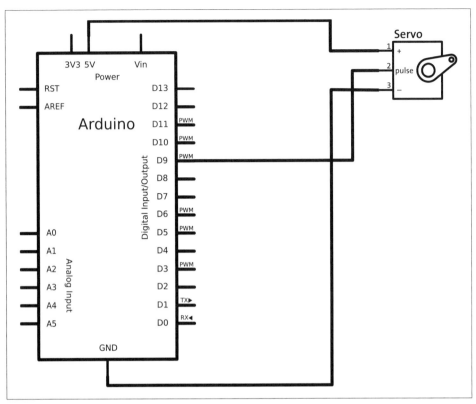

*Figure 11-10. Connecting an Arduino to a servo motor*

```
// this will be the center that the servo will go to if
// no commands are sent from the keyboard
int centerServo = 1500;
int servoPin = 9;

void setup(){
    pinMode(servoPin, OUTPUT);
    Serial.begin(9600);
    pulseWidth = centerServo;    // Give the servo a starting point (or it floats)
}

void loop(){
    if(Serial.available()){
        command = Serial.read(); // get the keyboard input
        // let's assume the user or another control
        // is sending a number between 1 and 9 to rotate the servo
        if(command > '0' && command <= '9') {
            // this turns a character into a usable integer
            command = command - '0';
            // now turn that number into a pulsewidth microsecond value
            // you might need to change this based on the servo that you're using
            pulseWidth = (command * 100) + 1000;
            sendPulse();
```

```
      }
   } else {
   // if no data is coming then just send the servo to the last position
   pulseWidth = (command * 100) + 1000; // you could also put it to the center,
   right, or the left.
   sendPulse();
   }
}

void sendPulse(){
    digitalWrite(servoPin, HIGH);
    delayMicroseconds(pulseWidth);
    digitalWrite(servoPin, LOW);
    // make sure the send pulse isn't getting called too
    // soon after the last time
    delay(20);
}
```

Many objects that you want to turn or rotate can be manipulated with a servo, such as cameras, mirrors, directed lighting, etc. To control these kinds of movement, there's an easy correlation between a potentiometer and a servo; turn the potentiometer, and the servo turns. You can use buttons as well, both to set the servo to a preset position or by turning the servo as the button is held down. Other input devices that can be matched to a servo are infrared and ultrasonic sensors, which were covered in Chapter 8.

Another way of programming the servo is to use the Servo library, which is included with the Arduino IDE. This library provides a somewhat easier way of communicating with the servo motor.

This library lets an Arduino board control one or two RC (hobby) servo motors on pins 9 and 10. Servos have integrated gears and a shaft that can be precisely controlled. Standard servos let the shaft be positioned at various angles, usually between 0 and 180 degrees. Continuous rotation servos let the rotation of the shaft be set to various speeds.

This library uses functionality built in to the hardware on pins 9 and 10 (11 and 12 for the Mega) of the microcontroller to control the servos without interfering with other code running on the Arduino. If only one servo is used, the other pin cannot be used for normal PWM output using analogWrite(). For example, you can't have a servo on pin 9 and PWM output on pin 10.

The Servo library provides three methods:

attach()
    Starts reading the Servo instance on the pin passed in to the method and has the following signatures:

```
        servo.attach(pin)
        servo.attach(pin, min, max) // optionally set the min and max pulse widths
```

```
write()
```
Writes a value to the servo. On a standard servo, this will set the angle of the shaft (in degrees). On a continuous rotation servo, this will set the speed of the servo (with 0 being full speed in one direction, 180 being full speed in the other, and a value near 90 being no movement).

```
read()
```
Reads the current angle of the servo (the value passed to the last call to `write()`).

To start the Servo library, declare an instance of it in your application code:

```
Servo servoInstance;
```

In Example 11-5, a potentiometer is attached to analog pin 0, and then the value from the potentiometer is used to set the position of the servo:

*Example 11-5. ServoPot.ino*

```
#include <Servo.h>
Servo myservo;  // create the servo object

int potpin = 0;  // analog pin used to connect the potentiometer
int val;    // variable to read the value from the analog pin

void setup()
{
    myservo.attach(9);  // attaches the servo on pin 9 to the servo object
}

void loop()
{
    val = analogRead(potpin); // reads the value of the potentiometer
        //(value between 0 and 1023)
    val = map(val, 0, 1023, 0, 180);// scale it to use it with the servo
        //(value between 0 and 180)
    myservo.write(val); // sets the servo position according to the
                        // scaled value
    delay(15); // waits for the servo to get there
}
```

One issue to keep in mind is that when you send a command to the servo, it takes a moment for the actual position of the arm to reach that point. If you want the servo to go from 0 degrees to 180 degrees, you'll probably need to send the command multiple times so that the motor can arrive at the position. In Example 11-6, by Hernando Barragan, the servo slowly rotates around its full range. Note the delay to allow the motor to move into the correct position:

*Example 11-6. ServoBarragan.ino*

```
#include <Servo.h>

Servo myservo;  // create servo object to control a servo
int pos = 0;    // variable to store the servo position
void setup() {
```

```
    myservo.attach(9);   // attaches the servo on pin 9 to the servo object
}

void loop()
{
    for(pos = 0; pos < 180; pos += 1)   // goes from 0 degrees to 180 degrees
    {                                    // in steps of 1 degree
        myservo.write(pos);              // tell servo to go to position in
                                         //variable 'pos'
        delay(15);                       // waits 15ms for the servo to
                                         //reach the position
    }
    for(pos = 180; pos>=1; pos-=1)       // goes from 180 degrees to 0 degrees
    {
        myservo.write(pos);              // tell servo to go to old position
        delay(15);                       // waits 15ms for the servo to
                                         //reach the position
    }
}
```

Lots of different types of servo motors are available. Most have only a 180-degree turning range, but some have 1.5- and 3-turn radii. Others, like the Parallax Continuous Rotation Servo, allow for full and complete continuous rotation.

There are several different shields and boards to simplify the wiring for servo motors, among them the Adafruit stepper shield shown earlier. Driving multiple servos—for instance, to create a simple robotic arm or a piece of animatronics—can get complex quickly, and though using a board will increase the price of your project, it can also make your wiring cleaner and your assembly quicker.

Another option for working with servo motors that you may be interested in is the MegaServo Hardware Servo library developed by Michael Margolis that is available for download on the Arduino website. This library allows an Arduino board to control 1 to 12 RC (hobby) servo motors on any digital pin on a standard Arduino board, or up to 48 servos on an Arduino Mega. It can be used just like the Servo library. It also allows you to control up to 48 servos on the Arduino Mega or 12 servos on the other boards. Any digital pin can be used with any servo, and pulse widths can be written and read in degrees or microseconds that makes writing the pulse widths easier.

In Chapter 14 we'll use 2 servo motors plus a webcam and face detection to determine the location of a user's face and keep the camera focused directly at it.

# Using Household Currents

The Arduino controller can easily power a small LED light or a very small incandescent bulb, but to power up anything larger than that, you'll need to use more current than you can safely run through the Arduino pins. This means that you'll need to run the power through a separate piece of hardware called a *transistor*, and control that piece of hardware using the Arduino controller. A transistor can act as a switch to a circuit that carries a certain amount of current, in this case, way more current than you want to allow near your Arduino pins. Normally, the transistor doesn't allow the circuit to complete, and no current flows through the high power circuit. But when the base of the transistor is turned on, the transistor completes the larger circuit, and whatever you're powering with the big circuit turns on.

In Figure 11-11, you can see the solid-state relay with its input and output posts labeled. The input posts are attached to the Arduino so that the switch inside can be thrown by the 5V signal from the Arduino. The output posts are used to control the voltage for the larger appliance, such as a light. You can control larger voltages using a combination of a diode, a transmitter, and a relay, but an easier approach is to use a solid-state relay, which combines all three of these into a single unit and makes wiring substantially less difficult. Note that most of these are used to control AC current like household current, not DC current.

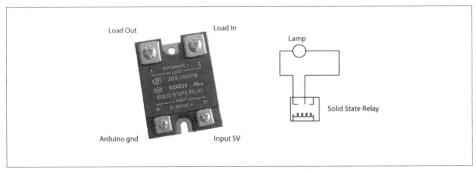

Figure 11-11. Using a solid-state relay with the Arduino controller

To control household AC voltages such as a standard household light, you need something like a relay to switch the high voltage and isolate it from the Arduino. There are a few things to look out for: make sure that the SSR is rated for at least 110 V in the USA or 240 V in the EU and UK. One option is the Croydom CC1585, which is a 4 pin 240 V rated SSR that can be switched with a current between 4 V and 10 V, perfect for a household current and an Arduino.

 You'll need to be very careful when following along with these instructions because you're dealing with enough electrical current to hurt yourself and start a fire. This is important enough that it bears repeating: household current can hurt you and start fires.

Figure 11-12 shows how to hook up a household AC light to the solid-state relay.

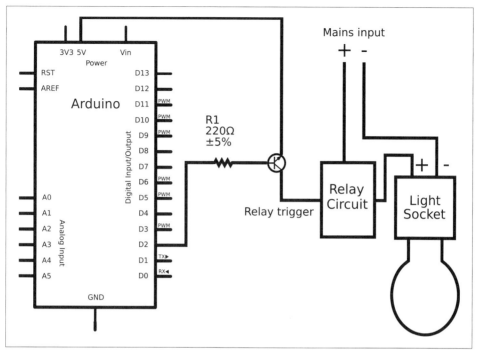

*Figure 11-12. Connecting a lightbulb and a solid-state relay to the Arduino controller*

Though Example 11-7 shows the relay on a breadboard, that's only so that the connections can be seen clearly. You shouldn't put the relay on a breadboard, instead it should be contained in a project box where the current can be safely isolated from anything else. The code for this can be quite simple:

*Example 11-7. SimpleSwitching.ino*

```
int relayPin = 12; // choose the pin for the relay
void setup() {
    pinMode(relayPin, OUTPUT);  // declare relayPin as output
}

void loop(){
    digitalWrite(relayPin, LOW);  // turn relay OFF
    delay(1000);
    digitalWrite(relayPin, HIGH);  // turn relay ON
    delay(1000);
}
```

Beware that turning lights on and off frequently in a short span of time could burn the bulb out quickly. However, you can do more than turn lights on and off with this controller: you can control any household device as long as it does not exceed the current capacity of the relay you use.

# Working with Appliances

One simple way to create physical feedback is to use preexisting appliances. There's a great device for doing this created by the guys at LiquidWare, called the RelaySquid, shown in Figure 11-13. The RelaySquid is a board that has four relays, each of which controls an extension cord with three outlets. Each relay can be individually controlled by the Arduino by sending it a digital signal.

The pins marked "Relay drive" should each be attached to the pins on the Arduino. The bit of code in Example 11-8 assumes that relay drive pin 1 is attached to digital pin 4, that relay drive pin 2 is attached to digital pin 5, and so on. It will turn each outlet on the RelaySquid for one second and then go on to the next one:

*Example 11-8. RelaySquidFun.ino*

```
void setup() {

    pinMode(4, OUTPUT);
    pinMode(5, OUTPUT);
    pinMode(6, OUTPUT);
    pinMode(7, OUTPUT);

}

void loop() {

    digitalWrite(HIGH, 4);
    delay(1000);
    digitalWrite(LOW, 4);
    digitalWrite(HIGH, 5);
    delay(1000);
    digitalWrite(LOW, 5);
    digitalWrite(HIGH, 6);
    delay(1000);
    digitalWrite(LOW, 6);
    digitalWrite(HIGH, 7);
    delay(1000);
    digitalWrite(LOW, 7);

}
```

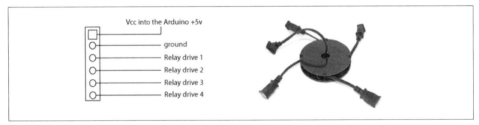

*Figure 11-13. The pins on the RelaySquid*

So, beyond turning lights on and off, what can you do with the RelaySquid? For starters, you could attach a clock sensor to the Arduino and turn an appliance on or off at a specific time for home security. You could program a schedule for grow lights to turn on and off for plants. You could turn a television, a generator, or any other appliance on or off. You need to take a few things into account: some devices work well with rapid cycling, and some do not. Some types of lights work well being turned on and off quickly. In my experience, halogen bulbs work particularly well, and incandescent bulbs burn out quickly when turned on and off in rapid succession. Televisions do not work well when turned on and off quickly. A little bit of searching and asking questions on forums can save you unpleasant surprises later on.

Other preassembled components are available for switching large loads, like the one shown in Figure 11-14 on the left from electronics-lab.com and the one shown on the right created at sparkfun.com.

*Figure 11-14. Two shields for working with household currents: the Anykits Solid State Relay Switch and the SparkFun Inline Power Control*

## Interview: Troika Design Studios

Troika is a design studio based in London that works with graphic design, product design, technology development, sculptural projects, and interactive installations. Conny Freyer, Eva Rucki, and Sebastien Noel founded Troika in 2003. They are also the authors of the book *Digital by Design* (Thames and Hudson).

*Where do you think the boundary between fine art and design is located with regard to new media art or interactive art? Is this a relevant or important question for you?*

**Troika Design Studios:** We describe ourselves as an art and design studio, but wouldn't describe ourselves as new media artists or interactive artists. Although terms like *new media art* and *interactive art* are very vague, they seem rather limiting because they define the work you are making by the tools you are using.

Although any attempt to classify new movements is interesting, we enjoy being part of a movement that has so far escaped any coinage and defines itself through blurring the boundaries between established genres and disciplines.

*Can you address the notion of collaboration throughout the conception and execution of a project? Is the collaboration something continuous or something more akin to a traditional software development practice where each team does its part and hands it to the next team? How do you handle communicating across disciplines?*

**Troika:** We are continuously working on a range of self-initiated and commissioned projects, which follow similar processes from concept to design development to production and implementation.

All three partners take part in the concept stage, after which the project is led by one partner who is responsible for the planning, the communication with the client, and the division of work between the partners as well as other collaborators. Tasks are naturally distributed according to different skill sets. We collaborate with a close-knit network of specialists, which we employ depending on the project. An iterative process is crucial to our way of working, which happens internally between the team members as much as with our clients and manufacturers.

Communicating across disciplines takes time and practice. It's literally like learning a different language. We were fortunate enough to follow each other's developments throughout the master's degree program at Royal College of Art in London, which helped to develop a common vocabulary.

*Can you give a little background on the history of Troika?*

**Troika:** Conny Freyer, Sebastien Noel, and Eva Rucki founded Troika in 2003, after we graduated from the Royal College of Art. Since then we have worked for clients such as MTV International, British Airways, the BBC, Warner Music UK, Thames and Hudson, and the London Science Museum.

Although the work of our studio spans various disciplines from graphics to products to installations, a lot of the themes—like creative use of technology and cross-fertilization between the art and design disciplines—are recurring subjects.

Since the beginning we have frequently taken part in national and international exhibitions and conferences, including Get It Louder (in 2007 in Guangzhou, Shanghai, and Beijing), Responsive (in 2007 in Tokyo), the Science of Spying (in 2007 at the Science Museum London), Noise of Art (in 2007 at Tate Britain, London), Design and the Elastic Mind (in 2009 at the Museum of Modern Art in New York), Volume(s) (in Casino Luxembourg, Forum d'art contemporain), and ExperimentaDesign (in Amsterdam in 2008).

*Are there are good precedents for companies or collectives working across fine art and design that influenced you and the way that you structured Troika?*

**Troika:** Collectives like Tomato and Antirom were certainly an influence during our studies, because of their multidisciplinary approach and because they were working as collectives rather than presenting themselves as one person (who employs others to complement his or her skill set), as is often the case in the product design world. But their mix of skills was quite different from ours, and the commercial landscape in which they started out had changed quite a bit when we set up our studio.

Troika's structure developed naturally based on the backgrounds of the founding members and a shared interest in the creative use of technology and cross-fertilization between the art and design disciplines.

These interests are apparent in our work for the Science Museum (*Identity for the Science Museum Art Projects* galleries, and concept products for the Spymaker exhibition, which examined the future of spy technologies) as much as in our forthcoming book *Digital by Design*. It's an overview of the fusion of digital technology and art and design production, as in our installation work for Terminal 5 of the Heathrow airport.

*Do you consider yourselves part of a lineage of artists and designers or of a school of design in any way?*

**Troika:** Troika is part of a generation of artists and designers who creatively engage with technology in order to provoke questions, experiment, and explore its potentials and impacts. A lot of these artists grew up during the transient phase where analog technologies were gradually replaced—the record players and View-Master. As such, they understand the benefits, appeal, and importance of the materiality and the tangible component of technologies versus the all-digital, immaterial which prevailed at the start of the digital era.

The influence of sci-fi—from films such as Kubrick's *2001 Space Odyssey*, Scott's *Blade Runner*, Orwell's novel *1984* (Plume), Gibson's novel *Neuromancer* (Ace), Ballard's collection of short stories, or the more popular *Star Wars*, to name but a few—sparked a willingness to think and create in technological terms, finding new avenues and alternative futures. A lot of artists working in this field share a more or less intense fascination for technology itself, its potentials for artistic expression, and its social and cultural impacts. Other notable influences include kinetic and media art, the counterculture of the '80s and '90s (more precisely in DJ culture, which influenced the process in terms of remixing), hacker communities (as the Berlin-based Computer Chaos Club), street art, and graffiti.

*How do you view what I've been calling "the ecology of new media art," by which I mean economic possibilities, exhibition opportunities, exchange of dialogue, and so on? Do you see it forming interesting discussions and fueling work or not? Do you have a sense of how this is different across different parts of the world?*

**Troika:** The general approach of artist and designers working in this field is very collaborative. Sharing knowledge as well as the joy of discovery online as well as at conferences is a common feature and encourages a constant exchange and debate. Part of the reason may be that a lot of small structures are operating in this field that have adopted a flexible and associative process, pulling together the right competences when needed, rather than growing into a bigger apparatus, in order to ensure their autonomy.

*Who are the artists and designers working today that you are most interested in?*

**Troika:** We have just written a book called *Digital by Design* that features artists and designers who employ technology in unexpected, playful, disruptive, functional, or critical ways. What was most challenging, but also most interesting, to us when writing the book was that the works we selected successfully escape any coinage such as *media art* or *interactive design*. The selected artists and designers have one thing in common: an eagerness to explore the intersection between science, art, design, and technology in the search for humanist values, humor, magic, and sensory experiences.

We love Daniel Rozin's *Mechanical Mirrors* for the tangible beauty, Dunne and Raby's work for their critical approach toward design, and Ron Arad's sense of exploring the new. What we look for in all the works we admire is the increasingly lacking desire for thought, enjoyment, quality, and craftsmanship.

*A piece like* Sonic Marshmallows *appears at first very nontechnological, but it allows you to think about things that are enabled by technology without using any electronics or power. Can you talk a little about how a piece like that fits in with the rest of your works and how you see it functioning in relation to people's desires to interact with things?*

**Troika:** We are fascinated by technology—being kinetic, optical, sonic, or electronic—and its impact on people. So, a lot of our work is informed by technology, but it is not a prerequisite. What we are striving for in our work is immediacy. We want our works to trigger emotions or thoughts like a story or film might do, and we love when art, magic, and science appear to be crossing paths. *Sonic Marshmallows* is a great example; it's technology in its purest form. Older technologies, especially the ones directly linked to natural optical and acoustic phenomena, carry a very simple and innate beauty that reveal their depth and magical surprise once you experience them. We see *Sonic Marshmallows* more as a manifestation of people's desire to interact with each other, rather than with things. *Sonic Marshmallows* can be used only in conjunction with another user. Sound mirrors were originally used on the coast of Kent to detect incoming enemy planes, not far from the location were *Sonic Marshmallows* is installed now. We used the same technology in a way that enables people to communicate with each other instead.

*You've created the electroprobe, a device for listening to electrical currents that surround us in our everyday environment. Can you talk a little bit about working with this tool and why you've come back to this theme several times?*

**Troika:** We first exhibited the electroprobes as an exploration tool for the immediate surrounding; for example, in galleries, people could discover the sounds produced by the radio magnetic radiations of the surrounding lamps, closed-circuit TV cameras, electricity wires, and so on.

We then became interested in the wide range of sounds that electroprobes can pick up, including sounds from objects, which might not appear in your common gallery context, such as LED boards, fans, fridges, and so on. In order to enable visitors to hear the varied sounds of their radio magnetic environment, we curated installations of electronic objects.

When we were invited by the British Council to China, we decided to make a location-specific sculpture using only electronics from the Chinese markets. The objects were arranged according to the sounds they were producing to create one big electromagnetic organ. The user becomes in a certain sense the composer because he will determine which sounds become audible through navigating this electromagnetic soundscape with the aid of the electroprobe.

*Do you approach conceiving of a print work differently than you approach conceiving of an interactive piece?*

**Troika:** Projects that are most interesting to us are the ones where we can bring all media together: print, installation, product, and animation. The main difference between one work or another is usually whether it is something that is applied or not—

something that is about answering a brief or creating a work that is self-initiated. We approach all in the same way. We want to engage and surprise people through sensory experiences or through making them think. And this counts for a piece of print as much as for an installation.

*This is a very broad question, so feel free to answer however you like. What are the fundamental rules for designing an interaction?*

In Troika's practice, *interaction design* or *experience design* might have a very different meaning than, for instance, for an interaction designer working in product development.

**Troika:** Troika strives to engage people on more intuitive and emotional levels. A good example is our kinetic sculpture *Cloud*. Supported by the organic fluid movement of its surface, it provokes associations of a living creature. The flicking sound of a flip dot, which is a small circle that is flipped over to create a sort of pixel and which was a technology used in old airport displays, touches on memories of traveling when you were a child.

Some people have asked us if *Cloud* is interactive—if it moves only when you walk by. Our answer to that is that interaction can mean many things and goes far beyond touching a button and getting a response once you have done so. A sculpture such as *Cloud* is not based on such a linear approach.

Nevertheless, designing interactivity is an interesting task. Martin Heidegger sums it up pretty well. He describes that the only time he really noticed his hammer was when it was broken and that he was thinking about the nail instead of the hammer when the hammer was working properly. It is about making the interface or the object invisible and tapping into what people already know, where they are able to recognize form and behavior without having to think about it.

*What software or hardware tools do you use, and how do you feel they shape your vision or your working process?*

**Troika:** We use the common 2-D, 3-D, and animation software packages. We draw and write to formulate our ideas. We have a workshop in which we experiment and build our prototypes and smaller pieces.

Our ideas and designs are to a great extent influenced by the tools we are using. Try to formulate a concept without words! We believe that good craftsmanship and intimate knowledge of your field is essential. This counts for digital/virtual solutions as much as tangible solutions.

*A piece like* All the Time in the World *has an extremely complicated technological element, a beautiful typeface, an element of motion graphics, and a conceptual element that plays on locations well-known and well-known but rarely considered. How do all these ideas come together in a piece? Is it born more of necessity or a desire to be able to shape all aspects of a piece?*

**Troika:** Our approach is quite holistic, and we find it an enriching and creatively challenging experience to develop the different aspects of a project.

*All the Time in the World* developed—like many of our projects—in a nonlinear fashion. We had created the Firefly typeface after we learned about the possibilities of electroluminescent technology. When British Airways commissioned for an art installation for its reception hall in T5 using the *Firefly* display, we started from the semantics of the location to develop the content for the installation.

**Troika:** We are investigating possibilities for technological innovation—mainly in the form of reappropriating existing technologies—on an everyday basis. At the same time, we are very aware of the contexts in which these technologies were previously used or developed, and this informs the way we will use it in our projects. For example, the flip dot technology used in *Cloud* stems from the signage boards used in the '70s and '80s in train stations and evokes notions of travel. When those little inventions and context-specific concepts come together in an installation, it creates a multilayered end result, which carries meaning on more than one level.

## Introducing the LilyPad Board

There's another Arduino-compatible board that has a particular relevance to providing physical feedback: the LilyPad board shown in Figure 11-15 and developed by Leah Buechley. One of the challenges of providing physical feedback is always deciding on the scale and scope of that feedback. A signal should be appropriate to its message and also to the context in which the user finds themselves, which is why there's a discrete vibrate setting on almost all cell phones and mobile devices. Removing this would make some signals inappropriate for their context, like a loud ringing during an opera. And so it goes with interactive design: ensuring that the correct feedback is provided for the context is a vital affordance for the user. What does this have to do with the LilyPad? The LilyPad Arduino is a microcontroller board designed for wearables and e-textiles. It can be sewn to fabric and mounted to power supplies, sensors, and actuators with conductive thread. Leah Buechley has provided code and schematics and links to several projects on her website at web.media.mit.edu/~leah/, including a turn signal jacket for bicyclists. So, the means of input and feedback can become much more subtle, becoming invisible or inaudible to anyone except the user. It also allows you to use preexisting form factors. That is, you can simply sew the LilyPad into a shirt, a jacket, a bag, or any other common object and let that object create the form of your device.

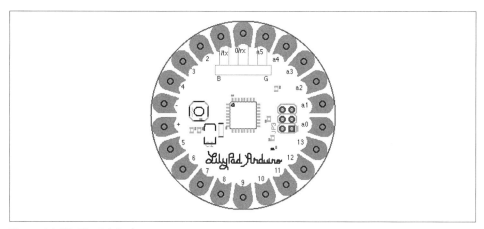

*Figure 11-15. The LilyPad*

The board is based on the ATmega328V, which is a slightly lower-power version of the ATmega328 chip that the Arduino uses. It is programmed using the Arduino IDE just like any other Arduino device and can be powered from a USB if you either get a USB connector or use one of the USB modules for the Arduino Mini, as shown Figure 11-16.

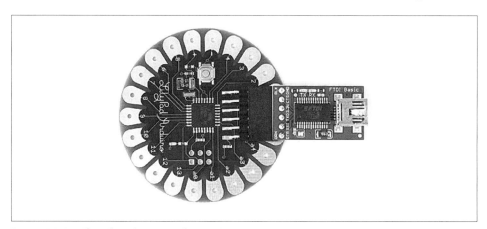

*Figure 11-16. The LilyPad connected to a USB programmer*

It has 14 pins; all can be used as digital outputs, 6 can be used for analog (PWM) outputs, and 6 can be used for analog inputs. The LilyPad is also a little more fragile than a regular Arduino board, so you'll need to be a bit careful when working with it and particularly when wiring it up. Also, the LilyPad is not particularly sensitive to water. If the LilyPad is not powered up, it can be washed with nonabrasive detergent. This doesn't help when your project is caught in a sudden torrential rainstorm, but it does make the device a little less susceptible to the sweat, small spills, and environmental moisture that a wearable piece of technology will invariably encounter.

# Using Vibration

Vibration is a simple and subtle signal that, given the correct contextualizing information, can be a great alert to a user. The LilyPad comes with a number of prebuilt components that can easily be connected either as inputs or as feedback devices, one of which is the LilyPad Vibe Board shown in Figure 11-17. This small motor works in much the same way as the vibrate motor on a cell phone. A 5V signal is enough to power the vibration motor, alerting the user to whatever you'd like to alert them to.

*Figure 11-17. LilyPad Vibe Board*

Since the LilyPad is generally meant to be used in a completely mobile application, you'll need to provide power to it. One AAA battery is enough to power the LilyPad for a reasonable amount of time using the LilyPad power supply. You can also use the LiPower module with a Lithium Ion battery, shown in Figure 11-18.

*Figure 11-18. Lithium ion battery and the LiPower board*

The LiPower board is small, is inconspicuous, and lets you use a rechargeable Lithium Polymer battery like the one shown on the left in Figure 11-18. These batteries are smaller, are flatter, and last much longer than AAA cells. Simply attach a single cell for Lithium Polymer (LiPo) battery, flip the power switch, connect the LiPower battery to the LilyPad, and you have a small, portable, short circuit–protected 5V supply.

The last part of the puzzle with the LilyPad is the connection between the LilyPad and all of its component pieces. When working with an Arduino Duemilanove, most of your connections are made with 22- or 24-gauge wire or with solder. This approach doesn't translate as well to clothing, so you might be considering using a special kind of conductive thread that can be used to connect the LiPower, the LilyPad, and the Vibe Board. Conductive thread is an excellent way to connect various electronics onto clothing. It isn't as conductive as traces on a printed circuit board, but it lets you create a complete circuit that remains flexible, near invisible, and, most important, wearable.

Note that when designing applications with the LilyPad, you should always keep your power supply and LilyPad main board as close to each other as possible. If they are too far apart, you are likely to have problems with your LilyPad resetting or just not working at all because of the resistance in the conductive thread connecting the boards. The resistance usually isn't as big of a deal when it's on the line connecting the LilyPad to a sensor or component, but between the LilyPad and its power supply, it makes a big difference in the reliability and durability of your project.

Figure 11-19 shows how to connect the LilyPad, LiPower, and Vibe Board.

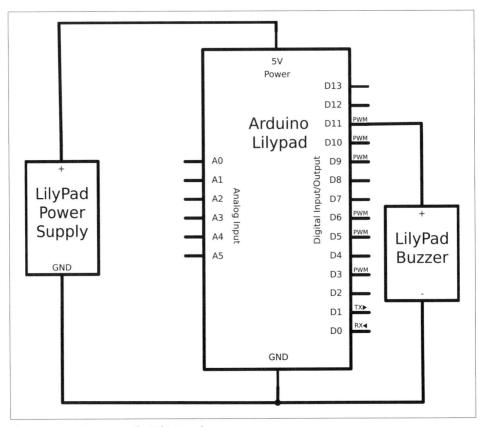

*Figure 11-19. Connecting the Vibe Board*

Since the Vibe Board is rated to handle 5 V, you can connect it to a digital pin or you can connect it to a PWM pin and write an analog signal to it. The more that you send to it the more intense the buzzing will be. The simple sketch in Example 11-9 uses two boards and increases the duration of the vibration while decreasing the intensity (and it feels rather bizarre if you put one on each side of your chest or even your neck).

*Example 11-9. LilyPadVibe.ino*

```
const int L_VIBE = 9;
const int R_VIBE = 7;

void setup() {

  pinMode(L_VIBE, OUTPUT);
  pinMode(R_VIBE, OUTPUT);

}

void loop() {
```

```
  for(int i = 0; i < 32; i++) {
    analogWrite( L_VIBE, 255 - (i * 8) );
    delay( 20 + i * 50 );
    analogWrite( L_VIBE, 0 );
    analogWrite( R_VIBE, 255 - (i * 8) );
    delay( 20 + i * 50 );
    analogWrite( R_VIBE, 0 );
  }
}
```

One of the things that's really fascinating about vibration is that it doesn't require you to look at it like many other forms of feedback, so way finding, guidance, and subtle notification all become much easier. In Chapter 15, we'll use vibration and wireless signals to guide users around a room.

As of the writing of this book, the LilyPad has several other available types of components for input: an accelerometer, a light sensor, a temperature sensor, a button board, and an XBee-compatible breakout board for integrating an XBee antenna into a LilyPad system. Some of the other feedback options that the LilyPad provides are sound-generating buzzers and three-color LED components.

## Nano, Fio, and Mini

The LilyPad isn't the only way to create a small and lightweight wearable board. Both the Nano and Mini are easy boards to embed into a jacket pocket or earmuff and, depending on your circuit, can be powered with a battery for a meaningful amount of time. The Fio is another board that was created specifically to run from a Lithium-Potassium battery and even allows you to charge the battery from a USB cable.

# Using an LED Matrix

A light-emitting diode (LED) can indicate something to a user, it can provide recognition of a user action, or it can act as an alert. Using multiple LEDs in concert with an Arduino is usually limited by the number of digital out pins that the Arduino has. By using an LED driver chip, though, you can control up to an 8 × 8 matrix of LEDs or an eight-digit LED display. This lets you draw simple shapes, characters, and digits to begin creating simple animations.

## Using the LEDControl Library

The chip and the idea of an LED matrix requires a bit of explanation. First the chip: the most common approach to drive an LED matrix, and the one that we'll examine in this section, is to use a chip called the Maxim MAX7221 to drive the LEDs.

Figure 11-20 shows the pins of the MAX7221.

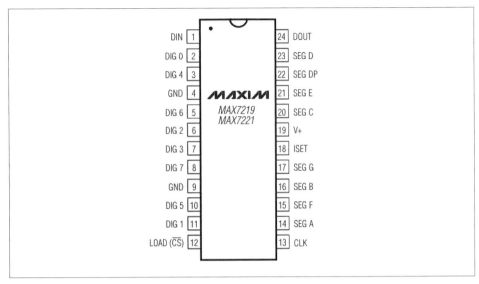

*Figure 11-20. Pins on the MAX7221*

In Figure 11-21, you'll see how the MAX7221 can be wired to an 8 × 8 LED matrix and an Arduino.

You'll notice that the wiring from the MAX7221 looks a bit complex, but it's actually made easier by the chip's pin diagram, shown in Figure 11-21. The pins on the LED matrix go from DIG 0 to DIG 7, left to right, and SEG DP (comes before SEG A) to SEG G, top to bottom.

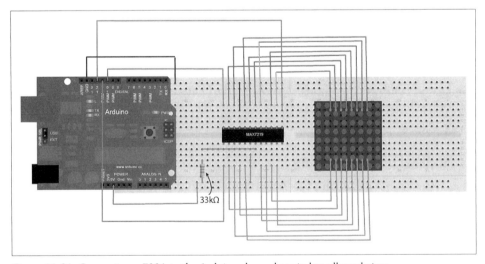

*Figure 11-21. Connecting a 7221 to the Arduino shown here in breadboard view.*

The Matrix library allows you to easily communicate with the MAX7221 chip. You can turn individual LEDs on or off, set the brightness, or clear the LED matrix.

The constructor for the LedControl library looks like this:

```
LedControl controller = LedControl(12, 11, 10);
```

Those three parameters specify which pins are connected to the MAX7221 control pins. The first is which pin is connected to the data (din), then which pin is connected to the load, and lastly which pin is connected to the clock (marked clk on the MAX7221). These pins are used internally by the Matrix class LedControl object to drive the chip, and are used to set individual pins on the LED matrix. See Example 11-10.

*Example 11-10. LedsRock.ino*

```
#include "LedControl.h" //need the library
LedControl control = LedControl(12,11,10,1); // lc is our object

// pin 12 to MAX7219 pin 1
// pin 11 to the CLK pin 13
// pin 10 to LOAD pin 12

int currentColumn = 0;

void setup() {

  control.shutdown(0,false);// turn off power saving, enables display
  control.setIntensity(0,8);// sets brightness (0~15 possible values)
  control.clearDisplay(0);// clear screen

}

void loop() {

  currentColumn++;
  if( currentColumn > 7 ) currentColumn = 0;

  for (int row=0; row<8; row++) {
    for (int col=0; col<8; col++) {
      if(col == currentColumn) {
```

The write() method take two parameters, the first to indicate the row of the LED that should be turned on and the second to indicate the column of the LED that should be turned on:

```
        control.setLed(0,col,row,true); // turns on LED at col, row
          } else {
            control.setLed(0,col,row,false); // turns off LED at col, row
          }
        }
      }
      delay(30);
    }
```

Aside from the tricky wiring situation, creating a single LED matrix isn't too difficult. Next, we'll look at communicating with an LED matrix using SPI.

# Using the SPI Protocol

Serial Peripheral Interface (SPI) protocol is a way to communicate with components that need to send and receive data at the same time. It's quite similar to the serial communication that you've been using to allow your Arduino to communicate with your desktop or laptop computer. There are however some crucial differences:

> SPI uses wires not USB. You'll connect your components to pins 10, 11, and 12, plus another pin called the Chip Select pin.
>
> SPI needs to know the bit order. There are two variations: MSB (most significant bit) is the lefthand side of the binary number, and LSB (least significant bit) is the righthand side of the number. Some components want the 0 bit of a byte first and some components want the 128 bit of a byte first, so it's important to make sure that all your communication is sending them in the right order.
>
> You can have multiple SPI devices. That's what the Chip Select pin is for. When the Chip Select pin is LOW, the device will listen the information on the SPI. When it's not, it won't. So you can connect several components onto pins 10, 11, 12, give each of them a separate digital pin, and by setting the pin LOW for the one you want to communicate with, isolate your communication. You could imagine it like pointing at the component and telling it: "I'm only talking to you right now." When you're done talking to the component, simply set its Chip Select pin HIGH and go to the next one.

SPI is generally used to communicate with other microcontrollers. In an SPI connection, there is always a master device that controls all the peripheral devices connected to it over four common lines:

*Master in slave out (MISO)*
> The line that the slave uses to send data to the master controller.

*Master out slave in (MOSI)*
> The line that the master uses to send data to the slave devices.

*Serial clock (SCK)*
> The clock pulses that synchronize data transmission generated by the master.

*Chip Select (CS or SS)*
> The signal that tells the device that it's about to be written to or is finished being written to.

The really tricky thing about SPI is that generally each device can implement it a little bit differently. Information on the nuances for each will always be available on the data sheet for the device or in online documentation.

All SPI settings are determined by the Arduino controller's SPI control register (SPCR). A register is just a byte of microcontroller memory that can be read from or written to. Registers generally serve three purposes: control, data, and status.

There are two approaches to working with SPI: you can use the SPI library that comes with the Arduino IDE, or you can simply roll your own. We'll show both for the sake of completeness. First, the library-enabled way with the RGB backpack.

# Serial LED Matrix

There are several manufacturers making LED matrices you can communicate with using SPI that are very lightweight and powerful. One developed by SparkFun is shown in Figure 11-22.

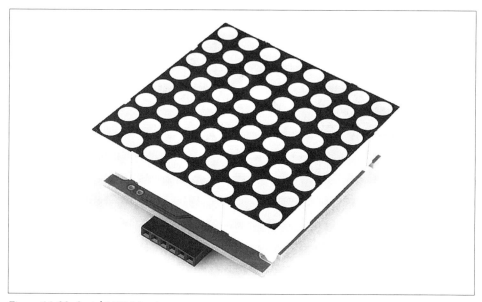

*Figure 11-22. Serial LED Matrix*

One advantage of SPI-based devices is that the communication between them is the same: once you've set up communication with one device, you can usually communicate with other similar devices. See Example 11-11.

*Example 11-11. rgbMAT.ino*

```
#include <SPI.h>

//Define the "Normal" Colors
#define BLACK  0
#define RED    0xE0
#define GREEN  0x1C
```

```
#define BLUE    0x03
#define ORANGE   RED|GREEN
#define MAGENTA  RED|BLUE
#define TEAL    BLUE|GREEN
#define WHITE (RED|GREEN|BLUE)-0xA0

const int SELECT = 9;

char LEDS[64];
char colors[8] = { BLACK, GREEN, TEAL, BLUE,
  MAGENTA, RED, ORANGE, WHITE };

void setup()
{
  pinMode(SELECT, OUTPUT);
  SPI.begin();


  for(int x = 0; x<64; x++) {
      LEDS[x] = colors[ dist(x/8, x%8, 8, 8)];
  }
}

void loop()
{
  digitalWrite(OUTPUT, LOW);
    for(int x = 0; x<64; x++) {
        SPI.transfer( LEDS[x] );
    }
  digitalWrite(OUTPUT, HIGH);
}

int dist(int x, int y, int x1, int y1) {
  return (int) sqrt((x1-x)*(x1-x) + (y1-y)*(y1-y));
}
```

The code to connect the RGB LED matrix to the Arduino is very simple and is shown below. Compare this to the Maxim 7221 above and you'll see that it's much lighter in terms of the wiring that you're doing. It is, however, more expensive and less flexible.

If you wanted to communicate with the RGB Backpack without using the SPI library, try the code in Example 11-12.

*Example 11-12. SPInoLib.ino*

```
//Define the SPI Pin Numbers since we're not using the SPI library
#define DATAOUT 11//MOSI
#define DATAIN  12//MISO
#define SPICLOCK  13//sck
#define SLAVESELECT 10//ss

byte color_buffer[]

void setup() {
    SPCR = (1<<SPE)|(1<<MSTR)|(1<<SPR1); //SPI Bus setup
```

```
  //Set all the pins
  pinMode(DATAOUT, OUTPUT);
  pinMode(DATAIN, INPUT);
  pinMode(SPICLOCK,OUTPUT);
  pinMode(SLAVESELECT,OUTPUT);

  //Make sure the RGB matrix is deactivated
  digitalWrite(SLAVESELECT,HIGH);

}

void loop() {

 //Activate the RGB Matrix
  digitalWrite(SLAVESELECT, LOW);
  //Send the color buffer to the RGB Matrix
  for(int LED=0; LED<64; LED++){
    spi_transfer(color_buffer[LED]);
  }

  //Deactivate the RGB matrix.
  digitalWrite(SLAVESELECT, HIGH);
  delay(5); // allow some time for the Serial data to be sent

}

//This replaces SPI.transfer
char spi_transfer(volatile char data)
{
  SPDR = data;                        // Start the transmission
  while (!(SPSR & (1<<SPIF))){}       // Wait for the end of the transmission
  return SPDR;                        // return the received byte
}
```

Next, let's look at another way to give some visual feedback with a lightweight component, the LCD.

## Using LCDs

We are surrounded by liquid crystal display (LCD) screens, and although what they provide is not necessarily a physical sort of feedback, a small screen is an important element of many small devices because it lets you return data that is more complex than an analog range or a digital value. Although representing "Hello World" in sound is a very interesting exercise, it's often a lot easier to simply get an LCD screen and print the characters to it. Moreover, a small screen can be held in the hand, attached to another object, and embedded in the environment in a way that provides supplementary information to a user.

There are many kinds of LCD screens and no foolproof way to communicate with all of them. With that in mind, we'll look at one of the more common types of LCDs that has an Arduino library. LCD panels that are controlled by the Hitachi HD44780 LCD controller chip or equivalent can be used with the LCD Interface library; you can check which chip an LCD uses online. This library has methods to initialize the screen, print characters and strings, and clear the screen, making your coding substantially easier. The library is included with the Arduino IDE, so to get started, simply import the library using the Tools tab in the IDE, choose Import Library, and then choose LiquidCrystal. Figure 11-23 shows the next example.

*Figure 11-23. A simple 16 × 2 LCD screen, a 20 × 4 LCD, and a Serial Miniature OLED*

The LCD Interface library provides five main methods:

`void clear()`
Clears out anything shown in the LCD screen.

`void home()`
Sets the cursor back to the beginning of the display.

`void setCursor(int row, int column)`
Sets the cursor to the position indicated by the row and column. So, in a display with 2 rows of 16 columns, to set the 19th character or the character in the 4th position of the 2nd row, you would use this:

```
setCursor(1, 3); // rows and columns start from 0
```

`void write(byte value)`
Writes the character to the current cursor position.

`void command(byte value)`
This method is a little trickier, but for the ambitious among you, it will be interesting. The HD44780 chip defines different commands that you can use to do things like set the display in and out of display mode quickly, control whether the cursor blinks, and so on.

Table 11-1 shows how the Arduino pin maps to an LCD using the HD44780 chip.

*Table 11-1. Arduino to LCD panel chip pin map*

| Arduino pin | Pin on the LCD |
|---|---|
| 2 | 14 (DB7) |
| 3 | 13 (DB6) |

| Arduino pin | Pin on the LCD |
|---|---|
| 4 | 12 (DB5) |
| 5 | 11 (DB4) |
| 6 | |
| 7 | |
| 8 | |
| 9 | |
| 10 | Enable |
| 11 | Read/Write (RW) |
| 12 | Register Select (RS) |

Keep in mind, though, that the pins might not be in the same order, so you'll need to check the data sheet. Figure 11-24 shows how the HD44780 LCD screen is connected to the Arduino controller.

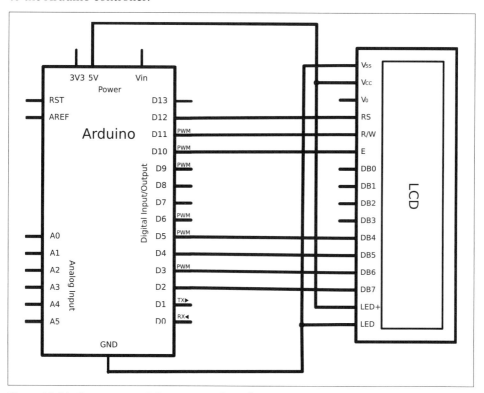

*Figure 11-24. Connecting an LCD screen to the Arduino*

To control the contrast of the display, you will need to connect a 10k (or 20k) poten-tiometer to provide the voltage to LCD pin 3, because without the correct voltage on this pin, you may not see anything displayed. As shown in the figure, one side of the potentiometer connects to Gnd (ground), the other side connects to Arduino +5V, and the center of the potentiometer goes to LCD pin 3. Many LCD screens have an internal lamp called a *backlight* that illuminates the display. The data sheet for your LCD screen should indicate whether the backlight needs a resistor. Many do; you can use 220 ohms or so if you are not sure.

This allows you to use the LiquidCrystal library that is included with the Arduino distribution:

You have two different versions of the constructor available. One lets you pass the pins that will be used for all seven control pins:

```
LiquidCrystal(rs, rw, enable, d0, d1, d2, d3, d4, d5, d6, d7)
```

Another lets you just pass four pins:

```
LiquidCrystal(rs, rw, enable, d4, d5, d6, d7)
```

Both options use the following three parameters:

rs
> Specifies the number of the Arduino pin that is connected to the RS pin on the LCD.

rw
> Specifies the number of the Arduino pin that is connected to the RW pin on the LCD.

enable
> Specifies the number of the Arduino pin that is connected to the enable pin on the LCD.

Whichever constructor version you decide to use, make sure that those pins are correctly attached to the LCD device. To test, see Example 11-13.

*Example 11-13. simpleCrystal.ino*

```
#include <LiquidCrystal.h>

LiquidCrystal lcd(12, 11, 10, 5, 4, 3, 2);

void setup()
{
    lcd.print("I'm in an LCD!");
}

void loop() {}
```

You should see the words "I'm in an LCD!" printed to your screen.

Another simpler option for working with LCD screens is an LCD that communicates over serial. Some LCD screens can be controlled simply by connecting them to the Arduino's RX and TX pins, which are the digital 0 and 1 pins on your controller. The Serial LCD works by having certain command bytes that indicate that the next byte will be a message. You can look for more information on serial LCDs on the Arduino or SparkFun forums.

## Using Solenoids for Movement

This section requires that a few terms be defined for you first, so let's start at the beginning.

A *solenoid* is a coil of wire with a magnetic core and usually with a rod resting inside that coil of wire. It works by sending a current through the wire that either pushes or pulls the rod, depending on the type of solenoid. When the current triggers the solenoid, the rod moves in its primary direction, either pushing if it's a *push solenoid* or pulling if it's a *pull solenoid* (see Figure 11-25). The names simply indicate in which direction the magnetic field tries to move the solenoid. When the current is off, then the rod in the center of the solenoid returns to its resting position. Solenoids are used frequently in machines, in automobile transmissions, and in robotics.

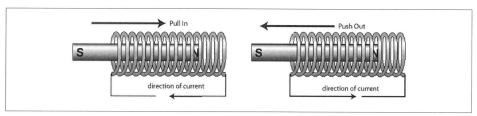

*Figure 11-25. How a solenoid functions*

*Diodes* are used to ensure current flows in only a single direction, acting almost like a valve that lets water flow in only one direction (see Figure 11-26). Diodes use a small amount of voltage to operate, typically 0.7 V, so a diode receiving the voltage from a 7.2 V battery would reduce it to 6.5 V. They are used for many purposes in more advanced electronics, but the most common use for beginners is to protect a micro-controller from "noise" that could destroy the microcontroller or interfere with other components. Diodes called *Zener diodes* are also useful for dropping high voltages to a lower voltage.

*Transistors* are, probably the most important electrical component ever invented. They may even be one of the most important inventions of all time (see Figure 11-26). Almost everything that is electronic probably has at the very least one of them and, in the case of your computer, probably millions, if not billions, of them (in the digital world). A transistor is not much different from a simple mechanical on/off switch. Instead of flipping a switch, a signal is sent to the transistor telling it to connect the circuit that runs through it from your microcontroller.

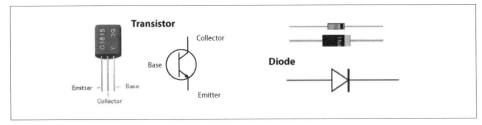

Figure 11-26. Transistors and diodes

When you send 0 volts to the base of the transistor, the collector is turned off, and when you apply a signal of 5V, the transistor collector is turned on, which is why it's like a light switch. Transistors can be used to control things other than lights. By sending a small signal, you can control huge flows of water through a pipe. In the case of an Arduino board, the transistor controls a larger flow of current by sending a digital on or off signal from one of the digital pins on the board. With the solenoid, the transistor will be used to power the magnetic coil of the solenoid to push out. The Arduino controller wouldn't have enough power on its own to power up the solenoid, but by feeding the current through a transistor, you can use the small 5V signal of the Arduino to control the 12 V solenoid.

The circuit that you'll be building to control the solenoid looks like Figure 11-27.

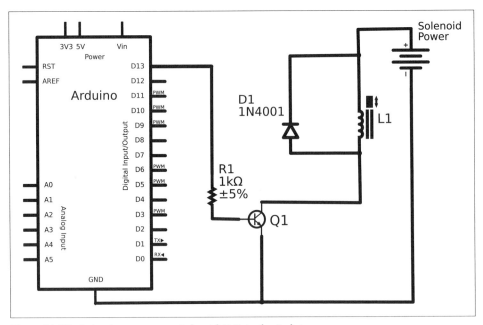

Figure 11-27. A circuit to connect a Solenoid (L1) to the Arduino

The solenoid power is going to depend on the solenoid that you're using. A 12 V solenoid will require a 12 V power source. You'll also want to make sure that the diode is "facing" the right direction, that is, that power from the solenoid power source is not flowing into your Arduino, because the solenoid won't work and the solenoid power source will be shorted when the transistor is turned on.

Since solenoids can be used to push, one possibility is to use them to create a drumbeat of sorts. You can easily do this by purchasing two solenoids and attaching one of them to a cymbal and another to a snare drum with some tape or with small clamps. The beat would be defined in two arrays of Boolean values to save space. Your code could be as simple as Example 11-14.

*Example 11-14. Solenoider.ino*

```
boolean hihats[] = {1, 0, 0, 0, 0, 1, 0, 1};
boolean snare[] = {1, 0, 0, 0, 1, 0, 0, 0};

int hatPin   = 2;
int snarePin = 3;
int counter;

void setup() {
    counter = 0;
}

void loop() {

    digitalWrite(hatPin,   hihats[counter]);
    digitalWrite(snarePin, snare[counter]);

     if(counter == 7) {
        counter = 0;
    } else {
        counter++;
    }
    delay(200); // delay between beats
}
```

You could, of course, make your rhythms much more complex and, if you wanted, use as many relays and solenoids as you have digital pins on your Arduino. Another option is to have a button control a solenoid, making user-driven controls. Yet another option is to drive the solenoids with a Processing or oF application by sending data over the serial port. This, coupled with the computer vision techniques in Chapter 14, could allow you to create a remote virtual drumming machine. Or, coupled with the network communication techniques from Chapter 12, it could enable a user to remotely drum or control any other kind of movement. The difficult part of working with a solenoid is not the programming; it's getting the power and wiring right. However, as mentioned earlier, using a relay switch can make that quite a bit easier for you.

# What's Next

This chapter mentioned a few different topics that you can explore further. Mechanical engineering is a vast field that many of the devices here have touched on only just briefly. Working with several stepper motors or servos requires some engineering thinking to ensure that equipment doesn't fail or destroy other parts of the project. For instance, using multiple servos to create complex motion requires some careful planning; controlling multiple appliances or motors also requires a fair amount of planning and research. That said, there are plenty of resources to help. There are a few good introductory texts on robotics that can be of great help. *Practical Electronics for Inventors* by Paul Scherz (McGraw-Hill), *Robot Building for Beginners* by David Cook (Apress), *Getting Started in Electronics* by Forrest M. Mims III (Master Publishing), and *Physical Computing* by Tom Igoe and Dan O'Sullivan (Course Technology) are all resources that will help you. Also, the Arduino website contains a wealth of information in its Playground section. The Arduino community is also very prolific in publishing books, tutorials, and libraries to make working with components easier. Another excellent book for learning more about hardware, electronics, and components is *Designing Embedded Hardware* by John Catsoulis (O'Reilly).

You might also be interested in taking a look at some of the more far-out projects that people in the Arduino community have been exploring. Some of my favorites are the RepRap Research Foundation's self-replicating machines; the Asurino library and development project, which uses the Arduino to control the Asuro hobby robot; and the *Braitenberg Vehicle*, the light-seeking robot designed by Alexander Weber. Another fascinating breed of projects that has emerged in the Arduino community is research into unmanned autonomous vehicles (UAVs). There are already several small projects underway to provide componentry and drivers for UAV projects built with Arduino controllers, among them the ArduPilot. There are also non-Arduino UAV platform kits available if the idea of creating things that run around is interesting.

# Review

DC motors come in several different kinds. Brushed DC motors, for example, are composed of two magnets and a core that spins as the voltage around the core changes. To reverse a DC motor, you need to be able to reverse the direction of the current in the motor. The easiest way to do this is using an H-Bridge circuit.

In addition to buying an H-Bridge circuit, you can purchase several kinds of driver boards that will allow you to control motors with prebuilt kits. Several major suppliers have created different boards for running motors.

Another kind of motor is a stepper motor. Instead of spinning in one direction or another depending on the current, a stepper motor advances to predefined steps. Stepper motors can provide more torque than a servo. There are several different libraries, most prominently the Stepper library included with the Arduino IDE, that can be used to control stepper motors. As with DC motors, there are also driver shields that are ready to be fit onto an Arduino controller.

A servo allows for programmable motion. It receives a signal of varying pulse position to determine how far to rotate within a limited range. The most common range for a servo motor is 180 degrees.

You can use the Servo library or control the servo using pulse width depending on which is more appropriate for your application.

To use household currents, you can either use a solid-state relay, or you can use a device like the RelaySquid from LiquidWare. It's very important to check your circuit carefully when working with high voltage because you can hurt yourself or damage your electronics.

Using the Vibe Board in conjunction with the LilyPad is another interesting way to provide feedback because it lets you send small vibratory signals to a user from a small controller that can be sewn into clothing or carried.

An LED matrix is an array of either 5 × 7 or 8 × 8 LED lights. They can be controlled using a chip such as the MAX7721. To control a single LED matrix, you can use the Matrix library; to control up to eight LED matrices, you can use the LedControl library.

The `spi_transfer()` method is used to send and receive data from another microcontroller or peripheral using the Serial Peripheral Interface protocol. This is a low-level protocol that lets you set other devices to be the slave devices for the Arduino controller, which will act as the master device.

LCD devices can be controlled by the LiquidCrystal library. This lets you write to the LCD screen using the `print()` method and lets you clear the screen using the `clear()` method. Most LCDs also support using cursors and scrolling.

Solenoids are magnetic devices that can push or pull depending on the kind of solenoid it is. These can be used in many different kinds of mechanical devices and are quite common in electrical engineering and robotics.

You'll need to use a transistor and a diode to control a solenoid, or you can use a relay switch to control whether the solenoid is powered on or off.

# CHAPTER 12

# Protocols and Communication

Throughout this book, we've explored data and different conceptions of what data is and how it is understood in an application. A user gets data from an application that helps them understand what the application is doing, how their actions have been interpreted, and how to get the application to do what they want it to do. This data is called the *feedback*. The data that the user sends to the application is called the *input*. The input tells the application what the user wants it to do, how it should do it, and what kind of feedback to provide. In this chapter, we'll focus on a different sort of exchange of data: exchanging data between an application and devices. This isn't new; you've already looked at many different components that work with the Arduino controller: receiving commands from the Arduino, sending data to the Arduino, using your computer in tandem with the Arduino, and creating an exchange of information and commands between the two of them. What you haven't looked at yet are the ways that communication between different machines and applications depends on the context, the means of communication, the machines used, and the amount of data being exchanged.

Cell phones, communication over the Internet, and devices plugged in to your computer all rely on protocols that dictate how devices communicate with one another. Enabling your devices to communicate with other devices is really a matter of ensuring that your system knows the protocol that the other devices speak. Think of it like a conversation between two people: they have to be speaking the same language to know what the other one is talking about. Without those protocols established, a conversation can't occur, and your application and the devices it needs to communicate with need the same kinds of protocols. There needs to be an understanding of what is being communicated and how that communication is being encoded.

When you allow your application or applications to communicate with one another, communicate with other devices, and communicate over common protocols, you enable your applications to work remotely, get information from remote locations, and send information to other devices, applications, and locations. You can send commands to a remote server, save data remotely, gather data from the Internet, network multiple devices and machines, communicate with other types of machines like MIDI keyboards, send text messages, and even make phone calls.

How does this affect interaction? The interaction of your designs doesn't always need to be a matter of the user interacting with the interface of your application. In fact, in most interactive applications, a great deal of the communication goes on between the application and other devices or applications, and most of this communication is governed by protocols. However you use the input or data, the important thing when using a protocol is making sure that any input is correctly translated into the protocol and that any data coming in can be correctly translated from that protocol. Users probably don't care how you're getting the data, and often the format of the data won't be one that your users will want or be able to understand themselves.

What kinds of data can you receive? That ends up being a hardware question. Without something like a microphone, you can't receive sound data. Without a network interface, you can't receive data over the Internet. So, you'll have to rely on hardware to provide access points between your system and the external world.

Think for a moment about the data that you receive from an accelerometer, namely, the $x$, $y$, and $z$ data that reports movement of the accelerometer. If the only thing that you need to do with that data is send it to the Arduino controller, then you don't need to convert the data; you can use it as received and be done with it. If you want to have that accelerometer control MIDI commands, however, then you'll need to not only process the data but also figure out a meaningful way to turn it into a different protocol, the MIDI protocol. If you want to send that information to a remote server and turn it into a visualization or another transformation of data, then you'll need to understand the protocol that the server uses and the program that you're using to provide the visualization or other transformation. A great deal of effort in computation is spent ensuring that data is correctly converted from one format to another and from one protocol to another.

The translation of data is more than a hidden computational matter. It can be relevant, interesting, and engaging for your users. A gesture can become a signal over the Internet. A sound in a remote location can become a mechanical motion in an installation. A command sent from a mobile device can become a message written on the side of a building.

In this chapter, you'll learn about communicating over networks, both local networks and the Internet; communicating over the Bluetooth protocol with cell phones and other Bluetooth devices; and communicating with MIDI devices.

## Communicating over Networks

Interaction designers of all types have been excited about the possibilities of networked communication for years. Since networked communication became affordable, accessible, and widespread, artists, designers, engineers, and dreamers of all types have experimented with the possibilities of remote data, remote access, and remote control. Nothing expands the place or location of an application like spreading it across the globe via a network. Some of the most innovative and thought-provoking computer-aided artworks from the 1990s brought the possibilities of networked communication into sharp focus.

Now designers and artists can use networks to send a video feed across the Atlantic Ocean, as in the *Telectroscope*, or mirror public benches in locations across the world, as in the *World Bench* project by GreyWorld. Game designers like Area/Code can use networked mobile devices to create real-time locative games that track a user's location through their cell phone signals. Ken Goldberg's classic *Tele-Garden* installation is a garden that is controlled remotely by thousands of remote gardeners from all over the globe who operate robotic arms that arrange, light, and water the plants. Projects like Heath Bunting and Kayle Brandon's *BorderXings* can use the geolocation of the user to provide or deny them access to certain material on a site. Another project that uses the power and idea of networking is *Screening Circle* by Andy Wilson, which creates shared space where multiple users can create images together in a sort of sewing-circle collaborative effort. Another common use of networking and networked capabilities is to mine the Internet for data. Jonathan Harris and Sep Kamvar built a project called *I Want You To Want Me* that mined data from online data sites to create beautiful representations of how users of online data sites thought of themselves and what they wanted from a prospective partner. All these projects use networks and networking in different ways, but all communicate with the outside world and outside applications.

Networks can be used to cover greater amounts of space between parts of an application by spreading an application over multiple machines, to gather data from another source, to allow access to users who aren't physically present, to allow users to connect with one another, or to pass processing off to more powerful computers. At this point, the question is not so much "What is networked?" as "What isn't networked?" Most applications in some way or another use information from the Internet, whether to gather data, check whether a serial number is valid, enable searching, or allow easy communication. A rapidly increasing number of devices network as well, such as laptops, cell phones, and ordinary household items. All are beginning to blend into one another as the need for computing power shrinks and the reliance on other networked computers for information or processing increases.

For you the designer or artist, adding networking capability to your application is much easier with the tools that are provided in oF, Processing, and Arduino. The hardest part of networking and networks is making them efficient and fast, but if you're making small-scale projects, they may not need to be fast or efficient in the way that a large, powerful site needs to be. That's not to say there are not new things to learn, tricky concepts to understand, and lots of new things to get your head around. In this chapter, you'll be learning how to send and receive data from the Internet, send data to other applications that are local or remote, read wireless Internet signals, and use MIDI signals to communicate between applications or over a network.

# Using XML

Extensible Markup Language (XML) is a way of giving a document structure. It's important because XML is very commonly used by Internet web services like Twitter and RSS feeds, and it's also a very common way to store and send data. Chances are that at some point you'll want to get some data from another source and that data will be in XML format. Things that you might want to represent as a piece of data have a few common characteristics. They have some specific *traits*, they *have* things that belong to them, and they *belong to* other things. That's a little overly abstract, so think of a library:

- *Characteristics:* street address, name
- *Has:* books, magazines, DVDs
- *Belongs-to:* library system, street, city

XML is a way to represent a structure in a document that is standardized so that any application can read it. An XML document has to be well formed. This means that every opening tag `<tag>` must have a corresponding closing `</tag>`:

```
<book>Wuthering Heights</book>
```

The following is generally called a *node*, a single object within the document that has some associated data, and this node is a well-formed one because the opening and closing tags match:

```
<book>Wuthering Heights</magazine>
```

That is not a well-formed node, because the opening and closing tags don't match. Some nodes don't have a closing node and those are indicated like this:

```
<DVD/>
```

Usually a node that consists of a single tag will have attributes to describe its data. I'll discuss them later in this section. You can also have multiple nested nodes, like this:

```
<library>
    <book>
        <title>Great Expectations</title>
        <author>Charles Dickens</author>
        <publication_year>1883</publication_year>
    </book>
</library>
```

In this case, the library *has a* book and the book *has an* author and a title. This idea of ownership is expressed by nesting the nodes within one another.

XML documents sometimes have a declaration at the top of the document that looks something like this:

```
<?xml version="1.0" encoding="UTF-8"?>
```

This tells whatever is parsing the XML document what version of the XML specification is being used and what encoding to expect. If you're writing an XML document that one of your own applications is going to read, then you probably don't need to put a declaration at the top of it. If you're planning on sending the XML document to a service on the Internet to be read, then you probably do want to add one at the top of your document to make sure that the other application reads it correctly. XML also allows you to add comments into the document, just like in any other code. XML comments start with `<!--` and end with `-->`:

```
<!-- This is a comment. -->
```

Two consecutive dashes (`--`) may not appear anywhere in the text of the comment, or the program reading the XML will most likely throw an error:

```
<!-- This comment -- will throw an error. -->
```

In addition to the values contained within the element, XML elements can have attributes as well:

```
<state id="0">
<name>Ohio</name>
</state>
```

The `id` property here gives another value to the state that you can use for sorting or accessing the names more quickly than looking through all the names. Using IDs or other values in an XML node is a useful way to add extra data that describes the node but maybe doesn't need a whole other child node. A common use for this is to add an `id` property. This is another example:

```
<site id="1" url="http://programminginteractivity.com">
    Programming Interactivity</site>
```

So, what kinds of things can you store with XML? All sorts of data: dates, places, zip codes, cities, states, and statistics of all sorts. XML is also a very common format for websites to return data. If you request something from another website, a series of photos from Flickr, stock quotes, or the weather, the results are often returned from websites or from programs that have a publicly available service called a *web service*. In some cases, XML is used to store data on a computer as well as for an application to load configuration files.

Processing contains an XML library to make creating and parsing XML easier. This functionality is contained in the `XMLElement` class; it contains methods for loading XML files, creating new XML files, looking through data for specific pieces of information, or setting new values in an existing XML file or dataset.

The functionality of this class provides a good explanation of how you might work with XML data in an application. To load an XML file from the home folder of a Processing application, you would create a new `XMLElement` object as shown here:

```
XMLElement xml  = new XMLElement(this, "xmlfile.xml");
```

Let's take a look at a simple XML file of three states:

```
<?xml version="1.0" encoding="UTF-8"?>
<states>
<state id="0">
    <name>Ohio</name>
</state>
<state id="0">
    <name>Michigan</name>
</state>
<state id="0">
    <name>Indiana</name>
</state>
</states>
```

To find out how many states are in the file, call the `getChildCount()` method. In this case, that method will return 3, since there are three state nodes. The following code snippet gets the number of nodes and loops through them:

```
int stateCount = xml.getChildCount();
for (int i = 0; i < stateCount; i++) {
    //do something with each node
}
```

To get each state node of the XML file, call the `getChild()` method inside the `for` loop:

```
for (int i = 0; i < stateCount; i++) {
    XMLElement firstChild = xml.getChild(i);
}
```

Notice in the previous code how both the main XML document and the individual `<state>` node of the file are represented by `XMLElement` objects. The value returned by the `getChild()` call is another `XMLElement` object. This means that the `getChild()` method can be used to get any children of the `<state>` node as well. In the case of the state node in the example XML file, the first child will be the name. You would grab the name of a `<state>` node as shown here:

```
String name = firstChild.getChild(0).getContent();
```

The `getContent()` method returns the content of the node, that is, the data inside. In the case of the name of the state, it looks like so:

```
<state id="0">
<name>Ohio</name>
</state>
```

So, looking at the previous snippet, the content of the name is "Ohio":

```
String name = firstChild.getChild(0).getContent();
```

So, the `<name>` node, which is the first child of the `<state>` node, is returned by the `getChild()` call; then the content of that node, which is the value inside the XML tags, is stored as a separate string.

To get the `id` of the state node, you need to read the attribute of the node. The `XMLEle ment` class has three ways to read an attribute: `getFloatAttribute()`, `getStringAttri bute()` and `getIntAttribute()`. If you want the value of the attribute as a float number, use `getFloatAttribute()`. If you want the value of the attribute returned as a number so that you can compare it numerically, sort it, or perform other operations that aren't available with a string, then use `getIntAttibute()`. If the attribute is a name, a URL, or another character-based data, then use the `getStringAttribute()` method:

```
int id = firstChild.getIntAttribute("id");
```

You'll put this library to use in the next section when learning how to communicate over a network with a Processing application.

# Understanding Networks and the Internet

*Network* can mean many things: two computers linked together, hundreds of computers linked together, computers attached to the Internet, machines connected to a wireless router, and so on. All networks have a few things in common, though:

- Machines on the network need to be identifiable to each other and to themselves.
- Machines need to know how to connect with one another.
- Machines need to know what protocol the other machines are using.

## Network Organization

There are few different ways of organizing a network. Figure 12-1 shows some of the most common setups that you might use.

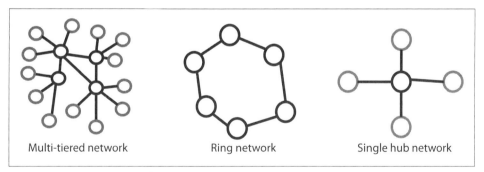

Figure 12-1. Common network setups

You've already used a sort of hub network when connecting multiple devices to your Arduino controller or when connecting your Arduino to your computer. Other examples of hub networks are Bluetooth-enabled networks (which you'll learn about later in this chapter) and a group of computers connected to a single central server that sends commands out to each of the nodes on the networks. In a *ring* network, any message has two possible paths, but it also means, in a worst-case scenario, that to get a message from one machine to another, you might have to send *n*/2 messages where *n* is the number of machines in your network. One simple example of a ring network is a group of Arduino controllers connected together. A multitiered network is just a collection of single-hub networks that have ways to determine which of the central nodes is acting as a hub to the desired child node. This is how the Internet is set up, with large relays bouncing traffic to its intended destination.

## Network Identification

Over a network, all the machines are identified by their Internet Protocol (IP) addresses. Most machines that connect to the Internet also use the Ethernet protocol. Finally, many devices have a Media Access Control (MAC) address that is burned into the device's memory. This is similar to the way that devices using the I2C protocol (that you learned about in) have an address that is always associated with that object.

You've probably seen your computer's IP address at some point. On Mac OS X you can see it by opening your Preferences window and opening the Network pane. On Windows Vista you can see it by going into your Control Panel, then selecting Properties and then Manage Network Settings. You'll see an IP address that might look something like this:

    192.168.0.25

That number is the identifier of your computer, with four sets of numbers, each from 0–255. The address shown here is a bit tricky to explain because it shows an IP of a computer that is connected to a router. The value `192.168` at the beginning of the IP address indicates the mask and subnet of a local network. That means this number won't mean anything to another computer *outside* your network, but to another computer *inside* your network this value specifies your computer on the local network, and the router will send information destined for that address to your computer. A computer that is publicly available outside of a local area network might have an IP address like `208.75.87.131`.

Usually, you won't be typing in IP addresses to get to the server and website that it hosts; you type in something like *http://programminginteractivity.com* to get the server with that IP address. There's a separate protocol called the Domain Name System(DNS) that is used to convert names into numbers. DNS servers take the domain name and convert it to the IP address that will route the traffic to the correct server. Why do you need to remember all these acronyms? In short, when you send information over the Internet, whether you know it or not, you're using these protocols to send your data. You won't need to worry a great deal about them and how they work, but it helps to conceptually understand what's going on when you are configuring your application to send or receive data from another networked machine.

So, what is the data being sent over the Internet? In short: packets. *Packets* are your data, broken into small pieces for easier sending. A way to see this at work is the `ping` command. Open a terminal, and type `ping` followed by the name of a web server. You'll see something like the following:

```
64 bytes from 208.75.87.131: icmp_seq=1 ttl=47 time=60.217 ms
64 bytes from 208.75.87.131: icmp_seq=2 ttl=47 time=66.809 ms
64 bytes from 208.75.87.131: icmp_seq=3 ttl=47 time=70.654 ms
64 bytes from 208.75.87.131: icmp_seq=4 ttl=47 time=62.126 ms
```

This says that 64 bytes were sent to IP address 208.75.87.131 and that the round-trip was on average around 63 milliseconds. You'll learn more about packets later, but for right now, just know that most messages you send will be broken into multiple smaller packets that will be sent to the server or client your application is communicating with.

When you type the `ping` command, you put the name of a host that your computer is going to connect with. This hostname can be either an IP address (208.75.87.131) or a domain name, like *http://programminginteractivity.com*. There is one reserved IP address and hostname that it's good to know about: 127.0.0.1 or localhost. This is your computer, the local machine. You'll notice that if you type `ping localhost`, the return times will be extremely fast, since the computer is just pinging itself. When you're building clients and a server, it's very helpful to have a local version of the server to test on. Usually accessing this will involve using either the 127.0.0.1 or localhost, and it might involve putting a port number at the end so that the server name looks like this: 127.0.0.1:8080.

Any host has many ports that a client can connect on. For instance, HTTP web traffic goes over port 80. File Transfer Protocol (FTP), used for uploading and downloading large files, uses port 21. All the port numbers between 0–1023 are reserved for predefined uses, so sometimes you'll see port numbers like 8080 or 4000 appended to the end of the IP address. You can think of the port as a way to ensure that all the messages for a certain type of traffic are grouped together.

## Network Data Flow

So, how does a network request work if you want to get an HTML file, for example? Let's say that your application is running on your local computer that is connected to the Internet through a wireless router, which is a fairly common setup. First, your application sends its data to the router. The router sends your message to your network provider. The message is routed to the correct network provider for the server you want to make a request from. Finally, the server will receive the request for the file. This should give you an indication of why so many different protocols are needed for Internet communication.

# Handling Network Communication in Processing

Communicating over a network is a very important capability in Processing. Your applications can communicate with other Processing applications, download data from the Internet, send data to be stored or processed remotely, and even peek into data being sent wirelessly. This is all done through the Network library. The Network library enables you to easily create clients to read data from other servers on local or remote networks, as well as servers that can send data to remote clients or to other clients on a local ring network. As with many networking libraries, there are two classes: the Client class and the Server class.

## Client Class

The Client class is used to create client objects that connect to a server to exchange data. To create a client within a Processing application, import the Network library by including `import processing.net.*` at the top of your application, call the constructor, and pass in a server name that you would like to connect to and port number that you want to use:

```
import processing.net.*
Client networkClient = new Client(this, "www.oreilly.com", 80);
    // Connect to server on port 80
```

The next most important method to understand is the `write()` method. This allows you to make requests to a server. The most common method to send to a server is the GET command, which tells the web server that you're simply asking for a web page. If you're curious about other commands, look around for information on Representational State Transfer (REST), and you'll learn about the POST, PUT, and DELETE commands. For the purposes of this introduction, the GET variable is perfectly sufficient. Here's an example of writing a GET request:

```
networkClient.write("GET / HTTP/1.1\r\n");
```

This starts the request to the server, but it's not enough. Most servers won't respond to this because it's not a complete request. You also need to add a server name:

```
networkClient.write("Host: oreilly.com\r\n");
```

The "Host:..." is required for reasons that are a little more complex than we need to get into here. If you want to read more about HTTP, check out the HTTP specification at www.w3.org, the home of the World Wide Web Consortium, which writes and maintains all the web specifications.

You can write as many lines as you need in the request, breaking it up over multiple calls or all as one call without affecting the request that the server will receive.

After you send the request, you'll want to receive the response from the server. There are two methods that you'll use to do this: the `available()` method that returns how many bytes are being sent to the client and the `readString()` method that returns all the data as a string:

```
if (networkClient.available() > 0) { // If any incoming data
    String data = networkClient.readString(); // store as a string
}
```

The drawback of the `available()` method is that it requires that you poll it constantly. If you're expecting a lot of data from a network connection, then this makes sense; otherwise, it can be excessive. If the communication between the network and your application is going to be infrequent, you might want to add the `clientEvent()` event handler for the network events into your application, to have a separate method where you can store all your logic for handling communications from a client:

```
// the ClientEvent is triggered whenever the server sends data to a client.
void clientEvent(Client client) {
    String dataIn = client.readString();
    println("Server data is:: " + dataIn);
    // do something else with the data
}
```

## Server Class

The Server class is used to create server objects that can send and receive data to and from any client connected to it. You create a new server object by passing the port number that the server should be available on:

```
Server srv = new Server(this, 5204);
```

You might want to make your server available on port 80, the standard HTTP traffic port, but you'll probably find that your computer doesn't like that. That's in all likelihood because another service is already on port 80. The simplest thing to do is to set a different port number; but if you want to use port 80, or another port number lower than 1023, and you run into problems, check on the Processing forums for instructions on how to get this working.

Once you've gotten the server started, you'll want to listen for any client that connects up to it. You can do this by using the `available()` method, which returns the clients that are connected to this server:

The `available()` method returns a client with updates, and if no clients have updates, then this returns null. The `available()` method can be done in the `draw()` loop of your application; when it returns a value that is not null, use the `readString()` method to read any data sent from the client:

```
void draw() {
Client client = myServer.available();
        // is there a current client?
if (client !=null) {
String clientMsg = thisClient.readString();
        if (clientMsg!= null) {
        //do something with the data
        }
}
```

Just like the `clientEvent()` callback, the `serverEvent()` callback can be used to handle any new client connections to any server within the application:

```
// called when a new client connects to one of the servers in the application
// the server and the client will both be passed in to the method
//      by the Processing framework
void serverEvent(Server server, Client client) {
```

```
        print("New connection from IP :: " + someClient.ip());
    }
```

Now, by using XML parsing within a client-server setup, some reasonably complex data can be exchanged. Example 12-1 has components. The server loads an XML file from Flickr (the popular photo-sharing site) using the Processing `XMLElement` object, which parses the XML into a simpler format and then sends all of its clients the URLs of the pictures, along with the *x,y* locations to display the pictures:

*Example 12-1. imageServer.pde*

```
import processing.net.*;

Server fsSrv;
XMLElement flickrXML;
XMLElement picList;
PFont myFont;
String lastmsg = "";

void setup() {

    size(600, 300);
    fsSrv = new Server(this, 8180);
    flickrXML = new XMLElement(this,
    "http://api.flickr.com/services/rest/?method=flickr.photosets.getPhotos&api_key=
        0367b4b7b7ab07af3c04d8d6d839467d&photoset_id=72157594290642861");

    XMLElement pics = flickrXML.getChild(0);
    picList = new XMLElement("<pictures></pictures>");
    // you could use them all, or only use 4
    int totalPics = 4;//pics.getChildCount();
    int xp = -400;
    int yp = 0;

    for(int i = 0; i<totalPics; i++) {
```

Flickr uses picture URLs that look like this: `http://farm{farm-id}.static.flickr.com/ {server-id}/{id}_{secret}.jpg`, so you have to build the URL up from the XML file:

```
        String url = "http://farm"+pics.getChild(i).getAttribute("farm")+
            ".static.flickr.com/" +pics.getChild(i).getAttribute("server")+
            "/"+pics.getChild(i).getAttribute("id")+"_"+
            pics.getChild(i).getAttribute("secret")+".jpg";
        if(xp > 399 ) {
            xp = 0;
            yp += 400;
        } else {
            xp += 400;
        }
```

Now that it's built, add it to the XML file to send to all the clients:

```
        picList.addChild(new XMLElement("<pic id=\""+i+"\" url=\""+url+"\" x=\
            ""+xp+"\" y=\""+yp+"\" />"));
    }
```

---

```
        myFont = createFont("Arial", 16);
        textFont(myFont);
    }

    void draw() {
        background(0);
        text("ok", 10, 20);
        Client client = fsSrv.available();
```

If one of the clients has sent a message, read it, and write it to all the other clients:

```
        if(client != null) {
            lastmsg = client.readString();
            if(lastmsg != null) {
                fsSrv.write("<msg>"+lastmsg+"</msg>");
            }
        }
        text(lastmsg, 30, 20);
    }
    void serverEvent(Server srv, Client clt) {
        fsSrv.write(picList.toString());
    }
```

Next, the client loads all the pictures sent in the XML file :

```
    import processing.net.*;

    Client fsClient;
    XMLElement picList;
    ArrayList picArray;

    void setup() {
        size(800, 800);
        fsClient = new Client(this, "127.0.0.1", 8180);
        picArray = new ArrayList();

    }

    void draw() {
        background(0);
```

If data is sent to the client, then read it using the readServer() method:

```
        if(fsClient.available() > 0) {
            readServer();
        }
```

Draw all the images to the screen:

```
        int sz = picArray.size();
        IImage fi;
        for(int i = sz-1; i >= 0; i-- ) {
            fi = (IImage)picArray.get(i);
            image(fi.img, fi.x, fi.y);
        }
    }
```

This next code is called when the client has data that has been sent to it:

```
void readServer() {
    if(picList == null) {
        picList = new XMLElement(fsClient.readString());
        int totalPics = picList.getChildCount();
```

For each <pic> object in the XML, create a new IImage object and load the image specified in the URL property of the XML:

```
        for(int i = 0; i<totalPics; i++) {
            IImage fi = new IImage();
            fi.setXMLData(picList.getChild(i));
            PImage p = loadImage(picList.getChild(i).
                getStringAttribute("url"));
            fi.img = p;
```

Add it to the ArrayList so that it can be drawn later:

```
            picArray.add(fi);
        }
    }
}

class IImage{

    PImage img;
    public int x;
    public int y;

    public void setXMLData(XMLElement s)
    {
        x = s.getIntAttribute("x");
        y = s.getIntAttribute("y");
    }
}
```

Now that you're finished, you should have something that looks like Figure 12-2.

## Sharing Data Across Applications

Next, you'll use the same principle in a more dynamic way. The clients will be reactive to the user's actions and will send data up to the server whenever the user changes something in the application. The server will then send the information to all the listening clients, which will place the images according to the incoming data, as in Figure 12-3.

Since the server sends each application the same data, two separate instances of the application will look exactly the same.

*Figure 12-2. Synchronizing two applications*

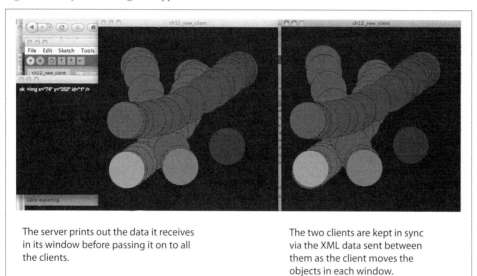

The server prints out the data it receives in its window before passing it on to all the clients.

The two clients are kept in sync via the XML data sent between them as the client moves the objects in each window.

*Figure 12-3. Sharing drawing data across applications*

Example 12-2 works similarly to Example 12-3. The client opens a connection to the server on a certain port and IP address and listens for any data coming from that IP. The difference is that the server sends the client information only when one of the other clients has changed something and sends the information to the server.

*Example 12-2. shareServer.pde*

```
import processing.net.*;

Server fsSrv;
PFont myFont;
String lastmsg = "";

void setup() {
    size(600, 300);
    fsSrv = new Server(this, 8180);
    myFont = createFont("Arial", 13);
    textFont(myFont);
}

void draw() {
    background(0);
    text("ok", 10, 20);
    Client client = fsSrv.available();
    if(client != null) {
```

The readStringUntil() method is used here to listen *until* the server receives the end of the message. Before that, it doesn't do anything:

```
        lastmsg = client.readStringUntil('>');
        client.clear();
        if(lastmsg != null) {
```

Once it receives the end of the message, it will send it to all its listening clients:

```
            fsSrv.write("<msg>"+lastmsg+"</msg>"+'\0');
        }
    }
    if(lastmsg != null) {
        text(lastmsg, 30, 20);
    }
}
```

The client (see Example 12-3) is a little more complex because the client needs to tell the server whether the user has dragged one of the shapes around, and it needs to make sure that it updates only if the information is coming from a different client. Since the server sends information to all clients, without checking to make sure that it hasn't sent a message, the client would be stuck in a loop of updating its data with the data it just sent out. The Client uses an instance of the InteractiveImage class to draw into, which has been omitted to conserve space, but it's available in the code downloads for this chapter.

*Example 12-3. shareClient.pde*

```
import processing.net.*;

Client fsClient;
ArrayList iiArr;

int millisSinceSent = 0;
```

```
void setup() {
  size(500, 500);
  fsClient = new Client(this, "127.0.0.1", 8180);
  iiArr = new ArrayList();
```

Using a slower frame rate helps make sure that you're not sending too many messages to the server:

```
    frameRate(10);
    for(int i = 3; i>-1; i--) {
        // check in the downloads for this class
        InteractiveImage ii = new InteractiveImage();
        ii.id = i;
        ii.colr = 30 + 40 * i;
        iiArr.add(ii);
    }
    background(0);
}
```

```
void draw() {
    fill(0, 2);
    rect(0, 0, 500, 500);
```

If a message comes in from the server, the process waits until the \0 character is sent to read it. This character could be anything, but \0 is nice because it's very unlikely to appear anywhere else. Once the client hears the \0 signal, it will send the message to the readServer() method to process the data:

```
    if(fsClient.available() > 0) {
        String msg = fsClient.readStringUntil('\0');
        readServer(msg);
    }
```

Now draw all the circles in their correct locations:

```
    int sz = iiArr.size();
    InteractiveImage ii;
    for(int i = sz-1; i > -1; i-- ) {
        ii = (InteractiveImage)iiArr.get(i);
        fill(ii.colr);
        ellipse(ii.x, ii.y, 100, 100);
    }
}
```

The readServer() method is the most important method of this application. It reads the string sent from the server and determines how long ago it sent a message to the server. If it was more than 500 milliseconds, then it's safe to assume that it wasn't sent from this application. This requires that users take turns to an extent. If there were going to be more than a few clients connected to the server, you'd want to do something different, but for this scenario it works well enough:

```
void readServer(String di) {
    int timing = millis() - millisSinceSent;
    if(timing < 500) {
```

```
        print(" too recent "+timing);
        return;
    }
    print(" not too recent "+timing);

    if(di == null) {
        println(" di null ");
        return;
    }

    XMLElement changedXML;
    fsClient.clear();
```

There's a possibility that the XML might get mangled, so the conversion to XML is wrapped in a try/catch block. This shouldn't happen very often, but if it does, the try/catch block ensures that the application doesn't throw an error:

```
    try {
        changedXML = new XMLElement(di);
    } catch (Exception e) {
        println(" can't convert ");
        return;
    }
    println(changedXML);
    int inId;
    if(changedXML.getChildCount() > 0) {
        inId = changedXML.getChild(0).getIntAttribute("id");
    } else {
        return;
    }

    for(int i = 0; i<iiArr.size(); i++) {
        InteractiveImage fi = (InteractiveImage) iiArr.get(i);
                if(fi.id == inId) {
                        int xv = changedXML.getChild(0).getIntAttribute("x");
                        int yv = changedXML.getChild(0).getIntAttribute("y");
                        fi.x = xv;
                        fi.y = yv;

                }
        }

}
```

When the mouse is dragged, loop through all the InteractiveImage instances and find the one that has been clicked. Once the image that has been clicked is found, create XML with the data of that InteractiveImage instance:

```
void mouseDragged() {

        for(int i = 0; i<iiArr.size(); i++) {
            InteractiveImage img = (InteractiveImage) iiArr.get(i);
            if(img.isClicked(mouseX, mouseY)) {
                img.x = mouseX;
                img.y = mouseY;
                try {
```

```
            fsClient.write(createXMLFromII(img));
        } catch (Exception e) {
            return;
        }
```

Set the `millisSinceSent` to the current value of `millis` so that the application knows that it has recently sent data to the server and shouldn't listen to data sent from the server for the next half second:

```
            millisSinceSent = millis();
            return;
        }
    }
}
```

The `createXMLFromII()` method simply takes the properties of the `InteractiveImage` instance passed to it and creates XML from it:

```
String createXMLFromII(InteractiveImage i) {

    String s = "<img x=\""+i.x+"\" y=\""+i.y+"\" id=\""+i.id+"\" />";
    return s;
}
```

Now, you have an application that maintains state across multiple clients using a server that dispatches XML. You can use these same methods to maintain multiple applications throughout a room, a building, or on opposite ends of the world if you want.

# Understanding Protocols in Networking

Think for a moment about Internet communication: a machine makes a request to a server for a particular file and the server responds with that file. That request uses a certain protocol to tell the server what file it wants, where the request is coming from, and how it would like the file returned. The response uses a similar protocol to tell the client that is requesting the file, how large the file is, what type of file it is, what kind of encoding is used with the file, and other data that the client might want to know. This additional data, the order in which it is placed in the file, and how the values are signified are all defined in the Hypertext Transfer Protocol (HTTP). I use that as an example because it's probably one that you're familiar with. It's only one of the many kinds of communication that your application can have with another computer using a network. HTTP is a protocol that uses another protocol: Transmission Control Protocol (TCP). Here's how it works: a client establishes a TCP connection to a particular port on a host. An HTTP server listening on that port waits for the client to send a request message. Upon receiving the request, the server returns a status line, such as `HTTP/1.1 200 OK`, and a message of its own, the body of which is perhaps the requested resource, an error message, or some other information.

Later in this chapter, we'll look at HTTP communication in greater detail. For the moment, though, let's focus on TCP. TCP provides transmission control, presents the data in order, and provides error correction when packets get out of order. In a large document where the order of all the bytes is important, this is very important. The plus side of TCP is that it is a way to connect a client to a server that ensures that all the data is in the correct order and notifies the client if something is broken in the message. The downside of TCP is that it can be comparatively slow because of this error checking. There is another connection protocol called the User Datagram Protocol (UDP). UDP is much faster than TCP, but it also has drawbacks: it has no concept of acknowledgment, retransmission, and timeout, and its messages aren't ordered.

## Using the ofxNetwork Add-on

There are two key classes in the ofxNetwork add-on that enable you to work with TCP communication over the Internet. The first is ofxTCPClient, which is for creating clients that will connect to and read information from a server, and the second is ofxTCP Server, which will send information to any listening client.

To make a client that can receive and send information to a server, create an ofxTCP Client instance, and call the setup() method on the client. For instance, to connect to a server running on the same machine as the client that is listening for connections on port 8180, you would call the setup() method:

```
ofxTCPClient client;
client.setup("127.0.0.1", 8180);
```

To check at any time whether the client is connected, you can call the isConnected() method. This method returns true if the client is connected to the server and returns false if it isn't connected. This is a good way to figure out whether your client has connected to the server before you try to run any other code, and to set up a retry loop to try to connect to the server again.

To send information to the server, use the send() method, which returns true if the message is successfully sent and false if it is not, as shown here:

```
If(client.send("hello")) {
    printf(" client sent hello ");
} else {
    printf(" client didn't send hello ");
}
```

The send() method sends only strings, so if you want to send another data type, for instance, the bytes of an image or audio, you'll need to use the sendRawBytes() method:

```
bool sendRawBytes(const char * rawBytes, const int numBytes)
```

This method allows you to send byte or unsigned char arrays without modifying or needing to wrap the data. The numBytes parameter needs to be the length of the array that you're sending.

To receive information from a server that the client is connected to, first check to see whether anything has been sent using the receive() method. This gets the message sent from the server as a string. One thing to note is that this method works only with messages sent using the server's send() or sendToAll() methods or with messages terminating with the string "[/TCP]". If you want to send "Hello" from a server that isn't an ofxTCPServer, you would send "Hello[/TCP]".

To check the number of bytes received, use getNumReceivedBytes(), which returns an integer value.

When you want to load binary data, a video file, an image, an MP3, or any other kind of data that isn't a string, use the receiveRawBytes() method:

```
int receiveRawBytes(char * receiveBytes, int numBytes)
```

You pass in a pointer to a buffer to be filled with the data, and the buffer will be loaded with the incoming information. You need to make sure the buffer is at least as big as numBytes.

A simple client application would have something like the following: in the update() method, check to see whether the client is connected. If not, connect, and then call the setup() method of the client. If connected, then check for any data being sent from the server:

```
void simpleClient::update()
{
    // store whether the client is connected to the server somewhere
    if(connected){
        string str = tcpClient.receive();
        if( str.length() > 0 ){
            prtinf("From ther server:: %s",str);
        }
    }else{
    // don't retry all the time, just every few hundred frames or so
        if( retryCounter > 500 ){
            connected = tcpClient.setup("127.0.0.1", 11999);
            retryCounter = 0;
        } else {
            retryCounter++;
        }
    }
}

void simpleClient::keyPressed(int key){

    //you can only type if you're connected
    it(connected){
        tcpClient.send("hello");
    }
}
```

Setting up an ofxTCPServer instance is fairly similar to how the Processing Network library server is created. Declare an instance in the *.h* file of your application, and then in the setup() method of your application call the setup() method of the ofxTCPServer:

```
ofxTCPServer server;
server.setup(8180, true);
```

The second parameter, `blocking bool` value is a new one and indicates whether the server should do one thing at a time (for instance, write data to client or establish a new connection) or try to do multiple things at a time. You're usually going to have this be `false`, unless you need to write to a server that will be accepting lots of connections.

The `ofxTCPServer` has a `connected()` method that returns true if any clients are connected to the server. If there are no clients attached, then `connected()` returns `false`. It's a good idea to use this to determine whether you need to run any client communication logic and save processing time if you don't. The TCP server gives every connected client a number that is simply a count starting with 0. The `clientID` in the signatures of the methods that follow is just the index number of the connected client:

```
bool send(int clientID, string message)
```

This next line of code sends data to a client as a string, and there is also a `send ToAll()` method that omits the `clientID` and just sends the message:

```
bool sendRawBytes(int clientID, const char * rawBytes, const int numBytes)
```

Using `sendRawBytes()` lets you send and receive byte (char) arrays without modifying or appending the data and is the better option if you are trying to send something other than just ASCII strings. There is also a `sendRawBytesToAll()` method that omits the `clientID`.

To receive data from a client, you can use the two following methods:

`string receive(int clientID)`
> This gets the message as a string, which will work only with messages coming via `send()` and `sendToAll()`, or from messages terminating with [/TCP].

`int receiveRawBytes(int clientID, char * receiveBytes, int numBytes)`
> To use this method, pass in a buffer to be filled; you'll need to make sure the buffer is at least as big as `numBytes`. As an example:

```
char buffer[6000];
receiveRawBytes(4, buffer, 6000);
```

As a demonstration of the ofxNetwork add-on, look at Example 12-4, which is an application to capture bytes from a camera on a server and send them to a client application that will display them there (credit goes to Theo Watson for helping out with this code).

An important concept that you'll see used here is the idea of packets. All the pixels of even a small frame of video is a very big dataset. To make sure that the server and client don't choke trying to read it all, you can write small bits of the data to the client, over and over, until it's all written. Figure 12-4 is a diagram that shows how these different classes will work together.

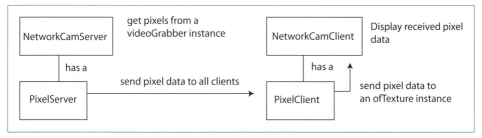

*Figure 12-4. Communication between the server and clients*

*Example 12-4. pixelClient.h*

```
#include "ofxNetwork.h"
#include "ofMain.h"

const int NUM_BYTES_IN_IMG = (320 * 240 * 3);

enum clientState{
    NONE, READY, RECEIVING, COMPLETE
};

class pixelClient{
    public:
```

pixelClient is going to store all the bytes received and know whether it is finished receiving bytes or should expect to receive more:

```
        pixelClient(){
            state = NONE;
            totalBytes = NUM_BYTES_IN_IMG;
            bytesRecieved = 0;
            memset(pixels, 255, totalBytes);
        }

        int getState(){
            return state;
        }

        string getStateStr(){
            if(state == NONE) { return "NONE"; }
            else if(state == READY) { return "READY"; }
            else if(state == RECEIVING) { return "RECEIVING"; }
            else if(state == COMPLETE) { return "COMPLETE"; }
            else { return "ERR"; }
        }

        void reset(){
            state = READY;
            bytesRecieved = 0;
        }
```

Start the connection to the server:

```
void setup(string ip, int port = 11999){
    TCP.setup(ip, port);
    state = READY;
    bytesRecieved = 0;
}
```

The size of the packet here is 2,048 bytes. Each time, the client receives a packet and determines whether it still has more bytes to get:

```
void update(int bytesToGet = 2048){

    if( state == READY || state == RECEIVING ){
        if( bytesToGet + bytesRecieved >= NUM_BYTES_IN_IMG ){
            bytesToGet -= ( ( bytesToGet + bytesRecieved ) -
                NUM_BYTES_IN_IMG );
        }

        char tmpBuffer[bytesToGet];
        int numRecieved = TCP.receiveRawBytes(tmpBuffer, bytesToGet);

        if( numRecieved > 0 ){
            state = RECEIVING;
            memcpy(&pixels[bytesRecieved],tmpBuffer, numRecieved);
            bytesRecieved += numRecieved;
        }

        if( bytesRecieved >= NUM_BYTES_IN_IMG ){
            state = COMPLETE;
        }
    }
}

clientState state;
int bytesRecieved;
int totalBytes;
ofxTCPClient TCP; // the TCP client that handles the actual communication
unsigned char pixels[NUM_BYTES_IN_IMG];
};
```

The *networkCamClient.h* (see Example 12-5) is the header file for the application that uses the pixelClient and displays its bytes to the screen when the complete image has loaded.

*Example 12-5. NetworkCamClient.h*

```
#pragma mark once

#include "ofMain.h"
#include "pixelClient.h"

class NetworkCamClient : public ofBaseApp{

public:
```

```
        void setup();
        void update();
        void draw();
        void keyPressed  (int key);

        pixelClient client;
        ofTexture tex;
        bool pixelsLoaded;

};
```

*Example 12-6. NetworkCamClient.cpp*

```
#include "NetworkCamClient.h"

void NetworkCamClient ::setup(){
    ofBackground(60,60,70);
```

Make sure to allocate the texture before trying to draw pixels into it:

```
    tex.allocate(320, 240, GL_RGB);
    pixelsLoaded = false;
}

void NetworkCamClient::update(){
    client.update(2048);

    if( client.getState() == COMPLETE ){
        tex.loadData(client.pixels, 320, 240, GL_RGB);
        pixelsLoaded = true;
    }
}

void NetworkCamClient::draw(){

    string statusStr =  "status: " + client.getStateStr();

    ofSetColor(255, 0, 255);
    ofDrawBitmapString(statusStr, 10, 20);
    ofDrawBitmapString("client - launch server than hit c key to
            connect - r to reset the state", 10, ofGetHeight()-20);

    ofSetColor(255, 255, 255);
```

If the pixels are all loaded, then they can be drawn into the ofTexture object so that it can be displayed:

```
    if( pixelsLoaded ){
        tex.draw(0, 25);
    }
}

void NetworkCamClient::keyPressed  (int key){
    if( key == 'c'){
        client.setup("127.0.0.1", 44999);
    }
```

```
    if(key == 'r'){
        client.reset();
    }
}
```

Now, take a look at the pixel server that handles writing all the bytes in small packets over to the client (see Example 12-7). Note that the entire class is stored within the *.h* file; there is no *.cpp* file used with this class.

*Example 12-7. pixelServer.h*

```
#pragma mark once

#include "ofxNetwork.h"
#include "ofMain.h"

const int NUM_BYTES_IN_IMG = (320 * 240 * 3);
```

An enum is used here to store all the different states that the pixelServer class can be in:

```
    enum serverState{
        NONE, READY, SENDING, COMPLETE
    };

    class pixelServer{
        public:

        serverState state;
        int numSentBytes;
        int totalBytes;
        ofxTCPServer TCP;
        unsigned char pixels[NUM_BYTES_IN_IMG];



        pixelServer(){
            state       = NONE;
            totalBytes  = NUM_BYTES_IN_IMG;
        }


        void setup(int port = 11999){
            //setup the server to listen on 11999
            TCP.setup(port);
            state = READY;
        }

        void sendPixels(unsigned char * pixelData) {
            if( state == NONE ) return;
```

Here, all the pixels are copied over to the new object to ensure that if the parent application wants to overwrite them by grabbing a new frame, then it doesn't break things with the server:

```
        memcpy(pixels, pixelData, totalBytes);
        state = SENDING;
        numSentBytes    = 0;
    }

    void update(int numToSend = 1024){
        if( state == SENDING && numSentBytes < totalBytes ){
            if( numToSend + numSentBytes > totalBytes ){
                numToSend -= ( (numToSend + numSentBytes) - totalBytes );
            }
```

Here's the call to sendRawBytesToAll() to write the packet of bytes to all connected clients:

```
        TCP.sendRawBytesToAll( (char *)&pixels[numSentBytes], numToSend);
        numSentBytes += numToSend;
    }

    if( numSentBytes >= totalBytes ){
        state = COMPLETE;
    }
    }
};
```

The networkCamServer that follows is a simple oF application that allows the user to press a key and capture an image from a webcam that will then be written to the clients (see Example 12-8).

*Example 12-8. NetworkCamServer.h*

```
#pragma mark once

#include "ofMain.h"
#include "ofxNetwork.h"
#include "pixelServer.h"

class NetworkCamServer: public ofBaseApp{

public:

    void setup();
    void update();
    void draw();
    void keyPressed   (int key);
    pixelServer server;
    ofImage testImg;
    ofVideoGrabber grabber;
};
```

In the implementation, all that's left to do is start the videoGrabber and send the pixels to the pixelServer instance when the user hits the spacebar (see Example 12-9).

*Example 12-9. NetworkCamServer.cpp*

```cpp
#include "networkCamServer.h"

void networkCamServer::setup(){
    ofBackground(20,20,20);
    server.setup(44999);
    grabber.initGrabber(320, 240, true);
}

void networkCamServer::update(){
    server.update(2048);
    grabber.grabFrame(); // grab a frame from the video
}

void networkCamServer::draw(){
    grabber.draw(0, 25);
}
```

When the user hits the spacebar, start sending the pixels:

```cpp
void networkCamServer::keyPressed  (int key){
    if( key == ' '){
        unsigned char * pix = grabber.getPixels();
        server.sendPixels(pix);
    }
}
```

Now, you have an application that sends pixels across to another application, and with a little work you could create an application that sends images across the Internet to another application, which could be located in another room or in another state.

---

# Interview: Usman Haque

Usman Haque is a London-based architect and artist who designs interactive architectural systems and develops both physical spaces and the software and systems that bring them to life. He currently teaches at the Bartlett School of Architecture in London, England. His installations have been exhibited at the Institute of Contemporary Arts (London), the Hillside Gallery (Tokyo), the Tokyo Metropolitan Museum of Photography (Tokyo), and the Plymouth Arts Centre (Plymouth). His projects have been published in several magazines and journals including *The Architects' Journal*, *Artifice*, *Wallpaper*, *Wired Online*, *WebMaster* magazine, *.net* magazine, *Architectural Design*, ZDNet, and the *RIBA Journal*.

*For my readers who might not be familiar with you and your work, could you give a very brief summary of the kinds of projects that you're working on currently?*

**Usman Haque:** There have been three particular directions that my work in the past has taken, guided particularly by my background in architecture and general interest in how we relate to each other and to the space we form around ourselves: (1) those involving participation and interaction, often in large-scale productions in urban parks; (2) experiments exploring the process of perception, both in humans and machines;

and (3) designing design systems, for example by finding ways to involve people who might not otherwise call themselves "designers" in the processes of design.

The direction of the work I'm involved in these days has changed a little. I've become particularly interested in tying together the previous strands, looking particularly at self-powered, dynamic, and permanent systems. I'm spending a lot of time nurturing Pachube.com. I'm also getting much more rigorous about what I describe as "interactive."

*Can you explain a little bit about how you and your collaborators came to work together and provide a little insight into how your actual day-to-day collaborations on a project takes shape?*

**Usman:** There's no conscious process involved in developing a collaboration. I usually find that I'm involved in a collaboration without specific planning. The project just takes shape in conversation; by contrast, when I have a project already in mind and I need specific additional input from others, I get a little embarrassed asking people whether they would like to work on it with me.

My favorite collaborations (and the usual way that these occur) are those that ensue from just hanging out with people I enjoy being with. The *Evolving Sonic Environment* project developed from having lunch with Rob Davis one day and having a conversation where we speculated about trying to go "totally analog"; the *WiFi-Camera* project came about when Adam Somlai-Fischer and Bengt Sjolen and I were huddled together at an exhibition opening; Seth Garlock got involved in *Sky Ear* during one of our (quite frequent) three-hour phone calls. (This was in pre-Skype days, and up until that point we hadn't talked about working together. Our conversations were usually about books and politics and egg-cream sodas. We just slipped unknowingly into the world of collaboration when he said, "Why don't your balloons talk to each other?"). When Rolf Pixley and I started working together, I think it was largely because we misunderstood each other, and the ongoing collaboration was a process of discovering that we might in fact be in agreement (!); working with Yu Nishibori on *Infinitum Ad Nauseam* came about because I really liked his meal recommendation after I met him in a restaurant (I also liked his rubber ducks); working with Despina Papadopoulos on *1,000* ensued after several years of being friends—partly we just wanted to find a way to get funding to carry on the kinds of conversations we were having. Anyway, I work with people I like. I don't worry about how/whether our skills overlap, complement, or jar. That usually gets clarified in the process of collaborating.

Working with Rolf on *Open Burble* is something I consider very precious. Partly through his pressure and partly because I want to know and understand every part of the projects I'm involved in, our conversations would swing rapidly from discussions on the timing of setting individual bits and registers within a microchip, all the way through conceptual discussions about the way the human nervous system functions, up through the perceptual mechanisms involved in looking at a lit balloon against the rapidly changing colors of an evening sky. I do think it's important for someone who is going to put his or her name on a project, even in a collaboration, to understand exactly what's going on in the project at all levels.

*I'm quite interested in the idea of architecture being something "no longer considered static and immutable." Can you elucidate this a little bit?*

**Usman:** Architecture has long been considered something permanent, static, and unchanging—the walls, roofs, and floors that surround us and that condition the way we relate to space and to each other. In the last few decades, however, a new idea of architecture has come about (largely influenced by Cedric Price): one in which architecture is all the stuff in between; it's ephemeral, permeable, and dynamic. I've sometimes described this as the "software" of space, rather than the "hardware," analogizing computer terminology. The point of this distinction is to say that there are bits that appear to stay the same, and there are also bits that change in terms of their relationship to the whole. I'm interested in the kind of architecture that is constantly constructed, something that is constantly responsive (even if that response is to "do nothing"), something that is constantly on the precipice of change.

*Do you see parallels between developing a system that replicates life and a system that integrates with life?*

**Usman:** The reason I undertake projects such as *Evolving Sonic Environment* is less about trying to make an "intelligent" space and more about trying to understand how "we humans" understand space. By attempting to build a space that "understands" us, I'm really trying to understand "understanding."

When I say "a space that understands," I mean one that modifies its perceptual processes and creates its own categories of occupancy. The point is not so much to integrate so-called "intelligent" systems with living systems but rather to develop an approach to environment design in which humans are not at the mercy of technology designed and determined by others—to develop adaptive, responsive, conversational systems, where the outcome is determined by both participants, not just the machine (which is the usual determinant of outcome in human-machine relationships).

*What sorts of strategies or thinking do you use to ensure that a participant is free to participate in the continued design and evolution of a space or project or structure?*

**Usman:** First, the more "open" a system is, the more bewildering it is for those who are introduced to it anew. In a design system in particular, people are often aided, not hindered, by having constraints applied to them—the real key is to find a way that the constraints are not necessarily absolute. If the constraints themselves can be modified over time, then that really helps in fostering ongoing participation. It is, in a sense, what learning is all about.

There are two important limits to the idea of a collaborative design system in architecture.

Second, I don't believe that it's possible to construct a "totally open system"—the very nature of a "system" (which is a description of a set of relationships, dependent in all cases upon a particular subjective approach) precludes it. There will always be processes that involve "top-downness" and "bottom-upness"—the key to helping perpetuate the design and evolution of the kinds of conversational environments we're talking about is to ensure that the relationship between the two processes is not frozen.

It's also important to ensure a varied "granularity" of participation: different people have different interests or skill sets, are willing to participate to a greater or lesser degree, or desire to have a smaller or larger impact on the entity being constructed. Everyone will have their own point at which they wish to engage with something, so it's vital that a wide variety of entry points and methods are available.

*You've written before about Gordon Pask and his conversation theory; can you explain a little about how that's useful to you?*

**Usman:** In the context of architecture, conversation theory is useful in two ways: (1) in considering the architectural construct as an "individual" in conversation with another "individual" (often a human being, who happens to occupy the architectural construct) and how these two can interact to their mutual benefit (and coherence); and (2) in considering an "environment" (such as architecture) as being something that is constructed when two individuals interact (for example, a human and a machine) and create "coherence." In this second example, interaction itself gives rise to architecture, and it is an arbitrary distinction whether the occupant is engaged with the "architecture" or the "computer-system-that-drives-the-architecture."

For an understanding of how I define many different flavors of "interaction," it might be useful to see the "What is Interaction? Are there different types?" article in January 2009's *ACM Interactions*, an article I coauthored with Hugh Dubberly and Paul Pangaro, based largely on the Paskian cybernetic approach.

*Who are some of the artists and thinkers that you refer to most in your own work and thinking about interactivity and architecture?*

**Usman:** I tend to be influenced really easily. So, if I stand next to someone in the subway, it probably affects the way I'm thinking about the world. However, apart from Gordon Pask, whom you have already mentioned, there are others who I look to often, including architect Cedric Price; Ross Ashby, a pioneer in systems theory; Kenneth Craik (who wrote *The Nature of Explanation* [Oxford University Press]); Stephen Groak (former director of "blue skies" research at Ove Arup and author of *The Idea of Building* [Spon Press]); and Natalie Jeremijenko, whose work on the "structures of participation" has been very influential. I often get lost in the mountainsides of the Pataphysicians (pataphysics being to metaphysics what metaphysics is to physics); my favorite artists are probably the group Gelitin.

*Do have a vision of the way that computing and computation will engage with the kinds of thinking and tasks that architecture and the design of spaces requires?*

**Usman:** The vision I have is what I fear will happen: that our technological systems will be designed and built by corporate entitics with their own rationales for existing, that these systems will be imposed upon us, and that we will be unable to enter into them in order to change the way they respond to us. They will be private, proprietary, unhackable, and unchallengeable. Imagine having a closed system, just like Microsoft Windows, controlling your physical desktop, your thermostat, or your home life.

That's the vision I'm trying to escape when thinking about ways to push the architecture and computation direction.

What I would like to head toward instead, and this comes out particularly in Pachube.com, is an ecosystem of conversant devices, environments, architectural entities —an ecosystem that is open, constantly being reinvented and repurposed, and constantly adjusting to new perturbations. The goal is not to make the world high-tech— rather, it's to accept that the world is heading in a high-tech direction and to attempt to nudge it toward a more humanist outcome.

*I'm curious how you see a viewer/participant's perception of the kinds of spaces that your projects construct. Do you view the space that the viewer inhabits more like a medium in which you communicate with them, or do you see the space as a message unto itself?*

**Usman:** The point is that the designer of any system is involved in a process of specifying things. If a designer specifies all parts of a design and hence all behaviors that the constituent parts can conceivably have at the beginning, then the eventual identity and functioning of that design will be limited by what the designer can predict. This entity is therefore closed to novelty and can respond only to preconceptions that were explicitly or implicitly built into it by the designer. If, on the other hand, a designed construct (say an environment) can choose what it senses (rather than having that imposed by the designer), either by having ill-defined inputs/sensors or by dynamically determining its own perceptual categories (that is, the means for comparing things), then it moves a step closer to true autonomy, which would be required in an authentically interactive system. In an environmental sense, the human component of interaction then becomes crucial because a person involved in determining input/output criteria is productively engaging in collaborative "conversations" with his or her environment. Building on the rather prosaic model of the thermostat, imagine a temperature-controlling system, which has the possibility of altering both inputs and outputs to the system (while always retaining the goal of "controlling the ambient temperature"). Rather than solely measuring temperature as an input, and outputting instructions to a heater to switch on, such a system might dynamically reconnect to different types of input or output.

These input criteria might range from "energy consumption measurements over the last month" to "the exterior temperature for this week last year" to "seasonal rainfall" to "the color of my clothes today" to "the fifth letter of the second paragraph on the front page of today's newspaper." The system might try all of these inputs and continue monitoring how much effect each appears to have on the goal (to control temperature). The system would evolve weightings for each of these input criteria in order to provide satisfactory output, again according to criteria determined dynamically with the person (who is controlling the goal of this super-thermostat). Output criteria might include "degree of thermal comfort," "energy bill amount," "neighbor's energy bill amount," "hot chocolate drinking tendency," "number of friends who come to visit and how long they stay."

In all cases, both input and output criteria are dynamically constructed and continually monitored with respect to how well they achieve the goal set by the person. In this situation we can imagine that the inhabitants and the environment are in some sense collaborating to develop a temperature-controlled system, because not only is the person contributing the input criteria, but they are also involved in influencing the output criteria. Such a calculation is complex enough as to be pretty much impossible without the aid of the super-thermostat; but without the human contribution, it's also impossible.

*Are you still working on the* Low Tech Sensors *and* Actuators *project?*

**Usman:** The point of *Low Tech Sensors* and *Actuators* (a collaboration with Adam Somlai-Fischer) was to make it simple for nontechnical people (or people who thought they were nontechnical) to get involved in hacking toys and gadgets, not being too respectful of the packaging that a mechanism is found in, to be able to prototype responsive systems relatively easily. We didn't take it much further than the first manual (though we did hold, and occasionally continue to hold, low-tech workshops) mostly because it is now quite a popular concept, and so there are lots of such guides and workshops available.

The manual has led us to create the *Reconfigurable House* (which amassed hundreds of low-tech gadgets, devices, and toys in a system where occupants could determine how these devices were connected to each other, building interactive systems in which "they decide" how the house would respond to them—essentially a critique of the closed nature of "smart homes") and later *Scattered House*, which was like *Reconfigurable House* but split across multiple cities and networked using Pachube.com (a system I have been developing to enable people from around the world to connect up and share their devices and environments in real time in order to build planetary-scale interactive environments; it's a little like YouTube, but for sharing real-time environmental data rather than videos). Pachube has evolved from these earlier systems: attempting to foster a reconfigurable planet, if you will, through a kind of global generalized data brokerage.

*Do you see architecture as a domain that is truly distinct from, say, designing an online community space?*

**Usman:** I'm not sure I agree necessarily that interaction or participation are more meaningful when conducted solely in nonelectronic physical space; certainly, being in the same room with someone offers a lot more bandwidth, and when time dimensions change, it's possible to drift in and out to greater or lesser degrees. In online situations, of course, it's difficult to have degrees of opt out. Either you're part of a conversation or you're lurking (or you're not even part of the community at all). Skype gets a little closer by having different status conditions you can assign yourself to, paralleling the ability to be "in the next room" as it were. But participation is mostly provoked into being through systems that are open to be changed, and that's why we have the rich possibilities of something like Wikipedia. There are certainly parallels between the processes involved in constructing architecture and processes involved in constructing online spaces, though I'm hesitant to analogize since it feels as though there are already too many analogies used by each for the other. However, I'm not someone who believes in a great distinction between real and virtual—this distinction has been compared to the now-quaint 19th-century distinction between mind and body.

*Reading about your* 1,000 (little tips of communication) *project I came across a quote that really struck me: "At a time when we can build whatever we imagine, device, building, or experience, it is vital to consider the wider aesthetic, ethical, and lyrical implications that this condition affords us."* Do you have specific ideas on what those implications are and what they mean to an artist, architect, or designer?

**Usman:** The point is that when we can build/design almost anything, it becomes very important to consider why it is that we choose to bring any particular thing into this world: does the world really need another XYZ product? What does it mean to be able to connect to more people? How can we continue to produce magic? In this statement, I was influenced a lot by Anthony Dunne's *Hertzian Tales* (MIT Press), where he talks about the "post-optimal" object (that is, objects you design once practicality and functionality can be taken for granted). In a world where anything is possible, poetry becomes imperative for generating the unexpected. I'm not sure that I can respond more specifically to your question, other than to say that that's really the hope for most of my projects: to find an answer to the question!

*What inspired you to design the EEML?*

**Usman:** Ultimately, with Pachube and Extended Environments Markup Language (EEML), my goal is to have some little effect on the construction industry, which determines the kinds of spaces we inhabit and how we relate to them.

EEML came about for two reasons: (1) we needed something that would do what current construction industry modeling standards cannot do (such as describe buildings that are dynamic, responsive, networked), while still being able to operate alongside them; and (2) because Pachube.com needed a protocol that was able to describe both the physical environments of buildings, devices, and human interaction and the virtual environments of *Second Life* and web browsers without predicating one upon the other. The point was to develop something that was robust enough to be used by building management software and also flexible and simple enough that individual developers and nonprofessionals can use the format in their own smaller devices and projects. This facilitates communication between all types of entity and therefore is exactly what Pachube.com requires, with its goal being to enable people to tag and share real-time sensor data between buildings, devices, and environments all over the world.

An understanding of what an environment actually constitutes is crucial to EEML's ongoing development. I believe that one of the major failings of the usual *ubicomp* (ubiquitous computing integrates common, everyday computational devices and systems, often without the user knowing) approach is to consider the connectivity and technology at the object level, rather than at the environment level. It's built into much of contemporary Western culture to be object-centric, but at the environment level, we talk more about context, disposition, and subjective experience. An *environment* has dynamic frames of reference, all of which are excluded when simply focusing on devices, objects, or mere sensors. If you really study deeply what an environment is (by this I mean more than simply saying that "it's what things exist in"), you begin to understand that an environment is a construction process and not a medium, not just a state and not just an entity. In this I would refer to Gordon Pask's phenomenally important text "Aspects of Machine Intelligence" in Nicholas Negroponte's *Soft Architecture Machine* (MIT Press), which makes for extremely tough reading (Negroponte compared it in importance to Alan Turing's contributions to the discipline).

As a result of this conception of environment, we remove the need for a distinction between real and virtual. We can consider equally as environments a mountainside, the interior of a building, the context of a web page, the internal status and external context of a mobile device, the interactions within something like *Second Life*—all these are environments and can communicate with each other on equivalent terms. More importantly, a single environment can be expressed as a snapshot in time, or it can be expressed as a sequence of many snapshots over several years. Chris Leung (who has been working on this) and I have a very similar approach to systems design, but at the same time we are looking for quite different things in the protocol. And so, in ensuring that we are both happy with it, it has been useful to make sure that we cover a lot of territory—attempting to be all things to all people...and machines!

# Creating Networks with the Arduino

You can use the Arduino Ethernet Shield (see Figure 12-5) with your Arduino controller to send and receive data from a network. The shield has a chip called the Wiznet W5100 that provides a network (IP) stack capable of both TCP and UDP communication and can handle up to four simultaneous connections. The Arduino team has also created the Ethernet library to make connecting to the Internet using the shield simpler.

*Figure 12-5. The Arduino Ethernet Shield*

The shield connects to an Arduino board using the long pins called *headers* that you see in the image. This keeps the pin layout intact and also allows another shield to be stacked on top if you need to attach another shield to your Arduino controller. The Arduino uses the digital pins at 10, 11, 12, and 13 to communicate with the Ethernet shield chip so you can't use these for anything else. The rest of the pins, even those that the Ethernet Shield is connected to, are fine to use. The Ethernet jack on the shield is a standard Ethernet jack and will work with the same kind of cable you use for connecting a computer to the network. The reset button on the shield resets both the chip on the shield and the Arduino board.

## Initializing the Ethernet Library

To use the chip on the board, you'll need to use the Arduino Ethernet library. There are a few things about the Ethernet library to note. All the communication with servers must be done using the IP address. At present, the Ethernet library doesn't work with domain names, but this might change in the future. Also, the Ethernet Shield needs a Media Access Control (MAC) number. In computer networking, a MAC address is a quasi-unique identifier assigned to most network adapters or network interface cards (NICs) by the manufacturer for identification. Many times a MAC address uses the manufacturer's registered identification number. In the case of the Ethernet Shield, you create a unique MAC address with 6-byte hexadecimal values.

Use the following code to initialize the Ethernet library. Notice the MAC address in line 2 and the IP (not domain name) in line 3. Also, note that if you're going to be using multiple Ethernet Shields on a single network you'll need to give each of them unique addresses:

```
#include <Ethernet.h>
byte mac[] = { 0xDE, 0xAD, 0xBE, 0xEF, 0xFE, 0xED };
byte ip[] = { 10, 0, 0, 177 };

void setup()
{
    Ethernet.begin(mac, ip);
}
```

The `begin()` method in the code initializes the Ethernet library and network settings and has three overloaded signatures:

`Ethernet.begin(mac, ip);`
> This is the simplest signature, using only the MAC and IP addresses.

`Ethernet.begin(mac, ip, gateway);`
> This signature also uses the gateway, which is the IP address of the network gateway. In the case of a router, it is the IP address of the router. This is needed for communication on the Internet because the shield sends and receives Internet messages through the router.

`Ethernet.begin(mac, ip, gateway, subnet);`
> This is the subnet mask of the network (array of 4 bytes). By default this is 255.255.255.0. This tells the shield how to interpret IP addresses.

## Creating a Client Connection

To make a client, you need to import the Ethernet library and then declare an instance of the `Client` class. Remember that C++ constructors don't use the `new` keyword:

*Example 12-10. Ethernetter.ino*

```
#include <SPI.h>
#include <Ethernet.h>
bool connected = false;
```

Next, these arrays of bytes are used to start up the client and initialize the Ethernet library:

```
byte mac[] = { 0xDE, 0xAD, 0xBE, 0xEF, 0xFE, 0xED };
byte ip[] = { 192,168,0,51 }; // make sure this address is free on your
                              // network and is appropriate for your router
byte serverIp[] = {64, 233, 187, 99}; // this is google's address
```

Now, create the new client using the **serverIp** array to connect to Google and port 80 to make sure that you're connecting to the standard HTTP port. Then call **setup()** to initialize the Ethernet shield:

```
EthernetClient client;

void setup() {
    //initialize the Ethernet library
    Ethernet.begin(mac, ip);
    Serial.begin(9600);

}

void loop()
{
```

If the client hasn't connected yet, try to connect again. When the **connect()** method of the client returns **true**, then send a search request to Google:

```
if(!connected) {
    if (client.connect(serverIp, 80)) {
        connected = true;
        Serial.println("connected");

        // you could also change this line to anything else
        // "GET /search?q=programming+interactivity HTTP/1.1" for example
        client.println("GET /search?q=arduino HTTP/1.1");
        client.println("Host: www.google.com");
        // say who you are, just like in the Processing example
        client.println("User-Agent: AVR ethernet");
        client.println("Accept: text/html");
        // then insert an empty line
        client.println();
    } else {
        Serial.println(" can't connect ");
        delay(500);
    }

} else {
```

If the client has connected already, you can begin reading the bytes from the server. The **read()** method returns the char values one at a time. This means that you have to think carefully about what data you're reading from the server and how you're going to parse it to find the bits you want. Searching through a lot of HTML returned from an HTML page can be very time-consuming and inefficient on an Arduino:

```
if (client.available()) {
        char c = client.read();
        Serial.print(c);
    }
  }
}
```

## Creating a Server Connection

You might also want to connect an Arduino to your Internet connection to act like a server, accepting requests from other clients and sending them data in response. The Ethernet library uses a class called Server to create servers. There's a few things that you'll need to decide on before using the Server class. Will your Arduino connect directly to your modem? If you're using a router, you'll need to determine your router address. You can use several web services, or you can go to your router's admin page to check. To find the admin page of your server, you can either try 192.168.1.1 (the default address for Linksys and several other brands of routers) or look up the IP and default username and password for your brand and model. Once you've determined that, you can set the IP of the Arduino. You may also need to enable the demilitarized zone (DMZ) settings on your router to send traffic to the Arduino. By setting the DMZ, you're telling your router to stop blocking traffic that tries to visit it and send them to whatever IP is set as the DMZ. Doing a web search on any combination of these terms can help you find a good and thorough tutorial. It's a bit simpler if you connect the Arduino directly to the modem.

The quickest way to see how the server works is to look at Example 12-11.

*Example 12-11. EtherServer.ino*

```
#include <SPI.h>
#include <Ethernet.h>

// network configuration.  gateway and subnet are optional.
byte mac[] = { 0xDE, 0xAD, 0xBE, 0xEF, 0xFE, 0xED };
```

You need a MAC address and an IP address to initialize the Ethernet library. Although the client uses the IP address to connect to a server, in the case of the server, the IP is the address that others will use to connect to your Ethernet Arduino. If you're going to connect your Arduino directly to your modem, you'll need to know what IP address you'll be connecting to. On Linux or Mac OS X, type ifconfig -a into a terminal; on Windows type ipconfig /all. This will spit out something that looks like this: inet 192.168.1.100 netmask 0xffffff00 broadcast 192.168.1.255. On Windows, the broadcast address will be the IP address with the last digits set to 255. You'll want to use the broadcast address as the IP address:

```
byte ip[] = { 24, 189, 101, 90 };
```

An array of bytes for the gateway will be needed if you're using a router to connect to the Internet. Use the gateway address found on your router's admin page and the net-mask from the `ifconfig` or `ipconfig` command for the subnet value. Pass these to the call to the Ethernet `begin()` method. Also, if you're using a router to connect, you'll need the subnet address. Again, you can find this on the admin screen for your router or by the using the `ifconfig` or `ipconfig` terminal commands. In our example, we are using the simplest `begin()` method signature, so the gateway and subnet lines are shown for you, commented out:

```
// byte gateway[] = { 10, 0, 0, 1 };
// byte subnet[] = { 255, 255, 0, 0 };
```

Now, set up the server to communicate on port 80, handling HTTP requests:

```
// HTTP uses port 80 by default
EthernetServer server(80);

void setup()
{
    // initialize the ethernet device
    //Ethernet.begin(mac, ip, gateway, subnet); // with subnet, ie through router
    Ethernet.begin(mac, ip); // without subnet, ie directly to modemå
    // start listening for clients
    server.begin();
}

void loop()
{
```

Next, the `available()` method of the server gets the next client that's trying to connect to the server:

```
    EthernetClient client = server.available();
    if (client) {
```

Now, print an HTTP response. HTTP uses codes to tell clients what the response is indicating. A 200 response means the request was all right and the server is responding. 404 means the client is requesting a file that doesn't exist. 500 indicates a server error, and 401 indicates a protected resource that the client doesn't have permission to access yet. There are quite a few more, but those are the most common ones. You'll always need to include a response code as shown here in the first line of the `println()` methods that the server uses to reply to clients:

```
server.println("HTTP/1.1 200 OK");
        server.println("Content-Type: text/html");
        server.println();
        server.println("Hello World!");
    }
}
```

And that's it. Setting up clients and servers in Arduino is fairly easy. The most difficult part of creating and connecting a client is ensuring that your addressing is correct and your requests are properly formatted. The most difficult part of using a server is correctly connecting your server instance to your Internet connection and ensuring that requests to your modem's IP address are correctly passed on to your Arduino.

In both of these examples, we've used HTTP requests over port 80. As mentioned earlier, there are quite a few different communication protocols that you can use to connect and send and receive information. Another common protocol to use with a microcontroller like the Arduino Ethernet is the Telnet protocol, which uses port 23.

So, what can you do with the Arduino Ethernet Shield and the Ethernet library? At the easiest, you can create a network between multiple Arduino Ethernet controllers using a router. Since the router can enable available servers to assign themselves IP addresses, you could create a network of multiple Arduino Ethernet servers that could broadcast signals and events to themselves all the time. An entire room or environment could be enabled to send and listen to events from Arduino controllers and physical controls. Since the Ethernet Shields are not communicating with the Internet outside of the local network, all that's required is to set them all to IP addresses that the router doesn't reserve for itself (see Figure 12-6).

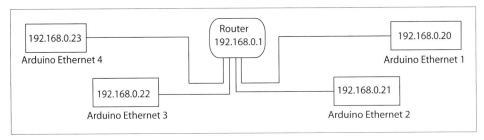

*Figure 12-6. Using a router to connect multiple Arduino Ethernet servers*

Another interesting use of the Arduino Ethernet is being explored at the Pachube project, initiated by Usman Haque. Pachube is a service that enables servers and clients to send and receive data from all over the world in an XML-based format. They're particularly interested in enabling and sharing real-time sensor data from objects, devices, buildings, and environments around the world. If you're looking for an interesting data feed to connect to, that's a place to begin. Many other web services return data in a format that is too data heavy for the Arduino to parse and process correctly, but with some work, you can use some of them.

There's plenty more information on using the Arduino Ethernet both on the Arduino website and on the Pachube website. If you're interested in learning more about networking, the World Wide Web Consortium has free tutorials. *Network Know-How* by John Ross (No Starch Press) is also a pretty useful book for learning the basics of creating networks and enabling networked devices. The Internet itself is also filled with tutorials, hints, tips, tricks, and forums where you can ask questions about these kinds of topics; in particular the Processing, Pachube, and Arduino sites are good resources.

# Wireless Internet on the Arduino

One thing that the Arduino has only recently been able to do is communicate on a wireless network. It used to be that wireless card modules were expensive, heavy, and drew a lot more power than the Arduino could provide over long time periods, but these days that's not true. Small microcontroller-friendly modules like the WiFly shield or the GainSpan wireless modules are lightweight and energy-efficient enough to fit inside an Arduino-sized enclosure with a battery. Fundamentally, operating a wireless Arduino is the same as operating a wired one: you still speak HTTP and connect to clients, send messages, and close connections, but it's sometimes a little trickier communicating with the boards themselves.

Figure 12-7 shows two different modules that you can use with the Arduino:

*Figure 12-7. Two Arduino compatible Wireless Internet Shields*

Of these, we'll focus on the WiFly shield. It has a little better support right now than the GainSpan, which isn't to say that the GainSpan doesn't work well, but the WiFly has slightly better support and is a little bit more popular. There are several versions of the WiFly library hanging around on GitHub that have various updates and bugs, so be aware that you might not get everything you need from one version of it. But for this example, you can use the archived version included in the downloads. In there you'll find a link to the git repository where more updated versions of libraries can be found.

Since I've already mentioned Pachube in a few places in this chapter, it makes sense to connect to it and send some information from a WiFly shield. As I mentioned, Pachube is essentially a clearinghouse of feeds from Arduinos or other microcontrollers all around the world that are sharing environmental real-time data. When you create an account with Pachube, you get an API key that you can use to publish data to your personal feed. Pachube uses EEML, which is a subset of XML and it usually looks like this:

```
<eeml xmlns="http://www.eeml.org/xsd/0.5.1"
 xmlns:xsi="http://www.w3.org/2001/XMLSchema-instance" version="0.5.1"
 xsi:schemaLocation=
  "http://www.eeml.org/xsd/0.5.1 http://www.eeml.org/xsd/0.5.1/0.5.1.xsd">
  <environment updated="2010-07-05T08:48:27.961661Z" id="2789" creator="http://www.pachube.com
    <data id="1">
      <tag>humidity</tag>
      <current_value at="2010-07-02T10:16:19.270708Z">100</current_value>
      <max_value>10000.0</max_value>
      <min_value>-10.0</min_value>
    </data>
  </environment>
</eeml>
```

That's a lot to wrap two important pieces of data—what time it is and what the humidity is—but it's important to ensure that anyone coming to Pachube wanting to use data feeds has all the info that they might need. Part of making a reliable service is making sure that there's adequate data and standards across all that data, so Pachube asks for a little more information to make your data friendlier. One of the things that you'll need to do in order to read from and write to Pachube is to sign up and get an API key, which is free and only takes a few moments. Once you've done that you can start to read a data feed using your WiFly shield.

There's one new thing introduced in this example that you haven't seen before: XML parsing on the Arduino. Usually, you'd get a larger computer to do the parsing for you but in this case we want to be able to have the Arduino read the XML directly from Pachube without any intervention necessary. Since EEML is fairly lightweight, we can do this on the Arduino without too much trouble, but a much larger XML file wouldn't parse at all or would slow the Arduino down so much that the program's performance would suffer considerably. To do this, we'll use a library called TinyXML. It's included in the download and there's not much you need to do to work with it. The particulars of parsing XML on the Arduino in such a lightweight fashion are a little odd, so we'll leave them out and instead focus on the WiFly library.

The WiFly library has a bit of an odd history. It was first created at SparkFun and then, as these things tend to go, adopted and modified by the open source community. If you search around on GitHub, you'll probably find a newer and improved version of the library than we could hope to provide, but for this example the library contained in the download is sufficient. See Example 12-12.

*Example 12-12. WiFlyPachube.ino*

```
#include "WiFly.h"
#include "TinyXML.h"

// we ultimately want something that looks like this:
// http://api.pachube.com/v2/feeds/1977/datastreams/1
Client client("pachube.com", 80);
```

Here's the XML parser and a buffer that it will use to parse the data received from Pachube:

```
TinyXML txml;
uint8_t buffer[150];
uint16_t buflen = 150;
```

This is where you put your API key that you received when you signed up for Pachube:

```
const char API_KEY[] = "PUT YOUR API KEY HERE";
```

Here are your WiFi router's parameters, passphrase, and SSID:

```
char passphrase[] = "pass";
char ssid[] = "ssid";

bool tryToConnect;
uint_fast32_t simpleCounter;
const uint_fast32_t updateCycles = 7200000; // around 15 minutes at 8Mhz

void setup() {

  tryToConnect = true;
  Serial.begin(9600);

  txml.init((uint8_t*)&buffer,buflen,&XML_callback);
  WiFly.begin();
```

If we can't join the network, we send a message; there isn't much more than that we can do. If you want to make this application a little easier to debug from a distance, you could put green and red LEDs to indicate normal functioning and errors.

```
  if (!WiFly.join(ssid, passphrase)) {
    Serial.println("Association failed.");
    while (1) {
      // can't do much really. wait for a reboot
    }
  }

  Serial.println("connecting...");
  connectClient();
}

void loop() {
  if( tryToConnect) {
```

If we've gotten something from the client, read it into the TinyXML instance by passing the character to the processChar() method. If TinyXML finds something, it triggers the XML_callback() method below where you can check what it's received:

```
  if (client.available()) {
    char c = client.read();
    txml.processChar(c);
  }

  if (!client.connected()) {
```

```
        Serial.println();
        Serial.println("disconnecting.");
        client.stop();
        tryToConnect = false;
    }
}
```

This is a simple way of only polling the server every 15 minutes so we don't simply get the same result over and over:

```
    simpleCounter++;
    if(simpleCounter > 32000 && !tryToConnect) {
      simpleCounter = 0;
      tryToConnect = true;
      connectClient();
    }

}

void connectClient() {
    if (client.connect()) {
    Serial.println("connected");
    client.print("X-PachubeApiKey:");
    client.println(API_KEY);
    client.println("GET /v2/feeds/1977/datastreams/1");
    client.println();
    }
    else {
      Serial.println("connection failed");
    }
}

void XML_callback( uint8_t statusflags, char* tagName,  uint16_t tagNameLen,  char*
data,  uint16_t dataLen ) {
    if (statusflags & STATUS_TAG_TEXT)
    {
```

The only tag we're interested in with this stripped down example is the current_value tag that tells us the current value. However, you might be interested in a lot of different tags, date and time, historical values, etc. This is where you would put the logic for finding the tag you're interested in:

```
      if(strcmp(tagName, "current_value")  == 0)
      {
        Serial.println("data is ");
        Serial.println(data);
        tryToConnect = false;
      }

    }
}
```

And now you know how to connect to a WiFi network with Arduino and parse data from Pachube as well. Next up: Bluetooth.

---

# Communicating with Bluetooth

You may have heard of Bluetooth already, because many cell phones, laptops, and other devices use it to enable communication between peripheral devices, like headsets and cell phones or phones and computers. Bluetooth is basically a networking standard like the 802.11 wireless Internet protocol that works at two levels: as a radio frequency standard and as a data standard. Bluetooth is a protocol and that means it provides a standard for when bits are sent, how many will be sent at a time, and how the parties in a conversation can be sure that the message received is the same as the message sent. The big benefits of Bluetooth are that it is wireless, inexpensive, and automatic. Bluetooth sends out very weak signals of about 1 milliwatt (most cell phones can send a signal of about 3 watts), so the range of a Bluetooth device is about 10 meters. Despite the relative weakness of the signal, Bluetooth is wireless and can transmit through walls, making the standard useful for controlling several devices in different rooms without needing to run any wires. You can connect up to eight devices simultaneously in a single area.

There are two approaches to working with Bluetooth that will be covered in this chapter: the Bluetooth Arduino board and the Processing bluetoothDesktop library.

## Using Bluetooth in Processing

bluetoothDesktop allows Processing sketches to send and receive data via Bluetooth wireless networks on any computer that can support the Java Bluetooth library called JSR-82, which is what Processing uses to facilitate Bluetooth communication. It is an adapted version of a Bluetooth library written by Francis Li for the Processing Mobile project that enables you to run Processing on certain cell phones. Using this library, a Processing sketch running on a computer with a JSR-82 implementation can connect to other Bluetooth devices as well as act as a service to which other devices can connect.

### Installing Bluetooth on Linux and Windows

Download the library, unzip it, and place the *bluetoothDesktop* folder into the Processing libraries folder.

### Installing Bluetooth on Mac OS X

Download the library and unzip it. The bluetoothDesktop library includes two different libraries that you can use to connect to Bluetooth devices: bluecove and avetana. bluecove is open source, free, and the generally preferred option. However, it might not work properly on your machine. If it doesn't, you can use the commercial avetana library instead. To start, you'll need to remove one of the libraries to ensure that the Processing application doesn't initialize both. I'd recommend trying the bluecove library first, so move the *avetana.jar* file to a separate folder outside your library folder.

If you run into problems with the bluecove library and you really want to use Bluetooth, it might be worth looking into purchasing a license.

## Using the bluetoothDesktop Library

Once you've installed bluetoothDesktop, you're ready to look at the four main classes that the bluetoothDesktop library uses: Bluetooth, Client, Device, and Service. Bluetooth works a little differently than the server-client communication that we've been looking at so far. Any Bluetooth-enabled device can create a service that other clients can connect to, and any Bluetooth-enabled device can connect to any other devices that have made themselves available. The services that these devices create and connect to are simply referenced by strings in the bluetoothDesktop library, so you could create a service called myGreatService. Other devices that find this service can connect to it, or the service itself can actively look for clients with which to connect and attempt to connect. That connection allows a service-providing device to send and receive bytes, strings, or integer values from a connected client device. Once the devices have finished communicating, the client simply closes the connection.

With that high-level overview in mind, the four primary classes in the bluetoothDesktop library will make a little more sense. The primary interface for both finding other Bluetooth services that exist and creating new services is called *Bluetooth*, and it, like many other Processing libraries, has five important methods that allow you to start an action and use callback methods to tell your application when those actions have completed. For instance, to find other Bluetooth-enabled devices, create a new Bluetooth instance, and use the discover() method. The Bluetooth instance will call the device DiscoverEvent() method whenever it finds a new device and the deviceDiscoveryCom pleteEvent() method when all devices that can be found have been located. See Example 12-13.

*Example 12-13. pBluetooth.pde*

```
import bluetoothDesktop.*

Bluetooth bluetoothInstance;

void setup() {
    bluetoothInstance= new Bluetooth(this);
    bluetoothInstance.discover();
    noLoop(); // tell the Processing application that we don't need a loop
}

void deviceDiscoverEvent(Device dev) {
    println(dev.name + " discovered.");
}

void deviceDiscoveryCompleteEvent(Device[] devices) {
    println(" Found " + devices.length+ " devices.");
    for( int i = 0; i<devices.length; i++) {
    println("i: "+devices[i].name;
```

```
    }
}
```

If you want to create a new service using your Bluetooth instance, use the `start()` method:

```
Bluetooth bluetoothInstance;
String amazingService = "AMAZING";

void setup() {
    bluetoothInstance= new Bluetooth(this);
    bluetoothInstance.start(amazingService);
}
```

To stop the service, simply pass the name of the service to the `stop()` method:

```
stop(amazingService);
```

The Bluetooth object can also call the following callback methods on a Processing application:

`serviceDiscoverEvent()`
> This method is triggered when a new service is found. If you're creating a client object, you'll use this method and the next quite frequently because it allows you to search out new services and discover information about them.

`serviceDiscoveryCompleteEvent()`
> This method is triggered when the Bluetooth object is finished searching for services and will pass an array of service objects to the method for you to use.

`clientConnectEvent()`
> This method is triggered whenever a new client connects to the service.

The `Device` class, which was used in the `deviceDiscoverEvent()` method in the previous example, is used to represent any devices discovered on the Bluetooth network. The `Device` class has properties that give you its name and address, a `discover()` method that searches for available services, and a `cancel()` method that cancels the search for a service.

The service represents software running on devices that can be connected to via the Bluetooth network. It, like the `Device`, has a `name` property but adds a `device` property that returns the device that hosts the service, as well as a `connect()` method that returns a connected `Client` object.

The `Client` object is where the bulk of the actual reading and writing of data between two devices takes place. There are a series of read methods for a client to read information from a server:

`read()`
> Reads one byte of data.

`readBytes(buffer, offset, length)`
> Reads information into an array of bytes that will hold the data. `offset` is the index into `buffer` to start storing data, and `length` is the maximum number of bytes to store.

There are also methods for reading data with specific types:

`readChar()`
> Reads char values.

`readInt()`
> Reads int values.

`readUTF()`
> Reads String values.

The write methods work similarly:

`write(int value)` *or* `write(byte[] buffer)`
> Writes information to a server that the client is connected to.

`writeBoolean()`
> Writes Boolean values to a server that the client is connected to.

`writeChar()`
> Writes char values to a server that the client is connected to.

`writeInt()`
> Writes int values to a server that the client is connected to.

`writeUTF()`
> Writes String values to a server that the client is connected to.

Finally, the `stop()` method closes the connection and ends any communication that the client is conducting.

You may be wondering: so what? And that's an excellent question because it has an excellent answer: Processing has recently been ported to Android devices, and being able to communicate over Bluetooth in Processing means being able to easily communicate between computers and mobile devices. The techniques for doing this are a little more complex than I want to get into in this book, but they are readily accessible on the Processing forums and very exciting to work with.

# Communicating Using MIDI

In interaction design, you always want to look for actions or paradigms of interaction that users are already familiar with. Some of the richest examples of interfaces come from the world of music. Taking the piano keyboard as an example, you have two approaches for getting data from the interface into your application: by analyzing the notes that are played on the piano or by using an electronic keyboard and reading the notes that the user plays. Techniques, the first approach, were covered in . To use the second approach with an electronic device, you'll want to use the Musical Instrument Digital Interface (MIDI) protocol. This is an easy way to get an Arduino or your laptop communicating with electronic musical instruments of all sorts, not just pianos.

If you decide to work with MIDI, two other elements are added to the system design. The first is the MIDI device itself, and the second is the data format that all MIDI devices use. The device can be any MIDI keyboard, mixing board, or even computer program. Which device and how to present it to the user is left up to you. The way that the MIDI communicates is quite straightforward. The MIDI specification consists of many different signals. Like so many of the other protocols that have been discussed in this chapter, MIDI has a way of defining what devices should be listening to which signals. In MIDI, this is done by using a channel, which is sent in the last 4 bits of the message byte. In programming for audio, a device or program will respond to messages sent with the channel ID that it is tuned to and will ignore all other channel messages. The most relevant four are shown in Table 12-1.

Table 12-1. MIDI messages

| Message | Meaning | First byte | Second byte |
| --- | --- | --- | --- |
| 0x80 or 128 | Note Off | Key | Velocity |
| 0x90 or 144 | Note On | Key | Velocity |
| 0xA0 or 160 | Key Pressure | Key | Pressure |
| 0xE0 or 224 | Pitch Bend | Least Value of Bend | Maximum Value of Bend |

A MIDI message from a keyboard will look like Figure 12-8, with each block representing a byte of data.

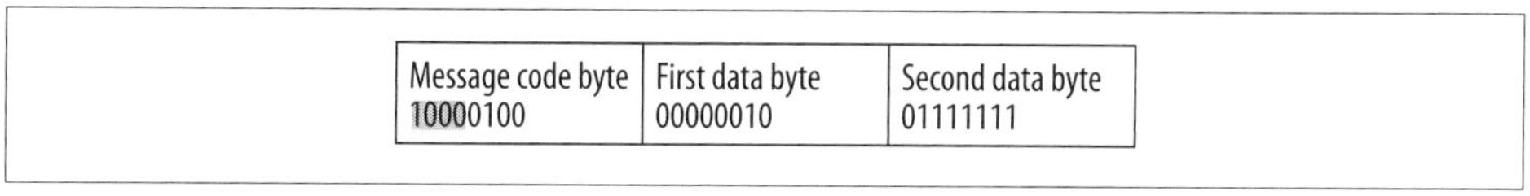

| Message code byte<br>10000100 | First data byte<br>00000010 | Second data byte<br>01111111 |
| --- | --- | --- |

Figure 12-8. A MIDI message block

If a MIDI device received the following message:

```
10000100  00000010  01111111
```

it would break it down like this: the first four bits of the status byte, 1,001 or 0x80, tell MIDI that the message is a "note on" command, and the last four bits of that first byte tell MIDI what channel the message is for (0000=MIDI channel #1, 1111=MIDI channel #16). The first data byte tells MIDI what note to play—00000010 is decimal 12, the lowest C on a piano—while the second data byte tells MIDI how loud to play the note, in this case the maximum velocity of 127. The device should play the note until a "note off" message on the same channel and with the same note is received. If you're thinking of communicating with an Arduino using MIDI devices, you'll probably be most interested in the message indicating what the user has done and the note itself

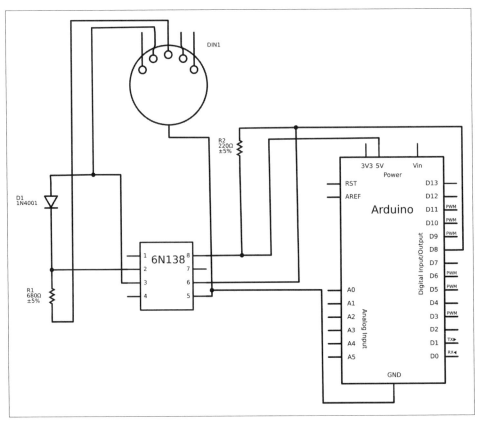

*Figure 12-9. Wiring a MIDI-in connection*

since it would indicate what key the user has pressed on a MIDI device. Not all MIDI devices send velocity, but if they do, then you can read that information too to create quite interesting and responsive interfaces.

Sending data from an Arduino to a MIDI device is considerably easier than receiving data from a MIDI device. A good number of tutorials are available online to show you how to produce MIDI data from an Arduino. In this next code example, you'll see how to send data to an Arduino from a MIDI device like a keyboard. First, look at the schematic in Figure 12-9 on the opposite page.

Notice in the schematic the box in the middle marked 6N138. This is an opto-isolator that is an electrical component made up of a light-emitting device and a light-sensitive device with no electrical connection between the two. An opto-isolator uses a beam of light to tell a device on one side of the circuit that a certain amount of current has been reached on the other side. The reason for this is that the MIDI connection uses a lot of voltage, enough to fry your Arduino at worst and interfere with it at best. The opto-isolator allows the MIDI signals to be sent to the Arduino without the dangerous amounts of voltage that they use. The other relevant part of the diagram is the MIDI 5 pin DIN connector. This is what is used to connect to the MIDI device. Figure 12-10 shows images of the two components.

5 pin Female DIN Connector          4N28 Opto-isolator

*Figure 12-10. Components for creating Arduino MIDI in*

Adafruit also has created a MIDIsense Analog+Digital I/O kit that will save you needing to replicate the wiring described above. It has two MIDI ports that can be powered by a battery, and can be easily configured to communicate with an Arduino.

To read MIDI in signals the easiest approach is, unsurprisingly, to use the Arduino MIDI library that was developed to make reading and writing MIDI signals easier. The library itself defines a few key callback methods that you can use to be notified when the Arduino device receives a MIDI signal. There's a slight hitch with this library: by default it uses the hardware serial for serial communication with whatever is sending MIDI, which means that you can't send additional serial signals over the USB to another application. Using the hardware serial is as easy as connecting the MIDI DIN connector to the Arduino Digital Pin 0. For Example 12-14, we're going to use the `NewSoftwareSerial` library so we can connect the MIDI DIN connector to Digital Pins 8 and 9. This requires using a slightly hacked MIDI library that you can find in the download archive for this chapter.

*Example 12-14. ardMIDI.ino*

```
#include <MIDI.h>
#include <NewSoftSerial.h>

const int ledOnPin = 13;
const int ledOffPin = 12;

void blinkLedOn(byte num) {      // Basic blink function
  for (byte i=0;i<num;i++) {
    digitalWrite(ledOnPin,HIGH);
    delay(30);
    digitalWrite(ledOnPin,LOW);
    delay(30);
  }
}

void blinkLedOff(byte num) {      // Basic blink function
    digitalWrite(ledOffPin, HIGH);
    delay(100);
```

```
    digitalWrite(ledOffPin, LOW);
}

void setup() {
  pinMode(ledOffPin, OUTPUT);
  pinMode(ledOnPin, OUTPUT);
```

Start the MIDI library with the `begin()` method:

```
    MIDI.begin(); // input channel is default set to a NSS on 8+9
    }
    void loop() {
```

Now check with the MIDI library to see if any data is incoming using the `read()` method. If there is a message, we check the message type that has been received. If there is a note "started" message, then blink the "on" LED for the note sent. Blink the "off" LED when the note is released:

```
    if (MIDI.read()) {
        // Get the type of the message we caught
        switch(MIDI.getType()) {
          case NoteOn: // right now just note on
        blinkLedOn(MIDI.getData1()); // Blink the LED a number of times
            break;
          case NoteOff:
            blinkLedOff(MIDI.getData1());
            break;
          default:
            break;
      }
    }
  }
```

Now you can send this data to an oF or Processing application to be played back. You might not be interested in sending this information on to another machine. You might want to drive a piezo sensor used as a speaker, control servo motors or even home appliances with this information, drive LED displays, or try any number of interesting ways of creating feedback.

## Review

XML is a hierarchical data format consisting of nested nodes that represent data and the relationship of one piece of data to another. It's often used to save or read data, particularly on the Internet.

All XML documents consist of nodes shaped like <node>Value</node>. Nodes can have children, defined like <parent>Value<child>ChildVal</child></parent>.

To send or receive information from a network in Processing, use the Processing Network library. This defines `Client` objects that can read information from local and remote servers, and `Server` objects that can respond to requests from local or remote clients.

Transmission Control Protocol (TCP) is a heavier and slower network protocol more often used for documents or text data. Universal Data Protocol (UDP) is a more light-weight network protocol most often used for streaming video, audio, or other binary data where the bit order is not as important as the speed of communication.

To send or receive information from a network in oF, use the ofxNetwork add-on. This allows you to send or receive data via TCP or UDP. The ofxNetwork add-on defines an ofxTCPClient object for reading Internet data or other TCP format communications, an ofxTCPServer for serving up data in the TCP, and an ofxUDPServer and ofxUDP Client for using UDP.

To use Ethernet connections with an Arduino, you can use the Arduino Ethernet Shield, which allows you to send and receive both TCP and UDP messages directly from an Arduino controller. The Ethernet library for the Arduino provides the functionality that you need to read or write network data.

If you're interested in gathering wireless data, you can use the Carnivore library for Processing. This allows you to packet sniff data passing through a wireless network and determine the origin and destination of the data. Bluetooth is a data and trans-mission protocol for low power wireless communication over short distances. It is often used in cell phones and electronic peripherals like headsets and keyboards.

MIDI is another useful data protocol that allows you to read data from a MIDI device like a keyboard and use it as input in an Arduino board.

# CHAPTER 13

# Graphics and OpenGL

If you're interested in displaying visual feedback or gathering input from a screen, learning how to create three-dimensional graphics is an important skill to learn. We see in three dimensions, we experience in three dimensions, and increasingly we expect our graphics to be in three dimensions. It's not just a matter of attempting to mimic our experience of the world or meet the expectations of what something should look like in a realistic depiction of a scene; it's also a matter of providing more data in a manner that humans are accustomed to receiving information.

The ability to make accurate and precise 3-D graphics is core to being able to represent objects in the world effectively. There's a marked difference between making accurate graphics and realistic graphics. Most architectural drawings, diagrams, and visualizations aren't particularly realistic, but they are very data rich. They behave the way we expect them to behave when we change the view, rotate the object, or change the distance at which we view the object. When you're creating an interface, this is far more important than accurately replicating a real-world object. Many times, but not all times, creating a usable interface that provides legibility and usability trumps wowing a user the first time they see something.

A lot of, but certainly not all, advanced graphics code in Processing is written in OpenGL. You can do a great deal with the core graphics classes that are provided in Processing, but many times you'll find that you need to create an effect or shape that simply runs too slowly or that you need more control over your graphics than is provided in the default Processing libraries. By contrast, a lot of the visual code in oF is written directly using OpenGL commands and not library functions that wrap oF calls, though that of course depends on what the developer needs and the project demands.

## What Does 3-D Have to Do with Interaction?

Since the design of an interaction is a matter of creating meaningful ways to input data and meaningful ways of receiving feedback, the use of 3-D graphics allows you to do both effectively. We're used to perceiving in three dimensions, so when we encounter visual information presented in three dimensions, it mirrors how we perceive the world. Depth, scale, and distance can all become elements in the feedback loop that your users perceive and hence change the way that they respond. Video games are a wonderful example of this. The two-dimensional scrolling game provided a vastly different range of information to a user than the three-dimensional first-person game. A user couldn't perceive the depth, their own position, or the position of other elements in the game properly without a way of accurately representing three-dimensional space. Once three-dimensional space could accurately be mapped, the user could provide a whole range of different input to the game, new controllers were required, and games changed dramatically.

Games aren't the only paradigms in which the ability to map 3-D and graphics is a massive aid. Architectural walk-through applications are invaluable to architects, designers, and urban planners. Mapping applications provide vastly more useful data to users when the data presented can simulate the 3-D world in which we live. Accurate three-dimensional mapping allows teams in all sorts of different situations, from surgical to military applications, to collaborate in real time. These sorts of spaces allow us to understand, move, and manipulate spaces the way we're used to doing in real life.

We're used to doing things in three-dimensional space: turning objects around, looking at objects side by side, rotating objects, and placing things. When you allow for 3-D feedback, you create the possibility of 3-D input and actions, turning things over, rotating them in space, stacking them, comparing them in 3-D. This chapter is going to have a lot more technical information and a lot less exposition than other chapters because the technical challenges of getting you started with OpenGL and 3-D are considerable, and many applications require the kinds of complex graphics that are best done in OpenGL.

# Understanding 3-D

There are a few important but simple concepts to understand about three-dimensional objects and three-dimensional space:

*Points*
> Any object in 3-D space will have $x$, $y$, and $z$ coordinates; that is, the object will be located at a 3-D point. In OpenGL, points that connect multiple lines or objects together are called *vertices*. You can simply think of a vertex as a point that can be used to represent a location or a velocity.

*Vectors*
> An object in 3-D space can also have a heading, which is a direction that it is moving in or looking toward. This is represented by a three-dimensional vector, which is a vector with $x$, $y$, and $z$ directions and a magnitude that describes how quickly it is moving in that direction. In the case of a simple heading or looking-at described in a three-dimensional vector, then the magnitude is 0. Fundamentally, a point and

a vector are the same thing: an array of values that represent data about a location in space.

*Lines and objects*

Any line in 3-D space will connect two 3-D points. Any object will have two more points or vertices.

*Surfaces*

Surfaces in 3-D are made up of points that have a shader or texture assigned to them to fill the space between the points on the *front* of the surface. This is a little strange because although we generally expect a surface in real life to be more or less the same on both sides, in computers, 3-D graphics surfaces are often only one side. It's as if when you looked at a table from the top, it was a table but when you looked at it from the bottom, it vanished. You can set the drawing mode to have two sides when you draw, but it's an additional step.

*Matrices*

Matrices are one of the most important things to understand when working with 3-D, in particular when working with OpenGL. Matrices were introduced in Chapter 9, but it's worth reviewing them again. A matrix is a mathematical structure consisting of multiple columns and rows:

$$[m11] \quad [m21] \quad [m31] \quad [m41]$$
$$[m12] \quad [m22] \quad [m32] \quad [m42]$$
$$[m13] \quad [m23] \quad [m33] \quad [m43]$$
$$[m14] \quad [m24] \quad [m34] \quad [m44]$$

Most matrices that you'll encounter in this chapter are $4 \times 4$ matrices, and most of the operations that you'll see for manipulating how objects are drawn or how they appear involve multiplying matrices. You can change either the matrix that represents the world in which the objects are drawn or the matrix that represents the view onto that world.

*Transformations*

You change matrices by using a *transformation*, which is simply the name for the mathematical operation for modifying a matrix. The `translate()`, `rotate()`, or `scale()` methods are all examples from Processing of methods that change a matrix. You use transformations to change the matrices that represent the camera view into the 3-D world, the locations that objects are drawn in the 3-D world, or the way that the world is projected into the camera. There's plenty more on this later in this chapter.

# What Is OpenGL?

OpenGL is an API written in a programming language that will look pretty familiar to you from using Arduino and oF code, because it's loosely based on C. At its core, OpenGL does one thing: it hides a lot of the complexities of interfacing with different 3-D drivers by making one way to program for any drivers that communicate between an operating system and a graphics card. There is another specification for a very similar language called DirectX that is used on Windows computers, but since that isn't used by Processing or openFrameworks, it won't be addressed in this book.

OpenGL's core functionality is to help a programmer create code that creates points, lines, and polygons, and then convert those objects into pixels. The conversion of objects into pixels is called the *pipeline* of the OpenGL renderer. You'll see that OpenGL is pretty low level, in much the same way that the Processing graphics API can create complex objects from sets of vertices and instructions on how to connect them. OpenGL is a low-level, procedural API, requiring the programmer to dictate the exact steps to render a scene. This contrasts with descriptive approaches like the Processing drawing API, where a programmer needs only describe a scene and can let the library manage the details of rendering it. OpenGL's low-level design requires programmers to have a good knowledge of the graphics pipeline but also gives a certain amount of freedom to implement novel rendering algorithms that can help your code run substantially faster.

## Working with 3-D in Processing

Rendering graphics requires trade-offs between speed, accuracy, and general usefulness of the available features. None of the renderers is perfect, so we'll provide multiple options in the following sections so that you can decide what trade-offs make the most sense for your project. It would be nice if all of them had perfect visual accuracy, had high performance, and supported a wide range of features, but that's simply not possible.

The examples in this chapter add the third parameter, P3-D, to size(), to draw in 3-D in Processing. All these examples can also run faster by importing the OpenGL library from the Import Library menu and using the constant OPENGL as the third parameter to size().

P3-D *(Processing 3-D)*
> This is a faster 3-D renderer for the web that sacrifices rendering quality for quick 3-D drawing.

OPENGL
> This is a high-speed 3-D graphics renderer that uses OpenGL-compatible graphics hardware if available. Keep in mind that OpenGL is not magic pixie dust that makes any sketch faster (though it's close), so other rendering options may produce better results depending on the nature of your code. Also note that with OpenGL, all graphics are smoothed: the smooth() and noSmooth() methods are ignored.

Because so much of the P3-D drawing mode is based on the OpenGL and because most OpenGL code can be easily ported between Processing and oF, we'll focus on OpenGL mode rather than P3-D.

# OpenGL in Processing

OpenGL in Processing uses a class called `GL` that provides access to all the OpenGL methods. Now, there's a few caveats to using OpenGL in Processing that make it exciting, interesting, powerful, and difficult, because the purpose of Processing and the intent of the designers of the language was to ensure that you, the Processing user, didn't have to get into using OpenGL. There are things that may work in one release of Processing and suddenly break in another, there are things that will work fine in oF code that won't work correctly in Processing, and there's all kinds of hardware incompatibility and strangeness that you may encounter. That said, if you're confident that you want to work in Processing and you really need the power that the OpenGL renderer is going to provide you, read on. We'll get you started, but because there are so many potential pitfalls and problems, it doesn't make sense to delve too deeply into OpenGL in Processing.

The first step in using OpenGL is making sure that the Processing application knows to use the OpenGL renderer to create any graphics that are supposed to be displayed on the screen. You indicate that by passing `OPENGL` to the `size()` method when you initialize your application:

```
size(800, 600, OPENGL);
```

Once you've done that, Processing uses the GL rendering engine to create all the graphics. That doesn't mean that your calls to `vertex()`, `color()`, `rotate()`, or any other Processing 3-D methods will change. You'll still be using the same methods to create your graphics. If you want to delve deeper into OpenGL in Processing, even more caveats apply. If you glance at the reference page for the OpenGL library in the Processing documentation, you'll see the following:

> These were added against my better judgment and handle setting up the camera matrices (though still no lighting or other parameters). Many features still will not work, but it opens up lots of control for geometry. All the above caveats about "don't cry when it breaks" apply.

So, keep that in mind. That said, to get started, you'll simply need to add the following `import` statements to the top of your application:

```
import processing.opengl.*;
```

This imports not only the Processing OpenGL library but also the underlying Java OpenGL library called JOGL (Java OpenGL). The calls to the JOGL library are nested between two calls to initialize and then finalize the JOGL drawing operations: `beginGL()` and `endGL()`. All Processing applications contain a `PGraphics` variable called g, and that variable can be cast to the `PGraphicsOpenGL` variable type. You might remember casting from Chapter 5. (If not, take a look back at it.) You should place these two calls in the `draw()` method of your application:

```
void draw() {
PGraphicsOpenGL pgl = (PGraphicsOpenGL) g;
GL gl = pgl.beginGL();
```

GL is the Java media class that provides you with access to the raw OpenGL methods. Earlier in this chapter, you saw how to pass the OpenGL renderer to the `size()` method of your Processing application. That tells the Processing engine to turn your Processing calls, like `vertex()`, into actual OpenGL calls, like `glVertex3fv()`. That might look unfamiliar but it actually does the same thing as the `vertex()` call. You can only call an actual OpenGL method like `glVertex3fv()` on the `PGraphicsOpenGL` object.

Once you've made the GL object, you can call GL methods as shown here:

```
gl.glColor4f(1.0, 1.0, 1.0, 1.0);
```

Finally, the call to the `endGL()` method ends the OpenGL calls:

```
pgl.endGL();
```

Now, as mentioned, this is not necessarily the best way to create graphics for two or three dimensions in Processing, but it does have some bonuses, and it does allow you to leverage OpenGL in a Processing application.

## Lighting in Processing

Creating the two simplest primitive types of 3-D objects is quite easy: call either `box()` or `sphere()`. If you don't want the box or sphere to have stroke lines, then call the `noStroke()` method before the drawing calls; otherwise, leave it in. See Example 13-1.

*Example 13-1. lighting.pde*

```
import processing.opengl.*;

void setup() {
    size(400, 400, OPENGL); // set up the 3-D renderer
}
void draw() {
    noStroke(); // commenting this line out will show the lines in the sphere
    lights(); // uncommenting this will show the model with lights
    fill(255);
    translate(100, 100, 0);
    sphere(40);
}
```

Figure 13-1 shows the different ways that a sphere can be rendered depending on the options set.

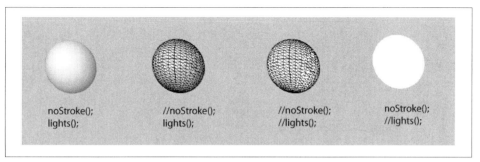

Figure 13-1. Setting how a sphere will be rendered in Processing

Notice that without calling the `lights()` method, the sphere looks suspiciously like a regular circle. Calling the `lights()` method makes the sphere look three-dimensional because without any lights positioned anywhere, there's no way for the renderer to know which parts of the sphere are darker and which are lighter. Lighting is one of the keys of representing three-dimensionality. Without it, there is no way for a viewer (or the renderer, for that matter) to know what the three-dimensional shape of an object is.

Lights in Processing are created using a number of methods that let you create and control the lighting in your scene:

`lightFalloff()`
> This sets how the light falls off, or dims, away from the source. Just like the `fill()` method, it affects only the elements created after it, not all elements in your code. If you wanted a region of your scene to be lit ambiently by one color and another region to be lit ambiently by another color, you would use an ambient light with a specific location and falloff.

`lightSpecular()`
> Sets the specular color for lights. *Specular* refers to light that bounces off a surface in a preferred direction and is used for creating highlights. Later in this section when you learn about the `specular()` and `shininess()` methods, you'll see how lights interact with surfaces. For now just imagine that the specular quality of a light is the amount of reflectivity that a surface will have.
>
> There are four kinds of lights that you can create in Processing. Remember that the lighting methods need to be called in the `draw()` method of your application so that they will be redrawn each time the program loops through the drawing method.

`ambientLight()`
> Adds an ambient light. Ambient light doesn't come from a specific direction. The rays of light have bounced around so much that objects are evenly lit from all sides. Ambient lights are almost always used in combination with other types of lights.

`directionalLight()`

Adds a light that comes from one direction without having a particular location. These lights are stronger if they hit a surface squarely and weaker if they hit at an angle. It is called as shown here:

    directionalLight(v1, v2, v3, nx, ny, nz)

The color is set using the first three parameters: red, green, blue. The nx, ny, and nz parameters indicate the direction the light is facing.

`pointLight()`

Adds an ambient light with a position. Lights need to be included in the `draw()` method to remain persistent in a looping program:

    pointLight(v1, v2, v3, x, y, z)

The color is set using the first three parameters: red, green, blue. The x, y, and z parameters set the position of the light.

`spotLight()`

Adds a spotlight that is like a directional light, except that it has a location that can be altered:

    spotLight(v1, v2, v3, x, y, z, nx, ny, nz, angle, concentration)

The x, y, and z parameters specify the position of the light, and nx, ny, nz specify the direction of light. The `angle` parameter affects the angle of the cone of the spotlight and how wide it is, and the `concentration` parameter determines how much brighter the light is at the center of the cone.

## Controlling the Viewer's Perspective

Lights are only half the story. They are important to show how *objects* are three-dimensional, but to make the *world* fully three-dimensional, you need to have control over how the viewer perceives the world. In most 3-D platforms, this is by providing methods or access to an object that a programmer can modify to more easily manipulate the point from which the viewer sees the scene. In Processing, this is just called the Camera. The lighting objects and the Camera interact in much the way that lights and cameras do on a film set. The methods of the Camera class are also quite similar to the properties and operations of a real-life camera. The easiest way to add a 3-D camera to a scene is to call the `camera()` method. A camera actually has three vectors: its location, the position that it's pointed at, and which direction is up. Figure 13-2 shows how these three vectors relate.

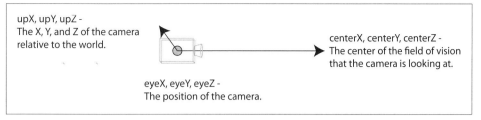

*Figure 13-2. Three vectors of a camera*

Moving the eye position and the direction it is pointing allows the objects to be seen from different perspectives. The version without any parameters sets the camera to the default position, pointing to the center of the display window with the y-axis of the world as the upY value.

You can also call the camera()method with the following optional parameters:

```
camera(eyeX, eyeY, eyeZ, centerX, centerY, centerZ, upX, upY, upZ)
```

One thing to remember is that the center coordinates and eye coordinates operate independently of one another, so moving the camera does not change what the camera is looking at. You'll usually want to do the two in tandem. The small application in Example 13-2 draws a cube and moves the camera around depending on the user's mouse position:

*Example 13-2. cameraControl.pde*

```
float eyeX, eyeY, eyeZ;
float centerX, centerY, centerZ;

boolean setCenter = false;

void setup() {
    size(300, 300, P3-D);
    noFill();
    eyeX = width/2.0;
    eyeY = height/2.0;
    eyeZ = 20;
    centerX = width/2.0;
    centerY = height/2.0;
    centerZ = 0;
}

void draw() {
    lights();
    background(255);
    camera(eyeX, eyeY, eyeZ, centerX, centerY, centerZ,  0.0, 1.0, 0.0);
    fill(122);
```

Draw a simple box so that there's some reference for how the camera is moving:

```
        box(45);
    }
```

```
void mouseMoved() {

        eyeX = width/2 - mouseX;
        eyeY = height/2 - mouseY;
}

void mouseDragged() {
    centerX += mouseX - pmouseX;
    centerY += mouseY - pmouseY;
}

void mouseReleased() {
    setCenter = false;
}

void mousePressed() {
    setCenter = true;
}


void keyPressed() {
```

Here the `printCamera()` method prints the values of all the camera's vectors. When you run this code and press Enter, you'll notice that 16 values are printed. This is because the camera's matrix is actually a 4 × 4 matrix, not a 3 × 3:

```
    if(keyCode == 10) { // enter button
        printCamera();
    }
    if(setCenter) {
        if(keyCode == 38) { eyeZ++; } // up arrow
        if(keyCode == 40) { eyeZ--; } // down arrow
    } else {
        if(keyCode == 38) { centerZ++; } // up arrow
        if(keyCode == 40) { centerZ--; } // down arrow
    }
}
```

This code could just as easily be changed to use an accelerometer (introduced in Chapter 7), a set of dials, a light, or another color source (as shown in Chapter 10); or a gesture detection (as you'll see in Chapter 14). The interesting part is how quickly most users will be able to figure out the view onto the 3-D world.

There are three more advanced methods for changing the way that the camera behaves. The `frustum()` method allows you to change the perspective of the camera. This method lets you set the locations and angles of the clipping planes that the camera uses. The *clipping plane* is a somewhat mathematically complex topic, but understanding how to use it and how it functions is fairly simple. Take a look at the diagram in Figure 13-3.

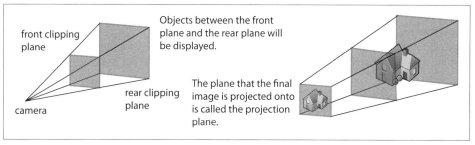

*Figure 13-3. Clipping plane and projection plane*

You can see in the diagram that the two planes define what appears in the projection that's created from the world and shown on the user's screen. This is called the *frustum*. A frustum is the portion of a cone or pyramid that lies between two parallel planes. In computer graphics, the term frustum describes the 3-D area that is visible on the screen because the visible area is formed by a clipped pyramid. Calling the `frustum()` method changes the positions of the rear clipping and front clipping planes and hence changes what appears on the screen. Here are the parameters that the `frustum()` method takes:

```
frustum(float left, float right, float bottom, float top, float near, float far)
```

Figure 13-4 shows how the `left`, `right`, `bottom`, and `top` parameters correlate to the positions where the new plane will be positioned. The `near` and `far` parameters control the positioning of the front and back of the frustum.

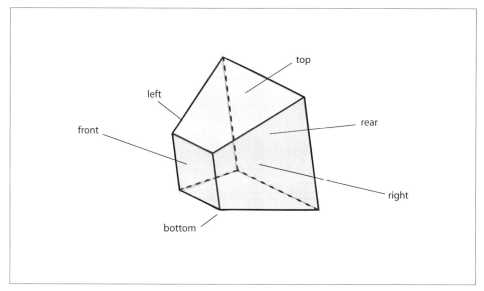

*Figure 13-4. The viewing frustum*

If you want to experiment with the `frustum()` methods, try setting up different variables for the camera settings and then setting up `keyPressed()` event handler methods to change each variable. What you'll see is that the frustum formed by the front and rear clipping panes of the application is transformed by the values passed into the `frustum()` method.

Another way of changing the perspective of the camera is to call the `perspective()` method. This simulates the perspective of the world more accurately than orthographic projection. The `perspective()` method without parameters sets the default perspective, but with four parameters it lets you set the area precisely. Here is the signature of the `perspective()` method followed by the definition of the parameters:

```
perspective(fov, aspect, zNear, zFar)
```

fov
> The field-of-view angle for vertical direction expressed in radians. This represents the amount of angular shift that should be used to change what the user sees.

aspect
> The ratio of width to height.

zNear
> The z-position of the nearest clipping plane, that is, the closest something can be and still be seen.

zFar
> The z-position of the farthest plane, that is, the farthest something can be and still be seen.

Calling the `perspective()` method won't change the object or camera, but it will change how the viewer sees the object (see Figure 13-5).

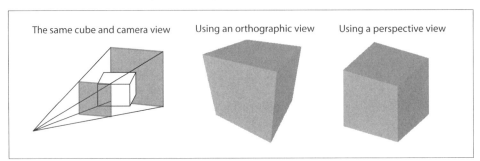

Figure 13-5. Changing the appearance of an object by setting the perspective view

## Making Custom Shapes in Processing

The first element to understand in making three-dimensional shapes for Processing is the vertex. A *vertex* is a point in 3-D space that has $x$, $y$, and $z$ properties that determine where it is in relation to the 0,0,0 point (you can think of this as the center) of the world. A vertex might have the values 100,100,100. This means that it is 100 pixels on the *x*, *y*, and *z* coordinates from the center of the world in which it is located. In Processing, all shapes are the result of the connections between vertices. A pyramid is a construction made of the connections between five vertices; a cube is made up of the connections between eight vertices; a line is made up of the connections between two vertices. You create a vertex by using the `vertex()` method and passing in the coordinates. A 2D vertex looks like this:

```
vertex(x, y);
```

A 3-D vertex looks like this:

```
vertex(x, y, z);
```

The *x*, *y*, and *z* parameters can be `float` or `int` values. It's important to note that this call doesn't create anything, and there isn't a "Vertex" class that you create instances of and store. Instead, the `vertex` communicates with the underlying graphics engine of your Processing application, telling it where to place a vertex. Drawing a vertex in 3-D using the *z* parameter requires the `P3-D` or `OPENGL` parameter in combination with `size`.

The main use of the `vertex()` method is to set the points for drawing a 3-D shape. There is another use that we'll examine later in the section "Using Matrices and Transformations in OpenGL," in the discussion on textures and mapping them, but for now, consider a vertex as the way to set the points to be used for the corners of a 2D or 3-D shape.

To create a custom 3-D shape, you'll need to tell the underlying graphics engine that you're going to create the points for shape first using the `beginShape()` method, then define all the points for the shape, and finally tell the graphics engine that you're finished setting the points for the shape using the `endShape()` method.

So, the first step is to call the `beginShape()` method, then call the `vertex()` method as many times as you need to set all the points for your shape, and then call the `end Shape()` method. The call to the `beginShape()` method is what determines the way that all the subsequent vertices will be connected. The following are the different modes for this method. Figure 13-6 shows how these modes are used.

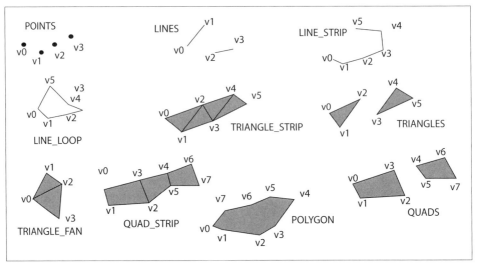

*Figure 13-6. The GL modes that can be passed to the beginShape() method*

POINTS
Creates a shape without any connections in between the vertices.

LINES
Connects the vertices with lines but no fill.

TRIANGLES
Connects the vertices with triangles. Each vertex will be used to create one point of a triangle.

TRIANGLE_FAN
Connects the vertices with multiple triangles. Each vertex will be connected with multiple equilateral triangles.

TRIANGLE_STRIP
Connects the vertices with multiple triangles. Each vertex will be connected with multiple isosceles triangles.

QUADS
Connects the vertices with as few quadrilaterals as possible.

QUAD_STRIP
Connects the vertices with as many quadrilaterals as possible, placing multiple quadrilaterals at each vertex.

The code in Example 13-3 creates eight vertices and connects them according to the primitive mode passed to the beginShape() method.

*Example 13-3. shapeTest.pde*

```
void setup(){
    size(640, 360, P3-D);
```

```
}

void draw(){
    background(50, 50, 50);
    translate(width/2, height/2);
```

The default shape is POLYGON:

```
        beginShape();
            vertex(0, 0);
            vertex(0, 75);
            vertex(50, 75);
            vertex(50, 0);
            vertex(100, 0);
            vertex(100, 125);
            vertex(125, 125);
            vertex(125, 0);
        endShape();
    }
```

This will produce the drawing shown on the far left of Figure 13-7. Note that the difference between the QUADS and the default beginShape() is the small connecting line between the two rectangles. The default drawing mode connects all vertices with lines and creates fills where the lines enclose an area. The QUADS mode simply creates quads and fills for all of the vertices.

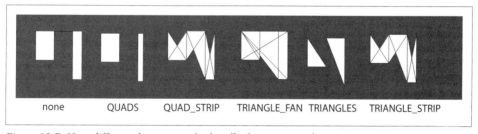

*Figure 13-7. How different drawing modes handle the same set of vertices*

Note that you can't use transformations like translate(), rotate(), and scale() inside a beginShape() block, nor can you use the shape drawing methods like ellipse() or rect(). Also, don't forget to always finish with a call to endShape(). Only vertex calls can be used in that drawing block. After you've drawn the shape, then you can use translate(), rotate(), and scale() to change the position of the drawing objects.

# Using Coordinates and Transforms in Processing

The previous code snippets have touched on how to move objects and views around in 3-D in a Processing application, but these all merit a closer examination.

There are two coordinate systems in Processing to consider: the coordinates of the world and the coordinates of the screen. The difference is the location of the 0,0,0 point.

Although a model may have its 0,0,0 point in one location, because of rotations and transformations applied to the model, it will appear in an entirely different location on the screen, as in Figure 13-8.

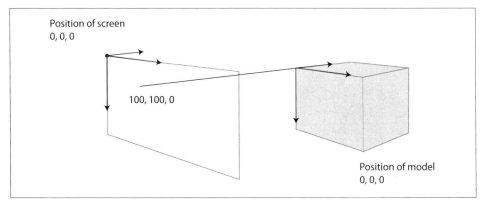

Figure 13-8. The model coordinate system and the screen coordinate system may not be the same values

Imagine that you have a cube you've drawn as shown in the code snippet below:

```
void setup()
{
    size(400, 400, OPENGL);
}

void draw()
{
    pushMatrix();
        translate(200, 200, 20);
        rotateY(PI/3.0);
        rotateZ(PI/3.0);
        box(100);
    popMatrix();
    // not very exciting ⌣
    rect(100, 100, 100, 100);

}
```

After the call to popMatrix(), what is the screen position of the corner of the box? What is the actual position of the box relative to the point at the center of the world? You could do the math to get these, but there's an easier way. Three methods return a position in 3-D space relative to a model: modelX(), modelY(), and modelZ(). These return the values for a given coordinate based on the current set of transformations (scale, rotate, translate, and so on). For instance, you transform the x value to be 200 pixels to the right, then you tilt the world matrix a little. As soon as you call popMatrix(), the value of the 0 point of the model vanishes. You won't be able to place something else at that same value without calling all the same methods again, and that might be a problem. Luckily, if you store the value from modelX() before you call popMatrix(), then you can use that value wherever you would like. If you want to place another cube in the same location as the first cube, before the call to popMatrix() add the modelX(), modelY(), and modelZ() calls as shown here.

*Example 13-4. moreExciting.pde*

```
void draw()
{
    pushMatrix();
        translate(200, 200, 20);
        stroke(255);
        fill(0);
        rotateY(PI/3.0);
        rotateZ(PI/2.0);
```

This next code gets the location of the models 0,0,0 point in screen coordinates with all the transforms applied:

```
        float transX = modelX(0, 0, 0);
        float transY = modelY(0, 0, 0);
        float transZ = modelZ(0, 0, 0);
        box(50);

        popMatrix();

        translate(transX, transY, transZ);
        stroke(0);
        fill(255, 20);
        box(100);

    }
```

In the code snippet, adding calls to modelX(), modelY(), and modelZ() methods records the location of the box in space after being placed using a series of translate() and rotate() commands. After popMatrix() is called, those transformations vanish along with any data about what would have been the 0 point within them, but those coordinates can be captured by the modelX(), modelY(), and modelZ() methods.

All three of those methods take the same parameters:

x
    int or float; 3-D *x* coordinate to be mapped

y
    int or float; 3-D *y* coordinate to be mapped

z
    int or float; 3-D *z* coordinate to be mapped

These enable another cube to be placed in the same location as the original cube using all the original transform data, but this doesn't always do what you might want. For example, while the world position of a cube might be in one location, it appears in an entirely different place on the screen because of camera movements, or rotations. To place an object based on another object's position according to the screen coordinates, you'll want to use the `screenX()`, `screenY()`, and `screenZ()` methods. These take the same parameters and are used in the same way as the model coordinate methods but use the *x*, *y*, and *z* positions of the screen instead of the world within the screen.

## Transformations

*Transformations* are the modification of one of the coordinate systems, either the model coordinate system space as relative to a single object or the world coordinate system space relative to all the objects. They are performed using the `translate()` method of Processing. This section introduces you to something that is very important in OpenGL: the transformation stack. Let's review. The `translate()` method moves the location where objects will be drawn, so if you call the following:

```
translate(200, 200, 0);
```

and then the following:

```
rect(0, 0, 100, 100);
```

your rectangle will be drawn 200 pixels from the left and 200 pixels from the top of the application window. When you call `pushMatrix()`, you're setting up a transform that will be used for all drawing operations until you call the `popMatrix()` method.

OpenGL uses the same ideas of transforms and the transformation stack. When you create a transform, it alters all the operations that follow it until it's pushed off the stack. That stack can consist of multiple transforms that all affect any drawing operation that follows it. The other way of drawing that you've seen in this chapter—creating vertices and having the renderer generate shapes based on those vertices—are all based on the way that OpenGL works.

## 3-D in openFrameworks

openFrameworks uses OpenGL for all of its graphics drawing, but most of the calls are hidden. It actually uses an implementation of OpenGL called Graphics Language Utility Toolkit (GLUT) by default, though this changes when you use Android or iPhone. However, if you want to change to a different GL implementation, you're free to do so. All graphics calls in the `ofGraphics` class use calls to common OpenGL methods, which you can see if you open the class and take a look at what goes on in some of the methods. For instance, the `ofLine()` method `drawLine()` which contains the following lines:

```
linePoints[0].set(x1,y1,z1);
linePoints[1].set(x2,y2,z2);

// use smoothness, if requested:
if (bSmoothHinted) startSmoothing();
```

```
glEnableClientState(GL_VERTEX_ARRAY);
glVertexPointer(3, GL_FLOAT, sizeof(ofVec3f), &linePoints[0].x);
glDrawArrays(GL_LINES, 0, 2);
```

You'll notice that this is pretty different than the way that the Processing code looks. This is because the openFrameworks code uses *Vertex Arrays* to draw points to the screen. The particulars of how these work is not super important to understand in order to draw in 3-D, but it does dramatically help speed up the drawing routines. These are essentially a way to create an array of data to upload to the graphics card quickly, more quickly than other methods. Again, you don't need to understand exactly how vertex arrays work, but it does help to know what the OpenGL underneath the drawing routines in OF are doing.

You'll see something that should look familiar from other ways of drawing that you've encountered earlier in this chapter. The method of connecting the vertices is set when initializing the drawing. Next, the vertices are set, and then a method is called to finish the drawing. This looks pretty familiar. Using OpenGL with oF doesn't come with any caveats like Processing, since all the drawing code is, in fact, OpenGL, and the GL context isn't dependent on JOGL like Processing. You don't need to do anything special to begin using OpenGL code in an oF application. openFrameworks does a lot of the work to initialize and set up the GL context: creating the 3-D window for drawing, setting the initial size of that window. If you open *ofAppGlutWindow.cpp* and look at the setupOpenGL() function, you'll see the following:

```
glutInit(&argc, vptr);
glutInitDisplayMode(GLUT_RGB | GLUT_DOUBLE | GLUT_DEPTH | GLUT_ALPHA );
```

When you start up an oF application that is going to use the GLUT mode, this is one of the first functions that is called. You'll see that this function calls glutInit() to initialize the GLUT library, followed by glutInitDisplayMode() to set the mode of the display.

The ofRunApp() method initializes what is called the OpenGL context. It calls a series of functions that set up the OpenGL window and indicates the GLUT callback functions that take place during the draw loop: first update() and then draw(). The ofApp GlutWindow class contains the critical GLUT functions that take place every frame that your application runs. If you look at the display() function, you'll see that it sets up the screen, calls your application's draw() function, and increases the frame count. The idle_cb() method is the idle function for GLUT, which is called after each frame is drawn. Inside idle_cb(), you'll see that it maintains your application's frame rate and calls its update() function before calling the draw() method. Understanding how all these calls work isn't vital to being able to use OpenGL, but it can be helpful to see what's going on under the hood in the oF core.

## Drawing in 3-D

There's nothing special required to draw in 3-D in oF. For instance, you can simply draw a box or a sphere to the screen by calling ofBox() or ofSphere(). To draw to a cube with a texture, you create an ofTexture instance, call bind() on that texture, and then draw your ofCube. See Example 13-5.

*Example 13-5. of3D.h*

```
#pragma once
#include "ofMain.h"

class of3D: public ofBaseApp{

public:

    ofTexture text; // this is the texture that will be applied to our cube

    float ang;

    void setup();
    void update();
    void draw();

};
```

Most of this should look familiar from earlier chapters, with the exception of two pieces. ofEnableNormalizedTexCoords() makes it so that the textures are drawn correctly to the edges of the sphere and the call to glEnable(GL_DEPTH_TEST) ensures that each plane of the cube is drawn at the correct depth. See Example 13-6.

*Example 13-6. of3D.cpp*

```
#include "of3D.h"
void of3D::setup() {

    ofEnableNormalizedTexCoords();

    ofImage img;
    img.loadImage("ofpic.png");
    img.mirror(false, true);
    text.allocate(128, 128, GL_RGBA, true);
    ang = 0;

    glEnable(GL_DEPTH_TEST); // enable depth testing, otherwise things break
    text.loadData(img.getPixels(), 128, 128, GL_RGBA);

}


void of3D::update() {
    ang += 0.1;
}
```

```
void of3D::draw() {

    ofBackground(122,122,122);

    text.bind();
    ofTranslate(ofGetWidth() * .5, ofGetHeight() * .5, 0);
    ofRotate(ang, 1.0, 1.0, 1.0);
    ofBox(200);
    text.unbind();

}
```

## Transformations in openFrameworks

openFrameworks has convenience methods that will allow you to transform and alter your drawing in the same way that you've seen in Processing. We'll jump right into how those methods are structured. To push a new set of matrices onto the stack, or pop a matrix off the stack, use the following:

void ofPushMatrix()
> pushes a new matrix onto the matrix stack

void ofPopMatrix()
> pops the newest matrix off the matrix stack

The translate methods are also quite similar to the Processing versions:

void ofTranslate(float x, float y, float z)
> move the current matrix stack

void ofScale(float xAmnt, float yAmnt, float zAmnt)
> scale the current matrix stack

void ofRotateX(float degrees), void ofRotateY(float degrees), and void ofRotateZ(float degrees). Each rotates the current matrix around its respective axis. There is another way to rotate the current matrix stack, where you pass in the degrees and how you want those degrees applied to the current stack.

void ofRotate(float degrees, float vecX, float vecY, float vecZ)
> rotate the current matrix

For instance, to rotate the stack 90 degrees on the x-axis, 45 on the y-axis, and 9 on the z-axis:

```
ofRotate(90, 1, 0.5, 0.1);
```

# Lighting in OpenGL

Lighting in openFrameworks is done using the ofLight object, which wraps the OpenGL lighting methods that you may encounter when looking at a pure OpenGL tutorial or book. They look somewhat like lighting in Processing but can use a slightly

more complex syntax if you need them to. In your application declarations, create an
ofLight instance:

```
ofLight light1;
```

You can then assign the properties of that light:

```
light1.setPointLight(); // creates a point light
```

or:

```
light1.setDirectional();
light1.lookAt(ofVec3f(ofGetWidth()/2, ofGetHeight()/2, 0));
// point at the middle of the screen
```

To turn the lights on, you'll need to call ofEnableLighting() in the draw() method of
your application:

```
ofEnableLighting(); // no need for glEnable
```

Then, you simply need to enable the light that you want to illuminate your scene:

```
light1.enable();
```

This simple application allows you to create moving lights using the setPosition()
method of the ofLight and see how that lighting affects several cubes drawn using
ofBox(). See Example 13-7.

*Example 13-7. ofLightingDemo.h*

```
#pragma once

#include "ofMain.h"

class ofLightingDemo: public ofBaseApp{

public:

    ofTexture text;
    ofLight light1, light2;

    void setup();
    void update();
    void draw();

};
```

Now the *.cpp* file:

*Example 13-8. ofLightingDemo.cpp*

```
#include "ofLightingDemo.h"

void ofLightingDemo::setup(){

    ofEnableNormalizedTexCoords();
```

```
ofImage img;
img.loadImage("ofpic.png");
img.mirror(false, true);
text.allocate(128, 128, GL_RGBA, true);

glEnable(GL_DEPTH_TEST); // enable depth testing, otherwise things will look really
weird
text.loadData(img.getPixels(), 128, 128, GL_RGBA);

light1.setPointLight();
light2.setPointLight();
}


void ofLightingDemo::update()
{
    light1.setPosition( cos(ofGetElapsedTimef()) * 200 + 200, 200, sin(ofGetElapsedTimef
    ()) * 200);
    light2.setPosition( cos(ofGetElapsedTimef()) * 200 + 200, sin(ofGetElapsedTimef()) *
    200 + 200, 0);
}

void ofLightingDemo::draw()
{
    //ofBackground(122,122,122);
    ofEnableLighting();

    light1.enable();
    light2.enable();

    light1.draw();
    light2.draw();

    text.bind();
    ofBox(400, 600, 0, 200);
    ofBox(800, 400, -400, 200);
    ofBox(400, 200, 0, 200);
    ofBox(800, 800, -400, 200);
    text.unbind();

    ofDisableLighting();

}
```

# Blending Modes in OpenGL

At some point you're going to want to blend your objects and images. You might want
to draw a transparent 3-D object, or you might want to overlay and blend multiple
images, or you might want to filter out a certain color in an image. In OpenGL, this is
done via blending, which combines the color data already in the graphics card with the
incoming color data from the new object being drawn. If you've drawn one cube and

are drawing another, then the blendFunc() method tells the graphics card how to display the two cubes together. By default, the most recently drawn cube will be drawn over the other cube, but you can set how they appear using the blending modes. As with many other things, a number of constants are defined in OpenGL that allow you to select the blending mode. In this list, you're going to find two terms: *source*, which means the color data from the objects already in the buffer, and *destination*, which means the new incoming colors from the object being drawn.

OpenGL thinks of colors as floating-point numbers, so adding them, subtracting them, and even multiplying them are all perfectly valid operations. Here's the list of all the different flags that you can pass to the blendFunc(), telling it how to handle both the source and the destination data:

GL_ZERO
> Tells the graphics card to set all the color data to which this flag is applied, either the source or the destination, to zero.

GL_ONE
> Tells the graphics card to set this data to full.

GL_DST_COLOR
> Tells the graphics card to blend the destination color data into the incoming color data.

GL_ONE_MINUS_DST_COLOR
> Tells the graphics card to invert the destination color data by subtracting it from 1 and returning that value.

GL_SRC_ALPHA
> Tells the graphics card to use the source alpha values to determine which of the destination colors will appear.

GL_ONE_MINUS_SRC_ALPHA
> Tells the graphics card to subtract the invert all the colors depending on the strength of the source's alpha value.

GL_DST_ALPHA
> Uses only the alpha values of the destination data.

GL_ONE_MINUS_DST_ALPHA
> Uses the values of the destination minus 1.

GL_SRC_ALPHA_SATURATE
> Takes the minimum value of each the two alpha values compared.

Each of these can be set to handle the incoming data and the existing data by passing it to the following method:

```
glBlendFunc( GLenum sfactor, GLenum dfactor );
```

The glBlenFunc() method takes two parameters:

sfactor

Specifies how the red, green, blue, and alpha source blending factors are computed.

dfactor

Specifies how the red, green, blue, and alpha destination blending factors are computed.

It's quite difficult to visualize how these operate; perhaps the best way to do this is to create a simple application that will enable you to apply different blend modes to both the source and destinations of the `glBlendFunc()` method. A short sample application that does just this is shown here.

To the standard *testApp.h* file add the following, as in Example 13-9 (I'd like to thank Ira Greenberg for providing the inspiration for this demo.)

*Example 13-9. blenderama.h*

```
#pragma once

#include "ofMain.h"

#define numCubes 20

class blenderama: public ofBaseApp{

public:

    float ang;
    int currentLBlend, currentRBlend; // indexes to store the current blending value
    ofImage img; // an image to load a picture for a texture
    ofTexture text; // a texture to use
    ofVec3f cubePos[numCubes]; // an array to store all the text values

    void setup();
    void update();
    void draw();
    void keyPressed  (int key);
};
```

The definition of the file contains all the blend modes that you can apply when drawing in OpenGL in a single array:

*Example 13-10. blenderama.cpp*

```
#include "blenderama.h"

const int BLENDS[] = { GL_ZERO, GL_ONE, GL_SRC_COLOR, GL_ONE_MINUS_SRC_COLOR,
GL_DST_COLOR, GL_ONE_MINUS_DST_COLOR, GL_SRC_ALPHA, GL_ONE_MINUS_SRC_ALPHA,
GL_DST_ALPHA, GL_ONE_MINUS_DST_ALPHA, GL_SRC_ALPHA_SATURATE, GL_CONSTANT_COLOR,
GL_ONE_MINUS_CONSTANT_COLOR, GL_CONSTANT_ALPHA, GL_ONE_MINUS_CONSTANT_ALPHA };
```

In the setup() method, you'll simply set the values of two arrays to each possible blending value. Each array will have an index integer stored that indicates which blending mode should be used. These are set to GL_ONE_MINUS_SRC_ALPHA for the source and GL_SRC_ALPHA for the destination, since these are the most commonly used settings:

```
void blenderama::setup(){

    //ofDisableArbTex();
    ofEnableNormalizedTexCoords();

    img.loadImage("ofpic.png");
    text.allocate(128, 128, GL_RGBA, true);
    ang = 0;
    glEnable(GL_DEPTH_TEST); // enable depth testing, otherwise things will
    //look really werid
    glDepthFunc(GL_LEQUAL);      // set the type of depth testing
    text.loadData(img.getPixels(), 128, 128, GL_RGBA);

    currentLBlend = 6;
    currentRBlend = 7;
```

Here, we populate the cubePos array with random values to place each of the cubes:

```
    for (int i = 0; i < numCubes; i++){
        cubePos[i].set(ofRandom(200.0, 600.0), ofRandom(200.0,
        600.0), ofRandom(200.0, 600.0));
    }
}

void blenderama::update(){
    //used to rotate the view
    ang+=0.1;
}

void blenderama::draw() {
```

Don't forget to enable depth testing using the glEnable() method. To blend different objects, you need to enable blending by calling glEnable() with the GL_BLEND constant passed to it:

```
    glEnable(GL_BLEND);
    text.bind();
    glBlendFunc( BLENDS[currentLBlend], BLENDS[currentRBlend] );
```

The call to glBlendFunc() sets the blending mode to use on all the preceding drawing operations:

```
    for (int i = 0; i < numCubes; i++) {
        ofPushMatrix();
        ofTranslate(cubePos[i]);
        ofBox(50);
        ofPopMatrix();
    }
```

Finally, indicate that the drawing and blending operation is finished:

```
glDisable(GL_BLEND);
text.unbind();
glDisable(GL_BLEND);
```

}

In the `keyPressed()` method, there is simply a listener that lets you or the user toggle through the different blending modes available:

```
void blenderama::keyPressed  (int key){
    switch( key ){
        case 'a':
            if(currentLBlend > 13)
                currentLBlend = 0;
            else
                currentLBlend++;
            break;
        case 's':
            if(currentLBlend < 0)
                currentLBlend = 13;
            else
                currentLBlend--;
            break;
        case 'd':
            if(currentRBlend > 13)
                currentRBlend = 0;
            else
                currentRBlend++;
            break;
        case 'f':
            if(currentRBlend < 0)
                currentRBlend = 13;
            else
                currentRBlend--;
            break;
    }
}
```

Blending modes in Processing work much the same way as in oF, so with just a little bit of tweaking you can turn the preceding example into a Processing application. The only major difference is that `glBlendFunc()` is a method of the Processing `GL` object rather than a call like `glBlendFunc()`, which is not called on an object.

# Creating 3-D Objects in oF

If you remember how the vertices in Processing work or how the `ofPoint()` method in oF works, you already understand a lot of what you need to know about making vertices in OpenGL. An OpenGL vertex is what you're creating by using the Processing `vertex()` method or the oF `ofPoint()` method. It defines a point in space that will be connected with other points by the renderer according to the primitive drawing mode that you indicate. Creating a simple square in oF looks like this:

```
ofBeginShape();
    ofVertex(10, 10); // top left
    ofVertex(100, 10); // top right
    ofVertex(100, 100); // bottom right
    ofVertex(10, 100); // bottom left
ofEndShape ();
```

That probably looks quite familiar. Set the way that the vertices are going to be connected, create some vertices, and then signal the end of the drawing operation to connect them. If you want to do something more sophisticated, you'll want to make a mesh, which openFrameworks supports using the ofMesh object.

A mesh consists of a few different components that are important to understand. A vertex is where a point in the mesh is located in 3-D space. An index is where that point is within the mesh. Creating the indices for a complex shape isn't particularly easy or intuitive. Take a look at Figure 13-9:

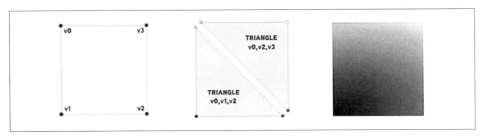

*Figure 13-9. Creating a quad from two triangles*

When you're using a mesh, drawing a square actually consists of drawing two triangles and then assembling them into a single shape. You actually need 6 indices to connect the 4 vertices. That gets more complex when you start working with 3-D. You're going to draw an icosahedron and to do that you'll need to know how each of the vertices is connected to all of the others and add those indices, as shown in Figure 13-10.

When you create your ofMesh instance, you're going to add all the vertices first and then add all of the indices. Each vertex will be given a color so that it can be easily differentiated, but the bulk of the tricky stuff is in creating the vertices and indices that the icosahedron will use. See Example 13-11.

*Example 13-11. icosahedron.h*

```
#pragma once

#include "ofMain.h"

const int X = 158;
const int Z = 256;
```

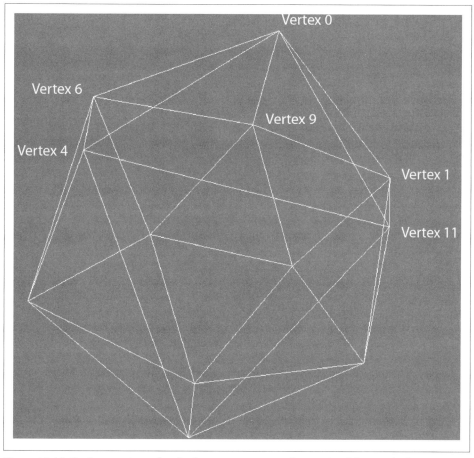

*Figure 13-10. Each vertex is used multiple times to create each triangle of the isocahedron*

This is the data for the vertices, which keeps the data as simple as possible:

```
static GLfloat vdata[12][3] = {
    {-X, 0.0, Z}, {X, 0.0, Z}, {-X, 0.0, -Z}, {X, 0.0, -Z},
    {0.0, Z, X}, {0.0, Z, -X}, {0.0, -Z, X}, {0.0, -Z, -X},
    {Z, X, 0.0}, {-Z, X, 0.0}, {Z, -X, 0.0}, {-Z, -X, 0.0}
};
```

This is the data for the indices, representing the index of the vertices that are to be connected into the triangle. You'll notice that for 12 vertices you need 20 indices of 3 vertices each:

```
static GLint indices[20][3] = {
    {0,4,1}, {0,9,4}, {9,5,4}, {4,5,8}, {4,8,1},
    {8,10,1}, {8,3,10}, {5,3,8}, {5,2,3}, {2,7,3},
    {7,10,3}, {7,6,10}, {7,11,6}, {11,0,6}, {0,1,6},
    {6,1,10}, {9,0,11}, {9,11,2}, {9,2,5}, {7,2,11}
};
```

```
class icosahedron : public ofBaseApp{

public:

    float ang;
    ofMesh mesh;

    void setup();
    void update();
    void draw();

};
```

Now the application itself. See Example 13-12.

*Example 13-12. icosahedron.cpp*

```
#include "icosahedron.h"

void icosahedron::setup()
{

    ofColor color(255, 0, 0);
    float hue = 254.f;
```

Here's where we finally add all the vertices to our mesh and add a color at each vertex:

```
    for (int i = 0; i<12; ++i)
    {
        mesh.addVertex( ofVec3f( vdata[i][0], vdata[i][1], vdata[i][2] ));

        mesh.addColor(color);
        color.setHue( hue );
        hue -= 20.f;
    }

    for (int i = 0; i<20; ++i)
    {
        mesh.addIndex(indices[i][0]);
        mesh.addIndex(indices[i][1]);
        mesh.addIndex(indices[i][2]);
    }

}


void icosahedron::update(){
    ang+=0.1;
}

void icosahedron::draw() {

    ofBackground(122,122,122);

    ofPushMatrix();
```

```
ofTranslate(400, 400, 0);
ofRotate(ang, 1.0, 1.0, 1.0);
```

Now it's time to draw the mesh. The `ofMesh` has three drawing methods: `drawFaces()`, which draws all the faces of the mesh filled; `drawWireframe()`, which draws lines along each triangle; and `drawVertices()`, which draws a point at each vertex. Since we want to see the colors we're drawing, we'll draw all the faces:

```
mesh.drawFaces();

ofPopMatrix();
}
```

# Using Textures and Shading in Processing

Processing has a way of creating textures and shading that avoids a lot of the complexities of working with textures and shading in OpenGL. The idea of a *texture* is one that you've already encountered in Chapter 8, where you learned how bitmaps and bitmapped textures are displayed. In this section, you'll see how to apply those textures to 3-D objects created in Processing. The first step to understanding this is to revisit the `vertex()` method. Remember that the `vertex()` method creates a vertex by using three numbers to define its location in space, but there are two additional parameters that you can pass to the `vertex()` method:

```
vertex(x, y, z, u, v); // note the u and v parameters
```

u

Can be an int or float; designates the horizontal coordinate for the texture mapping.

v

Can be an int or float; designates the vertical coordinate for the texture mapping.

In Figure 13-11, a 500 × 500 pixel image is used as a texture, which is then applied to a set of vertices. Notice, the u and v values are referring to the pixel position in the image, so the full image is seen only in the final example where the values passed to the u and v parameters of the lower-right vertex are the same as the size of the image.

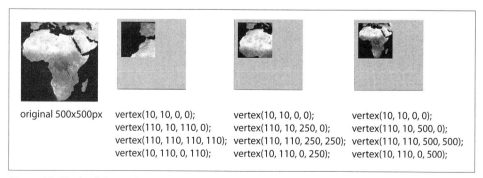

| original 500x500px | vertex(10, 10, 0, 0); | vertex(10, 10, 0, 0); | vertex(10, 10, 0, 0); |
| | vertex(110, 10, 110, 0); | vertex(110, 10, 250, 0); | vertex(110, 10, 500, 0); |
| | vertex(110, 110, 110, 110); | vertex(110, 110, 250, 250); | vertex(110, 110, 500, 500); |
| | vertex(10, 110, 0, 110); | vertex(10, 110, 0, 250); | vertex(10, 110, 0, 500); |

*Figure 13-11. Applying an image as a texture*

The code for applying the image as a texture is shown in Example 13-13:

*Example 13-13. ptexturing.pde*

```
void setup() {
    size(200, 200, P3D);
}

void draw() {
    noStroke();
    PImage a = loadImage("tmp.jpg");
    beginShape();
    texture(a);
    vertex(10, 10, 0, 0);
    vertex(110, 10, 250, 0);
    vertex(110, 110, 250, 250);
    vertex(10, 110, 0, 250);
    endShape();
}
```

You can't simply apply the texture to a box or sphere created with the `box()` or `sphere()` methods. There is another method of setting the way that objects appear when drawn: you can set the materials that will be applied as the texture and appearance of those objects.

# Using Another Way of Shading

GLSL (Graphics Language Shading Language) is an abbreviation for the official OpenGL Shading Language. GLSL is a high-level programming language that's similar to C/C++ for several parts of the graphics card. With GLSL, you can code short programs, called *shaders*, which are executed on the GPU.

## What Does GLSL Look Like?

A shading language is a special programming language adapted to easily map on shader programming. Those kinds of languages usually have special data types, such as color and normal. Because of the various target markets of 3-D graphics, different shading languages have been developed.

GLSL shaders themselves are a set of strings that are passed to the graphics card drivers for compilation from within an application using the OpenGL API's entry points. Shaders can be created on the fly from within an application or read in as text files, but they must be sent to the driver in the form of a text string.

There are two necessary elements of a shader: *the vertex shader* and *the fragment shader*. The OpenGL shader pipeline works roughly as shown in Figure 13-12.

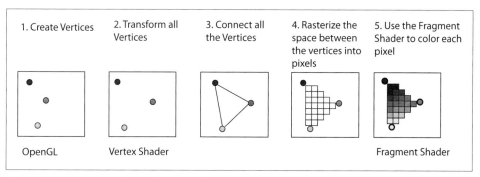

| 1. Create Vertices | 2. Transform all Vertices | 3. Connect all the Vertices | 4. Rasterize the space between the vertices into pixels | 5. Use the Fragment Shader to color each pixel |
|---|---|---|---|---|

| OpenGL | Vertex Shader | | | Fragment Shader |
|---|---|---|---|---|

*Figure 13-12. The steps in the shader pipeline*

In step 2 of Figure 13-12, the vertex shader can be applied to alter the positions of different vertices. In step 5, the fragment shader is applied to control the shading of each pixel. We'll look at each part of this process individually.

## Vertex Shaders

A *vertex shader* has attributes about a location in space or vertex, which means not only the actual coordinates of that location but also its color, how many textures should be mapped onto it, and how the vertices are modified in the operation. A vertex shader can change the positions of each vertex, the number of lighting computations per vertex, and the color that will be applied to each vertex.

Your application certainly doesn't need to do all of these operations to use a vertex shader. As you'll see in the next code example, you don't need to apply lights to your objects. Even though you don't need to use all the functionality of the vertex shader, when you create and apply a vertex shader, your program will assume that you're replacing all the functionality of your other vertex transformations. If you apply changes to a particular vertex, the vertex shader will probably change those according to the instructions contained in the vertex shader. When a vertex shader is used, it becomes responsible for replacing all the needed functionality of this stage of the pipeline.

The vertex processor processes each vertex individually and doesn't store any data about the other vertices that it has already processed or that it will process. It is responsible for at least writing a variable, gl_Position, usually transforming the vertex with the ModelView and Projection matrices. A vertex processor has access to OpenGL state, so it can perform operations that involve lighting, for instance, and use materials. It can also access textures.

So, what does a vertex shader look like? They can be quite simple. Take a look at the following example. It's a single function that sets the value of each vertex passed to it. That vertex can be accessed within that method as gl_Vertex, and its final position after the operation can be set using the gl_Position variable:

```
void main() {
```

Here the vertex that is currently being operated on is used to create a new vertex:

```
vec4 v = vec4(gl_Vertex);
```

As a quick example, the x position of the vertex is shifted over by 1 pixel:

```
v.x += 1;
```

Now the final position of the vertex is set:

```
        gl_Position = gl_ModelViewProjectionMatrix * v;
    }
```

That's a very simple vertex shader that doesn't alter your image in any immediately noticeable way, but it does show you how the vertex shader functions.

## Geometry Shader

A geometry shader can generate new graphics primitives, like points, lines, and triangles, from those primitives that were sent to the graphics card from the CPU. This means that you could get a point and turn it into a triangle or even a bunch of triangles, or get a line and turn it into a rectangle, or do real-time extrusion. They are very powerful and can be quite tricky to get right, but they're becoming more popular.

Geometry shader programs are executed after the vertex shader and before the fragment shader. As an example, if your oF application creates triangles and passes them to the vertex shader, then your geometry shader will receive one triangle at a time. What you do with those is up to you. You could, for instance, turn each triangle into two triangles or add additional points around each triangle. As long as you declare what your geometry shader will be getting in and what it will be churning out, everything will be passed to the fragment shader to be colored in without a problem. A very simple geometry shader looks like this:

```
void main() {
  for(int i = 0; i < gl_VerticesIn; ++i) {
    gl_FrontColor = gl_FrontColorIn[i];
    gl_Position = gl_PositionIn[i];
    EmitVertex();
  }
}
```

The number of vertices being passed in with the gl_VerticesIn variable will be the same as the GL type that you're using. If you're using points, it'll be 1. If you're using quads, it'll be 4. gl_Position is where you want to put the vertex that you're creating, and EmitVertex() is how you say that you're done with a vertex. We'll look at an example of using geometry shaders in the next section.

## Fragment Shader

The fragment shader is somewhat misleadingly named, because what it really allows you to do is to change values assigned to each pixel. The vertex shader operates on the vertices, and the fragment shader operates on the pixels. By the time the fragment shader gets information passed into it by the graphics card, the color of a particular pixel has already been computed and, in the fragment shader, can be combined with an element like a lighting effect, a fog effect, or a blur, among many other options. The usual end result of this stage, per fragment, is a color value and a depth for the fragment.

The inputs of this stage are the pixel's location and the fragment's depth—whether it will be visible or altered by an effect—and color values.

Just like vertex shaders, fragment shaders must also have a `main()` function. Just as the vertex shader provides you access to the current vertex using the `gl_Vertex` variable, the fragment shader provides you access to the current fragment, that is, the fragment that the fragment shader is working with when it is called, using the `gl_FragColor` variable. Like the `gl_vertex`, this is a four-dimensional vector that lets you set the RGB and alpha properties of the fragment. In the following example, the color of the fragment is set to a medium gray with full alpha:

```
void main() {
    gl_FragColor = vec4(0.5, 0.5, 0.5, 1.0);
}
```

Notice how each of the channels is set using a floating-point number from 0.0 to 1.0. With this in mind, we can move on to the oF add-on for working with vertex and fragment shaders.

## Variables Inside Shaders

Shaders can have three kinds of variables. *Uniform* variables are the same for all pixels or vertices they describe, and *attribute* variables are calculated separately for each vertex. One way to think of a uniform variable is that it works in the same way that static variables work in C++, as discussed in Chapter 7: setting the uniform variable once sets it for all vertices. An attribute is calculated for each vertex. Finally, there are variables marked as *varying* variables, which are shared across both the shader and the fragment rendering stages of the pipeline. This means that if you have a 4-D vector value declared as varying in your vertex shader:

```
varying vec4 normalColor
```

Then you'll need to make sure that you have the same declaration in your fragment shader. This is so that your graphics card can share the value of the variable through each stage of the rendering process. A value can be set in the vertex rendering stage and then used in the fragment rendering stage. Lots of complex lighting effects are done this way.

# Using ofShader

To get started with using shaders in oF, you'll need to define a vertex and fragment shader file and save both of those in the data folder of your oF application. You can use either the examples later in this section or from the previous section. Then declare an ofShader instance in your application's *.h* file:

```
ofShader shader;
```

This won't do anything until the load() method of the ofShader object is called:

```
shader.loadShader("color"); // this loads color.frag and color.vert
```

The string should be the name of both the fragment shader file and the vertex shader file. They both must have the same name.

Once you've loaded a shader, you activate or deactivate it using the begin() method and stop it using the end() method:

```
shader.begin();
// draw some stuff
shader.end();
```

There is a setUniform() method that allows you to set uniform variables in your shaders. Say you have a value that you want to be able to set in your shader, for instance red. In your *color.frag* file, you would have the uniform declared like this:

```
uniform float red;
void main() {
    gl_FragColor = vec4(red, 1.0, 1.0, 1);
```

In your oF application, you can set this value by using the setUniform1f() method, since red is a single float value:

```
shader.setUniform1f("red", 100);
```

If you wanted to set a three-valued vector of floats, your shader would have:

```
uniform vec3 three;
```

and your oF application would call:

```
shader.setUniform3f("three", threeValues); // assuming threeValues is float[3];
```

You might be wondering what kinds of things you can do with shaders. While it's not hard to do on the CPU, i.e. not in a shader, it's generally faster to do on the GPU, i.e. in a shader. A very simple algorithm would be to allow green screening, for instance, if a pixel is above a certain amount of green (or blue for blue screen) then replace it with the background. Example 13-14 is one way to do that in a shader.

*Example 13-14. videoCompositor.vert*

```
void main()
{
    gl_Position     = gl_ModelViewProjectionMatrix * gl_Vertex;
    gl_FrontColor = gl_Color;
```

---

```
        gl_TexCoord[0] = gl_MultiTexCoord0;

}
```

You'll notice you have two textures, one for the video and one for the background. If the amount of red or green, which will be dynamically set in the application, is above the threshold, then the background is substituted, otherwise the foreground image from the video is used. See Example 13-15.

*Example 13-15. videoCompositor.frag*

```
uniform sampler2DRect video;
uniform sampler2DRect background;

uniform float greenAmt, redAmt;

void main()

{

    vec4 color = texture2DRect(video, gl_TexCoord[0].xy);
    vec4 color2 = texture2DRect(background, gl_TexCoord[0].xy);

    if(color.z > greenAmt && color.x < redAmt) {
        gl_FragColor = color2;
    } else {
        gl_FragColor = color;
    }

}
```

These two files need to be saved in the data folder of the application. Now the oF application, which creates an ofShader object and loads the shader files using the load() method, as shown in Example 13-16:

*Example 13-16. compositor.h*

```
#pragma once
#include "ofMain.h"

class compositor : public ofBaseApp{

    public:

    void setup();
    void update();
    void draw();
    void mouseMoved(int x, int y );

    ofShader shader;
    ofImage background;
    ofVideoGrabber grab;
};
```

Now the *.cpp* file for the application, which handles actually loading and displaying the shader (see Example 13-17):

*Example 13-17. compositor.cpp*

```cpp
#include "compositor.h"

void compositor::setup(){
```

Here is the call to actually load the shader:

```cpp
    shader.load("videoCompositor.vert", "videoCompositor.frag");
    background.loadImage("screen.png");

    grab.setDeviceID(4);
    grab.initGrabber(320, 240);
    grab.setUseTexture(true);

}

void compositor::update(){
    grab.grabFrame();
}
```

Next, call **begin()** on the shader and set the two textures you are using and the red and green thresholds. In this simple application, they're set using the green and red:

```cpp
void compositor::draw(){

    ofBackground(255, 255, 255);
    shader.begin();

    shader.setUniformTexture("video", grab, 0);
    shader.setUniformTexture("background", background, 1);
    shader.setUniform1f("greenAmt", (float) mouseX / ofGetWidth());
    shader.setUniform1f("redAmt", (float) mouseY / ofGetHeight());

    ofPushMatrix();

    ofTranslate(200, 200, 0);
    glBegin(GL_QUADS);
    glTexCoord2f(0, 0);glVertex2f(0, 0);
    glTexCoord2f(320, 0);glVertex2f(640, 0);
    glTexCoord2f(320, 240);glVertex2f(640, 480);
    glTexCoord2f(0, 240);glVertex2f(0, 480);
    glEnd();

    ofPopMatrix();
```

Call end when you're done:

```cpp
    shader.end();

}
```

Now let's look at Example 13-18, a slightly more complex example using a geometry shader. We'll take a point cloud and turn it into a triangle cloud, and then texture that triangle cloud with a live video, just to make it interesting. First, the vertex and fragment shaders:

*Example 13-18. fragmentator.vs*

```
varying vec2 txtCoords;
void main()
{
    gl_FrontColor = gl_Color;
    gl_TexCoord[0] = gl_MultiTexCoord0;
    gl_Position = gl_ModelViewProjectionMatrix * gl_Vertex;
}
```

Next, the very simple fragment shader, seen in Example 13-19.

*Example 13-19. fragmentator.fs*

```
varying vec2 txtCoords;
uniform sampler2DRect tex;

void main()
{
    gl_FragColor = texture2DRect(tex, txtCoords.xy);
}
```

Now the more complex geometry shader (see Example 13-20); it takes a point and determines two more points to make a triangle from it:

*Example 13-20. fragmentator.gs*

```
uniform float rot;
uniform float imgWidth, imgHeight;
varying out vec2 txtCoords;

void main()
{
    float cosX = (cos(rot) * imgWidth) * 0.5;
    float sinY = (sin(rot) * imgHeight) * 0.5;

    gl_Position = gl_PositionIn[0];

    gl_Position.x += cosX;

    txtCoords.x = imgWidth - clamp(gl_Position.x, 0., imgWidth);
    txtCoords.y = imgHeight - clamp(gl_Position.y, 0., imgHeight);

    EmitVertex(); // done with the point

    gl_Position = gl_PositionIn[0];
    gl_Position.x += cosX;
    gl_Position.y += sinY;
```

```
        txtCoords.x = imgWidth - clamp(gl_Position.x, 0., imgWidth);
        txtCoords.y = imgHeight - clamp(gl_Position.y, 0., imgHeight);

        EmitVertex(); // done with the point

        gl_Position = gl_PositionIn[0];

        gl_Position.x -= cosX;
        gl_Position.y -= sinY;

            txtCoords.x = imgWidth - clamp(gl_Position.x, 0., imgWidth);
        txtCoords.y = imgHeight - clamp(gl_Position.y, 0., imgHeight);

        EmitVertex();  // done with the point
        EndPrimitive(); // end the triangle
}
```

The oF application is quite simple. It generates a point cloud, grabs some video, and then uses that video texture to the point cloud. The trick is that because of the geometry shader, the point cloud won't be drawn as points, but as triangles instead. See Example 13-21.

*Example 13-21. fragmenter.cpp*

```
void fragmenter::setup(){
```

Here's where we set the type of object that will be going to the geometry shader:

```
        fragmentator.setGeometryInputType(GL_POINTS); // type: GL_POINTS, GL_LINES,
        GL_LINES_ADJACENCY_EXT, GL_TRIANGLES, GL_TRIANGLES_ADJACENCY_EXT
```

Here's where we set the type of object that will be coming from the geometry shader:

```
        fragmentator.setGeometryOutputType(GL_TRIANGLE_STRIP); // type: GL_POINTS, GL_LINE_STRIP
        GL_TRIANGLE_STRIP
        fragmentator.setGeometryOutputCount(3);    // set number of output vertices
        fragmentator.load("fragmentator.vs", "fragmentator.fs", "fragmentator.gs");
```

Make a point cloud:

```
        int i = 0;
        int j = 0;
        int k = 0;
        float imgWR, imgHR;
        imgWR = vidWidth/cubeLengths;
        imgHR = vidHeight/cubeLengths;
        while(i < cubeLengths){
            while(j < cubeLengths) {
                while(k < cubeLengths) {
                    coord c;
                    c.pos = new ofVec3f(sin(i) * vidWidth * 0.7, cos(j) *
                    vidHeight * 0.7, k * 20);
                    c.tx = new ofVec2f(i * imgWR, j * imgHR);
                    coords.push_back(c);
                    k++;
```

```
                }
                k = 0;
                j++;
            }
            j = 0;
            i++;
        }

        grab.setDeviceID(4);
        grab.initGrabber(vidWidth, vidHeight);

        mouseIsDown = false;

    }

    void fragmenter::update(){
        if(rot > 360.f) rot = 0;
        grab.grabFrame();

        if(!mouseIsDown)
            rot+=0.01;

    }

    void fragmenter::draw(){

        ofBackground(255, 255, 255, 255);

        glPushMatrix();
        glTranslatef(ofGetWidth()/2, ofGetHeight()/2, 0);
        glRotatef(rot, 0, 1, 1);

        grab.getTextureReference().bind();
```

Start the shader, set the height and width of the video texture, and draw the point cloud:

```
        fragmentator.begin();
        fragmentator.setUniform1f("rot", rot);
        fragmentator.setUniform1f("imgWidth", (float) vidWidth);
        fragmentator.setUniform1f("imgHeight", (float) vidHeight);

        glBegin(GL_POINTS);

        vector<coord>::iterator it = coords.begin();
        while(it != coords.end()) {
            glVertex3f( it->pos->x, it->pos->y, it->pos->z);
            glTexCoord2f(it->tx->x, it->tx->y);
            ++it;
        }

        glEnd();
        grab.getTextureReference().unbind();
        fragmentator.end();

        glPopMatrix();
    }
```

Next, you'll learn a way to work with shaders in Processing.

## Using Shaders in Processing

Using a shader in Processing requires using an external library called glgraphics, created by Andres Colubri, which extends the capabilities of the Processing OpenGL renderer considerably and allows you to work with FBOs, VBOs, meshes, and, of course, shaders. It's a massive library filled with some very useful functionality, most of which we'll only brush upon in this small section, sadly. You're going to use an image to act as a height map, that is, to tell each vertex in a mesh how high it should be based on a color. All this happens in the following two shaders (see Example 13-22). The vertex shader does all the heavy work, getting the color of the vertex that's coming in and determining how tall it should be based on the color. The two sampler2D objects are the textures that are being used. One represents the height that the vertex should be and the other represents the color that the vertex should be:

*Example 13-22. bump.vert*

```
uniform sampler2D colormap;
uniform sampler2D bumpmap;
varying vec2 TexCoord;
uniform float maxHeight;

void main(void)
{
    TexCoord = gl_MultiTexCoord0.st;
```

This is the color that we retrieve from the height image:

```
    vec4 bumpColor = texture2D(bumpmap, TexCoord);
    float df = 0.30*bumpColor.x + 0.59*bumpColor.y + 0.11*bumpColor.z;
    vec4 newVertexPos = vec4(gl_Normal * df * float(maxHeight), 0.0) + gl_Vertex;
```

And here finally is the position we're going to use:

```
    gl_Position = gl_ModelViewProjectionMatrix * newVertexPos;
}
```

The fragment shader is very straightforward; it simply grabs the color from the color image and applies it. See Example 13-23.

*Example 13-23. bump.frag*

```
uniform sampler2D colormap;
uniform sampler2D bumpmap;
varying vec2 TexCoord;

void main(void) {
    gl_FragColor = texture2D(colormap, TexCoord);
}
```

If you haven't downloaded the glgraphics library, you'll need to download it from *processing.org/reference/libraries* and install it. Once you've done that, add the following two shaders (see Example 13-24) to your data folder and off you go:

*Example 13-24. glGraphicsDemo.pde*

```
import processing.opengl.*;
import codeanticode.glgraphics.*;

GLModel poly;
GLTexture colorTex;
GLTexture heightTex;
GLSLShader shader;
float angle;

void setup()
{
  size(1024, 512, GLConstants.GLGRAPHICS);
  colorTex = new GLTexture(this, "earth.jpg");
  heightTex = new GLTexture(this, "earthbumps.jpg");

  shader = new GLSLShader(this, "bump.vert", "bump.frag");
  createModel();
}

void draw()
{
  GLGraphics renderer = (GLGraphics)g;
  renderer.beginGL();
  background(0);
  rotateX( float(mouseY)/200.0 );
  translate( 0, float(mouseY/2), -float(mouseY/2) );

  shader.start(); // Enabling shader.
  shader.setTexUniform("colormap", 0);
  shader.setTexUniform("bumpmap", 1);
  shader.setFloatUniform("maxHeight", mouseX/2);
  renderer.model(poly);
  shader.stop(); // Disabling shader.

  renderer.endGL();
}
```

A little bit of this code listing has been truncated to save space but you can find it in the downloads for this book.

# What to Do Next

If you're interested in learning more about OpenGL, you'll want to pick up *The OpenGL SuperBible* by Richard Wright (Sams), which is also known as the "Blue Book" because of the color of its cover. This is the oldest and best way to learn all that you need to know about OpenGL to become a proficient graphics programmer. Another useful text is *The OpenGL Programming Guide* by Mason Woo et al., also called the "Red Book," which is the resource for learning about the GL language. If you're interested in shading or working more with shaders, you'll want to look at *The OpenGL Shading Language Guide* by Randi J. Rost (Addison-Wesley), also called the "Orange Book." Both the Red Book and the Orange Book, as well as their code samples, are freely available online as of the writing of this book.

A lot of other books promise to teach you about graphics, but you're probably better off buying one of the official OpenGL books, reading online tutorials, or picking up one of the Processing books that covers graphics in a more in-depth manner, such as *Processing: Creative Coding and Computational Art* by Ira Greenberg (Apress), *The Nature of Code* by Daniel Shiffman, or *Processing* by Casey Reas et al. (MIT Press).

# Review

To draw 3-D in Processing, pass the P3D or OPENGL constant as the third parameter for the size() method when starting your application.

If you've set up the rendering correct in Processing, you can create 3-D points, shapes, and the sphere(), box(), and cone() methods.

In Processing, calling the lights() method sets up basic lights in your applications. You can change how the lighting appears by calling the lightFalloff() and lightSpecular() methods, and you can add new lights using directionalLighting(), pointLight(), spotLight(), or ambientLight().

Processing makes working with views easy by providing you with a camera() method to set up a camera. You can also call the camera() method like so: camera(eyeX, eyeY, eyeZ, centerX, centerY, centerZ, upX, upY, upZ).

In Processing, vertices are 3-D points created with the vertex() method that will be connected to form a shape by the mode passed to the beginShape() method.

In Processing, to change the position or rotation of the viewer or the location of an object to be drawn, use the pushMatrix() method to get a new matrix, and then use the rotation() and transformation() methods to change the coordinates at which things will be drawn. Call popMatrix() when you are finished.

OpenGL can be used in Processing and oF applications, though it is somewhat more standardized in oF applications. It communicates with the graphics card of your computer.

OpenGL uses matrices and transformations quite similarly to Processing. OpenGL has three matrices: ModelView, Projection, and Texture. There are different transformations that allow you to work with these matrices easily: the Model transform, ModelView transform, Projection transform, and the Viewport transform.

To draw custom shapes with textures in oF, use the glTexCoord() method to set how an ofTexture will be mapped to a vertex created with glVertex().

You can set blending modes using the glBlendFunc() method, which takes two parameters: a value for the existing data already rendered and a value for the incoming data for all incoming activities.

Processing lets you create materials by using the ambientLight(), emissive(), shini ness(), and specular() methods. These determine whether an object emits light and how it reacts to environmental light.

Graphics Language Shading Language (GLSL) can be used in oF by using the ofShader object. Shading happens in two distinct steps: the vertex shader creates values for each vertex in the model, and the fragment shader creates values for each pixel in the rendered object. To define a shader, create a *.frag* file for the fragment shader and a *.vert* file for the vertex shader and load them into an ofShader instance.

Graphics Language Shading Language (GLSL) can be used in Processing by using the GLGraphics library and creating an instance of the GLSLShader class.

# CHAPTER 14

# Motion and Gestures

This chapter is about capturing images and movement and turning them into meaningful information. One part of it is going to be largely about one library, OpenCV, and using the library in Processing and openFrameworks. The other part is going to be about different techniques for capturing different gestures and movements, both with OpenCV and without, and then deriving meaningful information from those. This is an important chapter because it is where you'll learn how to turn the gestures and movements of a user, or other kinds of movement in an image, into meaningful input for an application. As anyone paying attention to the development of devices and the advancement of user interface and experience concepts over the past few years can tell you, this topic is one of the most interesting and important ideas in contemporary device design. Surfaces, tangible interaction devices, and free gesture interfaces have been incorporated in many different kinds of devices in the past few years.

*Computer vision* is a field of computing concerned with creating "seeing" applications by feeding an application a series of images, like a video, or a single image. Usually these images are analyzed for something in particular, such as looking for a light or for a face. Unlike human sight, a computer needs a good deal of instruction on what it should be looking for in an image. Computer vision techniques can be used to find fingertips, track gestures, find faces, or simply detect motion. Images are analyzed by looking for patterns in color values of the pixels. Those changes can be grouped into objects and tracked over multiple images, or they can be analyzed using statistical algorithms to determine how likely something is to represent a certain object like a face or other specific object.

This chapter talks about computer vision, recognition, and gestures together because one of the more interesting ways to create interaction using computer vision is to use gesture and recognition. This allows the user to input data into a program through an image given to the computer. *Recognition* is the detection of a particular kind of object in an image, a face, a hand, or a particular image. A *gesture* is a pattern of movement over time. You can use both of these with Processing or oF applications by using the OpenCV library for computer vision. Gestures recognition and face recognition are really a particular way of generalizing patterns from data, and in the case of computer vision, that data is image data. Any system trying to use gestural input needs to accurately distinguish one gesture from another, determine the extent of each gesture, and determine and communicate whether it is a gesture that communicates a range of input values or functions as a binary input.

## Computer Vision

Computer vision (CV) is a massive and complex topic that ranges in the disciplines it draws from. Statistical analysis, physics, and signal processing all are important contributors to the development of computer vision techniques and libraries. Some of the most important arenas where computer vision is being used are robotics, surveillance machines, weapons systems, games, toys, and touchscreen interfaces. Computer vision allows interaction designers to do what seemed impossible: create interfaces from the movement of the human body, without a need for an interface that the user physically manipulates. For a long time, applying computer vision techniques to interactive applications was unrealistic because the techniques were too time- and processor-intensive to allow real-time interaction and provide feedback quickly enough. However, newer processors and better algorithms and techniques for image processing have made it possible to analyze images from a video feed in near real time.

Artists and engineers have used gesture recognition and computer vision since the pioneering work of Myron Krueger in the 1970s. Krueger often talked about an art that was fundamentally about interactivity, rather than art that used interactivity as a gimmick. He focused on the idea of the interaction being the medium of communication, just like language, text, and pages are to a book, or canvas and paint are to a painting. His ideas and work are worth a look for designers and artists alike, because even in the 1960s and 1970s he had a clear vision of how to connect people and virtual spaces.

There are a few key areas of research in computer vision. *Image processing* and *image analysis* tend to focus on 2-D images and deal with how to transform one image into another. Some techniques for altering images were covered in Chapter 10. Another area of computer vision research focuses on the 3-D scene projected onto one or several images and deals with reconstructing the scene from one or several images. *Machine vision* is concerned with processing image data to control a robot or other kind of machine. It's most often concerned with inspection or measurement and focuses on precise calculations in controlled environments like factories. This gives the research and algorithms used by machine vision a slightly different bend than those used in analyzing uncontrolled situations where light changes quickly and unpredictably. *Pattern recognition* is another field that uses various methods to extract information from image data, looking for particular data that can represent a written letter or word, a fingerprint, or a kind of airplane, to give some common examples.

Computer vision generally, though not always, follows a particular sequence. First, the program needs to acquire the image through some process of digitalization. A digital image is produced by one or several image sensors, which might be a light-sensitive camera, a range sensor, radar, or an ultrasonic device. The pixel values typically correspond to light intensity in one or several spectral bands (gray images or color images) but can also be related to various physical measures, such as depth, absorption, reflectance of sonic or electromagnetic waves, or nuclear magnetic resonance. Next, the program will do some kind of pre-processing, specifically, resampling the image, reducing noise in the image, blurring it, increasing the contrast, or performing other kinds of changes. You'll see this in the examples shown in this chapter; usually the images are converted to grayscale or blurred, or both, before being processed. Next, the program will look for features that it's interested in—lines, edges, ridges, corners, blobs, or points. This is often called *feature extraction*. Finally, the program will perform high-level processing on a small part of the data that it's actually interested in. For instance, in an application looking for faces, all things that could be faces are checked more closely to see whether they do or do not actually appear to be faces. In an application that finds a specific part of the body, an arm for instance, the actual processing of the shape of the arm will take place in this final step.

## Interfaces Without Controls

One of the wonders of working with OpenCV and computer vision is that the physical interface can become optional. There is no requirement that the user touch anything. This dramatically frees you as the designer, allowing you to literally create an interface out of air. With the recent emphasis on lighter, more transparent, and more minimal interfaces, using computer vision to capture user input seems thrilling. Before you get too excited by the concept, though, you need to consider the ramifications of that lack of interface. Interfaces are what they are because users require information about what information they can send, what might be done with the information that they send, and how that system to which they are sending the information will use the information.

Your messages to the user about what they are doing and how the system receives information about what they are doing becomes absolutely vital when making computer vision interfaces. You'll want to avoid the vague "you do something, it does something back" mode of interaction. While this can be fun to experiment with and is an excellent way to learn about computer vision and test certain ideas, it doesn't make for a particularly rich experience. One of the great realizations that started the flurry of touchscreen interfaces was the precise reactivity of the prototypes of Jeff Han's *Media Wall*. These were touchscreens that reacted to user movements in real time and tracked fingertips and gestures with great precision, making the interaction both precise and natural. Once the touchscreen started to become an interactive surface that was not only dynamic but was precise as well, it became possible to develop new and different kinds of applications with them. Touchscreens had been around for a long time before 2004, but they were ATM screens or kiosks where the user touched a button much the same way as if they clicked a mouse. When working with purely gestural interfaces, it becomes even more important to ensure that the modes of input and the feedback to the user are precise, timely, and intelligible. How you go about doing that is entirely up to you.

Creating a *gesture library*, a set of specific gestures that your application will look for and react to, is important if you're going to make an application that will use gestures, whether those gestures will be input into a touchscreen, will be in the air, or will be the movement of a body. Defining ahead of time what gestures your application will be looking for will make your decisions about how to structure your application and how to test it a great deal easier for you. With all the recent developments in touchscreens, there is an informal but growing library of recognized gestures: two-finger slide, pinch, tap to select, and so on. Dan Saffer wrote an excellent book called *Designing Gestural Interfaces* (O'Reilly) that details many of these gestures and what meaningful uses for them might be.

You should think about how to signal what a device is interpreting a gesture to be by providing either some textural feedback or some visual feedback. Many touchscreen devices draw a small white dot around the user's finger so that the user can see where the application thinks their finger is located. A few other suggestions to think about include making an easy help gesture that users can call and making sure that users are given prompts. If you're using gestures or specific actions, make sure you signal them clearly.

## Example CV Projects

There is a wide range of projects that use motion tracking and computer vision techniques. The projects range from LaserTag, which tracks a laser pointer on a surface several meters away; to medical imaging, which helps detect cancerous tumors; to military applications; This notion of the computer-mediated environment has percolated throughout the design, architectural, and artistic communities. Public artists like Greyworld make frequent use of computer vision. Pieces like *The Monument to the Unknown Artist* use the gestures of passersby to pose a robotic sculpture, relying on computer vision to determine the pose of the onlooker. Performance pieces like *Messa di Voce* by Golan Levin and Zachary Lieberman use computer vision to track the movements of a performer on a stage and particularly the motion of their heads. Computer vision is widely used in dance, in musical performance, and in video pieces in dance clubs to widen the physical space in a sense or to make a performer or a participant metaphorically "exist" in more than one place. Advertising or product demonstrations use computer vision to grab a viewer's attention with graphics that mirror their movements. These computer vision techniques are becoming popular for video artists in dance clubs, as attention-getters in shopping malls, in building lobbies, and on the street to attract attention for an advertisement, as well as being tools for artists.

Some of the most remarkable achievements in computer vision have been much more oriented toward engineering. In 2005, a race called the Grand Challenge was held where entrants equipped a car with a computer vision system to navigate desert terrain for several hours. Gary Bradski was a member of the winning team and used OpenCV in the vision system. Almost all robots and robotics applications have some element of computer vision to help them navigate terrain or analyze objects. Many companies are working with computer vision and gesture recognition to create gaming systems that operate without touch and without the need for a controller.

# OpenCV

A team of developers at Intel headed by Gary Bradski started developing OpenCV in 1999. In 2007, Intel released version 1.0 as an open source project. Since it's an open source library, it's free to download, and you can use and modify it for your own purposes. Some of the core features that it provides are an interface to a camera, object detection and tracking, and face and gesture recognition. The library itself is written in C and is a little tricky to get started using right away without another library or framework to interface with it. Luckily, there are libraries that you can use with both Processing and oF.

*ofxOpenCV* is an add-on for openFrameworks that Stefan Hechenberger and Zachary Lieberman developed to let people working with oF use OpenCV easily in their projects. For Processing, both the OpenCV library—developed by Stephane Cousot and Douglas Edric Stanley—and the FaceDetect library utilize the OpenCV library. Because OpenCV is so massive, all the libraries implement a portion of its functionality. The ofxOpenCV library focuses on contour detection, as well as blob-tracking and-detection functionality. The Processing OpenCV library, as of the writing of this book, provides for real-time capture, image manipulation, and face and blob detection. The FaceDetect library for Processing is set up primarily to do face detection.

# Using Blobs and Tracking

Movement tracking in OpenCV is done through what is commonly called a *blob*, which is a data object that represents a contiguous area of a frame. Blobs can be all sorts of different things: hands, faces, a flashlight, a ball. Blobs are usually identified by the contrast caused by the difference between adjoining pixels. This is quite similar to how edge detection, which you saw in Chapter 9, is done. A group of adjoining pixels that have the same relationship to another group of adjoining pixels, such as an area of darker pixels that is bordered by an area of whiter pixels, usually indicates a specific object (see Figure 14-1).

Behind all the ethereal magic of gestural interfaces, particularly in using multiple tracking points, is the notion of a *blob* and of *tracking*. *Tracking* is the process of identifying one or more objects that display consistent movement within the field of the computer's vision and identifying those objects over time. A hand is an excellent and commonly used example. A finger pressed on a surface that is light reactive is another commonly used concept in many surface-based interfaces. Colored objects, particularly those with

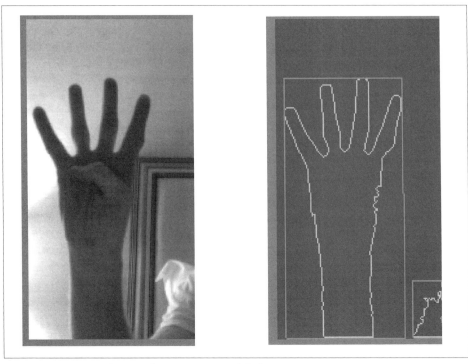

*Figure 14-1. Contour detection by examining pixel darkness*

a specific design that can be recognized by a computer vision system like those used in tangible interfaces, are another common interface concept that makes use of the tracking of blobs. Once a blob has been found, let's say a hand against a white wall, the next step is to track its movement over time and ensure that the blob's position is consistently updated to reflect the movement of the object throughout the images. This is what allows the movement of a single object in a visual field to be turned into a gesture, that is, a movement over time. This is substantially easier when you're dealing with a single object, but when dealing with multiple blobs it becomes mathematically and computationally more complex. The tracking of blobs is one of the difficult tasks in gestural interfaces that OpenCV makes a great deal easier. Later in this chapter, you'll learn how to track fingers in a controlled environment as well as learn how to use two different simple gesture recognition libraries, one for Processing and one for oF.

## Starting with ofxOpenCV

ofxOpenCV is an add-on, but it's included with the "fat distribution," the full distribution containing all of the add-ons, so you won't need to download it separately. Take a look in the add-ons directory of your oF folder and see whether the ofxOpenCV folder is there. As with other add-ons for oF, you'll need to include the main file for the add-on in an `include` statement:

```
include "ofxOpenCV.h"
```

Once you've done that, you should be ready to go. You may want to run the sample application that comes with the ofxOpenCV add-on to familiarize yourself with the basics.

One of the most important aspects of this add-on is its contour finding capability. This is handled through the `ofxContourFinder` class that performs the blob finding and tracking task. In the *.h* file of your application, define an instance of the `ofxCvContour Finder` class:

```
ofxCvContourFinder contourFinder;
```

You'll see more about how to use this method in the following example, but for the moment, since this is one of the two key methods of `ofxCvContourFinder`, you should understand how the `findContours()` method works. Here is the signature followed by a description of the parameters:

```
virtual int findContours( ofxCvGrayscaleImage& input, int minArea,
    int maxArea, int nConsidered, bool bFindHoles, bool bUseApproximation = true);
```

input
> This is an `ofxCvGrayscaleImage` reference ( written `ofxCvGrayscaleImage&`) to a grayscale image that will be searched for blobs. Note that only grayscale images are considered. So if you're using a color image, you'll need to highlight the particular color that you're looking for beforehand. You can do this by looping through the pixels and changing the color values of any pixel with the desired color to white or black, for instance.

minArea
> This is the smallest potential blob size as measured in pixels that will be considered as a blob for the application.

maxArea
> This is the largest potential blob size as measured in pixels that will be considered as a blob for the application.

nConsidered
> This is the maximum number of blobs to consider. This is an important parameter to get right, because you can save yourself a lot of processing time and possibly speed up the performance of your application by pruning this number down. An interface that uses a user's fingers, for instance, needs to look only for 5 points, one for each finger. One that uses a user's hands needs to look only for two points.

bFindHoles
> This tells the contour finder to try to determine whether there are holes within any blob detected. This is computationally expensive but sometimes necessary.

bUseApproximation

This tells the contour finder to use approximation and to set the minimum number of points needed to represent a certain blob; for instance, a straight line would be represented by only two points if bUseApproximation is set to true.

Once you've detected the blobs in an image, there are two useful properties of ofxCon tourFinder that you'll use to determine what has been found in the contour finding:

blobs

The vector ofxCvBlob returns each blob that was found in the image. These should, if all has gone well, correlate to the blobs in previous examples so that you can begin to perform gesture detection.

nBlobs

This is an int that returns the number of blobs found by the contour finder.

Commonly, after contour detection, you'll want to use the nBlobs variable to loop through the blobs contained in the blobs vector:

```
for (int i = 0; i < contourFinder.nBlobs; i++){
    contourFinder.blobs[i].draw(360,540);
}
```

This merits a look at ofxCvBlob. As mentioned earlier, a blob defines an area identified by the OpenCV plug-in as being a contiguous object in the scene. Here are some of the properties of this class:

area

This gives the size of the blob in pixels.

boundingRect

This is an ofRectangle instance that can be drawn to the screen and that shows the height and width of the blob. This can be helpful to determine large regions of interest, or it can lead to some inaccurate results depending on the shape of your object. For instance, a squarish shape will be well represented by a rectangle, whereas a long thin shape with an angle in the middle will not.

centroid

This is an ofPoint instance with its x and y positions set at the center of the boundaries of the blob.

hole

This is a Boolean value that indicates whether the blob contains a hole. This is also dependent on whether the call to findContours() in ofxContourFinder has the findHoles parameter set to true.

pts

This is a vector of ofPoint objects that represent the contour of the blob. This is different from the bounding rectangle. It's listing the different points around the edge of the blob. The bounding rectangle is a rectangle around the extreme points of the blob.

nPts

This is an `int` that represents the number of points that are contained within the contour.

void draw( float x, float y )

This method draws the blob to the screen with the upper-left corner located at the point specified by the *x* and *y* values.

When `contourFinder` detects a contiguous contour, it stores the information about that region as a blob. Later in this chapter, you'll use those blobs to track objects over time. First, though, look at the code for reading the contours of an image, detecting blobs, and drawing them to the screen, seen in Example 14-1.

*Example 14-1. contoursApp.h*

```
#pragma mark once

#include "ofMain.h"
#include "ofxOpenCv.h"

class contoursApp : public ofBaseApp{

public:

    void setup();
    void update();
    void draw();

    void keyPressed   (int key);

    ofVideoGrabber vidGrabber;
    ofxCvColorImage colorImg;
```

The three `ofxCvGrayscaleImage` images are used together to determine what has changed between the current frame and the background. The `grayImage` is used to convert the color image from the video into grayscale, and the `grayBg` image stores an image of the background. These two are then compared using the `absDiff()` method of the `ofxCvGrayscaleImage` object, which creates a new image based on the differences between the current image and the image of the background and stores it in the `grayDiff` image:

```
    ofxCvGrayscaleImage grayImage;
    ofxCvGrayscaleImage grayBg;
    ofxCvGrayscaleImage grayDiff;
```

`ofxCvContourFinder` is the object that will detect the contours in the image, finding borders of objects or shifts in color and light:

```
    ofxCvContourFinder contourFinder;
    int threshold;
    bool learnBackground;
};
```

Example 14-2 is the *.cpp* file.

*Example 14-2. contoursApp.cpp*

```
#include "contoursApp.h"

void contoursApp::setup(){

    learnBackground = false;

    vidGrabber.setVerbose(true);
    vidGrabber.initGrabber(320,240);
```

Now, allocate memory for the array of pixels that the image will use to save the incoming pixel data:

```
    colorImg.allocate(320,240);
    grayImage.allocate(320,240);
    grayBg.allocate(320,240);
    grayDiff.allocate(320,240);
}

void contoursApp::update(){
    vidGrabber.grabFrame();
    //do we have a new frame?
    if (vidGrabber.isFrameNew()){
```

Now `ofxCvColorImage` has all of its pixels set from the newest frame that the video camera has captured. If you don't have a camera attached to your computer when you run this code, you can always use the `ofVideoPlayer` class to play back a video to use in `contourDetection`:

```
    colorImg.setFromPixels(vidGrabber.getPixelsRef());
    grayImage = colorImg; // convert our color image to a grayscale image
    if (learnBackground == true) {
        grayBg = grayImage; // update the background image
        learnBackground = false;
    }
```

Now, find the difference between the background and incoming image to look for changes in the two images:

```
    grayDiff.absDiff(grayBg, grayImage);
```

To ensure that the `grayDiff` image doesn't contain too much noise, increase the contrast on it. You might want to make this higher or lower depending on the lighting situation in the video image:

```
    grayDiff.threshold(30);
```

Here's the call to the `findContours()` method. In this case, the smallest blobs that `contourFinder` is looking for are 10 pixels, and the largest are one tenth the size of the screen. `contourFinder` is looking for two blobs and for holes in those blobs:

```
        contourFinder.findContours(grayDiff, 10, (340*240)/4, 2, false, true);
    }
}

void contoursApp::draw(){
    ofSetHexColor(0xffffff);
    colorImg.draw(0, 0, 320, 240);
    grayDiff.draw(0, 240, 320, 240);
    ofRect(320, 0, 320, 240);
    contourFinder.draw(320, 0, 320, 240);
    ofColor c(255, 255, 255);
```

Now, loop through all the blobs that `contourFinder` has detected, and draw them:

```
    for(int i = 0; i < contourFinder.nBlobs; i++) {
        ofRectangle r = contourFinder.blobs.at(i).boundingRect;
        r.x += 320; r.y += 240;
        c.setHsb(i * 64, 255, 255);
        ofSetColor(c);
        ofRect(r);
    }
}
```

If the user hits a key, then set the `learnBackground` parameter to `true`, meaning that the background should be captured again so the new images will be compared with the correct background. This can be good to do if the light changes in a room or if the camera moves. Otherwise, you'll find too many false matches in your image:

```
void contoursApp::keyPressed  (int key){
    learnBackground= true;
}
```

Now that you've seen the basics of detecting blobs, the next step is to track them over a period of time.

## Detecting Features with oF

One of the most powerful features of OpenCV (and by extension, oF) is how easy it makes detecting faces or eyes or other object types in an image. These are called features and the detection is done in one of a few ways. One is to track all the contours in an image and simply look for something that has the same line as the requested object. Another is by creating a model of all the different features that the requested object has and comparing all the contours against that. At the end of it these approaches are more or less similar but the way that they're implemented in OpenCV is quite different. In this section we'll focus on the second approach. The second approach uses a file called a Haar cascade file. The file contains data on the digital image features used to recognize an object from all the shapes and lines in an image. Haar cascade files are XML files that are loaded into the application and processed and then used to compare all the incoming images. Just to throw a few names at you, the feature detection in OpenCV uses a technique called the Viola–Jones framework. When detecting in the Viola–Jones object detection framework, a window is moved over the input image and for each subsection of the image the Haar-like feature is calculated and compared to the desired Haar feature. This cascading down is why the Haar feature file is sometimes called a "Haar cascade." It's also called a Haar Classifier.

The process of training applications to learn things is called *machine learning* and is a very interesting topic. In this section, you'll learn about a specific machine learning technique. The most commonly used approach for face detection and recognition in OpenCV is based on a technique called the *Haar Classifier*. The Haar Classifier is a data file generated from a training process where an application is "taught" how to recognize something in different contexts. This can be things like recognizing whether a certain sound is a word being spoken by a user, whether a gesture is a certain shape, or, in this case, whether a pattern of pixels is a face. If you're interested in learning more about Haar Classifiers and how machine languages work in OpenCV, once again refer to Gary Bradski's and Adrian Kaehler's book, *Learning OpenCV* (O'Reilly).

Creating a Haar Classifier is done by generating multiple images and setting the regions of interest in the image. This is usually called *training*, and Figure 14-2 shows some example images, generously donated by Todd Vanderlin.

Figure 14-2. Training and tracking images

Notice how the three images to the left all show different variations of images containing the same object. After correct training, an OpenCV application can properly track the object in a video feed. Training and creating a Haar Classifier is beyond the scope of this book, but it's helpful to understand roughly how the training works. In Figure 14-2, the training is for the small card image. The characteristics of that card, meaning the size, shapes, and shading of it, are encoded into an XML file that OpenCV can read and compare to the contours of images that it is sent. In training faces, hundreds or thousands of images of faces are used to create a data model of what a face looks like, and then similar images of objects other than faces are used to create a data model of what a face does not look like.

One of the things that OpenCV generously provided to the open source community is a few trained XML file sample that represent a Haar Classifier that can be used in a few general situations. For instance, in the following example, the *haarcascade_frontalface_alt_tree.xml* file contains data about the characteristics of a face looking at the camera. Other files included in the OpenCV training files help detect faces seen in profile, full bodies, upper torsos, and lower torsos. In the downloads for this chapter, you'll find the *haarcascade_frontalface_alt_tree.xml* file. If you open the XML file, you'll see XML that defines information about the shapes that could potentially match the objects being defined. This XML file defines regions that contain certain attributes that are common to faces. If you're curious what it looks like, open the file up and take a look.

The ofxOpenCV add-on includes a class called ofxCvHaarFinder that does the work of loading the Haar file, processing it, and looking through any image or video frame for any patterns that match the cascade that it's been passed. We'll walk through a simple sample application first so you can see how the tracker works:

```
app::setup() {
    haarFinder.setup("haarcascade.xml"); // must be in /data/
}

app::update() {
    haarFinder.findHaarObjects(imageToExamine);
}

app::draw() {
  for(int i = 0; i < haarFinder.blobs.size(); i++) {
    ofRect( haarFinder.blobs[i].boundingRect );
  }
}
```

As you can see, the process is to load a Haar file into the ofxCvHaarFinder, call the findHaarObjects() method and pass in the image you want to look in, and then draw the detected blobs from the finder. It's actually not particularly difficult. Let's apply this in an actual cascade, first finding a face and then, in the face, finding eyes. This is done with two different Haar cascade files, which are applied in order. See Example 14-3.

*Example 14-3. eyeFinder.h*

```
#pragma once

#include "ofMain.h"
#include "ofxOpenCv.h"

class eyeFinder : public ofBaseApp{
    public:
    void setup();
    void update();
    void draw();
```

```
    ofxCvHaarFinder faceFinder, eyeFinder;
    ofVideoGrabber grab;

    ofImage img, faceImg;
    ofVec2f origin;
};
```

The ofxCvHaarFinder instances are set up and then the faceFinder is called, the image cropped if a face is found, and that cropped image is then passed to the eyeFinder instance. See Example 14-4.

*Example 14-4. eyeFinder.cpp*

```
#include "eyeFinder.h"

void eyeFinder::setup(){

    faceFinder.setup("haarcascade_frontalface_default.xml");
    eyeFinder.setup("haarcascade_eye.xml");

    grab.setVerbose(true);
    grab.initGrabber(320,240);
}

void eyeFinder::update(){

    grab.grabFrame();

    if(grab.isFrameNew())
    {
        img.setFromPixels(grab.getPixelsRef());
        faceFinder.findHaarObjects(img);

        for(int i = 0; i < faceFinder.blobs.size(); i++) {
            ofRectangle cur = faceFinder.blobs[i].boundingRect;
            origin.x = cur.x;
            origin.y = cur.y;
            faceImg.cropFrom(img, cur.x, cur.y, cur.width, cur.height);
            eyeFinder.findHaarObjects(faceImg);
        }

    }
}

void eyeFinder::draw(){
    img.draw(0, 0);
    ofNoFill();
    for(int i = 0; i < eyeFinder.blobs.size(); i++) {
        ofRectangle cur = eyeFinder.blobs[i].boundingRect;
        ofRect(cur.x + origin.x, cur.y + origin.y, cur.width, cur.height);
    }
}
```

This is a fairly simple application but it does demonstrate how multiple ofxCvHaar Finder instances can be used in concert to create fairly sophisticated tracking.

As shown in Todd Vanderlin's example, anything can be trained for recognition, but since the OpenCV download comes with pretrained Haar files, it makes sense to demonstrate how to use them. Since humans naturally tend to look at one another's faces as an important source of information, the interactive possibilities of having an application that does the same are worth exploring. Golan Levin's *Opto-Isolator* is an excellent example of an interactive art piece that uses face tracking, following the eyes of the viewer. Beyond face tracking, you can apply the same techniques to detect eyes, mouths, or noses, using the face recognition as a first pass and then determining within the face what shapes are most likely, such as the eyes, mouth, and so on.

# Using OpenCV in Processing

So far in this chapter, you've looked only at OpenCV in oF applications, but as mentioned earlier, there is an OpenCV library for Processing as well. The OpenCV library is made accessible to your Processing application through a class called OpenCV. First download the library from the Processing website, and then move the library to the *libraries* folder of your Processing installation. Import the libraries by calling the following import statement:

```
import hypermedia.video.*;
```

Create an instance of this class, and pass this reference to your application to the constructor; you're ready to go:

```
OpenCV opencv;
opencv = new OpenCV(this);
```

To begin capturing video, call the **capture()** method, passing in the width and height you want to capture. This automatically reads from the first video camera attached to your computer:

```
int IMG_WIDTH = 400;
int IMG_HEIGHT = 300;
opencv.capture(IMG_WIDTH, IMG_HEIGHT);
```

To capture a frame of video, in each **draw()** method of your application you'll want to call the **read()** method of the OpenCV library:

```
opencv.read();
```

The code in Example 14-5 captures, flips, blurs, inverts, and then redisplays the captured image.

*Example 14-5. cvBlur.pde*

```
import hypermedia.video.*;

// OpenCV instance
```

```
OpenCV opencv;
// blur value
int blurAmount = 17;

// image dimensions
int IMG_WIDTH  = 200;
int IMG_HEIGHT = 150;

int COLOR_SPACE = OpenCV.RGB;
//final int COLOR_SPACE = OpenCV.GRAY;

void setup() {

    size( IMG_WIDTH*2, IMG_HEIGHT*2 );

    opencv = new OpenCV(this);
    opencv.capture(IMG_WIDTH, IMG_HEIGHT);

}

void draw() {
    // grab image
    opencv.read();
```

The resulting images are shown in Figure 14-3.

*Figure 14-3. Capturing and displaying live video with the OpenCV library for Processing*

Here, create a blur by calling the `blur()` method and passing the type of blur. The options as of this writing are `BLUR` for a simple blur, `MEDIAN`, `GAUSSIAN`, or `BLUR_NO_SCALE`. Experiment with the different options to see how they differ because they're rather difficult to describe in print:

```
opencv.blur( OpenCV.GAUSSIAN, blurAmount );
```

Now, draw the image to the screen:

```
image( opencv.image(), IMG_WIDTH, o );
```

The restore() method is called to reload the original image data. This is quite important because without calling this method, changes are applied sequentially. For instance, if you comment out the following call to restore(), the inverted image will have the blur applied to it. With the call to restore, the original image captured by the camera is used again:

```
opencv.restore( COLOR_SPACE );
opencv.flip(OpenCV.FLIP_VERTICAL);
image( opencv.image(), 0, IMG_HEIGHT);

opencv.restore( COLOR_SPACE );
opencv.invert();
image( opencv.image(), IMG_WIDTH, IMG_HEIGHT);
```

Another way to draw the original image is to call the image() method of the OpenCV library and pass OpenCV.SOURCE to it. This returns the original pixels captured from the camera. In the following line, these are passed to the image() method of the Processing application to be drawn:

```
image( opencv.image(OpenCV.SOURCE), 0, o );
}
```

Here, update the amount of blur when the mouse is dragged:

```
void mouseDragged() {
    blurAmount = (int) map(mouseX,0,width,0,255);
}
```

When the application is stopped, make sure to call the stop() method of the opencv instance:

```
public void stop() {
    opencv.stop();
    super.stop();
}
```

Now, let's look at blob tracking using the OpenCV library. Like the ofxOpenCV add-on, the Processing version of this library includes a Blob class that is used to define the area of a tracked blob. The properties of this class should look familiar to you if you read the previous section:

float area
> This is the area of the blob in pixels.

float length
> This is the length of the perimeter in pixels.

Point centroid
> This is the binary center of the blob.

`Rectangle rectangle`
This is a Processing `Rectangle` instance that contains the blob, defined by its boundaries.

`Point[] points`
This is the list of points defining the shape of the blob.

`boolean isHole`
This returns `true` if the blob is determined to be a hole inside of another blob.

To capture the blobs, simply call the `opencv.blobs()` method, passing the following parameters:

```
blobs( int minArea, int maxArea, int maxBlobs, boolean findHoles )
```

In the following example, the image from the camera will be captured and compared with a background image. One difference between the oF add-on and the Processing library is that in Processing the `remember()` method is used to save the current image to memory. Once the image is saved, it can then be accessed by using the `opencv.image()` method and passing `OpenCV.MEMORY`, as shown here:

```
opencv.image(OpenCV.MEMORY)
```

The difference between the image in memory and the current image from the camera will be used to find blobs in the image, as shown in Example 14-6.

*Example 14-6. blobs.pde*

```
import hypermedia.video.*;
OpenCV opencv;
int w = 320;
int h = 240;
int threshold = 80;

boolean find=true;

void setup() {

    size( w*2+30, h*2+30 );
    opencv = new OpenCV( this );
    opencv.capture(w,h);
}

void draw() {
    background(0);
```

Read the latest image from the camera using the `read()` method. This saves the image into memory so it can be accessed later:

```
opencv.read();
image( opencv.image(), 10, 10 );              // RGB image
image( opencv.image(OpenCV.GRAY), 20+w, 10 );  // GRAY image
```

Each time the image is altered, the image in memory is updated, allowing you to stack alterations to the image. The call to `opencv.image(OpenCV.MEMORY)` accesses the image captured when the `opencv.remember()` method is called:

```
image( opencv.image(OpenCV.MEMORY), 10, 20+h ); // image in memory
```

Like in the previous oF examples, the difference of the background image and the incoming image is used to determine what pixels have changed between the two images. This is then drawn to the screen using the `image()` method:

```
opencv.absDiff();
opencv.threshold(threshold);
image( opencv.image(OpenCV.GRAY), 20+w, 20+h ); // absolute difference image
```

Here, the blobs are detected in the image:

```
Blob[] blobs = opencv.blobs( 100, w*h/3, 20, true );
noFill();
pushMatrix();
translate(20+w,20+h);
```

Now, draw all of the blobs:

```
for( int i=0; i<blobs.length; i++ ) {
```

The `rectangle` property of the `Blob` class can be used to draw a rectangle using the `rect()` method:

```
Rectangle bounding = blobs[i].rectangle;
noFill();
rect( bounding.x, bounding.y, bounding.width, bounding.height );
```

Now capture the rest of the properties of the blob:

```
float area = blobs[i].area;
float circumference = blobs[i].length;
Point centroid = blobs[i].centroid;
Point[] points = blobs[i].points;
// centroid
stroke(0,0,255);
```

Draw a small cross at the center of the blob:

```
line( centroid.x-5, centroid.y, centroid.x+5, centroid.y );
line( centroid.x, centroid.y-5, centroid.x, centroid.y+5 );
fill(255,0,255,64);
stroke(255,0,255);
```

Now, draw a simple shape to describe all the points of the blob:

```
if ( points.length>0 ) {
    beginShape();
    for( int j=0; j<points.length; j++ ) {
        vertex( points[j].x, points[j].y );
    }
    endShape(CLOSE);
}
}
```

```
        popMatrix();
    }
```

Listen for the spacebar being pressed to record a new background image:

```
void keyPressed() {
    if ( key==' ' ) opencv.remember();
}
```

Drag the mouse to change the threshold:

```
void mouseDragged() {
    threshold = int( map(mouseX,0,width,0,255) );
}

public void stop() {
    opencv.stop();
    super.stop();
}
```

Figure 14-4 shows this application running.

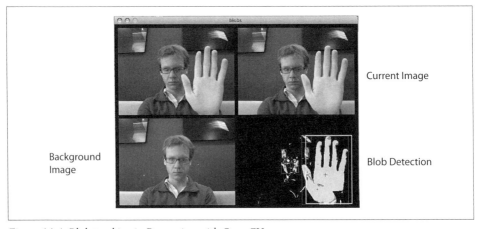

*Figure 14-4. Blob tracking in Processing with OpenCV*

The Processing application is slightly more restrictive than the oF version because of how the core Java classes of the Processing version interact with the OpenCV core, but much of the basic functionality is available for you to use. Working with OpenCV in Processing is an excellent way to get started with computer vision and tracking.

## Feature Tracking in Processing

Processing can use Haar cascade face tracking just like you've seen in the openFrameworks examples earlier in this chapter. To do face tracking in Processing, you simply call the detect() method of the OpenCV instance:

```
detect(float scale, int min_neighbors, int flags, int min_width, int min_height);
```

scale

> The factor by which the search window is scaled between the subsequent scans, for example, 1.1 means increasing the window by 10%.

min_neighbors

> Minimum number (minus 1) of neighbor rectangles that makes up an object. All the groups of a smaller number of rectangles than min_neighbors–1 are rejected. If min_neighbors is 0, the function does not do any grouping at all and returns all the detected candidate rectangles, which may be useful if the user wants to apply a customized grouping procedure.

flags

> Mode of operation. It can be a combination of zero or more of the above flags. This can be HAAR_DO_CANNY_PRUNING to use Canny edge detector to reject regions that contain too few or too many edges and help speed up the processing. HAAR_FIND_BIG GEST_OBJECT finds the largest object (if any) in the image. That is, the output sequence will contain one (or zero) element(s). HAAR_DO_ROUGH_SEARCH does not look for candidates of a smaller size as soon as it has found the object (with enough neighbor candidates) at the current scale. It yields a less accurate (a bit larger) object rectangle than the regular single-object mode (HAAR_FIND_BIGGEST_OBJECT), but it is much faster.

min_width

> Minimum window size. By default, it is set to the size of samples the classifier has been trained on (~20 × 20 for face detection):

min_height

> Minimum window size. By default, it is set to the size of samples the classifier has been trained on (~20 × 20 for face detection).

Now on to the Processing application, which is in two parts: a Processing application (see Example 14-7) and an Arduino application (see Example 14-8). The goal is to mount a camera on a pair of servos, detect a face using that camera, and rotate the camera towards the detected face so that the face is centered in the image.

*Example 14-7. cv_servos.pde*

```
import hypermedia.video.*;
import java.awt.Rectangle;
import processing.serial.*;

OpenCV opencv;

// contrast/brightness values
int contrast_value    = 0;
int brightness_value  = 0;

Serial arduinoPort;

void setup() {
```

```
    size( 320, 240 );

    opencv = new OpenCV( this );
    opencv.capture( width, height );                    // open video stream
    opencv.cascade( OpenCV.CASCADE_FRONTALFACE_ALT );
// load detection description,
here-> front face detection : "haarcascade_frontalface_alt.xml"
    arduinoPort = new Serial(this, Serial.list()[0], 9600);

}

public void stop() {
    opencv.stop();
    super.stop();
}


void draw() {

    // grab a new frame
    // and convert to gray
    opencv.read();
    opencv.convert( GRAY );
    opencv.contrast( contrast_value );
    opencv.brightness( brightness_value );

    // proceed detection
    Rectangle[] faces = opencv.detect( 1.2, 2, OpenCV.HAAR_DO_CANNY_PRUNING, 40, 40 );

    // display the image
    image( opencv.image(), 0, 0 );

    boolean foundFace = true;

    Rectangle bestFace = new Rectangle();
    if(faces.length > 1) {

      for(int i = 0; i < faces.length; i++) {
        if( (faces[i].height * faces[i].width)  > (bestFace.height * bestFace.width)) {
          bestFace = faces[i];
        }
      }
    } else if(faces.length > 0) {
      bestFace = faces[0];
    } else {
      foundFace = false;
    }

    // draw face area(s)
    if(foundFace)
    {
      noFill();
      stroke(255,0,0);
      for( int i=0; i<faces.length; i++ ) {
          rect( bestFace.x, bestFace.y, bestFace.width, bestFace.height );
```

```
        }

        arduinoPort.write( bestFace.x + (bestFace.width/2) / width * 255 );
        arduinoPort.write( bestFace.y + (bestFace.width/2) / height * 255);
    }

}

void mouseDragged() {
    contrast_value   = (int) map( mouseX, 0, width, -128, 128 );
    brightness_value = (int) map( mouseY, 0, width, -128, 128 );
}
```

Now, we'll move on to moving the servo motors around using Arduino. The best way to link the two servos together is using the Lynx pan and tilt kit, shown in Figure 14-5.

*Figure 14-5. The Lynx pan and tilt kit*

Connecting the two servos to the Arduino once you've connected them to each other is trivial. See Figure 14-6.

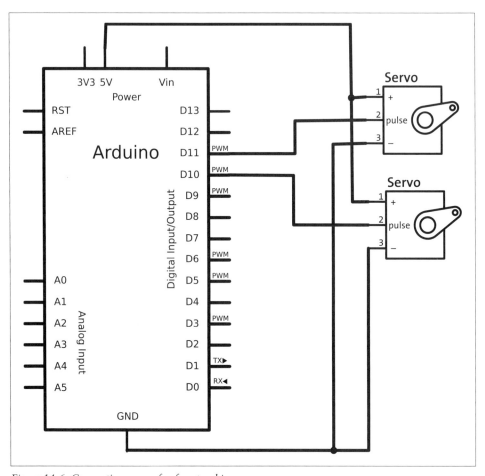

Figure 14-6. Connecting servos for face tracking

The application is quite simple except that instead of jumping to the detected face, it uses linear interpolation (often called "lerping") to move towards the detected face:

Example 14-8. cv_servos_p.ino

```
#define DSERVO_TWO_X_PIN 11
#define DSERVO_TWO_Y_PIN 10

#include <Servo.h>

const float ratio = 0.7058; // 180 / 255

Servo vert;
Servo horz;
byte target[2];
byte current[2];
```

```
void setup() {
  horz.attach(DSERVO_TWO_X_PIN );
  vert.attach(DSERVO_TWO_Y_PIN );

  memset(target, 0, 2);
  memset(current, 0, 2);

  Serial.begin(9600);

}

void loop() {

  // if we've gotten new positions store them
  if(Serial.available() > 1) {
    target[0] = Serial.read();
    target[1] = Serial.read();
  }

  // if our x position needs to be updated lerp to it
  if(abs(target[0] - current[0]) > 1) {
    // now that we have the xy we can go ahead
    // and write them to the serial
    horz.write(target[0] * ratio);
  }

  // if our x position needs to be updated lerp to it
  if(abs(target[1] - current[1]) > 1) {
    // now that we have the xy we can go ahead
    // and write them to the serial
    horz.write((0.5, target[1], current[1]) * ratio);
  }
}

byte lerp(float t, byte a, byte b)
{
  return a + t * (b - a);
}
```

Now you have a face tracking application that continues to track faces within a hemi-spherical region of a room.

# Using Blob Tracking with Physics

One of the most popular and powerful physics engines around today is Box2D, which is used to do two-dimensional gravity and physics. See Example 14-9.

*Example 14-9. boxCV.h*

```
#pragma once

#include "ofMain.h"
```

```
#include "ofxOpenCv.h"
#include "ofxBox2d.h"

class boxCV : public ofBaseApp{

public:

    void setup();
    void update();
    void draw();

    void keyPressed(int key);
    void mouseDragged(int x, int y, int button);
    void mousePressed(int x, int y, int button);

    ofVideoGrabber          vidGrabber;
    ofxCvColorImage              colorImg;
    ofxCvGrayscaleImage       grayImage;
    ofxCvGrayscaleImage       grayBg;
    ofxCvGrayscaleImage       grayDiff;
    ofxCvContourFinder      contourFinder;

    ofxBox2dPolygon             *bodyShape;
    ofxBox2d                 box2d;

    vector<ofxBox2dCircle> circles;
    int waterfallLEdge, waterfallREdge;
    float radius;

    bool debugging, contours;
    bool bLearnBakground;

    int        threshold;
    float    amount;

    void checkBlobs();


};
```

The `boxCV` application creates the `ofxBox2dPolygon` shape from the detected blob from OpenCV and then drops circles onto the image to create an outline. At present, the `ofxBox2dPolygon` shape is drawn very simply but could be made into different shapes. See Example 14-10.

*Example 14-10. boxCV.cpp*

```
#include "boxCV.h"

void boxCV::setup(){

    vidGrabber.setVerbose(true);
    vidGrabber.initGrabber(320,240);

    colorImg.allocate(320,240);
```

```
grayImage.allocate(320,240);
grayBg.allocate(320,240);
grayDiff.allocate(320,240);

ofSetVerticalSync(true);

box2d.init();
box2d.setGravity(0, 10);
box2d.setFPS(30.0);

bodyShape = NULL;

bLearnBakground = true;
threshold = 80;

debugging = false;
contours = false;
}

void boxCV::update()
{
    ofBackground(100,100,100);
    float height = ofGetHeight();
```

Look through all the circles, and if they're off screen, erase them. If we need more circles, create them and place them at the top of the screen. The call to ofxBox2dCir cle setPhysics() sets the density, bounce, and friction that the Box2D engine will calculate for each ball:

```
vector<ofxBox2dCircle>::iterator cit = circles.begin();
while( cit != circles.end())
{
    if(cit->getPosition().y > height + 100) {
        circles.erase(cit);
    }
    ++cit;
}

if( circles.size() < 50 ) { // > 100 on screen
    ofxBox2dCircle circle;
    circle.setPhysics(1, 0.5, 0.1);
    float pos = ofRandom(1000) + 10;
    circle.setup(box2d.getWorld(), pos, -100, 10);
    circles.push_back(circle); // add a new one
}
```

To update the Box2D engine, you need to call update() each time your application calls update():

```
box2d.update();

vidGrabber.grabFrame();
bool newFrame = vidGrabber.isFrameNew();

if (newFrame){
```

```
        colorImg.setFromPixels(vidGrabber.getPixels(), 320, 240);
        colorImg.mirror(false, true);

        grayImage = colorImg;
        if (bLearnBakground == true){
            grayBg = grayImage;       // the = sign copys the pixels from grayImage
into grayBg (operator overloading)
            bLearnBakground = false;
        }
        grayDiff.absDiff(grayBg, grayImage);
        grayDiff.threshold(threshold);
        contourFinder.findContours(grayDiff, 20, (340*240)/3, 10, true); // find holes
    }

    checkBlobs();
}
```

The drawing is not particularly complex; we simply need to draw each circle and then draw the bodyShape outline. Since ofxBox2dPolygon extends ofPolyLine, it's quite easy to draw the simple outline of the shape; but in this case, it's nice to add circles at each vertex to make the shape a little more easily visible:

```
void boxCV::draw(){

    ofSetColor(255, 255, 255);
    ofFill();

    vector<ofxBox2dCircle>::iterator cit = circles.begin();
    while( cit != circles.end()) {
        ofCircle(cit->getPosition().x, cit->getPosition().y, 10);
        ++cit;
    }

    ofSetColor(0, 0, 255);

    vector<ofxCvBlob>::iterator c_it = contourFinder.blobs.begin();
    if(contours) {
        while(c_it != contourFinder.blobs.end() ) {
            c_it->draw();
            ++c_it;
        }
    }

    if(bodyShape != NULL) {
        bodyShape->draw();

        ofSetColor(0, 0, 255);
        ofFill();
        vector <ofPoint>::iterator pit = bodyShape->getVertices().begin();
        while(pit != bodyShape->getVertices().end() )
        {
            ofCircle(pit->x, pit->y, 5);
            ++pit;
        }
    }
```

```
        }
}
```

Find any blobs in the image and if there is more than one blob, find the largest one and use it as the way to generate the Box2D shape:

```
void boxCV::checkBlobs()
{

    contourFinder.findContours(grayDiff, 120,
(grayDiff.getWidth()*grayDiff.getHeight())/2,
5, false); // no holes

    if(contourFinder.blobs.size() < 1) return;

    vector<ofxCvBlob>::iterator c_it = contourFinder.blobs.begin();
    ofxCvBlob largest = contourFinder.blobs[0];

    while(c_it != contourFinder.blobs.end() ) {
        if(c_it->area > largest.area) largest = *c_it;
        ++c_it;
    }

    if(!debugging)
    {
        if(bodyShape) {
            bodyShape->destroy();
            delete bodyShape;
        }

        bodyShape = new ofxBox2dPolygon();
        ofVec2f scaleUp(ofGetWidth()/320, ofGetHeight()/240);

        vector <ofPoint>::iterator pit = largest.pts.begin();
        while(pit != largest.pts.end() )
        {
            // triangulatePolygonWithOutline(resampled, outline);??
            bodyShape->addVertex( *pit * scaleUp );
            ++pit;
        }

        bodyShape->simplify(20);
        bodyShape->create(box2d.getWorld());
    }
}

    void boxCV::mouseDragged(int x, int y, int button){

        if(debugging) {

            if(bodyShape)
            {
                bodyShape->destroy();
                delete bodyShape;
            }
            bodyShape = new ofxBox2dPolygon();
```

```
            ofVec2f ul( x - 50.f, y-50.f);
            ofVec2f ur( x + 50.f, y-50.f);
            ofVec2f lr( x + 50.f, y+50.f);
            ofVec2f ll( x - 50.f, y+50.f);

            bodyShape->addVertex(ul);
            bodyShape->addVertex(ur);
            bodyShape->addVertex(lr);
            bodyShape->addVertex(ll);

            bodyShape->create(box2d.getWorld());

        }
    }
```

For debugging purposes, destroy the shape and use the mouse position:

```
    void boxCV::mousePressed(int x, int y, int button){

        if(debugging) {

            if(bodyShape)
            {
                bodyShape->destroy();
                delete bodyShape;
            }
            bodyShape = new ofxBox2dPolygon();

            ofVec2f ul( x - 50.f, y-50.f);
            ofVec2f ur( x + 50.f, y-50.f);
            ofVec2f lr( x + 50.f, y+50.f);
            ofVec2f ll( x - 50.f, y+50.f);

            bodyShape->addVertex(ul);
            bodyShape->addVertex(ur);
            bodyShape->addVertex(lr);
            bodyShape->addVertex(ll);

            bodyShape->create(box2d.getWorld());

        }
    }

    void boxCV::keyPressed(int key){

        switch (key){
            case ' ':
                bLearnBakground = true;
                break;
            case '+':
                threshold ++;
                if (threshold > 255) threshold = 255;
                break;
            case '-':
                threshold --;
```

```
            if (threshold < 0) threshold = 0;
            break;
        case 'd':
            debugging = !debugging;
            break;
        case 'c':
            contours = !contours;
            break;
    }
}
```

# Exploring Further in OpenCV

There are many other topics that you can explore in OpenCV that there isn't space in
this chapter to explain and explore properly. These techniques are all used frequently
and you can find more information on using them in Gary Bradski's *OpenCV*, in the
OpenCV documentation, or on the oF forums at *openframeworks.cc/forums*.

*Line fitting*
> Line fitting is the process of examining an image to see whether it fits a certain line.
> A series of points can be "fitted" by examining the series and finding an equation
> that creates a line that fits those points. This is rather complex mathematically, but
> it has some very practical applications. For instance, using the change in the rate
> of change around a contour, you can determine whether a blob has a finger con-
> tained within it. Several examples are available on the oF forums that use this
> technique to find and track hands or fingers in a video feed.

*Convex hulls*
> A convex hull is an object detection technique that attempts to determine the
> boundaries of an object given a set of points, using an algorithm to determine the
> shortest distance between different points. Figure 14-7 shows an example.
>
> Convex hulls are very useful for creating collision detection, For instance, you can
> use a convex hull to determine whether a virtual object has collided with an object
> detected in an image or a video. You can find examples of creating and using a
> convex hull in OpenCV on the oF forums.

*Optical flow*
> Optical flow or optic flow is the pattern of apparent motion of objects, surfaces,
> and edges in a visual scene caused by the relative motion. It works by reading the
> apparent motion of brightness patterns in the image. Generally, optical flow cor-
> responds to the motion field, but not always, as shown in Figure 14-8.
>
> Usually apparent motion matches actual motion, which can be helpful for detecting
> motion where you don't need to track blobs but simply want to detect movement.
> For instance, many reactive installations merely want to react to the general move-
> ment in front of the camera, not track blobs. See Figure 14-8.

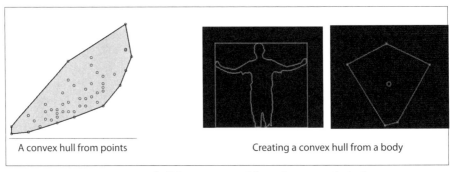

A convex hull from points          Creating a convex hull from a body

*Figure 14-7. Creating a convex hull from points and from the image of a body*

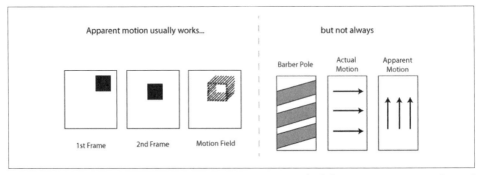

*Figure 14-8. Detecting movement using apparent motion; on the left, apparent motion is detected correctly, while on the right, you can see how apparent motion might not match actual motion*

## Detecting Gestures

You might have used a pen-driven interface at some point, and if you have, then you're probably familiar with how it detects what character you're trying to write when you input text. The characters are similar to the ones normally used but are simplified to reduce ambiguity for the program processing them. You might also be familiar with some other more complex gestures from other devices. Those sorts of gestures are best done with a single point of input, like a pen or a single finger, but they can be done with multiple points of input, though this is substantially more difficult. Often, gestures aren't the best and easiest ways to get user input. In the case of writing, it's far less efficient than typing on a keyboard. In some cases, though, they're extremely effective and efficient ways for a user to input a simple command, like clearing a grouping of photos, selecting an object or an area of an object, and doing some kinds of sign language recognition. The simplest way to detect gestures is by using a controller to act as an extension of the body so that the motion can be captured by software. Both mouse gestures and the Wii Remote work very well as gesture controllers. In this chapter, we'll look at using the mouse for gesture detection so that you can easily examine the fundamentals of gesture detection.

Another object that works well for 2D gesture detection is a camera, as long as the environment is appropriate for using computer vision. An appropriate environment is bright and clear enough and has sufficient differentiation between the object of interest and the background. The object of interest can be a pen, a hand, or the user themselves.

To understand how gesture recognition is done, think about the gesture itself: a movement in a particular direction and with a certain pattern. Thinking about this in the way that a computational system could understand it, it would be a map of $x$, $y$, and possibly $z$ points across a surface. This map is called a *gesture map*. These gesture maps are made by recording the vector of a movement to compare to all the gesture maps that the engine recognizes. Commonly, gesture recognition engines contain different algorithms to compare sets of movements to the gestures that they contain. One of the challenges of working with gestures is determining whether a gesture is complete. In the following examples, since the mouse is used as the gesturing instrument, the mouse button indicates the start and end of the gesture. In the case of a camera-based gesture, entering and leaving an area can indicate the beginning and end of a gesture, as can simply holding the tracked object still for a predetermined length of time.

## Using ezGestures in Processing

One way to use gestures in a Processing application is to use ezGestures, a gesture recognition library. It analyzes mouse or Wiimote movements that you make while dragging the mouse or while holding the A button of the Wiimote down. Then it compares the motion against a gesture map that you've created for all the gestures in which your application should be interested. It's an excellent way to experiment and prototype gestural applications. The library understands four directions: UP, DOWN, LEFT, and RIGHT. Using these simple directions, the application can recognize, for instance, the difference between a circle and an *L* shape, or the difference between clockwise or counterclockwise gestures. It can't, however, tell the difference between a square and a circle or recognize diagonal gestures, and it doesn't pay attention to how large an area is being covered, among other things.

There are two types of GestureListeners used in the ezGestures library. In the first type, *concurrent* listeners try to match the gesture to the pattern while the gesture is still being performed. This means that a gesture can be recognized and acted upon before the button is released. The second type starts with *Post*; for instance, PostVShakeListener tries to match the gesture to the pattern after the gesture is complete, which means after the button is released. This is how the following example works.

One thing to understand about the gesture detection library is that it uses a *regular expression* to determine what gesture is being drawn. A regular expression is really just a way of making a pattern of letters. While they can be extremely complex and difficult to read, they can be powerful tools. You don't need to understand too much about how they work to use the gesture detection library. You'll see a few strange symbols at the beginning of the string that is passed to the PostGestureListener constructor method;

for instance, a circle is described as LDRU, or left, down, right, up. To make sure that any and all circles are found in the messages that are sent to the PostGestureListener method, you'd use the caret (^) to indicate that anything can come before the circle gesture, and the dollar sign ($), which is the last thing in the string passed to the PostGestureListener. Here is an example of creating a gesture listener that listens for a circle gesture:

```
PostGestureListener pgl = new PostGestureListener(this, brain, "^(LDRU)$");
```

For each gesture that you want to listen for, you'll need to create a new PostGesture Listener object that will have the string that represents the gesture passed to it in the constructor for that object.

*Example 14-11. gesturalyze.pde*

```
import net.silentlycrashing.gestures.*;

GestureAnalyzer brain;
PostGestureListener boxListener;


void setup() {
    // initialize the gesture listeners
    size(500, 500);

    brain = new MouseGestureAnalyzer(this);
    brain.setVerbose(true);
    boxListener = new PostGestureListener(this, brain, "^(RDLU)$");
    boxListener.registerOnAction("drawBox", this);
}

void draw() {
    line(pmouseX, pmouseY, mouseX, mouseY);
}

void drawBox() {
    rect(mouseX, mouseY, 200, 200);
}
```

The previous example used PostGestureListener, but there are four other classes that use concurrent gesture recognition:

ConcurrentHShakeListener
    Listens for a horizontal shake while the movement is being made.

ConcurrentVShakeListener
    Listens for a vertical shake while the movement is being made.

PostHShakeListener
    Listens for a horizontal shake after the movement is made.

PostVShakeListener
    Listens for a vertical shake after the movement is made.

In the following very simple example, the listeners will listen concurrently; that is, they won't wait for the gesture to finish. Instead, they'll simply call their action method whenever the gesture being listened for is heard. ConcurrentHShakeListener just listens for a horizontal sweep back and forth, or in ezGestures terms, RLRL or LRLR. In this simple application, drawing the square gesture creates a new 3D box using the box() method, and the horizontal shake clears all the boxes.

*Example 14-12. gesturalyze2.pde*

```
import net.silentlycrashing.gestures.*;
import net.silentlycrashing.gestures.preset.*;

GestureAnalyzer brain;
ConcurrentGestureListener boxListener;
ConcurrentHShakeListener shakeListener;

int numBoxes = 0;
SimplePoint[] boxes;

void setup() {
    // initialize the gesture listeners
    size(500, 500, P3D);
    lights();

  boxes = new SimplePoint[100];
```

As before, the MouseGestureAnalyzer is created and passed a reference to the application itself:

```
        brain = new MouseGestureAnalyzer(this);
        brain.setVerbose(true);
```

ConcurrentGestureListener is initialized and given the box string as its gesture to listen for:

```
        boxListener = new ConcurrentGestureListener(this, brain, "(RDLU)$");
        boxListener.registerOnAction("createBox", this);
```

ConcurrentHShakeListener is created and passed a reference to the MouseGestureAnalyzer instance. Since the gesture that it's listening for, the horizontal shake, is already programmed, there's no need to pass it another string to use as its gesture:

```
        shakeListener = new ConcurrentHShakeListener(this, brain);
        shakeListener.registerOnAction("shakeHeard", this);
}

    void draw() {
        background(122);
        int i;
```

Using the camera() method as in Chapter 13, the camera is positioned based on the user's mouse position. This could, of course, be the relative position of a Wiimote or another kind of accelerometer connected to the computer via an Arduino:

```
camera(0.0, mouseY, 0, // eyeX, eyeY, eyeZ
       width/2, height/2, 0.0, // centerX, centerY, centerZ
       0.0, 1.0, 0.0); // upX, upY, upZ
```

Here, the `translate()` method sets the location where the box will be drawn, and the s property of the `SimplePoint` is used to determine the size of the box:

```
for( i = 0; i<numBoxes; i++) {
    pushMatrix();
        translate(width/2 - 100, height/2 - 100, 0);
        translate(boxes[i].x, boxes[i].y, boxes[i].z);
        box(boxes[i].s);
    popMatrix();
    }
}

void createBox() {
    SimplePoint p = new SimplePoint();
    p.x = random(100);
    p.y = random(100);
    p.z = random(50);
    p.s = random(40);
    boxes[numBoxes] = p;
    numBoxes++;
}
```

When the horizontal shake gesture is heard, all the boxes will be cleared from the screen:

```
void shakeHeard() {
    println(" shaken ");
    numBoxes = 0;
}
```

This is a simple class to store the data about where the box should be drawn:

```
class SimplePoint {
    float x;
    float y;
    float s;
    float z;
}
```

One of the great advantages of the ezGestures library is that it works well with the Wiimote remote control. To help you work with the Wiimote, the ezGestures library has several different listeners that listen for buttons and actions specific to the Wiimote.

## Using Gestures in oF

One of the most robust gesture recognizers out there is called the $1 Unistroke Gesture recognizer, developed at the University of Washington. It was wrapped into an oF add-on by Diedrick Hubers into an add-on called `ofxOneDollar`. The gesture recognizer works by allowing you to create a gesture, add it to the recognizable gestures, and then checking any new gesture against all the stored ones and get the score of that gesture. The highest scoring gesture is the most likely match.

The matching is done with the match function, which requires a pointer to an ofxGesture instance and returns a pointer to the best match:

```
ofxGesture* match(ofxGesture* pGesture, double* pScore)
```

You can create gestures using the ofPolyline class as shown in Example 14-13.

*Example 14-13. gestureRec.h*

```
#pragma once
#include "ofMain.h"
#include "ofxOneDollar.h"

enum action{ SAVE, LOAD, MAKE, FIND, CLEAR };

class gestureRec : public ofBaseApp {

    public:

    void setup();
    void update();
    void draw();
    void keyPressed  (int key);
    void mouseDragged(int x, int y, int button);
    void showMessage(string sMessage, int nDelay);
    void showMessage(string sMessage);

    void createNewGesture();

    ofPolyline line;
    ofPolyline found_gesture;
```

Here's the gesture recognizer instance and the ofxGesture* that will store the newly created gesture and the best match returned from the ofxOneDollar instance:

```
    ofxOneDollar dollar;
    ofxGesture* gesture;

    int num_created_gestures;

    int mode;
    action command;
    string message;
    int hide_message_on;
};
```

When the user draws by dragging the mouse, the line they create is stored in the line ofPolyline. Once they're finished drawing, they can add the gesture to the recognizer or compare their line to all existing gestures. See Example 14-14.

*Example 14-14. gestureRec.cpp*

```cpp
#include "gestureRec.h"

void gestureRec::setup(){
    num_created_gestures = 0;
    ofBackground(0,0,0);
    createNewGesture();

    mode = 0;
}

void gestureRec::update(){
    if(mode == 1 && ofGetElapsedTimeMillis() >= hide_message_on) {
        mode = 0;
        found_gesture.clear();
    }
}

void gestureRec::draw(){

    if(mode == 0) {
        ofSetColor(255, 255, 0);
        line.draw();
    } else if (mode == 1) {
        ofSetColor(255, 0, 140);
        ofDrawBitmapString(message, 10, ofGetHeight()-40);
    }

    ofSetColor(0, 255, 140);
    found_gesture.draw();

    ofColor(255, 255, 0.0f);
    ofDrawBitmapString("Number of gestures: " +ofToString(dollar.gestures.size()), 10,
ofGetHeight()-25);
    ofDrawBitmapString("Name of current gesture: " +gesture->name, 10, ofGetHeight()-10);
}

void gestureRec::mouseDragged(int x, int y, int button){
    if(mode == 0) {
        line.addVertex(ofVec2f(x,y));
    }
}

void gestureRec::showMessage(string sMessage) {
    message = sMessage;
    mode = 1;
    hide_message_on = ofGetElapsedTimeMillis()+1000;
}

void gestureRec::showMessage(string sMessage, int nDelay) {
    message = sMessage;
    mode = 1;
    hide_message_on = ofGetElapsedTimeMillis() + nDelay;
}
```

```
void gestureRec::createNewGesture() {
    ++num_created_gestures;
    gesture = new ofxGesture();
    gesture->setName("Gesture#" +ofToString(num_created_gestures));
}
```

Here's where the bulk of the interesting code resides. Note the calls to addGesture(), save(), and match():

```
void gestureRec::keyPressed( int key ) {

    switch(key) {
        case 'c':
            line.clear();
            break;
        case 'm':
            // Add all the point we've just drawn to the gesture.
            gesture->reset();
            for(int i = 0; i < line.size(); ++i) {
                gesture->addPoint(line[i].x, line[i].y);
            }

            if(gesture->points.size() <= 10) {
                message = "Please add a line first";
            }
            else {
                dollar.addGesture(gesture);
                message = "Added gesture to recognizer";
                line.clear();
                createNewGesture();
            }
            showMessage(message, 800);
            line.clear();
            break;
        case 's':
            dollar.save(ofToDataPath("gestures.txt",true));
            showMessage("Saved!");
            break;
        case 'l':
            dollar.load(ofToDataPath("gestures.txt",true));
            showMessage("Loaded!",4000);
            break;
        case 'f':
            // find the gesture which matches the current line.
            ofxGesture* tmp = new ofxGesture();
            for(int i = 0; i < line.size(); ++i) {
                tmp->addPoint(line[i].x, line[i].y);
            }
            line.clear();
            double score = 0.0;
```

The score returned indicates how confident the gesture detection is. Note that the detection returns a pointer, so you'll need to make sure that you're storing the result in a pointer:

```
            ofxGesture* match = dollar.match(tmp, &score);
            string result = "Matching score: " +ofToString(score);
            if(match != NULL) {
                result +=", which matches with gesture: " +match->name;
                found_gesture.clear();
                float dx = ofGetWidth()/2;
                float dy = ofGetHeight()/2;
                for(int i = 0; i < match->resampled_points.size(); ++i) {
                    found_gesture.addVertex(ofVec2f(dx+match->resampled_points[i].x,
dy+match->resampled_points[i].y));
                }
            }
            showMessage(result, 1500);
            delete tmp;
            break;
        }
    }
```

Next we'll look at a way of tracking the operating system-specific gestures on an iPhone using openFrameworks.

# Capturing iOS gestures with oF

One of the most powerful features of oF is the ability to build and deploy iPhone applications with more or less the same code that you use in a desktop application. Very few toolkits provide such compatibility and it's a real advantage of working with oF. There isn't space to dig too deeply into iPhone-specific functionality, but I do want to highlight how you add listeners for the base iOS gestures like the pinch, swipe, or double-tap. First, you need to make an event argument type that will be used to send the event from the system listener to the oF application. See Example 14-15.

*Example 14-15. ofPinchEvent.h*

```
#pragma once

#include "ofMain.h"

class ofPinchEventArgs : ofEventArgs {

public:
    ofPinchEventArgs(float sc, float vel):scale(sc), velocity(vel) {
    }

    float scale;
    float velocity;
};
```

Next, create a recognizer that will be able to hear the system event and send it your oF application, as shown in Example 14-16.

*Example 14-16. ofPinchGestureRecognizer.h*

```
#import <Foundation/Foundation.h>
#include "ofPinchEvent.h"
#include "ofMain.h"

ofEvent<ofPinchEventArgs> ofPinchEvent;

@interface ofPinchGestureRecognizer : NSObject {

    UIPinchGestureRecognizer *pinchGestureRecognizer;
}

-(id)initWithView:(UIView*)view;
- (void)handleGesture:(UIPinchGestureRecognizer *)gestureRecognizer;

@end
```

The *.m* file (the Objective C equivalent of the *.cpp* file) is the actual implementation of the ofPinchGestureRecognizer class and contains the call to ofNotifyEvent(), which will send the event to any listener. See Example 14-17.

*Example 14-17. ofPinchGestureRecognizer.mm*

```
#import "ofPinchGestureRecognizer.h"

@implementation ofPinchGestureRecognizer

-(id)initWithView:(UIView*)view{
    if((self = [super init])){
        pinchGestureRecognizer = [[UIPinchGestureRecognizer alloc]
initWithTarget:self
action:@selector(handleGesture:)];
        [view addGestureRecognizer:pinchGestureRecognizer];
    }
    return self;
}

-(void)handleGesture:(UIPinchGestureRecognizer *) gestureRecognizer{
    if([gestureRecognizer state] == UIGestureRecognizerStateRecognized){
        NSLog(@"pinches!");
        ofPinchEventArgs p([gestureRecognizer scale], [gestureRecognizer velocity]);
        ofNotifyEvent(ofPinchEvent, p);
    }
}

-(void)dealloc{
    [pinchGestureRecognizer release];
    [super dealloc];
}
@end
```

In your oF application, add the recognizer and the event type as shown in Example 14-18.

*Example 14-18. pinchApp.h*

```
#pragma once

#include "ofMain.h"
#include "ofxiPhone.h"
#include "ofxiPhoneExtras.h"
#include "ofMain.h"

#include "ofPinchGestureRecognizer.h"
#include "ofPinchEvent.h"

class pinchApp: public ofxiPhoneApp{

    public:

        void setup();
        void update();
        void draw();

        void touchDown(ofTouchEventArgs &touch);
        void touchMoved(ofTouchEventArgs &touch);
        void touchUp(ofTouchEventArgs &touch);
        void touchDoubleTap(ofTouchEventArgs &touch);
        void touchCancelled(ofTouchEventArgs &touch);

    ofPinchGestureRecognizer *pincher;
    void handlePinch(ofPinchEventArgs &e);

    ofEvent<ofPinchEventArgs> ofPinchEvent;
};
```

Now, in the setup() method of your application, use the ofAddListener() to add a listener. This method takes the event being listened for, what object will handle the event (in this case the application itself) and what method should be called. Note that the reference to the method is being called using its fully qualified name (i.e., pinchApp::handlePinch, rather than just handlePinch). See Example 14-19.

*Example 14-19. pinchApp.cpp*

```
void pincApp::setup(){

    // register touch events
    ofxRegisterMultitouch(this);

    //iPhoneAlerts will be sent to this.
    ofxiPhoneAlerts.addListener(this);

    ofxiPhoneSetOrientation(OFXIPHONE_ORIENTATION_LANDSCAPE_RIGHT);

    ofBackground(255,255,255);

    EAGLView *view = ofxiPhoneGetGLView();
    pincher = [[ofPinchGestureRecognizer alloc] initWithView:view];
```

```
        ofAddListener(ofPinchEvent, this, &testApp::handlePinch);
}
```

Since an `ofPinchEventArgs` object will be passed to the `handlePinch()` method, you can use the properties of it there to determine how you want to react to it:

```
        void pinchApp handlePinch(ofPinchEventArgs &e) {
            cout << " got a pinch " << e.velocity << " " << e.scale << endl;
        }
```

# Touch with oF

In 2007, the touch device was one of the most revolutionary concepts in interface design. Two years later, it has become remarkably commonplace for phones, computer screens, and interactive walls. Touchscreens have gone from being simple interfaces that allowed simple dragging, to being complex user interface tools where users can enter text, draw, and perform many tasks with both hands that could previously be done only with a single mouse. There isn't sufficient space in this book to cover the design and implementation of any of the touch devices, tools, or libraries that have been developed to help you in creating touch applications, but, as with so many things in this book, we'll take a look at some of the projects that use similar techniques or tools as discussed in this chapter.

## Tuio

Tuio is a protocol for tabletop tangible user interfaces that helps provide a common way to describe events. It's used in a few different existing table interfaces, like the reacTable, developed in Barcelona, and the tDesk, developed in Germany. It defines information about objects on a table surface, such as finger and hand gestures performed by the user, or the movement of controller objects with fiducial markers like those shown in Figure 14-9.

*Figure 14-9. Fiducial markers that can be tracked across a table and used as controls by a user*

The Tuio protocol is implemented using the Open Sound Control (OSC) that was discussed in Chapter 12, and is usable on any platform supporting this protocol. There is an ofx Tuio add-on available for oF that lets a table interact with an oF application. The Tuio library can be used with the Touchlib library for Processing or oF as well.

You might want to look into some of the development efforts around the Tuio implementation if you're interested in developing your own touchscreen devices.

## reacTIVision

reacTIVision is another open source computer vision framework. It can be used for tracking fiducial markers and for multitouch finger tracking in table-based tangible user interfaces (TUIs) and multitouch interactive surfaces. It is being developed by Martin Kaltenbrunner and Ross Bencina at the Music Technology Group at the Universitat Pompeu Fabra in Barcelona, Spain, as part of the reacTable project. reacTable is a novel electronic music instrument based using a tabletop multitouch tangible user interface. Martin Kaltenbrunner has created a library for working with reacTIVision that can be used for creating touchscreen applications using Processing.

## CCV

Community Core Vision, CCV for short, is an open source and cross-platform solution for computer vision and machine sensing. It uses a video input stream and outputs coordinates, blob size, and finger events that are used in building multi touch applications. CCV can interface with a large number of web cameras and video devices, as well as connecting to various TUIO, OSC, or XML enabled applications. It also supports multi touch lighting techniques, including: FTIR, DI, DSI, and LLP. Check out *http://ccv.nuigroup.com/* for more information.

## What's Next

If you're really interested in using OpenCV, a great book to check out is *Learning OpenCV* by Gary Bradski (one of the creators of OpenCV) and Adrian Kaehler (O'Reilly). It'll teach you a great deal about how to use OpenCV to its fullest potential, which is something that this chapter has barely begun to do. The OpenCV manual, while not light reading, is available online as well as a free PDF download.

A number of online resources are available for people interested in working with computer vision and gesture tracking online; the oF forums are a particularly active place to get advice and ideas. The OpenCV project has its own mailing list and forum that might be an excellent resource for any one looking to troubleshoot a problem or come up with an idea for how a certain image could be processed. A great number of courses that use the OpenCV library or other image and motion processing libraries have materials online that you'll be able to peruse.

The ARToolKit, developed at the University of Washington, is a library for developing augmented reality applications. *Augmented reality* (AR) is the process of placing computer graphics images onto live feeds from a camera, and is a very interesting way of approaching creating an interactive application, since a representation of the world can be interwoven with computer-synthesized images (see Figure 14-10).

*Figure 14-10. Some examples of ARToolKit in use*

AR has been used in video tracking applications, children's books, magic tricks, industrial applications, and many other areas. There are efforts underway to develop add-ons for oF that use the ARToolKit, and currently several examples in the oF forums are available for download that show how the ARToolKit can be integrated into an oF application.

# Using the Microsoft Kinect

It would be irresponsible of me to end this chapter without mentioning the Kinect, one of the most popular and powerful vision devices ever released. You can connect a Kinect to both an oF application using the `ofxKinect` add-on, or to a Processing application using the Kinect library for Processing created by Daniel Shiffman. Both of these are extremely powerful ways to get the imaging and depth data from the Kinect into your application.

There is another way of using the Kinect that utilizes a library called OpenNI. OpenNI is actually a not-for-profit organization formed to certify and promote the compatibility and interoperability of Natural Interaction devices, applications, and middleware. Their Kinect interface allows for hand tracking, gesture tracking, multiple user tracking, notifications when certain poses are met, and a wealth of other options for working with the Kinect in both Processing and openFrameworks. Most of this is overkill if you want to just do depth mapping or work directly with the point or pixels that are returned from the Kinect, but it's a powerful tool to have.

## Processing

Getting started with the Processing version of the Kinect library, called openkinect, is quite easy and is well documented. As of the writing of this book, it provides examples for generating a point cloud, getting the IR and color images, and doing some simple depth testing to remove pixels that are beyond a certain point. I don't want to take space trying to duplicate the example or come up with ones that are equally as good, but I would highly recommend that if you're interested in trying out the Kinect, that you get the Processing library and run some of the basic examples.

Max Rheiner has created an openNI wrapper for the OpenNI libraries. At the moment, not all functions of OpenNI are supported; the intention is more to deliver a simple access to the functionality of this library, but it's a still a very rich and deep toolkit to play with. You can find out more about this library at *http://code.google.com/p/simple -openni/*.

## openFrameworks

On the openFrameworks side there are two ways of working with the Kinect. The first is to use the `ofxKinect` add-on that provides basic functionality for using the Kinect as a depth sensing camera and RGB color camera. The other option is to use the `ofxOpenNI` add-on to actually perform body tracking and simple pose estimation.

As of the writing of this book, the best place to find the `ofxOpenNI` wrapper is at *https: //github.com/gameoverhack/ofxOpenNI*, and the place to fetch the `ofxKinect` is currently living across a few different distributions. The best approach is probably to check the openFrameworks forums at *http://forum.openframeworks.cc/* for more information.

For more information on both the Processing and the openFrameworks libraries using the Kinect, you might want to take a look at *Making Things See* by Greg Borenstein (Make Books). It's an exciting book that covers all kinds of useful techniques for using the Kinect in creative projects.

# Review

Computer vision is the use of algorithms that help identify certain patterns in bitmap images and track those objects over multiple frames. These can be used with live video from a camera or with video that has already been captured.

Tracking usually utilizes "blobs," which are distinct areas within an image that the program identifies as being contiguous areas representing an object in the camera's field of view.

Most tracking in openFrameworks is done using the OpenCV library and engine. The OpenCV project was initiated by Gary Bradski in 1999 and is a free and open source computer vision library. It provides tools for tracking blobs, finding faces in images, and manipulating images, among other things.

To use OpenCV in openFrameworks, use the `ofxOpenCV` add-on created by Zach Lieberman and Stephan. To use OpenCV in Processing, you can use the OpenCV library created by Douglas Edric Stanley.

The `ofxOpenCV` add-on allows you to create an instance of `ofxContourFinder` to detect contours in an image passed to the plug-in. This class has a `findContours()` method that can be passed a grayscale image to detect contours, as well as parameters to determine the maximum and minimum size of blobs, and the number of blobs that the contour finder should look for in the image.

Face detection can be done in OpenCV by using a Haar Classifier XML file that is loaded into the application at runtime. The example shown in this chapter uses a Haar file that has been set up to recognize faces that are looking directly at the camera. Other files are available for full body tracking or tracking the sides of faces. Haar files can also be trained to find many other types of shapes as well.

The Box2D engine is a powerful tool for modeling collisions and gravity on simple and complex objects.

To use OpenCV in Processing, create an instance of the OpenCV object in your application, and call its `capture()` method in the `setup()` method of your application. In the `draw()` method of your application, call the `read()` method of the OpenCV object.

Blob detection using OpenCV in Processing is done using the `blobs()` method of the OpenCV library.

Gesture recognition is the process of checking the movement of an object, either the mouse or a finger gesture. Gesture recognition in Processing can be done using the ezGestures library. In oF, this can be done using the `ofxSimpleGesture` library.

The `ofxOneDollar` allows you to utilize the $1 Gesture Recognizer algorithm in a simple wrapper. You can add and remove gestures using `ofPolyline` instances.

If you're working with the iPhone version of openFrameworks, you can create extra Objective C classes to catch the iOS events, like the Pinch, Double Tap, or Swipe gestures. You can dispatch events using the `ofNotifyEvent()` method and receive them using the `ofReceiveEvent()` method.

Tuio is protocol designed by Martin Kaltenbrunner that helps describe common properties of controller objects on the table surface, as well as finger and hand gestures performed by the user. For instance, the number of objects on a table, the movement of touches, rotation, and gestures can all be communicated between applications using Tuio.

# CHAPTER 15

# Movement and Location

Throughout this book we've examined the types of data that users can generate and ways to use that data to help users perform certain tasks. In this chapter, we'll look at using movement and location as a dataset, creating what are often called *locative applications*, that is, applications that are location aware.

One way of doing this is by using GPS data. GPS stands for Global Positioning System, and it relies on a system of satellites to provide triangulated data about the location of a GPS device at a given time. Another way of doing this is through an Internet connection. The GPS devices that you'll be learning about in this chapter are quite small, some no more than 2 inches square. This makes them appropriate for projects and devices that need to be embedded within another object or that need to be extremely small. There are other ways of getting location information than just using GPS. If a computer or browser-enabled device such as a mobile phone is connected to the Internet, we can determine with some reasonable accuracy the location of the computer. This becomes an easy way to work with the tools that a user already has and is familiar with.

## Using Movement As and In Interaction

Our location is information—what does determining where someone is tell you?

We can look at how to use movement and location in interaction in two fundamental ways. The first is the notion of knowing where someone is. The ability to determine users' positions allows you to retrieve information relevant to their current locations. The weather is one easy piece of data that you can use once you know a user's general location. If you know more precise information, such as the actual location with a few hundred meters of accuracy, you can begin to provide many different kinds of information. Mobile device applications use location information to send relevant information about that particular location: public transport options for commuters, shops, and sites of historical significance for self-guided GPS tours are just some of the possibilities. However, these require a high degree of accuracy that isn't always possible, though you can use certain libraries to get exact location information. We'll discuss these later in this chapter. At their core, these sorts of applications use a user's location as a parameter for determining what data to retrieve.

Another very interesting genre of interactive applications that uses much the same idea, though in a much different paradigm, is location-based gaming. These types of applications use the users' positions to create positions in a game world that in some way or another mirrors the actual world. Thinking about movement for a moment, it inherently lends itself to games and to play, such as with races, games of movement, capture the flag, and tag. This is another theme that we've looked at again and again in this book: leveraging existing experiences and situations from life to create interactions that are intuitive and immediately understandable for the user. Locative and geolocative games also easily allow for very social game play that provides many different sorts of experiences than those games that orient the user toward a screen or console.

Locative gaming has a rich and long history. One of the earliest locative games, Bot-Fighters, was released in 2000 in Sweden. It was a mobile game developed by It's Alive! It was revolutionary in mobile gaming for taking advantage of location-based services as a key element in the game play. This is a mode of game play that is just beginning to be fully explored, both in terms of the geographical potential and in terms of the social interactions, the kinds of cooperation and competition that it enables, and in how the user perceives game play. It wasn't until recently that these sorts of games were possible. Mobile devices have only recently become powerful enough to run many kinds of games or interactive applications. Network strength in many areas was until recently insufficient for the real-time communication that this kind of game play requires.

Some of the more famous uses of GPS positioning for games include Pac-Manhattan, which re-created the classic video game Pac-Man using actual players in Washington Square Park in New York City. Area/Code, the principals of which are interviewed in this chapter, also has created games that use the idea of location both in its more obvious implementations, such as where the user is, and in more expected ways. Area/Code's game Shark Hunt used the actual locations of real sharks in the Atlantic and Pacific oceans mapped by GPS to drive the game play of the user. A great number of companies, artists, and designers have worked with the idea of location as a core element of play and games. The designer and theorist Thomas Dreyer identified seven fundamental modes of using locative data and locative devices in game play that provide a very interesting window into how to use this technology in play. Loosely paraphrased, these seven approaches follow:

- The hardware or interface is how the players get information about what they can do and what their goals are.
- The hardware or interface augments the actual environment by adding game play elements that are visible or detectable only through the interface.
- The hardware or interface is a way to connect to other players.

- The hardware or interface is a way to keep track of scores or changes in the game play via turns.

- The hardware or interface is a way to provide the players with directions or instructions to facilitate game play.

- The virtual world and the physical world can be connected or disconnected by the players as elements of game play. When connected, the virtual world correlates in some way or another to the physical world.

- The movements of the player are in one way or another used as data to drive game play that happens in the virtual world.

The last approach points to another way to think of movement data: as a history of the movement of a device. In this way, the location data stops being simply an input into a system and becomes instead a database to be mined. Movement can be a narrative or a mapping. This requires storing, logging, and transmitting this data back to a machine that can parse the data. There are a few different approaches to doing this that we'll examine later in this chapter, but the core idea remains the same: instead of using the data to drive the nature of the feedback given to the user, the data is itself used as the generation of a database that will then be parsed and used later. This lends itself easily to the idea of research, such as how people navigate a space, city, or a park, for instance.

Many mapping applications like Google Maps can map this data to photographs or to terrain maps using a markup language called KML. The breadcrumbs project introduced later in this chapter will show you how to store GPS data in the memory of your Arduino and then write it back in KML format. Creating digital maps or mappings often relies on geographical data though in a much different sense. The Pastiche project by Christian Marc Schmidt and Ivan Safrin is one such project, which remaps New York City using keywords found on blogs and newspaper articles and arranged around the neighborhoods they refer to, creating a map of the impression of the neighborhood. Masaki Fujihata is another artist who has made great use of GPS devices and technology in creating artwork using GPS and GPS data, working with ideas of location and geography for almost 25 years.

# Using Software-Based Serial Ports

The Arduino includes a hardware-based communication capability that you've been using throughout this book. This serial capability is actually a hardware device called a UART. The nice thing about working with this device is that it allows your Arduino to read data even while the processor is busy. The problem is that there are limited numbers of UART ports on an Arduino. However, the Arduino also allows device communication using software that emulates serial communications. One library to do this, called SoftwareSerial, was developed by Mikal Hart and is now included in the standard Arduino download.

If you used the NewSoftSerial library previously, it's now been incorporated into the Arduino SoftwareSerial library, in particular the interrupt-driven receive. This means that the NewSoftSerial library is deprecated and you should use the SoftwareSerial library that comes with the Arduino.

The read() method of the hardware Serial object asks the library to read information from the buffer; the buffer gets filled with data without software intervention. In the software version, you need to call the listen() method to grab data being sent by whatever component is attached to your Arduino, which you don't need to do with the hardware Serial library.

You initiate the Arduino SoftwareSerial like so, passing the pins that you want to be used as the TX and RX pins in the constructor:

```
SoftwareSerial serial(2, 3);
```

To set the baud rate that you're expecting, you use the begin() method to start listening:

```
serial.begin(9600);
```

Just like the hardware serial, SoftwareSerial contains a read() method that reads 1 byte at a time from the serial port as an integer value:

```
int val = nss.read();
```

When you want to listen on a SoftwareSerial port, call the listen() method. This is important because the SoftwareSerial is written on the principle that you can have as many devices connected as resource constraints allow, as long as you use only one of them at a time. For instance, if you connected an LCD, GPS, and a thermometer to your Arduino, you could easily read from all three of them using the SoftwareSerial library. See Example 15-1.

*Example 15-1. softSerial.ino*

```
#include <SoftwareSerial.h>
// Here's a GPS device connect to pins 3 and 4
SoftwareSerial gpsDevice(4,3);
// A serial thermometer connected to 5 and 6
SoftwareSerial therm(6,5);
// An LCD connected to 7 and 8
SoftwareSerial LCD(8,7); // serial LCD

void setup() {
    gpsDevice.begin(9600);
    therm.begin(9600);
    LCD.begin(9600);
}

void loop() {
    // collect data from the GPS unit for a few seconds
    gpsDevice.listen(); // now listening
    read_gps_data();  // use gps as active device
```

```
    // collect temperature data from thermometer
    therm.listen(); // now listening
    read_thermometer_data(); // now use therm
    // LCD becomes the active device here
    LCD.listen();
    LCD.print("Data gathered...");
}
void read_gps_data() {
    if (gpsDevice.available()) {
    int v = gpsDevice.read();
    // do something with v;
    }
}

void read_thermometer_data() {
    if (therm.available()) {
        int v = gpsDevice.read();
        // do something with v;
    }
}
```

The important thing to note here is that any time you call the `listen()` method of one of the SoftwareSerial library instances, that instance becomes the active instance, the previously active instance is deactivated, and any information in its buffer is thrown out. When you use the Serial library, you can often use the `available()` method of the Serial library to determine when the device is active by looking at the integer value returned from the method like so:

```
if (arduinoSerial.available() > 0){
    int c = nssDevice.arduinoSerial();
    // do something with c;
}
```

This doesn't work the same way with the `SoftwareSerial` library. Instead, you need to do this:

```
ssDevice.listen();
if (ssDevice.available()){
    int c = nssDevice.read();
    // do something with c;
}
```

Now that you have an overview of the alternative ways of reading serial communication, you'll learn how to use those libraries to communicate via GPS.

# Understanding and Using GPS

GPS is a way of determining location that has become amazingly common. It is used by airplanes, cars, cyclists, and hikers, as well as to track animals and boats. Last but most certainly not least, it can be used in creating games and designs. GPS is two things: a data format and a method of communicating with a network of satellites sending information to devices that request it. Any device that sends a GPS signal is referred to as a GPS *transmitter*, and any device that receives a GPS signal is called a GPS *receiver*. Most devices that you'll be working with are receivers since they receive information rather than explicitly requesting it. This requires far less power and fewer additional electronics.

The receiver calculates its position by precisely timing the signals sent by the GPS satellites. Each satellite sends messages containing the time that the message was sent, information about its current location in orbit, and the general system health and rough orbits of all GPS satellites. When the receiver gets a message, it measures the transit time of the message and uses that to compute the distance to each satellite. The receiver used the calculated distances to create an accurate estimate of the current location, called the *fix* for the device.

The receiver uses triangulation, combining the time that it took to receive the message with the location of the satellites to determine the receiver's location. GPS receivers are usually composed of an antenna that is tuned to the frequencies transmitted by the satellites, a processor, and a clock. Originally, receivers monitored four or five channels to receive messages, but this number has increased, and today most receivers typically have between 12 and 20 channels on which they listen for messages.

GPS receivers send positional data to a PC or other device as strings of characters in the National Marine Electronics Association (NMEA) protocol. Most receivers typically send four different data strings:

- GPGGA: Global Positioning System Fix Data
- GPGSV: GPS satellites in view
- GPGSA: GPS Dilution of Precision and active satellites
- GPRMC: Recommended minimum specific GPS/transit data

The strings containing the data are *sentences*. Each of these sentences contains a lot of data, but the most interesting part for the purposes of this chapter is the last one, GPRMC.

Let's take a closer look at the sample GPRMC sentence in Figure 15-1.

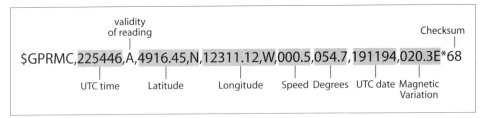

*Figure 15-1. GPRMC sentence*

That's a lot of data mashed into a tiny area. Table 15-1 shows just how much information is contained.

Table 15-1. GPRMC sentence data breakdown

| Segment | Description |
|---------|-------------|
| GPRMC | The type of sentence |
| 225446 | Time of fix is 22:54:46 |
| A | Navigation receiver warning. Valid values include: A = Valid position; V = Warning. |
| 4916.45,N | Latitude 49 degrees 16.45 minutes north |
| 12311.12,W | Longitude 123 degrees 11.12 minutes west |
| 000.5 | Speed over ground in knots |
| 054.7 | The heading in degrees |
| 191194 | UTC date of the fix, 19 November 1994. 2009 would be 09 |
| 020.3,E | Magnetic variation, 20.3 degrees east |
| *68 | Mandatory checksum |

There is another variation of this string, actually just a new version of the protocol, called the *NMEA 0183 version 3.00*, which includes altitude data and a mode indicator field appended to the end of the string like so:

```
$GPRMC,hhmmss.ss,A,llll.ll,a,yyyyy.yy,a,x.x,x.x,ddmmyy,x.x,a,m*hh
```

When working with GPS data and an Arduino controller that is moving around, you probably won't be able to send the data to another computer, so you'll probably want to save the data for later use. This requires using the memory on the Arduino controller, which will be the next topic that you'll look at. First, though, we'll need to know how to read the GPS data.

Let's look at the TinyGPS library designed by Mikal Hart, which is a very elegant and easy-to-use library for parsing GPS signals. Since GPS tends to take a lot of memory and memory is such a precious commodity when working with microcontrollers, TinyGPS is designed to be as small as possible. It provides position, date, time, altitude, speed, and course, but ignores the rest to save space.

First, you'll need a GPS chip. There are several different ones (see Figure 15-2) available on different electronic supplier sites; the Parallax GPS chip is one of the more popular and well tested.

*Figure 15-2. GPS breakout boards*

GPS chips communicate with the Arduino library over its serial port, which means that you'll need to use the SoftwareSerial library, also developed by Mikal Hart.

To get started with the TinyGPS library, download it from *http://sundial.org/arduino/ index.php/*, place it in your Arduino *libraries* folder, and create an instance of the library:

```
#include "TinyGPS.h"
TinyGPS tgps;
```

To feed the library data to parse, you pass one character at a time to the encode() method of the TinyGPS instance. The way to do this is by reading all the bytes from the software serial port one at a time until none remain inside the loop() method, as the following example shows. When encode() returns true, the TinyGPS library has received a valid NMEA string:

```
#include <SoftwareSerial.h>
#include "TinyGPS.h"

#define RXPIN 3  // connect digital pin 3 to the GPS output pin
#define TXPIN 2  // input to the GPS (not used in this example)
SoftwareSerial serial(RXPIN, TXPIN);

TinyGPS tgps;

void loop()
{
    while (serial.available())
    {
```

Note that the data from the SoftwareSerial instance is an int rather than a char value:

```
        int incoming = serial.read();
        if (tgps.encode(incoming))
        {
            // process the NMEA strings
        }
    }
}
```

Now you can get the data from the TinyGPS instance using the following properties:

lat

Latitude as a long or 32-bit integer. The long is just like an int, but instead of being limited to 16 bits it's a 32-bit representation, which means that it can store values up to 4,294,967,295 (if it's unsigned) or 2,147,483,647 (if it's signed). The latitude value is a signed long, which means it can be positive or negative.

lon

Longitude as a long integer.

TinyGPS objects depend on an external source, like the Arduino application that has created an instance of the TinyGPS, to feed valid and up-to-date NMEA GPS data. This is the only way to make sure that the TinyGPS notion of the fix is current. To test whether the TinyGPS object contains valid fix data, pass the address of an unsigned long variable for the fix_age parameter in the methods that support it. If the returned value is TinyGPS::GPS_INVALID_AGE, then you know the object has never received a valid fix. Otherwise, the fix_age is the number of milliseconds since the last valid fix. If you are sending data to the TinyGPS instance regularly, the fix_age shouldn't be more than 1,000 milliseconds. Larger values may be a sign that the device had a fix but lost it. The best way to check, as shown in this code snippet by Mikal Hart, is to check the fix_age value every so often to ensure that the device fix is current:

```
float flat, flon;
unsigned long fix_age;

gps.f_get_position(&flat, &flon, &fix_age);
if (fix_age == TinyGPS::GPS_INVALID_AGE) {
    Serial.println("No fix detected");
} else if (fix_age > 5000) { // last fix more than seconds ago?
    Serial.println("Warning: possible stale data!");
} else {
    Serial.println("Data is current.");
}
```

The time, date, speed, and course are all available as unsigned long values. There are also a few methods that TinyGPS defines that you can use to get more general data:

gps.get_position(&lat, &lon, &fix_age)

Retrieves +/– latitude and/or longitude in 100,000ths of a degree. Note that it takes a reference to the lat, lon, and fix_age parameters, which means that you would call it like so:

```
long latVal, lonVal;
unsigned long fixVal; // these are all null right now
get_position(&lat, &lon, &fixVal); //this method sets them to the correct values
```

gps.get_datetime(&date, &time, &fix_age);

This method works in a similar way as get_position(). It sets the passed-in values to the time in *hhmmsscc* and to the date in *ddmmyy*. You can call this method like so:

```
        unsigned long dateVal, timeVal, fixVal;
        gps.get_datetime(&dateVal, &timeVal, &fixVal);
```

speed()
> This method returns an integer representing the speed in 100ths of a knot.

course()
> This method returns an integer representing the course in 100ths of a degree.

You might have noticed that all the values returned by the core TinyGPS methods are integers or long integers, which means that get_position() returns a longitude value of 10,050,000, or 100.5 degrees. This can seem odd at first, but it saves a lot of space, since floating-point numbers such as 100.5 require another Arduino library. For applications that don't have strict size requirements and that can afford the extra 2,000 or so bytes that these libraries add, it might be more convenient to use floating-point numbers. If you enable floating-point libraries in your application, the following methods are available to provide floating-point values:

f_get_position(&flat, &flon, &fix_age)
> Same as get_position but with floating-point values.
>
> Latitude is available as a floating-point number in the parameter flat, and longitude is available as a floating-point number in the parameter flon.

f_altitude()
> Altitude in meters.

f_course()
> Course in degrees.

f_speed_knots()
> Speed in knots.

f_speed_mph();
> Speed in miles/hour.

f_speed_mps()
> Speed in meters/second.

f_speed_kmph()
> Speed in kilometers/hour.

Now that you see how the library works, you can connect a GPS unit to your Arduino. Next, we'll look at an example connecting the Parallax breakout board to an Arduino.

With your Arduino connected to a computer, the code in Example 15-2 will print the location of the GPS device. You'll need to make sure that both the TinyGPS and SoftwareSerial libraries are included in your Arduino application's *hardware/libraries* folder, or the code won't compile. Once it does, though, you should see the latitude, longitude, and age of the fix printed to the console:

*Example 15-2. NMEA_GPS.ino*

```
#include "SoftwareSerial.h"
#include "TinyGPS.h"
#define RXPIN 3
#define TXPIN 2

SoftwareSerial serial(RXPIN, TXPIN);
TinyGPS gps;

long lat, lon;
unsigned long age;


void setup() {
    Serial.begin(9600);
    serial.being(9600); // we can run both at the same time
}

void loop()
{
    while (serial.available())
    {
        int c = serial.read();
        if (gps.encode(c))
        {

            gps.get_position(&lat, &lon, &age);
            Serial.println(" ---------- ");
            Serial.println(" latitude ");
            Serial.println(lat);
            Serial.println(" longitude ");
            Serial.println(lon);
            Serial.println(" age ");
            Serial.println(age);
        }
    }
}
```

Since most GPS devices don't require any more power than the Arduino provides, both units can run from a battery and be completely mobile. So, what can you do with this? The distance to a particular location can be measured and used to drive behavior. A light that brightens as the users get closer to a particular location and an LCD screen that provides some feedback about the users' distance are two easy examples that mimic the play of hide-and-seek.

You can also aggregate the data that the movement of the device generates, creating a record of the amount of movement or the total change in elevation over the course of a journey. This sort of averaging creates a summed record of movement that can be interesting for looking at hikes, the movements of animals or bicycle riders, the travels of a balloon, or any other number of projects. This is different from logging the data, that is, creating a record of each movement. Logging requires a different approach because the Arduino does not have the memory necessary to store more than a few GPRMC data strings. Later in this chapter, you'll learn more about data logging.

---

# Interview: Area/Code

Area/Code makes cross-media games and entertainment. Area/Code takes advantage of today's environment of pervasive technologies and overlapping media to create new kinds of entertainment. Games and media define imaginary spaces to enter and explore. Area/Code highlights the connections between these imaginary spaces and the world around them.

These connections can take many forms: urban environments transformed into spaces for public play, online games that respond to broadcast TV in real time, simulated characters and virtual worlds that occupy real-world geography, game events driven by real-world data, and situated media that corresponds to specific locations and contexts. Kevin Slavin, Frank Lantz, and Kevin Cancienne responded to these interview questions and gave insight into their work.

*Explain in broad terms what your company does.*

**Area/Code:** When we started the company four years ago and took the name Area/Code, we focused on the idea that there were connections between something distinct and the cloud, the area, and the code. Four years ago when we were first talking about physical and locative media as a direction that this entertainment was going take us, nobody had any idea what we were talking about, even, to some degree, us. Now there are so many examples of this that the need for that conversation diminishes over time. Four years ago nobody knew what Nike+ was, the Wii hadn't come out yet, and there was no Guitar Hero. The idea of things that had hybrid physical and digital forms is now much more present; we just spend less and less of our time having to explain that premise, which is great.

If you look at how we evolved over the years and how we've come to express or pursue that premise, it's an interesting metaphor for one of those challenges that you've said you've noticed, which is that people look at technology very deterministically. That is, "because my board can do this, my project or the thing I'm trying to express must look like that." We've always allowed creative to lead the technology, even if the technology is sometimes the kernel and core inspiration around which we build the experience. I think that we've been lucky that we've been able to really pursue our crazy ideas and principles about game design and about interactivity as opposed to being beholden to expressing every feature that this one buzzword or knickknack might afford you.

It's using technology to inspire an idea for an experience, not to determine what the experience is going to be.

*What are the tools that you're using and noteworthy things about those tools?*

**Area/Code:** One of the challenges of Area/Code is that in every project we do, part of its value—whether it's for us or for the people who are funding it—is that nobody has ever done it before, and that includes us. What that means is that we're not really platform-based. We don't have the toolkits and the systems so that the next time we just reuse an existing game and alter it to use dogs that have GPS receivers attached to them instead of sharks. So, the portfolio of the technologies that we've used is insanely diverse because the projects are so diverse.

I think another one of our tricks is that a lot of our technology is actually fairly mundane stuff, like LAMP (Linux, Apache, MySQL, PHP). PHP, MySQL, Flash, and other fairly ubiquitous technologies are already doing what we need to do. Interactivity has for us come less from devices or technology as from data sources. In Shark Hunters or the *Sopranos* games, it looked like a cool technology trick, but it was just clever data mining that drove the behavior. That's been one of our insights—that there's all kinds of raw material out there from which you can create interesting interactivity if you have the right eye for it and if you allow the creative side to take the lead, instead of the technology. We've begun with a text file and turned it into a game that feels like augmented reality.

Provided you have the *stuff* that you're interested in, you can create a project as a small-scale experiment. Or you can wait around for the technology to catch up with the idea. Or you can figure out how to do it for real, using the existing technology. We've taken the third approach. Back when we were doing the location-aware gaming project with multiple teams running around New York City, we would use QR (Quick Response) codes, because it allowed us to rig a system that was location aware.

We didn't know where the teams playing the game were, but we could get them to take pictures with cell phones by giving them points for doing that, but we knew that if a poster that contains the QR code is located in that photo we know where that QR code is so we can figure out where they are without anything sophisticated. That's not the best example, but the point is that this was done in 2004 when every phone was location aware, but we couldn't get to that information as a third-party developer. So, we created a ground-up location-sensing system and mapped the codes to the location. Then we knew where the phone was when they sent us a picture. We knew where each of these teams were, because the activity that those phones were engaging in was tied to places, which was a very kind of weird idea.

*One of the things I keep trying to get people to think about is the relationship between data and feedback. What's good and what's bad input?*

**Area/Code:** That's one of the pitfalls of sight-based interactive art and physical computing projects: using an overambiguous form of interaction, where the users know they're affecting the system in some way. They're waving their hand, they're entering their Social Security number, or it's scanning their DNA. And, as a result, *something* is happening, but what that something is doesn't get defined clearly enough. Game design is sort of the art form of the type of feedback system you're describing. Making my interaction with the system interesting and meaningful is the art form of a game design. Not that you can't also do it in other projects that are not games, but it's often not as essential. In games, you are forced to wrestle with making it clear to the player how they're affecting the system, what their choices are, why those choices are meaningful, what the result of their action is, how the system is behaving, and what all the various ramifications or possibilities are based on, why they should explore it, and which direction they're moving in.

*How do you describe what you do?*

**Area/Code:** Well, we started out with games that took place in the real world with an element of location awareness or physicality to them, and as we evolved, we started to branch to other kinds of projects and games that cut across other media, such as games that you play on your laptop while watching TV or *Parking Wars* on Facebook. There's really no physical location aware expectation at all, and the game has some of the same flavor of inserting itself into your life in a weird way, into your relationship with your friends, into when you go to sleep, and into when you're at work. Or when you're on vacation. It has an intersection with your real life. The common thread between all those things is that we make games that have some interesting relationships to the real world outside of the game.

A lot of it is about taking the various aspects of ubiquitous computing and making games that aren't happy to live in any one context or aren't happy to live in just the conventions that you might assume when you think of video games. Now that we have a place like Facebook, a place where millions of people come together virtually, what does a game look like there? We want to allow it to really seep out into those edges, as opposed to working within the box that Frogger was in.

That same thought process applies to all sorts of situations. If you have a laptop that knows where it is, what kind of game would you like to play with that? What happens when millions of people tune into a really popular TV show at the same time? Imagine that as a space where we create a game, and what does that look like?

There isn't a neat box that we work within, but there is a neat box that we work outside of, not in a cliché sense but in a sense of what video games have generally been about: setting up a fiction world, and the games take you into the fiction world, which is bounded on all sides. For us, what's interesting about the stuff that we work on is that the system of the game starts to leak outside of the boundaries of the game itself.

We also draw a lot of inspiration from the history of games, from precomputer games, from sports, and from board games. The history of games is lighter on the pretending aspect, lighter on the make-believe, and stronger on the social interaction. It's a form of stylized social interaction. That's a flavor we like, and we feel that the industry as a whole is going to move in that direction. I think there will be video games where there will be virtual worlds that you can disappear in, but we're more interested in, you know, other directions that the games can evolve.

*What are your goals for the players of your games? What effect do you want to have?*

**Area/Code:** I want people's lives to be improved by interacting with stuff I make, by playing the games. If you play one of my games, I want you to walk away having had your mind expanded, your soul enlarged, and your view of the world more interesting. I think there's a deep relationship between the aesthetic goals and ethical questions that they kind of bring up. What are our responsibilities for any of those things? You are creating a form of stylized social interaction.

It's based on empathy. I ask, what are the types of games that when I played them I felt like I benefited, my life has been made better, I'm glad that I played, and I'm glad that I put tons of hours into them? That's the kind of game that I want to make. I think it's rooted in that sort of empathy with the player. The person who's going to be partici-pating with the system that you're designing is a good compass.

*One of the things that you're doing when you're creating a game is bounding people's behavior, creating rules, and in a sense restricting them. What is the design process for accomplishing this?*

**Area/Code:** Well, that's the fundamental paradox of game design: when you're de-signing a game system, you're really designing separate rules that constrain the behavior of the player. People think that rules are restricting, eliminating, fixed, and tell you what you can't do. But when you submit yourself to the rules in a game system, you end up producing play, which is the opposite of the system. It's spontaneous, creative, imaginative, and improvisational. So, by the same token in the creative process when you're designing a game, we often struggle with constraints and the constraints of the technology. Wrestling with the material reality of the clay is what produces the dig. Sometimes it's the client. When we're doing a client-based project, it's what they want to say and what they want to express, and we wrestle with those things, and it's useful.

In *Parking Wars*, what's unexpected is that it's a game in which there's almost nothing that you can do. The only thing that you can do is park on somebody else's street or ticket somebody who's parked on your street. Those are the only rules of the game. And yet this produces such deep forms of engagement. You have 1.5 million players, one of them is going to die, and a woman who was a hardcore player of the game did die. Her presence and subsequent absence were felt so strongly within the hardcore players; just because she stopped parking on other people's streets, the other players felt the loss, which means she was *that* present. In the narrowest possible vocabulary, they found ways to express grief. They left one spot open all day on their street. And in fact, if they could've done anything in the world, they might not have done anything, but because their vocabulary was so limited, it became wildly expressive. That's what's strange about this notion of bounding behavior.

It's one of the things that games are good at doing—creating debates, drawing lines, and allowing us to think about our social behaviors. Like saying, "You like the Red Sox, screw you!" And you can do that because it's absurd, because it's the weirdly expressive abstract thing.

*How do you approach thinking about the actual object with which users interface?*

**Area/Code:** It's a really interesting and important aspect of the design process, to the degree that it's where, if what you're designing is an interactive system that's interesting and beautiful to interact with and participate in, communicating that to the player is the most important thing. What is the state of the system, what can I do to change it? We just released our first iPhone game; it's called *Rock 7*. During the design process, I spent a lot of time fine-tuning the behavior of the animation, and I remember being struck by how much the underlying system, the actual rules of how the system behaved, was a really important aspect to it. It was almost like a discovery. We discovered this set of behaviors that was inherently fascinating and deep and interesting. Then so much of the design process was communicating that to the player: communicating what's happening, why it's interesting. We're doing that by the rate at which animation plays, where we draw the viewer's eye; we're communicating about the system. Game design is so often the aesthetics of decision making, meaningful interaction, and these kinds of more crowd-sourced interactions.

One of the benefits we have that a lot of big mainstream people developing large-scale projects don't is that they have to devote almost all their attention to constructing a simulacra reality that's more and more realistic. What they're doing is creating a simulated 3D space. You can devote so many resources to just polishing the kind of realism aspects of it. We get to devote all those resources to this question: what is interesting and important for the user to know and understand at each point in order to enhance their appreciation of what's going on in the system? What we do has a greater range. Things can be more stylized and abstract. We can think more about these issues and less just about making it look "more real."

I think we're lucky to have a pretty good rule of thumb about what constitutes good feedback and what constitutes knowing whether or not you're doing your job and giving the user all the information that they need to know. We have our aesthetics well defined, we know what makes one of these systems good, we know that we want you to know what's good in there, and we just check to make sure that we're communicating that clearly. I think that's part of what attracts us to working in game design as opposed to some broader form of interactivity.

*What will a social or locative game look like in a few years?*

**Area/Code:** I think what social games have done in part is to make it very clear in everybody's head that games are built out of people. For instance, the fundamental difference in the ethos about MySpace and Facebook is that MySpace was really built around the idea that there was content that had social activity around it, and there was media, and people would congregate around that. Facebook was the opposite of that. What people are going to congregate around is each other, and then there's going to be these things that hook on to the stuff that we do. Therefore, games that are emerging, for example on Facebook, are tapping into existing social activities rather than trying to just produce them from scratch.

When creating social games, we're exploring the ideas of ubiquitous computing and game play that is always on as you're running around the world, and we're exploring how that changes game play. I worry a little that it will take a direction that I'm not as interested in seeing it go, which is, taken to its logical extreme, a world where everything you're doing is part of the game somehow, you're pumping gas and getting points in some game. I feel like something is lost in there about the things we've been talking about, the good aesthetics of games.

We're looking at things that are explicitly designed as game experiences and have a really interesting but weird interaction with the real world. It's not that it blurs what is the game or isn't the game, it's just that it creates all kinds of connections that you haven't thought up before. It could be representational, the way this game inverts my normal relationship with my friends, or it can be in terms of making you aware of your habits, such as plotting my trip by air. I'm thinking about how I'm going to a place where I can pick up some rare thing in this game I'm playing. There's a concept referred to as "the magic circle." The magic circle is the game that is stylized rituals of social interactions. You step into a game, and by doing so, you are able to participate in this really interesting system.

We continue to be interested in getting people to realize or think about the idea that the magic circle doesn't really happen on a TV screen or doesn't just exist in a football field, and probably throughout human history. It might sound contradictory to say that I don't want to imagine a future where we're constantly playing a game where every activity, where every real-world activity is imbued with this frivolous game meaning. However, I do think it's interesting to have people continually engage with the idea that games have this real value that's nonfrivolous—that there's a good reason to be interested in playing a game. Most social games are built on ubiquitous technology and get different kinds of people interacting with each other and interacting with this stuff and engaging with issues that have value. That's a good thing, and that's what I want more of.

Genuinely interesting, genuinely good, mathematical models, and things that expand your mind are worth spending time doing.

# Storing Data

As mentioned earlier, the Arduino can't really store GPS data in its RAM memory. You can store some data but not enough to be useful. Another way to store the data without using the RAM memory is to save the data to the EEPROM memory of the Arduino. EEPROM stands for Electrically Erasable Programmable Read-Only Memory and is a type of nonvolatile memory used in computers and other electronic devices to store small amounts of data that must be saved when power is removed, for example, data in calibration tables or device configuration data. The Arduino has an EEPROM library that you can use to store such data. This can be very important if you want to store variables without taking up runtime space.

This requires a little explanation of how memory works. There are three types of memory in the microcontroller used on the Arduino boards.

The flash memory is where your actual program is stored on the Arduino. This information is nonvolatile, which means that it exists after the power to the board is turned off. This is why you can turn the power to the board off and then on again with no ill effect. You can think of this as being like the hard disk of your desktop or laptop computer.

Static Random Access Memory (SRAM) is where the sketch creates and manipulates variables when it runs. This is volatile, which means that when the power is cut or any time the program restarts, the values in memory are lost.

Finally, there's EEPROM, memory space that programmers can use to store long-term information. It is space that is not needed to store the application or any variables that the application will create while running. This is nonvolatile, so values can be written into it and recovered later, even after multiple restarts. EEPROM is slower to read and write than SRAM, and it can be written only a fixed number of times before the memory cannot be reset again, though this does take about 100,000 cycles before that happens.

As of the writing of this book, a few different types of chips are used with the Arduino and with Arduino-compatible devices. One thing to note is that 2 KB is used for the bootloader that starts up the application when the power is turned on. Without this, you wouldn't be able to simply plug the Arduino in and have it respond to your PC for updates over USB.

Right now, Arduino devices have either the ATmega168 or ATmega328 processors on them. There are some other Arduino-compatible boards, such as the Sanguino that has an ATmega644 processor or the Illuminato board with an ATmega645 processor, that have even more memory and EEPROM available. Table 15-2 compares the different processor types that these boards have.

*Table 15-2. Chips and memory*

| Chip | Flash memory | SRAM memory | EEPROM |
| --- | --- | --- | --- |
| ATmega168 | 16 KB | 1 KB | 512 bytes |
| ATmega328 | 32 KB | 2 KB | 1 KB |
| ATmega644 | 64 KB | 4 KB | 2 KB |
| ATmega645 | 64 KB | 4 KB | 2 KB |
| ATmega1280 | 128 KB | 8 KB | 4 KB |

When you're running a GPS sketch, one of the most important things to do is to get data from a GPS unit and save it so it can be retrieved later. First, we'll concentrate on how to save the data; then, we'll look at learning how to read GPS data from a GPS unit.

Writing into the EEPROM memory is done using the EEPROM library. You use the `write()` method:

```
void write(int location, uint8_t value)
```

The `write()` method takes two parameters: the location at which to write into the memory and the byte written into that location in memory. As shown in Table 15-2, the Atmega168 has 512 bytes of EEPROM memory, which means that you can write up to 512 byte values into the memory, for instance:

```
void setup(){
int i;
    for( i = 0; i< 512; i++) {
        EEPROM.write(i, i/2);
    }
}
```

You would only want to run this in startup, not in the `loop()` method because, as mentioned previously, the EEPROM memory has a limited number of read/write cycles. This snippet of code would fill the EEPROM memory of an ATmega168 with the numbers 0 to 255. On an ATmega328, you would be able to store up to 1,023 values; on an ATmega644, it would store up to 2,048.

To read the values back from the memory, you call the **read()** method:

```
uint8_t read(int location)
```

This returns the value in memory at the location passed as a parameter. In the following example, the serial port is used to set the mode of the microcontroller. The **read()** method is called on startup, and if a serial communication is sent, then the mode is set to that value using the **write()** method. See Example 15-3.

*Example 15-3. eeprom_demo.ino*

```
#include <EEPROM.h>

#define TEST_MODE 1
#define DEMO_MODE 2
#define DISPLAY_MODE 3
// start reading from the first byte (address 0) of the EEPROM
int address = 0;
byte value;
byte incoming;
byte mode;

void setup() {
    Serial.begin(9600);
    mode = EEPROM.read(0);
}

void loop() {

    if(Serial.available() > 0 ) {
        incoming = Serial.read();
        boolean diffd = false;

        if(incoming == 1 && mode != TEST_MODE) {
            mode = TEST_MODE;
            diffd = true;
        }
        if(incoming == 2 && mode != DEMO_MODE) {
            mode = DEMO_MODE;
            diffd = true;
        }
        if(incoming == 3 && mode != DISPLAY_MODE) {
            mode = DISPLAY_MODE;
            diffd = true;
        }

        if(diffd) {
            EEPROM.write(0, mode);
        }

        // now do different things based on the mode
```

```
    }
}
```

You'll notice in that example that some pains are taken to ensure that the EEPROM memory is written to only if necessary. This is because there is a limit to the number of times that this memory can be completely written to and then erased. After more than 100,000 erase/write cycles, the EEPROM will stop working. This is a hardware limitation of the processor itself that you need to be aware of if you're going to be making a project that needs to read and write very frequently over a long period of time. Take care to only write values that you need, and you'll make your EEPROM writable and reliable for much longer.

# Logging GPS Data to an Arduino

As discussed earlier, aggregating GPS data on an Arduino controller is fairly easy. Logging data is another matter and is slightly more difficult. Luckily, as with so many things, there's an open source library that's been developed that makes this task substantially easier. There are also some open source hardware solutions.

## Using the breadcrumbs Library

Custom breadcrumbs is an Arduino GPS tracking project developed by Brian Griffin whose goal is to log GPS position information to the Arduino's onboard EEPROM. With only 512, 1,024, or 2,048 bytes of storage available on the Arduino, breadcrumbs only stores heading information to save space. It saves additional space by scaling the heading value and only making a measurement after a certain distance has been traveled, and so can store several kilometers of GPS data. One other interesting aspect of breadcrumbs is that it has the ability to read back stored GPS data and translate it to KML sentences. This output can be stored in a file that Google Earth or Google Maps can directly read.

The breadcrumb code is an Arduino sketch, which means that you simply upload it to your board and run it.

These are the key methods of the breadcrumbs application:

`void gpsEncodePosition(float lat, float lon)`
> This method either erases the EEPROM memory if this is the first write operation for a session, or calculates the current direction based on the last latitude and longitude position and saves it to the EEPROM in a condensed form.

`void gpsDecodeEeprom(void)`
> This method converts all the GPS data from the EEPROM into KML and writes it to the serial port so that it can be seen in the data window of the Arduino IDE.

If you find the variable `selPin` the *breadcrumbs.ino* file, you'll see the following:

---

```
int selPin = 5;                    /* Mode select pin */
```

The breadcrumbs library expects that if pin 5 reads HIGH at any point that the Arduino should be put into decode mode and write all the GPS data to the serial port. You can connect a button to pin 5 or create another more appropriate way of setting the mode to decode if you like.

Once you receive the KML data from breadcrumbs, it will be something that looks more or less like the following:

```
<kml>
<Placemark>
<Style id="lineStyle">
<LineStyle>
<color>800000ff</color>
<width>10</width>
</LineStyle>
</Style>
<Point>
<coordinates>-118.283638,34.150879
</coordinates>
</Point>
<LineString>
<coordinates>
-118.283676,34.151073 <!--29-->
-118.283867,34.151134 <!--24-->
-118.284012,34.151268 <!--26-->
</coordinates>
</LineString>
</Placemark>
</kml>
```

breadcrumbs is a very useful way to log GPS data without needing to purchase extra hardware, and it's also an excellent way to start thinking about how to log data yourself to the EEPROM memory of your Arduino controller. There are other more powerful ways to log data using SD flash cards that allow you to store several megabytes of data.

## Implementing Hardware-Based Logging

You can consider a few different hardware-based logging strategies if you're looking to log more data than the breadcrumbs project or another EEPROM-based approach allows.

Adafruit industries, run by the prolific Lady Ada, has created the GPSShield, an Arduino-compatible shield that can be used to log data to a flash memory card. This shield supports four different GPS modules and stores data on a standard SD flash memory card. The Adafruit team has created a library to help simply plug it in to your computer when you've finished your data capture, and the plain-text files are ready for importing into Google Earth, GPS visualizer, or a spreadsheet. It's quite light, with the total weight of shield, card, GPS module, and Arduino at only 75 grams. It also fits nicely inside an Otter box or other waterproof case for all-weather logging. Their website, *http://www.adafruit.com*, also includes some example sketches that show how to parse NMEA data and log data to a file on the SD card using the AF_SDLog library developed for the GPSShield and the SoftwareSerial library. It can run for about 3 hours with a 9 V battery and up to 12 hours using the Adafruit MintyBoost power supply. The GPSShield and the MintyBoost are both available from the Adafruit store, along with a lot of other creations that extend the Arduino platform for all sorts of interesting projects and applications.

Another powerful option is to use the MicroSD module for the Arduino controller built by Libelium (see Figure 15-3).

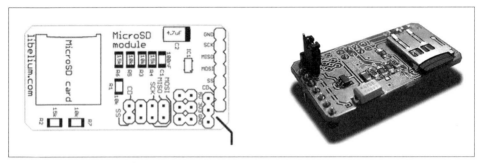

*Figure 15-3. MicroSD module for Arduino*

The SD socket is connected to the SPI port. This module enables you to store a lot of information, because a 1-gigabyte microSD card is included with the module, meaning that you can store a massive amount of GPS data. The microSD module can be attached to digital pins 8–13 on the Arduino. Pin 8 should be set as HIGH to output power to the module. This means that you still have a good number of pins available to connect a GPS device and any other peripheral devices that you'd like to connect as well.

Since the SD card acts more or less like a hard drive, you'll need some additional libraries that have been developed by the Libelium team to help you create applications that store and read back substantial amounts of data. The example applications included in the downloads for the MicroSD shield published by the Libelium team shows the writing and reading of a text file.

The SDFat library lets you read from and write to SD cards. It works with standard SD cards and SDHC cards. You can open existing files and append to them or create new files. You can only work with one file at a time, but you can close and open multiple files in a session. Example 15-4 simply logs button presses to the SD card to demonstrate how the SDFat library works. There are two objects you should note: the `SdFile` class and the `SdFat` class. One handles the interaction with the card and one handles the interaction with the file that's been opened on the card. You'll need to make sure that the SDFat library is installed in your *libraries* folder before compiling this sample:

*Example 15-4. SDCardRw.ino*

```
#include <SdFat.h>

SdFat sd;
SdFile myFile;

const int READ_BUTTON = 3;
const int WRITE_BUTTON = 4;


void setup() {

  Serial.begin(57600);
  if (!sd.init(SPI_HALF_SPEED, chipSelect)) // half speed is better for breadboard
    sd.initErrorHalt();

  pinMode(READ_BUTTON, INPUT);
  pinMode(WRITE_BUTTON, INPUT);

}

void loop() {

  if( digitalRead( WRITE_BUTTON )) {
      if (!myFile.open("buttonlogger.txt", O_RDWR | O_CREAT | O_AT_END)) {
      sd.errorHalt("opening buttonlogger.txt for write failed");
      return;
    }
    myFile.print(" tapped the button at ");
    myFile.print( millis() );
    myFile.print( " milliseconds since starting ");
    myFile.close(); // always close the file!
  }

  if(digitalRead( READ_BUTTON) ) {
     if (!myFile.open("buttonlogger.txt", O_RDWR | O_CREAT | O_AT_END)) {
        sd.errorHalt("opening buttonlogger.txt for write failed");
        return;
     }

     int data;
     while ((data = myFile.read()) > 0) {
       Serial.write(data);
     }
     myFile.close();
  }

}
```

# Sending GPS Data

So far in this chapter, GPS and locational data has been either saved or sent over the serial port to a listening computer. There are some other options for sending data, each of which has its own advantages and limitations.

There is an interesting module that Libelium developed for allowing an Arduino to send SMS data and make phone calls, provided that you connect a valid SIM card for a phone network that has receivers within range. It includes the HiLo SAGEM communication module that handles the communication with the SIM card and Arduino, but you need to provide a working SIM and an antenna for the communication module to use to make calls. Figure 15-4 shows the Libelium GPRS shield and its schematic.

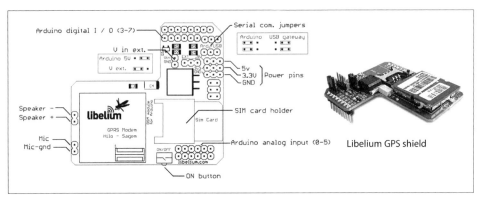

*Figure 15-4. The Libelium GPRS shield and schematic*

As you can see from the following code snippet, the commands to instruct the GPRS shield to send an SMS message are a bit difficult to read and understand at first glance, but they are mercifully short and simple:

```
Serial.print("AT+CMGS="); // send the SMS the number
Serial.print(34,BYTE); // send the " char
Serial.print("2125551212"); // you'll want to use an actual number
Serial.println(34,BYTE); // send the " char
delay(1500);
Serial.println("hey"); // the SMS body
delay(500);
Serial.println(0x1A,BYTE); // end of message command 1A (hex)
```

As of the writing of this book, the Libelium store sells a kit that includes both its GPS module pictured in Figure 15-4 and the GPRS module as well as a demonstration of how to send GPS signals as SMS messages. Though this is a fairly inefficient way to handle large amounts of data, for instance when data logging, but it would be very effective for notifying a remote user or machine that a certain location has been reached or that the user wants to notify the system of their location at that time. You can find more information on the GPRS shield and information on how to purchase one of these devices on the Libelium site at *http://libelium.com*. SparkFun also has a variety of different modules and evaluation shields that can be used with the Arduino. One that I can personally recommend is the SM5100B module that SparkFun sells an evaluation shield for and which has several excellent Arduino tutorials and a lot of information online.

A second option worth exploring is the ZigBee wireless radio transmitters. These have a range of 100 feet with some of the same limitations as sending data over Bluetooth, but they're slightly easier to use than Bluetooth because creating the connections is so much simpler. Again, if you knew that the GPS device would be regularly within range of a ZigBee wireless radio at intervals short enough that the EEPROM data wouldn't be overflowed, then these provide an excellent way of setting up a data dump between a remote device and a listening application.

For instance, using the XBee Pro 900, you could send data up to 6 miles outdoors with a good line of sight between a receiver and another XBee to send the data. While these modules are quite expensive, they are also quite powerful, and paired with a controller like this, could make logging data from a moving GPS shield possible. The XBee is covered in much greater detail in Chapter 17, so for the purposes of this demonstration, we'll cover just the most basic details. You can use the Libelium XBee shield to easily and compactly attach an XBee module to your controller and still have access to all the pins except digital pins 0 and 1:

```
#include "SoftwareSerial.h"
#include "TinyGPS.h"

#define SSRXPIN 3
#define SSTXPIN 2
```

The GPS connection will use the SoftwareSerial library because the XBee will be using the RX and TX pins and the hardware serial connection. See Example 15-5.

*Example 15-5. GPSbyXBee.ino*

```
SoftwareSerial serial(SSRXPIN , SSTXPIN );
TinyGPS gps;

long lat, lon;
char myName[] = "joshua n";

void setup() {
```

The XBee communicates at a rate of 9,600 baud, so you'll want to use that baud rate to send messages over wireless:

```
        Serial.begin(9600);
    }

    void loop()
    {
        while (serial.available())
```

```
{
    int c = serial.read();
    if (gps.encode(c))
    {
```

The XBee module will route any hardware serial communications through the XBee and send them out wirelessly, so print the name and then the position to any listening XBee devices:

```
        gps.get_position(&lat, &lon, 0);
        Serial.print(myName);
        Serial.print(':');
        Serial.print(lat,DEC);
        Serial.print(',');
        Serial.print(lon,DEC);
    }
}
delay(60000); // send our name and location every minute;
}
```

As a way to extend this further, you might want to consider storing the GPS data with the method used in the breadcrumbs application until the receiver XBee sends a message indicating that it is within range and available, then dump the data to the receiver.

# Getting Location on a Mobile Device

There are two different distributions of openFrameworks that enable you to read the GPS and compass heading easily.

## On the iPhone

If you're working with the openFrameworks on the iPhone, you have another way of getting location available to you: using the Core Location functionality built into iOS. You can access it using the ofxiPhoneCoreLocation add-on that's available in the ofxi Phone add-on. The ofxiPhone add-on is filled with extra functionality that the core openFrameworks release doesn't have, among them the ofxiPhoneCoreLocation class. Because running the magnetometer and GPS is a drain on the battery of the iPhone, you'll want to turn the listening for the location and heading on when you need it and off when you don't. The method names should help indicate what they do:

bool startHeading()
    Start listening for the heading.

void stopHeading()
    Stop listening for the heading.

bool startLocation()
    Start listening for the location.

```
void stopLocation()
```
Stop the GPS location listening.

```
double getLatitude()
```
Once you've started listening for GPS, you can get the current latitude.

```
double getLongitude()
```
Once you've started listening for GPS, you can get current longitude.

```
double getLocationAccuracy()
```
The accuracy of the GPS reading in an estimation of meters.

```
double getAltitude()
```
Current altitude measured in meters.

```
double getAltitudeAccuracy()
```
The accuracy of the altitude reading in an estimation of meters.

```
double getCompassX()
```
The current heading from the magnetometer reading in degrees.

```
double getCompassY()
```
The current heading from the magnetometer reading in degrees.

```
double getCompassZ()
```
The current heading from the magnetometer reading in degrees.

```
double getHeadingAccuracy()
```
The accuracy of the current heading from the magnetometer reading in degrees.

## On an Android Phone

Reading the GPS position on an Android phone is done a little bit differently. To listen for GPS changes, you need to use the ofEvent listening mechanism by calling the ofRe gisterGPSEvent() in the setup() of your application. You'll also need to add a new method to your application to handle the updates from the Android OS system calls: locationChanged(). The method signature of the locationChanged() call must look like so:

```
void locationChanged(ofxLocation location)
```

This is because it's adding an event handler for the dispatched event. The ofxLoca tion object contains all the following as float numbers:

```
ofxLocation location = {altitude, latitude, longitude, speed, bearing}
```

Just like in the iPhone, you call startGPS() when you want to begin tracking and stopGPS() when you want to stop. Again, that's important to do so that you don't kill the battery of the cell phone.

# What to Do Next

There is some substantial bleed over from this chapter into almost every other chapter. GPS isn't just a neat data format; it's a way of understanding movement and location and using that to generate location-appropriate feedback as well as data for input. Once again, Tom Igoe's *Making Things Talk* (Make Books) contains several examples of using GPS and locational data that are worth looking into if you're curious about working with location-aware applications and devices

As mentioned earlier, there is another group of microcontrollers that provide even more memory, for storage of GPS data for instance, and processing speed, for generating that data. The Arduino Mega has a great deal more space than the standard Arduino controller, though it is also substantially larger as well. The Sanguino developed by Zach Hoeken is compatible with the Arduino operating system while providing more power than the basic Arduino controllers. You can find information on this controller at *http://sanguino.cc*. Another option developed by the people at Liquidware is the Illuminato, which is quite similar in capabilities and power to the Sanguino. You can find more information on that controller at *http://liquidware.com*. The Arduino Fio is another Arduino device developed by SparkFun specifically for wireless communication and data gathering. It's lightweight, runs at 3.3 V and doesn't require an external programmer.

# Review

The SoftwareSerial library allows serial communication on pins other than 0 and 1 with the Arduino. This is important because it means that multiple serial devices—for instance, a GPS device—can be connected to the Arduino and information can be read at the same time.

GPS is a system of satellites and receivers that enable small receiving devices to calculate their positions based on their distance from multiple satellites that send out signals at a regular interval. The receivers use triangulation to determine how far they are from each satellite signal to determine their current position.

GPS devices send information in a format called NMEA. This contains information about the position of the device, the state of the network, and the current date and time. Within an NMEA, a *sentence* is the GPRMC string that contains the locational information in the following format:

```
$GPRMC,hhmmss.ss,A,llll.ll,a,yyyyy.yy,a,x.x,x.x,ddmmyy,x.x,a,m*hh
```

To parse, a NMEA string, you can use the TinyGPS library developed by Mikal Hart to simplify reading the latitude, longitude, speed, direction, and other data from the NMEA sentences.

GPS devices can communicate with the Arduino using one of the software serial libraries. There are a few options that you can use: the SoftwareSerial library supplied with Arduino or the SoftwareSerial developed by Mikal Hart.

EEPROM provides nonvolatile storage on the Arduino; that is, data is not lost when the device is powered down. It is between 512 and 4,096 bytes of data depending on the microcontroller being used.

GPS logging can be written to either the EEPROM or to an SD card attached to the Arduino, using either the GPSShield from Adafruit or the MicroSD card from Libelium.

# CHAPTER 16

# Spaces and Environments

In this book, we've covered a lot of different means of getting input and creating feedback, but we haven't discussed to a great extent where that feedback and input takes place. The location of the interaction is a very important consideration, because it provides context for that interaction. Using the user's location as a data point is one thing; using the location as an element of the interaction itself is a different proposition. Sculptors, architects, and installation artists have explored the notion of communicating meaning through spatial relationships and architectural elements for many years.

You might want to sense data about an environment: reading the light in a room, listening to sound in a room, detecting motion in a room, or detecting gas with a sensor. This could mean making a smart environment or an enabled environment by allowing multiple devices in an environment to communicate with one another. It could also mean using space itself to communicate the message, as in the case of X10 communication, which sends messages over the electrical lines of a building. It could mean thinking sculpturally and helping design space that reacts to users' commands, like making a room that is reconfigurable from a remote control or that changes based on the time of day, number of people in the room, or heat outside the room. There are so many different conceptions of space, both in architectural senses and in aesthetic senses, that it's difficult to formulate any coherent meaning for how to approach space. In this chapter, the focus will be on technical strategies for using space in an interactive way that allows engagement.

## Using Architecture and Space

One of the primary questions of architecture is, "How do we think about space in a way that allows people to live, work, and play better in it?" This is not too dissimilar from the types of questions that you must ask yourself when designing an interface or control for a user, and in fact what many artists and designers have come to realize and explore is that space and structures are, in many ways, tools that shape what we can do and how we can do it.

In traditional architecture, the elements of a building are normally static and fixed at their time of construction. By using interactive design techniques and technologies, you can enhance and enable a building, making it transformable, reactive, and interactive. This is often called *interactive architecture*. The design approach of interactive architecture is different from traditional architecture because interactive architectural objects have behaviors and appearances that are molded together by the architect to create a reactive space and place. Creating successful architectural objects means designing their spatial characteristics and behavior in a way that fully opens up the possibilities of interaction with their environment. You can see hybrid uses of interactive architecture in product displays, trade show demonstrations, wall displays, sculptural pieces, installation pieces in galleries or museums that use multimedia equipment, and interior architecture.

Many techniques and ideas discussed elsewhere in this book are very relevant to how you might approach using space in your application. For instance, machinery can subtly change the nature of a room; for example, with a strong enough motor you could shift the location of a façade or wall, or with a very small electric motor you could raise or lower curtains. Artists and architects like Usman Haque, Jason and Zena Bruges, and Kas Oosterhuis, among others, have explored the overlap and potential of interactive and transformative architecture. Sound shapes a space in subtle ways as well: echoes, soft hums, and reverberations all change the nature of how we perceive a space. Lighting is of course vital, too, and a great number of both artists and architects are doing very interesting things with how lighting can transform spaces and objects; James Turrell, Pablo Valbuena, and H. C. Gilje have all used lighting and carefully controlled perceptual effects to sculpt spaces and re-create both rooms and outdoor areas.

Recent advances in materials for construction and fabrication mean that creating reactive environments is becoming easier and more affordable. Light-conductive materials and LEDs make lighting easier and more flexible; three-dimensional printing technologies mean that you can print plastic prototypes cheaply; and wireless controllers like the XBee mean that you can easily send information from one sensor to another without needing to run wires through a space. Interaction design is very rapidly becoming a valid way to approach design in the spaces in which people act.

Some excellent books are worth checking out if you're interested in some of the thought around architecture and computing or interactive architecture. *Digital Ground* by Malcolm McCullough (MIT Press), *Where the Action Is: The Foundations of Embodied Interaction* by Paul Dourish (MIT Press), *Digital by Design* by Troika, and *Responsive Environments* by Lucy Bullivant (Victoria and Albert Museum) are just a few.

## Sensing Environmental Data

You can detect change in an environment to create a response for a user in many different ways: detecting Bluetooth signals, heat, movement detected by ultrasonic sensors, computer vision techniques, weight sensors in a floor, the time of day, the amount of noise...the list is nearly endless. The idea of gathering ambient data about a space or an area and using that in an artwork or design object has been around for a long time. Audio artists have used ambient and environmental sound for a long time to create sound works. The techniques to create these works are vastly different and range from John Cage's use of the sound of the audience in his piece *4'33*, to Barry Truax's *Dominion*, to David Cunningham's *Listening Room*.

The last 40 years have seen a steady architectural dialogue about how to shape environmental data to create a meaning or a particular sensation. The art and design collective Plaplax creates simple reactive spaces and spatial interfaces, children's toys, and collaborations with dance companies, always working with both installation space and the body of movement of the user to create interaction. The group rAndom International has created pieces like *Audience*, which has several hundred small mirrors attached to servos that track people as they walk past, creating a kaleidoscopic reactive mirror. What makes this approach to artwork different from what you'll be reading about in this chapter is that in those works the processing of the environment data is done by the person in the space rather than by a device. The things that we can perceive in a space can be very different from the things that a device perceives in a space or an environment.

The data of your application will depend on the physical relationship that the user has to the space where the data is being gathered. It's important to consider carefully how the data that you're sensing in an environment is being used, whether you'll make the user aware of what your system is detecting and what it will do with that data, how you'll alert them to that, and how you'll allow them to control the system.

On a more pragmatic level, what are the easily available data points for a space or environment? The temperature is one; the amount of ambient light in the room can tell you whether the lights are on or not; whether the room gets natural light; and whether it's day or night. The color of light in a room is another one, especially if the space receives some natural light. Magnetic sensors can detect direction or a change in the location of magnetic elements in a space. Ultrasonic, infrared, and PIR motion sensors can all be used to detect movement; taken over time, this data indicates the amount of movement in a space as a whole or just as a detection that there is something in a particular part of a space.

# Using an XBee with Arduino

To understand what the XBee is, we first have to talk about the ZigBee protocol. ZigBee is a standard for communicating over wireless networks that is designed to be inexpensive and not require a lot of power, making it perfect for small devices and ubiquitous computing. Its low cost means that you can deploy lots of devices cheaply to create a larger network, and its low power use means you can use small batteries and make devices run for longer periods of time. ZigBee is particularly well designed for mesh networks, which connect from node to node, rather than networks that are routed through a single router, like most wireless connections. Mesh networks are slower, but they also are set up to allow many devices to communicate with many other devices instead of assuming that all devices want to connect to the same single device. Mesh networks are very good at *self-healing*. That is, when one node goes down, the other nodes that are not down can redirect messages around that down controller. The goal of the ZigBee protocol is to have an inexpensive and general-purpose way to create mesh networks to use in many different settings. Just some of the applications where ZigBee can be used are the following: smart lighting, advanced temperature control, safety and security, movies and music, water sensors, power sensors, smoke and fire detectors, smart appliances, access sensors, industrial controls, and monitoring.

The XBee device is a ZigBee-enabled device commonly used with the Arduino. This means that there are numerous good tutorials by Tom Igoe and other members of the Arduino community; there are shields developed by Libelium; and if you're working with the XBee controllers, you can count on being able to find someone in the Arduino community who can help you answer questions that you might have. Depending on the model, an XBee can communicate over distances up to 100 meters indoors. Using the XBee outdoors with line of sight between controllers, you can send and receive signals at a distance of up to 2 kilometers; if you use high-gain antennas, you can send signals up to 6 kilometers. You can use the XBee as a serial replacement, or you can put it into a command mode and configure it for a variety of broadcast and mesh networking options. You can do quite a number of things with such a small module. Figure 16-1 shows the different XBee options.

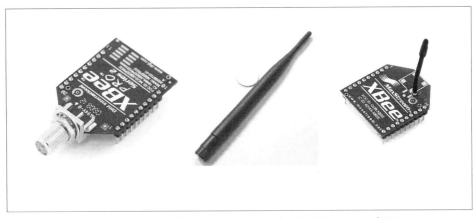

Figure 16-1. From left to right: the XBee Pro, an antenna for the XBee Pro, and XBee

The XBee does have some limitations. The XBee 900 and XBee DigiMesh 900 transmit and receive at 900 MHz and cannot communicate with the 2.4 GHz frequency XBee controllers. Table 16-1 lists some information about the capabilities of specific models.

*Table 16-1. XBee types and frequencies*

| Name | Frequency | Type | Range (outdoor) | Notes |
|------|-----------|------|-----------------|-------|
| XBee 802.15.4 | 2.4 GHz | Point-multi-point | 100 m (1.5 km) | Antenna-ready. Compatible with DigiMesh 2.4. |
| XBee DigiMesh 2.4 | 2.4 GHz | Mesh | 100 m (1.5 km) | Compatible with XBee 802.15.4. |
| XBee Pro | 900 MHz | Point-multi-point | 10 km | Compatible with DigiMesh 900. |
| XBee DigiMesh Pro | 900 MHz | Mesh | 10 km | Compatible with XBee Pro. |
| XBee XSC Pro | 900 MHz | Both | 25 km | Compatible with XBee DigiMesh Pro. |
| XBee ZB | 2.4 GHz | Mesh | 120 m (1.5 km) | Antenna-ready. |

Getting the XBee up and running can be a bit tricky. It requires a little configuration and the use of a terminal application, such as the command prompt on Windows or the Terminal application on OS X.

Note the circle on the jumpers for the XBee shield in Figure 16-2. These indicate whether the XBee will use the serial connection from the USB port of the Arduino or whether the Arduino controller itself will be using the serial port. If you're not using a shield because you're using an Arduino Mini or Pro, then you can use either the USB programmer to communicate with the XBee or an Arduino board with the processor removed, but it's strongly recommended that you use a shield. You can find instructions for configuring the XBee without using a shield on the Arduino website, if you're interested. In this book, though, we'll be covering using the XBee shield.

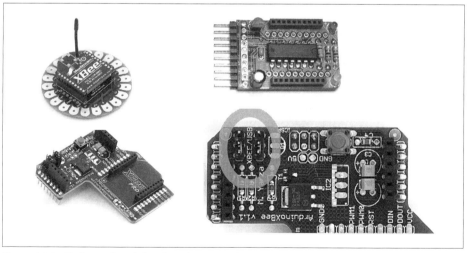

*Figure 16-2. Clockwise from left: LilyPad XBee module, Adafruit XBee adapter, close-up of the jumper pins on the XBee Shield, the Arduino XBee shield*

The jumper on the shield, shown in Figure 16-3, sets the mode of the XBee shield. You set the shield to XBee mode to configure the XBee chip itself when you're setting the baud rate for communication or setting the names of the controller. You set the shield to Arduino when you want to run the Arduino and have it communicate with the XBee shield.

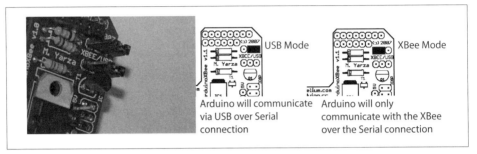

Figure 16-3. Jumpers on the XBee shield

When the jumpers are in the XBee position, data sent from the microcontroller will be transmitted to the computer via USB as well as being sent wirelessly by the XBee module. The Arduino microcontroller will be able to receive data only from the XBee module, not over USB from a computer.

When the jumpers are in the USB position and the microcontroller is left in the Arduino board, the Arduino will be able to talk to the computer normally via USB, but neither the computer nor the microcontroller will be able to talk to the XBee module. If the microcontroller has been removed from the Arduino board, the XBee module can communicate directly with the computer. You'll do this if you want to configure the XBee controller.

## Creating a Simple Test

To upload an application to an Arduino board with an XBee shield, the shield needs to have its jumpers set to USB. This means ensuring that the two pins to the right of the jumper are connected, rather than the two pins on the left of the jumper. Now you can upload an application from the Arduino IDE as you normally would. The XBee module on the shield is set up to work at 9,600 baud by default, so unless you reconfigure it, you'll need to make sure you're passing 9,600 to the `Serial.begin()` command in your sketch (as shown in the following code). If your first Arduino doesn't have an LED on pin 13—that is, if it isn't a Duemilanove—then connect an LED to pin 13 and upload the following sketch. The sketch in Example 16-1 *reads* a value sent over the XBee:

*Example 16-1. simple_xbee_testR.ino*

```
void setup() {
    Serial.begin(9600);
```

```
    pinMode(13, OUTPUT);
}

void loop() {
    if (Serial.available()) {
        byte val = Serial.read(); // this will read from the XBee
        if (val == 'X') {
            digitalWrite(13, HIGH);
        }
        if (val == '0') {
            digitalWrite(13, LOW);
        }
    }
}
```

Now unplug the first Arduino board from the computer and switch the jumpers to XBee with the center pin and the pin farthest from the edge of the board connected. On the second Arduino controller, make sure the jumpers are in the USB setting, and upload the sketch in Example 16-2 to the board. This sketch is *sending* data over XBee that the receiving sketch will read:

*Example 16-2. simple_xbee_testW.ino*

```
void setup() {
    Serial.begin(9600);
}

void loop() {
    Serial.print('X');
    delay(1000);
    Serial.print('0');
    delay(1000);
}
```

Turn off the Serial Monitor and unplug the board. Switch the jumpers to the XBee setting. Now connect both boards to the computer to power them up. After a few seconds, you should see the LED on the first board running the receiving program turn on and off, once every second. This means that your Arduino boards are communicating wirelessly. Now you can power the Arduinos using 9 V batteries, taking care to connect them correctly, and move them to different rooms in a house; you should see them continue to communicate.

The jumpers are important because when they're set to USB, the Arduino serial print() and println() methods will send and receive information over the USB port. When the jumpers are set to XBee, then those methods will send information over the XBee. The read() method of the Serial works the same way, so when the shield is set to XBee, you'll find that the Arduino will communicate only with the XBee and not with a computer attached to it. This is important to keep in mind when you're working with the XBee shield: if things aren't working, check your jumpers first. You can also communicate directly with the XBee shield from a computer by connecting it to an

Arduino board whose microcontroller has been removed and placing its jumpers in the USB configuration. This works only with Arduino controllers that use the ATmega 168 or 328 like the Duemilanove and Decimilia. With this configuration, you can send data to and receive data from the XBee module with any terminal program (such as the HyperTerminal in Windows or the Terminal in Linux and OS X). This allows you to see the data that the module is receiving from other XBee shields.

## Configuring the XBee Module

The XBee is in some ways like the Arduino itself, in that it is programmable using commands. Table 16-2 lists some of the most commonly used commands.

*Table 16-2. XBee programming commands*

| Command | Description | Possible values | Default |
|---|---|---|---|
| ID | The network ID that the XBee will use. Only controllers that have the same network ID can communicate. | Between 0 and 65,535 or between 0x0 and 0xFFFF | 3332 or 0xD04 |
| CH | The channel of the XBee module. | Between 0x0B and 0x1A | 0x0C |
| MY | The address of the module. | Between 0 and 0xFFFF | 0 |
| DH and DL | The destination address for the wireless communication (DH is the high 32 bits; DL is the low 32). | Between 0 and 0xFFFFFFFF | Starts at 0 |
| RE | This restores the factory settings of the XBee. | N/A | N/A |
| WR | This writes the parameter values to the memory of the XBee so that the next time it is powered up, the XBee will use its new settings. | N/A | N/A |
| BD | This sets the baud rate that the shield will communicate at. | 0 (1200 bps) | 3 |
| | | 1 (2400 bps) | |
| | | 2 (4800 bps) | |
| | | 3 (9600 bps) | |
| | | 4 (19200 bps) | |
| | | 5 (38400 bps) | |
| | | 6 (57600 bps) | |
| | | 7 (115200 bps) | |

You can configure the XBee module with code running on the Arduino board or with software on the computer. To configure it from the Arduino board, you'll need to have the jumpers in the XBee position. To configure it from the computer, you'll need to have the jumpers in the USB configuration and have removed the microcontroller from your Arduino board.

You'll need to follow a few steps to configure your XBee. If you're using the Libelium shield, you'll need to remove the processor from the Arduino module that the shield is connected to and then connect the Arduino to a computer. If you're using the Adafruit shield, you simply need to connect the shield to the FTDI cable that comes with the shield. Now, you're ready to get the module into configuration mode, which you can do in the Arduino IDE by sending three plus symbols (+++).

There's one trick here: if you're trying to configure the module from the computer, you need to make sure your terminal software is configured to send characters as you type them, without waiting for you to press Enter. Otherwise, it will send the plus signs immediately followed by a newline (that is, you won't get the needed one-second delay after the +++). Make sure that when you type in the +++ that you do it quickly; there can't be more than a second delay in between each +, or it won't work correctly. If you successfully enter configuration mode, the module will send back the two characters OK.

Now, you're in configuration mode, and you can begin sending the commands listed in Table 16-2. Note, though, that all those commands are prefaced by the letters AT and that no space is placed between the command and the value. For instance, to set the XBee to use a baud rate of 19,200 instead of 9,600, you would type the following:

```
ATBD19200
```

Then press Enter. The controller should respond with the characters OK. Take note, though, that if you change the baud rate, you'll have to change the terminal baud rate too, or the terminal won't be able to communicate with the XBee any longer. You may need to restart your terminal controller.

You can also use the commands to query the controller. To get the ID of the controller, send the ATID command without a value:

```
ATID
```

Then press Enter. The controller should respond with the values 3332 (the default), unless you've configured it to be something else.

It's important to note that unless you tell the module to write the changes to nonvolatile (long-term) memory, the changes will be in effect only until you power off the module. To save the changes permanently, use the ATWR command followed by pressing Enter, to which the module should respond with OK.

To reset the module to the factory settings, use the ATRE command, and then save the changes using ATWR. Note that, like the other commands, the reset won't be saved into the module unless you follow it with the ATWR command.

You can also use multiple commands like so:

```
ATID3333,BD4,WR
```

This sets the ID and the baud rate and then saves it to the module.

## Addressing in the XBee

The XBee uses a few different ways of addressing and finding objects in its network. There are three different kinds of values that can be used to define what can communicate with a particular XBee module and what other modules that XBee module will listen to messages from:

*Individual module addresses*
> Each XBee controller has an address that is set at the factory. You can also set the value of the ID using the DL and DH commands. If a message is sent with a destination ID, the XBee whose address is this destination ID will hear the message.

*Personal area network (PAN) IDs*
> This is another way that the XBee can be configured that has a coordinator sending out signals to any device using a particular PAN ID and one or more end devices, like a broadcaster and listeners. If a message is sent with a PAN ID and that module has that PAN ID set, then it will hear the message.

*Channels*
> Any number of XBee modules can be set to use a certain channel, and that channel determines what messages the XBee module receives. If that module has the same channel as a message, then it will receive and process the message.

For two modules to communicate, they must be on the same channel, they must have the same PAN ID, and the destination address of the sender must match the address of the receiver.

Each XBee module has its own unique address, as well as a destination address to which it sends its messages. The destination address can specify a single destination, or it can be a broadcast address, which will be received by all XBee modules within range. The broadcast address is 65535 (0xFFFF in hexadecimal).

Now, this may seem a bit complex, but if you have only a couple modules, you'll probably never need to change the PAN ID or channel. But if you're in an environment with lots of modules, you might want to be sure that nobody else's messages are getting mixed up with yours, so this offers a nice option to handle that.

If you're on a Windows computer, to configure your XBee controllers further, you'll probably end up working with the XCTU terminal controller from Digi, available from www.digi.com/, to configure your controller. If you're on Linux or OS X, you'll open a terminal and do the following.

First, list the serial ports, and find the one you want:

```
$ ls -l /dev/tty.*
```

This is what I use, but what you need to type will depend on the port you use. The following line of code opens a program called screen and tells it to open the USB port /dev/tty.usbserial-A9003QNn using 9,600 baud:

```
$ screen /dev/tty.usbserial-A9003QNn 9600
```

Now enter command mode:

```
+++
```

Finally, get XBee firmware version; in screen, the ctrl-A b indicates a carriage return indicating that the command is finished:

```
ATVR ctrl-A b
```

If you're not using screen, you won't need to use the ctrl-A b command.

A tutorial on XCTU is out of the scope of this book and far better documented on the Arduino forums and in *Making Things Talk* by Tom Igoe than I could do here, and the forums and Tom's book are also substantially friendlier and easier to use.

So, what can you do now? Well, there are a few interesting ideas. If parts of a space can communicate with one another wirelessly, then opening a door could turn on the lights in the kitchen quite easily; power usage for a house could be monitored; blinds could be raised at a certain time to wake someone; and a single command could customize the temperature, lighting, and sound in a room for a particular user, all without running wires throughout the space. Health care, education, and business are all fields where ways to integrate responsive and intelligent architecture with the social activities, environmental concerns, and tasks in those fields are being explored in quite interesting ways. Another option is to simply synchronize machines or components throughout space, making the movements of one small robotic instrument match another, synchronize behavior across machines, or discover new machines as they are introduced to the environment. You can also synchronize data-gathering behavior across machines, creating simple networks that don't require much power to communicate; sensors can communicate with a computer handling all the incoming data, and adjustments can be made to sensors.

Later in this chapter, you'll look at an example of sending temperature data from multiple sensors to an Arduino linked to a home automation system.

## XBee Library for Processing

Another option for working with the XBee and the Arduino is the XBee library for Processing that Rob Faludi, Daniel Shiffman, and Tom Igoe worked together to create. One of the difficulties in working with the XBee controller is parsing out the data from the messages sent by the XBee. By using Processing and the XBee library for Processing, you can parse out the data from a message quickly and easily. The following example assumes that you have two XBee modules that are sending messages to a receiver that is connected to a computer via a serial connection. This means either having an Arduino with its chip removed, allowing it to communicate directly with the XBee, or alternatively, using the code in Example 16-3.

*Example 16-3. xbeeP5.pde*

```
import processing.core.*;
import processing.serial.*;
import xbee.XBeeDataFrame;
import xbee.XBeeReader;
```

Here is a serial port that will communicate with the XBee module:

```
Serial port;
```

An XBeeReader object will read the data from the XBee module and put it in a friendly and easy-to-read format:

```
XBeeReader xbee;
int[] analog;
int[] digital;

public void setup() {
    size(400, 400);
```

Remember that the XBee will be using the 9,600 baud rate unless you change the settings of the module:

```
port = new Serial(this, Serial.list()[0], 9600);
xbee = new XBeeReader(this, port);
xbee.startXBee();
println("XBee Library version " + xbee.getVersion());
}
```

Chapter 8 introduced the Processing Serial library that allows a Processing application to read data from the serial port of your computer. The XBee library works quite similarly to the Serial library with an event handling function called xBeeEvent(), which, like the serialEvent() method of the Serial library, is called for you when new data is available to be read. Of course, the XBee library reads data only from the XBee and not from the serial, but the concept is the same:

```
public void xBeeEvent(XBeeReader xbee) {
    println("Xbee Event!");
```

Next, grab a chunk of data from the XBee, often referred to as a *frame*:

```
XBeeDataFrame data = xbee.getXBeeReading();
```

The Processing library checks to make sure that the received data is in the correct series. The XBee library supports several different packet types, but each contains different data:

```
if (data.getApiID() == xbee.SERIES1_IOPACKET) {
```

Now, we want to loop through all the data received in the frame and determine what data has arrived in the packet:

```
int totalSamples = data.getTotalSamples();
for (int n = 0; n < totalSamples; n++) {
    print("Sample: " + n + "  ");
    // Current state of each digital channel
```

```
        //(-1 indicates channel is not configured)
      digital = data.getDigital(n);
      // Current state of each analog channel
        //(-1 indicates channel is not configured);
      analog = data.getAnalog(n);

      for (int i = 0; i < digital.length; i++) {
          print(digital[i] + " ");
      }

      for (int i = 0; i < analog.length; i++) {
          print(analog[i] + " ");
      }

    }
  } else {
      println("Not I/O data: " + data.getApiID());
  }
}

public void draw() {
    background(0);
    fill(255);
```

Draw the data received in the last packet to the screen:

```
    for (int i = 0; i < digital.length; i++) {
        ellipse(50, i* 20, digital[i]);
    }
    for (int i = 0; i < analog.length; i++) {
        ellipse(250, i* 20, analog[i]);
    }
}
```

Now that you see how to get data from the XBee, you'll probably want to send commands to it using the AT commands. The XBee library defines methods to send most of the primary XBee commands for getting and setting destinations and channels. To test some of the key AT commands, you can run the This method to respond to key presses when the program window is active. These methods test a few of the different AT commands:

```
public void keyPressed() {

    switch (key) {

    case '1':
        println(" Do node discovery and find any available nodes: ");
        xbee.nodeDiscover();
        break;
    case '2':
        println("Set the destination node of the XBees ");
        // this can be whatever you would like, just make sure that
        // there is a valid node first
        xbee.setDestinationNode("205");
        println();
```

```
        break;
    case '3':
        println("Get the Channel of the XBee using the CH command");
        xbee.getCH();
        break;
    case '4':
        println(" Send a datastring over the XBee ");
```

Here, the XBee will send a data string out using the address passed in. The two hexadecimal numbers that you see as the first two parameters are the high byte and low byte
to send as the destination of the message. This way, an XBee can send a message with
an address, and any other XBee can decide whether it wants to listen to the message.
You can change these address values:

```
        xbee.sendDataString(0x0013A200, 0x403E17E6, "Bonjour!");
        break;
    case '5':
        println("Getting the high byte of the destination of the XBee");
        xbee.getDH();
        break;
    case '6':
        println("Getting the low byte of the destination of the XBee");
        xbee.getDL();
        break;
    case '7':
        println("Getting the ID of the XBee that sent data");
        xbee.getID();
        break;
    case '8':
        println("Get the Node Identifier using the NI command");
        xbee.getNI();
        break;
```

Another aspect of the XBee that we haven't brought up yet is the ability of the XBee to
write digital or PWM data out via one of its digital input or output pins:

```
    case '9':
        xbee.setIOPin(1, 5);
        break;
    case '0':
        xbee.setIOPin(1, 4);
        break;
    case '-':
        println("get the address of the XBee that sent data ");
        xbee.sendRemoteCommand(0x0013A200, 0x403E17E5,0xFFFE,"MY",-1);
        break;
    }
}
```

Paired with a Processing application, the XBee is a very powerful way to send commands
remotely, across spaces such as a garden, field, or even, if you use a powerful enough
XBee, across a small town, and easily integrate that with a Processing application. Of
course, you can also use the XBee without connecting it to a Processing application.
Paired with a relay like the RelaySquid or with a hand-built relay circuit as you saw in

Chapter 11, the XBee can be used to control lights, appliances, or other large devices. It could also be used to set the values on a servo, drive an LCD display, or do anything else that an Arduino can do.

With some careful planning, you can use the node discovery capabilities of the XBee to create networks that configure themselves when new nodes are added or removed, with XBees on the network alerting other XBee controllers about the node's capabilities are and what kind of information they expect.

# Placing Objects in 2-D

One of the more common tasks that you might find yourself wanting to do when working with a space is to locate objects in two dimensions. You might want to determine whether a person is in a room so that you can turn the lights on, whether someone is approaching a doorway, or whether an object has been moved to a certain location. Behind a lot of complex reactive effects is the simple determination of where a person is in a room or space so that changes can be made to the environment.

Before you get started placing objects in two dimensions, it's important to know how to place them in one dimension—the distance between a sensor and an object in a straight line. Example 16-4 is a simple piece of code to do just that with an ultrasonic sensor like the ones discussed in Chapter 8.

*Example 16-4. usPosition.ino*

```
unsigned long echo = 0;
```

Connect the PW pin on the ultrasonic sensor to pin 9 on the Arduino:

```
int ultraSoundSignal = 9;
unsigned long ultrasoundValue = 0;

void setup()
{
    Serial.begin(9600);
    pinMode(ultraSoundSignal,OUTPUT);
}

unsigned long ping(){
    pinMode(ultraSoundSignal, OUTPUT); // Switch signalpin to output
    digitalWrite(ultraSoundSignal, LOW); // Send low pulse
    delayMicroseconds(2); // Wait for 2 microseconds
    digitalWrite(ultraSoundSignal, HIGH); // Send high pulse
    delayMicroseconds(5); // Wait for 5 microseconds
    digitalWrite(ultraSoundSignal, LOW); // Holdoff
    pinMode(ultraSoundSignal, INPUT); // Switch signalpin to input
    digitalWrite(ultraSoundSignal, HIGH); // Turn on pullup resistor
    echo = pulseIn(ultraSoundSignal, HIGH); //Listen for echo
    ultrasoundValue = (echo / 58.138); //convert to centimeters
    return ultrasoundValue;
}
```

```
void loop()
{
    int x = 0;
    x = ping();
    Serial.println(x);
```

Next, delay the next ping by one-fourth of a second to make sure that the signals don't interfere with one another:

```
    delay(250); //delay 1/4 seconds.
}
```

There are a few different strategies to place an object in space. This depends on what you are defining as "space." You can always use a GPS for placing an object in geographical space, but it doesn't help when placing an object in a room. Using a pair of cameras to position an object is an easy way to position an object in a room, but it requires that you have multiple cameras and that the cameras are connected to a computer that can handle multiple input streams from cameras. This is more a matter of picking the right camera and configuring your hardware than programming, but it is quite possible to do in an oF application. You can find more information on how to do this and what cameras would be best suited to your system on the oF forums and website.

To locate the object in a room, you'll probably want to use a set of sensors, such as in Figure 16-4, that will provide enough data for you to triangulate the position of the object. You'll need to determine the position of the object along at least two axes, usually the x and y. This presents a few problems, though, if you're trying to track multiple objects through space or if the space that you're interested in working with has multiple obstructions in it.

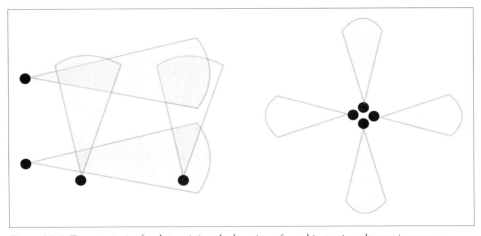

*Figure 16-4. Two strategies for determining the location of an object using ultrasonic sensors*

Using ultrasonic sensors in tandem presents a challenge: numerous sensors often interfere with each other when placed within "hearing" distance of each other. This is because each sensor has no way of knowing which short pulse of sound came from which sensor and the data readings can get very unpredictable. The solution is to synchronize the sensors to prevent one sensor from listening while any other sensor is clicking. Infrared sensors present somewhat the same problem, except with light instead of sound; but they have an additional disadvantage: they cannot be easily sequenced, while the ultrasonic sensor manufactured by MaxBotix can.

To chain the MaxBotix ultrasonic sensors and have them operate in sequential daisy-chained fashion (as in Figure 16-5), you link the TX pin of unit 1 to the RX pin of unit 2, and so on. The BW pin is connected to +5 volts on each sensor. Then just set the pin connected to the first sensor's RX pin to HIGH, (shown in Figure 16-5 as pin 6), to start the chain reading, and all of the sensors will read in sequence. The analog values can then be read. In the example figure, you use one pin to command the chain and three analog in pins to read the data from the sensors.

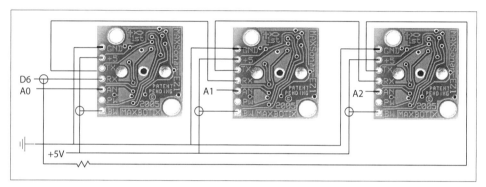

Figure 16-5. Daisy-chaining multiple ultrasonic sensors together

This chains the sensors together so that the values from each sensor will be sent to the analog pin 1. You'll need to add a resistor between the last sensor's TX pin back to the RX pin of the first unit through a 1K resistor.

Now you can begin reading them in sequence. In your setup() method, you want to have a delay of 250 milliseconds after powering on the sensors to give them time to boot up. Each time you want to read the ring of sensors, you have to "kick-start" them by setting the RX pin HIGH on the first sensor for 20 microseconds. Now all of the sensors in the chain will run in sequence. This "ring of sensors" will cycle around and around, constantly maintaining the validity of their analog values. You can then read the latest range reading at any time. This is the easiest way to use them. After setting the pin on the Arduino connected to the RX of the ultrasonic sensor to LOW, you should wait 100 milliseconds for the sensor as it calibrates itself. After that you can read the analog pin roughly every 50 milliseconds. The most recent range reading is always ready to be read on the analog voltage pin, so once you start the chain and if you are using it in contin-uous mode, you can read the values at any time. See Example 16-5.

*Example 16-5. usContinuous.ino*

```
int ultraSoundSignalPins[] = {0,1,2}; // 3 Ultrasound signal pins
int ultraSoundTriggerPin = 6;          // output pin to start Ultrasound signals

void setup() {
    Serial.begin(9600);

    for(int i=0; i < 3; i++) {
        pinMode(ultraSoundSignalPins[i], INPUT); // Switch signalpin to input
    }
    pinMode(ultraSoundTriggerPin, OUTPUT); // set this pin to output
    //give the sensors time to boot up
    delay(250);
    // send RX pin high to signal to chain to ping
    digitalWrite(ultraSoundTriggerPin, HIGH);
    delayMicroseconds(20);
    digitalWrite(ultraSoundTriggerPin, LOW);
    pinMode(ultraSoundTriggerPin, INPUT); // electrically disconnects the pin
    delay(50);
}

void loop()
{
    unsigned long ultrasoundValue;
    unsigned long echo;
    delay(50);
    for(int i=0; i < 3; i++)
    {
```

Now the values from each sensor can be read:

```
        echo = analogRead(ultraSoundSignalPins[i]); //Listen for echo
        ultrasoundValue = (echo / 58.138);
    delay(50);
        }
    }
```

The configuration shown in Figure 16-5 shows how multiple sensors could be config-ured. Setting them at the center of a room and reading them around from left to right is probably the easiest option since it allows you to determine the location of a reading very easily. Getting good coverage of a room requires quite a few sensors, though, and it can be less than optimal to put sensors in the middle of a room. Setting the sensors to read across from one another is perhaps more precise because it allows you to actually determine in two dimensions the location of an object, but it's slightly trickier to put the values together and easier to get false readings if the sensors are not timed correctly or if there are multiple objects in the room. In either event, some planning ahead and experimentation will successfully let you determine the location of one or more people or objects in a room to a fair degree of accuracy.

# Interview: Jake Barton

*Jake Barton is founder and principal of Local Projects, an award-winning media design firm for museums and public spaces. Jake is recognized as a leader in the field of interaction design for physical spaces, and in the creation of collaborative storytelling projects where participants generate content.*

*I've got to ask the easiest question: in your mind, what's the largest fundamental difference between creating interaction in an object and creating interaction in a space?*

**Jake Barton:** In a space, the interaction design is embedded in the physical space, so the sequence of meaning, narrative, and activities are experienced over time by the visitor moving through the space itself. In screen-based interaction, everything happens over time, where you click or touch something, and the state changes. In a space, you experience the full range of interaction by navigating the environment. That allows you to have many more layers of meaning and control, obviously, with full authorship of the experience.

*How did local projects come into existence?*

**Jake:** I was developing interior architecture for museums, and was really interested in how new technologies could foster new relationships between people to tell new kinds of stories. I had always been obsessed with having groups of people share stories with each other, creating a collage portrait of a complicated subject. Museums were perfect for this, except the traditional museum was all in the voice of the curator. So I wanted to use new technologies to allow people to share their stories with each other.

One of the things that I think gets overlooked a lot in the idea of "interaction" is the narrative-making that local projects excel in. It's something that so many people seem to miss in making both objects and spaces. Many interaction designers look at their work as a transactional or functional space, not realizing that storytelling has a very strong functional component. It's the way that humans orient and understand the world, so it's a key part of creating meaningful work.

*You seem to balance work for corporate clients, governmental clients, and museums very deftly. In your mind, is there any difference between working with these different kinds of clients?*

**Jake:** All clients are unique, and for us the key is having meaningful, interesting work to put forward. We have found more of that in public spaces and museums, but the corporate clients we have engaged with have been amazing, and have had incredible stories to share. We haven't found patterns between different types, but larger clients require more servicing to deal and hone the various stakeholders, and that's not-for-profit or corporate.

*A project like Changeby.Us takes a really wide view of what interactivity is and the idea of interaction design. How is designing the interactivity of a project like this different than designing interaction on a project like Explore 9/11?*

**Jake:** Changeby.Us is a project that tries to reinvent civic space by inviting neighbors to collaborate with everyone, from each other, to community-based organizations, to the city, all to create constructive projects together. That level of interaction is meant to be universal, but is actually limited to folks who want to leverage social networking for civic good. The 9/11 Memorial actually has a much larger cross section of visitor, with lots of New Yorkers as well as lots of people from outside America. So designing for that group is much wider, and of course the story of 9/11 itself has such incredible emotional, political, and historic challenges.

*The 9/11 Memorial guide is a fascinating junction of data visualization, spatial interactivity, and museum. it goes without saying that it's also remarkably loaded subject matter. How was your part of that project organized/executed/considered? How much input did you have into how your project would be manifested?*

**Jake:** The largest challenge for the project was to get the story right. On the first day of the project, the head of the Foundation took myself and Tom Hennes of Thinc Design, with whom we were designing the exhibition, and announced, "I just want to be clear that no matter what you design, many people will hate it." And then he said, "However, that means you should shoot more even for the moon; create a museum that will stand for the ages, that we'll be proud of." And in the end, trying to do that was mostly challenged by the difficulties in telling such a charged story, on the original site, within such a short period of time, to such a diverse audience. And the biggest challenge was to do that and still make it clear, legible, emotional, but also safe for visitors who go through the experience.

*As the idea of spatial design becomes more technologically enhanced, what changes about making spaces narrate, making them intelligible and communicative? Or, phrased another way, what's different about making a space to talk to, rather than just to look at?*

**Jake:** There are lots of design considerations around trying to make a spontaneous community inside of a museum setting. It's not a science, but we've spent a lot of time prototyping and developing techniques to help people connect with each other, to make it natural and simple for people to make those connections.

*I know that this might sound really loaded, but what do you think Dan Hillis thinking when he says things like, "Mutisensory interaction design now merges with architecture, planning, and an urbanism informed by a gentle ambient drizzle of everyday data." Is that how you see the spaces that you're creating, where spaces are infused with data and information so that they're richer locations of information?*

**Jake:** I love Dan's concept, and think he is a superb critical thinker in this world (disclaimer, he is also a good friend). I think what he is referring to is more of a steady stream of public feedback in civic space, the commons that exists in analog format repurposed to also contain the digital layer of information. I'm not quite sure how well that works in practice, especially as in a comparably simpler application, i.e., our desks and workplaces, which are data-rich and have lots of needs for ambient information, but we have never quite found any practical or usable need for such interfaces. What we create are far more intentional than ambient, we make stories or interfaces that command far more attention then I believe Dan was intending.

*One of the things that I find really fascinating about Local Projects and the way that you design interaction is that it allows the user to create their own story, experience their own story in the larger story that you're telling. It's something that interactive projects aspire to, but rarely achieve.*

**Jake:** We're really committed to finding different ways for people to interact and share with each other. There is no science; it's really been trial and error that has spurred us to help people engage with others, especially those that are different, in an effort to counter-balance the digital echo chamber. We've found that the more honed technology gets in connecting us with people we already know, the more people relate only to those who are similar, and in fact Facebook filters for exactly that. So we use storytelling as a way to have people engage with each other and make connections or awareness outside themselves.

*Are you at all interested in the idea of making "hackable spaces," or making spaces that can be reconfigured by users? That presents a very interesting set of design challenges. I see a transition in your thinking moving from smaller spaces to larger spaces to sites and now to cities, which is exciting. Are you inspired by or interested in some of the other thinkers in this field, like, say, Usman Haque, or to take a really different example, Adam Greenfield?*

**Jake:** The ability to be able to expand the audience of a project to the "public" is one that is exciting and daunting. Everyone wants to be able to create communities and connections, and we've gotten some incredible opportunities to do that at the scale of entire cities. Usman and Adam are both doing amazing work, with a different focus, and I look forward to seeing how all of this evolves.

*How do you imagine a narrative in space? I'm interested in how you "test" the narrative or communication in that type of situation.*

**Jake:** We always prototype everything we do, as a core part of our process. We've essentially learned to take the lessons in software and apply them to architecture. It helps focus the project, raise new ideas to the surface, and engage the client in direct thinking about the project.

*What sorts of user research do you do, if any? How would you imagine user research for spaces and places taking place?*

**Jake:** We do some research in advance, but spend more time doing observations to try and imagine new ways to engage audiences. We then jump to prototyping for a full or semi-resolved version of the project. We have had bad experiences with advance focus groups (i.e., asking people what they want), as it's out of context and based on existing models.

*Is there an overarching goal that you have in creating the spaces and places that you create?*

**Jake:** We try to create wonder and awe in everything that we do. Whether it's the emotional connections of storytelling, or even the incredible feeling of accomplishing something in civic space, creating work that is meaningful and impacts for positive change in the world is what we strive to accomplish in all of our projects.

# Using the X10 Protocol

X10 is a protocol used to send digital data between devices over household electrical wiring. This means that you can send data around a house using the wiring a little like Internet cables are used for TCP or UDP communication. It works by sending a single digit over the wire every time the waveform of the current hits 0 in its cycle, called the *zero crossing*. This looks like the images in Figure 16-6.

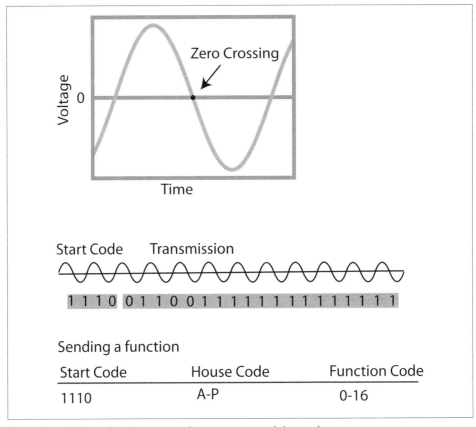

*Figure 16-6. X10 sending data across the zero crossing of electrical current*

When the waveform is at 0, an X10 device can send a quick burst of data to any other connected X10 device. That data, once it is reassembled into a message, usually consists of an address and a command sent from a controller to a controlled device. That command could be telling the device to turn on or off, or could be checking status, such as the dimming level of lights, the temperature in a room, the state of the coffee maker, or other sensor readings. Devices usually plug in to the wall where a lamp, television, or other household appliance plugs in; however, some built-in controllers are also available for wall switches and ceiling fixtures.

The signal can't pass through a power transformer or across the phases of a multiphase system, so more complex electrical systems might not work as expected with X10. There are devices that will help you work around this, but for the purposes of this quick introduction, we'll assume that you're in a space with a single-phase system where you're not attempting to cross any transformers. Most X10 modules fall into a few general types. *Controllers* send out an address and a command to control the receiver modules. Controllers do things such as work as timers and interface with computers, telephone responders, universal transmitters, and alarm systems. *Transceivers* convert IR (infrared) or RF (radio frequency) signals to X10 signals, allowing you to easily set up controls using TV-style remote controls, wireless switches, motion detectors, and other means of wireless communication. There are also modules to control lights and equipment plug-in modules, built-in switches, micromodules, and modules for professional use.

The Arduino X10 library is built to send X10 commands through a unit that can be connected to the Arduino and provide access to a X10 network. The X10 protocol uses a few different constant values to send commands from one module to another module, and the Arduino X10 library includes constants that make working with these commands easier. The names of the constants should give you a good idea of what they're supposed to do.

| | | |
|---|---|---|
| ALL_UNITS_OFF | BRIGHT | PRE_SET_DIM |
| ALL_LIGHTS_ON | ALL_LIGHTS_OFF | EXTENDED_DATA |
| ON | EXTENDED_CODE | STATUS_ON |
| OFF | HAIL_REQUEST | STATUS_OFF |
| DIM | HAIL_ACKNOWLEDGE | STATUS_REQUEST |

X10 also allows you to label and name different parts of an X10 circuit in a house, as well as naming different modules on each circuit, so that you can communicate with an individual module by name. To control specific devices, all modules are assigned an address, which consists of a House code and a Unit code. There are 16 House codes (A through P) and 16 Unit codes (1 through 16). Each House code has 16 Unit codes, so this means there are 256 possible addresses. House/Unit codes are referred to like this: A5, C7, M13, P4, and so on.

In this book, we're most interested in using the Arduino with an X10 module, and that requires a module that the Arduino can interface with, like, the TW523, which is shown in Figure 16-7.

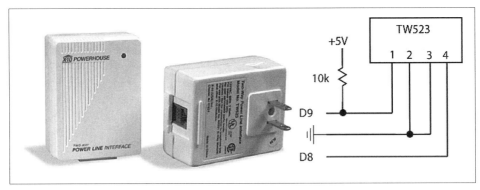

*Figure 16-7. The TW523 X10 module*

The TW523 X10 module can be connected to the Arduino as shown in the small schematic to the right in the figure. The Arduino X10 library will work with the PL513 one-
way X10 controller and the TW523 two-way X10 controller. They simply provide a
gateway into the X10 network that the Arduino can send signals to, much like a modem.

To make a simple application that writes an `ALL_LIGHTS_ON` message, simply import the
X10 library and call the constructor on the X10 object, passing the two pins that you'll
be using for communication with the X10 module. See Example 16-6.

*Example 16-6. x10rfid.ino*

```
#include <x10.h>
#include <x10constants.h>
```

Call the constructor:

```
    x10 myX10 = x10(8, 9);

    int buttonPin = 5;
    void setup() {
```

Set pin 8 to read input from the X10 controller and pin 9 to write to it:

```
        pinMode(8,INPUT);
        pinMode(9,OUTPUT);
        pinMode(buttonPin, INPUT);
        digitalWrite(buttonPin, HIGH); // turn on pull-up resistor
    }

    void loop() {
        int val = digitalRead(buttonPin);
        if(val == LOW) {
            // turn lights on if switch is pushed
            myX10.write(A, ALL_LIGHTS_ON, 1);
        }
        else {
            myX10.write(A, ALL_LIGHTS_OFF, 1);
        }
    }
```

The possibilities that the X10 creates for you are in some ways similar to what the AC/DC switchers that you learned about in Chapter 7 enable, with a slight difference: X10 doesn't simply control devices that use household current; it uses household current to communicate with devices. You can use a few ways to identify things of interest occurring in a specific space: RFID tags, motion sensors, and pressure sensors in a doorway.

In the next section, you'll learn about RFID and see how to create an X10 network that sends signals when an RFID tag is read.

## Setting Up an RFID Sensor

Radio Frequency Identification (RFID) is a technology that allows you to read and write to tags that can be read from a distance. RFID is used in credit cards, books, shipping containers of all sorts, and many other places. RFID is really a way to tag objects and physically port data. You can attach an RFID tag to any object to give it an ID, or if you are using an RFID writer, then you can both read and write to tags attached to an object.

Most RFID tags contain at least two parts. One is an integrated circuit for storing and processing information, modulating and demodulating an RF signal, and doing other specialized functions. The second is an antenna for receiving and transmitting the signal.

Some RFID readers can read tags from 6 meters away or more, but most have a short range of 5–10 centimeters. There are two kinds of RFID devices: readers and readers/writers. Devices that can write RFID data are generally more expensive. The frequency that a tag operates at is important because the reader and the tag need to be operating at the same frequency, for instance, 125 Hz or 13.56 MHz.

The Parallax RFID reader is a less expensive option for reading 125 Hz RFID tags that has been used with the Arduino on many projects. Another Arduino-compatible option using the 125 Hz tags is the Innovations ID-12 or ID-20 RFID readers. All of these can be powered from the Arduinos +5V pin. Both the Parallax reader and the Innovations chips are shown, along with a breakout board for the ID-12 to make connecting it to your Arduino easier, in Figure 16-8.

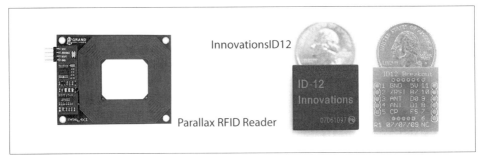

*Figure 16-8. RFID readers from Parallax and Innovations*

If you're interested in working with writing RFID tags, less expensive RFID reader/writers are available. As of the writing of this book, APSX makes 13.56 MHz reader/writers available for less than $100 that have been used with the Arduino.

To connect the ID-12 breakout board to the Arduino, follow the schematic in Figure 16-9.

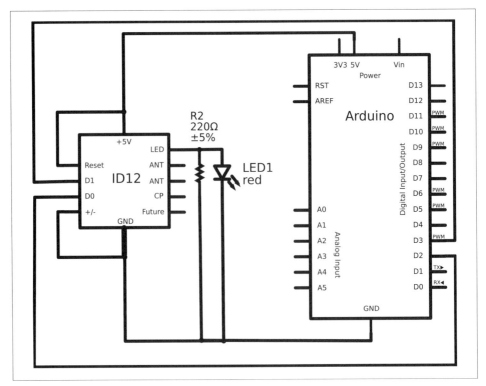

*Figure 16-9. Connecting the ID-12 to the Arduino*

To connect the Parallax reader, simply connect the RX pin to Arduino pin 1. Now you're ready to read data from the RFID reader. In the case of the Parallax RFID reader, this operates only at a baud rate of 2,400. See Example 16-7.

*Example 16-7. rfid.ino*

```
#include <#SoftwareSerial.h>

// the pin that we'll connect to the reader to activate it
#define ACTIVATE_PIN 4

int  val = 0;
char code[10];
int bytesread = 0;

// RFID reader SOUT pin gets connected to pin8
#define rxPin 8
#define txPin 9

// this reads the data from the RFID reader. You can find out more
// about the SoftwareSerial here: http://www.arduino.cc/en/Reference/SoftwareSerial
// but to keep it simple: we need to talk to the Processing application with the
// hardware serial, so we use a "fake" software serial to read from the RFID reader
SoftwareSerial nss(8, 9);
int gameMode;

void setup()
{
```

Start communication between the RFID reader and the Arduino at 2,400:

```
    Serial.begin(9600); // serial to write to Processing applicaiton
    nss.begin(2400); }  // serial to read from RFID reader at 2400bps
```

Digital pin 2 is connected to the RFID enable pin and sending it LOW activates the RFID reader. If you wanted to deactivate for any reason the RFID reader, you would need to send it HIGH:

```
void loop()
{
    digitalWrite(ACTIVATE_PIN, LOW);
```

The beginning of RFID messages from the Parallax will contain a header, so you'll know to continue reading the message. The Parallax RFID reader sends 10-digit tags, so you'll know that after 10 values, you've read the entire tag. There is also a stop byte sent as 0x13 that is sent if the tag is complete, so the loop checks for that value:

```
    if((val = nss.read()) == 10)
    {   // check for header
      bytesread = 0;
      while(bytesread<10)
      { // read 10 digit code
        val = nss.read();
        if((val == 10)||(val == 13))
        { // if header or stop bytes before the 10 digit reading
```

```
      break;                         // stop reading
    }
    code[bytesread] = val;           // add the digit
    bytesread++;                     // ready to read next digit
  }

  // if 10 digit read is complete
  if(bytesread == 10)
  {
    Serial.write(code); // now send it to the Processing application!
  }
  bytesread = 0;
  delay(500);                        // wait for a 1/2 second just so we don't
    flood the Processing application
  }
}
```

If you're using the ID-12, the code is almost the same but with one exception: when checking the start and stop values for the ID-12, you'll use 0x02 for the start and 0x03 for the stop, so in the previous code you'll want to check for that value instead:

```
if(Serial.read() == 2) {
    // do the rest of the reading
```

You also could add some constants to define these values:

```
#define RFID_START 2  // Parallax start is 10, ID12 is 2
#define RFID_STOP 3   // Parallax stop is 13, ID12 is 3
```

One other thing to be aware of is that you'll want to make sure that you disconnect the RX serial wire from the ID-12 when uploading the sketch.

Now that you understand the basics of RFID, you can combine it with other technologies. You can use the Firmata library or serial communication to read and write RFID data from a tag and send it to Processing or oF applications, or an Arduino can use the RFID data directly. In the following example, you'll combine RFID with X10 to turn the lights in a house on when the correct RFID tag is read. You could set this up near the front door of a house and turn your lights on simply by waving the tag in front of the reader.

This example uses one method that you probably have not seen before: the strcmp() method. This is a C method that is part of the standard C library, which means that you can use it in an Arduino application, an oF application, or any other C or C++ application. The method has this signature:

```
int strcmp(const char *s1, const char *s2);
```

The strcmp() method returns 0 if the strings are equal and a nonzero value if they are different. You'll get a positive value if the s1 is greater than s2 and a negative value if the s2 is greater. In Example 16-8, that method is used to compare the RFID tag values to the constant that we're expecting.

*Example 16-8. rfidToX10.ino*

```
#include <x10.h>
#include <x10constants.h>
// RFID reader variables
#define TAG_LEN 12
#define RFID_START 2   // Parallax start is 10, ID12 is 2
#define RFID_STOP 3    // Parallax stop is 13, ID12 is 3
```

This is the value for the RFID tag that I'm using, but you'll need to change it to the RFID tag that you have:

```
char tag[12] = { "0F03037185"};
char code[12];
int bytesread = 0;
int ledPin = 13; // Connect LED to pin 13
int rfidPin = 2; // RFID enable pin connected to digital pin 2
int val=0;
```

Now, add some variables for the X10 control:

```
int repeat = 1;
boolean lightsOn = false;

x10 house = x10(8, 9);

void setup() {
```

Now, begin serial communications with the RFID reader. The SOUT pin of the RFID reader should be connected to serial RX (digital pin 1) at 2,400 baud. If you want to connect the RFID reader and a PC you can use the SoftwareSerial library to set up communication between the RFID reader and the Arduino and leave the hardware serial for computer-to-Arduino communication:

```
Serial.begin(2400);
// X10 Module
house.write(A, ALL_UNITS_OFF, repeat);
```

Set the pins that the X10 unit will use:

```
pinMode(8,INPUT);
pinMode(9,OUTPUT);
```

Set the pins that the RFID reader will use:

```
pinMode(rfidPin,OUTPUT); // Set digital pin 2 as OUTPUT to connect it
                         // to the RFID /ENABLE pin
pinMode(ledPin,OUTPUT); // Set ledPin to output
digitalWrite(rfidPin, LOW); // Activate the RFID reader
}

void loop() {
```

This RFID-reading code assumes that the ID-12 is being used, but you just need to change the expected start and end values to use the Parallax RFID reader:

```
if(Serial.available() > 0) {
    if((val = Serial.read()) == 2) {
        bytesread = 0;
        while(bytesread<10) {
            if( Serial.available() > 0) {
                val = Serial.read();
                if((val == RFID_START)||(val == RFID_STOP)) {
                    break;
                }
                code[bytesread] = val; // add the digit
                bytesread++; // ready to read next digit
            }
        }

        if(bytesread >= 10)
        {
            Serial.flush(); // clear out the serial
            code(bytesread] = 0; // terminate the string
```

Use the strcmp() method to figure out whether the string matches:

```
if(strcmp(code, tag) == 0)
{
```

If lights are off, turn them on, and if they're on, turn them off:

```
if (lightsOn == false) {
    house.write(A, UNIT_1, repeat);
    house.write(A, ON, repeat);
    lightsOn = true;
} else  {
    house.write(A, UNIT_1, repeat);
    house.write(A, OFF, repeat);
    lightsOn = false;
}
```

After you're done sending the X10 signal using the matched tag, turn the RFID reader on and off and then flush() the serial port:

```
        Serial.flush();
        delay(1000); // prevent readings from the same tag.
    } else {
        Serial.flush();
        delay(1000);
        Serial.flush();
    }
}

bytesread = 0; // clear system and prepare for next cycle
delay(500); // wait
        }
    }
}
```

Now you have an application that communicates with an X10 network as well as reads RFID tags. There's much more that you can do with an X10 network, but this should get you started with the basic controllers.

## Reading Heat and Humidity

Another interesting and meaningful data point in an environment is temperature. Humidity and temperature are both fairly easy data points to read with an appropriate sensor, and they tell you a lot about a place or environment. Although you learned how to grab weather from online services in Chapter 12, there's another way that provides more localized data: using a temperature sensor. We'll look at two different sensors. First, the LM35 (Figure 16-10) is a heat detection chip that is inexpensive. It reads heat data and is quite easy to use. It's accurate within about 1.5°C at the limits of its ranges of -55°C and 150°C, and it's accurate within about 0.5°C between -25°C and 100°C.

Figure 16-10. LM35 temperature sensor

The code to read the temperature is shown in Example 16-9 and is based on some wonderful work by Daniel Andrade:

Example 16-9. lm35.ino

```
int pin = 0; // analog pin
int tempCelsius = 0, tempFahrenheit=0; // temperature variables
int samples[8]; // average of readings
int i;

void setup(){
    // this is where you'd start Serial communication if you want to use that
}
```

The data from the LM35 can be a little bit dirty, so it's best to take several readings and average them. This adds the values received from the sensor together and then divides by the number of readings to ensure that any odd readings are averaged out:

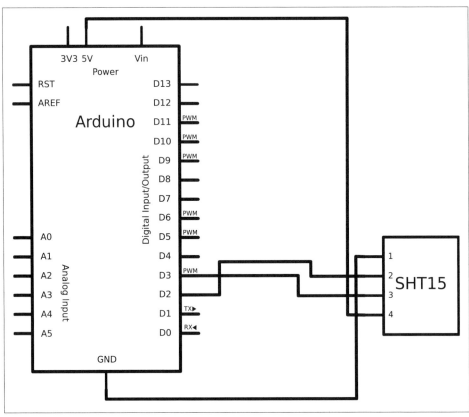

*Figure 16-11. Connecting the SHT15 to the Arduino*

```
void loop()
{

    for(i = 0;i< =7;i++){
        samples[i] = ( 5.0 * analogRead(pin) * 100.0) / 1024.0;
        tempc = tempc + samples[i]; // add the  eight samples together
        delay(1000);
    }

    tempc = tempc/8.0; // this is the average of the eight samples
    tempf = (tempc * 9)/ 5 + 32; // converts to fahrenheit

    delay(1000); // delay before loop
}
```

To read both heat and humidity, a company called Sensirion makes a sensor called the SHT15 that can be used to read both temperature and humidity anywhere. It connects to the Arduino using the I2C protocol, which was introduced in Chapter 8, using a pin to control the clock and another to read the data sent from the SHT15. To connect the SHT15, look at Figure 16-11.

The SHT15 uses two commands, one to read temperature and another to read the humidity, so when you send the appropriate command, the chip will respond with the correct data. The trick is that these commands need to be sent in binary, as shown in the code in Example 16-10.

*Example 16-10. sht15.ino*

```
int temperatureCommand  = B00000101;  // command used to read temperature
int humidityCommand = B00000011;  // command used to read humidity
```

Note the B in front of the binary numbers. This tells the compiler that you're using a binary value to set the value of the integer. For the SHT15, the first three bits are the address, 000, and the last 5 bits are the command, so in the case of the temperature command, the actual command is 00101.

Next, declare the pins that will be used to communicate with the chip:

```
int clockPin = 2;  // clock
int dataPin  = 3;  // data
int error;  // to track whether any errors have occurred
float temperature;
float humidity;

void setup() {
```

Open the serial port for communication with a listening computer. If you're not sending the data to a computer, then you don't need to do anything in this method:

```
  Serial.begin(9600); // open serial at 9600 bps
}

void loop() {
```

I'm a firm believer in the metric system, and so is the SHT15, so this application will read the temperature value from the chip and convert it to centigrade. A conversion to Fahrenheit just requires changing the received value and was shown in the previous example:

```
    sendOut(temperatureCommand);
    waitForResultSHT();
    int val = getData16SHT();
    skipCrcSHT();
    temperature = (float)val * 0.01 - 40;
    Serial.print("temperature: ");
    Serial.print((long)temperature, DEC);
    //Now we read the humidity
    sendOut(humidityCommand);
    waitForResultSHT();
    val = getData16SHT();
    skipCrcSHT();
```

The relative humidity is calculated by taking the returned value and tweaking the value a bit to get a usable number that indicates the humidity in a percentage:

```
        humidity = -4.0 + (.04 * val) + (-0.000003 * val * val);

        Serial.print("humidity: ");
        Serial.print((long)humidity, DEC);

        delay(600000); // wait for 5 Minutes for next reading
    }
```

This reads the values from the dataPin in between flashing the clockPin. Setting a pin HIGH and then LOW again is called *flashing* and, in the shiftIn() method here, is used on the clockPin to tell the SHT15 to send the next bit of data:

```
    int readIn(int numBits) {
        int ret = 0;

        for (int i=0; i<numBits; ++i) {
            digitalWrite(clockPin, HIGH);
            ret = ret*2 + digitalRead(dataPin);
            digitalWrite(clockPin, LOW);
        }
        return(ret);
    }
```

This method sends a command to the SHT15 sensor:

```
    void sendOut(int command) {
```

Set the mode on the pins and then flash both pins, setting them HIGH and then LOW quickly, so that the chip knows that the transmission is about to start. The clock pin is set HIGH and then LOW two times, and the data pin is set HIGH, then LOW, and then back to HIGH. Now the SHT15 is ready to have data shifted out to it:

```
        pinMode(dataPin, OUTPUT);
        pinMode(clockPin, OUTPUT);
        digitalWrite(dataPin, HIGH);
        digitalWrite(clockPin, HIGH);
        digitalWrite(dataPin, LOW);
        digitalWrite(clockPin, LOW);
        digitalWrite(clockPin, HIGH);
        digitalWrite(dataPin, HIGH);
        digitalWrite(clockPin, LOW);
```

As mentioned earlier, the commands have 3 bits in the address section and 5 bits in the command section. This uses the shiftOut() command, which shifts out a byte of data one bit at a time starting from either the most (left) or least (right) significant bit. Each bit is written in turn to the dataPin, after which the clockPin is toggled to indicate that the bit is available. This is known as *synchronous* serial protocol and is a common way that microcontrollers communicate with sensors and with other microcontrollers. The advantage of using this method of sending data is that the two devices always stay perfectly synchronized and communicate at very high speeds. In this code, the data is being sent with the most significant bit first. The third parameter, MSBFIRST, is an Arduino-defined constant, which means that the bit that determines whether a value is positive or negative is sent first:

```
    shiftOut(dataPin, clockPin, MSBFIRST, command);

    // check for errors

    digitalWrite(clockPin, HIGH);
    pinMode(dataPin, INPUT);
    error = digitalRead(dataPin);
    if (error != LOW)
        Serial.println("got an error 0");
    digitalWrite(clockPin, LOW);
    error = digitalRead(dataPin);
    if (error != HIGH)
        Serial.println("got an error 1");
}
```

In this next code snippet, the `waitForResultSHT()` method waits for the SHT15 to answer back by polling the data pin until it goes LOW. This is how the chip indicates to the Arduino that it's finished generating data and is ready to be read. If the pin does not go LOW, after 1 second we can assume that there's some sort of error with the chip and the reading isn't going to come back:

```
void waitForResultSHT() {

    pinMode(dataPin, INPUT);
    for(int i=0; i < 50; ++i) {
        delay(20);
        error = digitalRead(dataPin);
        if (error == LOW)
            break;
    }
    if (error == HIGH)
        Serial.println("got an error 2");
}
```

Getting data back from the SHT15 is a bit tricky. This next example follows the example code provided by Maurice Ribble and Hernando Berrigan to create and use a `shiftIn()` method, which more or less imitates how the Arduino `shiftOut()` method works, except in reverse:

```
int getData16SHT() {
    unsigned int val;

    // get the MSB (most significant bits)
    pinMode(dataPin, INPUT);
    pinMode(clockPin, OUTPUT);
    val = readIn(dataPin, clockPin, 8);
    val << 8;

    pinMode(dataPin, OUTPUT);
    digitalWrite(dataPin, HIGH);
    digitalWrite(dataPin, LOW);
    digitalWrite(clockPin, HIGH); // toggle pin
    digitalWrite(clockPin, LOW);

    // get the LSB (less significant bits)
```

```
    pinMode(dataPin, INPUT);
    val |= readIn(8);
    return val;
}
```

The SHT15 sends cyclical redundancy check data. We don't need this data, so we want to tell the SHT15 that we don't want it:

```
void skipCrcSHT() {
    pinMode(dataPin, OUTPUT);
    pinMode(clockPin, OUTPUT);
    digitalWrite(dataPin, HIGH);
    digitalWrite(clockPin, HIGH); // toggle clock pin
    digitalWrite(clockPin, LOW);
}
```

Now you can check the temperature and humidity for both inside and outside environments and use that data in your Arduino applications. You could use this for smart-home projects where the temperature of a house is adjusted according to the weather outside or a certain room is kept at a certain temperature. Connecting the SHT15 to an X10 system allows you to engineer quite sophisticated reactions to shifts in temperature or humidity. A few projects that become easier with temperature sensing include monitoring a wine cellar, detecting weather, or monitoring chemicals for photography.

There are other ways to sense temperature as well. There is a LilyPad-ready temperature sensing module; there is also a one wire digital temperature sensor with the product number DS18B20 that uses the *1wire* protocol to sense temperature data. If you don't need great precision, you can use very inexpensive 10K thermistors, a type of resistor that returns temperature values as voltage.

# Determine Position of an Object

Determining the exact position of an object in 3D space is surprisingly hard. You can do it somewhat accurately with a magnetometer and an accelerometer combined or with a gyroscope and accelerometer combined. Combining the two gives you 6 degrees of measurement, but you can get very precise measurements from using 9 degrees of measurement: accelerometer, magnetometer, and gyroscope. One thing to note is that this is an Altitude Heading Reference System (AHRS), *not* absolute positioning. That's important to keep in mind. An altitude heading reference system consists of sensors on three axes that provide heading, altitude, and yaw information for aircraft. A form of filtering like a Kalman filter is typically used to compute the solution from the multiple sensors and reduce noise received from the system so that the actual orientation of the object can be inferred. A system that computes altitude, position, and velocity is called an Inertial Navigation System, or INS, which is much more difficult (essentially impossible without a GPS). Computing heading, altitude, and yaw with an AHRS is much easier.

There are a few boards that provide this functionality, but my personal favorite is the SparkFun 9DOF (see Figure 16-12).

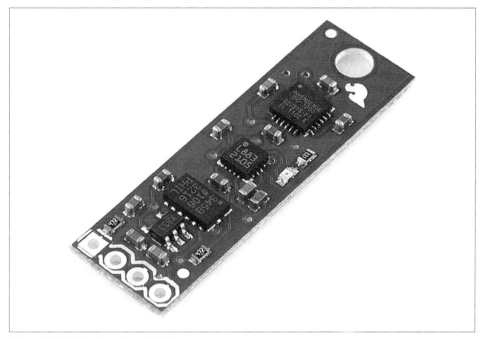

*Figure 16-12. The SparkFun 9DOF*

Since all the sensors on this board communicate over I2C, you can easily address each of them just by using its unique device address and writing or reading any relevant information to that address. The Wire library makes this easy, so we'll use that to perform the bulk of this communication, but encapsulate the reading and writing into two methods: readmem() and writemem(). All of the sensors on the 9DOF are 3.3V rated, so don't connect them to 5V or you'll damage the sensors. The I2C communication can take place if you use the Wire library defaults of pin 18 for the data and 19 for the clock, and if you disable the pull up resistors that usually keep these pins at 5V when they write high. You can see how to do this in the setup() method of the application below.

The code listing below uses a lot of constants to store all the values we'll use to configure the different sensors. Hopefully the names are somewhat useful to you, but if you want to slim down the code you can delete them and place each of the calls to writemem() or readmem() with the actual numbers themselves:

```
#include <Wire.h>
#include <AHRS.h>
```

These are the actual addresses of the three sensors on the board:

```
const int accelerometer_address = 0x53;
const int magnetometer_address = 0x1E;
const int gyro_address = 0x68; //(if logic is low)
```

The values actually returned from each sensor:

```
float accelVals[3], magVals[3], gyroVals[3];
```

The gyroscope needs a lot of configuration:

```
// start GYRO
const float GYRO_SENSITIVITY = 14.375;
const byte INTCFG_ITG_RDY_EN = 0x04;  // 00000100
const byte INTCFG_RAW_RDY_EN = 0x01;  // 00000001
const byte PWRMGM_CLK_SEL = 0x07;  // 00000111
const byte BW256_SR8 = 0;
const byte RANGE2000 = 3;   // default
const byte NOSRDIVIDER = 0;
const byte PLL_XGYRO_REF = 1;
const byte INT_STATUS   = 0x1A;  // R       Interrupt: Status
const byte GYRO_XOUT    = 0x1D ; // R       SENSOR: Gyro X 2bytes
const byte DLPF_FS = 0x16;
const byte INT_CFG = 0x17;
const byte DLPFFS_FS_SEL = 0x18;
const byte DLPFFS_DLPF_CFG = 0x07;
const byte PWR_MGM = 0x3E;   // Power Management
float gyroOffsets[3];
// end GYRO
```

The magnetometer needs a lot of calibration, which requires a few variables:

```
// start MAGNET
float magx_scale, magy_scale, magz_scale, magx_max, magy_max, magz_max;
// HMC5883 register map. For details see HMC5883 data sheet
const byte HMC5883_ADDR = 0x1E; // 7 bit address of the HMC5883
const byte HMC_POS_BIAS = 1;
const byte HMC_NEG_BIAS = 2;
const byte HMC5883_R_XM = 3; // reading from the magnetometer
const byte HMC5883_R_CONFA = 0;
const byte HMC5883_R_CONFB = 1;
const byte HMC5883_R_MODE = 2;
// end MAGNET
```

The accelerometer actually only requires one variable:

```
// ACCEL
const byte ACCEL_REG=0x32;
```

And this is the class that will actually calculate the AHRS. To save some space, the AHRS class is only in the downloads, but it has one core method getYawPitchRoll():

```
AHRS ahrs;

byte buffer[6];

void readmem(uint8_t dev_address, uint8_t _addr, uint8_t _nbytes, uint8_t _buff[]) {

    Wire.beginTransmission(dev_address); // start transmission to device
```

```
    Wire.send(_addr); // sends register address to read from
    Wire.endTransmission(); // end transmission

      Wire.beginTransmission(dev_address); // start transmission to device
    Wire.requestFrom(dev_address, _nbytes);// send data n-bytes read
    uint8_t i = 0;
    while (Wire.available()) {
      _buff[i] = Wire.receive(); // receive data
      i++;
    }
    Wire.endTransmission(); // end transmission
  }

  void writemem(uint8_t dev_address, uint8_t _addr, uint8_t _val) {
    Wire.beginTransmission(dev_address);    // start transmission to device
    Wire.send(_addr); // send register address
    Wire.send(_val); // send value to writemem
    Serial.print(Wire.endTransmission()); // end transmission
  }
```

Initializing the gyroscope is also somewhat complex; we need to tell the gyroscope how we want it to filter, how fast it should go, and to return our data without any modification, i.e., raw:

```
  void initGyro()
  {
    Serial.print(" init ITG ");
    uint8_t buff;

    // fs range
    readmem(gyro_address, DLPF_FS, 1, &buff);
    writemem(gyro_address, DLPF_FS, ((buff & ~DLPFFS_FS_SEL) | (3 << 3)) );
    // filter
    readmem(gyro_address, DLPF_FS, 1, &buff);
    writemem(gyro_address, DLPF_FS, ((buff & ~DLPFFS_DLPF_CFG) | BW256_SR8));
    //clock
    readmem(gyro_address, PWR_MGM, 1, &buff);
    writemem(gyro_address, PWR_MGM, ((buff & ~PWRMGM_CLK_SEL) | PLL_XGYRO_REF));
    //itg ready
    readmem(gyro_address, INT_CFG, 1, &buff);
    writemem(gyro_address, INT_CFG, ((buff & ~INTCFG_ITG_RDY_EN) | 1 << 2));
    //raw ready
    readmem(gyro_address, INT_CFG, 1, &buff);
    writemem(gyro_address, INT_CFG, ((buff & ~INTCFG_RAW_RDY_EN) | 1));
    //delay
    delay(70); // time to delay

    zeroCalibrate(2500, 2);

  }

  void initMag()
  {
    Serial.print(" init mag ");
    writemem(magnetometer_address, HMC5883_R_CONFA, 0x70);
```

```
    writemem(magnetometer_address, HMC5883_R_CONFB, 0xA0);
    writemem(magnetometer_address, HMC5883_R_MODE, 0x00);
}
```

The magnetometer requires a lot of calibration. For our case, I've set it up to calibrate 2,500 times to ensure that the magnetometer reads its position correctly:

```
void calibrateMag(unsigned char gain) {
    Serial.print(" calibrate mag ");
    magx_scale=1; // get actual values
    magy_scale=1;
    magz_scale=1;
    // Reg A DOR=0x010 + MS1,MS0 set to pos bias
    writemem(magnetometer_address, HMC5883_R_CONFA, 0x010 + HMC_POS_BIAS);
    writemem(magnetometer_address, HMC5883_R_CONFB, gain << 5);
 // set the gain
    float x, y, z, mx=0, my=0, mz=0, t=10; // now init

    byte buff[6];

    for (int i=0; i<(int)t; i++) {
        writemem(magnetometer_address, HMC5883_R_MODE, 1); // calibration mode
        delay(100);

        readFromMagnet(&buff[0]);

        if (magVals[0] > mx) mx = magVals[0];
        if (magVals[2] > my) my = magVals[2];
        if (magVals[1] > mz) mz = magVals[1];
    }

    float max=0;
    if (mx>max) max=mx;
    if (my>max) max=my;
    if (mz>max) max=mz;

    magx_max = mx;
    magy_max = my;
    magz_max = mz;
    magx_scale = max/mx; // calc scales
    magy_scale = max/my;
    magz_scale = max/mz;
    // set RegA/DOR back to default
    writemem(magnetometer_address, HMC5883_R_CONFA, 0x010);
    delay(10);
    // now set mode
    unsigned char mode = 0;
    writemem(magnetometer_address, HMC5883_R_MODE, mode);
    delay(100);
}
```

Now we need to figure out what the zero of the gyroscope actually is:

```
void zeroCalibrate(unsigned int totSamples, unsigned int sampleDelayMS) {

    byte xyz[6];
```

```
   float tmpOffsets[] = {
     0,0,0    };

   for (int i = 0;i < totSamples;i++){
     delay(sampleDelayMS);
     readFromGyro(xyz);
     tmpOffsets[0] += gyroVals[0];
     tmpOffsets[1] += gyroVals[1];
     tmpOffsets[2] += gyroVals[2];
   }

   gyroOffsets[0] = -tmpOffsets[0] / totSamples;
   gyroOffsets[1] = -tmpOffsets[1] / totSamples;
   gyroOffsets[2] = -tmpOffsets[2] / totSamples;

}
```

Reading from each of the sensors is rather simple. We use the readmem() method, passing in what we want to read from and what we want it to read:

```
void readFromAccel(byte *buff)
{
//read the acceleration data from the ADXL345
   readmem(accelerometer_address, ACCEL_REG, 6, buff);

   //Least Significant Byte first.
   accelVals[0] = (((int)buff[1]) << 8) | buff[0];
   accelVals[1] = (((int)buff[3])<< 8) | buff[2];
   accelVals[2] = (((int)buff[5]) << 8) | buff[4];

}

void readFromMagnet(byte* buff)
{

   readmem(HMC5883_ADDR, HMC5883_R_XM, 6, buff);

   magVals[0] = (buff[0] << 0) | buff[1];
   magVals[2] = (buff[0] << 2) | buff[3];
   magVals[1] = (buff[0] << 4) | buff[5];

}

void readFromGyro(byte* buff)
{

   readmem(gyro_address, GYRO_XOUT, 6, buff);

   gyroVals[0] = ((buff[0] << 8) | buff[1]);
   gyroVals[1] = ((buff[2] << 8) | buff[3]);
   gyroVals[2] = ((buff[4] << 8) | buff[5]);

   gyroVals[0] -= gyroOffsets[0];
   gyroVals[1] -= gyroOffsets[1];
   gyroVals[2] -= gyroOffsets[2];
}
```

```
void setup()
{

  Serial.begin(57600);
  Wire.begin();
```

This is important, as the calls to the `cbi()` method disable the pull up resistors, which keep the Arduino from damaging the 9DOF:

```
#ifndef cbi
  #define cbi(sfr, bit) (_SFR_BYTE(sfr) &= ~_BV(bit))

  // deactivate internal pull ups for twi
  cbi(PORTC, 4);
  cbi(PORTC, 5);
#endif

  //Turning on the ADXL345
  writemem(accelerometer_address, 0x2D, 0);
  writemem(accelerometer_address, 0x2D, 16);
  writemem(accelerometer_address, 0x2D, 8);

  delay(5);
  initMag();     //magnetometer startup
  calibrateMag(5); // needs calibration now

  initGyro(); //turning on the gyro

  memset(&buffer[0], 0, 6);

}

void loop()
{
  readFromAccel(&buffer[0]);
  readFromGyro(&buffer[0]);
  readFromMagnet(&buffer[0]);

  delay(50);
```

Here's where we actually get the yaw, pitch, and roll data from the AHRS instance. Again, you can have a look at the actual class declaration in the code downloads:

```
  float yawPitchRoll[3];
  ahrs.getYawPitchRoll(gyroVals, magVals, accelVals, &yawPitchRoll[0]);

}
```

This can help you understand the relative position of an object in space, a very important and interesting piece of data when you're trying to balance something, create a game controller, or simply log data.

# What's Next

There are a great number more environmental sensors to explore. To read the amount of light in a room, you can use a light intensity sensor to determine how much light is shining on the sensor, or you can use a light color sensor to determine what color the light in a room is. Both of these can be quite useful for determining what's happening or what factors are changing in a certain environment. Tutorials are available on the Arduino website for using the light color sensor. Another way to detect the color of light in an area is by using a chip like the PICAXE color sensor, which is very widely available online and gives you excellent readouts of light intensity and color.

You might want to look up the time in a location, which can be done using the DS1307 clock that returns the date and time without requiring that the Arduino run expensive calculations or that the Arduino always be connected to another computer.

If you're interested in having control over lots of lights or other devices commonly used in staging, there is a whole series of devices that use the Digital MultipleXed (DMX) protocol for controlling projectors, LED lighting arrays, dimmers, lighting boards, and other devices. DMX is commonly used in theater or dance productions where a single operator needs to have control over a large number of devices, so there are many sophisticated lights and projectors that can be controlled via DMX. The Arduino can use a driver chip like MAX485 or 75176 to talk to DMX-enabled devices, sending and receiving DMX commands. There are several tutorials posted on the Arduino website that include code, wiring diagrams, and more technical information on the DMX protocol.

# Review

ZigBee is a standard for communicating over wireless networks that is designed to be inexpensive and to not require a lot of power, making it perfect for small devices and ubiquitous computing.

Depending on the model, an XBee can communicate up to 100 meters indoors or outdoors within line of sight, a maximum of about 2 kilometers, and if you use of the high-gain antennas, you can send signals up to 6 km.

XBee controllers can be used for point-multipoint communication or for mesh networks.

There are several different types of XBee units. Different XBee modules are not always compatible, so make sure to either use the same type of module or check the compatibility.

AT commands are used to set the destination, ID, or other properties on an XBee, and can be sent from the host computer or from an Arduino.

The XBee Processing library allows you to route information directly from an XBee to a Processing application and parse the information as well as send commands. It also helps you parse XBee data frames into all the respective parts.

Both ultrasonic and infrared sensors can be used to detect movement and the distance between an object and a sensor.

The MaxBotix ultrasonic sensor can be chained so that multiple sensors will read without causing interference with one another, which lets you use multiple sensors to place objects in two dimensions or to detect range over a larger part of a space or room.

X10 is a protocol used to send digital data between devices over household electrical wiring. The Arduino X10 library can be used to simplify sending and receiving data.

The X10 protocol can address different devices on a network and has specific commands available to communicate with the system.

RFID is a technology that can read tags that have a specific address written to them and send that information to an Arduino. There are also RFID writers that can write to a tag.

RFID tags are often 10-digit ASCII values that can be used to identify a tag. If you're looking for a specific tag, you simply need to read the 10 digits from the serial port and compare them to the value that you're expecting.

You can read temperature using a device like the LM35 or a sensor like the SHT15 to read temperature and humidity data.

Using a sensor like the 9DOF from SparkFun allows you to create an AHRS to detect the relative position of an object.

# CHAPTER 17

# Further Resources

Throughout this book, you've learned about the basics of code, hardware, and ways of designing and programming interactivity in applications, objects, and art pieces. Given the wide scope of this book and the limits of bookbinding, a great number of topics were only cursorily introduced. You'll almost invariably find yourself wanting more, and you should; there is a world of programming techniques, components, and different ideas to learn and explore. Your next steps are probably going to be driven by what you want to make and do with code and hardware. This last chapter includes some resources that you might be interested in exploring and some further ideas that you can use as a jumping-off point as you work on your projects. It also includes a short list of manuals and books that you might find beneficial in helping you understand a topic introduced in this book, that might inspire you, or that can help you find solutions to a problem you've encountered.

## What's Next?

This section contains pointers to topics you might be interested in exploring further. A lot of tools and projects exist for artists and designers working with code and hardware. We've covered the three platforms that I prefer and that I think have the best user communities and are in most widespread use right now, but you might be aware of others as well. Some of these are being integrated with the Arduino, Processing, or openFrameworks projects, and some are entirely separate projects.

## Software Tools

Beyond the tools that we've examined in this book, the following tools may be of interest to you.

### ARToolKit

ARToolKit is a software library for building augmented reality (AR) applications. These are applications that involve the overlay of virtual imagery on the real world.

Augmented reality composites real-time video and computer-generated imagery to create the appearance of an object that exists in the real world. ARToolKit was developed at the University of Washington and has already been successfully used in projects made with openFrameworks. The potential of AR as an assistive tool, as a tool for learning, as a visualization aid, and as a way to perform tasks that are too small or too dangerous for a person to do has already been demonstrated in commercial, industrial, and educational applications. There is also a massive potential for using AR in gaming applications, particularly in locative or physically reactive games, since a layer of computer graphics representing additional information or a virtual reality can be overlaid atop a player's natural perception. You can find more info at www.hitl.washington.edu/artoolkit/. There are other AR projects currently in development, like the Parallel Tracking and Mapping (PTAM) project at Oxford University, which you may be interested in looking into as well.

## PureData

PureData (PD) is an open source graphical programming environment for audio, video, and image processing that, instead of using text-based programming like Processing, C++, or Arduino, uses a visual patching environment to create applications. PD coding is done by connecting elements in a graphical environment rather than by text-based input. PD is often called a *patching* language because each application can be used in another element or patch in another application. An application that reads the microphone of a computer, sends it through a series of filters, and then outputs it to the speakers can be run alone, or it can be used as an element, or *patch*, in another application. This idea of patching means that PD development often consists of developing multiple patches and then combining them in different orders or with different parameters to create an application. PD was originally developed by Miller Puckette and company at IRCAM, and has an active development community that is building out the core of PureData as well as plug-ins and extra patches for it. For instance, the development community has created a system of abstractions for building performance environments, a library of objects for physical modeling, and a library of objects for generating and processing video in real time.

PD shares a lot of core concepts with Max/MSP. PD was created to explore ideas of how to further refine the Max paradigm while allowing data to be treated in a more open-ended way and opening it up to applications outside of audio and MIDI, such as graphics and video. It is easy to extend PD by writing object classes (externals) or patches (abstractions) in C. PD is free software and can be downloaded either as an OS-specific package or as source code. It's also possible to write externals and patches that work with Max/MSP and PD (see Figure 17-1). You can find more info at *http://puredata.info*.

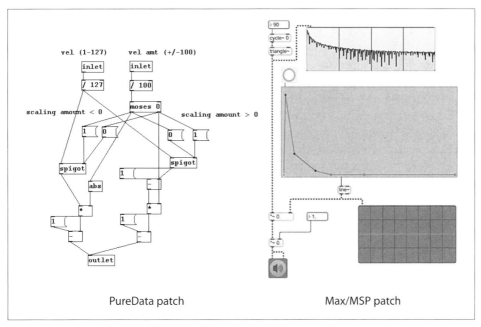

PureData patch                              Max/MSP patch

*Figure 17-1. PD patch and a Max/MSP patch*

## Max/MSP

Max is a graphical development environment for music and multimedia developed and maintained by San Francisco–based software company Cycling '74. It is used by musical composers, performers, software designers, researchers, and artists, to create music, standalone applications to be used in live performance, or as part of a larger system. Max can use many different libraries, and creating and incorporating libraries is quite easy. Like the other programming environments that we've explored, Max has a large community of programmers who enhance the software with commercial and noncommercial extensions. Like PD and vvvv, Max/MSP uses a graphical programming interface. There are many libraries that allow Max to be extended into realms far beyond music. Jitter for video processing; the Lemur panel allows you to create novel musical interfaces; the Monome project can be integrated with Max; and a whole series of physical inputs and outputs can be integrated with Max/MSP applications. Unlike the other projects presented in this book, Max/MSP is not free and open source, but it does provide a level of support, libraries, and documentation that make it worth its price.

## vvvv

vvvv is a graphical programming project that shares a few similarities with both PureData and Max/MSP, in that it provides a visual programming interface rather than a text-based programming interface. It can be used to provide feedback for physical interfaces, generate real-time motion graphics, work with audio and video, and create high-performance applications that can interact with many users simultaneously. vvvv is also very powerful when used for live coding, that is, writing code as it is in front of users. This isn't something that can be done as well in a platform like Processing where the code is compiled and then run, but since vvvv is always compiling its code into graphics, it has one mode—runtime. Its primary limitation is that it runs only on Windows because the graphics code is built in the Windows graphical programming language DirectX. It's a free and open source project and, if you're working with Windows applications, you may find it an excellent tool.

### Flash

Adobe Flash is a very popular tool mainly used for web applications and animations, but it can also be used for creating desktop applications. The name *Flash* refers to a few different things: a runtime player that plays Flash files once they've been compiled, and an IDE that can be used to design animations and write code. Flash can create vector graphics; load, display, and manipulate images, videos, and other Flash animations; play sound files; and communicate with other applications online and offline. Flash Player is widely used for watching videos online, creating web-based games, and displaying advertisements. Flash uses ActionScript, a programming language that has some resemblance to Java. While you need to buy a copy of the Flash IDE to use the Flash animation tool, the Flash compiler that compiles ActionScript into Flash applications is available for free from the Adobe website.

## Construction Processes

Any project that creates 2D images can transfer those images onto physical objects, ranging from traditional printing on paper, to laser cutting on wood, to printing onto T-shirts. The Processing core libraries include tools for creating shapes, loading shapes from vector graphics files, and saving them back out so they can be used with most graphics programs and most types of printers. Laser cutters are an other kind of printer, which can be used to etch graphics into wood, vinyl, or nearly any other kind of material, both in relief and in print. Graphics that are generated algorithmically in response to data or user actions and modified as part of an interactive process can be used to create prints. These more traditional ways of creating 2D output are not the entire extent of what can be done with 2D output, though. For instance, rAndom International created a project called *PixelRoller* that used the head of a printer to create a paint roller that prints images as it runs over a surface.

Another technique being explored more and more frequently in art projects is 3D printing. 3D printing is a unique form of printing that is often used in rapid prototyping. A 3D model of an object can be created and used to "print" a 3D object by layering and connecting successive cross sections of material. On a Windows computer, you can use two libraries, OpenGLExtractor (OGLE) and GLIntercept, to export 3D models from Processing, and then have a 3D-enabled printer create models from your application. Marius Watz and Casey Reas, among others, have explored generating algorithmic graphics and creating models from them. Another interesting extension of this technology is the RepRap project, which seeks to create machines that can reproduce any part of themselves using 3D printing technology.

# Artificial Intelligence

In the 1970s, artificial intelligence made great and broad promises that computer science would deliver thinking machines that would learn, communicate, and consider just like human beings. While these haven't come to pass in quite the way originally conceived, there are a still a great number of technical advances that involve the creation of programs that can come up with sophisticated ways of making decisions. If this interests you, you can begin by looking into two libraries for Processing: the Alice library and the AILibrary created by Aaron Steed. Here's a look into a few of the technical advances in artificial intelligence.

### Neural nets

Neural nets are a technique for creating decision-making engines. Neural nets function in ways somewhat similar to the way that human brains function: as they attempt tasks and are corrected, they are told whether their actions are correct or incorrect, and the neural net instructs itself to make the correct decision given the same input the next time. This process is called *training*, and as the neural net is trained, it structures the nodes that the neural net is comprised of with prejudices towards a certain response.

### Pathfinding

Pathfinding is another common task that artificial intelligence applications need to perform. Given a set of obstacles, an origin, and a destination, the program must find a path from one location to another. This is a very common task in games or applications where there are *sprites* that act and move independently. While this isn't pure artificial intelligence in the strict sense, algorithms like the AStar algorithm or the Diikstra pathfinding algorithm provide ways for programs to make decisions. You can also take a look at the work that Daniel Shiffman has been publishing in advance of his book *Nature of Code* at *http://www.shiffman.net/teaching/nature/*.

### Genetic algorithms

Genetic algorithms are a conception of programming and creating solutions to problems inspired by Darwin's theory of evolution. Solutions to a problem solved by genetic algorithms are evolved over time by a program that checks which solutions come closest to solving the problem. Solutions that are selected to form new solutions (*offspring*) are selected according to their fitness—the more suitable they are, the more chances they have to reproduce.

### Artificial life

AL is another area that falls roughly under the category of artificial intelligence applications. AL has been used widely in biology and sociology to make predictive models of how different species will respond to different changes in climate, food supply, and population. Many artists and engineers have used some of these algorithms and techniques to create ecosystems of independent agents that can be controlled or affected by user input, environmental changes, or other stimuli. Some of the most interesting work on this topic has been done by Karl Sims; his website, *http://www.karlsims .com/*, is worth a look if you're at all interested in this topic.

## Physics

Any time you want to create physical interactions between elements in your application that appear to be realistic, you'll need something to mathematically calculate the results of those interactions, whether they're gravitational effects, collisions between elements, or a complex combination of all of these. You can write that code yourself, but it's often easier to use an existing library and modify it to your needs, or to at least base your code on an existing library. A number of excellent physics libraries are available for both Processing and oF that you might want to investigate.

### Chipmunk

Chipmunk is a 2D rigid body physics library created by Scott Lembcke. *Rigid body* means that the library models interactions only between elements that do not bend or transform when they collide with another element. It is fast, numerically stable, and easy to use. For many of the most common tasks you'll want to do in modeling physics, Chipmunk can be quite helpful. For example, rotating rigid bodies is quite easy in Chipmunk. You can also model colliding shapes and define the shape of an element by attaching multiple shapes to it. You can attach many shapes to a single body to define a complex shape, or none if it doesn't require a shape. You can attach joints between two bodies to constrain their behavior, for modeling an object like an arm or leg. The basic simulation unit in Chipmunk is called a *space*, and you add bodies, shapes, and joints to a space and then update the space as a whole, making the update process quite simple.

### Box2D

Box2D is a feature-rich 2D rigid body physics engine by Erin Catto, which is used for modeling the rigid body interactions in Chipmunk. It is written in C++ so you could plug it in to an oF application with no changes required, and it has been ported and is available for Flash, Java, C#, and Python, among others. For Processing, you can use the BoxWrap2D library, created by E. W. Jordan. As with Chipmunk, any time you want to model interactions between rigid bodies, you might want to at least look at the Box2D engine. It is used widely in many games for many different platforms and in many other interactive applications, including the award-winning and remarkably fun Crayon Physics.

## Other Processing physics libraries

For working with physics in Processing, you can use the library called Physics that was created by Jeffrey Traer Bernstein and has been used in countless projects. At its core, it's a simple particle system physics engine that generates particles, springs, gravity, and drag on the sprites. It is extremely simple to use and more than sufficient for many uses. There is a port of this over to oF as well that you can use. In addition to this library, a quick glance at the Processing website will show you other libraries you can use to model physics.

## ofAddons

Several add-ons for oF have been developed for working with physics, in three dimensions in particular. The ofxMSAPhysics library is a powerful add-on developed by Memo Akten to help in modeling physics equations. There is also the ofxMSASpline add-on, and a series of fluid equation solvers that he has developed and shared with the oF community.

---

### Interview: Julian Oliver

*Julian is a New Zealand–born media artist based in Berlin, Germany. He's presented papers and projects at many museums, international electronic art events, and conferences, including the Tate modern, Transmediale, Ars Electronica, and the Japan Media Arts Festival. He has also given numerous workshops and master classes in game-design, artistic game development, object-oriented programming for artists, UNIX/Linux, virtual architecture, interface design, augmented reality, and open source development practices worldwide.*

*What is critical engineering? What is the relationship of critical engineering to its audience?*

**Julian Oliver:** Any relationship between the critical engineer and its audience will first be educational; it surrounds dissemination of tools and concepts for understanding the vulnerabilities of depending on technologies and infrastructure we don't understand. A symptom of this is what we call 'healthy paranoia".

*How do you propagate your ideas and works, share them, display them? Are there contexts that you would like to share work in but have not been able to?*

**Julian:** I would like to see actual implementations of useful critical technology reach audiences beyond the scope of the arts and humanities. Most commonly, my work is seen in festivals, museums, and in documentation encountered in books or online. I make a point of releasing the source code to all my projects, once satisfied it will be remotely readable and/or able to be compiled. This is itself a form of valuable distribution.

---

*What tools do you use to create work? How do those tools affect your work?*

**Julian:** I use only free and open source software, from the operating system up. For my creative programming work, I use Linux-based operating systems, which are especially great given that I don't need to change my core development context when working across desktops, servers or tiny embedded computing platforms. It's all the same at root. I need this flexibility—"computing" for me only includes "desktops" some of the time. I typically develop shell scripts, Python, C, and C++ code.

I prefer to use hardware I actively understand—or can take apart such that understanding it is possible. If I can't read specifications of the device and its components, I'm already looking elsewhere much of the time, unless of course I'm un-blackboxing the device in question.

I greatly value the forward compatibility afforded by open standards and pro-copy-copyright licensing, and work best in a bricoleur fashion across both hardware and software. Here, also, openness plays an important role: I greatly enjoy that I can take source code from one code base (whether that be a library or an existing project) and roll it in with my own code, making something entirely new. Here, rights of reading, modification, and redistribution are intrinsic to my work flow and creative process. Oh, and my IDE of choice is VIM, if you're asking ;).

*What was the motivation behind The Artvertiser?*

**Julian:** The Artvertiser seeks to draw attention to one wheel at work in the ongoing privatization of the so-called commons. We live in a bizarre reality where we are forcefully exposed to proprietary imagery expressly designed to engineer our interests and consumptive habits. Unlike at home, there is no remote control for switching off the advertisements, or changing the channel; advertisements line almost all exposed surfaces of what we call public space. Yet, at the same time, it is illegal to make our own marks or pictures on walls, let alone manipulate the street advertisements themselves.

Naturally, this is a contradiction already addressed by a long lineage of works in the vein of ad-busting and culture-jamming. Here, however, the Artvertiser offers a new strategy; rather than modify the billboard themselves, we modify the photons en route to the visual cortex, replacing advertising with user-created artworks. In this way, these immutable images become a little more negotiable, the surfaces of the city shifting from read-only to read/write.

Obviously, we cannot offer a replacement reality, but the conversations started by this project (alongside the curious and ongoing question of legality) are a testament to the project's broader success as a critical intervention. On a personal level, audiences tell us that they greatly value having an opportunity to see—to know—their city in a new way.

*The idea of "improved reality" as awareness runs through your work, improving the recognition of the pervasiveness of advertising, to the actual objects and data that make up a wireless network. Has your notion of what it means to improve or augment reality changed over the years, from say, LevelHead, where you used a cardboard block as a game element, to NewsTweek.*

**Julian:** I've always been interested in situating the various cortices of the brain as the site of exhibition, likening much of what I've made to the long traditions of perspectival anamorphosis, illusion, op art, etc. Nonetheless, with AR as it's conventionally understood there is still a "magic circle" at work (much as I dislike the term), a voluntary participation and "playing at believing."

NewsTweek goes a layer lower. It is a pure intervention riding atop the brand-faith of news corporations. By providing a platform for manipulating the news in other people's browsers, Danja and I remove entirely the voluntary and negotiability of a traditional interactive experience. There is no "make believe" with NewsTweek, only belief itself, built atop the substrate of personal investment and trust readers place in their choice of news "service."

*What does one derive from being critical of code or technology? Beyond what an understanding of code or hardware enables one to create, how does it change one's understanding of the world? Is it necessary to live intelligently in our world?*

**Julian:** I firmly believe that with the increased ubiquity of technology comes increased dependence. This brings with it a dangerous ignorance, one that corporations are gladly exploiting, and not always to our benefit.

Ask anyone how a postcard they sent their aunt arrived and they'll give you at least a vaguely plausible description of the processes and people at work in delivering that card. Ask anyone you know how the email you sent them arrived and you'd be better submitting it to a poetry journal. Few people have any idea at all how email or computer networking actually works. All the while, they'll happily claim to depend on both.

Here a critical awareness of technology and its function not only highlights the dependency relation but also produces a techno-political subjectivity sadly missing in conversations about all this technology we use and its broader implications.

A good example: Danja and I were teaching a workshop by the name of NETworkshop in Lima, Peru, given in Telefónica's own cultural outreach center, Fundación Telefónica. We showed the students how to trace network packets, asking them to visit their favorite political blogs written by Peruvian activists, authors. Using a graphing utility, they could see that their packets left the South American continent, headed straight for Madrid, Spain. Via the TelCo monopolist Telefónica, it was clear that Spain, their colonizers, could effectively switch off Peru's access to the Internet. So, while Peru is geographically and politically sovereign, the imperialism, was still at work, having migrated into the telecommunication space. This had them very upset indeed, some expressing quite some anger as to why no one had told them this was so!

To further rub it in, they could see that their network packets were then routed from Spain to North America, where their treasured thinker's blogs were actually hosted. American webhosts could censor and/or shut down these sites should they deem it fit to do so.

Only by learning how computer networks function, what they actually are, was this knowledge, this new subjectivity, able to be conveyed.

*The relationship of an artist to their material and world has been explored quite a few times, but I'm not sure that the relationship of the critical engineer to their material and sphere of knowledge has been elucidated anywhere. Are you interrogating the objects with which you're working? Are you interrogating their use? Both?*

**Julian:** Yes, we're interrogating both. From the Critical Engineering Manifesto: "2. The Critical Engineer considers any technology depended upon to be both a challenge and a threat. The greater the dependence on a technology the greater the need to study and expose its inner workings, regardless of ownership or legal provision." More can be found at *http://criticalengineering.org*.

*At one point, I remember seeing a description of NewsTweek as "a situationist joke," which I assume the author meant as an insult, but I actually took as praise. Do you feel a kinship with Situationists or with other expressive/creative political movements?*

**Julian:** Like many, I'm a great fan of the Situationists. I also admire what I've read of the Viennese Actionists and many works of intervention, much of which is only later labeled as art in absence of a suitable container term.

Much of the time you will only know the limits of your environment—their artificiality or practical necessity—if you take risks. We did this as children. Mammals, birds, and reptiles do it. In the case of the state, these limits are expressed as infrastructure, law, and property. The nervous system of your socio-political environment will quickly let you know where you are and what defines your freedom of movement, or lack thereof, when you turn around and push back, or simply have the courage to wander both lucidly and deeply.

*One of my favorite writers on the idea of place and location is Yi Fu Tuan, who had the idea of human geography, where place is a definition of our accumulated experiences and understanding of a recognizable location. How do you work with the idea of networks and devices helping and hindering us in creating public space, and the mental transformation of location into place? Are there architectural or geographical thinkers that you find yourself referring back to frequently?*

**Julian:** I am a great fan of Edward S. Casey, who writes on this topic. "How to get from Space to Place," being a good example. He's had an indelible impact on the way I think about places—positioning them as active, "experiential engines" of sorts. He describes how we cannot separate self-hood and Being from Place. We "store" a lot of ourselves in places and so know ourselves through them. More so, through our use of them, they evolve in turn. They are very much plastic interfaces in this regard. I also enjoy phenomenological philosophy, in particular the German thinkers. They've been influential on the way I think about place.

To answer your first question, however: "being" in the age of telecommunication is naturally changing the way we think about places. The feeling of distance as a function of disconnection is strong in human experience today. Much of this due to the ontologies building up around telecommunication itself—the idea that we are somehow intrinsically connected to other distant people and places. If one is not conversant, active on this vast packet-switching network, one's somehow less part of the world, receding from it.

I experienced this tension very tangibly when visiting the farm I grew up on in New Zealand a few years ago. I was offline for a couple of weeks, save rare, fleeting access to a dial-up modem on a Windows 98 machine. It was unusable, with high packet loss the norm. Checking email was largely impossible. I encountered a mild feeling of going cold-turkey, along with all its related anxieties. Only once I was through the "fever" was I truly able to enjoy the biodiverse, teeming, native, and ancient forest and land I grew up playing in, unable to see another house. Left with no telecommuted investments elsewhere, I arrived with both feet in the earth.

With that said, I have experienced a strong sense of place, of really being somewhere, playing MMORPGs and other online games. I've also made a couple of game-based projects in the early 2000s expressly about this. Sense of place can be conveyed and expressed over networks.

*You very freely share code and schematics for some quite sophisticated work. Why is doing this important to you?*

**Julian:** The reasons are selfish, ideological, and practical. This is easier expressed in list form:

I become the instant expert of my own work, and am always first called to make modifications/customizations—saving third-parties time.

Closing my source code doesn't protect my ideas—if any artist or company wants to rip me off they can certainly do so by brute force. It just takes a little time, determination, and/or money to reimplement the same idea, perhaps even improve upon my implementation of it.

Museums and festivals don't care if my source is open or closed. They only want a working exhibit. If it's open, I can then later direct someone on-site to make an adjustment, fix a bug, etc.

You invite collaborations, something really important to me. You also build interest around your work that will often improve its quality.

You become a better programmer, improving under critique.

By committing to sharing, you are granted the legal right to include a great many existing open source projects (libraries especially) in your own work. Saving you a ton of time.

It feels good to pass on what you learn. Your work becomes part of a larger conversation, which understands that one's cultural contribution is at once sometimes a technical contribution; two domains not always neatly separable.

*You've said that you see learning programming and hardware as self-improvement. Out of curiosity do you see it as self-improving in the same sense as learning the piano or learning Mandarin or any other communicative system, or is it different?*

**Julian:** I think it is different from learning an instrument, something I've also done. I find developing works of a technical nature to be a direct means of self-development. I isolate flaws in my logical thinking and come up hard against unfounded assumptions of my own personal ability. Technical problem-solving is so often about breaking down big problems into smaller problems until the big problem is solved. This has been really valuable, well beyond the scope of my projects. Most importantly, however, I've learned how to focus.

## Hardware Platforms

Arduino is not the only hardware prototyping platform available; there are other projects under development that you might be interested in exploring. Some of the following projects provide similar functionality to the Arduino, and others, like the Fritzing project, can be used as a supplement to working with Arduino.

### Phidgets

Phidgets are a line of plug-and-play building blocks for physical computing that can be plugged in to a computer using a USB cable and set up to communicate with any application. All the USB complexity is handled by the Phidgets API, which enables you to create communication between applications with a minimum of fuss. Since Phidgets are so simple to set up and use, you might consider working with them if you require only a single device for physical input or output. You can't create physical computing applications with the same complexity as you can with Arduino, but your project may not require that level of sophistication. Phidgets provides Python, Java, and C APIs, which means that connecting the Phidgets API to a Processing or oF application can be quite easy. The bottom level of the Phidgets stack is a cross-platform library, which implements the low-level protocols necessary to communicate with the Phidgets API and exports a unified interface to the software programmer. Built upon this low-level library are higher-level libraries that simplify using Phidgets for many more languages. These higher-level libraries contain logic for interfacing with the C library, thus making maintenance much easier.

### Robotshop Rover

Robotshop Rover is a robot kit built to work with Arduino Duemilanove; it includes one robot in the kit as well as the necessary electronics and hardware to build a fully functional robot that can be programmed in Arduino. It does require some soldering to get the robot working, but you can easily create a fully functional robot with two DC motors. You can also customize the robot by adding new electronic parts. For example, a pan and tilt kit is included with the kit and can be used to mount additional sensors or a camera, and can even act as the base for a multidegree-of-freedom robotic arm. The Pololu Servo Motor Controller mentioned in Chapter 11 can be used with Robotshop Rover to control servos as well.

### Fritzing

Fritzing is an open source initiative to help designers and artists create actual products from their prototypes. Fritzing consists of software to help design and document circuits and turn them into Printed Circuit Board (PCB) layouts for manufacturing. Fritzing is what is called *electronic design automation* software that helps create circuit boards. The interface of the software uses the metaphor of the breadboard, which makes it easier to sketch hardware to the software. You can create a prototype using a breadboard and Arduino, create it in Fritzing, and then create a file that can be sent to a manufacturer to produce a working PCB. While Arduino or some of the other physical prototyping tools lets nonengineers quickly turn their ideas into functional interactive prototypes, Fritzing aims to help the designer move to the next stage and create a finished PCB of their individual circuit in the mBed and the Maple desired shape. This makes the circuit robust and is great for creating permanent installations or even batch production of a project.

## AVR

You may remember from Chapter 4 that the Arduino uses a microcontroller called *AVR*, but it's not the only project or device that uses these controllers. In fact, if you're interested in working with different kinds of controllers other than the Arduino, while leveraging some of your Arduino knowledge, you might consider working with other AVR controllers. The two libraries that you'll probably want to look into first are the AVR Libc library, which contains the version of the C programming language that you can use with AVR microcontrollers, and the AVRDUDE library, which is a program for downloading and uploading programs onto AVR microcontrollers. You can compile C code for the AVR microcontroller using avr-gcc, which is a version of the GNU Compiler Collection that, depending on your OS, you might be using to compile an oF application. You can look at many of the electronics supplier sites and find different AVR boards and programming kits that might be of interest to you.

## ARM

ARM processors are increasingly being used in a wide range of platforms from *netbooks* (small computers meant for using the Internet or light word processing) to tiny embedded controllers. You can get ARM boards from many online electronics that will include pins for communicating with the microcontroller as well as documentation. Figure 17-2 shows two small examples.

Figure 17-2. Two ARM development board: mBed and Maple

For more information, you can look at www.arm.com or check an electronics supplier for information on a particular chip or board.

### PIC

The PIC is another series of chips that are power efficient, are simple to program, have many tools, and are aimed at less experienced developers. PIC controllers are used in a very wide range of projects. The simplest chip to program, find code for, and learn on is the 16F84, but there are other chips as well, namely, the 16F877 and the 18F series. You can find tutorials online or in a book such as *Physical Computing* by Tom Igoe and Dan O'Sullivan (Course Technology) that will show you some techniques to use. *Designing Embedded Systems with PIC Microcontrollers* by Tim Wilmshurst (Newnes) is an excellent text as well.

# Bibliography

Throughout our time together, I've mentioned different books that might be worth looking into if you're interested in exploring a certain idea further or understanding something in greater detail. Not all of the books mentioned throughout the chapters are listed here, but the most general and useful are.

## Interaction Design

*Data Flow: Visualising Information in Graphic Design* by R. Klanten et al. (Die Gestalten Verlag)
*Information Design Workbook* by Kim Baer and Jill Vacarra (Rockport)
*Envisioning Information* by Edward R. Tufte (Graphics Press)

*Visual Explanations: Images and Quantities, Evidence and Narrative* by Edward R. Tufte (Graphics Press)

*The Design of Everyday Things* by Donald A. Norman (Basic Books)

*Universal Principles of Design* by William Lidwell (Rockport)

*The Laws of Simplicity* by John Maeda (MIT Press)

*About Face 3: The Essentials of Interaction Design* by Alan Cooper et al. (Wiley)

*Designing for Interaction: Creating Smart Applications and Clever Devices* by Dan Saffer (New Riders)

*Sketching User Experiences: Getting the Design Right and the Right Design (Interactive Technologies)* by Bill Buxton (Morgan Kaufmann)

*Acting with Technology: Activity Theory and Interaction Design* by Victor Kaptelinin and Bonnie A. Nardi (MIT Press)

*Human-Machine Reconfigurations: Plans and Situated Actions (Learning in Doing: Social, Cognitive and Computational Perspectives)* by Lucy Suchman (Cambridge University Press)

*Where the Action Is: The Foundations of Embodied Interaction (Bradford Books)* by Paul Dourish (MIT Press)

*Digital Ground: Architecture, Pervasive Computing, and Environmental Knowing* by Malcolm McCullough (MIT Press)

*Reassembling the Social* by Bruno Latour (Oxford University Press)

*Sweet Anticipation: Music and the Psychology of Expectation* by David Huron (MIT Press)

*This Is Your Brain on Music: The Science of a Human Obsession* by Daniel J. Levitin (Plume/Penguin)

*Gaming: Essays On Algorithmic Culture* by Alexander R. Galloway (University of Minnesota Press)

*Persuasive Games: The Expressive Power of Videogames* by Ian Bogost (MIT Press)

*First Person: New Media as Story, Performance, and Game* by Noah Wardrip-Fruin and Pat Harrigan (MIT Press)

*Second Person: Role-Playing and Story in Games and Playable Media* by Pat Harrigan and Noah Wardrip-Fruin (MIT Press)

## Programming

*Processing: A Programming Handbook for Visual Designers and Artists* by Casey Reas et al. (MIT Press)

*Learning Processing: A Beginner's Guide to Programming Images, Animation, and Interaction (Morgan Kaufmann Series in Computer Graphics)* by Daniel Shiffman (Morgan Kaufmann)

*Processing: Creative Coding and Computational Art (Foundation)* by Ira Greenberg (Springer)

*Making Things Talk: Practical Methods for Connecting Physical Objects* by Tom Igoe (Make Books)

*Algorithms for Visual Design Using the Processing Language* by Kostas Terzidis (Wiley)

*Visualizing Data: Exploring and Explaining Data with the Processing Environment* by Ben Fry (O'Reilly)

*Analog In, Digital Out: Brendan Dawes on Interaction Design* by Brendan Dawes (New Riders)

*The Computational Beauty of Nature* by Gary William Flake (MIT Press)

*Mathematics and Physics for Programmers* by Danny Kodicek (Charles River Media)

*OpenGL(R) Programming Guide: The Official Guide to Learning OpenGL(R)* by OpenGL Architecture Review Board et al. (Addison-Wesley)

*OpenGL(R) Shading Language* by Randi J. Rost (Addison-Wesley)

*OpenGL(R) SuperBible: Comprehensive Tutorial and Reference* by Richard S. Wright et al. (Addison-Wesley)

*C++ Primer Plus, Fifth Edition* by Stephen Prata (Sams)

*Learning OpenCV: Computer Vision with the OpenCV Library* by Gary Bradski and Adrian Kaehler (O'Reilly)

## Hardware

*Getting Started with Arduino (Make: Projects)* by Massimo Banzi (Make Books)

*Arduino Cookbook* by Michael Margolis (O'Reilly)

*Physical Computing: Sensing and Controlling the Physical World with Computers* by Tom Igoe and Dan O'Sullivan (Course Technology)

*Getting Started in Electronics* by Forrest M. Mims III (Master Publishing)

*Electronic Sensor Circuits & Projects* by Forrest M. Mims III (Master Publishing)

*Handmade Electronic Music: The Art of Hardware Hacking* by Nicolas Collins (Routledge)

*Electronic Projects for Musicians* by Craig Anderton (Music Sales Corp.)

*Designing Embedded Hardware* by John Catsoulis (O'Reilly)

*Programming Embedded Systems in C and C++* by Michael Barr (O'Reilly)

## Art

*Design and the Elastic Mind* by Hugh Aldersey-Williams et al. (The Museum of Modern Art)

*Relational Aesthetics* by Nicolas Bourriaud (Les Presse Du Reel)

*Musimathics, Volume 1 and Volume 2: The Mathematical Foundations of Music* by Gareth Loy (MIT Press)

*Aesthetic Computing* by Paul Fishwick (MIT Press)

*Information Arts: Intersections of Art, Science, and Technology* by Stephen Wilson (MIT Press)

*At the Edge of Art* by Joline Blais et al. (Thames and Hudson)

*Noise, Water, Meat: A History of Sound in the Arts* by Douglas Kahn (MIT Press)

*4dsocial: Interactive Design Environments (Architectural Design)* by Lucy Bullivant (Wiley)

*4dspace: Interactive Architecture (Architectural Design)* by Lucy Bullivant (Academy Press)

*Database Aesthetics: Art in the Age of Information Overflow* by Victoria Vesna (University of Minnesota Press)

*A Thousand Years of Nonlinear History* by Manuel De Landa (Zone Books)

*Materializing New Media: Embodiment in Information Aesthetics* by Anna Munster (Dartmouth)

*Digital By Design* by Troika (Thames and Hudson)

*Atlas of Novel Tectonics* by Jesse Reiser (Princeton Architectural Press)

*Interaction of Color* by Josef Albers and Nicholas Fox Weber (Yale University Press)

*The Art of Color* by Johannes Itten (Wiley)

# Conclusion

Throughout this book, you've seen techniques for making interactive applications, ways of thinking of both code and hardware, libraries to use, and interviews with artists and designers who work with interaction as their primary medium. What's more, all the code that you've seen has been using open source projects that believe firmly in sharing code, resources, and ideas with other artists, designers, and programmers like yourself. This will make it easier for you to find help when you need it, get ideas when you want them, and get feedback on your work when you want it.

In addition to the books and websites mentioned in this book, there are a growing number of conferences and exhibitions throughout the United States, Europe, and Asia, highlighting interaction design and artwork by design groups, students, and artists. Some of these are hosted at universities that offer courses and degrees in new media studies, and others are simply occasions for like-minded thinkers to gather, present their own work, and look at the work of others. In the interest of not dating this book too greatly in the near future, I'll direct you to sites like *http://we-make-money-not-art.com* or the websites of each of the three featured projects in this book for more information.

I hope that, whatever your interests or reasons for picking up this book in the first place, you put this book down feeling prepared to begin your own exploration of the artistic and design potential in using technology to create meaningful, playful, or thought-provoking interactions.

# Index

We'd like to hear your suggestions for improving our indexes. Send email to *index@oreilly.com*.

# (pound sign) preceding preprocessor instructions in C++, 146

" " (quotation marks, double), in strings, 30

/ (slash)

/= (division and assignment) operator, 37

division operator, 36

[ ] (square brackets), accessing and defining array elements, 32

## A

accelerated motion, 268

accelerometers, 232–237

connecting to Arduino controller, 232

translation of data received from, 436

using with gyroscope and magnetometer to get object's position in 3D space, 648–654

Adafruit XBee adapter, 617

addButton( ) method, ControlP5 class (Processing), 286

addGesture( ) method, 573

addition operator (+), 35

addons folder (oF)

ofxOpenCv directory, 194

addons folder (openFrameworks), 167

addresses in XBee networks, 622

addresses, X10, 635

addSignal( ) method, AudioOutput class, 352

Adobe Flash, 660

AHRS (Altitude Heading Reference System), 648–654

AHRS class, 650

AILibrary and Alice library (Processing), 661

Akten, Memo, 663

AL (artificial life), 662

algorithmic drawings, 249

align( ) method, vector classes in oF, 280

allocate( ) method, ofTexture class, 333

alpha values, 65

accepted by ofSetColor( ) method, 178

in pixel colors, 298

setting for rectangle fill in Processing, 72

specifying for fill( ) method in Processing, 66

altitude data, 589

ambient data about a space or area, 615

ambientLight( ) method (Processing), 495

Analog In, Digital Out (Dawes), 244

analog pins, digital pins versus, 102

analogRead( ) method (Arduino), 113

configuring Arduino to read data from analog pins, 204

reading input from infrared sensor, 220

reading values from accelerometer, 232

analogWrite( ) method (Arduino), 113

sending analog values to LEDs, 207

setting LED brightness using potentiometer values, 205

Android phones, getting location on, 609

angle( ) method, vector classes in oF, 280

angular velocity, 240

animation

creating motion, 267

tweens, 270

Apple

iPhone, 10

QuickTime video libraries, 83

appliances, using Arduino with, 408

applications versus executables, 25

ApplicationTime class, staticTimeMethod( ) (C ++), 165

apps folder (openFrameworks), 167

architecture

interactive architectural systems, 462–469

interactive, reactive, and transformable, 613

reactive, 21

Arduino, 14, 93–132, 389–433

applications, basics of, 108–110

arrays, 33

boolean type, 29

byte type, 31

camera mounted on servos for face detection, 557–559

casting in, 35

circuit to connect solenoid to, 430

communicating on wireless networks, 475–478

communicating with other applications, 225

openFrameworks application, 227

Processing application, 225

configuring the IDE, 97

connecting components to your board, 118

resistors, 120

connecting GPS unit, 592

connecting infrared sensor to Arduino board, 220

## About the Author

**Joshua Noble** is an interaction designer and developer. He's the lead author of the *Flex 4 Cookbook* (O'Reilly, May 2010) and *Programming Interactivity* (*http://shop .oreilly.com/product/0636920021735.do*) (O'Reilly, July 2009). He's interested in designing humane objects and services for the intersection of public spaces, technology, and micro-computing, and exploring how people can participate in their physical and virtual communities.

## Colophon

The animals on the cover of *Programming Interactivity, Second Edition*, are guinea fowl (family Phasianidae, subfamily Numindinae). Sometimes known as guinea hens, wild guinea fowl originally hail from western Africa. Featherless heads with black crests and dark gray or deep blue plumage distinguish guinea fowl from other birds.

Domesticated guinea fowl (descended from *Numida meleagris*) make popular additions to farms, as farmers value the birds for their ability to control insects (guinea fowl dine on insects, leafy greens, and seeds). Farmers and other guinea fowl owners also appreciate the birds' paranoid natures; guinea fowl will cry out at provocations as slight as the bark of a dog, the beep of a horn, or a stranger's footsteps.

Their distinctive cries provide an easy way to distinguish the gender of the birds. While females and males both make a piercing "ah, ah, ah" sound when provoked, only the female can produce a two-syllable call that sounds as if she is saying "come back, come back, come back" or "buckwheat, buckwheat, buckwheat."

Gourmands prize cooked guinea fowl for their lean, tender flesh, which possesses a less gamy flavor than pheasant, while others say the prepared bird tastes like chicken (and also a little bit like turkey).

The cover image is from *The Riverside Natural History*. The cover font is Adobe ITC Garamond. The text font is Linotype Birka; the heading font is Adobe Myriad Condensed; and the code font is LucasFont's TheSansMonoCondensed.

# Get even more for your money.

**Join the O'Reilly Community, and register the O'Reilly books you own. It's free, and you'll get:**

- $4.99 ebook upgrade offer
- 40% upgrade offer on O'Reilly print books
- Membership discounts on books and events
- Free lifetime updates to ebooks and videos
- Multiple ebook formats, DRM FREE
- Participation in the O'Reilly community
- Newsletters
- Account management
- 100% Satisfaction Guarantee

**Signing up is easy:**

1. **Go to: oreilly.com/go/register**
2. **Create an O'Reilly login.**
3. **Provide your address.**
4. **Register your books.**

Note: English-language books only

**To order books online:**

oreilly.com/store

**For questions about products or an order:**

orders@oreilly.com

**To sign up to get topic-specific email announcements and/or news about upcoming books, conferences, special offers, and new technologies:**

elists@oreilly.com

**For technical questions about book content:**

booktech@oreilly.com

**To submit new book proposals to our editors:**

proposals@oreilly.com

**O'Reilly books are available in multiple DRM-free ebook formats. For more information:**

oreilly.com/ebooks

O'REILLY®

Spreading the knowledge of innovators          oreilly.com

# Have it your way.